Breaking Tolerance to Antibody-Mediated Immunotherapy

RESISTANCE TO ANTI-CD20 ANTIBODIES AND APPROACHES FOR THEIR REVERSAL

VOLUME 2

Breaking Tolerance to Antibody-Mediated Immunotherapy

Series Editor: Benjamin Bonavida, PhD

Volume 1: Novel Sensitizing Agents for Therapeutic Anti-EGFR Antibodies
Edited by Shi Hu, MD, PhD

Volume 2: Resistance to Anti-CD20 Antibodies and Approaches for Their Reversal
Edited by William C.S. Cho, PhD

Upcoming Volumes:

Overcoming Cancer Resistant to HER-2 Antibodies
Edited by Benjamin Bonavida, PhD

New Combination Approaches to Enhance Rituximab-Based Lymphoma Therapies
Edited by Benjamin Bonavida, PhD

Breaking Tolerance to Antibody-Mediated Immunotherapy

RESISTANCE TO ANTI-CD20 ANTIBODIES AND APPROACHES FOR THEIR REVERSAL

VOLUME 2

Edited by

WILLIAM C.S. CHO, PHD
Department of Clinical Oncology, Queen Elizabeth Hospital, Hong Kong

Academic Press is an imprint of Elsevier
125 London Wall, London EC2Y 5AS, United Kingdom
525 B Street, Suite 1650, San Diego, CA 92101, United States
50 Hampshire Street, 5th Floor, Cambridge, MA 02139, United States
The Boulevard, Langford Lane, Kidlington, Oxford OX5 1GB, United Kingdom

ISBN: 978-0-443-19200-5

For information on all Academic Press publications
visit our website at https://www.elsevier.com/books-and-journals

Publisher: Stacy Masucci
Senior Acquisitions Editor: Linda Versteeg-Buschman
Editorial Project Manager: Samantha Allard
Production Project Manager: Punithavathy Govindaradjane
Cover Designer: Vicky Pearson

Typeset by STRAIVE, India

Cover Image Insert

A schematic diagram showing CD20 antibodies bind to the targeted cell.

Aims and Scope of Series "Breaking Tolerance to Antibody-Targeted Therapies"

The role of the immune system in the eradication of cancer has been the subject of numerous controversial reports. In particular, the role of anticancer antibodies in the prevention and treatment of established cancers in experimental animal models has resulted often in both the protection and the rejection of various experimental tumors; however, the clinical findings in humans were not encouraging and yielded poor responses. It is worth noting that, in 1997, the FDA approved the first chimeric anti-CD20 monoclonal antibody, rituximab, or Rituxan, for the treatment of resistant non-Hodgkin's lymphoma. The clinical responses achieved were very good for a subset of patients, who were treated with a single agent alone, though the clinical response rates were significantly improved with the combination of rituximab and chemotherapy. As a result of the initial successful finding of the therapeutic efficacy of rituximab, in the subsequent years, a large number (greater than 25) of FDA-approved monoclonal antibodies were generated against various cancers, the majority of which was directed and targeting the cancer cells and a few were targeting noncancerous cells. However, it was found that not all patients respond to antibody treatment initially and many responding patients develop resistance to further treatments. Therefore, it was important to develop novel strategies to treat the unresponsive patients. Analyses of the various underlying mechanisms of antibody resistance in various cancers have revealed a number of gene products and resistant factors, which can be targeted by various specific interventions, namely, small molecules that can be termed sensitizing agents. In many cases, the combination of sensitizing agents and antibody therapy resulted in the reversal of resistance in various experimental models and also clinically.

The main aim of the new series "Breaking Cancer Resistance to Therapeutic Antibodies" is to develop highly focused volumes, each of which will review the role of particular and specific sensitizing agents that reverse the resistance of various therapeutic antibodies in different cancers. In each volume, the chapter reviews will have a detailed discussion on the underlying biochemical, molecular, and genetic underlying by which the sensitizing agents mediate their effects when used alone or in combination with a therapeutic antibody.

The scope of the series is to provide scientists and clinicians with updated basic, fundamental, and clinical findings. Such updated information will be helpful for further investigations and the development of more potent and different antibody-sensitizing agents for various cancers.

Benjamin Bonavida, PhD (Series Editor)

About the Series Editor

Dr. Benjamin Bonavida, PhD, Series Editor, is currently Distinguished Research Professor at the University of California, Los Angeles (UCLA). He is affiliated with the Department of Microbiology, Immunology, and Molecular Genetics, UCLA David Geffen School of Medicine. His research career, thus far, has focused on investigations in the fields of basic immunochemistry and cancer immunobiology. His research investigations have ranged from the biochemical, molecular, and genetic mechanisms of cell-mediated killing and tumor cell resistance to chemo-immuno-cytotoxic drugs. The reversal of tumor cell resistance was investigated using various selected sensitizing agents based on molecular mechanisms of resistance. In these investigations, there was the newly characterized dysregulated NF-κB/Snail/YY1/RKIP/PTEN loop in many cancers that was reported to regulate cell survival, proliferation, invasion, metastasis, and resistance. Emphasis was focused on the roles of the tumor suppressor Raf kinase inhibitor protein (RKIP), the tumor promoter Yin Yang 1 (YY1), and the role of nitric oxide as a chemo-immunosensitizing factor. Many of the aforementioned studies are centered on the clinically challenging features of cancer patients' failure to respond to both conventional and targeted therapies.

Dr. Benjamin Bonavida has been active in the organization of regular sequential international mini conferences that are highly focused on the roles of YY1, RKIP, and nitric oxide in cancer and their potential therapeutic applications. Several books edited or coedited by him have been published. In addition, he has been Series Editor of books (more than 23) published by Springer series *Resistance to Anti-Cancer Targeted Therapeutics*. In addition, he is presently Series Editor of three series published by Elsevier/Academic Press: *Chemotherapy-Sensitizing Agents for Cancer, Sensitizing Agents for Cancer Resistance to Antibodies*, and *Breaking Tolerance to Anti-Cancer Immunotherapy*. Last, Dr. Benjamin Bonavida is Editor-in-Chief of the journal *Critical Reviews in Oncogenesis*. He has published more than 500 research publications and reviews in various scientific journals of high impact.

Acknowledgments: Dr. Benjamin Bonavida acknowledges the excellent editorial assistance of Ms. Inesa Navasardyan, who has worked diligently in the completion of this volume, namely, in both the editing and formatting of the various contributions of this volume. Ms. Navasardyan has recently graduated from UCLA (June 2020) and has also contributed a review chapter in this volume: Triple Negative Breast Cancer.

Dr. Benjamin Bonavida acknowledges the Department of Microbiology, Immunology, and Molecular Genetics and the UCLA David Geffen School of Medicine for their continuous support. He also acknowledges the assistance of Mr. Rafael Teixeira, Acquisitions Editor for Elsevier/Academic Press, and the excellent assistance of Ms. Samantha Allard, Editorial Project Manager for Elsevier/Academic Press, for their continuous cooperation throughout the development of this book.

Aims and Scope of the Volume

Anti-CD20 antibodies are used to deplete B-cells and to treat B-cell disorders. Over the past two decades, anti-CD20 antibodies have revolutionized the treatment of all B-cell malignancies. However, some patients either do not respond to initial treatment or experience a rapid relapse. The precise mechanism behind drug resistance remains unclear. In recent years, many next-generation anti-CD20 therapies, such as bispecific antibodies, have been developed. Nevertheless, predicting and reversing drug resistance remains a challenging task. Consequently, the question arises: what are the treatment options for patients who are resistant to rituximab? These areas are under active research and represent the potential for improved anti-CD20 therapies. This book aims to understand and reverse resistance to anti-CD20 monoclonal antibody (mAb) therapy through a multifaceted analysis and multidisciplinary approach.

Anti-CD20 mAbs were originally developed for the treatment of B-cell proliferative disorders, including non-Hodgkin's lymphoma and chronic lymphocytic leukemia. Subsequently, they have also been employed in the treatment of autoimmune and renal diseases. The clinical efficacy of anti-CD20 antibodies, immune monitoring of patients receiving anti-CD20 therapy, and kinetic exclusion assays using cell membranes to measure the affinity of anti-CD20 antibodies will be discussed in detail. At present, a variety of anti-CD20 mAbs have been approved for the treatment of neurological and neuromuscular diseases, with good clinical efficacy. The underlying mechanisms, developments, and current evidence for anti-CD20 therapies in neurological and neuromuscular diseases will be elaborated.

This book serves as the pioneering professional resource on the topic of anti-CD20 antibody resistance and its reversal, compiling subjects of interest pertaining to anti-CD20 antibody therapy and drug resistance from opinion leaders in the field.

William C.S. Cho, PhD

About the Volume Editor

William C.S. Cho, PhD, RCMP, FHKIMLS, FHKSMDS, Chartered Scientist (UK), FIBMS (UK).

Department of Clinical Oncology, Queen Elizabeth Hospital, Hong Kong.

Dr. Cho's primary research interests focus on cancer research to discover biomarkers for cancer diagnosis, treatment prediction, and prognosis. As a seasoned researcher, Dr. Cho has conducted cancer research using molecular biology, proteomics, genomics, immunology, bioinformatics, and next-generation sequencing technologies.

Dr. Cho has published more than 600 peer-reviewed papers (*Lancet*, *Lancet Oncology*, *Annals of Oncology*, *Lancet Gastroenterology & Hepatology*, *Advanced Science*, *Nature Communications*, *PNAS*, *Molecular Cancer*, *Journal of Thoracic Oncology*, *Journal of the National Cancer Institute*, *Journal of Extracellular Vesicles*, *Clinical Cancer Research*, *Clinical Chemistry*, *Theranostics*, etc.) covering cancer biomarkers, proteomics, noncoding RNA, traditional Chinese medicine, and dozens of books (including *An Omics Perspective on Cancer Research*, *MicroRNAs in Cancer Translational Research*, *Drug Repurposing in Cancer Therapy: Approaches and Applications*, *Supportive Cancer Care with Chinese Medicine*, etc.). The cumulative impact factor of journals exceeds 4500. Furthermore, Dr. Cho's papers have garnered significant attention within the scientific community, having been cited over 25,000 times. These achievements have also led to Dr. Cho's recognition as one of the top 2% most influential scientists in the world.

In addition, Dr. Cho has served as a research grant reviewer for many international research funds, including the Hope Funds for Cancer Research (United States), Cancer Research (United Kingdom), National Medical Research Council (Singapore), etc.

Preface

Since the FDA approved the first chimeric anti-CD20 monoclonal antibody (rituximab) for the treatment of non-Hodgkin's lymphoma, research on anti-CD20 antibodies and their clinical response has made significant progress. This is a book dedicated to anti-CD20 antibody resistance and how to reverse it. This book brings together an unparalleled topic of interest to anti-CD20 antibody resistance from opinion leaders in the field. Each chapter contains the latest commentary and expert views on the topic.

This professional book aims to present state-of-the-art discoveries of anti-CD20 antibodies in cancer treatment. It explores possible mechanisms of drug resistance and strategies for reversing it, as well as the combination of anti-CD20 antibodies with other treatment modalities. The scientific and medical communities in dire need of up-to-date information supported by specific laboratory evidence or clinical trials. This book fills that gap by offering experimental and clinical evidence of anti-CD20 antibody resistance and its reversal. For example, understanding the mechanisms of resistance and how to reverse them is critical to improving the efficacy of anti-CD20 therapies. This volume covers timely content based on current research, critical analysis, in-depth literature reviews, and anti-CD20 antibody resistance perspectives aimed at providing solutions to current clinical issues. A large number of diagrams are used to visually illustrate complex content, and numerous tables are used to summarize important information.

This book provides essential information and clinical studies for scientists/experts in the field. In addition, cancer patients undergoing or considering anti-CD20 antibody therapy and their families will find this book helpful in understanding and choosing treatment options. Clinicians, translational scientists, academics, and graduate students in related disciplines such as oncology, hematology, immunology, and pharmacy will be the primary audience. Since CD20 antibodies are also increasingly used to deplete B-cells in patients with autoimmune diseases (such as rheumatoid arthritis and systemic lupus erythematosus) or multiple sclerosis, rheumatologists, neurologists, and nephrologists will also be interested in this book. I envision this book will bring some solutions and insights to address clinical issues, ultimately leading to improved patient outcomes.

William C.S. Cho

Department of Clinical Oncology, Queen Elizabeth Hospital, Hong Kong

Contents

5. Targeted therapies for follicular lymphoma

Radhika Takiar and Tycel J. Phillips

6. Treatment of relapsed follicular lymphoma

Silvia Montoto

7. New monoclonal antibodies for the treatment of acute lymphoblastic leukemia

Mark Gurney and Mark R. Litzow

8. Clinical relevance and therapeutic implications of CD20 expression in Hodgkin's lymphoma

Marcelo Antônio Oliveira Santos Veloso and Rafael Pinheiro dos Santos

II

Resistance and affinity determination of anti-CD20 antibodies

9. Therapeutic options for rituximab-resistant patients

Jing Wang, Ran Qin, Yanling Jin, Bili Xia, and Jianqing Xu

10. Mechanisms of resistance to anti-CD20 antibodies in lymphoid malignancies

Anne Bordron, Marie Morel, and Cristina Bagacean

11. Kinetic exclusion assay using cellular membranes for affinity determination of anti-CD20 antibody

Madelynn Grier, Helen J. McBride, Thomas R. Glass, and Qing Chen

III

Therapeutic anti-CD20 antibodies against noncancer diseases

12. Clinical efficacy of anti-CD20 antibodies in autoimmune diseases

Zeineb Zian, Abubakar Umar Anka, Hamisu Abdullahi, Emna Bouallegui, Shayan Maleknia, and Gholamreza Azizi

13. B-cell depletion with obinutuzumab for the treatment of proliferative lupus nephritis

Matthew Salvatore Snyder and Richard Furie

14. Anti-CD20 antibodies in glomerular diseases, their resistance and reversal approaches

Lakshmi Kannan

15. Adverse events following rituximab therapy in pemphigus patients

Sahar Dadkhahfar

16. Immune monitoring of patients treated with anti-CD20 therapeutic monoclonals for autoimmune disorders

Bruno Brando and Arianna Gatti

17. Clinical efficacy of anti-CD20 antibodies in neurological and neuromuscular diseases

Yuan-teng Fan, Tao-xiang Chen, Yu-min Liu, and Bi-wen Peng

18. Reversal of resistance to anti-CD20 antibody therapies: Conclusions and future perspectives

Benjamin Bonavida

Contributors

Hamisu Abdullahi Department of Immunology, School of Medical Laboratory Sciences, Usmanu Danfodiyo University Sokoto, Sokoto, Nigeria

Sharafudeen Dahiru Abubakar Division of Molecular Pathology, Research Institute for Biomedical Sciences, Tokyo University of Science, Tokyo, Japan; Department of Medical Laboratory Science, College of Medical Science, Ahmadu Bello University, Zaria, Nigeria

Mansur Aliyu Department of Immunology, School of Public Health, Tehran University of Medical Sciences, Tehran, Iran; Department of Medical Microbiology, Faculty of Clinical Science, College of Health Sciences, Bayero University, Kano, Nigeria

Abubakar Umar Anka Department of Medical Laboratory Science, College of Medical Sciences, Ahmadu Bello University Zaria, Zaria, Nigeria

Gholamreza Azizi Non-communicable Diseases Research Center, Alborz University of Medical Sciences, Karaj, Iran; Department of Neurology, Thomas Jefferson University, Philadelphia, PA, United States

Cristina Bagacean LBAI, UMR1227, Univ Brest, Inserm; Department of Clinical Hematology, University Hospital of Brest; UMR 1304, GETBO, Univ Brest, Inserm, Brest, France

Benjamin Bonavida Department of Microbiology, Immunology & Molecular Genetics, David Geffen School of Medicine, Jonsson Comprehensive Cancer Center, University of California at Los Angeles, Los Angeles, CA, United States

Anne Bordron LBAI, UMR1227, Univ Brest, Inserm, Brest, France

Emna Bouallegui Ministry of public health Qatar MOPH, Doha, Qatar

Bruno Brando Hematology Laboratory and Transfusion Center, Western Milan Hospital Consortium, Legnano General Hospital, Legnano, Milano, Italy

Federica Cavallo Division of Hematology, Department of Molecular Biotechnology and Health Sciences, University of Torino, A.O.U. Città della Salute e della Scienza di Torino, Turin, Italy

Qing Chen Amgen Inc., Thousand Oaks, CA, United States

Tao-xiang Chen Department of Physiology, School of Basic Medical Sciences, Wuhan University, Wuhan, China

William C.S. Cho Department of Clinical Oncology, Queen Elizabeth Hospital, Hong Kong

Michele Clerico Division of Hematology, Department of Molecular Biotechnology and Health Sciences, University of Torino, A.O.U. Città della Salute e della Scienza di Torino, Turin, Italy

Sahar Dadkhahfar Skin Research Center, Shahid Beheshti University of Medical Sciences, Tehran, Iran

Rafael Pinheiro dos Santos Mauricio de Nassau University, School of Medicine, Recife, Brazil

Yuan-teng Fan Department of Neurology, Zhongnan Hospital, Wuhan University, Wuhan, China

Richard Furie Division of Rheumatology, Department of Medicine, Donald and Barbara Zucker School of Medicine at Hofstra/Northwell, Great Neck, NY, United States

Arianna Gatti Hematology Laboratory and Transfusion Center, Western Milan Hospital Consortium, Legnano General Hospital, Legnano, Milano, Italy

Thomas R. Glass Sapidyne Instruments Inc., Boise, ID, United States

Madelynn Grier Sapidyne Instruments Inc., Boise, ID, United States

Mark Gurney Division of Hematology, Department of Internal Medicine, Mayo Clinic, Rochester, MN, United States

Stella Amarachi Ihim Department of Molecular and Cellular Pharmacology, University of Shizuoka, Shizuoka, Japan; Department of Pharmacology and Toxicology & Department of Science Laboratory Technology, University of Nigeria, Nsukka, Nigeria

Yanling Jin Shanghai Public Health Clinical Center, Fudan University, Shanghai, China

Ying Jin Department of Hematology, Affiliated Hospital and Medical School of Nantong University, Nantong, Jiangsu, China

Lakshmi Kannan Pikeville Medical Center, Adjunct Clinical Faculty, University of Pikeville Kentucky College of Osteopathic Medicine, Pikeville, KY, United States

Mohammad Aqueel Khan Computer Aided Drug Design and Molecular Modelling Lab, Department of Bioinformatics, Science Block, Alagappa University, Karaikudi, Tamil Nadu, India

Mark R. Litzow Division of Hematology, Department of Internal Medicine, Mayo Clinic, Rochester, MN, United States

Yu-min Liu Department of Neurology, Zhongnan Hospital, Wuhan University, Wuhan, China

Shayan Maleknia Biopharmaceutical Research Center, AryoGen Pharmed Inc., Alborz University of Medical Sciences, Karaj, Iran

Helen J. McBride TORL Biotherapeutics, Culver City, CA, United States

Silvia Montoto Department of Haemato-Oncology, St Bartholomew's Hospital, Barts Health NHS Trust, London, United Kingdom

Marie Morel LBAI, UMR1227, Univ Brest, Inserm, Brest, France

Umesh Panwar Computer Aided Drug Design and Molecular Modelling Lab, Department of Bioinformatics, Science Block, Alagappa University, Karaikudi, Tamil Nadu, India

Bi-wen Peng Department of Physiology, Hubei Provincial Key Laboratory of Developmentally Originated Disease, School of Basic Medical Sciences, Wuhan University, Wuhan, China

Tycel J. Phillips Division of Lymphoma, Department of Hematology & Hematopoietic Cell Transplantation, City of Hope, Duarte, CA, United States

Ran Qin Shanghai Public Health Clinical Center, Fudan University, Shanghai, China

Simone Ragaini Division of Hematology, Department of Molecular Biotechnology and Health Sciences, University of Torino, A.O.U. Città della Salute e della Scienza di Torino, Turin, Italy

Mohammad Saffarioun Biopharmaceutical Research Center, AryoGen Pharmed Inc., Alborz University of Medical Sciences, Karaj, Iran

Chandrabose Selvaraj Center for Transdisciplinary Research, Department of Pharmacology, Saveetha Dental College and Hospitals, Saveetha Institute of Medical and Technical Sciences (SIMATS), Saveetha University, Chennai, Tamil Nadu, India

Sanjeev Kumar Singh Computer Aided Drug Design and Molecular Modelling Lab, Department of Bioinformatics, Science Block, Alagappa University, Karaikudi, Tamil Nadu; Department of Data Sciences, Centre of Biomedical Research, Lucknow, Uttar Pradesh, India

Matthew Salvatore Snyder Division of Rheumatology, Department of Medicine, Donald and Barbara Zucker School of Medicine at Hofstra/Northwell, Great Neck, NY, United States

Guoqi Song Department of Hematology, Affiliated Hospital and Medical School of Nantong University, Nantong, Jiangsu, China

Radhika Takiar Division of Hematology and Oncology, Department of Internal Medicine, University of Michigan, Ann Arbor, MI, United States

Marcelo Antônio Oliveira Santos Veloso Hospital Alfa, Division for Internal Medicine; Department of Therapeutic Innovation, Federal University of Pernambuco, Center for Biosciences; Mauricio de Nassau University, School of Medicine, Recife, Brazil

Cheng Wang Department of Hematology, Affiliated Hospital and Medical School of Nantong University, Nantong, Jiangsu, China

Jing Wang Shanghai Public Health Clinical Center, Fudan University, Shanghai, China

Bili Xia Shanghai Public Health Clinical Center, Fudan University, Shanghai, China

Jianqing Xu Shanghai Public Health Clinical Center; Zhongshan Hospital and Institutes of Biomedical Science, Fudan University, Shanghai, China

Li Yang Department of Hematology, Affiliated Yancheng NO.1 People's Hospital, Yancheng, Jiangsu, China

Zeineb Zian Biomedical Genomics and Oncogenetics Research Laboratory, Faculty of Sciences and Techniques of Tangier, Abdelmalek Essaadi University, Tetouan, Morocco

PART I

Therapeutic anti-CD20 antibodies against cancers and escape

CHAPTER

1

Therapeutic antibodies against cancer—A step toward the treatment

Umesh Panwar[a], *Mohammad Aqueel Khan*[a], *Chandrabose Selvaraj*[b], *and Sanjeev Kumar Singh*[a,c]

[a]Computer Aided Drug Design and Molecular Modelling Lab, Department of Bioinformatics, Science Block, Alagappa University, Karaikudi, Tamil Nadu, India [b]Center for Transdisciplinary Research, Department of Pharmacology, Saveetha Dental College and Hospitals, Saveetha Institute of Medical and Technical Sciences (SIMATS), Saveetha University, Chennai, Tamil Nadu, India [c]Department of Data Sciences, Centre of Biomedical Research, Lucknow, Uttar Pradesh, India

Abstract

The second-greatest cause of death in the world is cancer, resulting in a significant issue that has an impact on the health of all human communities. Recently, the growth of recombinant antibody technology has made antibody therapeutics the most powerful and quickly spreading class of drugs that offer significant patient advantages, particularly in the treatment of cancer. The utilization of mAbs has seen significant progress in recent years for cancer therapy after its first approval by the United States Food and Drug Administration (US FDA) in 1986. It belongs to a promising family of targeted anticancer agents that improve the function of the immune system to inhibit the activity of cancer cells and eradicate cancer cells. Hence, the market for therapeutic antibodies has experienced explosive growth as a novel drug against different human diseases. Therefore, in this chapter, we provide a comprehensive overview of therapeutic antibodies, including their structural format, mechanism of action, and design strategies. Also, we discuss the importance of CD20 as a potential target for therapeutic antibodies and the resistance issues that arise during treatment. Computational techniques for designing therapeutic antibodies and the availability of antibody databases are also highlighted. In addition, the advantages and disadvantages of therapeutic antibodies along with their possible side effects as well as current limitations with production costs are discussed. The chapter concludes with a discussion on the approaches to overcoming mechanisms of resistance to therapy, the future of therapeutic antibodies, and the potential of predictive biomarkers for a therapeutic response against cancer. Overall, this chapter provides valuable insights into the current state of therapeutic antibodies and opportunities in the development of novel antibody treatment strategies in the field of medicine.

https://doi.org/10.1016/B978-0-443-19200-5.00001-4

Abbreviations

ADCC antibody-dependent cellular cytotoxicity
B-AL B-cell acute leukemia
CDC complement-dependent cytotoxicity
CLL chronic lymphocytic leukemia
FDA Food and Drug Administration
Ig immunoglobulins
IMGT International Immunogenetics Information System
mAb monoclonal antibody
NHL non-Hodgkin's lymphoma
RA rheumatoid arthritis
TABS Therapeutic Antibody Databases
TR T-cell receptors
WHO World Health Organization

Conflict of interest

No potential conflicts of interest were disclosed.

Introduction

Cancer is described by the uncontrolled development and spread of unusual cells in the body. At present, it is a major issue and extraordinary challenge in front of the scientific community, has surpassed cardiovascular infections as the second biggest reason for mortality around the world. There are various kinds of cancer such as breast cancer, colon cancer, lung cancer, prostate cancer, and others, each with remarkable causes and side effects. The principal focus in cancer therapy is to decrease the number of infected cells, slow down their development, and forestall the spread of the disease to different parts of the body. This therapy relies on a couple of factors, including the sort and long period of cancer growth, the patient's overall health, and own inclinations. There are a few therapies including medical procedures, radiation treatment, chemotherapy, immunotherapy, and therapeutic antibodies treatment that offer extraordinary and dependable clinical capacities in different cancers [1–4]. Among these, therapeutic monoclonal antibodies (mAbs) are the classes of drugs that have dramatically evolved and encountered the fastest development after their first approval in 1986 by the United States Food and Drug Administration (US FDA). They are authorized for the therapy of various signs, including the administration of immune system issues and diseases. Coming up next are a portion of the key motivations behind the significance of therapeutic antibodies in disease treatment [5–11] are as follows:

- Target specific: Therapeutic antibodies may explicitly target substances or cells engaged with the beginning or movement of disease. The likelihood of injury to healthy cells, which is much of a concern with traditional medicines such as chemotherapy, is diminished by this tailored approach.
- High specificity: Antibodies have a high tendency for their target, which empowers them to tie to a specific compound or sort of cell with incredible accuracy. This is particularly vital in conditions like a disease when it's fundamental to dispose of infected cells with minimal harm to healthy cells.

- Long half-life: Antibodies stay in the body for a more drawn-out measure of time than numerous other therapeutic agents because of their more extended half-life. By doing so, the treatment's benefits might be delayed, and treatment frequency or dosage might be reduced.
- Effective in treating chronic conditions: Therapeutic antibodies have been shown to be valuable in treating chronic illnesses, including immune system issues and a few types of cancer growth. These can offer long-term benefits to patients by focusing on the fundamental reasons for specific diseases.
- Fewer side effects: Compared to standard treatments such as chemotherapy, therapeutic antibodies are more averse to having large numbers of secondary effects that are related to them. Thus, patients who are looking for a more satisfactory and secure treatment might have them as a better option.
- Improving patient outcomes: Patients suffering from various issues are presently encountering improved results because of the advancement of therapeutic antibodies. For example, the utilization of antibodies in the therapy of autoimmune diseases and malignant growth has expanded patient survival rates and quality of life.

Today's scenario represents antibody-based targeted therapy as an appealing choice for treating disease since it is frequently less harmful than other medicines and may have less side effects. Since the therapeutic antibodies have changed and secured patients with more powerful and advantageous treatment options. Here is a brief timeline of the key events in the history of fruitful innovation and the improvement of therapeutic antibodies approved [12–20], as shown in Table 1.

TABLE 1 A brief timeline of a therapeutic antibody.

1975	Initial mAbs were produced by B cells that target antigens. The first hybridoma technique was established by Köhler and Milstein
1981	A successful testing of antilymphoma antibody was done
1984	Antibody chimerization
1986	The first mAb therapy, muromonab-CD3 (Orthoclone OKT3), is approved for use in transplantation
1990	First clinical trial of bispecific antibody was performed
1994	The US Food and Drug Administration (FDA) approved the first chimeric antibody, abciximab [anti-GPIIb/IIIa antigen-binding fragment (Fab)], which inhibits platelet aggregation in cardiovascular disorders, in 1994
1997	Rituximab (Rituxan), a chimeric anti-CD20 mAb, developed and approved for use in the treatment of non-Hodgkin's lymphoma (NHL)
1998	Trastuzumab (Herceptin) became the second mAb approved for the treatment of a malignant condition of metastatic breast cancer
2000	The development of humanized and fully human mAbs begins, with the goal of improving the safety and efficacy of these treatments

Continued

TABLE 1 A brief timeline of a therapeutic antibody—cont'd

2002	Adalimumab (Humira; Abbott) is approved as an antiinflammatory cytokine TNF-α for the treatment of moderate to severe rheumatoid arthritis
2003	Omalizumab was approved as an anti-IgE (Xolair) to treat the asthma patient. Additionally, Efalizumab is approved for the treatment of psoriasis against the cell adhesion molecule CD11a
2004	Bevacizumab as anti-VGFR and Cetuximab as an anti-EGFR antibody to guide the treatment of CRC
2005	EMA approval for the first bispecific mAb
2006	Panitumumab was approved for use in metastatic CRC, and in the same year, Ranibizumab injection was first approved for wet age-related macular degeneration
2007	Eculizumab was approved as anti-C5 to treat the Paroxysmal nocturnal hemoglobinuria
2009	Ustekinumab as anti-IL-12/23 for Psoriasis
2010	Denosumab is approved as an anti-RANKL for the treatment of bone loss
2011	The development of brentuximab vedotin was approved for use in relapsed Hodgkin lymphoma and systemic anaplastic large-cell lymphoma
2012	Trastuzumab emtansine was established to treat patients with HER2-positive breast cancer
2014	Siltuximab, a humanized monoclonal antibody was developed to treat a rare blood disorder called multicentric Castleman's disease (MCD). Also, Nivolumab and Pembrolizumab were discovered to treat the Melanoma in same year
2015	Dinutuximab for Neuroblastoma, Evolocumab for high cholesterol, and Mepolizumab for severe eosinophilic asthma were approved
2016	Atezolizumab is a cancer immunotherapy treatment for nonsmall cell lung cancer after surgery and chemo with stage IIA, stage IIB, or stage IIIA cancer Reslizumab is an IL-5 antagonist specifically used to treat patient with severe eosinophilic asthma
2017	Many therapeutics like Avelumab to treat metastatic Merkel cell carcinoma, Emicizumab for the treatment of hemophilia A, and Gemtuzumab ozogamicin to treat acute myeloid leukemia that is CD33 positive were approved this year
2018	Discovery of Burosumab for X-linked hypophosphatemia and Erenumab to prevent migraine headaches
2019	Crizanlizumab was discovered to treat sickle cell disease and reduce the pain
2021	Casirivimab and imdevimab are the recombinant human monoclonal antibodies (IgG1κ and IgG1λ, respectively) for the treatment or postexposure prevention of COVID-19
2022	Bebtelovimab was approved by FDA to the treat COVID-19

Antibodies have turned into a pivotal part of modern biomedicine for various therapies against cancer growth, immune disorders, infectious infections, blood-related diseases, neurological diseases, hereditary issues, etc. As of July 1, 2022, there were 165 therapeutic antibodies authorized or undergoing regulatory reviews worldwide, as indicated by data given by the Antibody Society [21]. Fig. 1 portrays the total rundown of approved antibody medicines maintained by the Antibody Society.

The major objective of cancer treatment is to give better results to the patients by diminishing the side effects of cancer growth, prolonging survival, and improving the quality

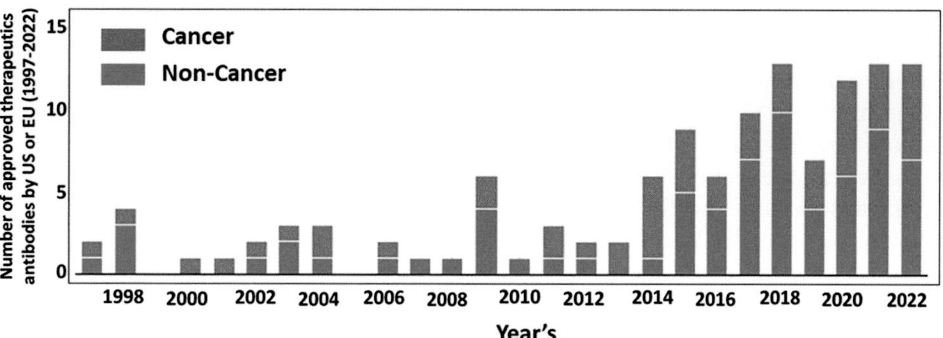

FIG. 1 Graphical representation of therapeutics antibodies first approvals in either the US or EU (1997–2022) (www.antibodysociety.org/antibody-therapeutics-product-data/).

of life. The determination of the most appropriate therapies requires cautious thought of the individual needs and characteristics, as well as the latest developments in cancer research and treatment. This section provides a thorough overview of therapeutic antibodies, their significance, current difficulties, and potential future applications with reference to developing novel antibody treatments.

Search strategy and selection criteria

In general, the keywords "Cancer and their target," "therapeutic antibodies," "CD20 as a target," "anti-CD20 antibodies," "Resistance of therapeutic antibodies in Cancer," "Reversal of antibodies," "biological mechanism of CD20," "Computational importance to design the therapeutic antibody," "Antibody therapeutics approved by US FDA," "Production Cost of therapeutic antibodies," and an "Antibody therapeutics approved by European Medicines Agency" were used to search for and select content. All the research articles, reviews, and other published research works in peer-reviewed publications were retrieved. This tactic offered useful knowledge on therapeutic antibodies and their application in cancer treatment.

Structural format of therapeutic antibodies and their mechanism

Immunoglobulins (Ig), well known as antibodies, are vital proteins for the immune system. In response to the presence of foreign substances such as microbes and infected cells, these antibodies are developed by the B cells of the immune system. Antibodies have exceptional underlying attributes that empower them to perceive and destroy these particles. Four polypeptide chains, two indistinguishable heavy chains, and two indistinguishable light chains develop the fundamental structure of an antibody. Most of the atomic load of the antibody is contributed by the heavy chains, though the light chains are more modest. Disulfide bonds tie together the heavy and light chains. The antigen-binding site is the region of the antibody that manages to distinguish and connect to the foreign particle. This area, which incorporates a variable region that is specific to every antibody, is found at the tips of the heavy and light chains. The amino acid sequence of the variable district is incredibly inconsistent, empowering the development of a huge scope of antibodies with different binding specificities. One fragment crystallizable region (Fc) and two antigen-binding regions (Fab) fragments complete the antibody with the most biological underlying configuration. The H and L chain variable sections (VH and VL) that tight the spot to the antigen's related surface are significant parts of the Fab. The complementarity-determining region (CDRs) that are characterized by the VH-VL and contain a large part of the antigen-binding are displayed in Fig. 2A. Antibodies could recognize and connect to specific antigens found on the outer layer of foreign substances, which thusly sets off various immune responses that can either kill or annihilate them. For example, antibodies can draw the immune system response to the disease site, such as phagocytes, where they can ingest and kill the foreign substance. Furthermore, supplements, a bunch of blood proteins that can straightforwardly destroy foreign particles, are activated by antibodies. Antibodies could kill infected explicit cells such as cancer cells by connecting and inactivating them, which hold the host back from enduring harm. By and large, antibodies have designs that empower the human body system, for example, restricting foreign particles, and rescuing the immune system cells. It can effectively shield the host from the dangerous response of upcoming foreign particles. These biologic medications known as therapeutic mAb are customized and made to look like the body's own regular antibodies. At the point when foreign substances target healthy cells, these administered therapeutic antibodies fortify the immune system to forestall the impacts of these particles and enroll the assistance of other immune systems to kill the antigen-containing cells. As displayed in Fig. 2B, these may have a particular binding to a protein on a specific kind of

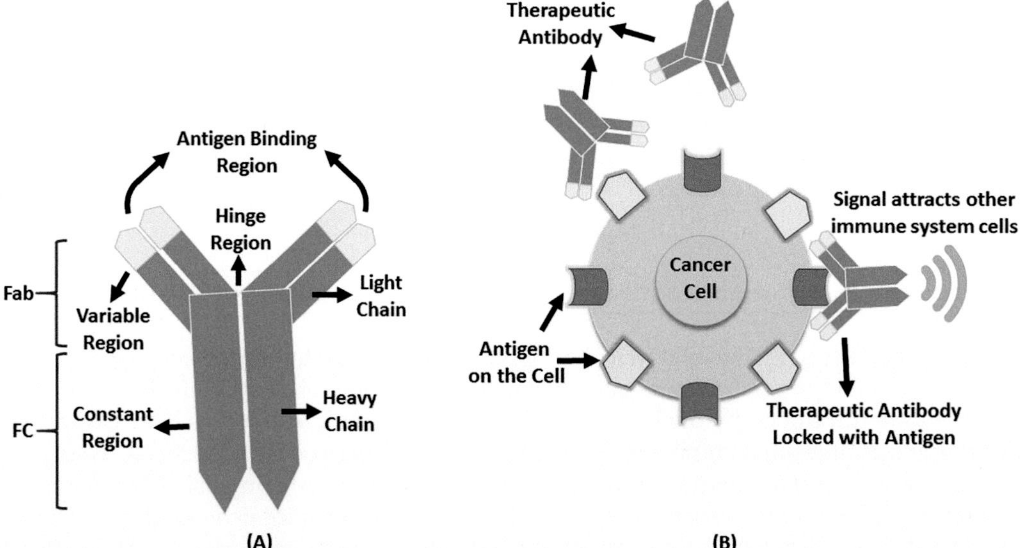

FIG. 2 Schematic representation of (A) the antibody structure, and (B) general perspective view of therapeutic antibodies mechanism.

cell (for instance, a cancer cell), making the cell pass on or be gone after by the body's immune system [7,22–27].

Designing of chimeric, humanized, and human antibodies

During the 1990s, progress in molecular biology made it conceivable to clone the qualities of IgG particles, introducing the period of antibody designing and considering the adaptable improvement of recombinant antibodies. The capacity to deliver various kinds of antibodies was a huge utilization of antibody engineering. Afterward, the antibody engineering refreshed the different kinds of antibodies that may be utilized in the therapy against various diseases including cancer, as follows [28–33].

- Chimeric antibodies: Both mouse and human antibodies are utilized to make chimeric antibodies. They are delivered through the splicing of human and mouse antibody genes. Chimeric antibodies have a mouse-constant region that permits them to enact the immune system and a human antigen-binding region that empowers them to tie to focuses on the outer layer of cancer cells.
- Humanized antibodies: To develop humanized antibodies, chimeric antibodies are additionally changed by exchanging the mouse-constant region for a human-constant region. Subsequently, the antibody looks like human antibodies more intently and is less inclined to cause an immunological response.
- Human antibodies: Human antibodies are made by genetic engineering strategies such as phage display to generate human antibodies that explicitly tie to a target antigen. Since there are no animal components in these antibodies, they are more averse to getting an immunological response.
- These various sorts of antibodies offer a scope of remedial choices, taking into consideration the specific disease-based treatment to individual patient requirements.
- mAb treatments are commonly administered intravenously and can be utilized in combination with other cancer therapies, such as chemotherapy or radiation treatment. They have turned into a significant treatment with various therapies against infectious diseases.

CD20 as a potential target, the resistance of therapeutic antibody against it, and the importance of computational role

CD20 is a protein (33–37 kDa) that has a valuable place with the nonglycosylated transmembrane phosphoprotein from the membrane-spanning 4-A (MS4A) family. It is essentially found on the outer layer of immune system cells known as B cells. B cells assume a significant part in the body's immune reaction and are associated with creating antibodies that assist with battling diseases. CD20 is viewed as a possible target for cancer growth treatment since it is available in mostly 95% of B cell-related diseases, including NHL, CLL, and a few kinds of lymphoma. Hardly any new medical effect the ideal models as the production of mAb against CD20. The *Period of Rituximab* has been utilized with regard to hematology and oncology since the FDA endorsed rituximab in 1997. This is particularly obvious in the administration of B-cell malignancies, since anti-CD20 is highly specific to cancer cells and does not damage healthy cells, lessening the aftereffects related to chemotherapy [6,34–39]. Rituximab's exceptional clinical performance has ignited the making of another class of anti-CD20 mAbs for therapeutic purposes (e.g., Obinutuzumab, Ofatumumab, Veltuzumab, and Ocrelizumab). Their effectiveness and safety in contrast with rituximab are yet easily proven wrong, and rituximab keeps on having an ordering position in acknowledged norms of care. A few anti-CD20 mAb's are introduced in Table 2 [40–52].

Relapsed and refractory disease keeps on representing a huge treatment challenge regardless of late progressions. It is imagined that one powerful method for improving existing medicines is to upgrade CD20-designated immunotherapies. The absence of preclinical models that precisely address the complex connection between the immune system and

TABLE 2 List of approved therapeutic antibodies (1997–2022).

Anti-CD20 mAb	Source	Mechanisms of action	Use in	Company	Approval year
Rituximab	Chimeric IgG1	CDC, ADCC, PCD, & ADCP	NHL	Biogen Inc./Roche, F. Hoffmann-La Roche Ltd./Genentech Inc.	1997
Ibritumomab tiuxetan	Murine IgG1κ	High CDC, low ADCC	NHL	Biogen IDEC Pharmaceuticals Corp.	2002
Tositumomab	Murine IgG2aλ	High PCD, low CDC	NHL	Corixa, Glaxo Smithkline	2003
Reditux	Murine IgG1	CDC, ADCC, PCD, and ADCP	NHL	Dr. Reddy Laboratories	2007
Ofatumumab	Fully human IgG1 κ	High CDC	CLL	Genmab A/S/GlaxoSmithKline/Novartis	2009
Obinutuzumab	Humanized IgG2κ	High PCD/ADCC, low CDC	CLL	Biogen Inc./Roche, F. Hoffmann-La Roche, Ltd./Genentech Inc.	2013
Ublituximab	Chimeric; IgG1 Glycoengineered	High ADCC	CLL, NHL	GTC Biotherapeutics, LFB Biotechnologies	Phase I
PRO131921	Humanized IgG1	High CDC, low ADCC	NHL	Genentech	Phase I/II
TRU-015	SMIL	High ADCC, low CDC	RA	Trubion Pharmaceuticals Inc.	Phase II
Veltuzumab	Humanized IgG1	High CDC	CLL, NHL	Immunomedics USA	Phase II
Ocaratuzumab	Fully human IgG1 κ	High ADCC	CLL, FL	Mentrik Biotech	Phase II
Ocrelizumab	Humanized IgG1	High ADCC, low CDC	MS	Biogen Inc./Roche Ltd./Genentech Inc.	Phase III

cancer has notwithstanding confined studies. However, the development of resistance to these treatments is yet an issue. Resistance can be welcomed based on the activation of the immune evasion mechanism, overexpression of alternative signaling pathways, and the generation of drug resistance. The new anti-CD20 mAb, the utilization of combined treatments, and the revelation of intracellular resistance mechanisms that can be focused on are all drives being required to resolve these issues. To foster a fruitful anti-CD20, it is vital to better describe and comprehend the jobs that antibodies play in the immune system. This research has featured the difficulties in such a manner. Generally, the utilization of anti-CD20 antibodies to treat cancer growth has progressed altogether, and investigation into ways of defeating protection from these medicines is yet continuous. Recent scenario reports that the production of therapeutic antibodies as a treatment against various diseases depends significantly on computational methodologies. These techniques are utilized to configure, investigate, and upgrade their qualities. The utilization of antibodies is helpful and relies on additional compelling strategies for manufacturing. Considering that they produce results more rapidly than the arduous trial strategies that are currently the best quality level in antibody advancement. Computational methodologies show a guarantee for facilitating the discipline. Rational antibody design approaches utilize now deep-rooted primary bioinformatics procedures including protein interactions, homology modeling, and protein interface examinations. Computational techniques with a pharmaceutical focus can likewise be used to assess the immunogenicity and biophysical qualities of antibodies. The introduction of next-generation sequencing (NGS) of B-cell receptor decisions is especially notable for the most recent decade. The approach of computational antibody procedures can possibly be utilized with novel antibody designs, for example, nanobodies, which have better biophysical properties naturally. By and large, computational antibody examination procedures have been created to the point that they might be utilized even more broadly in the advancement of therapeutics [53–58].

What do we now know about anti-CD20 and its importance?

Anti-CD20 mAbs are fruitful at bringing down cancer growth and upgrading clinical results in an assortment of B-cell malignancies, including NHL, CLL, and other hematological malignancies, as exhibited by clinical preliminaries and certifiable experience. The consumption of B lymphocytes communicating the CD20 antigen has been shown to be brought about by anti-CD20 mAb antibody-dependent cellular cytotoxicity (ADCC) and complement-dependent cytotoxicity (CDC). The deletion or downregulation of the CD20 antigen on growth cells or the initiation of intracellular flagging pathways that help cell endurance and expansion are two reasons that specific patients might experience resistance against CD20 mAbs. The innovation of cutting-edge enemy of CD20 mAbs and blend treatments that attention to a few flagging channels are two current drives to battle anti-CD20 mAb obstruction. By and large, the utilization of anti-CD20 mAbs has extraordinarily improved the restorative choices and guesses for patients with B-cell malignancies, and continuous exploration is proceeding to sharpen and upgrade their clinical application [59–64].

How do cancer cells become resistant to mAbs after receiving treatment?

While it is obvious that the mAbs contribution has a lot of experience in treating cancer patients and has shown the ability to control those types of cancer which could not be cured by traditional treatments. The therapeutic response of mAbs is in this manner obliged by mechanisms of resistance, which straightforwardly affect treatment efficacy whether they are given as single agents or in combination. There is an urgent need to more likely comprehend the reason why cancer cells are resistant to mAbs or how they become resistant to mAbs after treatment, and which strategies could be utilized to get around these resistance mechanisms in patients, as shown in Fig. 3. These kinds of resistance can be intrinsic or acquired. Here are the several ways in which cancer cells can become resistant to mAbs [65–70]:

- Alterations in the target protein: Cancer cells might go through hereditary changes that outcome in modifications of the target protein that the mAb is intended to tie to. These changes can lessen the limiting binding affinity of the mAb to the targeted protein, which diminishes the adequacy of the treatment.
- Activation of alternative pathways: Cancer cells can activate the alternative signaling pathways that bypass the target antigen and advance cell survival and multiplication.
- Modulation of the tumor microenvironment: The tumor microenvironment can assume a basic part in intervening protection from mAb treatments. These cancer cells can change

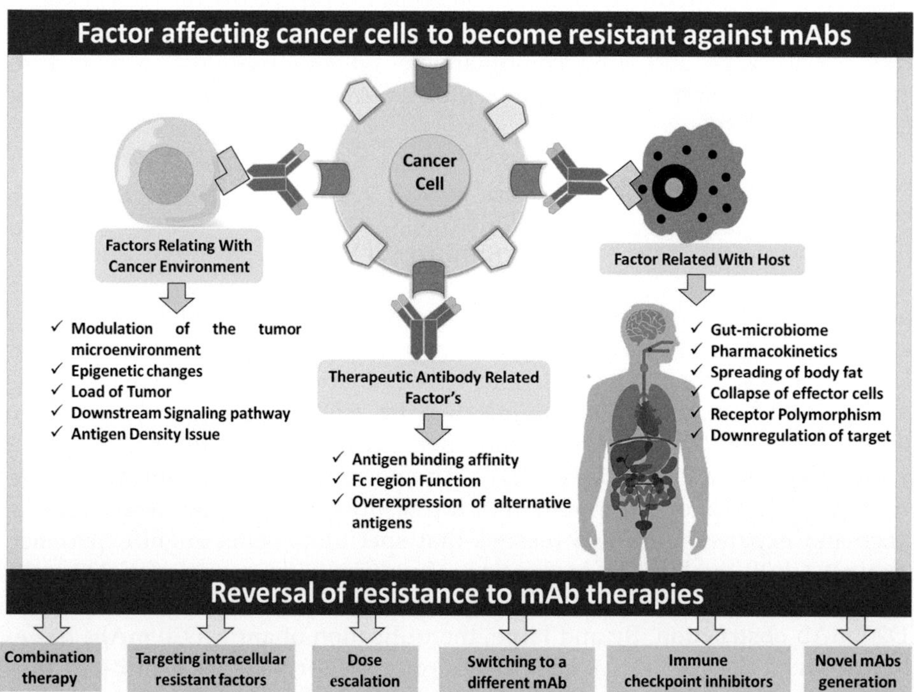

FIG. 3 Factor related to resistance against mAb, and their reversal.

the microenvironment to evade the immune system or may advance the growth of tumor, which can decrease the adequacy of mAb treatments that depend on immune activation.

- Epigenetic changes: Epigenetic changes, such as DNA methylation or histone modifications, can alter gene expression and promote the development of resistance to mAb therapies.
- Antibody clearance: The rapid clearance of therapeutic antibodies from the body can decrease their efficacy and may limit their duration of action. It can occur via various mechanisms, including antibody binding to circulating proteins such as complement or Fc receptors, or antibody-mediated clearance by the reticuloendothelial system.

Resistance issue with anti-CD20 therapies and potential strategies for reversing their effect

A class of immunotherapy drugs called anti-CD20 mAb is utilized to treat different B-cell malignancies, for example, NHL and CLL. Albeit these meds are often very helpful, some individuals in the end become impervious to the treatment. The following are some of the main causes of anti-CD20 mAb resistance [71–83]:

- Downregulation of CD20 expression—One of the primary ways that anti-CD20 mAb capability is by connecting to the CD20 antigen on the outer layer of B-cells, which brings about their downfall. Nonetheless, over the long haul, some disease cells may downregulate or lessen the expression of CD20, making them more resistant to the medicine's belongings.
- Altered glycosylation of CD20—The way CD20 is glycosylated can affect how well the anti-CD20 mAb works. Decreased efficacy might result from changes in the glycosylation pattern of CD20, which can make it more challenging for antibodies to append to the antigen.
- Genetic mutations—Genetic changes in the cancer cells might make them become resistant to anti-CD20 mAb. For instance, TP53 gene alterations have been connected to a decreased response to these medications.
- Immune system dysfunction—Anti-CD20 mAb assault cancer cells by enrolling immune cells to do as such, but immunological dysfunction can make this approach less productive. For example, the immunological function might be compromised in individuals with CLL, making it harder for the immune system to foster a strong reaction to the medicine.
- Overexpression of alternative antigens—Cancer cells periodically overexpress alternative antigens to compensate for lost CD20 expression. These alternative antigens might decrease the intensity of anti-CD20 mAb by acting as immune system targets.

Despite these mAbs' initial efficiency, some cancer cells may eventually develop resistance, decreasing the treatment's effectiveness. Anti-CD20 mAb resistance formation is a multistep process that may entail several mechanisms. To circumvent these mechanisms of resistance and enhance the long-term prognoses of patients with B-cell malignancies, researchers are attempting to develop novel therapeutics and therapy combinations. Numerous techniques have been examined to overcome resistance to anti-CD20 mAb treatments [71,84–90].

- Combination therapy: One strategy to reverse resistance to anti-CD20 mAb is to use combination therapy. This approach includes combining anti-CD20 mAbs with chemotherapy, radiation treatment, or different immunotherapies. This combination of therapies can prompt a more thorough attack on the malignant cells, decreasing the risk of resistance and improving the probability of progress. For instance, the combination of rituximab (an anti-CD20 mAb) and lenalidomide (an immunomodulatory drug) has been demonstrated to be powerful in patients with rituximab-refractory follicular lymphoma.
- Targeting intracellular resistant factors: One more technique for reversing resistance to anti-CD20 is to target intracellular resistant factors. This includes recognizing the molecular mechanisms that drive resistance and developing drugs that focus on these mechanisms. For instance, some cancers may develop resistance to anti-CD20 mAbs through changes in the CD20 antigen, making it less accessible to the mAbs. In these cases, drugs that focus on the intracellular mechanisms liable for these progressions could be utilized to overcome resistance.
- Dose escalation: Another methodology is to expand the dose of anti-CD20 mAb, which might overcome resistance at times. This system has been effective in patients with follicular lymphoma who develop resistance to standard dosages of rituximab.
- Switching to a different anti-CD20 mAb: If a patient develops resistance to anti-CD20 mAb, changing to an alternate one might be viable. For instance, patients with follicular lymphoma who developed resistance to rituximab have been shown to respond to ofatumumab.
- Modifying the Fc portion of the mAb: The Fc portion of a mAb assumes a vital role in its effector capabilities, including ADCC and CDC. Changing the Fc portion of an anti-CD20 mAb can upgrade its effector functions and overcome resistance. For instance, obinutuzumab has been demonstrated to be more powerful than rituximab in patients with chronic lymphocytic leukemia.
- Immune checkpoint inhibitors: Immune checkpoint inhibitors, such as anti-PD-1 and anti-CTLA-4 antibodies, can improve the antitumor immune response and reverse resistance to anti-CD20 mAb treatment. This approach has shown promising outcomes in preclinical studies and early-phase clinical trials.
- New anti-CD20 mAbs: Also, the advancement of new anti-CD20 mAbs with further developed strength and particularity could assist with overcoming resistance. For instance, specialists are investigating the utilization of bispecific antibodies, which are intended to combine the CD20 antigen and one more target on the cancer cell. These bispecific antibodies can possibly expand the power and particularity of anti-CD20 mAb treatments, diminishing the risk of resistance.

Reversing resistance to anti-CD20 mAb therapy requires a multidisciplinary approach, in which, further examination is expected to decide the ideal procedures for individual patients and to foster new treatments that can overcome resistance.

Computational techniques to design the therapeutic antibody

Recently, several proteomic techniques have been applied to the study of cancer to better comprehend and provide a more thorough interpretation. Computational strategies assume a pivotal role in the age of therapeutic antibodies against cancer. These strategies are utilized to design, predict, and enhance the properties of therapeutic antibodies [91–99].

- Design of therapeutic antibodies—Computational procedures are utilized to anticipate the construction of the antigen-binding site on antibodies, which is the region that ties to the target antigen on disease cells. This data is utilized to plan antibodies with explicit binding properties, such as high specificity and affinity for the target antigen.
- Predictive modeling—Predictive models are utilized to reproduce the communications between therapeutic antibodies and their target antigens. These models help to foresee the binding affinity, specificity, and adequacy of the antibodies in obstructing the target antigen. This data is used to advance the design of the antibodies and select the most encouraging candidate for further events.
- Optimization of antibody properties—Computational methods are useful to upgrade the properties of therapeutic antibodies, such as stability, half-life, and immunogenicity. This data is utilized to work on the pharmacokinetics and pharmacodynamics of the antibodies and make them more compelling as cancer medicines.
- Virtual screening—Virtual screening is a computational method used to recognize and focus on possible therapeutic antibodies from huge libraries of antibody sequences. This data is utilized to choose the most encouraging candidates for further development and testing.

Availability of antibody databases

The availability of datasets is a prerequisite for computational tools to assess and develop antibodies. There are numerous databases for therapeutic antibodies that offer thorough details on the traits and attributes of various antibody-based treatments. Many other sources can be categorized according to whether their information consists of either in the form of sequences/structures or experimental data; some of the most well-known therapeutic antibody databases are as follows [92,100–105]. Along with these, there are some examples of databases mentioned in Table 3.

TABLE 3 A list of antibodies databases available online.

Database name	Server link
International Immunogenetics Information System (IMGT)	http://www.imgt.org/
SAbDab-therapeutic antibodies	http://opig.stats.ox.ac.uk/webapps/sabdab-sabpred/Therapeutic.html
Antibodypedia	https://www.antibodypedia.com/
TABS (Therapeutic Antibody Database)	https://tabs.craic.com/users/sign_in
DrugBank database	https://go.drugbank.com/
Thera-SAbDab: the Therapeutic Structural Antibody Database	http://opig.stats.ox.ac.uk/webapps/therasabdab

International Immunogenetics Information System (IMGT)

An excellent integrated knowledge source in immunogenetics and immunoinformatic is the IMGT. The Montpellier, France-based Laboratoire d'ImmunoGénétique Moléculaire (LIGM) developed it in 1989. The naming of sequence analysis, and comparison of immunoglobulins (IG) T-cell receptors (TR) from human and other vertebrate species are provided by IMGT in a consistent manner. The system includes several databases, including the IMGT/LIGM-DB, IMGT/mAb-DB, IMGT/GENE-DB, IMGT/PRIMER-DB, IMGT/CLL-DB, IMGT/2Dstructure-DB, and IMGT/3Dstructure-DB, which contains a significant amount of nucleotide, protein sequences, gene, primer, and their associated information with 2D/3D structure, as well as the IMGT/Collier de which displays the amino acid sequences of the variable domains of IG and TR in a schematic representation. Greater decisions can be made while developing cutting-edge diagnostic tools and therapies with a better understanding of the molecular underpinnings of disease. Thus, IMGT offers tools for sequence comparison and alignment as well as for the prediction of functional traits such as antigen-binding affinity. To assist researchers in learning about immunogenetics and immunoinformatics, IMGT also offers a variety of educational resources in addition to its databases, tools, including tutorials and webinars. Numerous characteristics of IMGT make it a useful tool for researchers working in the areas of immunology and immunogenetics. The approach provides uniform terminology for IG and TR genes, alleles, and domains, making it easier to compare data from various studies. The data and tools from IMGT have aided in various studies in immunology, and it is now a widely utilized and regarded resource for the scientific community. Also, IMGT collaborates closely with NCBI, EBI, and DDBJ. Overall, IMGT is essential to the organization and analysis of immunogenetics data, and its thorough and standardized methodology has advanced our knowledge of the immune system and its function in both health and illness [101].

Antibodypedia (an examination of antibodies against the human proteome from the perspective of the chromosome)

It is crucial to confirm an antibody for the application and sample before utilizing it in an experiment. As a result, in 2008, Antibodypedia, an online database with 3900 antibodies and validation categories, was launched that offers thorough information about antibodies and their uses in research. The Human Protein Atlas project, an international effort to map the human proteome using various omics technologies, oversees keeping it up to date. To give users the required information and an overview of all antibodies available against a certain biomolecule of research interest, the database is well-organized in a gene-centric manner. A user-friendly and open-source tool called Antibodypedia has a sizable database of antibodies from various sources. The database contains comprehensive details about the antibodies, such as their targets, immunogen sequences, validation information, and suggested uses. Based on the inclusion of peer-reviewed antibody validation data that helps to assure the experimental design in a well manner, is one of the important characteristics of Antibodypedia. It allows users to choose an antibody with high dependability and repeatability of research findings. By allowing users to contribute both conclusive and inconclusive information to the portal, Antibodypedia encourages the user community to be engaged and share their findings. The data set gives a thorough rundown of the immune response, including the quantity of antibodies that are as of now accessible for each target protein and the level of quality antibodies. To find top-notch antibodies for a range of applications, including Western blotting, flow cytometry, and immune histochemistry, researchers often use Antibodypedia. The database is also beneficial for antibody suppliers, who may use the data to identify gaps in the market and produce novel products to meet the prospects of the scientific community. The database is an important element for scientists because it is frequently updated with new data and features [102].

TABS (Therapeutic Antibody Database)

An exhaustive online resource that offers details on therapeutic antibodies is called TABS. It includes specific details of the chemical composition, mode of action, and clinical utilization of both authorized as well as scrutinized therapeutic antibodies. A wide assortment of diseases, including cancer, immune system problems, irresistible illnesses, and inflammatory issues, are focused on the antibodies in the database. Each entry for an antibody in the data set accompanies complete insights about the therapeutic target, clinical sign, and phase of research. This data set's consideration of information on the development of therapeutic antibodies is one of its unique viewpoints. For drug designers, realizing this data is critical because the assembling system affects the consistency and nature of the completed item. For investors and medication developers who need to assess the business feasibility of a specific substance, it contains data about the patent status of helpful antibodies. In general, it is a valuable device for academicians, experts, and the pharma industry keen on these antibodies and their clinical applications. It also offers current information regarding the pharmacological and chemical qualities of therapeutic antibodies, making them a significant asset for clinical examination and medication improvement [92,103].

DrugBank

The broad web data set DrugBank offers subtleties on prescriptions and therapeutic targets. The data set remembers careful subtleties for the pharmacology, clinical applications, and chemical composition of drugs, including therapeutic antibodies. It records remedial antibodies as per their medication target, which can be the two proteins and different atoms embroiled in disease pathways. Every therapeutic immune response in the data set has a unique ID number, alongside thorough subtleties on its chemical makeup, method of activity, and clinical application. Its consideration of information on the pharmacokinetics and pharmacodynamics of therapeutic antibodies is one of its standout attributes. To ensure that the treatment is both protected and successful for the objective patient populace, this data is critical for both the advancement of new medications and their clinical application. DrugBank offers different information with respect to pharmacological targets and disease pathways notwithstanding data about unambiguous remedial antibodies. Specialists that are attempting to track down creative therapeutic targets and foster new meds will find this information advantageous. Analysts, doctors, and medication engineers who are keen on therapeutic antibodies and their clinical use can benefit significantly from the therapeutics antibodies in the DrugBank database. It also offers exhaustive and current information with respect to the pharmacological and chemical qualities of helpful antibodies, making it a significant asset for clinical exploration and medication improvement [104].

Thera-SAbDab: The Therapeutic Structural Antibody Database

Currently, it is possible to see and download specific bound and unbound antibody structures from various antibody data sources. Additionally, most databases provide extra metadata for their therapeutic entries, including target specificity, firms involved in the development, clinical trial status, and other names. However, the structural coverage of treatments that has been published is quite limited, and bispecific immunotherapeutics have also received no reports of known structural information. To address these issues, Thera-SAbDab database was created by researchers at the University of Toronto it is a comprehensive database of therapeutic antibodies and contains detailed information about the structures including functions of a wide range of therapeutic antibodies standards by the WHO, that locates structures precise or nearly perfect variable domain sequence matches in the Structural Antibody Database (SAbDab). It is freely available to the scientific community that offers a plethora of knowledge about therapeutic antibodies, including details on their target antigens, therapeutic uses, the status of clinical trials, and structural characteristics. The database furthermore contains comprehensive data on the antigen-binding domains of antibodies, as well as details on their effector activities and structural stability. It can be searched by the name of a therapeutic, by a set of metadata, or by a variable domain sequence, which returns all treatments that fall inside a given sequence identity. These sequences can be downloaded along with the necessary metadata. Thera-interactive SAbDab's visualization tool, which enables users to examine the structures of antibodies and their binding to antigens, is one of its primary advantages. The database also contains data on antigen epitopes, which is essential for the creation of novel treatments that target certain areas of disease-related proteins. Overall, it is a package of valuable tools for the scientific community which mainly offers a vast and easily searchable library of therapeutic antibodies that can be utilized to increase our knowledge of the immune system and its function [105].

Advantages and disadvantages of therapeutic antibodies

MAbs are versatile molecules with significant purposes in the medical field. Due to their steadiness, tolerance, usefulness, and capacity to be designed to improve different advantageous attributes, such as diminished immunogenicity, longer half-lives, higher affinities, and better effector capabilities, mAbs are engaging as remedial up-and-comers notwithstanding their utilization in symptomatic applications. MAbs have thrived as a class of physiologically dynamic mixtures for treatments from the most recent couple of many years. Utilizing therapeutic antibodies has advantages and disadvantages regardless of their viability in treating an assortment of diseases. Nevertheless, the proceeded with advancement of these therapies holds a guarantee for working on the prognosis for patients with cancer and other diseases. There are some advantages and disadvantages as follows [9,53,74–77,106–111].

Advantages

- The way that therapeutic antibodies offer an engaged sort of treatment is one of their key advantages. Unlike chemotherapy and radiation therapy in both healthy and infected cells, therapeutic antibodies are produced to explicitly target and bind to explicit antigens on the outer member of only infected cells, decreasing the risk of off-target impacts.
- Certain types of cancer have been shown to answer very well to these therapeutic antibodies, especially when combined with different treatments such as immunotherapy. Therapeutic antibodies regularly produce long-lasting effects and raise the overall guess for infected patients.
- Therapeutic antibodies are less harmful than chemotherapy and radiation therapy. This is on the grounds that they have a lesser effect on healthy cells such as targeted disease cells.
- It is more compelling than different medications at diminishing inflammation. Additionally, they have strong purity and an infinite capacity with respect to production.

Disadvantages

- The cost of therapeutic antibodies is one of their key downsides. These treatments can be expensive, especially for patients who require extended treatment. A few patients might encounter access challenges subsequently, which might restrict their ability to seek important treatment.
- It can require years and millions of dollars to develop therapeutic antibodies, which makes it challenging to acquaint novel medicines with the market rapidly.
- One more disadvantage of therapeutic antibodies is that a cancer cell may ultimately develop resistance to them. Subsequently, the viability of the treatment might be decreased, and more risky cancer cells may manifest.

Possible side effects

Because of their distinct specificity, toleration, and lengthy half-life, antibodies are the best therapeutic agents. Antibody treatments are now legal against cancer, autoimmune infections, and other infectious diseases. To develop efficient antibody-based therapeutics and to combine medications with chemotherapy or hormone therapy, a physiologic understanding of the ailment states is needed. Because mAb can be directly injected intravenously, in which allergic responses might occasionally occur. The exact mAb being administered, and its intended target largely determines any side effects. The issues occur more frequently when it delivers to the patient for the first time. High temperature, weakness, chills, changes in blood pressure, exhaustion, muscle aches, shortness of breath, headaches, skin rashes, a slow or rapid heartbeat, diarrhea, etc. are examples of possible adverse effects. However, it is unknown whether the frequency and seriousness of these adverse effects are influenced by the pharmacological characteristics of the antibodies [112–115]. For instance:

- Rituximab and Ofatumumab are primarily used to treat cancers such as NHL, mature B-cell acute leukemia (B-AL), and CLL, respectively. These medications may have side

effects such as infusion, which are mild and temporary, postural hypotension, allergies, blurred vision, facial swelling, a warm sensation, lower back or side pain, nausea, or vomiting [116,117].
- Avastin (bevacizumab) targets the VEGF protein, which can result in adverse effects including increased blood pressure, bleeding, inadequate wound healing, blood clots, and kidney damage [118–120].
- Erbitux (cetuximab) targets the EGFR protein, which can result in severe rashes [121,122].

Current limitations with production cost

Therapeutic antibody manufacture and their use are dependent on various limitations, including their significant expense and certain restricted viability. The significant expense of manufacturing is one of the principal downsides of therapeutic antibodies. A single antibody particle can cost countless dollars to develop and deliver, due to the extreme expense, patients, and medical services suppliers much of the time cannot manage the cost of these medicines. This is on the grounds that developing antibodies in high amounts requires work escalated and costly assembling techniques, for example, the utilization of cell lines and bioreactors, purging strategies, as well as quality control checks. Therapeutic antibodies may not work for all patients, which is another downside. Although antibodies are extremely specific to their objective and may not find success for different patients because of hereditary or different irregularities. It limits the use of certain antibodies to specific patient gatherings or disease subtypes. Other likely adverse consequences of therapeutic antibodies incorporate infusion reactions, hypersensitivity, or immunogenicity. Certain antibodies will most likely be unable to be utilized due to these incidental effects, or they might require cautious oversight while getting treatment. Specialists and developers are investigating new advancements and strategies to limit the expense of producing antibodies and to build their viability as well as well-being with an end goal to get past these imperatives. The improvement of new antibody-based drugs, for example, bispecific antibodies and antibody-drug conjugates, is being finished to build the power and selectivity of existing antibody-based drugs. For example, improvements in genetic engineering and cell line development have delivered more compelling and adaptable production methods. Therapeutic antibodies, in conclusion, are an important class of drugs that have reformed the treatment of various diseases, yet their high development expenses and cutoff points as far as viability and well-being keep on being critical deterrents to their expanded utilization. To address these issues and increase the accessibility and affordability of antibody-based therapeutics, further research and innovation are required [106–111,123–126].

Future

Therapeutic antibodies have revolutionized the treatment of different diseases and have become one of the quickest-developing classes of biologics. Currently, these therapies have shown extraordinary commitment to treating cancer and have worked on the anticipation for various patients. The future of therapeutic antibody treatments holds a lot of commitment, as researchers keep on investigating better approaches to upgrade and work on these medicines. Presently, most therapeutic antibodies focus on a single protein or receptor on a cell surface. However, as to how we might interpret the biological mechanism of diseases and their cell signaling pathways, there is potential to at the same time develop antibodies that focus on numerous proteins or pathways. This could prompt more successful therapies for complex diseases such as cancer. One more area of advancement is the utilization of new innovations to work on the production and delivery of therapeutic antibodies. One arising innovation is the utilization of gene editing to produce antibodies straightforwardly in cells, which could build the effectiveness and adaptability of the production cycle. Furthermore, advances in drug delivery systems, for example, nanoparticles could empower more exact focusing on and further developing viability of therapeutic antibodies. With the rising accessibility of patient information and advances in innovations, for example, genomics, it might be feasible to develop antibodies that are tailored to individual patients based on their genetic makeup or disease characteristics. There are a few likely progressions of anti-CD20 response that holds a lot of commitment, as scientists keep on investigating better approaches to upgrade and work on these medicines [127–130].

- Combination therapy: Anti-CD20 antibody treatments are probably going to be utilized in combination with different therapies, such as chemotherapy, radiation treatment, and immunotherapy. This approach has been demonstrated to be exceptionally successful in treating cancer and improving the overall prognosis for patients [84].
- Optimization of antibodies: Research is continuous to streamline anti-CD20 antibodies, making them more viable and decreasing their true capacity for side effects. This might include the advancement of new antibodies with further developed particularity or the utilization of existing antibodies in new ways [131].
- Personalized therapy: There is additional potential for the improvement of personalized therapeutic antibodies. It might include the utilization of prescient biomarkers to decide the best treatment approach for every patient and the improvement of new, more designated medicines with less incidental effects [132–134].

At long last, the use of therapeutic antibodies becomes more widespread, there will be a continued focus on improving the safety and cost-effectiveness of these medications. This could include the advancement of more vigorous security profiles for new antibodies, as well as endeavors to decrease the general expense of creation and dissemination. In general, the future of therapeutic antibodies looks encouraging, with numerous possible headways and enhancements for the skyline. Therapeutic antibodies will probably assume an undeniably significant part in the treatment of many diseases.

Predictive biomarkers—A therapeutic response against cancer

Researchers are developing new strategies and technologies to combat these resistance mechanisms, such as the development of bispecific antibodies, combination therapy, and the use of novel targets. These approaches are designed to enhance the efficacy and specificity of therapeutic antibodies as well as circumvent resistance mechanisms. Furthermore, ongoing research aims to comprehend the underlying mechanisms of resistance and find biomarkers that might forecast treatment response and direct the development of more efficient therapies. The development and refinement of therapeutic antibodies for the treatment of cancer require the use of predictive biomarkers as key tools. Biomarkers are quantifiable traits that can reveal the existence, severity, or course of a disease as well as the propensity for a therapeutic response. The following list of putative biomarkers for predicting therapy response and patients' prognosis in cancer [135–142].

- Tumor biomarker—Tumor biomarkers are substances that can be detected in blood, urine, or tissue samples and are mainly produced by tumor cells. Various distinct tumor markers have been recognized and are being utilized in clinical processes. Some are associated with a single type of cancer, whereas others are with multiple types. For instance, HER2 for breast cancer, CA 19-9 for pancreatic cancer, and PSA for prostate cancer as well as CA125 for lung cancer. These can be utilized to track the effectiveness of treatment, find cancer recurrence, and forecast the prognosis.
- Genetic biomarker—These are mutations or alterations in DNA sequence that can be detected in tumor cells associated with susceptibility to disease. They can contribute to cancer pathogenesis, progression, and response to therapy. Ex. BRAF mutations in melanoma, EGFR mutations in lung cancer, and KRAS mutations in colon cancer.
- Immune biomarker—These are markers of immune activity that can be recognized in blood or tissue samples. For instance, PD-L1 expression and tumor-infiltrating lymphocytes (TILs). Immune biomarkers can be used to anticipate the response to immunotherapy, which works by activating the immune system to attack cancer cells.
- Imaging biomarker—An imaging biomarker is the feature of an image related to a patient's diagnosis. These are characteristics of tumors that can be detected by using imaging techniques for example MRI, CT, or PET scans. Examples mainly include tumor size, shape, and metabolic activity. Imaging biomarkers can be used to monitor treatment response and detect recurrence.

Translational research fills the gap between the growing understanding of the characteristics of biomarkers linked to cancer or noncancerous infections and the clinical outcomes of such patients in the current era of precision medicine. It is crucial that biomarkers undergo thorough review, including analytical validation, clinical validation, and appraisal of clinical utility, prior to being included in normal clinical care because of the crucial role they play at all stages of disease.

Conclusions

A growing awareness of the numerous immunological functions that antibodies perform over the past 35 years has sparked the development of innovative and varied targeted techniques for the treatment of human diseases. Therapeutic antibodies are the best therapeutic agents because of their distinct selectivity, tolerability, and long half-life. Effective antibody-based therapeutics must consider the physiology of certain disease states, and this knowledge must be paired with biophysical considerations for the design and production of these complex proteins. The recent recognition of mAb therapy's efficacy has prompted serious consideration of novel therapeutic combinations that combine immunotherapy and conventional chemotherapy to offer a combined strategy that may improve therapeutic responsiveness while minimizing adverse side effects. These antibodies are increasingly demonstrating their ability to prolong overall survival, ensure disease-free survival, and slow the course of certain cancers. MAb therapy stands out from other forms of treatment due to its complex mode of action and target specificity, which also emphasizes the capacity of antibodies to produce potent antitumor effects with a minimum amount of side effects. Even though nanobodies and other antibody types have been created for this use, mAb has so far undergone an extraordinary metamorphosis from a useful scientific tool to a valuable medicine for human therapies. In conclusion, anti-CD20 antibody therapeutics have a promising future as long as scientists keep finding innovative ways to enhance and advance them. Since, most of the new clinical approvals for biotherapeutics are still for therapeutics antibodies, which continue to rule the pharmaceutical market. The bulk of molecules created to date have been used in surface display and animal vaccination technologies, and current strategies for bringing these agents to the market have remained experimentally oriented. The development of computational antibody design approaches is facilitated by the growth of antibody-specific data in the public repository, which leads to a greater uptake as part of standard pharmaceutical discovery processes. In addition, the current scenario uses the enormous amount of data produced by NGS technology which makes it easier to derive more trustworthy profiles to direct the development of antibody therapeutics. Existing computational methods and knowledge for designing antibodies may be useful for developing biotherapeutic agents such as antibodies, including nanobodies. Nevertheless, rigorous benchmarking will still be required to ascertain if the development of nanobodies may benefit from computational antibody methods in their current form or whether they need to be modified accordingly, despite the similarities between antibodies and nanobodies. Because it may be difficult to point out that computational technologies will completely replace the discovery process. In fact, their main contribution will still be in the form of time and money-saving strategies for directing experimental approaches. Antibody-specific benchmarking challenges will highlight the drawbacks and benefits of each approach and allow for the concentrated improvement of each approach, particularly its utility in the therapeutic development process. By taking part in data sharing and benchmarking initiatives, various research groups active in the discovery and development of antibody treatments have a unique potential to accelerate the development of computational antibody approaches. Faster and more precise computational methods are expected to be even more tightly incorporated into therapeutic development procedures as the value of antibodies as therapies develop, speeding up the delivery of new medications to patients. In the upcoming years, there will probably be a lot of attention paid to the use of combination therapy, antibody optimization, tailored therapy, and the expansion to other tumors. The prognosis for people with cancer and other disorders may be improved because of these discoveries.

Acknowledgments

SKS and UP thankfully acknowledge the DST-PURSE 2nd Phase Programme grant [No. SR/PURSE Phase 2/38 (G); DST-FIST Grant [(SR/FST/LSI—667/2016)]; MHRD RUSA-Phase 2.0 grant sanctioned vide Letter no. [F.24-51/2014-U, Policy (TN Multi-Gen), Department of Education, Govt of India]; Tamil Nadu State Council for Higher Education (TANSCHE) under [No. AU: S.O. (P&D): TANSCHE Projects: 117/ 202, File No. RGP/2019-20/ALU/

HECP-0048]; DBT-BIC, New Delhi, under Grant/Award [No. BT/PR40154/BTIS/137/ 34/2021, dated 31.12.2021]; and DBT-NNP Project, New Delhi, under Grant/Award [No. BT/PR40156/BTIS/54/2023 dated 06.02.2023] for providing the research grant and infrastructure facilities in the lab. CS thankfully acknowledges Saveetha University for providing the infrastructure facilities to perform this work. MAK thankfully acknowledges the Alagappa University for providing the RUSA 2.0 Senior Research Fellowship [Alu/RUSA/SRF-Bioinformatics/4156/2022 dated 30.11.2022].

References

[1] Siegel RL, Miller KD, Fuchs HE, Jemal A. Cancer statistics, 2022. CA Cancer J Clin 2022;72(1):7–33.

[2] Hassanpour SH, Dehghani M. Review of cancer from perspective of molecular. J Cancer Res Pract 2017;4 (4):127–9.

[3] Meacham CE, Morrison SJ. Tumour heterogeneity and cancer cell plasticity. Nature 2013;501(7467):328–37.

[4] Fisher R, Pusztai L, Swanton C. Cancer heterogeneity: implications for targeted therapeutics. Br J Cancer 2013;108(3):479–85.

[5] Nelson AL, Dhimolea E, Reichert JM. Development trends for human monoclonal antibody therapeutics. Nat Rev Drug Discov 2010;9(10):767–74.

[6] Casan JM, Wong J, Northcott MJ, Opat S. Anti-CD20 monoclonal antibodies: reviewing a revolution. Hum Vaccin Immunother 2018;14(12):2820–41.

[7] Suzuki M, Kato C, Kato A. Therapeutic antibodies: their mechanisms of action and the pathological findings they induce in toxicity studies. J Toxicol Pathol 2015;28(3):133–9.

[8] Makowski EK, Kinnunen PC, Huang J, Wu L, Smith MD, Wang T, Desai AA, Streu CN, Zhang Y, Zupancic JM, Schardt JS. Co-optimization of therapeutic antibody affinity and specificity using machine learning models that generalize to novel mutational space. Nat Commun 2022;13(1):3788.

[9] Chames P, Van Regenmortel M, Weiss E, Baty D. Therapeutic antibodies: successes, limitations and hopes for the future. Br J Pharmacol 2009;157(2):220–33.

[10] Oldham RK, Dillman RO. Monoclonal antibodies in cancer therapy: 25 years of progress. J Clin Oncol Off J Am Soc Clin Oncol 2008;26(11):1774–7.

[11] Liu L, Chen J. Therapeutic antibodies for precise cancer immunotherapy: current and future perspectives. Med Rev 2023;2:555–69.

[12] Lu RM, Hwang YC, Liu IJ, Lee CC, Tsai HZ, Li HJ, Wu HC. Development of therapeutic antibodies for the treatment of diseases. J Biomed Sci 2020;27(1):1–30.

[13] Milstein C, Kohler G. Continuous cultures of fused cells secreting antibody of predefined specificity. Nature 1975;256(5517):495–7.

[14] Kaplon H, Reichert JM. Antibodies to watch in 2019. MAbs 2019;11(2):219–38.

[15] The Antibody Society. Approved antibodies., 2019, https://www.antibodysociety.org/. [Accessed 15 July 2019].

[16] Liu JK. The history of monoclonal antibody development–progress, remaining challenges and future innovations. Ann Med Surg 2014;3(4):113–6.

[17] Sodoyer R. The history of therapeutic monoclonal antibodies. In: Biosimilars of monoclonal antibodies: a practical guide to manufacturing, preclinical, and clinical development, 14. Wiley; 2016. p. 1–62.

[18] Rees A. Antibodies: a history of their discovery and properties. In: Introduction to antibody engineering. Springer; 2021. p. 5–39.

[19] Herman GA, O'Brien MP, Forleo-Neto E, Sarkar N, Isa F, Hou P, Chan KC, Bar KJ, Barnabas RV, Barouch DH, Cohen MS. Efficacy, and safety of a single dose of casirivimab and imdevimab for the prevention of COVID-19 over an 8-month period: a randomised, double-blind, placebo-controlled trial. Lancet Infect Dis 2022;22 (10):1444–54.

[20] Hentzien M, Autran B, Piroth L, Yazdanpanah Y, Calmy A. A monoclonal antibody stands out against omicron subvariants: a call to action for a wider access to bebtelovimab. Lancet Infect Dis 2022;22(9):1278.

[21] The Antibody Society. Therapeutic monoclonal antibodies approved or in review in the EU or US, www.antibodysociety.org/resources/approved-antibodies.

[22] Sun Y, Xu J. Emerging antibodies in cancer therapy. Adv NanoBiomed Res 2023;3(1):2200083.

[23] Briney B, Inderbitzin A, Joyce C, Burton DR. Commonality despite exceptional diversity in the baseline human antibody repertoire. Nature 2019;566(7744):393–7.

[24] Bannas P, Hambach J, Koch-Nolte F. Nanobodies and nanobody-based human heavy chain antibodies as antitumor therapeutics. Front Immunol 2017;8:1603.
[25] Chothia C, Lesk AM. Canonical structures for the hypervariable regions of immunoglobulins. J Mol Biol 1987;196 (4):901–17.
[26] Chiu ML, Goulet DR, Teplyakov A, Gilliland GL. Antibody structure and function: the basis for engineering therapeutics. Antibodies 2019;8(4):55.
[27] Redman JM, Hill EM, AlDeghaither D, Weiner LM. Mechanisms of action of therapeutic antibodies for cancer. Mol Immunol 2015;67(2):28–45.
[28] Chames P, Baty D. Antibody engineering and its applications in tumor targeting and intracellular immunization. FEMS Microbiol Lett 2000;189(1):1–8.
[29] Winter G, Milstein C. Man-made antibodies. Nature 1991;349(6307):293–9.
[30] Almagro JC, Daniels-Wells TR, Perez-Tapia SM, Penichet ML. Progress and challenges in the design and clinical development of antibodies for cancer therapy. Front Immunol 2018;8:1751.
[31] Jarchum I. To humans, and beyond! Nat Immunol 2016;17(Suppl 1):S16.
[32] Mallbris L, Davies J, Glasebrook A, Tang Y, Glaesner W, Nickoloff BJ. Molecular insights into fully human and humanized monoclonal antibodies: what are the differences and should dermatologists care? J Clin Aesthet Dermatol 2016;9(7):13.
[33] Vaswani SK, Hamilton RG. Humanized antibodies as potential therapeutic drugs. Ann Allergy Asthma Immunol 1998;81(2):105–19.
[34] Pierpont TM, Limper CB, Richards KL. Past, present, and future of rituximab—the world's first oncology monoclonal antibody therapy. Front Oncol 2018;8:163.
[35] Cragg MS, Walshe CA, Ivanov AO, Glennie MJ. The biology of CD20 and its potential as a target for mAb therapy. Curr Dir Autoimmun 2005;8:140–74.
[36] Oldham RJ, Cleary KL, Cragg MS. CD20 and its antibodies: past, present, and future. Onco Therapeutics 2014;5 (1–2):7–23.
[37] Gürcan HM, Keskin DB, Stern JN, Nitzberg MA, Shekhani H, Ahmed AR. A review of the current use of rituximab in autoimmune diseases. Int Immunopharmacol 2009;9(1):10–25.
[38] Ishibashi K, Suzuki M, Sasaki S, Imai M. Identification of a new multigene four-transmembrane family (MS4A) related to CD20, HTm4 and β subunit of the high-affinity IgE receptor. Gene 2001;264(1):87–93.
[39] Kuijpers TW, Bende RJ, Baars PA, Grummels A, Derks IA, Dolman KM, Beaumont T, Tedder TF, van Noesel CJ, Eldering E, van Lier RA. CD20 deficiency in humans results in impaired T cell-independent antibody responses. J Clin Invest 2010;120(1):214–22.
[40] Kimby E. Tolerability and safety of rituximab (MabThera®). Cancer Treat Rev 2005;31(6):456–73.
[41] Feugier P. A review of rituximab, the first anti-CD20 monoclonal antibody used in the treatment of B non-Hodgkin's lymphomas. Future Oncol 2015;11(9):1327–42.
[42] Marcus R, Davies A, Ando K, Klapper W, Opat S, Owen C, Phillips E, Sangha R, Schlag R, Seymour JF, Townsend W. Obinutuzumab for the first-line treatment of follicular lymphoma. N Engl J Med 2017;377 (14):1331–44.
[43] Keating MJ, Dritselis A, Yasothan U, Kirkpatrick P. Ofatumumab. Nat Rev Drug Discov 2010;9(2):101–2
[44] Rizzieri D. Zevalin®(ibritumomab tiuxetan): after more than a decade of treatment experience, what have we learned? Crit Rev Oncol Hematol 2016;105:5–17.
[45] Syed YY. Ocrelizumab: a review in multiple sclerosis. CNS Drugs 2018;32(9):883–90.
[46] Ganjoo KN, de Vos S, Pohlman BL, Flinn IW, Forero-Torres A, Enas NH, Cronier DM, Dang NH, Foon KA, Carpenter SP, Slapak CA. Phase 1/2 study of ocaratuzumab, an Fc-engineered humanized anti-CD20 monoclonal antibody, in low-affinity FcγRIIIa patients with previously treated follicular lymphoma. Leuk Lymphoma 2015;56(1):42–8.
[47] Goldenberg DM, Morschhauser F, Wegener WA. Veltuzumab (humanized anti-CD20 monoclonal antibody): characterization, current clinical results, and future prospects. Leuk Lymphoma 2010;51(5):747–55.
[48] Babiker HM, Glode AE, Cooke LS, Mahadevan D. Ublituximab for the treatment of CD20 positive B-cell malignancies. Expert Opin Investig Drugs 2018;27(4):407–12.
[49] Srinivasan A, Mukherji SK. Tositumomab and iodine I 131 tositumomab (Bexaar). Am J Neuroradiol 2011;32 (4):637–8.
[50] Flores-Ortiz LF, Campos-García VR, Perdomo-Abúndez FC, Pérez NO, Medina-Rivero E. Physicochemical properties of rituximab. J Liq Chromatogr Relat Technol 2014;37(10):1438–52.

[51] Cang S, Mukhi N, Wang K, Liu D. Novel CD20 monoclonal antibodies for lymphoma therapy. J Hematol Oncol 2012;5(1):1–9.
[52] Rubbert-Roth A. TRU-015, a fusion protein derived from an anti-CD20 antibody, for the treatment of rheumatoid arthritis. Curr Opin Mol Ther 2010;12(1):115–23.
[53] Payandeh Z, Bahrami AA, Hoseinpoor R, Mortazavi Y, Rajabibazl M, Rahimpour A, Taromchi AH, Khalil S. The applications of anti-CD20 antibodies to treat various B cells disorders. Biomed Pharmacother 2019;109:2415–26.
[54] Lim SH, Beers SA, French RR, Johnson PW, Glennie MJ, Cragg MS. Anti-CD20 monoclonal antibodies: historical and future perspectives. Haematologica 2010;95(1):135.
[55] Chen Z, Kankala RK, Yang Z, Li W, Xie S, Li H, Chen AZ, Zou L. Antibody-based drug delivery systems for cancer therapy: mechanisms, challenges, and prospects. Theranostics 2022;12(8):3719.
[56] Prabakaran P, Glanville J, Ippolito GC. Next-generation sequencing of human antibody repertoires for exploring B-cell landscape, antibody discovery and vaccine development. Front Immunol 2020;11:1344.
[57] Xu Z, Ismanto HS, Zhou H, Saputri DS, Sugihara F, Standley DM. Advances in antibody discovery from human BCR repertoires. Front Bioinform 2022;2, 1044975.
[58] Młokosiewicz J, Deszyński P, Wilman W, Jaszczyszyn I, Ganesan R, Kovaltsuk A, Leem J, Galson JD, Krawczyk K. AbDiver: a tool to explore the natural antibody landscape to aid therapeutic design. Bioinformatics 2022;38 (9):2628–30.
[59] Marshall MJ, Stopforth RJ, Cragg MS. Therapeutic antibodies: what have we learnt from targeting CD20 and where are we going? Front Immunol 2017;8:1245.
[60] Cree BA. All anti-CD20 monoclonal antibodies have similar efficacy and safety risks: yes. Mult Scler J 2022;28 (12):1843–4.
[61] Degn SE, Thiel S. Humoral pattern recognition and the complement system. Scand J Immunol 2013;78(2):181–93.
[62] Merle NS, Church SE, Fremeaux-Bacchi V, Roumenina LT. Complement system part I–molecular mechanisms of activation and regulation. Front Immunol 2015;6:262.
[63] Wang SY, Weiner G. Complement and cellular cytotoxicity in antibody therapy of cancer. Expert Opin Biol Ther 2008;8(6):759–68.
[64] Teeling JL, French RR, Cragg MS, van den Brakel J, Pluyter M, Huang H, Chan C, Parren PW, Hack CE, Dechant M, Valerius T. Characterization of new human CD20 monoclonal antibodies with potent cytolytic activity against non-Hodgkin lymphomas. Blood 2004;104(6):1793–800.
[65] Labrie M, Brugge JS, Mills GB, Zervantonakis IK. Therapy resistance: opportunities created by adaptive responses to targeted therapies in cancer. Nat Rev Cancer 2022;22(6):323–39.
[66] Wu P, Gao W, Su M, Nice EC, Zhang W, Lin J, Xie N. Adaptive mechanisms of tumor therapy resistance driven by tumor microenvironment. Front Cell Dev Biol 2021;9, 641469.
[67] Dagogo-Jack I, Shaw AT. Tumour heterogeneity and resistance to cancer therapies. Nat Rev Clin Oncol 2018;15 (2):81–94.
[68] Hayashi T, Konishi I. Correlation of anti-tumour drug resistance with epigenetic regulation. Br J Cancer 2021;124 (4):681–2.
[69] von Manstein V, Min Yang C, Richter D, Delis N, Vafaizadeh V, Groner B. Resistance of cancer cells to targeted therapies through the activation of compensating signaling loops. Curr Signal Transduction Ther 2013;8(3):193–202.
[70] Emran TB, Shahriar A, Mahmud AR, Rahman T, Abir MH, Faijanur-Rob-Siddiquee M, Ahmed H, Rahman N, Nainu F, Wahyudin E, Mitra S. Multidrug resistance in cancer: understanding molecular mechanisms, immunoprevention, and therapeutic approaches. Front Oncol 2022;23:2581.
[71] Navasardyan I, Bonavida B. Reversal of resistance to anti-CD20 antibody therapies: targeting intracellular resistant factors. Crit Rev Oncog 2020;25(3):275–90.
[72] Chao MP. Treatment challenges in the management of relapsed or refractory non-Hodgkin's lymphoma—novel and emerging therapies. Cancer Manage Res 2013;23:251–69.
[73] Perez-Callejo D, Gonzalez-Rincon J, Sanchez A, Provencio M, Sanchez-Beato M. Action and resistance of monoclonal CD20 antibodies therapy in B-cell non-Hodgkin lymphomas. Cancer Treat Rev 2015;41(8):680–9.
[74] Hiraga J, Tomita A, Sugimoto T, Shimada K, Ito M, Nakamura S, Kiyoi H, Kinoshita T, Naoe T. Down-regulation of CD20 expression in B-cell lymphoma cells after treatment with rituximab-containing combination chemotherapies: its prevalence and clinical significance. Blood 2009;113(20):4885–93.
[75] Pavlasova G, Mraz M. The regulation and function of CD20: an "enigma" of B-cell biology and targeted therapy. Haematologica 2020;105(6):1494.

[76] Michot JM, Buet-Elfassy A, Annereau M, Lazarovici J, Danu A, Sarkozy C, Chahine C, Bigenwald C, Bosq J, Rossignol J, Romano-Martin P. Clinical significance of the loss of CD20 antigen on tumor cells in patients with relapsed or refractory follicular lymphoma. Cancer Drug Resist 2021;4(3):710.

[77] Hollander N, Haimovich J. Altered N-linked glycosylation in follicular lymphoma and chronic lymphocytic leukemia: involvement in pathogenesis and potential therapeutic targeting. Front Immunol 2017;8:912.

[78] Tomita A. Genetic and epigenetic modulation of CD20 expression in B-cell malignancies: molecular mechanisms and significance to rituximab resistance. J Clin Exp Hematop 2016;56(2):89–99.

[79] Johnson NA, Leach S, Woolcock B, deLeeuw RJ, Bashashati A, Sehn LH, Connors JM, Chhanabhai M, Brooks-Wilson A, Gascoyne RD. CD20 mutations involving the rituximab epitope are rare in diffuse large B-cell lymphomas and are not a significant cause of R-CHOP failure. Haematologica 2009;94(3):423.

[80] Reslan L, Dalle S, Dumontet C. Understanding and circumventing resistance to anticancer monoclonal antibodies. MAbs 2009;1(3):222–9.

[81] Aldeghaither DS, Zahavi DJ, Murray JC, Fertig EJ, Graham GT, Zhang YW, O'Connell A, Ma J, Jablonski SA, Weiner LM. A mechanism of resistance to antibody-targeted immune attack. Cancer Immunol Res 2019;7 (2):230–43.

[82] Smith CC, Selitsky SR, Chai S, Armistead PM, Vincent BG, Serody JS. Alternative tumour-specific antigens. Nat Rev Cancer 2019;19(8):465–78.

[83] Bernard A, Boidot R, Végran F. Alternative splicing in cancer and immune cells. Cancers 2022;14(7):1726.

[84] Mokhtari RB, Homayouni TS, Baluch N, Morgatskaya E, Kumar S, Das B, Yeger H. Combination therapy in combating cancer. Oncotarget 2017;8(23):38022.

[85] Stolz C, Schuler M. Molecular mechanisms of resistance to rituximab and pharmacologic strategies for its circumvention. Leuk Lymphoma 2009;50(6):873–85.

[86] Song Y, Guo Y, Wang Z, Wu M, Peng W, Sun L, Sun J, Li M, Zhu J. A dose escalation phase Ia study of anti-CD20 antibody drug conjugate, MRG001 in relapsed/refractory advanced non-Hodgkin lymphom. Blood 2021;138:2490.

[87] Juárez-Salcedo LM, Conde-Royo D, Quiroz-Cervantes K, Dalia S. Use of anti-CD20 therapy in follicular and marginal zone lymphoma: a review of the literature. Drugs Context 2020;9:1–12.

[88] Liu R, Oldham RJ, Teal E, Beers SA, Cragg MS. Fc-engineering for modulated effector functions—improving antibodies for cancer treatment. Antibodies 2020;9(4):64.

[89] Seidel JA, Otsuka A, Kabashima K. Anti-PD-1 and anti-CTLA-4 therapies in cancer: mechanisms of action, efficacy, and limitations. Front Oncol 2018;8:86.

[90] Bonavida B, Chouaib S. Resistance to anticancer immunity in cancer patients: potential strategies to reverse resistance. Ann Oncol 2017;28(3):457–67.

[91] Selvaraj C, Panwar U, Ramalingam KR, Vijayakumar R, Singh SK. Exploring the macromolecules for secretory pathway in cancer disease. Adv Protein Chem Struct Biol 2022;133:55–83.

[92] Norman RA, Ambrosetti F, Bonvin AM, Colwell LJ, Kelm S, Kumar S, Krawczyk K. Computational approaches to therapeutic antibody design: established methods and emerging trends. Brief Bioinform 2020;21(5):1549–67.

[93] Hummer AM, Abanades B, Deane CM. Advances in computational structure-based antibody design. Curr Opin Struct Biol 2022;74, 102379.

[94] Panwar U, Chandra I, Selvaraj C, Singh SK. Current computational approaches for the development of anti-HIV inhibitors: an overview. Curr Pharm Des 2019;25(31):3390–405.

[95] Panwar U, Singh SK. An overview on Zika Virus and the importance of computational drug discovery. J Explor Res Pharmacol 2018;3(2):43–51.

[96] Raybould MI, Marks C, Krawczyk K, Taddese B, Nowak J, Lewis AP, Bujotzek A, Shi J, Deane CM. Five computational developability guidelines for therapeutic antibody profiling. Proc Natl Acad Sci 2019;116 (10):4025–30.

[97] Baran D, Pszolla MG, Lapidoth GD, Norn C, Dym O, Unger T, Albeck S, Tyka MD, Fleishman SJ. Principles for computational design of binding antibodies. Proc Natl Acad Sci 2017;114(41):10900–5.

[98] Zhao J, Nussinov R, Wu WJ, Ma B. In silico methods in antibody design. Antibodies 2018;7(3):22.

[99] Selvaraj C, Dinesh DC, Panwar U, Boura E, Singh SK. High-throughput screening and quantum mechanics for identifying potent inhibitors against Mac1 Domain of SARS-CoV-2 Nsp3. IEEE/ACM Trans Comput Biol Bioinform 2020;18(4):1262–70.

[100] Wilton EE, Opyr MP, Kailasam S, Kothe RF, Wieden HJ. sdAb-DB: the single domain antibody database. ACS Synth Biol 2018;7(11):2480–4.
[101] Lefranc MP, Giudicelli V, Duroux P, Jabado-Michaloud J, Folch G, Aouinti S, Carillon E, Duvergey H, Houles A, Paysan-Lafosse T, Hadi-Saljoqi S. IMGT®, the international ImMunoGeneTics information system® 25 years on. Nucleic Acids Res 2015;43(D1):D413–22.
[102] Björling E, Uhlén M. Antibodypedia, a portal for sharing antibody and antigen validation data. Mol Cell Proteomics 2008;7(10):2028–37.
[103] Van Montfort RL, Workman P. Structure-based drug design: aiming for a perfect fit. Essays Biochem 2017;61 (5):431–7.
[104] Wishart DS, Feunang YD, Guo AC, Lo EJ, Marcu A, Grant JR, Sajed T, Johnson D, Li C, Sayeeda Z, Assempour N. DrugBank 5.0: a major update to the DrugBank database for 2018. Nucleic Acids Res 2018;46(D1):D1074–82.
[105] Raybould MI, Marks C, Lewis AP, Shi J, Bujotzek A, Taddese B, Deane CM. Thera-SAbDab: the therapeutic structural antibody database. Nucleic Acids Res 2020;48(D1):D383–8.
[106] Modjtahedi H, Ali S, Essapen S. Therapeutic application of monoclonal antibodies in cancer: advances and challenges. Br Med Bull 2012;104(1):41–59.
[107] Arias-Pinilla GA, Modjtahedi H. Therapeutic application of monoclonal antibodies in pancreatic cancer: advances, challenges and future opportunities. Cancers 2021;13(8):1781.
[108] Loisel S, Ohresser M, Pallardy M, Daydé D, Berthou C, Cartron G, Watier H. Relevance, advantages and limitations of animal models used in the development of monoclonal antibodies for cancer treatment. Crit Rev Oncol Hematol 2007;62(1):34–42.
[109] Elgundi Z, Reslan M, Cruz E, Sifniotis V, Kayser V. The state-of-play and future of antibody therapeutics. Adv Drug Deliv Rev 2017;122:2–19.
[110] Rizzo A, Mollica V, Santoni M, Massari F. Cancer immunotherapy: current and future perspectives on a therapeutic revolution. J Clin Med 2021;10(22):5246.
[111] Hernandez I, Bott SW, Patel AS, Wolf CG, Hospodar AR, Sampathkumar S, Shrank WH. Pricing of monoclonal antibody therapies: higher if used for cancer. Am J Manag Care 2018;24(2):109–12.
[112] Hansel TT, Kropshofer H, Singer T, Mitchell JA, George AJ. The safety and side effects of monoclonal antibodies. Nat Rev Drug Discov 2010;9(4):325–38.
[113] Guan M, Zhou YP, Sun JL, Chen SC. Adverse events of monoclonal antibodies used for cancer therapy. Biomed Res Int 2015;2015, 428169.
[114] Kong DH, Kim MR, Jang JH, Na HJ, Lee S. A review of anti-angiogenic targets for monoclonal antibody cancer therapy. Int J Mol Sci 2017;18(8):1786.
[115] Bonanni A, Calatroni M, D'Alessandro M, Signa S, Bertelli E, Cioni M, Di Marco E, Biassoni R, Caridi G, Ingrasciotta G, Bertelli R. Adverse events linked with the use of chimeric and humanized anti-CD20 antibodies in children with idiopathic nephrotic syndrome. Br J Clin Pharmacol 2018;84(6):1238–49.
[116] Chen LY, Shah R, Cwynarski K, Lambert J, McNamara C, Mohamedbhai SG, Virchis A, Townsend W, D'Sa S, Ardeshna KM. Ofatumumab is a feasible alternative anti-CD20 therapy in patients intolerant of rituximab. Br J Haematol 2019;184(3):462–5.
[117] Kasi PM, Tawbi HA, Oddis CV, Kulkarni HS. Clinical review: serious adverse events associated with the use of rituximab-a critical care perspective. Critical Care 2012;16(4):1–10.
[118] Garcia J, Hurwitz HI, Sandler AB, Miles D, Coleman RL, Deurloo R, Chinot OL. Bevacizumab (Avastin®) in cancer treatment: a review of 15 years of clinical experience and future outlook. Cancer Treat Rev 2020;86, 102017.
[119] Kamba T, McDonald DM. Mechanisms of adverse effects of anti-VEGF therapy for cancer. Br J Cancer 2007;96 (12):1788–95.
[120] Subramani M, Ponnalagu M, Krishna L, Jeyabalan N, Chevour P, Sharma A, Jayadev C, Shetty R, Begum N, Archunan G, Das D. Resveratrol reverses the adverse effects of bevacizumab on cultured ARPE-19 cells. Sci Rep 2017;7(1):1–6.
[121] Štulhofer Buzina D, Martinac I, Ledić Drvar D, Čeović R, Bilić I, Marinović B. Adverse reaction to cetuximab, an epidermal growth factor receptor inhibitor. Acta Dermatovenerol Croat 2016;24(1):70–2.
[122] Bou-Assaly W, Mukherji S. Cetuximab (erbitux). Am J Neuroradiol 2010;31(4):626–7.
[123] Matte A. Recent advances and future directions in downstream processing of therapeutic antibodies. Int J Mol Sci 2022;23(15):8663.
[124] Jacquemart R, Vandersluis M, Zhao M, Sukhija K, Sidhu N, Stout J. A single-use strategy to enable manufacturing of affordable biologics. Comput Struct Biotechnol J 2016;14:309–18.

[125] Hummel J, Pagkaliwangan M, Gjoka X, Davidovits T, Stock R, Ransohoff T, Gantier R, Schofield M. Modeling the downstream processing of monoclonal antibodies reveals cost advantages for continuous methods for a broad range of manufacturing scales. Biotechnol J 2019;14(2):1700665.
[126] Mahal H, Branton H, Farid SS. End-to-end continuous bioprocessing: impact on facility design, cost of goods, and cost of development for monoclonal antibodies. Biotechnol Bioeng 2021;118(9):3468–85.
[127] Tsumoto K, Isozaki Y, Yagami H, Tomita M. Future perspectives of therapeutic monoclonal antibodies. Immunotherapy 2019;11(2):119–27.
[128] Wei J, Yang Y, Wang G, Liu M. Current landscape and future directions of bispecific antibodies in cancer immunotherapy. Front Immunol 2022;13:6573.
[129] Shin C, Kim SS, Jo YH. Extending traditional antibody therapies: novel discoveries in immunotherapy and clinical applications. Mol Ther Oncolytics 2021;22:166–79.
[130] Carter PJ, Rajpal A. Designing antibodies as therapeutics. Cell 2022;185(15):2789–805.
[131] Wang B, Gallolu Kankanamalage S, Dong J, Liu Y. Optimization of therapeutic antibodies. Antibody Ther 2021;4(1):45–54.
[132] Gambardella V, Tarazona N, Cejalvo JM, Lombardi P, Huerta M, Roselló S, Fleitas T, Roda D, Cervantes A. Personalized medicine: recent progress in cancer therapy. Cancers 2020;12(4):1009.
[133] Gasser M, Waaga-Gasser AM. Therapeutic antibodies in cancer therapy. Adv Exp Med Biol 2016;917:95–120.
[134] Jain KK, Jain KK. Personalized immuno-oncology. Med Princ Pract 2021;30(1):1–16.
[135] Novak D, Utikal J. New biomarkers in cancers. Cancers 2021;13(4):708.
[136] Liu D. Cancer biomarkers for targeted therapy. Biomark Res 2019;7:1–7.
[137] Pal M, Muinao T, Boruah HP, Mahindroo N. Current advances in prognostic and diagnostic biomarkers for solid cancers: detection techniques and future challenges. Biomed Pharmacother 2022;146, 112488.
[138] Rao Bommi J, Kummari S, Lakavath K, Sukumaran RA, Panicker LR, Marty JL, Yugender Goud K. Recent trends in biosensing and diagnostic methods for novel cancer biomarkers. Biosensors 2023;13(3):398.
[139] Singh V, Guleria P, Malik PS, Mohan A, Thulkar S, Pandey RM, Luthra K, Arava S, Ray R, Jain D. Epidermal growth factor receptor (EGFR), KRAS, and BRAF mutations in lung adenocarcinomas: a study from India. Curr Probl Cancer 2019;43(5):391–401.
[140] Li ZN, Zhao L, Yu LF, Wei MJ. BRAF and KRAS mutations in metastatic colorectal cancer: future perspectives for personalized therapy. Gastroenterol Rep 2020;8(3):192–205.
[141] van de Donk PP, de Ruijter LK, Lub-de Hooge MN, Brouwers AH, van der Wekken AJ, Oosting SF, Fehrmann RS, de Groot DJ, de Vries EG. Molecular imaging biomarkers for immune checkpoint inhibitor therapy. Theranostics 2020;10(4):1708.
[142] Bai R, Lv Z, Xu D, Cui J. Predictive biomarkers for cancer immunotherapy with immune checkpoint inhibitors. Biomark Res 2020;8:1–7.

CHAPTER

2

Anti-CD20 antibody treatment for B-cell malignancies

Sharafudeen Dahiru Abubakar[a,b], *Stella Amarachi Ihim*[c,d], *Mansur Aliyu*[e,f], *Mohammad Saffarioun*[g], *and Gholamreza Azizi*[h,i]

[a]Division of Molecular Pathology, Research Institute for Biomedical Sciences, Tokyo University of Science, Tokyo, Japan [b]Department of Medical Laboratory Science, College of Medical Science, Ahmadu Bello University, Zaria, Nigeria [c]Department of Molecular and Cellular Pharmacology, University of Shizuoka, Shizuoka, Japan [d]Department of Pharmacology and Toxicology & Department of Science Laboratory Technology, University of Nigeria, Nsukka, Nigeria [e]Department of Immunology, School of Public Health, Tehran University of Medical Sciences, Tehran, Iran [f]Department of Medical Microbiology, Faculty of Clinical Science, College of Health Sciences, Bayero University, Kano, Nigeria [g]Biopharmaceutical Research Center, AryoGen Pharmed Inc., Alborz University of Medical Sciences, Karaj, Iran [h]Non-Communicable Diseases Research Center, Alborz University of Medical Sciences, Karaj, Iran [i]Department of Neurology, Thomas Jefferson University, Philadelphia, PA, United States

Abstract

B-cell malignancies account for the majority of non-Hodgkin's lymphomas and approximately 2.8% of all cancer cases. CD20 is a prominent surface marker molecule expressed in most stages of B-cell development. The observation of the high expression of CD20 on many B-cell neoplasms led to its utility as a target for cancer management. Many monoclonal anti-CD20 antibodies were licensed and some were being researched; they employ varying degrees of the antibody-mediated killing of their target, which includes antibody-dependent cell-mediated cytotoxicity (ADCC), antibody-dependent cell-mediated phagocytosis (ADCP), complement-dependent cytotoxicity (CDC), induction of apoptosis, direct cell death, increased expression of reactive oxygen species, and other nonapoptotic cell death mechanisms. Rituximab, an anti-CD20 monoclonal antibody, was the first FDA-approved CD20-based agent for cancer management with huge success. However, there exist some poor outcomes among some patients and in certain B-cell cancer types. Despite anti-CD20 combination therapy with chemotherapy and radiotherapy in B-cell non-Hodgkin's lymphoma, refractory cases arise, which were thought to be caused by mutations in CD20 signaling pathways. Currently, combining

https://doi.org/10.1016/B978-0-443-19200-5.00019-1

anti-CD20 with other monoclonal antibodies has yielded promising results in some B-cell neoplasms. In this chapter, we carefully scrutinized and reviewed the most recent classification of B-cell malignancies and available anti-CD20-based agents. We discussed the origin, mechanism of action, efficacy, and side effects of CD20-based agents in the management of B-cell malignancies. We also show how these shortcomings could be remedied from knowledge obtained from recent advances in molecular, genomic, and clinical studies.

Abbreviations

ADCC	antibody-dependent cell-mediated cytotoxicity
ADCP	antibody-dependent cell-mediated phagocytosis
AEs	adverse effects
BCR	B-cell receptor
BL	Burkitt lymphoma
CDC	complement-dependent cytotoxicity
CHOP	cyclophosphamide/doxorubicin/vincristine/prednisone
CLL/SLL	chronic lymphocytic leukemia/small lymphocytic lymphoma
CSR	class switch recombination
CVP	cyclophosphamide/vincristine/prednisone
DHAP	dexamethasone/cytarabine/cisplatin
DLBCL	diffuse large B-cell lymphoma
FFS	failure-free survival
FL	follicular lymphoma
HCL	hairy cell lymphoma
ICE	ifosfamide/carboplatin/etoposide
LPL	lymphoplasmacytic lymphoma
mAb	monoclonal antibody
MCL	mantle cell lymphoma
MZL	marginal zone lymphoma
PCM	plasma cell myeloma
PFS	progression-free survival
SEER	surveillance, epidemiology, and end results
SHM	somatic hypermutation

Conflict of interest

No potential conflicts of interest were disclosed.

Introduction

Cancers are heterogenous multilineage cells whose dynamic relationship with one another and their microenvironment favors cellular proliferation, differentiation, and movement while restricting cell death and environmental stability [1]. Several theories—the somatic mutation theory [2], the tissue organization field theory [3], and the atavistic theory of cancer [4] have contributed to our knowledge of carcinogenesis. Each has its own strengths and weaknesses. However, by unifying these theories, we see that the mutations in DNA and epigenetic alterations caused by a number of factors disrupt the balance between cell proliferation, cell death, and immune response [5–7] leading to proliferative malignant tumors which can arise from any nucleated cell or tissue.

B lymphocytes (B cells) are a key component of the adaptive immune system tasked with the humoral response—antibody secretion [8]. B cells originate in the bone marrow from the common lymphoid progenitor [9]. Their development into mature B cells involves different gene and surface marker expressions with the rearrangement of their immunoglobulin H chain and L chain gene loci in a process called V(*D*)J recombination [10]. In increasing order of maturity from the common lymphoid progenitor, we have pre-pro B cell, early pro-B cell, late pro-B cell, large pre-B cell, small pre-B cell, immature B cell, and mature B cell [11]. Strong B-cell receptor (BCR) signaling commits B cells into Follicular B cells which reside in primary follicles and can migrate from secondary lymphoid organs to bone marrow in both directions via blood and the lymphatic system. Follicular B cells interact with follicular T helper cells (Tfh) and undergo class switching and somatic hypermutation (SHM) to produce high-affinity antibodies with subsequent development into memory B cells [11,12]. On the other hand, weaker BCR signaling gives rise to marginal zone B cells, which reside primarily between the marginal sinus and the red pulp of the spleen [11,13,14].

Among the surface markers expressed by B cells during development, CD20 is expressed starting from late pre-B cells (pre-pro B cells and early pro-B cells lack this expression) up to memory B cells but lost in plasmablasts and plasma cells [15,16]. CD20 belongs to the membrane-spanning 4-domain family A (MS4A) protein family [17]. MS4A1 gene, a 16 kb long gene with 8 exons, codes for the CD20 protein. Several CD20 mRNA transcripts have been identified which all translate to identical CD20 proteins [18]. The CD20 protein has four hydrophobic transmembranes with both N and C terminals located in the cytoplasm. These four transmembrane domains are linked by one intracellular loop and two extracellular domain which form small and large loops with the complex existing as homodimers [17]. Apart from membrane CD20, circulating CD20 has also been identified in certain B-cell malignancies [19].

CD20 interacts with the BCR, functions as a calcium channel, and is involved in B-cell activation [20]. CD20 is expressed on both normal [21] and malignant B cells, but its expression in malignant conditions varies within and among tumors [22,23] and even predicts survival in patients [24,25]. This high expression of CD20 in malignant tumors makes it a therapeutic target, and hence anti-CD20 antibodies were born [26]. Rituximab was the first anti-CD20 monoclonal antibody approved for treatment which proved to be quite a success in the management of B-cell malignancies [27]. Rituximab was recently discovered to target an intraclonal BCR signaling mediated by CD20 [28] supporting data that showed that alternate CD20 mRNA transcripts were associated with rituximab resistance [18,29].

We investigate current classifications of B-cell malignancies and carcinogenesis in this chapter. We then examine the available anti-CD20 monoclonal antibodies, their efficacy, and their role in the treatment of B-cell malignancies.

B-cell malignancies

The World Health Organization (WHO) provides a multidisciplinary approach to classify tumors in their regularly updated series of tumor classifications. The 5th edition of the WHO classification of hematolymphoid tumors: lymphoid neoplasm [30] categorizes B-cell malignancies (Table 1) into tumor-like lesions with B-cell predominance, precursor B-cell neoplasms, mature B-cell neoplasms, and plasma cell neoplasms, comprising more than 70 distinct entities grouped into families, tumors, and tumor subtypes [30]. An analysis of the surveillance, epidemiology, and end results (SEER) database, which is drawn from the cancer registry of 185 countries [79], reveals that B-cell malignancies (which account for the majority of the non-Hodgkin's Lymphoma [NHL]) account for about 2.8% of cancer cases [80], with

TABLE 1 Types of B-cell malignancies as per recent WHO classification of hematolymphoid tumors, 5th edition [30].

Family	Tumor type(s)	Tumor subtype(s)	Recommended CD20-based agent used in the treatment
Tumor-like lesions with B-cell predominance			
Tumor-like lesions with B-cell predominance	Reactive B-cell-rich lymphoid proliferations that can mimic lymphoma		Not applicable [31]
	IgG4-related disease		Rituximab [32,33]
	Castleman disease	Unicentric, Idiopathic multicentric, KSHV/HHV-8-associated	Rituximab [34,35]
Precursor B-cell neoplasms			
B-cell lymphoblastic leukemia/ lymphoma	B-cell lymphoblastic leukemia/ lymphoma (BLL)	BLL with high hyperdiploidy, hypoploidy, iAMP21, BCR-ABL1 fusion, BCR-ABL1-like fusion, KMT2A rearrangement, ETV6-RUNX1 fusion, ETV6-RUNX1-like fusion, TCF3-PBX1 fusion, IGH-IL3 fusion, TCF3-HLF fusion, other defined genetic abnormalities NOS	Rituximab [36,37]
Mature B-cell neoplasms			
Preneoplastic and neoplastic small lymphocytic proliferations	Monoclonal B-cell lymphocytosis		Rituximab, obinutuzumab [38,39]
	Chronic lymphocytic leukemia/ small lymphocytic lymphoma (CLL/SLL)		

Splenic B-cell lymphomas and leukemias	Hairy cell leukemia		Rituximab [40,41], obinutuzumab [42]
	Splenic marginal zone lymphoma		Rituximab, obinutuzumab, [43,44]
	Splenic diffuse red pulp B-cell lymphoma		Rituximab [45,46]
	Splenic B-cell lymphoma/ leukemia with prominent nucleoli		
Lymphoplasmacytic lymphoma	Lymphoplasmacytic lymphoma		Rituximab [47,48]
Marginal zone lymphoma	Extranodal marginal zone lymphoma of mucosa-associated lymphoid tissue	Primary cutaneous, other mucosa-associated lymphoid tissues	Rituximab, obinutuzumab, [43,44]
	Nodal marginal zone lymphoma	Adult, pediatric	
Follicular lymphoma	Follicular lymphoma	In situ follicular B-cell neoplasm, follicular lymphoma pediatric-type, duodenal-type	Rituximab, obinutuzumab [49,50]
Cutaneous Follicle Center Lymphoma	Primary cutaneous follicle center lymphoma		Rituximab [51,52]
Mantle cell lymphoma	Mantle cell lymphoma	In situ mantle cell neoplasm, mantle cell lymphoma leukemic nonmodal	Rituximab [53,54]
Transformation of indolent B-cell lymphomas	Transformation of indolent B-cell lymphomas		Rituximab [55,56]
Large B-cell lymphomas	Diffuse large B-cell lymphoma (DLBCL)	DLBCL with MYC and BCl2 rearrangement, EBV-positive, associated chronic inflammation, primary cutaneous leg type, DLBCL NOS	Rituximab [57], Ofatumumab, obinutuzumab [58]

Continued

TABLE 1 Types of B-cell malignancies as per recent WHO classification of hematolymphoid tumors, 5th edition [30]—cont'd

Family	Tumor type(s)	Tumor subtype(s)	Recommended CD20-based agent used in the treatment
	Large B-cell lymphoma	T-cell/histiocyte-rich, ALK-positive, with IRF4 rearrangement, High-grade B-cell lymphoma with 11q aberration fibrin-associated, fluid overload-associated, intravascular, primary mediastinal, High-grade B-cell lymphoma, NOS	Rituximab [59]
	Primary large B-cell lymphoma of immune-privileged sites	CNS, Vitreo-retina, Testis	Rituximab [60]
	Lymphomatoid granulomatosis		Rituximab [61]
	Plasmablastic lymphoma		No standard regiment [30]
Burkitt lymphoma	Burkitt lymphoma	Endemic, sporadic, immunodeficiency-associated	Rituximab [62,63]
Hodgkin lymphoma	Hodgkin lymphoma	Classic, Nodular lymphocyte predominant	Rituximab [64,65] based on CD20 expression of subtype
KSHV-/HHV8-associated B-cell lymphoid proliferations and lymphoma	Primary effusion lymphoma		Failure due to CD20 negativity [30]
	KSHV-/HHV8-positive DLBCL		Same as DLBCL
	KSHV-/HHV8-positive germinotropic lymphoproliferative disorder		CHOP due to CD20 negativity [30]
Lymphoid proliferations and lymphomas associated with immune deficiency and dysregulation	Primary immunodeficiency associated	Inborn error of immunity-associated lymphoid proliferations and lymphoma	Rituximab [66,67] (based on CD20 expression)

	Immune deficiency/ dysregulation-associated such as posttransplantation	Hyperplasia, polymorphic lymphoproliferative disorders, lymphomas	
	EBV-positive mucocutaneous ulcer		Rituximab [68]
Plasma cell neoplasms and other diseases with paraproteins			
Monoclonal gammopathies	Monoclonal gammopathy of undetermined significance	IgM type, Non-IgM type	Rituximab [47,48]
	Monoclonal gammopathy of renal significance		Rituximab [69]
	Cold agglutinin disease		Rituximab [70]
Diseases with monoclonal immunoglobulin deposition	Immunoglobulin-related Amyloidosis		Rituximab [71,72]
	Monoclonal immunoglobulin deposition disease		Rituximab [73,74]
Heavy chain diseases	Alpha heavy chain disease Gamma heavy chain disease Mu heavy chain disease		Rituximab [75,76] (based on CD20 expression)
Plasma cell neoplasms	Plasmacytoma		Surgery or radiotherapy due to CD20 negativity [30]
	Plasma cell myeloma		Bortezomib. CD20-based agents are not recommended due to failure [77,78]
	Plasma cell neoplasms with associated paraneoplastic syndrome	POEMS syndrome TEMPI syndrome, AESOP syndrome	Immunomodulatory antibodies to other detected antigens. CD20 negativity [30]

KSHV, Kaposi's sarcoma-associated herpesvirus; HHV8, human herpesvirus 8; BCR, B-cell receptor; iAMP21, intrachromosomal amplification of chromosome 21; ABL1, abelson tyrosine-protein kinase 1; KMT2A, lysine (K)-specific methyltransferase 2A; ETV6, ETS variant transcription factor 6; RUNX1, runt-related transcription factor 1; TCF3, transcription factor 3; PBX1, PBX Homeobox 1; IGH, immunoglobulin heavy chain; IL. Interleukin; HLF, hepatic leukemia factor; NOS, nitric oxide synthase; MYC, myelocytomatosis; EBV, Epstein-Barr virus; ALK, anaplastic lymphoma kinase; IRF4, interferon regulatory factor 4; CNS, central nervous system; POEMS, polyneuropathy, organomegaly, endocrinopathy, monoclonal protein, skin changes; TEMPI, telangiectasias, elevated erythropoietin level and erythrocytosis, monoclonal gammopathy, perinephric fluid collections, and intrapulmonary shunting; AESOP, adenopathy and an extensive skin patch overlying a plasmacytoma.

diffuse large B-cell lymphoma (DLBCL) representing around 30% of all cases [81]. CD20 expression in B-cell malignancies is a good justification for using anti-CD20 monoclonal antibodies in the treatment of these disorders, but it is usually used in conjunction with other antineoplastic agents [82,83]. With a large number of distinct entities both rare and common (Table 1), we summarize the more common B-cell malignancies while highlighting the molecular features and anti-CD20-based biologic used in their management. Hence, Table 1 highlighted different types and subtypes of B-cell NHL neoplasms with their corresponding treatment guidelines, which take into account not only anti-CD20 mAbs but also the currently recommended chemotherapy combination and radiotherapy for the afflicted patients.

Diffuse large B-cell lymphoma (DLBCL)

DLBCL is the most common type of adult lymphoma worldwide [84], with millions suffering considerable disease-related socioeconomic burden [85]. It also occurs in children, can arise de novo, or arise as a result of the transformation of a less aggressive lymphoma [86,87]. The neoplastic cells seen in DLBCL based on molecular and phenotypic subtyping can originate from the germinal center (germinal center B cells, GCB) or the cells that have already undergone SHM (activated B cells, ABC) [88,89]. Deregulation and chromosomal rearrangement of *BCL6*, *BCL2*, and *MYC* genes have been shown to significantly contribute to the pathogenesis of DLBCL [30]. The epigenetic factors *KMT2D* and *CREBBP*, tumor suppressor gene *TP53*, antigen presentation factor B2M, and some signal transduction and transcription factors such as STAT6 and FOXO1 are sometimes mutated in DLBCL [90,91]. Since receiving approval from the US Food and Drug Administration (FDA), rituximab, a CD20-directed agent, has been the first line of treatment for DLBCL [57]. Poor outcomes for some patients receiving rituximab led to the generation and subsequent approval of newer CD20 monoclonal antibodies such as ofatumumab and obinutuzumab [58,92].

Follicular lymphoma (FL)

Follicular lymphoma (FL) is the most common lymphoma and is usually indolent [93,94]. As the name implies, it arises from the germinal center in the follicles of lymphoid organs [95,96]. They are usually asymptomatic (indolent) and hence commonly diagnosed at later stages. FL is mostly characterized by the t(14;18)(q32;q21) translocation between the IGH locus and the *BCL2* gene [50,95] with a host of heterogenous mutations in epigenetic genes—*KMT2D*, *CREBBP*, *EP300*, *EZH2* [97,98] —and other transcription factors involved in JAK-STAT and mTORC pathways [49,99]. *BCL2* overexpression and other associated mutations lead to the blocking of apoptosis and other pathological derangement seen in FL [100]. In situ and duodenal FL usually have the t(14,18) translocation while the other subtypes do not have this chromosomal abnormality [101]. The CD20-based agents approved for the management of FL are rituximab and obinutuzumab [49,50].

Chronic lymphocytic leukemia/small lymphocytic lymphoma (CLL/SLL)

Chronic lymphocytic leukemia (CLL), otherwise called small lymphocytic lymphoma (SLL), is the most common leukemia affecting the elderly [102,103]. In many cases, CLL is preceded by an asymptomatic and unnoticed preliminary stage with the proliferation of clonal B cells, which is known as monoclonal B-cell lymphocytosis that in itself is a separate entity [104,105]. It was assumed to have no chromosomal or genetic alterations, but recent studies have shown it to encompass a heterogeneity of genetic mutations [106,107]. Of note is the role of *TP53* mutations [108,109] and the contributions of a complex aberrant karyotype as detected by fluorescent in situ hybridization (FISH) [109,110]. Another important prognostic marker is the status of the *IGHV* gene [111,112] with a mutation indicating a favorable prognosis [113]. The *TP53* and *IGHV* mutational status [113] assists in the choice of therapy, which in this case includes rituximab and obinutuzumab [38,39].

Mantle cell lymphoma (MCL)

Mantle cell lymphoma (MCL) is a naïve B-cell-derived malignancy that exhibits a range of indolent to aggressive behavior [114]. The oncogenetic highlight of MCL is the translocation—t(11;14)(q13;q32) that juxtaposes the *CCND1* gene on chromosome 11 to the IGH regulatory region during the pro/pre-B stage leading to cyclin D1 overexpression [115,116]. Cyclin D1 overexpression deregulates the cell cycle leading to malignant transformation irrespective of the chromosomal alteration [117,118]. Mutations in the *IGHV* and *SOX11* expression [119,120] gene have been used to classify MCL—minimally mutated $SOX11^+$ nodal MCL and *IGHV* mutated $SOX11^-$ nonnodal MCL [121,122]. *TP53* (17p deletion) and *CDKN2A* (9p deletion) mutation usually represent a poorer prognosis [123,124]. Rituximab is the CD20-based agent of choice in the management of MCL [53,54].

Marginal zone lymphomas (MZLs)

Marginal zone lymphoma (MZL) is a relatively common lymphoma that is derived from postgerminal center memory B cells present in the marginal zone of lymphoid organs [125,126]. The three types of MZLs are primary extranodal MZL, extranodal MZL of mucosa-associated lymphoid tissues (MALTs), and nodal MZL [43,127]. Chronic immune stimulation appears to be a significant risk factor for the development of MZL [128,129]. A small population of patients with MZL undergoes transformation into DLBCL [130], which shows an even worse prognosis [131]. The majority of patients with MZL have an aberrant karyotype [132] with 7q deletion being the most common [133]. Mutations in *TP53*, *NOTCH2*, and *KLF2* are associated with poorer prognosis [134]. Rituximab and obinutuzumab are usually recommended in MZL treatment regimens [43,44].

Burkitt lymphoma (BL)

Burkitt lymphoma (BL) is an aggressive B-cell malignancy that affects both children and adults and has a doubling time of about 24 h [135,136]. Three subtypes of BL have been described—endemic, sporadic, and immunodeficiency-associated [137,138]. The most common chromosomal aberration in BL is the *IGH-MYC* gene rearrangement—t(8;14)(q24;q32) and less common is the *IGL-MYC* rearrangement—t(8;22)(q24;q11) and the *IGK-MYC* rearrangement—t(2;8)(p12;q24) [139–141]. The dysregulation of the *MYC* gene (not restricted to BL) and accompanying mutations to *ID3* and *CCND3* affecting the TCF pathway have been implicated in the pathogenesis of BL [140,142,143]. Uncommonly, *MYC* disruption may be absent in some rare variants of BL which present with changes in 11q [144,145], but no mutations in the *TCF3* pathway or *TP53* [146,147]. BL responds very well to treatment; rituximab is broadly included in treatment regimens and shows superior outcomes when included in regimens across all subtypes [62,63].

Lymphoplasmacytic lymphoma (LPL)

Lymphoplasmacytic lymphoma (LPL) is an indolent lymphoproliferative tumor of the bone marrow with abundant monoclonal IgM secreting small B cells which is commonly termed Waldenström macroglobulinemia [92,148]. About 2% of LPL arises from IgM monoclonal gammopathy of undetermined significance (IgM-MGUS) [48,149], which is characterized by the presence of 6q deletion, which is linked to the likelihood of transformation and symptomatic LPL [150,151]. Consequently, 6q deletions are the most common chromosomal alteration in LPL; this deleted region codes for regulatory factors for NF-kappa B signaling, apoptosis, and plasma cell differentiation, which helps to explain its pathophysiology [151,152]. More than 90% of LPL harbors the L265P mutation in the *MYD88* gene and 30% possesses the nonsense S338X mutation in the *CXCR4* gene, which contribute to the pathogenesis and prognosis of LPL patients [153,154]. *TP53* mutations have also been associated with a poorer prognosis even though they have not yet been clinically evaluated [148,155,156]. Rituximab-based therapy is the gold standard for the management of LPL and related disorders [47,48].

Hairy cell leukemia (HCL)

Hairy cell leukemia (HCL) is a rare indolent B-cell malignancy characterized by cells with fine hairy-like cytoplasmic projections and hence their name [157,158]. Annexin A1 is commonly upregulated in HCL [159,160], but recent findings reveal some patients do not express this phospholipid-binding protein [161,162]. HCL features a heterogenous chromosomal abnormality profile [163], but the key molecular identifier is the V600E mutation in the *BRAF* gene, which permanently activates the RAS-RAF-MEK-ERK pathway and is seen in about 90% of patients [164–166]. CDNK1B and KLF2 mutations are also seen albeit less commonly [167,168]. A variant form of HCL lacking these mutations has been described with SHM in the *IGHV* locus [169,170]. Therapy with other agents followed by rituximab [41,171] or concurrently with rituximab [40,172] is recommended for management of HCL depending on the clinician's preferences. Obinutuzumab [42,173] is currently being used successfully in some patients.

Primary large B-cell lymphoma of immune-privileged sites

Primary B-cell lymphoma of the eye (vitreo-retina), testis, and the central nervous system (CNS) have been reclassified as primary large B-cell lymphoma of the immune-privileged sites in the recent fifth WHO classification of hematolymphoid tissues [30]. They have similar features [174] and can easily spread from one site to the other [175]. The most common histological and genetic features of these entities are quite similar to those of DLBCL [176] but possess unique characteristics such as loss of HLA class I and II expression [177] and mutations in the *CD37* gene [178]. Genetic profiles that differentiate the different sites are the BTG2 mutation in the testicular type [179], CD79B mutation in the vitreo-retina type [180], and PIM1 and/or CD79B mutation in the CNS type [181,182]. The treatment strategy is similar to DLBCL due to their similar features; hence, rituximab is used as a standard approach [60].

Plasma cell myeloma (PCM)

Plasma cell myeloma (PCM), otherwise called multiple myeloma (MM), is a clonal B-cell malignancy characterized by the accumulation of mature plasma cells in the bone marrow and various tissues leading to elevated serum monoclonal immunoglobulins [183]. Recent studies have shown novel mutations, biallelic hits in tumor suppressor genes, and segmental copy number changes which might contribute to the pathogenesis of PCM [184,185]. Hyperdiploidy [186,187] and six cytogenetic indicators—t(4;14), del(17p), trisomy 5, trisomy 21, 1q gain, and del(1p32)—are used in the diagnostic, prognostic, and therapeutic assessment of PCM [188,189]. More than half of the patients have a mutation affecting components of the NFκB and MEK-ERK pathway, which is believed to be significant in the choice of therapy [190,191]. 1q gain, del(17p), and t(4;14) have been generally agreed upon to signify a worse prognosis [192,193]. All patients with t(11;14) have CD20 expression [183,194]; this suggests that rituximab could be useful for its therapy. Unfortunately, rituximab use has shown a relatively "limited efficacy" [77,78].

Mechanism of B-cell carcinogenesis/lymphomagenesis

B cells develop from bone marrow-derived hematopoietic stem cells via the common lymphoid progenitor [9,195]. Development into matured B cells involves several stages as outlined earlier with each B cell acquiring a specific BCR through V(*D*)J recombination [10,196]. V(*D*)J recombination involves rearrangement of the IGH and IGL or IGK loci where "positively" selected cells enter into the circulation and into secondary lymphoid organs [10,197]. An encounter of the BCR of a naïve B cell with cognate antigen causes differentiation [198] into extrafollicular B cells [199] or germinal center B cells that undergo a process called SHM [200]. SHM involves point mutations, deletions, insertions, and duplications in the genes of the IGH and IGL or IGK and is mediated by activation-induced cytidine deaminase (AID) [201] which converts cytidine to uracil. The constant region of the immunoglobulin heavy chain undergoes class switch recombination (CSR) in order to produce different subtypes of immunoglobulins [202].

A host of factors—chromosomal aberrations, genetic mutations, epigenetic alterations, infections, and immune alterations (Fig. 1)—singly or in combination could potentially affect BCR signaling, thereby favoring cellular proliferation, inhibiting apoptosis, and ultimately supporting progression to malignancy [203]. We first describe the overall disruption in BCR signaling in B-cell malignancies before elucidating the various factors. An appraisal of the pathophysiology and mechanism of malignant transformation can reveal the many targets that can be utilized in the management of B-cell malignancies.

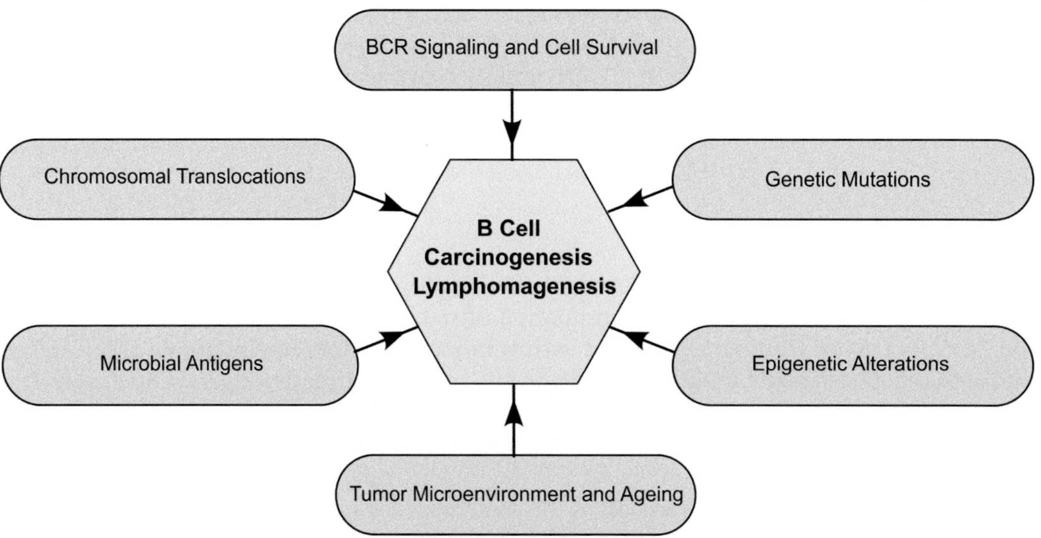

FIG. 1 Mechanisms involved in B-cell carcinogenesis/lymphomagenesis. A diagram depicting the several factors that contribute to the development of B-cell malignancies.

BCR signaling and cell survival in B-cell malignancies

BCR expression and signaling are fundamental to B-cell survival [204]. BCR signaling normally involves an antigen-dependent mechanism that primarily involves the NF-kappa-B pathway and is called active BCR signaling [205]. This signaling pathway involves a broad network of genes including NF-kappa B and is essential for the formation of normal B cells [206]. B cells that display high-affinity BCR are sustained by the expression of additional receptors, including CD40, TNF receptor superfamily member 13C, and Toll-like receptors (TLRs), which all lead to the activation of NF-kappa B in what is called affinity-based selection [207]. Constitutive activation of the NF-kappa B pathway is necessary for malignant B cell survival. The consistent activation of this pathway is mediated by alterations in the components of the NF-kappa B pathway such as activating mutations in CD79A and CD79B [208], mutations in MYD88 [209,210], or mutations in TNF alpha-induced protein 3, a negative modulator of the NF-kappa B signaling pathway [211]. BCR signaling can also occur independently of antigen engagement (tonic BCR signaling) with the engagement of the phosphatidylinositol 3-kinase (PI3K)-mediated activation of the AKT serine/threonine kinase (AKT) instead of NF-kappa B signaling [203,212]. Mounting evidence has suggested the role of tonic signaling in many B-cell malignancies [208,213] and appears to be sustained in several B-cell malignancies which are believed to be essential for the proliferation of leukemic cells [16,214].

Oncogenic mimicry is a strategy where B cell cancers acquire BCR survival signals by oncogenic BCR expression and activation instead of a functional BCR [215,216]. In precursor B-cell neoplasms, defective BCR expression is a result of a little or absent V(*D*)J recombination and subsequent Igα and Igβ downregulation [217,218]; it usually bears *VPREB1* deletion [219] and aberrant splicing of Bruton Tyrosine Kinase (BTK) [220] or, in some cases, *BLNK* alterations [221]. These inactivating genetic alterations affect components of the BCR-ABL1 tyrosine kinase in Philadelphia chromosome-positive cancers [222,223], JAK-STAT signaling [224], and the RAS pathway [225,226]. On the other hand, in most mature B-cell neoplasms, abnormal BCR signaling is often a result of the dysfunctional V(*D*)J recombination acquired during affinity maturation in GCs [215]. In malignancies with functional BCRs, the BCR could be autoreactive [213] or highly sensitive to a myriad of agents such as the fungal antigen—β-[1,6]-glucan [227], the viral protein—E2 envelope protein from HCV [228], the bacterial antigen(s) from *Helicobacter pylori* [229], and parasitic antigen(s) from *Plasmodium falciparum* [230,231]. In mature B-cell neoplasms with nonfunctional or absent BCR expression, Kaposi's sarcoma-associated herpesvirus (KSHV) K1 protein [232,233], and Epstein-Barr virus (EBV) LMP2A protein [234,235] have been reported to serve as oncogenic mimics of BCR signaling [216].

Several BCR-related transcriptional networks are also hijacked during lymphomagenesis and one of the most commonly identified factors is the involvement of the *MYC* gene. MYC is a transcription factor that regulates many targets, including DNA replication and the cell cycle [236,237]. MYC is needed only in the initial phases of GC formation' then it is downregulated via repression by BLC6 [238,239]. The ectopic expression of MYC usually via chromosomal translocation is a common feature of most GC-derived B-cell malignancies where it favors cell proliferation [203]. Forkhead box O1 (FOXO1) is a transcription factor that also negatively regulates cellular activation and differentiation [240]. FOXO1 mutations are frequently seen in GC-derived B-cell lymphomas and promote lymphomagenesis due to defective AKT targeting [241,242].

BCL6 is a transcriptional factor with a myriad of targets; it represses premature activation and differentiation of GC B cells by restraining the DNA damage response and modulating apoptosis [243,244]. Dysregulated expression of BCL6 is common in GC-derived lymphomas with features such as replacement of the regulatory region with the IGH locus [245] or mutations in the IRF4 binding site [246]. BCL6 expression can also be affected indirectly by mutations in modulators of BCL6 such as MEF2B [247,248], FBXO11 [88], CREB binding protein (CREBBP) [249,250], and E1A binding protein p300 (EP300) [251]. Mutations affecting *TCF3* and *ID3* genes also help to maintain the survival of lymphoma cells by promoting tonic BCR signaling and CCND3 transactivation [252,253]. Other mutations that aid in lymphomagenesis is the *BLIMP1* mutation, which inhibits the ability of B cells to differentiate terminally [254,255]. Some epigenetic factors such as EZH2 [256,257] and KMTs2D [258] have also been implicated to contribute to malignant cell proliferation by interfering in signaling in the B-cell germinal center.

Chromosomal translocations, a survival factor in B-cell malignancies

One key characteristic of many B-cell lymphomas is chromosomal translocations between an immunoglobulin locus and another gene, usually a proto-oncogene [259]. These translocations arise as derivatives of V(*D*)J recombination, SHM, and CSR [260,261]. The IG locus in B cells is rich with highly active enhancers; when a proto-oncogene is translocated into an IG locus, the proto-oncogene becomes continuously expressed, which stimulates downstream activities of the oncogene. The translocated BCL2 on the IGH locus found in FL [50,96], the translocated MYC on the IGH or IGL found in BL [63], and the translocated CCND1 on the IGH locus found in MCL and PCM [116,262] all favor cellular proliferation and cause uncontrolled proliferation of the cells harboring the respective translocation [263]. Another type of translocation involves the fusion of two genes. This leads to the transcription of fusion transcripts involving two genes and the translation of proteins that combine parts of two separate genes [259]. An example is the API2-MALT1 fusion in MALT lymphoma where the translated protein consists of an API2 amino region and a MALT1 carboxy region, a feature making it capable of activating NF-kB by cleaving MAP3K14, hence inhibiting apoptosis [264,265]. Other proto-oncogenes translocated in several IG loci include BCL6-IGH in DLBCL [266]; BCL10-IGH, MALT1-IGH, and FOXP1-IGH in MALT lymphoma [267]; PAX5-IGH in LPL [268] as well as FGFR3-IGH and MAF-IGH in PCM [269].

Microbial antigens in B-cell malignancies

Antigens from microorganisms have been identified as culprits in the pathogenesis of B-cell lymphomas [259,270]. EBV, Human Herpes 8 virus (HHV8), and KSHV are the most well recognized and characterized oncogenic viruses in B-cell malignancies [271–273]. These viruses typically exhibit latent infections. In EBV, for example, the ENV nuclear antigen 1 (EBNA1) codes the two latent proteins—LMP1 and LMP2a—which mimic the active CD40 receptor and active BCR, respectively. This provides two critical survival signals that prevent apoptosis and favor cell proliferation [274–276]. EBNA2 is also found to favor the proliferation of malignant B cells [277]. As for HHV8, the protein LNA1 has been reported to inhibit p53 and Rb, a viral cyclin, and favors malignant transformation [278]. The two KSHV proteins K1 and K15 have also been shown to be functional homologues of EBV LMP2a [279]. Overall, these latent viral infections mimic BCR signaling and promote tumorigenesis.

The hepatitis C virus (HCV) does not cause a latent infection. Rather, it drives malignant transformation by serving as a source of chronic antigen stimulation and upregulating AID, the key enzyme required for SHM. The E2 envelope protein [228] has been shown to be responsible for this stimulus. These two factors increase the likelihood of both an excess production of reactive oxygen species (ROS) and a chromosomal translocation [280,281] without affecting other driver mutations such as TP53 or BCL6 [282]. Other viruses with possible links to B-cell malignant tumors are the human herpesvirus 6-variant (HHV6) [283] and gamma-herpesvirus [284]. Chronic bacterial infections, such as *H. pylori*-induced gastric ulcer, have been linked to the development of gastric MALT lymphoma [285] and gastric DLBCL [286], where they serve as a source of consistent BCR stimulation [229]. The malaria parasite *P. falciparum* has been implicated as a chronic BCR stimulant in the pathogenesis of endemic BL [230,231]. It was clearly shown that this risk factor did not apply to other Plasmodium species, further solidifying the over 50-year association between endemic BL and *P. falciparum* [287,288].

DNA repair and B-cell malignancies

We have seen many mutations in several pathways that contribute to dysfunctional BCR signaling and favor malignant transformation in the previous sections. A cell with a mutated gene is normally repaired; otherwise, it is eradicated; a breakdown of this process can affect many physiological processes as well as initiate the transformation to malignancy [289,290]. In most cancers, including B-cell malignancies, DNA repair pathways are frequently affected [291], and the most commonly mutated gene is the *TP53* gene, which codes for the p53 proteins and is called the guardian of the genome [292]. p53 has a dual role as a genomic guardian and as a master regulator of stress. Abnormalities in the p53 pathway are present in virtually all cancer cells and are associated with poorer outcomes [2]. The p53 pathway is a complex pathway with more than 50 genes. In lymphoid malignancies, the dysregulation might arise from reversible or irreversible alterations of factors upstream or downstream of p53 and is not limited to a loss of function in p53, ATM, and $P14^{ARF}$ and a gain of function in RAS, MYC, and MDM2 [293,294]. The dysregulation in p53 is highly varied between different cancers. P53 activates DNA repair, arrests the cell cycle, and initiates apoptosis if DNA repair fails [295]. The serine/threonine kinase ATM is activated upon DNA double-strand breaks to initiate DNA repair and also phosphorylates p53 [296,297]. $P14^{ARF}$, on the other hand, regulates cell cycle activity and inhibits MDM2, thus promoting p53 [298]. MDM2 negatively regulates p53 [299], while the *RAS* genes (*HRAS*, *KRAS*, and *NRAS*) and the *MYC* genes (*C-MYC*, *L-MYC*, and *N-MYC*) favor cell growth, differentiation, and survival [300,301]. This failure of DNA repair accompanied by cell cycle inhibition and deficient apoptosis is one of the defining features of cancers.

Role of epigenetic mechanisms in B-cell malignancies

DNA methylation and histone modification are key epigenetic mechanisms that can induce functional alteration in the genome without affecting the nucleotide sequence [302]. Almost all the B-cell malignancies studied have exhibited some epigenetic changes [303], as have other solid cancers [304]. DNA hypomethylation is common in B-cell malignancies [305,306], and it has been shown to increase mutation rates [307] and perhaps lead to a higher cancer risk. On the other hand, DNA hypermethylation is also common in B-cell malignancies and is mediated by polycomb repression via EZH2 methyltransferase [308]. Numerous studies have shown that altered DNA alteration aggregates at enhancers in B-cell malignancies [309], with the majority being DNA hypomethylation except in PCM, which shows DNA hypermethylation [310]. The focal sites for these methylations have also been shown to be intragenic rather than intergenic [311]. These epigenetic changes are not necessarily seen at a particular stage in malignant diseases and their pattern changes during the course of a disease and its relapse [303,312,313]. This might mean there exists some form of dynamic relationship between epigenetics, mutations, and the tumor microenvironment. More research is needed to investigate how the epigenome affects mutational status in B-cell malignancies and how it can be used to manage the disease.

Tumor microenvironment and aging facilitates the progression of carcinogenesis

After malignant transformation, the growth, progression, and metastatic potential of cancer cells are greatly influenced by the tumor microenvironment [314]. The tumor microenvironment is a complex ecosystem consisting of tumors, other cells, extracellular components, and a rich vascular network [315]. Current experimental data have further shown that the soluble and insoluble factors in the tumor microenvironment, the stroma, and the agents inducing DNA damage, such as ROS, all impact the neoplastic potential [316]. Inflammatory agents, chemokines, and cytokines by virtue of their influence on cells have also been shown to be a promoter of cancer progression [317,318]. These findings about the interrelationship between tumors and their microenvironment have led to the discovery of molecular targets that could be beneficial in the management of cancers [319].

The risk of many diseases increases with age, and cancer is no exception [320]. Aging reflects the time-dependent accumulation of genetic and environmental injuries with features of genomic instability, telomere dysfunction, epigenetic alterations, and many other changes [321]. This loss of fitness might create a favorable condition for aberrant neoplastic proliferation or malignant transformation to occur [322]. Of note is the alteration to the functions of the immune system known as immunosenescence [323]. Strong evidence for the involvement of aging and immunosenescence in the development of B-cell malignancies comes from the observation that lymphomas are more common in elderly people [324,325] despite the absence of any inherited propensity or risk factors [326]. Sufficient data linking immunosenescence and lymphomagenesis on a global scale with specific interpopulation peculiarities is still lacking and needs to be investigated [327,328].

Anti-CD20 antibodies

CD20 is a 33–37 kDa phosphoprotein expressed on the surface of normal and malignant B lymphocytes. It is present at the pre-B-cell stage until differentiation into plasma cells. The combination of this and the upregulation of CD20 expression on malignant B cells provides the much-needed therapeutic target [83]. The introduction and approval of the anti-CD 20 antibody rituximab by the FDA in 1997 improved the outlook of patients with CD20-positive B-cell malignancies. Subsequently, following the success of rituximab, other anti-CD20 monoclonal antibodies such as ofatumunab and obinutuzumab were developed. Three isoforms of CD20 (33, 35, and 37 kDa) have been identified to result from CD20 phosphorylation, which is higher in proliferating malignant B cells than in normal resting cells. It contributes to cell signal transduction by being present on the cell surface and forming homodimeric and homotetrameric oligomers with other cell surface and cytoplasmic proteins. Anti-CD20 mAbs have been broadly divided into two types, I and II.

Type 1: These antibodies are characterized by the induction of the translocation of CD20 into lipid rafts within the plasma membrane upon binding, thus enhancing the recruitment and activation of the complement [329]. Hence, they are associated with enhanced complement-dependent cytotoxicity (CDC) and antibody-dependent cell-mediated cytotoxicity/phagocytosis (ADCC/ADCP). Rituximab is a type I anti-CD20 mAb that engages fragment crystallizable (Fc) receptors on macrophages and natural killer (NK) cells inducing direct proapoptotic, antiproliferative effects and facilitating CDC and ADCC/ADCP activities [330–333]. Other type I anti-CD20 mAbs include ofatumumab and ublituximab, which may differ from rituximab with respect to the modification of their Fc domains by glycoengineering to enhance ADCC and ADCP effects.

Type II: These antibodies are associated with suppressed CDC effect, retained ADCC/ADCP effect, and strongly enhanced direct cell death. Compared to type I, type II antibodies more potently induce homolytic adhesion and direct cell death. Although this form of cell death was previously described to be apoptotic, recent studies indicate that it does not show classical signs of apoptosis-like DNA laddering. Instead, it may follow an action-dependent enhancement of cell-to-cell contact resulting in the rupture of lysosomes within the cytoplasm and the production of ROS. Obinutuzumab is a type II mAb associated with direct cell death induction and works by the induction of CDC through the clustering of CD20 in lipid rafts and by ADCC [331–334]. Generally, the second-generation anti-CD20 mAbs are humanized to reduce immunogenicity. Table 2 shows an overview of the basic characteristics of available anti-CD20 monoclonal antibodies.

TABLE 2 The characteristics of anti-CD20 monoclonal antibodies [83,335–340].

Type	mAb	Status/indication	Characteristics	Mechanism	Epitope
I	Rituximab	FDA approved for NH; ADCP/ALCL; relapsed/refractory FL (1998). Rituximab-CHOP (patients of DLBCL). Off-label use—MCL	Mouse/human chimeric IgG1	ADCP (+), ADCC (++), CDC (++), PCD (+), direct cell death induction (+)	Class 1, large extracellular loop, core epitope ANPS region. Contact region (positions 165–182)
I	Ocrelizumab (2H7)	In the phase 3 trial for relapsed/refractory FL	Humanized IgG1	ADCC (++++), CDC (low)	Class 1, large extracellular loop, core epitope ANPS region.
I	Ofatumumab	Frontline for CLL (2009); Ofatumumab-CHOP (Untreated FL)	Human IgG1	ADCC (++), CDC (++++), direct cell death induction (+)	Class 1, large extracellular loop, core epitope ANPS region. Contact region (positions 165–180)
I	Ublituximab	In phase 3 trial for NHL; phase 2 for CLL	Chimeric IgG1	ADCC (++++), CDC (++), direct cell death induction (+)	Class 1, large extracellular loop, core epitope ANPS region
I	Veltuzumab (immu-06; hA20)	Approved for FL, NHL, DLBCL (2009); in phase 2 trial for NHL	Humanized IgG1 kappa	ADCC (++), CDC (++), direct cell death induction (+)	Identical to rituximab
I	Ocaratuzumab (AME-D, AME-133)	In the phase 2 trial for NHL and relapsed/refractory FL	Humanized IgG1	ADCC (++), CDC (+++), direct cell death induction (+)	Identical to rituximab
I	Pro131921 (rhumAbv114)	Discontinued	Humanized IgG1		Same as 2H7/ocrelizumab

Continued

TABLE 2 The characteristics of anti-CD20 monoclonal antibodies [83,335–340]—cont'd

Type	mAb	Status/indication	Characteristics	Mechanism	Epitope
I	TRU-015	Discontinued	Single chain CD20 targeting protein derived from 2H7 and with a human IgG1 hinge	ADCC (high), CDC (low)	Same as 2H7/ ocrelizumab
I	Ibritumomab	Approved for rituximab refractory FL (2002)	Murine IgG1kappa	ADCC (high), CDC (low)	Identical to rituximab
II	Obinutuzumab (GA101)	Approved for refractory NHL (2013), obinutuzumab-CHOP (relapsed/refractory FL), Obinutuzumab-Fc (relapsed/ refractory FL) (2003)	Humanized IgG1	ADCC (++++), direct cell death induction (++++)	Class II, large extracellular loop, core epitope: 172–176 region
II	Tositumomab (Bexxar)	Approved orphan status in FL	Murine IgG2a	PCD (high), CDC (low)	Class II, large extracellular loop, core epitope: ANPS, contact region: 170–182 positions
Unclear	hoUBM 316	Preclinical	Humanized IgG1kappa		Large extracellular loop

FDA, food and drug administration; NH, non-Hodgkin's; ADCP, antibody-dependent cell-mediated phagocytosis; ADCC, antibody-dependent cell-mediated cytotoxicity; CDC, complement-dependent cytotoxicity; ALCL, anaplastic large cell lymphoma; PCD, programmed cell death; ANPS, alanine asparagine, proline serine; CHOP, cyclophosphamide, doxorubicin, vincristine, prednisolone; FL, follicular lymphoma; MCL, mantle cell lymphoma; CLL, chronic lymphocytic leukemia; NHL, non-Hodgkin's lymphoma.

Mechanism of action of anti-CD20 antibodies

CD20 mAbs generally destroy B cells through various mechanisms. Unlike type II, type I mAbs are capable of inducing the redistribution of CD20 into small heterogenous lipid-protein microdomains (lipid rafts) that are important for signal transduction and have significant implications for the mAb effector function. In addition, type 1 mAbs bind twice as many molecules per target cell with respect to the mode of cell killing compared to type II mAbs. It is important to note that the killing of cells by mAbs acts by direct cell death induction and via indirect mechanisms that are mediated by the Fc portion of mAbs and include CDC as well as ADCC and ADCP [341,342]. The following key mechanisms shown in Fig. 2 underlie the functions and effects of anti-CD20 mAbs.

(A) ADCC: Macrophages, monocytes, neutrophils, and NK cells are the effector cells involved in ADCC. It is a lytic mechanism of cell-mediated immune defense through which Fc receptors bearing effector cells of the immune system can recognize and kill

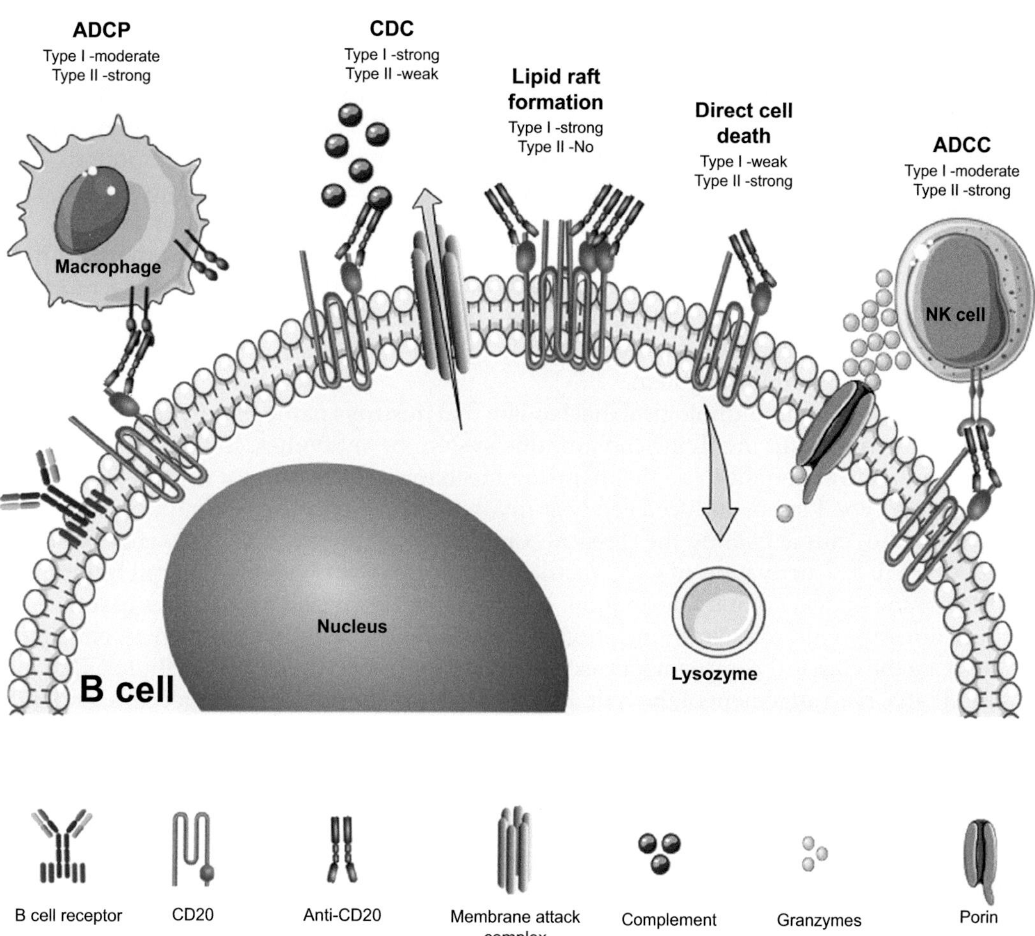

FIG. 2 Mechanism of action of Anti-CD20 Antibodies. Type I (rituximab, ofatumumab, obinutuzumab) and type II (obinutuzumab) anti-CD20 mAbs share similar mechanisms of action, but differ significantly for each modality. Type I anti-CD20 exhibits moderate ADCP, robust CDC, form lipid rafts with CD20, poor direct cell killing, and moderate ADCC. While type II anti-CD20 has a high ADCP, it has a weak CDC, does not form lipid rafts, but causes a powerful direct cell killing and ADCC. ADCC, antibody-dependent cell-mediated cytotoxicity; ADCP, antibody-dependent cell-mediated phagocytosis; CDC, complement-dependent cytotoxicity.

target cells. Effector cells express activating Fcγ receptors (FcγRs) with varying affinity for different IgG subclasses (FcγRs are surface receptors for IgG expressed on leukocytes). The signal transducing γ-chain is usually associated with FcγRs (FcγRγ-chain) and is required for surface expression [343]. It is worthy of note that functionally FcγRs can be grouped into inhibiting and activating receptors depending on their signals. Generally, preclinical and clinical evidence indicates that the Fcγ receptors of effector cells bind to the Fc component of mAbs when both Fab components are bound to CD20 molecules on the surface of B cells and their interaction is important for the functioning of therapeutic CD20 mAbs. The match between the antibody's Fcγ component and that of Fcγ receptors on the cell, as well as polymorphism, determines the efficiency of ADCC [344,345]. For instance, NK cells following stimulation through FcγRIIIa prompt the attack of opsonized (target cells coated with antibodies) targets by the release of cytolytic compounds (perforin and granzyme B) through the ADCC process [346]. Signaling through FcγR on macrophages, neutrophils, and monocytes following opsonization stimulates engulfment and target cell destruction through the fusion of the phagosome with the effector cell's lysosome through the process of ADCP [347]. The identified Fcγ receptors were CD64 (high-affinity FcR1), CD16 (low-affinity FcRIII), and CD32 (inhibitory FcRII). Because of its dependence on prior antibody response, ADCC is considered a component of the adaptive immune system.

(B) CDC: a molecular immunological mechanism that destroys pathogens by disrupting their membranes without involving the immune system or antibodies. Initially, CDC was predominantly thought to be the mainstay mechanism of antitumor activity. Rituximab and other type 1 mAbs-induced cell lysis involve the ability of the Fc component of mAbs to bind C1q, thus activating the classical complement pathway, ultimately generating the CDC [345]. The activation of CDC manifests as increased phagocytosis, cell bursting membrane attack, complex formation, and increased expression and upregulated recruitment of alternate immune effector cells [348]. These type 1 mAbs may effectively activate the classical complement cascade due to their potential to redistribute CD20 into lipid rafts, rearrangement of the type 1 CD20 mAbs on the surface of target cells, and tight clustering which allows for improved interaction with C1q [82,349]. Type 1 anti-CD20 mAbs promote the effects of complements, but not by redistributing CD20 molecules [350]. Ofatumumab has been noted to more potently stimulate the complement pathway than rituximab due to its ability to bind both extracellular loops of CD20, increasing closer proximity to the cell membrane surface, optimizing the Fc:FcγRIIIa interaction that benefits effector molecule recruitment [351].

Numerous studies have supported the beneficial role played by the complement during type 1 CD20 mAbs interaction [351–353]; however, some other studies do not support the involvement of the complement. In a preclinical murine model study for normal or malignant B-cell depletion using Cobra venom factor (CVF)-depleted mice or mice deficient in complement factors C1q, C3, or C4, no role was found for the complement [354,355]. Overall, the role of the complement is controversial and may require more studies and investigation. Other studies have indicated that the complement is involved in B-cell lysis by both type I and II anti-CD antibodies [356].

(C) Apoptosis: target B cells can be activated by type 1 mAbs like rituximab until they undergo apoptosis. Initially, it was postulated that the clustering and migration of CD20 molecules to lipid rafts, where transduction enzymes are aggregated, was a significant and essential prerequisite to apoptosis. However, this is different with type II mAbs, which induce apoptosis without the transfer of CD20 to lipid rafts [82,357–359]. Type 1 CD20 mAbs can produce a form of caspase-dependent apoptotic cell death resulting from a hyper-cross-linking phenomenon [360,361]. Another form of hyperlinked caspase-independent direct killing related to extracellular calcium influx and ROS has also been described [82,362].

(D) Fab-mediated direct induction of cell death: Type II CD20 mAbs, unlike type 1, can induce direct cell death when bound to CD20 [363]. This direct cell death induction of programmed cell death (PCD) is independent of BCL-2 and caspases, but necessitates the activities of lysosomal enzymes [364].

(E) ROS-dependent nonapoptotic cell death: anti-CD20 antibodies also induce their function through this mechanism. Here the excess amount of ROS could cause irreversible oxidative damage to lipids, proteins, and DNA, which ultimately induces cell death. A role for ROS has also been described in inducing nonapoptotic PCD including cyclophilin D-dependent mitochondrial necrosis and autophagic cell death [365].

(F) Homotypic adhesion and lysosome-mediated nonapoptotic cell death: homotypic adhesion involves the interaction of a specific cell with an identical cell, whereas lysosome-mediated nonapoptotic cell death is independent of caspases and BCL-2 control. The phenomenon involves the swelling of lysosomes releasing their contents, including cathepsin B, into the surrounding environment and cytoplasm, resulting in cell death. Tositumomab, a type II anti-CD20 mAb, may induce its activities through caspase-independent cell death and homotypic adhesion [365].

Efficacy of anti-CD20 antibodies therapy for B-cell malignancies and clinical trials

Rituximab

Following preliminary animal studies, rituximab was tested in humans. A total of 47 patients were enrolled in the phase I/II study; 16 were included in the pharmacokinetic analysis where 125 mg/m^2, 250 mg/m^2 and 375 mg/m^2 were administered to three, four and nine patients, respectively. Rituximab revealed strong activity and its serum levels were higher for responders than for nonresponders [366]. In another phase II trial, strong activity of the use of rituximab alone in indolent B NHL, especially in patients with FL, was demonstrated. The most utilized dose schedule was 375 mg/m^2 4× weekly. Rituximab serum concentration was also reported to correlate with clinical response in a study of 166 patients with low-grade or follicular NHL. The medium serum concentration of rituximab was higher in responders than in nonresponders between 4 and 13 weeks after treatment [367]. So far, rituximab is the most effective anti-CD20 mAb.

Two pivotal phase III randomized trials established R-CHOP therapy (rituximab-CHOP [Cyclophosphamide, Doxorubicin, Vincristine, and prednisolone] chemotherapy) as a treatment standard for elderly patients with DLBCL. In the study, 560 untreated elderly patients with DLBCL were enrolled and randomized to receive either R-CHOP or CHOP therapy, followed by the randomization of responders to rituximab maintenance therapy or observation. Results indicated that the proportion of patients with failure-free survival (FFS) at 3 years was significantly higher with R-CHOP than CHOP and the second randomization was 76% for rituximab maintenance therapy compared with 61% for observation [368,369]. In the United States and Europe, rituximab administered intravenously was approved for the treatment of patients with previously untreated and refractory/relapsed CLL [370]. The concurrent administration of rituximab plus FC (rituximab plus fludarabine and cyclophosphamide, R-FC) compared with FC alone was performed in CLL patients in two large phase III randomized studies based on the findings from the trial of R-FC, which became the first-choice treatment for patients with newly diagnosed or relapsed $CD20^+$ CLL patients [371]. A multicenter randomized trial compared six cycles of rituximab plus fludarabine and cyclophosphamide (R-FC) with six cycles of fludarabine and cyclophosphamide (FC) in patients with previously treated CLL. The study enrolled 552 patients. Rituximab significantly improved progression-free survival (PFS) in patients with previously treated CLL. Event-free survival, response rate, complete response rate, duration of response, and time to new CLL treatment or death were all significantly improved [371].

In another study, 454 patients with extranodal MZL of MALT (IELSG-19 phase III study) were randomly assigned to receive either chlorambucil monotherapy or a combination of chlorambucil and rituximab. At a median follow-up of 7.4 years, the addition of rituximab to chlorambucil significantly enhanced PFS and treatment outcomes such as overall survival (OS) and efficacy [372]. Since the first approval over two decades ago, rituximab has changed the treatment for patients with B-cell malignancies, reduced mortality, and improved clinical prognosis. Extensive clinical data has also confirmed the efficacy of rituximab.

Tositumomab

A phase II trial (S9911) was conducted among 90 patients with previously untreated advanced-stage FL; they received a 3-weekly CHOP chemotherapy repeated in six cycles followed by tositumomab/iodine-131(I^{131}) after 4–8 weeks. Results indicated that the overall response rate (ORR) was 91%, including a 69% complete remission rate. Following a median follow-up time of 5.1 years, the estimated 5-year OS rate was 87% and the PFS rate was 67% [373]. In another multicenter phase II study, the efficacy and safety of cyclophosphamide, vincristine, and prednisolone (CVP) followed by tositumomab and I^{131} among 306 enrolled patients with untreated low-grade FL were evaluated. The response rate after therapy completion was 100% with 28 patients achieving a complete response and only two patients achieving a partial response, indicating that the regimen represents a highly active treatment for first-line therapy of follicular NHL [374]. Tositumomab and I^{131} were administered to 41 patients with indolent or transformed indolent B-cell lymphoma following their first or second recurrence: an open-label phase II trial to determine tositumomab efficacy and safety. Results showed that 31 patients responded, with either a confirmed or unconfirmed full remission occurring in 20 cases. Eleven patients experienced total remission, with associated mild and manageable toxicity [375].

Ofatumumab

This is a fully humanized type I anti-CD20 IgG1 kappa mAb that binds to both small and large extracellular loops of the CD20 molecule. A phase II trial was conducted to assess the dose of ofatumumab combined with cyclophosphamide ($750\,mg/m^2$), doxorubicin ($50\,mg/m^2$), prednisolone (100 mg), and vincristine ($1.4\,mg/m^2$) as frontline treatment for the treatment of FL. In all, 59 patients with previously untreated FL were randomized to ofatumumab 500 or 100 mg with CHOP. The ORR was 90% for the 500 mg group and 100% for the 100 mg group. Overall, O-CHOP was safe and efficacious [340]. In another prospective phase 3 open-label trial, 27 patients with rituximab-refractory FL were randomized to receive 8 weekly infusions of ofatumumab. Results indicated that 46% of patients demonstrated tumor reduction 3 months after the initiation of therapy, suggesting that ofatumumab may have a role in FL [376]. After randomization, 61 patients with untreated CLL participated in an international phase II trial utilizing ofatumumab (500 or 1000 mg) in combination with fludarabine and cyclophosphamide to evaluate its use as frontline therapy. Results demonstrated that O-FC is effective and safe in treating CLL naïve patients, including those at high risk [377]. The efficacy and safety of ofatumumab monotherapy were evaluated in a phase 2 trial (Hx-CD20-415) involving 81 heavily pretreated patients with $CD20^+$ relapsed/progressive DLBCL after failing autologous stem cell transplantation (ASCT) or being ineligible for ASCT. In 57 evaluable patients, ofatumumab was well tolerated, and the primary endpoint was 11% [378]. Similarly, ofatumumab was evaluated in combination with chemotherapy in DLBCL in a phase II trial investigating ofatumumab plus ifosfamide/carboplatin/etoposide (ICE) or dexamethasone/cytarabine/cisplatin (DHAP). Of the 61 patients with relapsed/refractory aggressive B-cell lymphoma, 47 patients had DLBCL while 12 patients had transformed low-grade FL. The primary endpoint was promising (61%) across 59 evaluated patients; the treatment was well tolerated with no unexpected toxicity. The safety and activity of ofatumumab in combination with chemotherapy in patients with Philadelphia chromosome (pH)-negative $CD20^+$ B-cell acute lymphoblastic leukemia (ALL) were investigated in a single-arm phase 2 trial. In all, 69 patients with B-cell ALL and 2 patients with B-cell lymphoblastic lymphoma were enrolled and treated with hyper-CVAD regimen (hyperfractionated cyclophosphamide, vincristine, doxorubicin, and dexamethasone) alternating with high dose methotrexate and cytarabine in combination with ofatumumab. Results showed that the combination of hyper-CVAD plus ofatumumab is safe and active in adult patients with Ph-negative $CD20^+$ B-cell ALL [379].

Veltuzumab

Veltuzumab is a humanized second-generation anti-CD20 mAb. In a phase I/II trial of veltuzumab and milatuzumab among 35 enrolled patients with relapsed or refractory cell NHL, the results showed that no dose-limiting toxicities were observed in the phase I study. Of these, 29% of patients completed the therapy (36 weeks) and the ORR was 24%. Hence, combination therapy with veltuzumab and milatuzumab showed activity in a population of patients with relapsed or refractory indolent NHL [380]. In a multicenter phase I/II study among 82 patients with relapsed/refractory B-cell NHL, veltuzumab (80–750 mg/m^2) was assessed for safety and efficacy. The result showed that veltuzumab appeared safe and active at all tested doses. In FL, 44% of patients had objective responses with 27% complete responses [381].

Ublituximab

The safety of Umbralisib, a PI3k-delta inhibitor plus ublituximab was evaluated in 75 patients with CLL or NHL in a phase I/Ib study. Ublituximab was administered IV (NHL, 900 mg, CLL, 600 or 900 mg) for 12 cycles. Results showed that neither the CLL cohort nor the NHL cohort achieved the maximum tolerable dose, and that just one dose-limiting toxicity was noticed, suggesting that the combination's initial efficacy is encouraging and should be the subject of future study. The ORR for all patients was 46% with 17% complete responses and the combination therapy was well tolerated [382].

Side effects and prerequisites related to anti-CD20 antibodies therapy in B-cell malignancies

The development of anti-CD20, mAb biological agents represents a major breakthrough in the treatment of B-cell disorders. Given their functional differences, engineered Fc regions, and other peculiarities, distinct safety profiles can be expected for each of these agents [383].

In four randomized control trials (RCTs) with a total of 3465 patients, obinutuzumab was compared with rituximab in induction therapy of CD20-positive B-cell non-Hodgkin's lymphomas ($CD20^+$ B-NHL) [384]. Metaanalyses showed that compared with rituximab with respect to the incidences of adverse effects (AEs), obinutuzumab had higher incidences of total AEs, grade 3–5 AEs, serious AEs, fatal AEs, total infusion-related reaction (IRR), grade 3–5 IRR, all grades of neutropenia, grade 3–5 neutropenia, grade 3–5 thrombocytopenia, pyrexia, diarrhea, headache, grade 3–5 infections, chills, and insomnia. In the two arms, the incidences of other AEs were comparable [384]. In a randomized phase II trial (GAUSS) involving 175 patients with relapsed indolent iNHL, wherein patients received either rituximab ($375\,mg/m^2$) or obinutuzumab (1000 mg/week) for up to 2 years, the safety analysis population included 87 and 86 patients in the obinutuzumab and rituximab arms, respectively [385]. Although most AEs occurred at a similar rate, a higher rate of IRRs and cough was observed in the obinutuzumab versus the rituximab arm. Most episodes of IRRs were grade 1–2. In another trial for FL, patients receiving Obinutuzumab also had more AEs compared to rituximab either at first-line therapy [386] or even in previously untreated patients [387,388]. A similar pattern of AEs distribution was also seen in clinical trials in patients with DLBCL [389,390].

In another metaanalysis study in which two RCTs with 854 patients compared ofatumumab with rituximab in induction therapy of relapsed/refractory $CD20^+$ B-NHL, with respect to the incidences of AEs, ofatumumab was associated with higher incidences of infusion-related AEs, grade 3–5 infusion-related AEs, gastrointestinal disorders, AEs leading to dose interruptions and rash, but lower incidences of pyrexia. The incidences of other AEs were comparable between arms [391]. Another phase III randomized study—the HOMER study—also compared ofatumumab and rituximab without observing any superiority between their efficacies. However, AEs were higher in ofatumumab patients than among rituximab patients [376].

In three RCTs with a total of 769 patients, the efficacy and safety of ^{131}I-tositumomab were compared with rituximab in induction therapy of $CD20^+$ B-NHL [392–394]. Metaanalyses showed that with the incidences of AEs, the ^{131}I-tositumomab arm was associated with higher incidences of total grade 3–5 AEs, grade 3–5 thrombocytopenia, grade 3–5 febrile neutropenia, and grade 3–5 mucositis. Other AEs were comparable between these two arms. The findings were generally similar between DLBCL [392] and FL [393,394], as stated above.

Similarly, a multicenter phase III trial compared 90Y-ibritumomab tiuxetan with rituximab in induction therapy of $CD20^+$-low grade or B-NHL. There were no significant differences between the two arms regarding the incidences of nonhematologic AEs except for higher incidences of nausea and vomiting in the 90Y-ibritumomab tiuxetan arm [395,396]. Another randomized clinical trial investigated the outcomes and AEs between rituximab and 90Y-ibritumomab tiuxetan with a similar finding to the previously stated study in terms of efficacy and AEs [397]. Overall, most anti-CD20 mAbs have tolerable AEs [384].

Biomarkers for responsive anti-CD20 antibody therapy and solutions for refractory cases

As B-cell malignancies are characterized by deranged B-cell homeostasis and metabolism, several markers related to B-cell development and signaling are used in the assessment of clinical response to treatment or the presence of resistance. As stated previously, BCL2 and BCL6 are inherently linked with B-cell signaling and were one of the earliest biomarkers used in prognosis [398] together with LMO2, FN1, CCND2, and SCYA3 27,825,111. They served as indicators of B-cell "immortality" and have shown some clinical utility. Some researchers have used the proportion of other myeloid cells in blood as a prognostic marker in successful therapy, particularly myofibroblasts, dendritic cells, and $CD4^{+}$ T cells [399]. In clinical trials, macrophages associated with lymphomas have recently been shown to be predictive [400]. Immune checkpoint molecules like PD1/PDL1 might also serve as a biomarker(s) for successful therapy [401]. Since all cancers have a high replicative ability, Ki67 was also shown to be a predictive biomarker in a metaanalysis, but its use depends on the tumor type [402]. Circulating free DNA [403] as well as some small noncoding microRNAs [404,405] have also shown to be a valuable biomarker for therapeutic success since they are a product of apoptotic or dysregulated B cells. In summary, several biomarkers could be useful for prognosis and monitoring treatment success; however, care should be taken not to generalize the utility of a biomarker to all tumor types [406].

B-cell malignancies, like other cancers, are polyclonal and have a varying number of mutations [407,408]. As a result, it has been clinically observed that about 60% of patients do not have long remission and experience refractory disease [409]. These findings have been linked to mutations in some pathways that may affect CD20 signaling. STAT6 mutation is a common alteration affecting the JAK/STAT pathway in some B-cell malignancies [410] that renders them "resistant" to the traditional regimen. However, they show sensitivity to JAK2 inhibitors [411] and a novel target PARP14 [412]. Another common reason for refractory disease is a mutation to Myd88 and CD79B which are critical for CD20 signaling [413]. In this case, the treatment of choice is targeting BCR signaling via inhibiting BTK. The BTK inhibitor of choice is Ibrutinib [414] for most B-cell refractory B-cell malignancies. However, recent clinical trials favor newer BTK inhibitors such as Acalabrutinib for refractory CLL [415], Zanubrutinib for DLBCL and MCL [416], and Tirabrutinib for LPL [417], CNS lymphomas [418], and plasma cell malignancies [419]. In other cases of refractory disease, another immunotherapeutic target is CD19, which is similar to CD20, and the antibody of choice is loncastuximab [420], which has shown relative success in most B-cell lymphomas.

It is also common for unresponsive or refractory or even recurrent B-cell lymphoma treatments to use certain targeted therapies with success. Alemtuzumab [421] is an anti-CD52 antibody present on cells in CLL [422] which has been used with some success. PI3K dysfunction has been implicated in some cancers [423] and has been an attractive target for B-cell malignancies. Copanlisib, a PI3K inhibitor, is also used in combination with other anti-CD20 antibodies as first-line therapy in refractory disease [424,425]. Idelalisib is another Pi3K inhibitor commonly recommended for refractory disease [426]. Gene therapies have also been used in treating cancers and chimeric antigen receptor (CAR) T cells stand out for their allogeneicity and can be personalized to each patient [427]. Axicabtagene Ciloleucel, a CD19 targeting CAR T cell with a CD3 and CD28 signaling domain [428], is an FDA-approved therapy for refractory B-cell malignancies with documented success [429,430].

Future perspectives

With the success of rituximab, considerable efforts have been initiated to develop improved agents. Currently, there are a considerable number of new anti-CD20 mAbs in clinical use and development with many more in preclinical evaluation. The newly developed mAbs have been modified and engineered for prospective advantages over rituximab of the first generation, which are intended to enhance therapeutic performance by enhancing their effector activities. It will be fascinating to determine if the lysis potency associated with the mechanism of action of certain anti-CD20 antibodies can be accomplished in vivo. The ability to activate the complement as a specific mechanism for certain anti-CD20 antibodies has not been associated with more toxicity in patients, but remains a potential concern knowing the toxicity associated with systemic complement activation.

It will also be interesting to see if combination chemotherapy with certain anti-CD20 antibodies will produce higher responses (clinical efficacy and safety) than those observed with that of a single agent. For instance, although rituximab was used as a single agent, patients with relapsed or refractory low-grade NHL demonstrated ORR of 40%–50%, with a median time to progression (TTP) of approximately 9 months [431]. The combination of rituximab and CHOP chemotherapy (R-CHOP) produced a higher ORR of 95%, with a median TTP of 82 months. Further, the addition of rituximab to standard frontline chemotherapy regimens significantly improves ORR in low-grade NHL [432] and newly diagnosed patients with DLBCL [433]. The mechanism of this synergistic activity as well as numerous other effective combination therapies is not clear.

It is also important to explore whether the superior performance of Type II mAb is due to their direct cell killing by PCD, their failure to promote CDC when compared with Type I mAb, or other undefined differences. Bi-specific antibodies combining CD20 and other markers could prove to be beneficial in the long run.

Conclusions

CD20 is a major marker expressed on all B-cell surfaces. Hence, anti-CD20 antibodies were widely targeted for B-cell malignancies therapy. Numerous clinical evidences indicate that these different generations of anti-CD20 antibodies are associated with effectiveness in the treatment of diverse B-cell disorders. For over 20 years, the anti-CD20 mAbs have been around and their development has contributed to our current knowledge of their effectiveness as therapeutic targets. Therefore, anti-CD20 mAb therapy has initiated a new era of B-cell malignancy therapy. A major aspect of the development involves an in-depth understanding of the disease microenvironment. Indeed, the introduction of rituximab has laid the foundation for mAb therapy, and it is interesting to note that attention is now geared toward mAb therapy to many other different targets. The lessons learned from rituximab are necessary for the use of future mAbs. The future anticipates an era of combination and improved engineering of antibodies to improve patients' responses. Combination therapy, for instance, the combination of chemotherapy and anti-CD20 mAbs, has pointed to the possibility of improved remission of disease duration and survival. It also appears that the design and production of new generation anti-CD20 antibodies could contribute to better therapeutic outcomes, especially in relation to the reduced side effects in the treatment of B-cell disorders. Questions still abound regarding the dosing schedule of anti-CD20 therapy, the specific mechanism of action when used solely or in combination with chemotherapeutic agents or other drugs, the limitation of the use of anti-CD20 as a single agent, and many more. Although anti-CD20 therapy (types 1 and II) may facilitate cell killing through diverse mechanisms, including immune-mediated responses (CDC, ADCC, ADPC), and direct death cell signaling, it is still not yet understood which mechanism plays the most significant role in vivo or why only a portion of patients achieve lasting responses. Finding biomarkers that accurately predict which patients will benefit from a specific anti-CD20 single drug or its inclusion in combination therapy remains an unmet need.

Despite the issues on the ground, giant strides have been reached, especially with the introduction of the newer engineered Fc region anti-CD20 mAbs, which are in the clinical trial or currently in use and offer numerous benefits over rituximab. Furthermore, another main success of anti-CD20 mAbs has been in combination with chemo- or radiotherapy.

References

[1] Tlsty TD, Coussens LM. Tumor stroma and regulation of cancer development. Annu Rev Pathol 2006;1:119–50.

[2] Hanahan D, Weinberg RA. Hallmarks of cancer: the next generation. Cell 2011;144(5):646–74.

[3] Soto AM, Sonnenschein C. The tissue organization field theory of cancer: a testable replacement for the somatic mutation theory. BioEssays 2011;33(5):332–40.

[4] Davies PC, Lineweaver CH. Cancer tumors as Metazoa 1.0: tapping genes of ancient ancestors. Phys Biol 2011;8 (1), 015001.

[5] Tomasetti C, Li L, Vogelstein B. Stem cell divisions, somatic mutations, cancer etiology, and cancer prevention. Science 2017;355(6331):1330–4.

[6] Vyatkin AD, Otnyukov DV, Leonov SV, Belikov AV. Comprehensive patient-level classification and quantification of driver events in TCGA PanCanAtlas cohorts. PLoS Genet 2022;18(1), e1009996.

[7] Majérus M-A. The cause of cancer: the unifying theory. Adv Cancer Biol 2022;4:100034.

[8] Cooper MD. The early history of B cells. Nat Rev Immunol 2015;15(3):191–7.

[9] Kondo M. Lymphoid and myeloid lineage commitment in multipotent hematopoietic progenitors. Immunol Rev 2010;238(1):37–46.

[10] Pelanda R, Torres RM. Central B-cell tolerance: where selection begins. Cold Spring Harb Perspect Biol 2012;4 (4), a007146.

[11] Wang Y, Liu J, Burrows PD, Wang JY. B cell development and maturation. Adv Exp Med Biol 2020;1254:1–22.

[12] Pillai S, Cariappa A. The follicular versus marginal zone B lymphocyte cell fate decision. Nat Rev Immunol 2009;9(11):767–77.

[13] Cerutti A, Cols M, Puga I. Marginal zone B cells: virtues of innate-like antibody-producing lymphocytes. Nat Rev Immunol 2013;13(2):118–32.

[14] Aliyu M, Zohora F, Saboor-Yaraghi AA. Spleen in innate and adaptive immunity regulation. AIMS Allergy Immunol 2021;5(1):1–17.

[15] Schuh E, Berer K, Mulazzani M, Feil K, Meinl I, Lahm H, et al. Features of human CD3+CD20+ T cells. J Immunol 2016;197(4):1111–7.

[16] Pavlasova G, Mraz M. The regulation and function of CD20: an "enigma" of B-cell biology and targeted therapy. Haematologica 2020;105(6):1494–506.

[17] Eon Kuek L, Leffler M, Mackay GA, Hulett MD. The MS4A family: counting past 1, 2, and 3. Immunol Cell Biol 2016;94(1):11–23.

[18] Gamonet C, Bole-Richard E, Delherme A, Aubin F, Toussirot E, Garnache-Ottou F, et al. New CD20 alternative splice variants: molecular identification and differential expression within hematological B cell malignancies. Exp Hematol Oncol 2015;5:7.

[19] Manshouri T, Do KA, Wang X, Giles FJ, O'Brien SM, Saffer H, et al. Circulating CD20 is detectable in the plasma of patients with chronic lymphocytic leukemia and is of prognostic significance. Blood 2003;101(7):2507–13.
[20] Polyak MJ, Li H, Shariat N, Deans JP. CD20 homo-oligomers physically associate with the B cell antigen receptor. Dissociation upon receptor engagement and recruitment of phosphoproteins and calmodulin-binding proteins. J Biol Chem 2008;283(27):18545–52.
[21] Kuijpers TW, Bende RJ, Baars PA, Grummels A, Derks IA, Dolman KM, et al. CD20 deficiency in humans results in impaired T cell-independent antibody responses. J Clin Invest 2010;120(1):214–22.
[22] Olejniczak SH, Stewart CC, Donohue K, Czuczman MS. A quantitative exploration of surface antigen expression in common B-cell malignancies using flow cytometry. Immunol Investig 2006;35(1):93–114.
[23] Fang C, Zhuang Y, Wang L, Fan L, Wu YJ, Zhang R, et al. High levels of CD20 expression predict good prognosis in chronic lymphocytic leukemia. Cancer Sci 2013;104(8):996–1001.
[24] Johnson NA, Boyle M, Bashashati A, Leach S, Brooks-Wilson A, Sehn LH, et al. Diffuse large B-cell lymphoma: reduced CD20 expression is associated with an inferior survival. Blood 2009;113(16):3773–80.
[25] Prevodnik VK, Lavrencak J, Horvat M, Novakovic BJ. The predictive significance of CD20 expression in B-cell lymphomas. Diagn Pathol 2011;6:33.
[26] Rafiq S, Butchar JP, Cheney C, Mo X, Trotta R, Caligiuri M, et al. Comparative assessment of clinically utilized CD20-directed antibodies in chronic lymphocytic leukemia cells reveals divergent NK cell, monocyte, and macrophage properties. J Immunol 2013;190(6):2702–11.
[27] Salles G, Barrett M, Foa R, Maurer J, O'Brien S, Valente N, et al. Rituximab in B-cell hematologic malignancies: a review of 20 years of clinical experience. Adv Ther 2017;34(10):2232–73.
[28] Pavlasova G, Borsky M, Svobodova V, Oppelt J, Cerna K, Novotna J, et al. Rituximab primarily targets an intraclonal BCR signaling proficient CLL subpopulation characterized by high CD20 levels. Leukemia 2018;32(9):2028–31.
[29] Henry C, Deschamps M, Rohrlich PS, Pallandre JR, Remy-Martin JP, Callanan M, et al. Identification of an alternative CD20 transcript variant in B-cell malignancies coding for a novel protein associated to rituximab resistance. Blood 2010;115(12):2420–9.
[30] Alaggio R, Amador C, Anagnostopoulos I, Attygalle AD, Araujo IBO, Berti E, et al. The 5th edition of the World Health Organization Classification of Haematolymphoid Tumours: lymphoid neoplasms. Leukemia 2022;36(7):1720–48.
[31] Hussein MR. Atypical lymphoid proliferations: the pathologist's viewpoint. Expert Rev Hematol 2013;6(2):139–53.
[32] Johnston J, Allen JE. IgG4-related disease in the head and neck. Curr Opin Otolaryngol Head Neck Surg 2018;26(6):403–8.
[33] Backhus J, Neumann C, Perkhofer L, Schulte LA, Mayer B, Seufferlein T, et al. A follow-up study of a European IgG4-related disease cohort treated with rituximab. J Clin Med 2021;10(6):1329.
[34] El-Osta HE, Kurzrock R. Castleman's disease: from basic mechanisms to molecular therapeutics. Oncologist 2011;16(4):497–511.
[35] Kaegi C, Wuest B, Schreiner J, Steiner UC, Vultaggio A, Matucci A, et al. Systematic review of safety and efficacy of rituximab in treating immune-mediated disorders. Front Immunol 2019;10:1990.
[36] Maury S, Chevret S, Thomas X, Heim D, Leguay T, Huguet F, et al. Rituximab in B-lineage adult acute lymphoblastic leukemia. N Engl J Med 2016;375(11):1044–53.
[37] Samra B, Jabbour E, Ravandi F, Kantarjian H, Short NJ. Evolving therapy of adult acute lymphoblastic leukemia: state-of-the-art treatment and future directions. J Hematol Oncol 2020;13(1):70.
[38] Hallek M. Chronic lymphocytic leukemia: 2020 update on diagnosis, risk stratification and treatment. Am J Hematol 2019;94(11):1266–87.
[39] Hallek M, Al-Sawaf O. Chronic lymphocytic leukemia: 2022 update on diagnostic and therapeutic procedures. Am J Hematol 2021;96(12):1679–705.
[40] Kreitman RJ. Hairy cell leukemia: present and future directions. Leuk Lymphoma 2019;60(12):2869–79.
[41] Maitre E, Cornet E, Troussard X. Hairy cell leukemia: 2020 update on diagnosis, risk stratification, and treatment. Am J Hematol 2019;94(12):1413–22.
[42] Pott C, Sehn LH, Belada D, Gribben J, Hoster E, Kahl B, et al. MRD response in relapsed/refractory FL after obinutuzumab plus bendamustine or bendamustine alone in the GADOLIN trial. Leukemia 2020;34(2):522–32.

[43] Sindel A, Al-Juhaishi T, Yazbeck V. Marginal zone lymphoma: state-of-the-art treatment. Curr Treat Options in Oncol 2019;20(12):90.

[44] Herold M, Hoster E, Janssens A, McCarthy H, Tedeschi A, Pocock C, et al. Immunochemotherapy and maintenance with obinutuzumab or rituximab in patients with previously untreated marginal zone lymphoma in the randomized GALLIUM trial. Hemasphere 2022;6(3), e699.

[45] Julhakyan HL, Al-Radi LS, Moiseeva TN, Danishyan KI, Kovrigina AM, Glebova SM, et al. A single-center experience in splenic diffuse red pulp lymphoma diagnosis. Clin Lymphoma Myeloma Leuk 2016;16(Suppl): S166–9.

[46] Yilmaz E, Chhina A, Nava VE, Aggarwal A. A review on splenic diffuse red pulp small B-cell lymphoma. Curr Oncol 2021;28(6):5148–54.

[47] Pophali PA, Bartley A, Kapoor P, Gonsalves WI, Ashrani AA, Marshall AL, et al. Prevalence and survival of smouldering Waldenstrom macroglobulinaemia in the United States. Br J Haematol 2019;184(6):1014–7.

[48] Bustoros M, Sklavenitis-Pistofidis R, Kapoor P, Liu CJ, Kastritis E, Zanwar S, et al. Progression risk stratification of asymptomatic Waldenstrom macroglobulinemia. J Clin Oncol 2019;37(16):1403–11.

[49] Matasar MJ, Luminari S, Barr PM, Barta SK, Danilov AV, Hill BT, et al. Follicular lymphoma: recent and emerging therapies, treatment strategies, and remaining unmet needs. Oncologist 2019;24(11):e1236–50.

[50] Freedman A, Jacobsen E. Follicular lymphoma: 2020 update on diagnosis and management. Am J Hematol 2020;95(3):316–27.

[51] Fernandez-Guarino M, Ortiz-Romero PL, Fernandez-Misa R, Montalban C. Rituximab in the treatment of primary cutaneous B-cell lymphoma: a review. Actas Dermosifiliogr 2014;105(5):438–45.

[52] Lang CCV, Ramelyte E, Dummer R. Innovative therapeutic approaches in primary cutaneous B cell lymphoma. Front Oncol 2020;10:1163.

[53] Silkenstedt E, Linton K, Dreyling M. Mantle cell lymphoma—advances in molecular biology, prognostication and treatment approaches. Br J Haematol 2021;195(2):162–73.

[54] Silkenstedt E, Dreyling M. Mantle cell lymphoma—advances in molecular biology, prognostication and treatment approaches. Hematol Oncol 2021;39(Suppl 1):31–8.

[55] Montoto S, Fitzgibbon J. Transformation of indolent B-cell lymphomas. J Clin Oncol 2011;29(14):1827–34.

[56] Demirdas S, Hense J, Duhrsen U, Huttmann A. Treatment outcome in patients with primary or secondary transformed indolent B-cell lymphomas. Oncol Res Treat 2019;42(11):580–8.

[57] Miao Y, Medeiros LJ, Li Y, Li J, Young KH. Genetic alterations and their clinical implications in DLBCL. Nat Rev Clin Oncol 2019;16(10):634–52.

[58] Flinn IW, Erter J, Daniel DB, Mace JR, Berdeja JG. Phase II study of bendamustine and ofatumumab in elderly patients with newly diagnosed diffuse large B-cell lymphoma who are poor candidates for R-CHOP chemotherapy. Oncologist 2019;24(8):1035–e623.

[59] Crombie JL, Armand P. Diffuse large B-cell lymphoma and high-grade B-cell lymphoma: genetic classification and its implications for prognosis and treatment. Surg Oncol Clin N Am 2020;29(1):115–25.

[60] Ollila TA, Olszewski AJ. Extranodal diffuse large B cell lymphoma: molecular features, prognosis, and risk of central nervous system recurrence. Curr Treat Options in Oncol 2018;19(8):38.

[61] Melani C, Jaffe ES, Wilson WH. Pathobiology and treatment of lymphomatoid granulomatosis, a rare EBV-driven disorder. Blood 2020;135(16):1344–52.

[62] Evens AM, Danilov A, Jagadeesh D, Sperling A, Kim SH, Vaca R, et al. Burkitt lymphoma in the modern era: real-world outcomes and prognostication across 30 US cancer centers. Blood 2021;137(3):374–86.

[63] Crombie J, LaCasce A. The treatment of Burkitt lymphoma in adults. Blood 2021;137(6):743–50.

[64] Saini KS, Azim Jr HA, Cocorocchio E, Vanazzi A, Saini ML, Raviele PR, et al. Rituximab in Hodgkin lymphoma: is the target always a hit? Cancer Treat Rev 2011;37(5):385–90.

[65] Ansell SM. Hodgkin lymphoma: a 2020 update on diagnosis, risk-stratification, and management. Am J Hematol 2020;95(8):978–89.

[66] Kiykim A, Eker N, Surekli O, Nain E, Kasap N, Akturk H, et al. Malignancy and lymphoid proliferation in primary immune deficiencies; hard to define, hard to treat. Pediatr Blood Cancer 2020;67(2), e28091.

[67] Sharma S, Pilania RK, Anjani G, Sudhakar M, Arora K, Tyagi R, et al. Lymphoproliferation in inborn errors of immunity: the eye does not see what the mind does not know. Front Immunol 2022;13, 856601.

[68] Roberts TK, Chen X, Liao JJ. Diagnostic and therapeutic challenges of EBV-positive mucocutaneous ulcer: a case report and systematic review of the literature. Exp Hematol Oncol 2015;5:13.

[69] Leung N, Drosou ME, Nasr SH. Dysproteinemias and glomerular disease. Clin J Am Soc Nephrol 2018;13 (1):128–39.

[70] Berentsen S. How I treat cold agglutinin disease. Blood 2021;137(10):1295–303.

[71] Palladini G, Foli A, Russo P, Milani P, Obici L, Lavatelli F, et al. Treatment of IgM-associated AL amyloidosis with the combination of rituximab, bortezomib, and dexamethasone. Clin Lymphoma Myeloma Leuk 2011;11 (1):143–5.

[72] Manwani R, Sachchithananthам S, Mahmood S, Foard D, Sharpley F, Rezk T, et al. Treatment of IgM-associated immunoglobulin light-chain amyloidosis with rituximab-bendamustine. Blood 2018;132(7):761–4.

[73] Rudnicki M. Rituximab for treatment of membranoproliferative glomerulonephritis and C3 Glomerulopathies. Biomed Res Int 2017;2017:2180508.

[74] Maharjan R, Wang JW, Shrestha IK. The efficacy of rituximab in the treatment of membranous nephropathy. J Nepal Health Res Counc 2021;18(4):580–7.

[75] Bianchi G, Anderson KC, Harris NL, Sohani AR. The heavy chain diseases: clinical and pathologic features. Oncology (Williston Park) 2014;28(1):45–53.

[76] Singer S, Efebera Y, Bumma N, Khan A, Devarakonda S, Chaudhry M, et al. Heavy lifting: nomenclature and novel therapy for gamma heavy chain disease and other heavy chain disorders. Clin Lymphoma Myeloma Leuk 2020;20(8):493–8.

[77] Sherbenou DW, Behrens CR, Su Y, Wolf JL, Martin 3rd TG, Liu B. The development of potential antibody-based therapies for myeloma. Blood Rev 2015;29(2):81–91.

[78] Schelker RC, Grube M, Reichle A, Wagner B, Herr W, Evert M, et al. Detection of hemophagocytic extremely multinucleated giant plasma cells after rituximab/low-dose lenalidomide treatment in CD20(+) multiple myeloma. Leuk Lymphoma 2019;60(9):2331–3.

[79] Bray F, Ferlay J, Soerjomataram I, Siegel RL, Torre LA, Jemal A. Global cancer statistics 2018: GLOBOCAN estimates of incidence and mortality worldwide for 36 cancers in 185 countries. CA Cancer J Clin 2018;68 (6):394–424.

[80] Sung H, Ferlay J, Siegel RL, Laversanne M, Soerjomataram I, Jemal A, et al. Global cancer statistics 2020: GLOBOCAN estimates of incidence and mortality worldwide for 36 cancers in 185 countries. CA Cancer J Clin 2021;71(3):209–49.

[81] Li S, Young KH, Medeiros LJ. Diffuse large B-cell lymphoma. Pathology 2018;50(1):74–87.

[82] Casan JML, Wong J, Northcott MJ, Opat S. Anti-CD20 monoclonal antibodies: reviewing a revolution. Hum Vaccin Immunother 2018;14(12):2820–41.

[83] Klein C, Jamois C, Nielsen T. Anti-CD20 treatment for B-cell malignancies: current status and future directions. Expert Opin Biol Ther 2021;21(2):161–81.

[84] Siegel RL, Miller KD, Jemal A. Cancer statistics, 2019. CA Cancer J Clin 2019;69(1):7–34.

[85] Morrison VA, Bell JA, Hamilton L, Ogbonnaya A, Shih HC, Hennenfent K, et al. Economic burden of patients with diffuse large B-cell and follicular lymphoma treated in the USA. Future Oncol 2018;14(25):2627–42.

[86] Rossi D, Spina V, Gaidano G. Biology and treatment of Richter syndrome. Blood 2018;131(25):2761–72.

[87] Schmitz R, Wright GW, Huang DW, Johnson CA, Phelan JD, Wang JQ, et al. Genetics and pathogenesis of diffuse large B-cell lymphoma. N Engl J Med 2018;378(15):1396–407.

[88] Basso K, Dalla-Favera R. Germinal centres and B cell lymphomagenesis. Nat Rev Immunol 2015;15(3):172–84.

[89] Chapuy B, Stewart C, Dunford AJ, Kim J, Kamburov A, Redd RA, et al. Molecular subtypes of diffuse large B cell lymphoma are associated with distinct pathogenic mechanisms and outcomes. Nat Med 2018;24(5):679–90.

[90] Karube K, Enjuanes A, Dlouhy I, Jares P, Martin-Garcia D, Nadeu F, et al. Integrating genomic alterations in diffuse large B-cell lymphoma identifies new relevant pathways and potential therapeutic targets. Leukemia 2018;32(3):675–84.

[91] Grimm KE, O'Malley DP. Aggressive B cell lymphomas in the 2017 revised WHO classification of tumors of hematopoietic and lymphoid tissues. Ann Diagn Pathol 2019;38:6–10.

[92] Wang L, Li LR, Young KH. New agents and regimens for diffuse large B cell lymphoma. J Hematol Oncol 2020;13(1):175.

[93] Swerdlow SH, Campo E, Pileri SA, Harris NL, Stein H, Siebert R, et al. The 2016 revision of the World Health Organization classification of lymphoid neoplasms. Blood 2016;127(20):2375–90.

[94] Sud A, Chattopadhyay S, Thomsen H, Sundquist K, Sundquist J, Houlston RS, et al. Analysis of 153 115 patients with hematological malignancies refines the spectrum of familial risk. Blood 2019;134(12):960–9.

[95] Pasqualucci L, Khiabanian H, Fangazio M, Vasishtha M, Messina M, Holmes AB, et al. Genetics of follicular lymphoma transformation. Cell Rep 2014;6(1):130–40.
[96] Takata K, Miyata-Takata T, Sato Y, Yoshino T. Pathology of follicular lymphoma. J Clin Exp Hematop 2014;54 (1):3–9.
[97] Okosun J, Bodor C, Wang J, Araf S, Yang CY, Pan C, et al. Integrated genomic analysis identifies recurrent mutations and evolution patterns driving the initiation and progression of follicular lymphoma. Nat Genet 2014;46 (2):176–81.
[98] Green MR, Kihira S, Liu CL, Nair RV, Salari R, Gentles AJ, et al. Mutations in early follicular lymphoma progenitors are associated with suppressed antigen presentation. Proc Natl Acad Sci U S A 2015;112(10):E1116–25.
[99] Okosun J, Wolfson RL, Wang J, Araf S, Wilkins L, Castellano BM, et al. Recurrent mTORC1-activating RRAGC mutations in follicular lymphoma. Nat Genet 2016;48(2):183–8.
[100] Green MR. Chromatin modifying gene mutations in follicular lymphoma. Blood 2018;131(6):595–604.
[101] Qu X, Li H, Braziel RM, Passerini V, Rimsza LM, Hsi ED, et al. Genomic alterations important for the prognosis in patients with follicular lymphoma treated in SWOG study S0016. Blood 2019;133(1):81–93.
[102] Dighiero G, Hamblin TJ. Chronic lymphocytic leukaemia. Lancet 2008;371(9617):1017–29.
[103] Kikushige Y. Pathogenesis of chronic lymphocytic leukemia and the development of novel therapeutic strategies. J Clin Exp Hematop 2020;60(4):146–58.
[104] Strati P, Shanafelt TD. Monoclonal B-cell lymphocytosis and early-stage chronic lymphocytic leukemia: diagnosis, natural history, and risk stratification. Blood 2015;126(4):454–62.
[105] Galigalidou C, Zaragoza-Infante L, Iatrou A, Chatzidimitriou A, Stamatopoulos K, Agathangelidis A. Understanding monoclonal B cell lymphocytosis: an interplay of genetic and microenvironmental factors. Front Oncol 2021;11, 769612.
[106] Damm F, Mylonas E, Cosson A, Yoshida K, Della Valle V, Mouly E, et al. Acquired initiating mutations in early hematopoietic cells of CLL patients. Cancer Discov 2014;4(9):1088–101.
[107] Fabbri G, Dalla-Favera R. The molecular pathogenesis of chronic lymphocytic leukaemia. Nat Rev Cancer 2016;16(3):145–62.
[108] Baliakas P, Moysiadis T, Hadzidimitriou A, Xochelli A, Jeromin S, Agathangelidis A, et al. Tailored approaches grounded on immunogenetic features for refined prognostication in chronic lymphocytic leukemia. Haematologica 2019;104(2):360–9.
[109] Baliakas P, Jeromin S, Iskas M, Puiggros A, Plevova K, Nguyen-Khac F, et al. Cytogenetic complexity in chronic lymphocytic leukemia: definitions, associations, and clinical impact. Blood 2019;133(11):1205–16.
[110] Herling CD, Klaumunzer M, Rocha CK, Altmuller J, Thiele H, Bahlo J, et al. Complex karyotypes and KRAS and POT1 mutations impact outcome in CLL after chlorambucil-based chemotherapy or chemoimmunotherapy. Blood 2016;128(3):395–404.
[111] Baliakas P, Agathangelidis A, Hadzidimitriou A, Sutton LA, Minga E, Tsanousa A, et al. Not all IGHV3-21 chronic lymphocytic leukemias are equal: prognostic considerations. Blood 2015;125(5):856–9.
[112] Jeromin S, Haferlach C, Dicker F, Alpermann T, Haferlach T, Kern W. Differences in prognosis of stereotyped IGHV3-21 chronic lymphocytic leukaemia according to additional molecular and cytogenetic aberrations. Leukemia 2016;30(11):2251–3.
[113] Eichhorst B, Robak T, Montserrat E, Ghia P, Niemann CU, Kater AP, et al. Chronic lymphocytic leukaemia: ESMO clinical practice guidelines for diagnosis, treatment and follow-up. Ann Oncol 2021;32(1):23–33.
[114] Dreyling M, Campo E, Hermine O, Jerkeman M, Le Gouill S, Rule S, et al. Newly diagnosed and relapsed mantle cell lymphoma: ESMO clinical practice guidelines for diagnosis, treatment and follow-up. Ann Oncol 2017;28(Suppl 4):iv62–71.
[115] Albero R, Enjuanes A, Demajo S, Castellano G, Pinyol M, Garcia N, et al. Cyclin D1 overexpression induces global transcriptional downregulation in lymphoid neoplasms. J Clin Invest 2018;128(9):4132–47.
[116] Navarro A, Bea S, Jares P, Campo E. Molecular pathogenesis of mantle cell lymphoma. Hematol Oncol Clin North Am 2020;34(5):795–807.
[117] Wlodarska I, Meeus P, Stul M, Thienpont L, Wouters E, Marcelis L, et al. Variant t(2;11)(p11;q13) associated with the IgK-CCND1 rearrangement is a recurrent translocation in leukemic small-cell B-non-Hodgkin lymphoma. Leukemia 2004;18(10):1705–10.
[118] Marrero WD, Cruz-Chacon A, Cabanillas F. Mantle cell lymphoma with t(11;22) (q13;q11.2) an indolent clinical variant? Leuk Lymphoma 2018;59(10):2509–11.

[119] Vegliante MC, Palomero J, Perez-Galan P, Roue G, Castellano G, Navarro A, et al. SOX11 regulates PAX5 expression and blocks terminal B-cell differentiation in aggressive mantle cell lymphoma. Blood 2013;121 (12):2175–85.
[120] Palomero J, Vegliante MC, Eguileor A, Rodriguez ML, Balsas P, Martinez D, et al. SOX11 defines two different subtypes of mantle cell lymphoma through transcriptional regulation of BCL6. Leukemia 2016;30(7):1596–9.
[121] Cheah CY, Seymour JF, Wang ML. Mantle cell lymphoma. J Clin Oncol 2016;34(11):1256–69.
[122] Puente XS, Jares P, Campo E. Chronic lymphocytic leukemia and mantle cell lymphoma: crossroads of genetic and microenvironment interactions. Blood 2018;131(21):2283–96.
[123] Eskelund CW, Dahl C, Hansen JW, Westman M, Kolstad A, Pedersen LB, et al. TP53 mutations identify younger mantle cell lymphoma patients who do not benefit from intensive chemoimmunotherapy. Blood 2017;130 (17):1903–10.
[124] Martin P, Ruan J, Leonard JP. The potential for chemotherapy-free strategies in mantle cell lymphoma. Blood 2017;130(17):1881–8.
[125] Maes B, De Wolf-Peeters C. Marginal zone cell lymphoma—an update on recent advances. Histopathology 2002;40(2):117–26.
[126] Nakamura S, Ponzoni M. Marginal zone B-cell lymphoma: lessons from Western and Eastern diagnostic approaches. Pathology 2020;52(1):15–29.
[127] Raderer M, Kiesewetter B, Ferreri AJ. Clinicopathologic characteristics and treatment of marginal zone lymphoma of mucosa-associated lymphoid tissue (MALT lymphoma). CA Cancer J Clin 2016;66(2):153–71.
[128] Perrone S, D'Elia GM, Annechini G, Pulsoni A. Infectious aetiology of marginal zone lymphoma and role of anti-infective therapy. Mediterr J Hematol Infect Dis 2016;8(1), e2016006.
[129] Sriskandarajah P, Dearden CE. Epidemiology and environmental aspects of marginal zone lymphomas. Best Pract Res Clin Haematol 2017;30(1–2):84–91.
[130] Xing KH, Kahlon A, Skinnider BF, Connors JM, Gascoyne RD, Sehn LH, et al. Outcomes in splenic marginal zone lymphoma: analysis of 107 patients treated in British Columbia. Br J Haematol 2015;169(4):520–7.
[131] Florindez JA, Alderuccio JP, Reis IM, Lossos IS. Splenic marginal zone lymphoma: a US population-based survival analysis (1999–2016). Cancer 2020;126(21):4706–16.
[132] Zinzani PL. The many faces of marginal zone lymphoma. Hematology Am Soc Hematol Educ Program 2012;2012:426–32.
[133] Salido M, Baro C, Oscier D, Stamatopoulos K, Dierlamm J, Matutes E, et al. Cytogenetic aberrations and their prognostic value in a series of 330 splenic marginal zone B-cell lymphomas: a multicenter study of the splenic B-cell lymphoma group. Blood 2010;116(9):1479–88.
[134] Parry M, Rose-Zerilli MJ, Ljungstrom V, Gibson J, Wang J, Walewska R, et al. Genetics and prognostication in splenic marginal zone lymphoma: revelations from deep sequencing. Clin Cancer Res 2015;21(18):4174–83.
[135] Jacobson C, LaCasce A. How I treat Burkitt lymphoma in adults. Blood 2014;124(19):2913–20.
[136] Kalisz K, Alessandrino F, Beck R, Smith D, Kikano E, Ramaiya NH, et al. An update on Burkitt lymphoma: a review of pathogenesis and multimodality imaging assessment of disease presentation, treatment response, and recurrence. Insights Imaging 2019;10(1):56.
[137] Painschab MS, Westmoreland KD, Kasonkanji E, Zuze T, Kaimila B, Waswa P, et al. Prospective study of Burkitt lymphoma treatment in adolescents and adults in Malawi. Blood Adv 2019;3(4):612–20.
[138] Bouda GC, Traore F, Couitchere L, Raquin MA, Guedenon KM, Pondy A, et al. Advanced Burkitt lymphoma in Sub-Saharan Africa pediatric units: results of the third prospective multicenter study of the Groupe Franco-Africain d'Oncologie Pediatrique. J Glob Oncol 2019;5:1–9.
[139] Aukema SM, Theil L, Rohde M, Bauer B, Bradtke J, Burkhardt B, et al. Sequential karyotyping in Burkitt lymphoma reveals a linear clonal evolution with increase in karyotype complexity and a high frequency of recurrent secondary aberrations. Br J Haematol 2015;170(6):814–25.
[140] Haberl S, Haferlach T, Stengel A, Jeromin S, Kern W, Haferlach C. MYC rearranged B-cell neoplasms: impact of genetics on classification. Cancer Genet 2016;209(10):431–9.
[141] Zayac AS, Olszewski AJ. Burkitt lymphoma: bridging the gap between advances in molecular biology and therapy. Leuk Lymphoma 2020;61(8):1784–96.
[142] Rohde M, Bonn BR, Zimmermann M, Lange J, Moricke A, Klapper W, et al. Relevance of ID3-TCF3-CCND3 pathway mutations in pediatric aggressive B-cell lymphoma treated according to the non-Hodgkin lymphoma Berlin-Frankfurt-Munster protocols. Haematologica 2017;102(6):1091–8.

[143] Panea RI, Love CL, Shingleton JR, Reddy A, Bailey JA, Moormann AM, et al. The whole-genome landscape of Burkitt lymphoma subtypes. Blood 2019;134(19):1598–607.

[144] Salaverria I, Martin-Guerrero I, Wagener R, Kreuz M, Kohler CW, Richter J, et al. A recurrent 11q aberration pattern characterizes a subset of MYC-negative high-grade B-cell lymphomas resembling Burkitt lymphoma. Blood 2014;123(8):1187–98.

[145] Grande BM, Gerhard DS, Jiang A, Griner NB, Abramson JS, Alexander TB, et al. Genome-wide discovery of somatic coding and noncoding mutations in pediatric endemic and sporadic Burkitt lymphoma. Blood 2019;133(12):1313–24.

[146] Wagener R, Seufert J, Raimondi F, Bens S, Kleinheinz K, Nagel I, et al. The mutational landscape of Burkitt-like lymphoma with 11q aberration is distinct from that of Burkitt lymphoma. Blood 2019;133(9):962–6.

[147] Gonzalez-Farre B, Ramis-Zaldivar JE, Salmeron-Villalobos J, Balague O, Celis V, Verdu-Amoros J, et al. Burkitt-like lymphoma with 11q aberration: a germinal center-derived lymphoma genetically unrelated to Burkitt lymphoma. Haematologica 2019;104(9):1822–9.

[148] Dimopoulos MA, Kastritis E. How I treat Waldenstrom macroglobulinemia. Blood 2019;134(23):2022–35.

[149] Kyle RA, Therneau TM, Rajkumar SV, Remstein ED, Offord JR, Larson DR, et al. Long-term follow-up of IgM monoclonal gammopathy of undetermined significance. Blood 2003;102(10):3759–64.

[150] Paiva B, Corchete LA, Vidriales MB, Garcia-Sanz R, Perez JJ, Aires-Mejia I, et al. The cellular origin and malignant transformation of Waldenstrom macroglobulinemia. Blood 2015;125(15):2370–80.

[151] Guerrera ML, Tsakmaklis N, Xu L, Yang G, Demos M, Kofides A, et al. MYD88 mutated and wild-type Waldenstrom's macroglobulinemia: characterization of chromosome 6q gene losses and their mutual exclusivity with mutations in CXCR4. Haematologica 2018;103(9):e408–11.

[152] Treon SP, Xu L, Guerrera ML, Jimenez C, Hunter ZR, Liu X, et al. Genomic landscape of Waldenstrom macroglobulinemia and its impact on treatment strategies. J Clin Oncol 2020;38(11):1198–208.

[153] Hunter ZR, Xu L, Tsakmaklis N, Demos MG, Kofides A, Jimenez C, et al. Insights into the genomic landscape of MYD88 wild-type Waldenstrom macroglobulinemia. Blood Adv 2018;2(21):2937–46.

[154] Kaiser LM, Hunter ZR, Treon SP, Buske C. CXCR4 in Waldenstrom's macroglobulinema: chances and challenges. Leukemia 2021;35(2):333–45.

[155] Poulain S, Roumier C, Bertrand E, Renneville A, Caillault-Venet A, Doye E, et al. TP53 mutation and its prognostic significance in Waldenstrom's macroglobulinemia. Clin Cancer Res 2017;23(20):6325–35.

[156] Gustine JN, Tsakmaklis N, Demos MG, Kofides A, Chen JG, Liu X, et al. TP53 mutations are associated with mutated MYD88 and CXCR4, and confer an adverse outcome in Waldenstrom macroglobulinaemia. Br J Haematol 2019;184(2):242–5.

[157] Grever MR, Abdel-Wahab O, Andritsos LA, Banerji V, Barrientos J, Blachly JS, et al. Consensus guidelines for the diagnosis and management of patients with classic hairy cell leukemia. Blood 2017;129(5):553–60.

[158] Angelova EA, Medeiros LJ, Wang W, Muzzafar T, Lu X, Khoury JD, et al. Clinicopathologic and molecular features in hairy cell leukemia-variant: single institutional experience. Mod Pathol 2018;31(11):1717–32.

[159] Falini B, Tiacci E, Liso A, Basso K, Sabattini E, Pacini R, et al. Simple diagnostic assay for hairy cell leukaemia by immunocytochemical detection of annexin A1 (ANXA1). Lancet 2004;363(9424):1869–70.

[160] Weston-Bell NJ, Hendriks D, Sugiyarto G, Bos NA, Kluin-Nelemans HC, Forconi F, et al. Hairy cell leukemia cell lines expressing annexin A1 and displaying B-cell receptor signals characteristic of primary tumor cells lack the signature BRAF mutation to reveal unrepresentative origins. Leukemia 2013;27(1):241–5.

[161] Simonetti E, Ascani S, Volpetti S, Sabattini E, Falini B, Tiacci E. A BRAF-mutated case of hairy cell leukaemia lacking Annexin-A1 expression. Br J Haematol 2018;183(5):702.

[162] Wang HY, Heyman BM. Annexin A1—but CD10+ hairy cell leukemia. Blood 2022;139(12):1924.

[163] Durham BH, Getta B, Dietrich S, Taylor J, Won H, Bogenberger JM, et al. Genomic analysis of hairy cell leukemia identifies novel recurrent genetic alterations. Blood 2017;130(14):1644–8.

[164] Waterfall JJ, Arons E, Walker RL, Pineda M, Roth L, Killian JK, et al. High prevalence of MAP2K1 mutations in variant and IGHV4-34-expressing hairy-cell leukemias. Nat Genet 2014;46(1):8–10.

[165] Falini B, Martelli MP, Tiacci E. BRAF V600E mutation in hairy cell leukemia: from bench to bedside. Blood 2016;128(15):1918–27.

[166] Maitre E, Bertrand P, Maingonnat C, Viailly PJ, Wiber M, Naguib D, et al. New generation sequencing of targeted genes in the classical and the variant form of hairy cell leukemia highlights mutations in epigenetic regulation genes. Oncotarget 2018;9(48):28866–76.

[167] Piva R, Deaglio S, Fama R, Buonincontri R, Scarfo I, Bruscaggin A, et al. The Kruppel-like factor 2 transcription factor gene is recurrently mutated in splenic marginal zone lymphoma. Leukemia 2015;29(2):503–7.
[168] Dietrich S, Hullein J, Lee SC, Hutter B, Gonzalez D, Jayne S, et al. Recurrent CDKN1B (p27) mutations in hairy cell leukemia. Blood 2015;126(8):1005–8.
[169] Xi L, Arons E, Navarro W, Calvo KR, Stetler-Stevenson M, Raffeld M, et al. Both variant and IGHV4-34-expressing hairy cell leukemia lack the BRAF V600E mutation. Blood 2012;119(14):3330–2.
[170] Tiacci E, Park JH, De Carolis L, Chung SS, Broccoli A, Scott S, et al. Targeting mutant BRAF in relapsed or refractory hairy-cell leukemia. N Engl J Med 2015;373(18):1733–47.
[171] Chihara D, Kantarjian H, O'Brien S, Jorgensen J, Pierce S, Faderl S, et al. Long-term durable remission by cladribine followed by rituximab in patients with hairy cell leukaemia: update of a phase II trial. Br J Haematol 2016;174(5):760–6.
[172] Visentin A, Imbergamo S, Frezzato F, Pizzi M, Bertorelle R, Scomazzon E, et al. Bendamustine plus rituximab is an effective first-line treatment in hairy cell leukemia variant: a report of three cases. Oncotarget 2017;8(66):110727–31.
[173] Sadeghi N, Li HC. MRD-negative complete remission in relapsed refractory hairy cell leukemia with bendamustine and obinutuzumab. Ann Hematol 2018;97(4):723–4.
[174] Booman M, Douwes J, Legdeur MC, van Baarlen J, Schuuring E, Kluin P. From brain to testis: immune escape and clonal selection in a B cell lymphoma with selective outgrowth in two immune sanctuaries [correction of sanctuariesy]. Haematologica 2007;92(6):e69–71.
[175] Kridel R, Telio D, Villa D, Sehn LH, Gerrie AS, Shenkier T, et al. Diffuse large B-cell lymphoma with testicular involvement: outcome and risk of CNS relapse in the rituximab era. Br J Haematol 2017;176(2):210–21.
[176] King RL, Goodlad JR, Calaminici M, Dotlic S, Montes-Moreno S, Oschlies I, et al. Lymphomas arising in immune-privileged sites: insights into biology, diagnosis, and pathogenesis. Virchows Arch 2020;476(5):647–65.
[177] Riemersma SA, Oudejans JJ, Vonk MJ, Dreef EJ, Prins FA, Jansen PM, et al. High numbers of tumour-infiltrating activated cytotoxic T lymphocytes, and frequent loss of HLA class I and II expression, are features of aggressive B cell lymphomas of the brain and testis. J Pathol 2005;206(3):328–36.
[178] Elfrink S, de Winde CM, van den Brand M, Berendsen M, Roemer MGM, Arnold F, et al. High frequency of inactivating tetraspanin C D37 mutations in diffuse large B-cell lymphoma at immune-privileged sites. Blood 2019;134(12):946–50.
[179] Guo D, Hong L, Ji H, Jiang Y, Lu L, Wang X, et al. The mutation of BTG2 gene predicts a poor outcome in primary testicular diffuse large B-cell lymphoma. J Inflamm Res 2022;15:1757–69.
[180] Kirkegaard MK, Minderman M, Sjo LD, Pals ST, Eriksen PRG, Heegaard S. Prevalence and prognostic value of MYD88 and CD79B mutations in ocular adnexal large B-cell lymphoma: a reclassification of ocular adnexal large B-cell lymphoma. Br J Ophthalmol 2021;107:576–81.
[181] Garcia-Reyero J, Martinez Magunacelaya N, Gonzalez Perena A, Marcos Gonzalez S, Teran-Villagra N, Azueta A, et al. Clonal evolution in primary diffuse large B-cell lymphoma of the central nervous system. Appl Immunohistochem Mol Morphol 2020;28(8):e68–71.
[182] Zhou J, Zuo M, Li L, Li F, Ke P, Zhou Y, et al. PIM1 and CD79B mutation status impacts the outcome of primary diffuse large B-cell lymphoma of the CNS. Front Oncol 2022;12, 824632.
[183] Yavasoglu I, Sargin G, Kadikoylu G, Doger FK, Bolaman Z. Immunohistochemical evaluation of CD20 expression in patients with multiple myeloma. Rev Bras Hematol Hemoter 2015;37(1):34–7.
[184] Maura F, Bolli N, Angelopoulos N, Dawson KJ, Leongamornlert D, Martincorena I, et al. Genomic landscape and chronological reconstruction of driver events in multiple myeloma. Nat Commun 2019;10(1):3835.
[185] Boyle EM, Deshpande S, Tytarenko R, Ashby C, Wang Y, Bauer MA, et al. The molecular make up of smoldering myeloma highlights the evolutionary pathways leading to multiple myeloma. Nat Commun 2021;12(1):293.
[186] Shah V, Sherborne AL, Walker BA, Johnson DC, Boyle EM, Ellis S, et al. Prediction of outcome in newly diagnosed myeloma: a meta-analysis of the molecular profiles of 1905 trial patients. Leukemia 2018;32(1):102–10.
[187] Lakshman A, Paul S, Rajkumar SV, Ketterling RP, Greipp PT, Dispenzieri A, et al. Prognostic significance of interphase FISH in monoclonal gammopathy of undetermined significance. Leukemia 2018;32(8):1811–5.
[188] Moreau P, San Miguel J, Sonneveld P, Mateos MV, Zamagni E, Avet-Loiseau H, et al. Multiple myeloma: ESMO clinical practice guidelines for diagnosis, treatment and follow-up. Ann Oncol 2017;28(Suppl 4):iv52–61.
[189] Perrot A, Lauwers-Cances V, Tournay E, Hulin C, Chretien ML, Royer B, et al. Development and validation of a cytogenetic prognostic index predicting survival in multiple myeloma. J Clin Oncol 2019;37(19):1657–65.

[190] Lionetti M, Neri A. Utilizing next-generation sequencing in the management of multiple myeloma. Expert Rev Mol Diagn 2017;17(7):653–63.

[191] Pawlyn C, Davies FE. Toward personalized treatment in multiple myeloma based on molecular characteristics. Blood 2019;133(7):660–75.

[192] Merz M, Jauch A, Hielscher T, Bochtler T, Schonland SO, Seckinger A, et al. Prognostic significance of cytogenetic heterogeneity in patients with newly diagnosed multiple myeloma. Blood Adv 2018;2(1):1–9.

[193] Kumar SK, Rajkumar SV. The multiple myelomas—current concepts in cytogenetic classification and therapy. Nat Rev Clin Oncol 2018;15(7):409–21.

[194] Robillard N, Avet-Loiseau H, Garand R, Moreau P, Pineau D, Rapp MJ, et al. CD20 is associated with a small mature plasma cell morphology and t(11;14) in multiple myeloma. Blood 2003;102(3):1070–1.

[195] Fischer U, Yang JJ, Ikawa T, Hein D, Vicente-Duenas C, Borkhardt A, et al. Cell fate decisions: the role of transcription factors in early B-cell development and leukemia. Blood Cancer Discov 2020;1(3):224–33.

[196] Martensson IL, Almqvist N, Grimsholm O, Bernardi AI. The pre-B cell receptor checkpoint. FEBS Lett 2010;584 (12):2572–9.

[197] Harwood NE, Batista FD. Early events in B cell activation. Annu Rev Immunol 2010;28:185–210.

[198] Yuseff MI, Pierobon P, Reversat A, Lennon-Dumenil AM. How B cells capture, process and present antigens: a crucial role for cell polarity. Nat Rev Immunol 2013;13(7):475–86.

[199] Nutt SL, Hodgkin PD, Tarlinton DM, Corcoran LM. The generation of antibody-secreting plasma cells. Nat Rev Immunol 2015;15(3):160–71.

[200] Shlomchik MJ, Weisel F. Germinal center selection and the development of memory B and plasma cells. Immunol Rev 2012;247(1):52–63.

[201] Pavri R, Nussenzweig MC. AID targeting in antibody diversity. Adv Immunol 2011;110:1–26.

[202] Laffleur B, Bardet SM, Garot A, Brousse M, Baylet A, Cogne M. Immunoglobulin genes undergo legitimate repair in human B cells not only after cis- but also frequent trans-class switch recombination. Genes Immun 2014;15(5):341–6.

[203] Basso K. Biology of germinal center B cells relating to lymphomagenesis. Hemasphere 2021;5(6), e582.

[204] Kraus M, Alimzhanov MB, Rajewsky N, Rajewsky K. Survival of resting mature B lymphocytes depends on BCR signaling via the Igalpha/beta heterodimer. Cell 2004;117(6):787–800.

[205] Treanor B. B-cell receptor: from resting state to activate. Immunology 2012;136(1):21–7.

[206] Kaileh M, Sen R. NF-kappaB function in B lymphocytes. Immunol Rev 2012;246(1):254–71.

[207] Heise N, De Silva NS, Silva K, Carette A, Simonetti G, Pasparakis M, et al. Germinal center B cell maintenance and differentiation are controlled by distinct NF-kappaB transcription factor subunits. J Exp Med 2014;211 (10):2103–18.

[208] Davis RE, Ngo VN, Lenz G, Tolar P, Young RM, Romesser PB, et al. Chronic active B-cell-receptor signalling in diffuse large B-cell lymphoma. Nature 2010;463(7277):88–92.

[209] Ngo VN, Young RM, Schmitz R, Jhavar S, Xiao W, Lim KH, et al. Oncogenically active MYD88 mutations in human lymphoma. Nature 2011;470(7332):115–9.

[210] Phelan JD, Young RM, Webster DE, Roulland S, Wright GW, Kasbekar M, et al. A multiprotein supercomplex controlling oncogenic signalling in lymphoma. Nature 2018;560(7718):387–91.

[211] Compagno M, Lim WK, Grunn A, Nandula SV, Brahmachary M, Shen Q, et al. Mutations of multiple genes cause deregulation of NF-kappaB in diffuse large B-cell lymphoma. Nature 2009;459(7247):717–21.

[212] Srinivasan L, Sasaki Y, Calado DP, Zhang B, Paik JH, DePinho RA, et al. PI3 kinase signals BCR-dependent mature B cell survival. Cell 2009;139(3):573–86.

[213] Duhren-von Minden M, Ubelhart R, Schneider D, Wossning T, Bach MP, Buchner M, et al. Chronic lymphocytic leukaemia is driven by antigen-independent cell-autonomous signalling. Nature 2012;489(7415):309–12.

[214] Sharma S, Pavlasova GM, Seda V, Cerna KA, Vojackova E, Filip D, et al. miR-29 modulates CD40 signaling in chronic lymphocytic leukemia by targeting TRAF4: an axis affected by BCR inhibitors. Blood 2021;137 (18):2481–94.

[215] Muschen M. Autoimmunity checkpoints as therapeutic targets in B cell malignancies. Nat Rev Cancer 2018;18 (2):103–16.

[216] Chan LN, Murakami MA, Robinson ME, Caeser R, Sadras T, Lee J, et al. Signalling input from divergent pathways subverts B cell transformation. Nature 2020;583(7818):845–51.

[217] Geng H, Hurtz C, Lenz KB, Chen Z, Baumjohann D, Thompson S, et al. Self-enforcing feedback activation between BCL6 and pre-B cell receptor signaling defines a distinct subtype of acute lymphoblastic leukemia. Cancer Cell 2015;27(3):409–25.
[218] Schjerven H, Ayongaba EF, Aghajanirefah A, McLaughlin J, Cheng D, Geng H, et al. Genetic analysis of Ikaros target genes and tumor suppressor function in BCR-ABL1(+) pre-B ALL. J Exp Med 2017;214(3):793–814.
[219] Mangum DS, Downie J, Mason CC, Jahromi MS, Joshi D, Rodic V, et al. VPREB1 deletions occur independent of lambda light chain rearrangement in childhood acute lymphoblastic leukemia. Leukemia 2014;28(1):216–20.
[220] Feldhahn N, Rio P, Soh BN, Liedtke S, Sprangers M, Klein F, et al. Deficiency of Bruton's tyrosine kinase in B cell precursor leukemia cells. Proc Natl Acad Sci U S A 2005;102(37):13266–71.
[221] Ta VB, de Haan AB, de Bruijn MJ, Dingjan GM, Hendriks RW. Pre-B-cell leukemias in Btk/Slp65-deficient mice arise independently of ongoing V(D)J recombination activity. Leukemia 2011;25(1):48–56.
[222] Roberts KG, Li Y, Payne-Turner D, Harvey RC, Yang YL, Pei D, et al. Targetable kinase-activating lesions in Ph-like acute lymphoblastic leukemia. N Engl J Med 2014;371(11):1005–15.
[223] Chen Z, Shojaee S, Buchner M, Geng H, Lee JW, Klemm L, et al. Signalling thresholds and negative B-cell selection in acute lymphoblastic leukaemia. Nature 2015;521(7552):357–61.
[224] Schwartzman O, Savino AM, Gombert M, Palmi C, Cario G, Schrappe M, et al. Suppressors and activators of JAK-STAT signaling at diagnosis and relapse of acute lymphoblastic leukemia in down syndrome. Proc Natl Acad Sci U S A 2017;114(20):E4030–9.
[225] Teodorovic LS, Babolin C, Rowland SL, Greaves SA, Baldwin DP, Torres RM, et al. Activation of Ras overcomes B-cell tolerance to promote differentiation of autoreactive B cells and production of autoantibodies. Proc Natl Acad Sci U S A 2014;111(27):E2797–806.
[226] Irving J, Matheson E, Minto L, Blair H, Case M, Halsey C, et al. Ras pathway mutations are prevalent in relapsed childhood acute lymphoblastic leukemia and confer sensitivity to MEK inhibition. Blood 2014;124(23):3420–30.
[227] Hoogeboom R, van Kessel KP, Hochstenbach F, Wormhoudt TA, Reinten RJ, Wagner K, et al. A mutated B cell chronic lymphocytic leukemia subset that recognizes and responds to fungi. J Exp Med 2013;210(1):59–70.
[228] Quinn ER, Chan CH, Hadlock KG, Foung SK, Flint M, Levy S. The B-cell receptor of a hepatitis C virus (HCV)-associated non-Hodgkin lymphoma binds the viral E2 envelope protein, implicating HCV in lymphomagenesis. Blood 2001;98(13):3745–9.
[229] Kuo YC, Yu LY, Wang HY, Chen MJ, Wu MS, Liu CJ, et al. Effects of *Helicobacter pylori* infection in gastrointestinal tract malignant diseases: from the oral cavity to rectum. World J Gastrointest Oncol 2022;14(1):55–74.
[230] Robbiani DF, Deroubaix S, Feldhahn N, Oliveira TY, Callen E, Wang Q, et al. Plasmodium infection promotes genomic instability and AID-dependent B cell lymphoma. Cell 2015;162(4):727–37.
[231] Kugelberg E. Tumour immunology: malaria alters B cell lymphomagenesis. Nat Rev Immunol 2015;15(9):528.
[232] Katano H. Pathological features of Kaposi's sarcoma-associated herpesvirus infection. Adv Exp Med Biol 2018;1045:357–76.
[233] Choi UY, Lee JJ, Park A, Zhu W, Lee HR, Choi YJ, et al. Oncogenic human herpesvirus hijacks proline metabolism for tumorigenesis. Proc Natl Acad Sci U S A 2020;117(14):8083–93.
[234] Portis T, Longnecker R. Epstein-Barr virus (EBV) LMP2A mediates B-lymphocyte survival through constitutive activation of the Ras/PI3K/Akt pathway. Oncogene 2004;23(53):8619–28.
[235] Anderson LJ, Longnecker R. EBV LMP2A provides a surrogate pre-B cell receptor signal through constitutive activation of the ERK/MAPK pathway. J Gen Virol 2008;89(Pt 7):1563–8.
[236] Dominguez-Sola D, Ying CY, Grandori C, Ruggiero L, Chen B, Li M, et al. Non-transcriptional control of DNA replication by c-Myc. Nature 2007;448(7152):445–51.
[237] Eilers M, Eisenman RN. Myc's broad reach. Genes Dev 2008;22(20):2755–66.
[238] Dominguez-Sola D, Victora GD, Ying CY, Phan RT, Saito M, Nussenzweig MC, et al. The proto-oncogene MYC is required for selection in the germinal center and cyclic reentry. Nat Immunol 2012;13(11):1083–91.
[239] Calado DP, Sasaki Y, Godinho SA, Pellerin A, Kochert K, Sleckman BP, et al. The cell-cycle regulator c-Myc is essential for the formation and maintenance of germinal centers. Nat Immunol 2012;13(11):1092–100.
[240] Wang Y, Zhou Y, Graves DT. FOXO transcription factors: their clinical significance and regulation. Biomed Res Int 2014;2014, 925350.
[241] Trinh DL, Scott DW, Morin RD, Mendez-Lago M, An J, Jones SJ, et al. Analysis of FOXO1 mutations in diffuse large B-cell lymphoma. Blood 2013;121(18):3666–74.
[242] Kabrani E, Chu VT, Tasouri E, Sommermann T, Bassler K, Ulas T, et al. Nuclear FOXO1 promotes lymphomagenesis in germinal center B cells. Blood 2018;132(25):2670–83.

[243] Basso K, Dalla-Favera R. Roles of BCL6 in normal and transformed germinal center B cells. Immunol Rev 2012;247(1):172–83.

[244] Huang C, Hatzi K, Melnick A. Lineage-specific functions of Bcl-6 in immunity and inflammation are mediated by distinct biochemical mechanisms. Nat Immunol 2013;14(4):380–8.

[245] Pasqualucci L, Migliazza A, Basso K, Houldsworth J, Chaganti RS, Dalla-Favera R. Mutations of the BCL6 proto-oncogene disrupt its negative autoregulation in diffuse large B-cell lymphoma. Blood 2003;101 (8):2914–23.

[246] Willis SN, Good-Jacobson KL, Curtis J, Light A, Tellier J, Shi W, et al. Transcription factor IRF4 regulates germinal center cell formation through a B cell-intrinsic mechanism. J Immunol 2014;192(7):3200–6.

[247] Ying CY, Dominguez-Sola D, Fabi M, Lorenz IC, Hussein S, Bansal M, et al. MEF2B mutations lead to deregulated expression of the oncogene BCL6 in diffuse large B cell lymphoma. Nat Immunol 2013;14 (10):1084–92.

[248] Brescia P, Schneider C, Holmes AB, Shen Q, Hussein S, Pasqualucci L, et al. MEF2B instructs germinal center development and acts as an oncogene in B cell lymphomagenesis. Cancer Cell 2018;34(3). 453–65e9.

[249] Jiang Y, Ortega-Molina A, Geng H, Ying HY, Hatzi K, Parsa S, et al. CREBBP inactivation promotes the development of HDAC3-dependent lymphomas. Cancer Discov 2017;7(1):38–53.

[250] Zhang J, Vlasevska S, Wells VA, Nataraj S, Holmes AB, Duval R, et al. The CREBBP acetyltransferase is a haploinsufficient tumor suppressor in B-cell lymphoma. Cancer Discov 2017;7(3):322–37.

[251] Meyer SN, Scuoppo C, Vlasevska S, Bal E, Holmes AB, Holloman M, et al. Unique and shared epigenetic programs of the CREBBP and EP300 acetyltransferases in germinal center B cells reveal targetable dependencies in lymphoma. Immunity 2019;51(3):535–47 e9.

[252] Schmitz R, Young RM, Ceribelli M, Jhavar S, Xiao W, Zhang M, et al. Burkitt lymphoma pathogenesis and therapeutic targets from structural and functional genomics. Nature 2012;490(7418):116–20.

[253] Richter J, Schlesner M, Hoffmann S, Kreuz M, Leich E, Burkhardt B, et al. Recurrent mutation of the ID3 gene in Burkitt lymphoma identified by integrated genome, exome and transcriptome sequencing. Nat Genet 2012;44 (12):1316–20.

[254] Mandelbaum J, Bhagat G, Tang H, Mo T, Brahmachary M, Shen Q, et al. BLIMP1 is a tumor suppressor gene frequently disrupted in activated B cell-like diffuse large B cell lymphoma. Cancer Cell 2010;18 (6):568–79.

[255] Calado DP, Zhang B, Srinivasan L, Sasaki Y, Seagal J, Unitt C, et al. Constitutive canonical NF-kappaB activation cooperates with disruption of BLIMP1 in the pathogenesis of activated B cell-like diffuse large cell lymphoma. Cancer Cell 2010;18(6):580–9.

[256] Beguelin W, Popovic R, Teater M, Jiang Y, Bunting KL, Rosen M, et al. EZH2 is required for germinal center formation and somatic EZH2 mutations promote lymphoid transformation. Cancer Cell 2013;23(5):677–92.

[257] Caganova M, Carrisi C, Varano G, Mainoldi F, Zanardi F, Germain PL, et al. Germinal center dysregulation by histone methyltransferase EZH2 promotes lymphomagenesis. J Clin Invest 2013;123(12):5009–22.

[258] Zhang J, Dominguez-Sola D, Hussein S, Lee JE, Holmes AB, Bansal M, et al. Disruption of KMT2D perturbs germinal center B cell development and promotes lymphomagenesis. Nat Med 2015;21(10):1190–8.

[259] Seifert M, Scholtysik R, Kuppers R. Origin and pathogenesis of B cell lymphomas. Methods Mol Biol 2019;1956:1–33.

[260] Kuppers R, Dalla-Favera R. Mechanisms of chromosomal translocations in B cell lymphomas. Oncogene 2001;20(40):5580–94.

[261] Matthews AJ, Zheng S, DiMenna LJ, Chaudhuri J. Regulation of immunoglobulin class-switch recombination: choreography of noncoding transcription, targeted DNA deamination, and long-range DNA repair. Adv Immunol 2014;122:1–57.

[262] Polonis K, Schultz MJ, Olteanu H, Smadbeck JB, Johnson SH, Vasmatzis G, et al. Detection of cryptic CCND1 rearrangements in mantle cell lymphoma by next generation sequencing. Ann Diagn Pathol 2020;46, 151533.

[263] Meng X, Min Q, Wang JY. B cell lymphoma. Adv Exp Med Biol 2020;1254:161–81.

[264] Dierlamm J, Baens M, Wlodarska I, Stefanova-Ouzounova M, Hernandez JM, Hossfeld DK, et al. The apoptosis inhibitor gene API2 and a novel 18q gene, MLT, are recurrently rearranged in the t(11;18)(q21;q21) associated with mucosa-associated lymphoid tissue lymphomas. Blood 1999;93(11):3601–9.

[265] Hosokawa Y. Anti-apoptotic action of API2-MALT1 fusion protein involved in t(11;18)(q21;q21) MALT lymphoma. Apoptosis 2005;10(1):25–34.

[266] Wagner SD, Ahearne M, Ko Ferrigno P. The role of BCL6 in lymphomas and routes to therapy. Br J Haematol 2011;152(1):3–12.

[267] Du MQ. MALT lymphoma: genetic abnormalities, immunological stimulation and molecular mechanism. Best Pract Res Clin Haematol 2017;30(1–2):13–23.
[268] Okuyama K, Strid T, Kuruvilla J, Somasundaram R, Cristobal S, Smith E, et al. PAX5 is part of a functional transcription factor network targeted in lymphoid leukemia. PLoS Genet 2019;15(8), e1008280.
[269] Walker BA, Mavrommatis K, Wardell CP, Ashby TC, Bauer M, Davies FE, et al. Identification of novel mutational drivers reveals oncogene dependencies in multiple myeloma. Blood 2018;132(6):587–97.
[270] Pagano JS, Blaser M, Buendia MA, Damania B, Khalili K, Raab-Traub N, et al. Infectious agents and cancer: criteria for a causal relation. Semin Cancer Biol 2004;14(6):453–71.
[271] Gonzalez-Farre B, Martinez D, Lopez-Guerra M, Xipell M, Monclus E, Rovira J, et al. HHV8-related lymphoid proliferations: a broad spectrum of lesions from reactive lymphoid hyperplasia to overt lymphoma. Mod Pathol 2017;30(5):745–60.
[272] Vega F, Miranda RN, Medeiros LJ. KSHV/HHV8-positive large B-cell lymphomas and associated diseases: a heterogeneous group of lymphoproliferative processes with significant clinicopathological overlap. Mod Pathol 2020;33(1):18–28.
[273] Schuhmachers P, Munz C. Modification of EBV associated lymphomagenesis and its immune control by co-infections and genetics in humanized mice. Front Immunol 2021;12, 640918.
[274] Kuppers R. B cells under influence: transformation of B cells by Epstein-Barr virus. Nat Rev Immunol 2003;3 (10):801–12.
[275] Kieser A, Sterz KR. The Latent Membrane Protein 1 (LMP1). Curr Top Microbiol Immunol 2015;391:119–49.
[276] Albanese M, Tagawa T, Hammerschmidt W. Strategies of Epstein-Barr virus to evade innate antiviral immunity of its human host. Front Microbiol 2022;13, 955603.
[277] Kempkes B, Ling PD. EBNA2 and its coactivator EBNA-LP. Curr Top Microbiol Immunol 2015;391:35–59.
[278] Mohanlal RD, Pather S. Variability of HHV8 LNA-1 immunohistochemical staining across the 3 histologic stages of HIV-associated mucocutaneous Kaposi sarcoma: is there a relationship to patients' CD4 counts? Am J Dermatopathol 2015;37(7):530–4.
[279] Steinbruck L, Gustems M, Medele S, Schulz TF, Lutter D, Hammerschmidt W. K1 and K15 of Kaposi's sarcoma-associated herpesvirus are partial functional homologues of latent membrane protein 2A of Epstein-Barr virus. J Virol 2015;89(14):7248–61.
[280] Machida K, Cheng KT, Sung VM, Lee KJ, Levine AM, Lai MM. Hepatitis C virus infection activates the immunologic (type II) isoform of nitric oxide synthase and thereby enhances DNA damage and mutations of cellular genes. J Virol 2004;78(16):8835–43.
[281] Couronne L, Bachy E, Roulland S, Nadel B, Davi F, Armand M, et al. From hepatitis C virus infection to B-cell lymphoma. Ann Oncol 2018;29(1):92–100.
[282] Tucci FA, Broering R, Johansson P, Schlaak JF, Kuppers R. B cells in chronically hepatitis C virus-infected individuals lack a virus-induced mutation signature in the TP53, CTNNB1, and BCL6 genes. J Virol 2013;87 (5):2956–62.
[283] Lacroix A, Collot-Teixeira S, Mardivirin L, Jaccard A, Petit B, Piguet C, et al. Involvement of human herpesvirus-6 variant B in classic Hodgkin's lymphoma via DR7 oncoprotein. Clin Cancer Res 2010;16 (19):4711–21.
[284] Preiss NK, Kang T, Usherwood YK, Huang YH, Branchini BR, Usherwood EJ. Control of B cell lymphoma by Gammaherpesvirus-induced memory CD8 T cells. J Immunol 2020;205(12):3372–82.
[285] Salar A. Gastric MALT lymphoma and *Helicobacter pylori*. Med Clin (Barc) 2019;152(2):65–71.
[286] Paydas S. *Helicobacter pylori* eradication in gastric diffuse large B cell lymphoma. World J Gastroenterol 2015;21 (13):3773–6.
[287] Thorley-Lawson D, Deitsch KW, Duca KA, Torgbor C. The link between *Plasmodium falciparum* malaria and endemic Burkitt's lymphoma-new insight into a 50-year-old enigma. PLoS Pathog 2016;12(1), e1005331.
[288] Quintana MDP, Smith-Togobo C, Moormann A, Hviid L. Endemic Burkitt lymphoma—an aggressive childhood cancer linked to *Plasmodium falciparum* exposure, but not to exposure to other malaria parasites. APMIS 2020;128(2):129–35.
[289] Broustas CG, Lieberman HB. DNA damage response genes and the development of cancer metastasis. Radiat Res 2014;181(2):111–30.
[290] Jeggo PA, Pearl LH, Carr AM. DNA repair, genome stability and cancer: a historical perspective. Nat Rev Cancer 2016;16(1):35–42.
[291] Supek F, Lehner B. Clustered mutation signatures reveal that error-prone DNA repair targets mutations to active genes. Cell 2017;170(3):534–47 e23.

[292] Toufektchan E, Toledo F. The guardian of the genome revisited: p53 downregulates genes required for telomere maintenance, DNA repair, and centromere structure. Cancers (Basel) 2018;10(5):135.

[293] Tessoulin B, Eveillard M, Lok A, Chiron D, Moreau P, Amiot M, et al. p53 dysregulation in B-cell malignancies: more than a single gene in the pathway to hell. Blood Rev 2017;31(4):251–9.

[294] Cencini E, Fabbri A, Raspadori D, Gozzetti A, Bocchia M. Tp53 disruptions: is there a marker of poor prognosis in chronic lymphoproliferative disorders? Blood Res 2021;56(4):333–4.

[295] Lacroix M, Riscal R, Arena G, Linares LK, Le Cam L. Metabolic functions of the tumor suppressor p53: implications in normal physiology, metabolic disorders, and cancer. Mol Metab 2020;33:2–22.

[296] Bakkenist CJ, Kastan MB. DNA damage activates ATM through intermolecular autophosphorylation and dimer dissociation. Nature 2003;421(6922):499–506.

[297] Hall MJ, Bernhisel R, Hughes E, Larson K, Rosenthal ET, Singh NA, et al. Germline pathogenic variants in the Ataxia telangiectasia mutated (ATM) gene are associated with high and moderate risks for multiple cancers. Cancer Prev Res (Phila) 2021;14(4):433–40.

[298] Abida WM, Gu W. p53-dependent and p53-independent activation of autophagy by ARF. Cancer Res 2008;68 (2):352–7.

[299] Ebrahim M, Mulay SR, Anders HJ, Thomasova D. MDM2 beyond cancer: podoptosis, development, inflammation, and tissue regeneration. Histol Histopathol 2015;30(11):1271–82.

[300] Zaravinos A. Oncogenic RAS: from its activation to its direct targeting. Crit Rev Oncog 2017;22(3–4):283–301.

[301] Dhanasekaran R, Deutzmann A, Mahauad-Fernandez WD, Hansen AS, Gouw AM, Felsher DW. The MYC oncogene—the grand orchestrator of cancer growth and immune evasion. Nat Rev Clin Oncol 2022;19(1):23–36.

[302] Rabajante JF, Babierra AL. Branching and oscillations in the epigenetic landscape of cell-fate determination. Prog Biophys Mol Biol 2015;117(2–3):240–9.

[303] Oakes CC, Martin-Subero JI. Insight into origins, mechanisms, and utility of DNA methylation in B-cell malignancies. Blood 2018;132(10):999–1006.

[304] Hansen KD, Timp W, Bravo HC, Sabunciyan S, Langmead B, McDonald OG, et al. Increased methylation variation in epigenetic domains across cancer types. Nat Genet 2011;43(8):768–75.

[305] Kretzmer H, Bernhart SH, Wang W, Haake A, Weniger MA, Bergmann AK, et al. DNA methylome analysis in Burkitt and follicular lymphomas identifies differentially methylated regions linked to somatic mutation and transcriptional control. Nat Genet 2015;47(11):1316–25.

[306] Wedge E, Hansen JW, Garde C, Asmar F, Tholstrup D, Kristensen SS, et al. Global hypomethylation is an independent prognostic factor in diffuse large B cell lymphoma. Am J Hematol 2017;92(7):689–94.

[307] Chen RZ, Pettersson U, Beard C, Jackson-Grusby L, Jaenisch R. DNA hypomethylation leads to elevated mutation rates. Nature 1998;395(6697):89–93.

[308] Schlesinger Y, Straussman R, Keshet I, Farkash S, Hecht M, Zimmerman J, et al. Polycomb-mediated methylation on Lys27 of histone H3 pre-marks genes for de novo methylation in cancer. Nat Genet 2007;39(2):232–6.

[309] Ntziachristos P, Abdel-Wahab O, Aifantis I. Emerging concepts of epigenetic dysregulation in hematological malignancies. Nat Immunol 2016;17(9):1016–24.

[310] Agirre X, Castellano G, Pascual M, Heath S, Kulis M, Segura V, et al. Whole-epigenome analysis in multiple myeloma reveals DNA hypermethylation of B cell-specific enhancers. Genome Res 2015;25(4):478–87.

[311] Jeziorska DM, Murray RJS, De Gobbi M, Gaentzsch R, Garrick D, Ayyub H, et al. DNA methylation of intragenic CpG islands depends on their transcriptional activity during differentiation and disease. Proc Natl Acad Sci U S A 2017;114(36):E7526–35.

[312] Oakes CC, Claus R, Gu L, Assenov Y, Hullein J, Zucknick M, et al. Evolution of DNA methylation is linked to genetic aberrations in chronic lymphocytic leukemia. Cancer Discov 2014;4(3):348–61.

[313] Smith EN, Ghia EM, DeBoever CM, Rassenti LZ, Jepsen K, Yoon KA, et al. Genetic and epigenetic profiling of CLL disease progression reveals limited somatic evolution and suggests a relationship to memory-cell development. Blood Cancer J 2015;5, e303.

[314] Hinshaw DC, Shevde LA. The tumor microenvironment innately modulates cancer progression. Cancer Res 2019;79(18):4557–66.

[315] Tamma R, Ranieri G, Ingravallo G, Annese T, Oranger A, Gaudio F, et al. Inflammatory cells in diffuse large B cell lymphoma. J Clin Med 2020;9(8), 2418.

[316] Anuja K, Roy S, Ghosh C, Gupta P, Bhattacharjee S, Banerjee B. Prolonged inflammatory microenvironment is crucial for pro-neoplastic growth and genome instability: a detailed review. Inflamm Res 2017;66(2):119–28.

[317] Suarez-Carmona M, Lesage J, Cataldo D, Gilles C. EMT and inflammation: inseparable actors of cancer progression. Mol Oncol 2017;11(7):805–23.

[318] Khandia R, Munjal A. Interplay between inflammation and cancer. Adv Protein Chem Struct Biol 2020;119:199–245.
[319] Ingravallo G, Tamma R, Opinto G, Annese T, Gaudio F, Specchia G, et al. The effect of the tumor microenvironment on lymphoid neoplasms derived from B cells. Diagnostics 2022;12(3):573.
[320] Fulop T, Dupuis G, Witkowski JM, Larbi A. The role of Immunosenescence in the development of age-related diseases. Rev Investig Clin 2016;68(2):84–91.
[321] Fulop T, Dupuis G, Baehl S, Le Page A, Bourgade K, Frost E, et al. From inflamm-aging to immune-paralysis: a slippery slope during aging for immune-adaptation. Biogerontology 2016;17(1):147–57.
[322] Falandry C, Bonnefoy M, Freyer G, Gilson E. Biology of cancer and aging: a complex association with cellular senescence. J Clin Oncol 2014;32(24):2604–10.
[323] Caruso C, Accardi G, Virruso C, Candore G. Sex, gender and immunosenescence: a key to understand the different lifespan between men and women? Immun Ageing 2013;10(1):20.
[324] Morton LM, Wang SS, Devesa SS, Hartge P, Weisenburger DD, Linet MS. Lymphoma incidence patterns by WHO subtype in the United States, 1992–2001. Blood 2006;107(1):265–76.
[325] Monabati A, Safaei A, Noori S, Mokhtari M, Vahedi A. Subtype distribution of lymphomas in South of Iran, analysis of 1085 cases based on World Health Organization classification. Ann Hematol 2016;95(4):613–8.
[326] Morton LM, Slager SL, Cerhan JR, Wang SS, Vajdic CM, Skibola CF, et al. Etiologic heterogeneity among non-Hodgkin lymphoma subtypes: the InterLymph non-Hodgkin lymphoma subtypes project. J Natl Cancer Inst Monogr 2014;2014(48):130–44.
[327] Sarkozy C, Salles G, Falandry C. The biology of aging and lymphoma: a complex interplay. Curr Oncol Rep 2015;17(7):32.
[328] Mancuso S, Carlisi M, Santoro M, Napolitano M, Raso S, Siragusa S. Immunosenescence and lymphomagenesis. Immun Ageing 2018;15:22.
[329] Polyak MJ, Deans JP. Alanine-170 and proline-172 are critical determinants for extracellular CD20 epitopes; heterogeneity in the fine specificity of CD20 monoclonal antibodies is defined by additional requirements imposed by both amino acid sequence and quaternary structure. Blood 2002;99(9):3256–62.
[330] Browne K, Freeling P. The doctor-patient relationship. X. The analysis of the transaction. Practitioner 1966;197 (180):562–7.
[331] Al-Sawaf O, Fischer K, Engelke A, Pflug N, Hallek M, Goede V, et al. Obinutuzumab in chronic lymphocytic leukemia: design, development and place in therapy. Drug Des Devel Ther 2017;11:295.
[332] Freeman CL, Sehn LH. A tale of two antibodies: obinutuzumab versus rituximab. Br J Haematol 2018;182(1):29–45.
[333] Pescovitz MD. Rituximab, an anti-cd20 monoclonal antibody: history and mechanism of action. Am J Transplant 2006;6(5 Pt 1):859–66.
[334] Garnica AD, Chan WY, Rennert OM. Trace elements in development and disease. Curr Probl Pediatr 1986;16 (2):45–120.
[335] Klein C, Lammens A, Schafer W, Georges G, Schwaiger M, Mossner E, et al. Epitope interactions of monoclonal antibodies targeting CD20 and their relationship to functional properties. MAbs 2013;5(1):22–33.
[336] Du FH, Mills EA, Mao-Draayer Y. Next-generation anti-CD20 monoclonal antibodies in autoimmune disease treatment. Auto Immun Highlights 2017;8(1):12.
[337] Chamarthy MR, Williams SC, Moadel RM. Radioimmunotherapy of non-Hodgkin's lymphoma: from the 'magic bullets' to 'radioactive magic bullets'. Yale J Biol Med 2011;84(4):391–407.
[338] Fisher RI, Kaminski MS, Wahl RL, Knox SJ, Zelenetz AD, Vose JM, et al. Tositumomab and iodine-131 tositumomab produces durable complete remissions in a subset of heavily pretreated patients with low-grade and transformed non-Hodgkin's lymphomas. J Clin Oncol 2005;23(30):7565–73.
[339] Leonard JP, Coleman M, Kostakoglu L, Chadburn A, Cesarman E, Furman RR, et al. Abbreviated chemotherapy with fludarabine followed by tositumomab and iodine I 131 tositumomab for untreated follicular lymphoma. J Clin Oncol 2005;23(24):5696–704.
[340] Czuczman MS, Hess G, Gadeberg OV, Pedersen LM, Goldstein N, Gupta I, et al. Chemoimmunotherapy with ofatumumab in combination with CHOP in previously untreated follicular lymphoma. Br J Haematol 2012;157 (4):438–45.
[341] Golay J, Introna M. Mechanism of action of therapeutic monoclonal antibodies: promises and pitfalls of in vitro and in vivo assays. Arch Biochem Biophys 2012;526(2):146–53.
[342] Hassenruck F, Knodgen E, Gockeritz E, Midda SH, Vondey V, Neumann L, et al. Sensitive detection of the natural killer cell-mediated cytotoxicity of anti-CD20 antibodies and its impairment by B-cell receptor pathway inhibitors. Biomed Res Int 2018;2018:1023490.
[343] Boross P, Leusen JH. Mechanisms of action of CD20 antibodies. Am J Cancer Res 2012;2(6):676–90.

[344] Weng WK, Levy R. Two immunoglobulin G fragment C receptor polymorphisms independently predict response to rituximab in patients with follicular lymphoma. J Clin Oncol 2003;21(21):3940–7.

[345] Renaudineau Y, Devauchelle-Pensec V, Hanrotel C, Pers JO, Saraux A, Youinou P. Monoclonal anti-CD20 antibodies: mechanisms of action and monitoring of biological effects. Joint Bone Spine 2009;76(5):458–63.

[346] Pross HF, Maroun JA. The standardization of NK cell assays for use in studies of biological response modifiers. J Immunol Methods 1984;68(1–2):235–49.

[347] Gul N, van Egmond M. Antibody-dependent phagocytosis of tumor cells by macrophages: a potent effector mechanism of monoclonal antibody therapy of cancer. Cancer Res 2015;75(23):5008–13.

[348] Marshall MJE, Stopforth RJ, Cragg MS. Therapeutic antibodies: what have we learnt from targeting CD20 and where are we going? Front Immunol 2017;8:1245.

[349] Golan MD, Burger R, Loos M. Conformational changes in C1q after binding to immune complexes: detection of neoantigens with monoclonal antibodies. J Immunol 1982;129(2):445–7.

[350] Beurskens FJ, Ruuls SR, Engelberts PJ, Vink T, Mackus WJ, van de Winkel JG, et al. Complement activation impacts B-cell depletion by both type I and type II CD20 monoclonal antibodies. Blood 2008;112(10):4354–5 [author reply 5-6].

[351] Teeling JL, Mackus WJ, Wiegman LJ, van den Brakel JH, Beers SA, French RR, et al. The biological activity of human CD20 monoclonal antibodies is linked to unique epitopes on CD20. J Immunol 2006;177(1):362–71.

[352] Golay J, Zaffaroni L, Vaccari T, Lazzari M, Borleri GM, Bernasconi S, et al. Biologic response of B lymphoma cells to anti-CD20 monoclonal antibody rituximab in vitro: CD55 and CD59 regulate complement-mediated cell lysis. Blood 2000;95(12):3900–8.

[353] Treon SP, Mitsiades C, Mitsiades N, Young G, Doss D, Schlossman R, et al. Tumor cell expression of CD59 is associated with resistance to CD20 serotherapy in patients with B-cell malignancies. J Immunother 2001;24 (3):263–71.

[354] Uchida J, Hamaguchi Y, Oliver JA, Ravetch JV, Poe JC, Haas KM, et al. The innate mononuclear phagocyte network depletes B lymphocytes through Fc receptor-dependent mechanisms during anti-CD20 antibody immunotherapy. J Exp Med 2004;199(12):1659–69.

[355] Minard-Colin V, Xiu Y, Poe JC, Horikawa M, Magro CM, Hamaguchi Y, et al. Lymphoma depletion during CD20 immunotherapy in mice is mediated by macrophage FcgammaRI, FcgammaRIII, and FcgammaRIV. Blood 2008;112(4):1205–13.

[356] Beum PV, Lindorfer MA, Beurskens F, Stukenberg PT, Lokhorst HM, Pawluczkowycz AW, et al. Complement activation on B lymphocytes opsonized with rituximab or ofatumumab produces substantial changes in membrane structure preceding cell lysis. J Immunol 2008;181(1):822–32.

[357] Pedersen IM, Buhl AM, Klausen P, Geisler CH, Jurlander J. The chimeric anti-CD20 antibody rituximab induces apoptosis in B-cell chronic lymphocytic leukemia cells through a p38 mitogen activated protein-kinase-dependent mechanism. Blood 2002;99(4):1314–9.

[358] Dykstra M, Cherukuri A, Sohn HW, Tzeng SJ, Pierce SK. Location is everything: lipid rafts and immune cell signaling. Annu Rev Immunol 2003;21:457–81.

[359] Shan D, Ledbetter JA, Press OW. Apoptosis of malignant human B cells by ligation of CD20 with monoclonal antibodies. Blood 1998;91(5):1644–52.

[360] Janas E, Priest R, Wilde JI, White JH, Malhotra R. Rituxan (anti-CD20 antibody)-induced translocation of CD20 into lipid rafts is crucial for calcium influx and apoptosis. Clin Exp Immunol 2005;139(3):439–46.

[361] Ghetie MA, Bright H, Vitetta ES. Homodimers but not monomers of Rituxan (chimeric anti-CD20) induce apoptosis in human B-lymphoma cells and synergize with a chemotherapeutic agent and an immunotoxin. Blood 2001;97(5):1392–8.

[362] Bellosillo B, Villamor N, Lopez-Guillermo A, Marce S, Esteve J, Campo E, et al. Complement-mediated cell death induced by rituximab in B-cell lymphoproliferative disorders is mediated in vitro by a caspase-independent mechanism involving the generation of reactive oxygen species. Blood 2001;98(9):2771–7.

[363] Beers SA, Chan CH, French RR, Cragg MS, Glennie MJ. CD20 as a target for therapeutic type I and II monoclonal antibodies. Semin Hematol 2010;47(2):107–14.

[364] Ivanov A, Beers SA, Walshe CA, Honeychurch J, Alduaij W, Cox KL, et al. Monoclonal antibodies directed to CD20 and HLA-DR can elicit homotypic adhesion followed by lysosome-mediated cell death in human lymphoma and leukemia cells. J Clin Invest 2009;119(8):2143–59.

[365] Payandeh Z, Bahrami AA, Hoseinpoor R, Mortazavi Y, Rajabibazl M, Rahimpour A, et al. The applications of anti-CD20 antibodies to treat various B cells disorders. Biomed Pharmacother 2019;109:2415–26.

[366] Sacchi S, Federico M, Dastoli G, Fiorani C, Vinci G, Clo V, et al. Treatment of B-cell non-Hodgkin's lymphoma with anti CD 20 monoclonal antibody rituximab. Crit Rev Oncol Hematol 2001;37(1):13–25.

[367] Berinstein NL, Grillo-Lopez AJ, White CA, Bence-Bruckler I, Maloney D, Czuczman M, et al. Association of serum rituximab (IDEC-C2B8) concentration and anti-tumor response in the treatment of recurrent low-grade or follicular non-Hodgkin's lymphoma. Ann Oncol 1998;9(9):995–1001.

[368] Pfreundschuh M, Trumper L, Osterborg A, Pettengell R, Trneny M, Imrie K, et al. CHOP-like chemotherapy plus rituximab versus CHOP-like chemotherapy alone in young patients with good-prognosis diffuse large-B-cell lymphoma: a randomised controlled trial by the MabThera International Trial (MInT) Group. Lancet Oncol 2006;7(5):379–91.

[369] Kluin-Nelemans HC, Hoster E, Hermine O, Walewski J, Trneny M, Geisler CH, et al. Treatment of older patients with mantle-cell lymphoma. N Engl J Med 2012;367(6):520–31.

[370] Eichhorst B, Robak T, Montserrat E, Ghia P, Hillmen P, Hallek M, et al. Chronic lymphocytic leukaemia: ESMO clinical practice guidelines for diagnosis, treatment and follow-up. Ann Oncol 2015;26(Suppl 5):v78–84.

[371] Robak T, Dmoszynska A, Solal-Celigny P, Warzocha K, Loscertales J, Catalano J, et al. Rituximab plus fludarabine and cyclophosphamide prolongs progression-free survival compared with fludarabine and cyclophosphamide alone in previously treated chronic lymphocytic leukemia. J Clin Oncol 2010;28(10):1756–65.

[372] Zucca E, Conconi A, Martinelli G, Bouabdallah R, Tucci A, Vitolo U, et al. Final results of the IELSG-19 randomized trial of mucosa-associated lymphoid tissue lymphoma: improved event-free and progression-free survival with rituximab plus Chlorambucil versus either Chlorambucil or rituximab monotherapy. J Clin Oncol 2017;35(17):1905–12.

[373] Press OW, Unger JM, Braziel RM, Maloney DG, Miller TP, Leblanc M, et al. Phase II trial of CHOP chemotherapy followed by tositumomab/iodine I-131 tositumomab for previously untreated follicular non-Hodgkin's lymphoma: five-year follow-up of Southwest Oncology Group Protocol S9911. J Clin Oncol 2006;24(25):4143–9.

[374] Link BK, Martin P, Kaminski MS, Goldsmith SJ, Coleman M, Leonard JP. Cyclophosphamide, vincristine, and prednisone followed by tositumomab and iodine-131-tositumomab in patients with untreated low-grade follicular lymphoma: eight-year follow-up of a multicenter phase II study. J Clin Oncol 2010;28(18):3035–41.

[375] Davies AJ, Rohatiner AZ, Howell S, Britton KE, Owens SE, Micallef IN, et al. Tositumomab and iodine I 131 tositumomab for recurrent indolent and transformed B-cell non-Hodgkin's lymphoma. J Clin Oncol 2004;22(8):1469–79.

[376] Maloney DG, Ogura M, Fukuhara N, Davis J, Lasher J, Izquierdo M, et al. A phase 3 randomized study (HOMER) of ofatumumab vs rituximab in iNHL relapsed after rituximab-containing therapy. Blood Adv 2020;4(16):3886–93.

[377] Wierda WG, Kipps TJ, Durig J, Griskevicius L, Stilgenbauer S, Mayer J, et al. Chemoimmunotherapy with O-FC in previously untreated patients with chronic lymphocytic leukemia. Blood 2011;117(24):6450–8.

[378] Gupta IV, Jewell RC. Ofatumumab, the first human anti-CD20 monoclonal antibody for the treatment of B cell hematologic malignancies. Ann N Y Acad Sci 2012;1263:43–56.

[379] Jabbour E, Richard-Carpentier G, Sasaki Y, Konopleva M, Patel K, Roberts K, et al. Hyper-CVAD regimen in combination with ofatumumab as frontline therapy for adults with Philadelphia chromosome-negative B-cell acute lymphoblastic leukaemia: a single-arm, phase 2 trial. Lancet Haematol 2020;7(7):e523–33.

[380] Christian BA, Poi M, Jones JA, Porcu P, Maddocks K, Flynn JM, et al. The combination of milatuzumab, a humanized anti-CD74 antibody, and veltuzumab, a humanized anti-CD20 antibody, demonstrates activity in patients with relapsed and refractory B-cell non-Hodgkin lymphoma. Br J Haematol 2015;169(5):701–10.

[381] Morschhauser F, Leonard JP, Fayad L, Coiffier B, Petillon MO, Coleman M, et al. Humanized anti-CD20 antibody, veltuzumab, in refractory/recurrent non-Hodgkin's lymphoma: phase I/II results. J Clin Oncol 2009;27(20):3346–53.

[382] Lunning M, Vose J, Nastoupil L, Fowler N, Burger JA, Wierda WG, et al. Ublituximab and umbralisib in relapsed/refractory B-cell non-Hodgkin lymphoma and chronic lymphocytic leukemia. Blood 2019;134(21):1811–20.

[383] Puxeddu I, Caltran E, Rocchi V, Del Corso I, Tavoni A, Migliorini P. Hypersensitivity reactions during treatment with biological agents. Clin Exp Rheumatol 2016;34(1):129–32.

[384] Luo C, Wu G, Huang X, Ma Y, Zhang Y, Song Q, et al. Efficacy and safety of new anti-CD20 monoclonal antibodies versus rituximab for induction therapy of CD20(+) B-cell non-Hodgkin lymphomas: a systematic review and meta-analysis. Sci Rep 2021;11(1):3255.

[385] Sehn LH, Goy A, Offner FC, Martinelli G, Caballero MD, Gadeberg O, et al. Randomized phase II trial comparing Obinutuzumab (GA101) with rituximab in patients with relapsed CD20+ indolent B-cell non-Hodgkin lymphoma: final analysis of the GAUSS study. J Clin Oncol 2015;33(30):3467–74.
[386] Marcus R, Davies A, Ando K, Klapper W, Opat S, Owen C, et al. Obinutuzumab for the first-line treatment of follicular lymphoma. N Engl J Med 2017;377(14):1331–44.
[387] Davies A, Trask P, Demeter J, Florschutz A, Hanel M, Kinoshita T, et al. Health-related quality of life in the phase III GALLIUM study of obinutuzumab- or rituximab-based chemotherapy in patients with previously untreated advanced follicular lymphoma. Ann Hematol 2020;99(12):2837–46.
[388] Hong X, Song Y, Shi Y, Zhang Q, Guo W, Wu G, et al. Efficacy and safety of obinutuzumab for the first-line treatment of follicular lymphoma: a subgroup analysis of Chinese patients enrolled in the phase III GALLIUM study. Chin Med J 2021;135(4):433–40.
[389] Vitolo U, Trneny M, Belada D, Burke JM, Carella AM, Chua N, et al. Obinutuzumab or rituximab plus cyclophosphamide, doxorubicin, vincristine, and prednisone in previously untreated diffuse large B-cell lymphoma. J Clin Oncol 2017;35(31):3529–37.
[390] Sehn LH, Martelli M, Trneny M, Liu W, Bolen CR, Knapp A, et al. A randomized, open-label, phase III study of obinutuzumab or rituximab plus CHOP in patients with previously untreated diffuse large B-cell lymphoma: final analysis of GOYA. J Hematol Oncol 2020;13(1):71.
[391] van Imhoff GW, McMillan A, Matasar MJ, Radford J, Ardeshna KM, Kuliczkowski K, et al. Ofatumumab versus rituximab salvage Chemoimmunotherapy in relapsed or refractory diffuse large B-cell lymphoma: the ORCHARRD study. J Clin Oncol 2017;35(5):544–51.
[392] Vose JM, Carter S, Burns LJ, Ayala E, Press OW, Moskowitz CH, et al. Phase III randomized study of rituximab/carmustine, etoposide, cytarabine, and melphalan (BEAM) compared with iodine-131 tositumomab/BEAM with autologous hematopoietic cell transplantation for relapsed diffuse large B-cell lymphoma: results from the BMT CTN 0401 trial. J Clin Oncol 2013;31(13):1662–8.
[393] Quackenbush RC, Horner TJ, Williams VC, Giampietro P, Lin TS. Patients with relapsed follicular lymphoma treated with rituximab versus tositumomab and iodine I-131 tositumomab. Leuk Lymphoma 2015;56(3):779–81.
[394] Shadman M, Li H, Rimsza L, Leonard JP, Kaminski MS, Braziel RM, et al. Continued excellent outcomes in previously untreated patients with follicular lymphoma after treatment with CHOP plus rituximab or CHOP plus (131)I-Tositumomab: long-term follow-up of phase III randomized study SWOG-S0016. J Clin Oncol 2018;36(7):697–703.
[395] Witzig TE, Gordon LI, Cabanillas F, Czuczman MS, Emmanouilides C, Joyce R, et al. Randomized controlled trial of yttrium-90-labeled ibritumomab tiuxetan radioimmunotherapy versus rituximab immunotherapy for patients with relapsed or refractory low-grade, follicular, or transformed B-cell non-Hodgkin's lymphoma. J Clin Oncol 2002;20(10):2453–63.
[396] Gordon LI, Witzig T, Molina A, Czuczman M, Emmanouilides C, Joyce R, et al. Yttrium 90-labeled ibritumomab tiuxetan radioimmunotherapy produces high response rates and durable remissions in patients with previously treated B-cell lymphoma. Clin Lymphoma 2004;5(2):98–101.
[397] Chahoud J, Sui D, Erwin WD, Gulbis AM, Korbling M, Zhang M, et al. Updated results of rituximab pre- and post-BEAM with or without (90)yttrium ibritumomab tiuxetan during autologous transplant for diffuse large B-cell lymphoma. Clin Cancer Res 2018;24(10):2304–11.
[398] Lossos IS, Czerwinski DK, Alizadeh AA, Wechser MA, Tibshirani R, Botstein D, et al. Prediction of survival in diffuse large-B-cell lymphoma based on the expression of six genes. N Engl J Med 2004;350(18):1828–37.
[399] Ciavarella S, Vegliante MC, Fabbri M, De Summa S, Melle F, Motta G, et al. Dissection of DLBCL microenvironment provides a gene expression-based predictor of survival applicable to formalin-fixed paraffin-embedded tissue. Ann Oncol 2018;29(12):2363–70.
[400] Staiger AM, Altenbuchinger M, Ziepert M, Kohler C, Horn H, Huttner M, et al. A novel lymphoma-associated macrophage interaction signature (LAMIS) provides robust risk prognostication in diffuse large B-cell lymphoma clinical trial cohorts of the DSHNHL. Leukemia 2020;34(2):543–52.
[401] Keane C, Vari F, Hertzberg M, Cao KA, Green MR, Han E, et al. Ratios of T-cell immune effectors and checkpoint molecules as prognostic biomarkers in diffuse large B-cell lymphoma: a population-based study. Lancet Haematol 2015;2(10):e445–55.
[402] He X, Chen Z, Fu T, Jin X, Yu T, Liang Y, et al. Ki-67 is a valuable prognostic predictor of lymphoma but its utility varies in lymphoma subtypes: evidence from a systematic meta-analysis. BMC Cancer 2014;14:153.
[403] Eskandari M, Manoochehrabadi S, Pashaiefar H, Zaimy MA, Ahmadvand M. Clinical significance of cell-free DNA as a prognostic biomarker in patients with diffuse large B-cell lymphoma. Blood Res 2019;54(2):114–9.

[404] Zheng B, Xi Z, Liu R, Yin W, Sui Z, Ren B, et al. The function of MicroRNAs in B-cell development, lymphoma, and their potential in clinical practice. Front Immunol 2018;9:936.

[405] Kersy O, Salmon-Divon M, Shpilberg O, Hershkovitz-Rokah O. Non-coding RNAs in Normal B-cell development and in mantle cell lymphoma: from molecular mechanism to biomarker and therapeutic agent potential. Int J Mol Sci 2021;22(17), 9490.

[406] Papageorgiou SG, Thomopoulos TP, Katagas I, Bouchla A, Pappa V. Prognostic molecular biomarkers in diffuse large B-cell lymphoma in the rituximab era and their therapeutic implications. Ther Adv Hematol 2021;12. 20406207211013987.

[407] Morin RD, Mendez-Lago M, Mungall AJ, Goya R, Mungall KL, Corbett RD, et al. Frequent mutation of histone-modifying genes in non-Hodgkin lymphoma. Nature 2011;476(7360):298–303.

[408] Morin RD, Mungall K, Pleasance E, Mungall AJ, Goya R, Huff RD, et al. Mutational and structural analysis of diffuse large B-cell lymphoma using whole-genome sequencing. Blood 2013;122(7):1256–65.

[409] Kuruvilla J, MacDonald DA, Kouroukis CT, Cheung M, Olney HJ, Turner AR, et al. Salvage chemotherapy and autologous stem cell transplantation for transformed indolent lymphoma: a subset analysis of NCIC CTG LY12. Blood 2015;126(6):733–8.

[410] Yildiz M, Li H, Bernard D, Amin NA, Ouillette P, Jones S, et al. Activating STAT6 mutations in follicular lymphoma. Blood 2015;125(4):668–79.

[411] Ritz O, Rommel K, Dorsch K, Kelsch E, Melzner J, Buck M, et al. STAT6-mediated BCL6 repression in primary mediastinal B-cell lymphoma (PMBL). Oncotarget 2013;4(7):1093–102.

[412] Mentz M, Keay W, Strobl CD, Antoniolli M, Adolph L, Heide M, et al. PARP14 is a novel target in STAT6 mutant follicular lymphoma. Leukemia 2022;36(9):2281–92.

[413] Morin RD, Assouline S, Alcaide M, Mohajeri A, Johnston RL, Chong L, et al. Genetic landscapes of relapsed and refractory diffuse large B-cell lymphomas. Clin Cancer Res 2016;22(9):2290–300.

[414] Wilson WH, Young RM, Schmitz R, Yang Y, Pittaluga S, Wright G, et al. Targeting B cell receptor signaling with ibrutinib in diffuse large B cell lymphoma. Nat Med 2015;21(8):922–6.

[415] Byrd JC, Woyach JA, Furman RR, Martin P, O'Brien S, Brown JR, et al. Acalabrutinib in treatment-naive chronic lymphocytic leukemia. Blood 2021;137(24):3327–38.

[416] Yuan X, Li X, Huang Y, Jin X, Liu H, Zhao A, et al. Zanubrutinib plus salvage chemotherapy for relapsed or refractory diffuse large B-cell lymphoma. Front Immunol 2022;13:1015081.

[417] Saburi M, Saburi Y, Kawano K, Sato R, Urabe S, Ohtsuka E. Successful treatment with tirabrutinib for relapsed lymphoplasmacytic lymphoma complicated by Bing-Neel syndrome. Int J Hematol 2022;115(4):585–9.

[418] Narita Y, Nagane M, Mishima K, Terui Y, Arakawa Y, Yonezawa H, et al. Phase I/II study of tirabrutinib, a second-generation Bruton's tyrosine kinase inhibitor, in relapsed/refractory primary central nervous system lymphoma. Neuro-Oncology 2021;23(1):122–33.

[419] Sekiguchi N, Rai S, Munakata W, Suzuki K, Handa H, Shibayama H, et al. A multicenter, open-label, phase II study of tirabrutinib (ONO/GS-4059) in patients with Waldenstrom's macroglobulinemia. Cancer Sci 2020;111 (9):3327–37.

[420] Hamadani M, Radford J, Carlo-Stella C, Caimi PF, Reid E, O'Connor OA, et al. Final results of a phase 1 study of loncastuximab tesirine in relapsed/refractory B-cell non-Hodgkin lymphoma. Blood 2021;137(19):2634–45.

[421] Skoetz N, Bauer K, Elter T, Monsef I, Roloff V, Hallek M, et al. Alemtuzumab for patients with chronic lymphocytic leukaemia. Cochrane Database Syst Rev 2012;2012(2), CD008078.

[422] Piccaluga PP, Agostinelli C, Righi S, Zinzani PL, Pileri SA. Expression of CD52 in peripheral T-cell lymphoma. Haematologica 2007;92(4):566–7.

[423] Fruman DA, Chiu H, Hopkins BD, Bagrodia S, Cantley LC, Abraham RT. The PI3K pathway in human disease. Cell 2017;170(4):605–35.

[424] Munoz J, Follows GA, Nastoupil LJ. Copanlisib for the treatment of malignant lymphoma: clinical experience and future perspectives. Target Oncol 2021;16(3):295–308.

[425] Matasar MJ, Capra M, Ozcan M, Lv F, Li W, Yanez E, et al. Copanlisib plus rituximab versus placebo plus rituximab in patients with relapsed indolent non-Hodgkin lymphoma (CHRONOS-3): a double-blind, randomised, placebo-controlled, phase 3 trial. Lancet Oncol 2021;22(5):678–89.

[426] Ghia P, Pluta A, Wach M, Lysak D, Kozak T, Simkovic M, et al. ASCEND: phase III, randomized trial of Acalabrutinib versus Idelalisib plus rituximab or Bendamustine plus rituximab in relapsed or refractory chronic lymphocytic leukemia. J Clin Oncol 2020;38(25):2849–61.

[427] Dotti G, Gottschalk S, Savoldo B, Brenner MK. Design and development of therapies using chimeric antigen receptor-expressing T cells. Immunol Rev 2014;257(1):107–26.

[428] Wang K, Wei G, Liu D. CD19: a biomarker for B cell development, lymphoma diagnosis and therapy. Exp Hematol Oncol 2012;1(1):36.

[429] Neelapu SS, Locke FL, Bartlett NL, Lekakis LJ, Miklos DB, Jacobson CA, et al. Axicabtagene Ciloleucel CAR T-cell therapy in refractory large B-cell lymphoma. N Engl J Med 2017;377(26):2531–44.

[430] Locke FL, Miklos DB, Jacobson CA, Perales MA, Kersten MJ, Oluwole OO, et al. Axicabtagene ciloleucel as second-line therapy for large B-cell lymphoma. N Engl J Med 2022;386(7):640–54.

[431] McLaughlin P, Grillo-Lopez AJ, Link BK, Levy R, Czuczman MS, Williams ME, et al. Rituximab chimeric anti-CD20 monoclonal antibody therapy for relapsed indolent lymphoma: half of patients respond to a four-dose treatment program. J Clin Oncol 1998;16(8):2825–33.

[432] Herold M, Haas A, Srock S, Neser S, Al-Ali KH, Neubauer A, et al. Rituximab added to first-line mitoxantrone, chlorambucil, and prednisolone chemotherapy followed by interferon maintenance prolongs survival in patients with advanced follicular lymphoma: an East German Study Group Hematology and Oncology Study. J Clin Oncol 2007;25(15):1986–92.

[433] Coiffier B, Lepage E, Briere J, Herbrecht R, Tilly H, Bouabdallah R, et al. CHOP chemotherapy plus rituximab compared with CHOP alone in elderly patients with diffuse large-B-cell lymphoma. N Engl J Med 2002;346(4):235–42.

CHAPTER

3

Anti-CD20 antibody treatment for diffuse large B cell lymphoma: Genetic alterations and signaling pathways

Ying Jin[a], *Cheng Wang*[a], *Li Yang*[b], *William C.S. Cho*[c], *and Guoqi Song*[a]

[a]Department of Hematology, Affiliated Hospital and Medical School of Nantong University, Nantong, Jiangsu, China [b]Department of Hematology, Affiliated Yancheng NO.1 People's Hospital, Yancheng, Jiangsu, China [c]Department of Clinical Oncology, Queen Elizabeth Hospital, Hong Kong

Abstract

Diffuse large B cell lymphoma (DLBCL) is the most common non-Hodgkin's lymphoma with high heterogeneity [1]. The standard first-line treatment regimen is R-CHOP (rituximab-cyclophosphamide + adriamycin + vincristine + prednisone), with 5-year survival rates of 60%–70% [2], but more than 30% of patients will still develop relapsed/refractory DLBCL due to resistance to targeted and chemotherapeutic agents, resulting in poor prognosis [1,2]. Scholars have investigated the mechanism of resistance to rituximab, but a conclusive understanding is yet to be established. Anti-CD20 antibodies, drug resistance, genetic alterations, and molecular mechanisms are the main topics of this chapter.

Abbreviations

4EBP1	4E-binding protein 1
5′-UTR	5′-untranslated regions
ABC	activated B-cell
ADCC	antibody-dependent cellular cytotoxicity
ADCP	antibody-dependent cellular phagocytosis
AP-1	activator protein-1
B2M	beta2-microglobulin
Bcl2	B-cell lymphoma protein 2
BCR	B-cell receptor
BTK	Bruton's tyrosine kinase

https://doi.org/10.1016/B978-0-443-19200-5.00002-6

C3b	complement fraction 3b
CAF	cancer-associated fibroblasts
CAR-T	chimeric antigen receptor (CAR) T cell
CDC	complement-dependent cytotoxicity
CDKN1A	cyclin-dependent kinase inhibitor 1A
cIAP	calf intestinal alkaline phosphatase
CIITA	class II transactivators
CLL	chronic lymphocytic leukemia
CREBBP	CREB-binding protein
CRISPR	clustered regularly interspaced short palindromic repeats
DAF	decay accelerating factor
DC	dendritic cells
DHL	double-hit lymphoma
DLBCL	diffuse large B cell lymphoma
DNMT1	DNA methyltransferase 1
DZ	dark zone
EBNA	Epstein-Barr nuclear antigen
ECM	extracellular matrix
ERK1/2	extracellular signal-regulated kinase 1/2
EZH2	enhancer of zeste homolog 2
FcRs	Fc receptors
Gal-1	galactose lectin-1
GC	germinal center
GCB	germinal center B-cell
H3K27	histone H3 Lys-27-specific trimethylation
H3K4me3	tri-methylation of lysine 4 on histone H3
HAT	histone acetyltransferase
HGBL	high-grade B-cell lymphoma
HL	Hodgkin's lymphoma
HSCT	hematopoietic stem cell transplantation
ICI	immune checkpoint inhibitor
IGF1	insulin-like growth factor 1
IKK	inhibitor of kappa B kinase
IL-10	interleukin 10
JAK2	Janus kinase 2
JNK	c-Jun N-terminal kinase
LCR	locus control region
LME	lymphoma microenvironment
LMP	latent membrane protein
LZ	light zone
MACs	membrane attack complexes
MAPK	mitogen-activated protein kinase
MDSC	marrow-derived suppressor cell
MEK	mitogen-activated extracellular signal-regulated kinase
MHC-II	major histocompatibility complex class II
MLL	mixed lineage leukemia
MM	multiple myeloma
mTOR	mammalian target of rapamycin
NF-κB	nuclear factor-kappa B
NHL	non-Hodgkin's lymphoma
NIK	NF-κB-inducible kinase
NK	natural killer
OFA	ofatumumab

OS	overall survival
PBL	plasmablastic lymphoma
PD-1	programmed cell death protein 1
PI3K	phosphatidylinositol 3-kinase
PIP3	phosphatidylinositol (3,4,5)-trisphosphate
PKC	protein kinase C
PRC	polycomb repressive complex
PTEN	phosphate and tension homology deleted on chromosome ten
Raf	rapidly accelerated fibrosarcoma
Ras	rat sarcoma
RTX	rituximab
Smac	second mitochondrial-derived activators of caspases
SNP	single-nucleotide polymorphisms
Sp1	specific protein 1
STAT	signal transducer and activator of transcription
Syk	splenic tyrosine kinase nucleases
TALENs	transcription activator-like effector
TAM	tumor-associated macrophages
TAN	tumor-associated neutrophils
THL	triple-hit lymphoma
TME	tumor microenvironment
TNF	tumor necrosis factor
TP53	tumor protein 53
TRAFS	TNFR-associated factors
UHRF1	ubiquitin-like, PHD and Ring Finger-containing 1
YY1	Yin and Yang 1
ZAFNs	zinc finger nuclease

Conflict of interest

No potential conflicts of interest were disclosed.

Introduction

Lymphoma is a cancer of the lymphatic system and is classified into two categories according to histopathologic changes: non-Hodgkin's lymphoma (NHL) and Hodgkin's lymphoma (HL). They can be divided into B-cell, T-cell, and natural killer (NK)-cell lymphomas, in accordance with the origin of the lymphocytes. According to the 2016 World Health Organization (WHO) reclassification of hematopoietic and lymphoid tissue tumors [3], lymphomas are mostly B-cell in origin. Lymphoma is becoming more common accounting for 11%–13% of all malignant tumor mortality, which is similar to leukemia, and the existing treatment options have not improved the outcomes [1].

The lymphatic circulation permits lymphoma to assault all tissues and organs throughout the body, so the medical signs and symptoms of lymphoma at different sites are ordinarily similar. However, the treatment consequences and prognosis of lymphoma range broadly in accordance with the pathological classification and clinical stage. A combination of chemotherapy and radiotherapy, surgery, hematopoietic stem cell transplantation (HSCT) and biological therapy are the main treatments. Biological therapies, in which monoclonal antibodies are secreted by B-lymphocyte clones that can only target specific antigenic determinants, have gained popularity in tumor treatment in recent years. Nevertheless, due to the development of medication resistance and individual specificity, the therapeutic efficacy of monoclonal antibodies varies [2]. This chapter focuses on the mechanism of anti-CD20 monoclonal antibodies in B-lymphocytic tumors and explores the reasons for the development of drug resistance.

Mechanisms of rituximab

Tumor cell activation through antibody-mediated complement activation results in the following three mechanisms of action: modulation of C3 fragments with target cells [4], recruitment and activation of multiple immune cells by the allergenic toxins C3a and C5a [5], and formation of membrane attack complexes (MACs) that lyse tumor cells [6]. In addition, cell-binding C3 metabolites (iC3b/C3d) recognize immune-responsive cells via complement 3 (CR3, CD11b/CD18), produce complement-dependent cytotoxicity (CDC), and enhance antibody-dependent cytotoxicity [7].

The study on the function of the CD20 antibody can provide a theoretical basis for the development of drug resistance. It has been demonstrated that the direct or indirect interaction of rituximab with CD20 is responsible for cell death. Rituximab is a mouse-human anti-CD20 monoclonal antibody, which can specifically bind to the CD20 antigen on the cell membrane and is the most common anti-CD20 antibody. The CD20 protein, encoded by the MS4A1 gene located on chromosome 11q12 [8], is expressed only on the surface of mature B cells and is absent in the early or late stages of B-cell differentiation such as pre-B cells and plasma cells. Rituximab can directly inhibit cell growth, induce cell apoptosis, and improve the sensitivity of cells to chemotherapy. It also has indirect effects through CDC and antibody-dependent cellular cytotoxicity (ADCC) [9]. In B-cell malignancies, abnormal CD20 protein expression, alterations in the structure of the CD20 antibody-binding site, or alterations in the cell membrane (e.g., lipid raft reorganization) may contribute to resistance to it [10–13].

Complement-dependent cytotoxicity

CDC refers to the binding of specific antibodies to antigens on the cell membrane surface, resulting in the formation of a complex, while the Fc terminus of the antibody contains a binding site for serum protein C1q [14], which activates the traditional complement pathway and, in a series of actions, produces a membrane attack complex that causes tumor cells lysis, allowing C3b to be deposited on the cell surface. In patients with chronic lymphocytic leukemia (CLL), the rapid and substantial depletion of complement fractions due to rituximab infusion suggests that complement activation may be a part of rituximab therapy [15]. The efficacy of antibodies is limited by their resistance to complement attack due to overexpression of one or more membrane complement regulatory proteins (mCRPs) [16]. mCRPs are expressed in most cancer cells, and CD46 (membrane cofactor protein), CD55 (decay accelerating factor, DAF), and CD59 (membrane inhibitor of reactive cleavage) are negatively correlated with CDC [17]. Overexpression of CD59 can inhibit the efficacy of rituximab in patients with B-cell malignancies. Mamidi et al. [18] significantly increased RTX, ofatumumab (OFA)-induced CDC by mCRPs-specific siRNA or neutralizing antibodies. The results showed that by inhibiting the expression of mCRPs, the sensitivity of leukemic cells to drugs could be enhanced, which elevated the CDC effect of plasmablastic lymphoma (PBL) and macrophages. Many researchers have found that neutralization of complement regulators by inhibitors can improve the sensitivity of RTX-mediated CDC and thus its antitumor effects in vivo and in vitro [19–21].

Antibody-dependent cellular cytotoxicity

ADCC refers to cytotoxic cells such as NK cells, granulocytes, and macrophages, which recognize Fc fragments on antigens through Fc receptors (FcRs) on their surface, activate target cells, and mediate cytotoxic effects against the target. The efficacy of rituximab, a constant region of its heavy chain that allows it to interact with host cell IgG (FcγRIIIa) Fc receptors, is associated with single-nucleotide polymorphisms in FcrRs. The polymorphism only affected patients who had received rituximab, suggesting that ADCC plays an important role in the treatment of anti-CD20. Fc-γ-IIb can inhibit or eliminate the activity of effector cells, while FC-γ-RIIa and FC-γ-RIIIa can activate effector cells around the target cells. FcrRIIIa exhibits a dimorphic state because the valine (V) at position 158 within the transcriptionally synthesized receptor protein is replaced by a phenylalanine (F). Hatjiharissi et al. [22] observed that FcγRIIIa transcript levels were higher in individuals with FcγRIIIa-158 V/V compared to individuals with FcγRIIIa-158 V/F or F/F genotypes and that rituximab-binding capacity and its mediated ADCC were enhanced with the presence of at least one valine, and that ADCC action was also associated with the number of cell surface CD16 receptors. Elvington et al. [7] established a mouse fusion protein of CR2Fc that targets C3 activation products and enhances mAb-dependent complement activation as well as tumor cell lysis in vitro. The CR2Fc construct significantly enhances the efficacy of monoclonal antibodies via macrophage-dependent Fcγ R-mediated ADCC and CDC.

Induction of apoptosis

Studies [23–25]have shown that rituximab causes apoptosis in several B-cell lines and that the Fc function of rituximab is not associated with this immunochemical sensitization [26]. Most cytotoxic chemotherapeutic agents utilize caspase-dependent pathways to regulate apoptosis, and modulation of these pathways is an important pathway leading to chemoresistance. Some investigators [27] will argue that an important factor in the induction of apoptosis by rituximab is caspase activation, while rituximab-mediated caspase-dependent apoptosis is caused by three major pathways: activation of Src family tyrosine kinases (Lyn, Fyn, Lck), activation of Fas apoptotic signaling, and inhibition of major survival pathways: p38 mitogen-activated protein kinase (MAPK), extracellular signal-regulated kinase 1/2 (ERK1/2), nuclear factor-kappaB (NF-κB), AKT. However, other studies [28,29] have reported that the function of rituximab is independent of caspase-induced apoptosis. In addition, some scholars have proposed that the rituximab-induced apoptotic pathway is involved through proteins in the Bcl-2 gene family. It contains both pro-apoptotic and antiapoptotic proteins, and cells are sensitive to apoptosis in part because of the balance between mutual interference signals. Overexpression of Bcl-2 in NHL is a manifestation of aggressive disease, chemotherapy resistance, and poor prognosis [30], and rituximab can overcome this resistance (Table 1, Fig. 1) [31].

TABLE 1 Mechanisms of rituximab.

Mechanisms of rituximab		References
Complement-dependent cytotoxicity	Membrane complement regulatory proteins (mCRPs)	[14–21]
Antibody-dependent cellular cytotoxicity	FcrR single-nucleotide polymorphisms (SNP)	[7,22]
Induction of apoptosis	Imbalance of antiapoptotic or apoptotic proteins	[26–31]

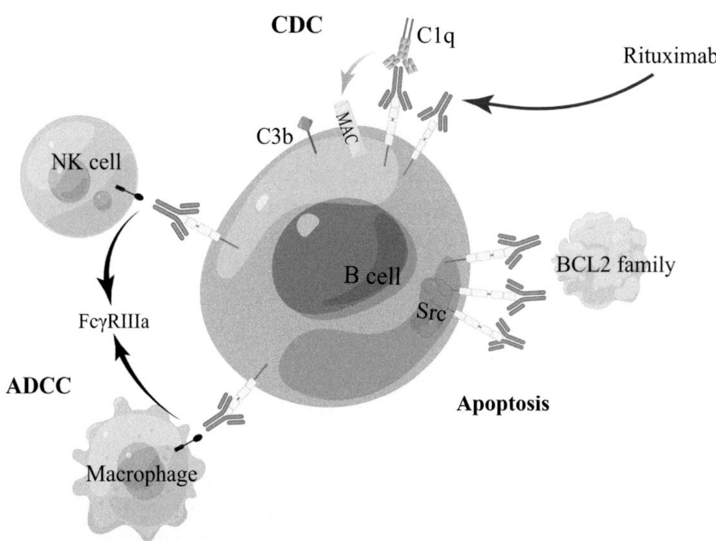

FIG. 1 Rituximab can not only directly induce cell apoptosis, but can also resist tumor cell growth through ADCC, CDC, and other pathways. Fc terminus of the antibody contains a binding site for serum protein C1q, which activates the traditional complement pathway and produces a membrane attack complex that causes tumor cells lysis, allowing C3b to be deposited on the cell surface. NK cells, macrophages, and so on can recognize the Fc fragment on the antigen through the Fc receptor, which activates the target cell, resulting in antibody-dependent cellular cytotoxicity. The rituximab-induced apoptotic pathway may be involved through proteins in the Bcl-2 gene family or caspase activation.

Genetic alterations and molecular mechanisms

DLBCL is divided into two main subtypes: activated B-cell (ABC) and germinal center B-cell (GCB) [32]. ABC DLBCL has a lower overall survival (OS) rate compared to GCB DLBCL. Morin et al. [33] found that the most frequently mutated genes in ABC rrDLBCL were PIM1 (38%), MYD88 (31%), MLL3 (23%), and CD79B (23%). In contrast, the most enriched mutations in GCB rrDLBCL were CREBBP (45%), STAT6 (36%), and FOXO1 (36%), followed by BCL2 and EZH2 (27%). The most frequent non-COO-specific mutations were TP53 (32%), MLL2 (KMT2D) (28%), and FAS (16%). In addition, mutations that may affect sensitivity to new therapies, such as MYD88 and CD79B mutations in the ABC subtype and recurrent STAT6 mutations affecting D419 in the GCB subtype, have been detected in rrDLBCL patients. The D419 mutation, present only in GCB-rrDLBCL, is associated with activated JAK/STAT signaling, increased phospho-STAT6 protein expression, and increased STAT6 target gene expression, suggesting that JAK/STAT signaling may serve as a novel therapeutic target for these patients. Jazirehi et al. [34] studied that NF-κB, ERK1/2, p38MAPK, and PI3K/AKT pathways were highly activated in RR cell lines and that the antiapoptotic gene products Bcl-2 and Bcl-xL were overexpressed, leading to chemosensitization and reversal of drug resistance.

Cell signaling

Rituximab can inhibit key pro-survival pathways (including NF-κB, p38MAPK, Raf/MEK/ERK, and PI3K/AKT/mTORC1 pathways) to induce apoptosis, and acts in synergy with different chemotherapeutic agents.

The NF-κB pathway

NF-κB is a family of transcription factors including RelA, RelB, c-Rel, p50, and p52 that are involved in the proliferation and survival of B cells. NF-κB is activated mainly through two pathways (canonical and noncanonical), while the downstream effects of the noncanonical pathway cause B-cell maturation and lymphoid organ formation. The NF-κB pathway is highly targeted due to its interconnection with many pathways, such as the receptors of B cells, the PI3K/Akt/mTOR pathway. Inhibitors of apoptosis protein calf intestinal alkaline phosphatase 1 (cIAP1) and cIAP2 have increased the copy number and expression levels in primary DLBCL tissues, while a second mitochondrial-derived activators of caspases (Smac) were designed to antagonize cIAP proteins. Smac mimicry-induced cIAP depletion leads to the accumulation of NF-κB-inducible kinase (NIK). Tumor necrosis factor (TNF) α, a well-described NF-κB target gene, overbinds to cell surface receptors and induces receptor-mediated cell death, further enhancing apoptotic cell death [35]. Rituximab reduced the phosphorylation of NIK, Iκ B kinase (IKK), and IκB-α (IκB) and decreased the binding activity of NF-κB DNA. In addition, rituximab significantly increased the expression of RKIP, which in turn blocked the NF-κB signaling pathway, while inhibiting the downregulation of Bcl-xL. By inducing the expression of RKIP, its physical binding to NIK, IKK, and TAK1 could be increased, resulting in a decrease in NF-κB pathway activity and a decrease in NF-κB DNA-binding activity [36]. These studies suggest that rituximab can act through the NF-κB pathway or interfere with RKIP and that it may be a potential target for therapeutic intervention.

The MAPK pathway and the Ras/Raf/MEK/ERK pathway

MAPK consists of ERK 1/2, c-Jun N-terminal kinase (JNK), p38, and ERK5 members [37]. Vega et al. [38] found that rituximab can exert antitumor effects through inhibition of the p38MAPK pathway. The p38MAPK pathway activates Sp1 and then reduces the transcriptional level of tumor-derived IL-10, while inhibition of the IL-10 autocrine/paracrine loop results in reduced STAT3 activity, reduced Bcl-2 expression, and sensitization to drug-induced apoptotic responses. The main downstream molecule of MAPK is JNK, which activates phosphorylation of the dominant substrate c-Jun and is involved in cell survival and apoptosis and oxidative damage (e.g., ROS generation) pathways [39,40]. In DLBCL, c-Jun/JNK signaling plays an important role in its development [41]. He et al. [6] transfected OCI-LY8 and NU-DU-L1 cells with si-JNK, thereby inhibiting their expression. The results of western blotting, cell viability inhibition, and changes in DNA damage indicated that rafoxinib had an inhibitory effect on PTEN/PI3K/AKT and JNK/c-Jun pathways, which contributed to the antiproliferative effect.

The Ras/Raf/MEK/ERK signaling cascade is commonly found in growth factors and mitogens, regulating gene expression and preventing apoptosis through signaling. Activation of AKT can phosphorylate and inactivate Rafs, resulting in the suppression of the Raf/MEK/ERK cascade response, while TP53 promotes Raf/MEK/ERK expression. Inhibition of NF-κB and ERK1/2 pathways is manifested by reduced phosphorylation of signaling molecules and kinase activity, such as reduced expression of the κ-2 family of antiapoptotic proteins and reduced DNA-binding capacity of NF-κB and activator protein-1 (AP-1), along with reduced expression of their common downstream target Bcl-xL [Bcl-2-related gene (long alternatively spliced variant of the Bcl-x gene)] [42,43]. Activation of NF-κB and ERK1/2 pathways is gradually becoming a major mechanism of drug resistance in tumor cells, enabling them to evade drug-killing effects while it is through inhibition of NF-κB and extracellular signal-regulated kinase 1/2 (ERK1/2) mitogen-activated protein kinase (MAPK) pathways that rituximab exerts its antitumor effects, sensitizing cells to drug-induced apoptosis.

The PI3K/AKT/MTOR pathway

Phosphate and tension homology deleted on chromosome ten (PTEN) is the only lipid phosphatase currently found to dephosphorylate phosphatidylinositol (3,4,5)-trisphosphate (PIP3), the lipid product of PI3K, and its protein expression and B-cell receptor (BCR) surface density may influence the clinical response to therapeutic inhibition of tonic (antigen-independent) BCR signaling in DLBCL. Tonic BCR signaling primarily activates the phosphatidylinositol 3-kinase (PI3K)/AKT/mTOR pathway, while alternative AKT activation induced by mTORC2, incomplete activation of mTORC1 downstream inhibitory effector eukaryotic translation initiation factor 4E-binding protein 1 (4EBP1) and a negative feedback loop as well as activation of parallel pathways make patients resistant to the antibody. mTOR, a serine/threonine kinase, is a complex of two subunits, mTORC1 and mTORC2. mTORC1 induces phosphorylation of eukaryotic translation initiation factor 4EBP1 and inhibits its negative regulation of transcription initiator eIF4E, allowing long 5-untranslated regions (5-UTR) containing complex RNA secondary structures of mRNAs containing complex RNA secondary structures (e.g., MYC) proceeds in translation [44]. Thus, inhibition of the

PI3K/AKT/mTOR pathway can significantly reduce MYC levels. In GCB-DLBCL cell lines, AKT activation is an important role in the BCR signaling pathway, which protects GCB-DLBCL cell lines from the BCR or the 2 BCR signaling carriers SYK and CD19. PTEN is a negative regulator of AKT activation, and PTEN regulates cell proliferation and DNA repair by antagonizing PI3K/AKT signaling. It was found that PTEN deficiency leads to abnormal expression of PI3K/AKT pathway proteins, which is important in terms of tumor growth, cell proliferation, and survival of DLBCL patients [45,46]. The relative decline in the GCB-DLBCL profile caused by KO of SYK or CD19 is usually similar to that produced by BCR KO and rescued by PTEN KO [47].

The JAK-STAT pathway

The JAK/STAT signaling pathway, also known as the IL-6 signaling pathway, is involved in a variety of important biological processes such as cell proliferation, differentiation, apoptosis, and immune regulation [48]. Ligands such as cytokines and growth factors bind to the receptor and activate the JAK kinase, resulting in phosphorylation of the receptor as well as its main substrate STAT. Phosphorylated STAT forms a dimer with other members of the STAT family with a conserved SH2 structural domain, which translates into the nucleus and binds to a specific regulatory region in the DNA sequence, resulting in activation or repression of transcription of the target gene. JAK kinase is an activator of the PI3K/AKT signaling pathway, and phosphorylation of JAK activates PI3K, thereby activating the PI3K/AKT/mTOR pathway. It was shown that SOCS1 gene expression induced by activation of the JAK/STAT signaling pathway has an impact on the efficacy of elderly DLBCL patients treated with R-CHOP [49].

Barbarino et al. [50] evaluated the combination of a Bruton tyrosine kinase inhibitor ibrutinib and monoclonal antibody by macrophage-mediated antibody-dependent cytophagy (ADCP) and found a significant reduction in Janus kinase2 (JAK2). Meanwhile, inhibition of JAK and knockdown of JAK2 using CRISPR-Cas9 resulted in increased ADCP and prolonged survival. The consequences recommend that the JAK-STAT signaling pathway can also serve as a new goal for B-cell malignant diseases. Furthermore, JAK2 was significantly absent only under ibrutinib treatment, with no significant difference in ADCP augmentation using the second-generation Bruton's tyrosine kinase (BTK) which means that ibrutinib increases ADCP is independent of BTK Inhibition. Analysis of kinase activity revealed that JAK2 and JAK3 may be off-target kinases of ibrutinib for a macrophage-mediated increase in phagocytosis, while ADCP augmentation is mediated by targeting the malignant B-cell compartment and causes macrophage activation by the induction of secretory components in malignant B cells.

BCR signaling

BCR is a B-cell surface immunoglobulin that specifically recognizes and binds antigens, causing the aggregation of multiple BCR complexes on the B-cell surface, phosphorylation of CD79A and CD79B in the cytoplasm, and activation of various signaling molecules, such as splenic tyrosine kinase (Syk), which activates MAPK, triggering a signaling cascade that generates transcription factors such as NF-κB and NFAT, thereby regulating gene transcription in B cells [51].

Thieme et al. [52] demonstrated that a dual BTK/SYK inhibitor, CG-806 (lusefenib), downregulates the antiapoptotic proteins Mcl-1 and Bcl-xL, disrupts BCR signaling, and induces metabolic reprogramming and apoptosis in MCL. BTK/SYK inhibition leads to mitochondrial membrane depolarization accompanied by mitochondrial autophagy and metabolic reprogramming to glycolysis. BCR cross-linking promotes the interaction between SRC family kinases (e.g., LYN) and CD79A/B, which induces activation of SYK. BCR signaling is a key driver of NF-κB, which in turn induces Bcl-2 protein, and the Bcl-2 network is a key mediator of sensitivity to CG-806. CG-806 targets the key BCR-associated kinases LYN, SYK and BTK, a BCR signal-driven kinase that recruits BTK to trigger distinct downstream events leading to propagation of AKT, MAPK, and NF-κB signaling and upregulation of Bcl-2 family proteins. Loss of BAX, a direct activator of apoptosis, confers resistance to CG-806 resistance, reflecting the importance of antiapoptotic Bcl-2 family members and MOMP in CG-806-induced apoptosis. Inactivation of type I interferon and cell cycle control pathways as well as Wnt/β-linked protein and mTOR signaling pathways promotes CG-806 resistance. NFKBIA is a negative regulator of NF-κB signaling and BAX is a direct apoptosis activator, and their knockdown reduced the sensitivity of MCL cells to CG-806, confirming the role of the NF-κB pathway and the Bcl-2 family network in the resistance to dual BTK/SYK inhibition.

Fas/FasL apoptotic pathway

Fas (Apo-1, CD95) and FasL receptor (FasL, CD95L) are typical members of the TNF receptor and TNF ligand families, which play important roles in the regulation of apoptosis. They can induce apoptosis, mediate T-lymphocyte-induced cytotoxicity, and monitor tumor cells. There is increasing evidence that Fas activation also leads to nonapoptotic responses, such as cell proliferation or NF-κB activation. The initiation of Fas signaling is associated with the polymerization of the Fas complex, and the activation of effector caspases is caused by two main pathways, leading to apoptosis. Vega et al. [53] showed that rituximab treatment of B NHL cell lines 2F7, Ranmos and Raji inhibited the constitutive NF-κB and induced an apoptotic sensitization response of cells to CH-11 (FasL-activated monoclonal antibody). It has been shown that this effect depends on elevated Fas levels, which occur within 6 h, and that transcriptional repressor Yin and Yang 1 (YY1) DNA binds to the silent region of the Fas promoter to inhibit Fas transcription. YY1 is located downstream of NF-κB and is regulated by NF-κB activity; therefore, rituximab, which inhibits NF-κB, may also inhibit YY1, rendering NHL cell lines sensitive to FASL-induced apoptosis. Part of the reason why some patients do not respond to rituximab may be that tumor cells are not sensitive to immune-mediated apoptosis, which can be attributed to Fas gene variation. Data have shown that approximately 20% of B-cell lymphomas originating from postgerminal central B cells have been found to carry mutations or defects in Fas expression levels (Fig. 2).

MYC, BCL2, BCL6

MYC protein expression is high in DLBCL (~40%) and is associated with the concomitant expression of BCL-2. DLBCL carrying MYC, BLC2, and/or BCL6 translocations is known as "double-hit" lymphoma (DHL) or triple-hit lymphoma (THL) [54], collectively referred to as high-grade B-cell lymphoma (HGBL). MYC, BCL2, and/or BCL6 rearrangements and protein expression levels have been identified as prognostic factors in DLBCL, with MYC being the most common [55–57].

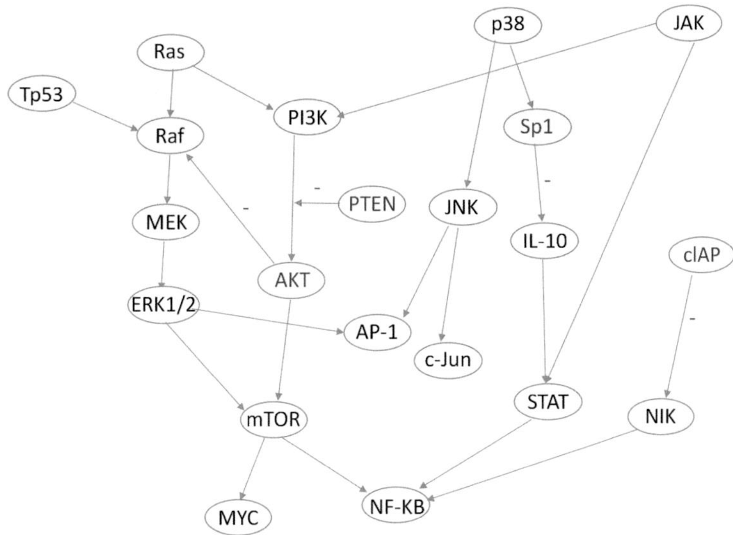

FIG. 2 Cell signaling. "-" means inhibiting effect and *red color* means genes act as inhibitor. Rituximab induces apoptosis, with the main pathways being inhibition of NF-κB, p38MAPK, Ras/Raf/MEK/ERK, JAK/STAT, and PI3K/AKT/mTORC1 pathways. The genes involved in these reaction steps are shown in this figure. Activation of AKT can phosphorylate and inactivate Rafs, resulting in a suppression of the Raf/MEK/ERK cascade response. PTEN is a negative regulator of AKT activation, and PTEN regulates cell proliferation and DNA repair by antagonizing PI3K/AKT signaling. The p38MAPK pathway activates Sp1 and then reduces the transcriptional level of tumor-derived IL-10, while inhibition of the IL-10 autocrine/paracrine loop results in reduced STAT3 activity, reduced Bcl-2 expression, and sensitization to drug-induced apoptotic responses. Smac mimicry-induced cIAP depletion leads to the accumulation of NIK.

MYC

MYC proto-oncogene is located on chromosome 8q24. MYC is a major oncogenic transcription factor that regulates the expression of several cell cycle kinases. AuroraA and AuroraB are a class of serine/threonine kinases with antitumor activity, playing an important regulatory role in the eukaryotic cell cycle. Activation or overexpression of MYC leads to a significant increase in the levels and activity of Aurk A and Aurk B in vivo and in vitro. Overexpression of Aurk A, especially Aurk B, is a hallmark of MYC-driven B-cell lymphoma [58]. Overexpression of MYC in normal cells upregulates the pro-apoptotic protein BIM and indirectly downregulates BCL2, BCL-xL, and MCL1, while enhancing the sensitivity of cells to different types of apoptosis-inducing factors, which in turn induces apoptosis. MYC in turn promotes TP53 expression and inhibits apoptosis in tumor cells, so mutations in the TP53 gene and overexpression of BCL2 may counteract the pro-apoptotic effect of MYC cells [59].

EBV viruses switch from lysis to latency to evade host immune intervention, and depletion of MYC or factors affecting MYC expression drives EBV viruses to reenter lysis. Guo et al. [60] performed a genomic screen using CRISPR-Cas9 in Burkitt's lymphoma B cells and identified an MYC-centered gene network in which MYC and endoglin, FACT, STAGA, and the mediator collaborate to repress transcription of the BZLF1 promoter. BZLF1 primarily regulates B-cell lysis, and its transcription causes the expression of more than 30 early lytic genes, including viral DNA polymerase, the synthesis factor BMRF1, kinases, and other factors important for cleaved DNA replication. The expression of Epstein-Barr nuclear antigen (EBNA), latent membrane protein (LMP), and BZLF1 was reduced after the knockdown of Ubiquitin-like, PHD, and Ring Finger-containing 1(UHRF1), DNA methyltransferase 1 (DNMT1), and polycomb repressive complex 1 (PRC1) by Guo et al. [61]. The incapability of the immune system to recognize the EBV virus led to a long-term latent infection in the host. Sidorov et al. [62] investigated the impact of IgH/c-myc translocation in primary B cells with the use of the CRISPR-Cas9 knock-in method and confirmed that CD4+ T cells inhibit EBL by using killing pre-EBL cells lacking IgH/c-myc translocation in vitro on the one hand; on the other hand, by means of reducing the expression of EBNA2 promoter, they induce EBV transition between latency III and latency I, thereby indirectly stimulating EBL development. EBNA2 has an antiapoptotic effect, but its loss can lead to decreased viability of the LCL. CD4+ T lymphocytes increased the expression of BCL6 mRNA in the LCL, which is an important marker of EBL.

BCL2

The Bcl-2 family plays an important role in apoptosis, with conserved structural domains such as BH1, BH2, BH3, and BH4. The Bcl-2 family can be divided into two major groups; one is antiapoptotic, mainly Bcl-2, Bcl-xL, Bcl-W, Mcl-1, CED9, etc., and the other is apoptotic, mainly including Bax, Bak, Bcl-XS, Bad, Bik, Bid, etc. BCL2 is widely expressed in immature B cells and memory B cells with potent antiapoptotic functions, and its expression level is elevated in patients with relapsed DLBCL. BCL2 translocation, t(14;18) (q32; q21), is observed in approximately 15%–20% of DLBCL cases and approximately 80%–90% of FL cases [63]. Overexpression of antiapoptotic BCL-2 proteins may cause dysregulation of apoptosis, and BCL-2 proteins can isolate a number of pro-apoptotic BH3 proteins (BIM, BID), thereby preventing oligomerization of pore-forming proteins (BAX, BAK) and subsequent mitochondrial outer membrane permeabilization. Inhibition of BCL2 by BCL6 causes a transient decrease in BCL2 expression in GC B cells. MYC can interact with the antiapoptotic network through the BCL2 family of proteins, which can regulate the intrinsic mitochondrial pathway of apoptosis [64]. Members of the BCL2 family are known to render hematologic malignancies resistant to various chemotherapeutic agents [65,66], and thus they are likely to be associated with drug resistance and relapse of R-CHOP.

BCL6

DLBCL originates in the germinal center (GC) stage of B-cell differentiation [67], and BCL6, a core transcription factor of the GC response, has been shown to be an oncogene that can develop into lymphoma. The BCL6 translocation, t(3q27), occurs in approximately 35% of DLBCL patients and is the highest translocation gene [68]. BCL6 is a member of the BCL family of proteins encoding BTB/POZ zinc finger transcription factors that act as an inhibitor by recruiting corepressor molecules in cell cycle control, proliferation and differentiation, apoptosis, and DNA damage response. BCL6 gene expression is tightly regulated during the differentiation of mature B cells and is essential for the development of germinal centers in B cells by inhibiting P53, MYC, and BCL2 family proteins, cyclin dependent kinase inhibitor 1A (CDKN1A). CD40 plays a major role in B-cell development, activation, and germinal center responses. Low CD40 activity leads to immunodeficiency, while its overexpression leads to autoimmunity and lymphoma. CD40 stimulation of B-cell lymphoma cells downregulates BCL6 and induces the expression of the BCL6 target gene CD23b. Activated CD40 recruits TNFR-associated factors (TRAFs) to three CD40 cytoplasmic tail structural domains to activate the NF-κB, MAPK, and PI3K pathways, while NF-κB-induced IRF4 binds to IRF4-responsive elements in the BCL6 promoter and represses BCL6 transcription [69]. The locus control region (LCR) is positioned 150kb upstream of BCL6 on chromosome 3q26 and acts appreciably on adjoining and distal genes consisting of the BCL6 proto-oncogene and its function is GC-specific [70]. Chu et al. [71] observed that CRISPR interference with gRNA targeting OCT2 and OCA-B both resulted in a significant reduction in BCL6 mRNA levels. Furthermore, BCL6 and its adjacent LCR can function in vivo only if they are located on the same chromosome, reflecting the direct *cis*-regulatory role of the LCR in the induction of Bcl6 and GC formation. The sequential function of these factors may be particularly important in that BCL6 is repressed early in transcription, i.e., when located in the promoter region, and is activated as cells migrate and form nascent GCs [72,73]. Thus, a hierarchical model of BCL6 regulation by progressive activation of the LCR can be proposed.

Mutations in epigenetically regulated genes

One of the main factors in the pathogenesis of DLBCL is epigenetic dysregulation. For example, genes encoding histone methyltransferases (e.g., EZH2 and KTM2D) or acetyltransferases (e.g., CREBBP and EP300) are frequently altered.

EZH2 and MLL

Activation mutation and overexpression of enhancer of zeste homolog 2 (EZH2) are common in NHL, especially in GC-induced lymphoma. EZH2 regulates cell cycle progression and is mainly involved in cell proliferation, apoptosis, and senescence. EZH2 mutation is an influencing factor of relapse in patients with DLBCL [74], and its frequency is increased in R/R DLBCL [75]. EZH2 is the catalytic subunit of polycomb repressive complex 2 (PRC2), whose SET structural domain acts as a histone methyltransferase and represses gene expression by histone H3 lysine 4 trimethylation (H3K27), in contrast to methylating mixed lineage leukemia (MLL) that induces tri-methylation of lysine 4 on histone H3 (H3K4me3). Small molecule inhibitors of EZH2 methyltransferase activity reduce overall H3K27me3 levels, activate silent target genes of EZH2, and inhibit the proliferation of diffuse large B lymphomas with EZH2 mutations in vitro. A somatic heterozygous mutation in the catalytic SET domain of histone methyltransferase EZH2 at codon 641 (Y641) was found to increase the expression level of histone H3 Lys-27-specific trimethylation (H3K27me3), thereby enhancing its suppressive effect on the gene in lymphoma [76]. CD58 is a receptor for CD2 in NK cells or T cells, and EZH2 inhibitors reverse the epigenetic silencing of CD58 [77]. The histone lysine methyltransferase gene KMT2D, also known as MLL2, is one of the most common relapse-associated genetic variants, and clonal expansions of KMT2D have been identified in relapsed

DLBCL, with KMT2D mutations occurring in approximately 44% of DLBCL patients, with R/R DLBCL patients being more common [75,78]. KMT2D and ASC2 form ASCOM (ASC-2 Complex) and MLL3/4, acts as a p53 coactivator, is required for H3K4-trimethyation and expression of endogenous p53-target genes in response to the DNA damaging agent doxorubicin [79].

CREBBP and EP300

CREB-binding protein (CREBBP) and EP300 belong to the KAT3 family of histone/protein lysine acetyltransferases. CREBBP and EP300 modify lysine residues on histone and nonhistone nuclear proteins and transcriptionally coactivate multiple signaling factors [80,81]. CREBBP and EP300 are tumor suppressors and the genes encoding histone acetyltransferases (HATs). CREBBP and EP300 are recurrently mutated in ABC and GCB subtypes of DLBCL and significantly associated with poor prognosis, the gene products of which contribute to histone H3 acetylation and promote active transcription in DLBCL cells and affects the expression of many genes, most notably the MHCII gene, which participates in tumor immune escape. Specific deficiency of CREBBP in the germinal center B-cell compartment also results in loss of its MHCII expression and demonstrates hyperproliferation of germinal center B cells upon immunization, which predisposes them to MYC-driven lymphoma [82,83]. The effect of CREBBP loss was confirmed by MHCII deficiency in spontaneous and sequential transplantation models of MYC-driven lymphomas, supporting the idea of the notion that CREBBP mutational inactivation promotes immune escape. CREBBP used to be proven to be a regulator of the enhancer/superenhancer network, inhibiting enhancer activity via the BCL6/SMRT/HDAC3 complex and regulating GC and plasma cell development as well as antigenic rapture to result in formed lymphomas [82,83]. Mutations in CREBBP and EP300 genes can promote the development of DLBCL by activating the signaling pathway of NOTCH through the negative regulation of FBXW7, the major blocking factor of NOTCH [84].

Other frequent gene mutations

TP53

The TP53 gene encodes the p53 tumor suppressor and is the most frequently mutated gene in malignant tumors [85]. The TP53 gene responds to DNA damage by initiating a DNA repair program and cell cycle arrest to maintain genomic stability. TP53 mutations are present in approximately 20% of DLBCL, and most TP53 mutations are accompanied by loss of p53 function, which is associated with poor survival in DLBCL patients [86]. Cells express major histocompatibility complex class II (MHC-II), and there is a link between p53 and MHC-I/II expression [87]. The interference of the p53 signaling pathway significantly reduces the MHC-II gene, which may partly lead to the deterioration of tumor prognosis. It has been shown that TP53 mutations are more common in MYC/BCL2 DHL than in classical DLBCL or DHL with MYC/BCL6 rearrangements [88] and that both TP53 mutations and p53 overexpression may lead to a poorer prognosis in DLBCL patients, but DLBCL patients with MYC rearrangements and TP53 mutations have worse survival rates than MYC/BCL2 DHL patients [89]. Caeser et al. [90] used steady Cas9 reverse transcription in primary, human GC B cells and proved that can be used for gRNA targeted targeting. In the CRISPR-Cas9 screen TP53, GNA13, CDKN2A, ATRX, NFKBIA, ZFP36L1, ZNF281, PTEN, FBXO11, FUBP1, S1PR2, and NFKBIE have been strongly enriched and most elements are tumor suppressors. While tumor cell proliferation used to be enhanced by TSG inactivation.

PIM1

PIM1 belongs to the PIM kinase family, which includes three highly conserved oncogenes, PIM1, PIM2, and PIM3, and is a new class of serine/threonine kinases, whose unique molecular and biochemical properties regulate various cancer pathways, such as hypoxia response, cell cycle regulation, and resistance to apoptosis. PIM1 expression is associated with poor prognosis in various leukemias [91], lymphomas [92], and DLBCL [93]. JAK-STAT [94] and NF-κB [95] are the most prominent pathways for activating PIM1 expression. Szydlowski et al. [96] investigated the mechanism of the pro-survival effect of PIM kinase and the toxicogenic effect of PIM inhibition in DLBCL by blocking PIM in the chemical and genetic ways. The expression of several MYC-dependent genes was downregulated in DLBCL cells treated with SEL24/MEN1703 (a pan-PIM inhibitor), including those involved in cell cycle control and proliferation, such as PLK1 (a major regulator of mitosis). MYC represses the MS4A1 gene encoding the CD20 surface antigen by two mechanisms: direct repression of the MS4A1 promoter and induction of MS4A1/CD20 targeting miR-222. The expression of CD20 is elevated in DHL4 and RAJI cells after siRNA knockdown of MYC, indicating that the PIM-MYC axis suppressed CD20 expression in B-cell lymphomas. PIM inhibition enhances the two major mechanisms of action of rituximab, CDC and ADCP, and also affects the activity of important regulators of protein translation and apoptosis, including 4EBP1, RPS6, and BAD, whose blockade also reduces the expression of the antiapoptotic BCL2 family member MCL1.

FOXO1

FOXO plays an important role in determining the fate of mature B cells, is required for dark zone (DZ) formation, and contributes to the LZ-DZ (light zone-dark zone) transition [97], acting as a tumor suppressor by regulating DNA repair, cell cycle, and apoptosis [98,99]. FOXO1 mutations have been recently reported in DLBCL [100], and in addition, FOXO1 mutations have been associated with decreased overall survival in DLBCL patients treated with R-CHOP combination therapy [101]. Pyrzynska et al. [102] first discovered FOXO1 negatively regulates CD20 transcription in NHL and human lymphoma specimens carrying FOXO1 mutations. Knockdown of the FOXO1 gene using CRISPR-Cas9 gene editing technology revealed a more than threefold increase in surface CD20 levels, suggesting that FOXO1 expression was suppressed and could improve the effect of rituximab. FOXO1 is a transcription factor to decrease CD20 after incubation with BTK, SYK, PI3K, and AKT inhibitors. The use of two inhibitors, MK-2206 (a metastable inhibitor of AKT) and GDC-0068 (an ATP-competitive AKT inhibitor) at nontoxic concentrations, resulted in dephosphorylation and nuclear accumulation of FOXO1 in the Raj and SU-DHL4 cell lines, downregulating CD20 levels in both cell lines. In addition, the expression of FOXO1 exogenous mutants and inhibition of AKT both activated FOXO1, enhancing its binding to the promoter of MS4A1 and reducing CD20 expression.

Abnormal structure and function of CD20

CD20 expression can be down-regulated at the DNA,RNA and protein levels before rituximab binds to CD20, such as CD20 gene mutation, abnormal splicing of CD20 mRNA, abnormal expression of CD20 protein, etc. Mutations in the MS4A1 gene, which encodes the CD20 protein, affect protein expression levels. Mutations at positions 170–173 and 182–185 significantly reduced rituximab's ability to bind to the extracellular portion of CD20 [103]. The missense mutation in MS4A1 may directly lead to a decrease in its CD20 expression and/or stability. Genetic mutations in the CD20 coding sequence, which result in amino acid changes located in the second transmembrane domain and the C-terminal intracellular domain, may lead to resistance or relapse to rituximab treatment. Terui et al. [11] found genetic variants in 11 of 50 patients, C-terminal gene deletion in four RD/PD patients, and a significant decrease in CD20 gene expression, suggesting that the development of rituximab resistance is closely associated with C-terminal deletion. Mishima et al. [12] demonstrated that loss of the CD20 C terminus may be associated with a large reduction in the extracellular loop on the cell membrane and may contribute to rituximab resistance. The abnormal expression of CD20 gene splice variants may cause a change in the structure of the rituximab-binding epitope and the change of the CD20 gene position on the cell membrane [104]. In addition, epigenetic effects can regulate CD20 expression, and it has been shown that the histone deacetylase inhibitor suberoylanilide hydroxamine acid regulates the expression of apoptosis-related genes [105], while the acetylase inhibitor trigonelline A increases the expression of CD20 mRNA and protein in CD20-negative cell lines, thereby increasing their sensitivity to drugs [106].

Other possible mechanisms of rituximab resistance

Immune escape

In DLBCL tumorigenesis, interference with antigen presentation and impairment of T-cell recognition lead to immune escape, a process that involves multiple mechanisms, with mutations in HLA genes [107] and class II transactivators (CIITA) encoding activators of MHC-II gene expression [108] being reported to re-enrich the HLA gene. In HLA type I and II molecules, CD8 and CD4 T lymphocytes are important components of tumor immune surveillance [109].

B2M gene

Immune escape is an important aspect of DLBCL tumorigenesis progression, which involves several mechanisms, and many studies have found an increased incidence of mutations or recurrence-specific mutations in the Beta2-microglobulin (B2M) gene, which disrupt MHC class I folding and transport to the cell surface, while MHC class I assists the immune system in recognizing its own cells and causes antigen degradation by interacting with cytotoxic T cells and thus allowing immune escape [110]. It enables tumor cells to escape recognition by immune cells, and promoting cancer progression which is a new direction in the treatment and prediction of B-cell lymphoma. Sorigue et al. [111] found that B2M was a strong predictor of OS and was the only variable that independently predicted PFS in follicular lymphoma. Decreased B2M expression may also have important implications for immune checkpoint inhibitor (ICI) therapy, as ICIs require tumor antigen presentation to function, and immune escape strategies involve interfering with antigen presentation [112]. One of the most successful innovations in the area of hematology is the CRISPR-Cas9-edited chimeric antigen receptor (CAR) T cell (CAR-T cell), which is additionally a primary leap forward in the area of immunotherapy and was approved by the FDA for the treatment of leukemia and lymphoma [113,114]. Eshhar et al. [115] suggested that delivery of bound CAR and CRISPR RNA through electroporation with lentivirus leads to injury of TCR and B2M genes, ensuing in homozygous CAR-T cells missing TCR, HLA type I molecules and PD1, which can effectively inhibit the response of allogeneic T cells, reduce rejection of the host, and prolong their duration of action [116].

PD-1 and PD-L1

Programmed cell death protein 1 (PD-1) is a surface inhibitory receptor for macrophages, dendritic cells, and T cells. The PD-1 pathway allows tumor cells to escape immune surveillance during normal chemotherapy and thus generate resistance to it, making anti-PD-1/PD-L1 antibodies a highly promising therapeutic approach. Griffin et al. [117] observed that 64% of malignant B cells had PD-L1/PD-L2 copy amplification or associated PD-L1 expression, and secondly, tumor microenvironment (TME) contained a large number of PD-L1-expressing TAMs and PD-1+ T cells, which were distributed according to tumor-specific, spatially resolved immune properties. The results suggest that TCRLBCL malignant B lymphocytes evade antitumor immunity through the PD-1/PD-L1 signaling pathway. PD-1 blockade has been shown to cooperate with anti-CD20-mediated lymphoma cell depletion. CD47 and PD-L1 are common immunoregulatory factors, and their expression is regulated by MYC. Inhibition of MYC with BET inhibitors (e.g., JQ1) has been shown to reduce the programmed death of PD-L1 and CD47 [118]. The efficacy of treatment by blocking immune checkpoints in lymphomas varies widely between types [119,120]; for example, in relapsed/refractory DLBCL, anti-PD-1 alone is poorly effective [121]. In addition, changes in PD-L1 were associated with poor PFS after R-CHOP. Anti-CD20 mAbs can eliminate tumor cells, while anti-PD-1 mAbs can block immune checkpoints, thereby enhancing immune cell invasion. CTLA-4, PD-1, LAG-3, and TIM-3 are T-cell suppressor receptors or signaling molecules whose expression induces T-cell failure [116,122,123]; therefore, knockdown of these elements through CRISPR-Cas9 can decrease T-cell apoptosis and amplify CAR-T cells and thereby decorate their function.

Changes in the TME

The TME is an immune microenvironment composed of immune cells and a nonimmune microenvironment composed of fibroblasts constitutes a complex network that forms a physical barrier around the tumor cells [124,125]. The immune microenvironment consists of T and B lymphocytes, tumor-associated macrophages (TAM), bone marrow-derived suppressor cells (MDSC), tumor-associated neutrophils (TAN), NK cells, and dendritic cells (DC). The nonimmune microenvironment consists mainly of stromal cells, including cancer-associated fibroblasts (CAFs), an extracellular matrix (ECM), pericytes, mesenchymal stromal cells, and other secreted molecules, including growth factors, cytokines, chemokines, and extracellular vesicles. TME can be involved in a variety of biological mechanisms, including pathogenesis, progression, metastasis, and drug resistance [126]. It has been shown that the TME is involved in the development of disease and drug resistance in B lymphocytes, thus avoiding the immune recognition of tumor cells and contributing to tumor growth. TME plays an important role in the formation and maintenance of cancer [124], and is a new direction in the treatment and prediction of prognosis of tumors.

The TME-mediated therapeutic resistance acts mainly through soluble factors, cell adhesion effects, and immune responses [127]. The therapeutic strategy consists mainly in depleting the cells already present, preventing their entry into the tumor region, and reconstituting them into antitumor subtypes. In the TME, cytokine alterations activate oncogenes or inactivate tumor suppressor genes, while environmentally mediated resistance (EM-DR) tends to be transient, occurring only when tumor cells are in contact with the microenvironment, and regains sensitivity to drugs once removed from the microenvironment [128]. Insulin-like growth factor 1 (IGF1), VEGF, and IL-6 promote MAPK, PI3K, and protein kinase C (PKC) signaling, thereby promoting multiple myeloma (MM) cell survival, metastasis, and infiltration [129–131]. The role of cytosine methylation in lymphoma cells may be responsible for the depletion of the lymphoma microenvironment (LME). Treatment of an A20 homozygous B lymphoma model with the hypomethylating agent azacitidine or vector for 4 days and then analyzed by RNA-seq and DNA methylation sequencing showed that cytosine methylation may be responsible for the depletion of LME in lymphoma cells [132]. Galactose lectin-1 (Gal-1) expression levels in the tumor microenvironment is strongly correlated with immunotherapy resistance, and its expression inhibits antibody-dependent phagocytic activity and sensitivity to CD20 immunotherapy (Table 2) [133].

TABLE 2 Genetic alterations and molecular mechanisms.

Genetic alterations and molecular mechanisms			References
Cell signaling	The NF-κB pathway		[36]
	The MAPK pathway and the Ras/Raf/MEK/ERK pathway		[37–43]
	The PI3K/AKT/MTOR pathway		[44–47]
	The JAK-STAT pathway		[48–50]
	B-cell receptor (BCR) signaling		[51,52]
	Fas/FasL apoptotic pathway		[53]
Genetic alterations	MYC		[59–62]
	BCL2		[63–66]
	BCL6		[67–73]
	Tp53		[85–90]
	PIM1		[91–96]
	FOXO1		[97–101]
Mutations in epigenetically regulated genes	Histone methyltransferases	EZH2	[74–79]
		MLL	
	Acetyltransferases	CREBBP	[80–84]
		EP300	
Abnormal structure and function of CD20	CD20 gene mutation		[11,12,103–106]
	Abnormal splicing of CD20 mRNA		
	Abnormal expression of CD20 protein		
Other possible mechanisms	Immune escape	Beta2-microglobulin(B2M) gene	[110–116]
		PD-1 and PD-L1	[116–123]
	Changes in the tumor microenvironment		[124–133]

Conclusions

For the time being, R-CHOP is the standard first-line treatment regimen for DLBCL, disease control and patients' survival can be improved, researchers want to cure the disease from the root, i.e., at the genetic level. Miller et al. [134] developed zinc finger nucleases (ZFNs) to target genes, and with the rapid development of science and technology, transcription activator-like effector nucleases (TALENs) [135,136] and CRISPR-Cas9 [137,138] have emerged one after another, with CRISPR-Cas9 being the most thoroughly studied and commonly used. CRISPR-Cas9 technology has the potential to permanently destroy tumor genes, it opens new avenues for the study of tumor pathogenesis, screening of drug-acting gene targets and precision medicine. Researchers can combine this with related research on B-cell lymphoma to discover new targets for targeting and knocking out pathogenic genes to cure the disease.

References

[1] Barré FPY, Claes BSR, Dewez F, Peutz-Kootstra C, Munch-Petersen HF, Grønbæk K, et al. Specific lipid and metabolic profiles of R-CHOP-resistant diffuse large B-cell lymphoma elucidated by matrix-assisted laser desorption ionization mass spectrometry imaging and in vivo imaging. Anal Chem 2018;90(24):14198–206.

[2] Crump M, Neelapu SS, Farooq U, Van Den Neste E, Kuruvilla J, Westin J, et al. Outcomes in refractory diffuse large B-cell lymphoma: results from the international SCHOLAR-1 study. Blood 2017;130(16):1800–8.

[3] Arber DA, Orazi A, Hasserjian R, Thiele J, Borowitz MJ, Le Beau MM, et al. The 2016 revision to the World Health Organization classification of myeloid neoplasms and acute leukemia. Blood 2016;127(20):2391–405.

[4] Perlmann H, Perlmann P, Schreiber RD, Muller-Eberhard HJ. Interaction of target cell-bound C3bi and C3d with human lymphocyte receptors. Enhancement of antibody-mediated cellular cytotoxicity. J Exp Med 1981;153(6):1592–603.

[5] Markiewski MM, DeAngelis RA, Benencia F, Ricklin-Lichtsteiner SK, Koutoulaki A, Gerard C, et al. Modulation of the antitumor immune response by complement. Nat Immunol 2008;9(11):1225–35.

[6] He W, Xu Z, Song D, et al. Antitumor effects of rafoxanide in diffuse large B cell lymphoma via the PTEN/PI3K/Akt and JNK/c-Jun pathways. Life Sci 2020;243:117249. https://doi.org/10.1016/j.lfs.2019.117249

[7] Elvington M, Huang Y, Morgan BP, Qiao F, van Rooijen N, Atkinson C, et al. A targeted complement-dependent strategy to improve the outcome of mAb therapy, and characterization in a murine model of metastatic cancer. Blood 2012;119(25):6043–51.

[8] Tedder TF, Disteche CM, Louie E, Adler DA, Croce CM, Schlossman SF, et al. The gene that encodes the human CD20 (B1) differentiation antigen is located on chromosome 11 near the t(11,14)(q13;q32) translocation site. J Immunol 1989;142(7):2555–9.

[9] Ziepert M, Hasenclever D, Kuhnt E, Glass B, Schmitz N, Pfreundschuh M, et al. Standard International prognostic index remains a valid predictor of outcome for patients with aggressive CD20+ B-cell lymphoma in the rituximab era. J Clin Oncol 2010;28(14):2373–80.

[10] Small GW, McLeod HL, Richards KL. Analysis of innate and acquired resistance to anti-CD20 antibodies in malignant and nonmalignant B cells. PeerJ 2013;1, e31.

[11] Terui Y, Mishima Y, Sugimura N, Kojima K, Sakurai T, Mishima Y, et al. Identification of CD20 C-terminal deletion mutations associated with loss of CD20 expression in non-Hodgkin's lymphoma. Clin Cancer Res 2009;15(7):2523–30.

[12] Mishima Y, Terui Y, Takeuchi K, Matsumoto-Mishima Y, Matsusaka S, Utsubo-Kuniyoshi R, et al. The identification of irreversible rituximab-resistant lymphoma caused by CD20 gene mutations. Blood Cancer J 2011;1(4), e15.

[13] Czuczman MS, Olejniczak S, Gowda A, Kotowski A, Binder A, Kaur H, et al. Acquirement of rituximab resistance in lymphoma cell lines is associated with both global CD20 gene and protein down-regulation regulated at the pretranscriptional and posttranscriptional levels. Clin Cancer Res 2008;14(5):1561–70.

[14] Idusogie EE, Presta LG, Gazzano-Santoro H, Totpal K, Wong PY, Ultsch M, et al. Mapping of the C1q binding site on rituxan, a chimeric antibody with a human IgG1 Fc. J Immunol 2000;164(8):4178–84.

[15] Kennedy AD, Beum PV, Solga MD, DiLillo DJ, Lindorfer MA, Hess CE, et al. Rituximab infusion promotes rapid complement depletion and acute CD20 loss in chronic lymphocytic leukemia. J Immunol 2004;172(5):3280–8.

[16] Geller A, Yan J. The role of membrane bound complement regulatory proteins in tumor development and cancer immunotherapy. Front Immunol 2019;10:1074.

[17] Dzietczenia J, Wróbel T, Mazur G, Poreba R, Jaźwiec B, Kuliczkowski K. Expression of complement regulatory proteins: CD46, CD55, and CD59 and response to rituximab in patients with CD20+ non-Hodgkin's lymphoma. Med Oncol 2010;27(3):743–6.

[18] Mamidi S, Hone S, Teufel C, Sellner L, Zenz T, Kirschfink M. Neutralization of membrane complement regulators improves complement-dependent effector functions of therapeutic anticancer antibodies targeting leukemic cells. Oncoimmunology 2015;4(3), e979688.

[19] Golay J, Zaffaroni L, Vaccari T, Lazzari M, Borleri GM, Bernasconi S, et al. Biologic response of B lymphoma cells to anti-CD20 monoclonal antibody rituximab in vitro: CD55 and CD59 regulate complement-mediated cell lysis. Blood 2000;95(12):3900–8.

[20] Stadlbauer K, Andorfer P, Stadlmayr G, Rüker F, Wozniak-Knopp G. Bispecific mAb(2) antibodies targeting CD59 enhance the complement-dependent cytotoxicity mediated by rituximab. Int J Mol Sci 2022;23(9):5208.

[21] Treon SP, Mitsiades C, Mitsiades N, Young G, Doss D, Schlossman R, et al. Tumor cell expression of CD59 is associated with resistance to CD20 serotherapy in patients with B-cell malignancies. J Immunother 2001;24 (3):263–71.

[22] Hatjiharissi E, Xu L, Santos DD, Hunter ZR, Ciccarelli BT, Verselis S, et al. Increased natural killer cell expression of CD16, augmented binding and ADCC activity to rituximab among individuals expressing the Fc {gamma}RIIIa-158 V/V and V/F polymorphism. Blood 2007;110(7):2561–4.

[23] Hofmeister JK, Cooney D, Coggeshall KM. Clustered CD20 induced apoptosis: src-family kinase, the proximal regulator of tyrosine phosphorylation, calcium influx, and caspase 3-dependent apoptosis. Blood Cells Mol Dis 2000;26(2):133–43.

[24] Shan D, Ledbetter JA, Press OW. Apoptosis of malignant human B cells by ligation of CD20 with monoclonal antibodies. Blood 1998;91(5):1644–52.

[25] Mathas S, Rickers A, Bommert K, Dorken B, Mapara MY. Anti-CD20- and B-cell receptor-mediated apoptosis: evidence for shared intracellular signaling pathways. Cancer Res 2000;60(24):7170–6.

[26] Vega MI, Huerta-Yepez S, Martinez-Paniagua M, Martinez-Miguel B, Hernandez-Pando R, Gonzalez-Bonilla CR, et al. Rituximab-mediated cell signaling and chemo/immuno-sensitization of drug-resistant B-NHL is independent of its Fc functions. Clin Cancer Res 2009;15(21):6582–94.

[27] Byrd JC, Kitada S, Flinn IW, Aron JL, Pearson M, Lucas D, et al. The mechanism of tumor cell clearance by rituximab in vivo in patients with B-cell chronic lymphocytic leukemia: evidence of caspase activation and apoptosis induction. Blood 2002;99(3):1038–43.

[28] Chan HT, Hughes D, French RR, Tutt AL, Walshe CA, Teeling JL, et al. CD20-induced lymphoma cell death is independent of both caspases and its redistribution into triton X-100 insoluble membrane rafts. Cancer Res 2003;63(17):5480–9.

[29] van der Kolk LE, Evers LM, Omene C, Lens SM, Lederman S, van Lier RA, et al. CD20-induced B cell death can bypass mitochondria and caspase activation. Leukemia 2002;16(9):1735–44.

[30] Shivakumar L, Armitage JO. Bcl-2 gene expression as a predictor of outcome in diffuse large B-cell lymphoma. Clin Lymphoma Myeloma 2006;6(6):455–7.

[31] Mounier N, Briere J, Gisselbrecht C, Emile JF, Lederlin P, Sebban C, et al. Rituximab plus CHOP (R-CHOP) overcomes bcl-2-associated resistance to chemotherapy in elderly patients with diffuse large B-cell lymphoma (DLBCL). Blood 2003;101(11):4279–84.

[32] Hans CP, Weisenburger DD, Greiner TC, Gascoyne RD, Delabie J, Ott G, et al. Confirmation of the molecular classification of diffuse large B-cell lymphoma by immunohistochemistry using a tissue microarray. Blood 2004;103(1):275–82.

[33] Morin RD, Assouline S, Alcaide M, Mohajeri A, Johnston RL, Chong L, et al. Genetic landscapes of relapsed and refractory diffuse large B-cell lymphomas. Clin Cancer Res 2016;22(9):2290–300.

[34] Jazirehi AR, Vega MI, Bonavida B. Development of rituximab-resistant lymphoma clones with altered cell signaling and cross-resistance to chemotherapy. Cancer Res 2007;67(3):1270–81.

[35] Yang Y, Kelly P, Shaffer 3rd AL, Schmitz R, Yoo HM, Liu X, et al. Targeting non-proteolytic protein ubiquitination for the treatment of diffuse large B cell lymphoma. Cancer Cell 2016;29(4):494–507.

[36] Yeung KC, Rose DW, Dhillon AS, Yaros D, Gustafsson M, Chatterjee D, et al. Raf kinase inhibitor protein interacts with NF-kappaB-inducing kinase and TAK1 and inhibits NF-kappaB activation. Mol Cell Biol 2001;21 (21):7207–17.

[37] Santen RJ, Song RX, McPherson R, Kumar R, Adam L, Jeng MH, et al. The role of mitogen-activated protein (MAP) kinase in breast cancer. J Steroid Biochem Mol Biol 2002;80(2):239–56.

[38] Vega MI, Huerta-Yepaz S, Garban H, Jazirehi A, Emmanouilides C, Bonavida B. Rituximab inhibits p38 MAPK activity in 2F7 B NHL and decreases IL-10 transcription: pivotal role of p38 MAPK in drug resistance. Oncogene 2004;23(20):3530–40.
[39] Cargnello M, Roux PP. Activation and function of the MAPKs and their substrates, the MAPK-activated protein kinases. Microbiol Mol Biol Rev 2011;75(1):50–83.
[40] Muniyappa H, Das KC. Activation of c-Jun N-terminal kinase (JNK) by widely used specific p38 MAPK inhibitors SB202190 and SB203580: a MLK-3-MKK7-dependent mechanism. Cell Signal 2008;20(4):675–83.
[41] Leventaki V, Drakos E, Karanikou M, Psatha K, Lin P, Schlette E, et al. c-JUN N-terminal kinase (JNK) is activated and contributes to tumor cell proliferation in classical Hodgkin lymphoma. Hum Pathol 2014;45 (3):565–72.
[42] Jazirehi AR, Vega MI, Chatterjee D, Goodglick L, Bonavida B. Inhibition of the Raf-MEK1/2-ERK1/2 signaling pathway, Bcl-xL down-regulation, and chemosensitization of non-Hodgkin's lymphoma B cells by Rituximab. Cancer Res 2004;64(19):7117–26.
[43] Sevilla L, Zaldumbide A, Pognonec P, Boulukos KE. Transcriptional regulation of the bcl-x gene encoding the anti-apoptotic Bcl-xL protein by Ets, Rel/NFkappaB, STAT and AP1 transcription factor families. Histol Histopathol 2001;16(2):595–601.
[44] Wullschleger S, Loewith R, Hall MN. TOR signaling in growth and metabolism. Cell 2006;124(3):471–84.
[45] Pfeifer M, Grau M, Lenze D, Wenzel SS, Wolf A, Wollert-Wulf B, et al. PTEN loss defines a PI3K/AKT pathway-dependent germinal center subtype of diffuse large B-cell lymphoma. Proc Natl Acad Sci U S A 2013;110 (30):12420–5.
[46] Uddin S, Hussain AR, Siraj AK, Manogaran PS, Al-Jomah NA, Moorji A, et al. Role of phosphatidylinositol 3′-kinase/AKT pathway in diffuse large B-cell lymphoma survival. Blood 2006;108(13):4178–86.
[47] Havranek O, Xu J, Kohrer S, Wang Z, Becker L, Comer JM, et al. Tonic B-cell receptor signaling in diffuse large B-cell lymphoma. Blood 2017;130(8):995–1006.
[48] Bolli R, Dawn B, Xuan YT. Role of the JAK-STAT pathway in protection against myocardial ischemia/reperfusion injury. Trends Cardiovasc Med 2003;13(2):72–9.
[49] Tiacci E, Ladewig E, Schiavoni G, Penson A, Fortini E, Pettirossi V, et al. Pervasive mutations of JAK-STAT pathway genes in classical Hodgkin lymphoma. Blood 2018;131(22):2454–65.
[50] Barbarino V, Henschke S, Blakemore SJ, Izquierdo E, Michalik M, Nickel N, et al. Macrophage-mediated antibody dependent effector function in aggressive B-cell lymphoma treatment is enhanced by ibrutinib via inhibition of JAK2. Cancers (Basel) 2020;12(8):2303.
[51] Treanor B. B-cell receptor: from resting state to activate. Immunology 2012;136(1):21–7.
[52] Thieme E, Liu T, Bruss N, Roleder C, Lam V, Wang X, et al. Dual BTK/SYK inhibition with CG-806 (luxeptinib) disrupts B-cell receptor and Bcl-2 signaling networks in mantle cell lymphoma. Cell Death Dis 2022;13(3):246.
[53] Vega MI, Jazirehi AR, Huerta-Yepez S, Bonavida B. Rituximab-induced inhibition of YY1 and Bcl-xL expression in Ramos non-Hodgkin's lymphoma cell line via inhibition of NF-kappa B activity: role of YY1 and Bcl-xL in Fas resistance and chemoresistance, respectively. J Immunol 2005;175(4):2174–83.
[54] Karube K, Campo E. MYC alterations in diffuse large B-cell lymphomas. Semin Hematol 2015;52(2):97–106.
[55] Aukema SM, Siebert R, Schuuring E, van Imhoff GW, Kluin-Nelemans HC, Boerma EJ, et al. Double-hit B-cell lymphomas. Blood 2011;117(8):2319–31.
[56] Rosenthal A, Younes A. High grade B-cell lymphoma with rearrangements of MYC and BCL2 and/or BCL6: double hit and triple hit lymphomas and double expressing lymphoma. Blood Rev 2017;31(2):37–42.
[57] Riedell PA, Smith SM. Double hit and double expressors in lymphoma: definition and treatment. Cancer 2018;124(24):4622–32.
[58] den Hollander J, Rimpi S, Doherty JR, et al. Aurora kinases A and B are up-regulated by Myc and are essential for maintenance of the malignant state. Blood. Sep 2 2010;116(9):1498–505. https://doi.org/10.1182/blood-2009-11-251074.
[59] Wang XJ, Medeiros LJ, Bueso-Ramos CE, Tang G, Wang S, Oki Y, et al. P53 expression correlates with poorer survival and augments the negative prognostic effect of MYC rearrangement, expression or concurrent MYC/BCL2 expression in diffuse large B-cell lymphoma. Mod Pathol 2017;30(2):194–203.
[60] Guo R, Jiang C, Zhang Y, Govande A, Trudeau SJ, Chen F, et al. MYC controls the Epstein-Barr virus lytic switch. Mol Cell 2020;78(4):653–69. e658.
[61] Guo R, Zhang Y, Teng M, Jiang C, Schineller M, Zhao B, et al. Author correction: DNA methylation enzymes and PRC1 restrict B-cell Epstein-Barr virus oncoprotein expression. Nat Microbiol 2022;7(6):928.

[62] Sidorov S, Fux L, Steiner K, Bounlom S, Traxel S, Azzi T, et al. CD4+ T cells are found within endemic Burkitt lymphoma and modulate Burkitt lymphoma precursor cell viability and expression of pathogenically relevant Epstein-Barr virus genes. Cancer Immunol Immunother 2022;71(6):1371–92.
[63] Scarfo L, Ghia P. Reprogramming cell death: BCL2 family inhibition in hematological malignancies. Immunol Lett 2013;155(1–2):36–9.
[64] Topham C, Tighe A, Ly P, Bennett A, Sloss O, Nelson L, et al. MYC is a major determinant of mitotic cell fate. Cancer Cell 2015;28(1):129–40.
[65] Garcia-Aranda M, Perez-Ruiz E, Redondo M. Bcl-2 inhibition to overcome resistance to chemo- and immunotherapy. Int J Mol Sci 2018;19(12):3950.
[66] Khan N, Kahl B. Targeting BCL-2 in hematologic malignancies. Target Oncol 2018;13(3):257–67.
[67] Basso K, Dalla-Favera R. Germinal centres and B cell lymphomagenesis. Nat Rev Immunol 2015;15(3):172–84.
[68] Wlodarska I, Nooyen P, Maes B, Martin-Subero JI, Siebert R, Pauwels P, et al. Frequent occurrence of BCL6 rearrangements in nodular lymphocyte predominance Hodgkin lymphoma but not in classical Hodgkin lymphoma. Blood 2003;101(2):706–10.
[69] Polo JM, Ci W, Licht JD, Melnick A. Reversible disruption of BCL6 repression complexes by CD40 signaling in normal and malignant B cells. Blood 2008;112(3):644–51.
[70] Bunting KL, Soong TD, Singh R, Jiang Y, Beguelin W, Poloway DW, et al. Multi-tiered reorganization of the genome during B cell affinity maturation anchored by a germinal center-specific locus control region. Immunity 2016;45(3):497–512.
[71] Chu CS, Hellmuth JC, Singh R, Ying HY, Skrabanek L, Teater MR, et al. Unique immune cell coactivators specify locus control region function and cell stage. Mol Cell 2020;80(5):845–61. e810.
[72] Calado DP, Sasaki Y, Godinho SA, Pellerin A, Köchert K, Sleckman BP, et al. The cell-cycle regulator c-Myc is essential for the formation and maintenance of germinal centers. Nat Immunol 2012;13(11):1092–100.
[73] Dominguez-Sola D, Victora GD, Ying CY, Phan RT, Saito M, Nussenzweig MC, et al. The proto-oncogene MYC is required for selection in the germinal center and cyclic reentry. Nat Immunol 2012;13(11):1083–91.
[74] Greenawalt DM, Liang WS, Saif S, Johnson J, Todorov P, Dulak A, et al. Comparative analysis of primary versus relapse/refractory DLBCL identifies shifts in mutation spectrum. Oncotarget 2017;8(59):99237–44.
[75] Rushton CK, Arthur SE, Alcaide M, Cheung M, Jiang A, Coyle KM, et al. Genetic and evolutionary patterns of treatment resistance in relapsed B-cell lymphoma. Blood Adv 2020;4(13):2886–98.
[76] Yap DB, Chu J, Berg T, Schapira M, Cheng SW, Moradian A, et al. Somatic mutations at EZH2 Y641 act dominantly through a mechanism of selectively altered PRC2 catalytic activity, to increase H3K27 trimethylation. Blood 2011;117(8):2451–9.
[77] Otsuka Y, Nishikori M, Arima H, Izumi K, Kitawaki T, Hishizawa M, et al. EZH2 inhibitors restore epigenetically silenced CD58 expression in B-cell lymphomas. Mol Immunol 2020;119:35–45.
[78] Juskevicius D, Lorber T, Gsponer J, Perrina V, Ruiz C, Stenner-Liewen F, et al. Distinct genetic evolution patterns of relapsing diffuse large B-cell lymphoma revealed by genome-wide copy number aberration and targeted sequencing analysis. Leukemia 2016;30(12):2385–95.
[79] Lee J, Kim DH, Lee S, Yang QH, Lee DK, Lee SK, et al. A tumor suppressive coactivator complex of p53 containing ASC-2 and histone H3-lysine-4 methyltransferase MLL3 or its paralogue MLL4. Proc Natl Acad Sci U S A 2009;106(21):8513–8.
[80] Goodman RH, Smolik S. CBP/p300 in cell growth, transformation, and development. Genes Dev 2000;14 (13):1553–77.
[81] Bannister AJ, Kouzarides T. The CBP co-activator is a histone acetyltransferase. Nature 1996;384(6610):641–3.
[82] Jiang Y, Ortega-Molina A, Geng H, Ying HY, Hatzi K, Parsa S, et al. CREBBP inactivation promotes the development of HDAC3-dependent lymphomas. Cancer Discov 2017;7(1):38–53.
[83] Zhang J, Vlasevska S, Wells VA, Nataraj S, Holmes AB, Duval R, et al. The CREBBP acetyltransferase is a haploinsufficient tumor suppressor in B-cell lymphoma. Cancer Discov 2017;7(3):322–37.
[84] Yeh CH, Bellon M, Nicot C. FBXW7: a critical tumor suppressor of human cancers. Mol Cancer 2018;17(1):115.
[85] Bykov VJN, Eriksson SE, Bianchi J, Wiman KG. Targeting mutant p53 for efficient cancer therapy. Nat Rev Cancer 2018;18(2):89–102.
[86] Xu-Monette ZY, Wu L, Visco C, Tai YC, Tzankov A, Liu WM, et al. Mutational profile and prognostic significance of TP53 in diffuse large B-cell lymphoma patients treated with R-CHOP: report from an International DLBCL Rituximab-CHOP Consortium Program Study. Blood 2012;120(19):3986–96.
[87] Zeki K, Tanaka Y, Morimoto I, Nishimura Y, Kimura A, Yamashita U, et al. Induction of expression of MHC-class-II antigen on human thyroid carcinoma by wild-type p53. Int J Cancer 1998;75(3):391–5.

[88] Gebauer N, Bernard V, Gebauer W, Thorns C, Feller AC, Merz H. TP53 mutations are frequent events in double-hit B-cell lymphomas with MYC and BCL2 but not MYC and BCL6 translocations. Leuk Lymphoma 2015;56 (1):179–85.
[89] Clipson A, Barrans S, Zeng N, Crouch S, Grigoropoulos NF, Liu H, et al. The prognosis of MYC translocation positive diffuse large B-cell lymphoma depends on the second hit. J Pathol Clin Res 2015;1(3):125–33.
[90] Caeser R, Di Re M, Krupka JA, Gao J, Lara-Chica M, Dias JML, et al. Genetic modification of primary human B cells to model high-grade lymphoma. Nat Commun 2019;10(1):4543.
[91] Amson R, Sigaux F, Przedborski S, Flandrin G, Givol D, Telerman A. The human protooncogene product p33pim is expressed during fetal hematopoiesis and in diverse leukemias. Proc Natl Acad Sci U S A 1989;86(22):8857–61.
[92] Hsi ED, Jung SH, Lai R, Johnson JL, Cook JR, Jones D, et al. Ki67 and PIM1 expression predict outcome in mantle cell lymphoma treated with high dose therapy, stem cell transplantation and rituximab: a Cancer and Leukemia Group B 59909 correlative science study. Leuk Lymphoma 2008;49(11):2081–90.
[93] Mahadevan D, Spier C, Della Croce K, Miller S, George B, Riley C, et al. Transcript profiling in peripheral T-cell lymphoma, not otherwise specified, and diffuse large B-cell lymphoma identifies distinct tumor profile signatures. Mol Cancer Ther 2005;4(12):1867–79.
[94] Miura O, Miura Y, Nakamura N, Quelle FW, Witthuhn BA, Ihle JN, et al. Induction of tyrosine phosphorylation of Vav and expression of Pim-1 correlates with Jak2-mediated growth signaling from the erythropoietin receptor. Blood 1994;84(12):4135–41.
[95] Zhu N, Ramirez LM, Lee RL, Magnuson NS, Bishop GA, Gold MR. CD40 signaling in B cells regulates the expression of the Pim-1 kinase via the NF-kappa B pathway. J Immunol 2002;168(2):744–54.
[96] Szydlowski M, Garbicz F, Jablonska E, Gorniak P, Komar D, Pyrzynska B, et al. Inhibition of PIM kinases in DLBCL targets MYC transcriptional program and augments the efficacy of anti-CD20 antibodies. Cancer Res 2021;81(23):6029–43.
[97] Dominguez-Sola D, Kung J, Holmes AB, Wells VA, Mo T, Basso K, et al. The FOXO1 transcription factor instructs the germinal center dark zone program. Immunity 2015;43(6):1064–74.
[98] Reagan-Shaw S, Ahmad N. The role of Forkhead-box Class O (FoxO) transcription factors in cancer: a target for the management of cancer. Toxicol Appl Pharmacol 2007;224(3):360–8.
[99] Maiese K, Chong ZZ, Shang YC. OutFOXOing disease and disability: the therapeutic potential of targeting FoxO proteins. Trends Mol Med 2008;14(5):219–27.
[100] Xie L, Ushmorov A, Leithäuser F, Guan H, Steidl C, Färbinger J, et al. FOXO1 is a tumor suppressor in classical Hodgkin lymphoma. Blood 2012;119(15):3503–11.
[101] Naka K, Hoshii T, Muraguchi T, Tadokoro Y, Ooshio T, Kondo Y, et al. TGF-beta-FOXO signalling maintains leukaemia-initiating cells in chronic myeloid leukaemia. Nature 2010;463(7281):676–80.
[102] Pyrzynska B, Dwojak M, Zerrouqi A, Morlino G, Zapala P, Miazek N, et al. FOXO1 promotes resistance of non-Hodgkin lymphomas to anti-CD20-based therapy. Oncoimmunology 2018;7(5), e1423183.
[103] Binder M, Otto F, Mertelsmann R, Veelken H, Trepel M. The epitope recognized by rituximab. Blood 2006;108 (6):1975–8.
[104] Henry C, Deschamps M, Rohrlich PS, Pallandre JR, Remy-Martin JP, Callanan M, et al. Identification of an alternative CD20 transcript variant in B-cell malignancies coding for a novel protein associated to rituximab resistance. Blood 2010;115(12):2420–9.
[105] Zhao WL, Wang L, Liu YH, Yan JS, Leboeuf C, Liu YY, et al. Combined effects of histone deacetylase inhibitor and rituximab on non-Hodgkin's B-lymphoma cells apoptosis. Exp Hematol 2007;35(12):1801–11.
[106] Tomita A, Hiraga J, Kiyoi H, Ninomiya M, Sugimoto T, Ito M, et al. Epigenetic regulation of CD20 protein expression in a novel B-cell lymphoma cell line, RRBL1, established from a patient treated repeatedly with rituximab-containing chemotherapy. Int J Hematol 2007;86(1):49–57.
[107] Nijland M, Seitz A, Terpstra M, van Imhoff GW, Kluin PM, van Meerten T, et al. Mutational evolution in relapsed diffuse large B-cell lymphoma. Cancers (Basel) 2018;10(11):459.
[108] Isaev K, Ennishi D, Hilton L, Skinnider B, Mungall KL, Mungall AJ, et al. Molecular attributes underlying central nervous system and systemic relapse in diffuse large B-cell lymphoma. Haematologica 2021;106(5):1466–71.
[109] Rooney MS, Shukla SA, Wu CJ, Getz G, Hacohen N. Molecular and genetic properties of tumors associated with local immune cytolytic activity. Cell 2015;160(1–2):48–61.
[110] Williams DB, Barber BH, Flavell RA, Allen H. Role of beta 2-microglobulin in the intracellular transport and surface expression of murine class I histocompatibility molecules. J Immunol 1989;142(8):2796–806.

[111] Sorigue M, Bishton M, Domingo-Domenech E, McMillan A, Prusila R, Garcia O, et al. Refractoriness to rituximab-based therapy and elevated serum B2-microglobulin predict for inferior survival in marginal zone lymphoma. Leuk Lymphoma 2019;60(10):2524–31.

[112] Garrido F, Aptsiauri N, Doorduijn EM, Garcia Lora AM, van Hall T. The urgent need to recover MHC class I in cancers for effective immunotherapy. Curr Opin Immunol 2016;39:44–51.

[113] Braendstrup P, Levine BL, Ruella M. The long road to the first FDA-approved gene therapy: chimeric antigen receptor T cells targeting CD19. Cytotherapy 2020;22(2):57–69.

[114] Roex G, Feys T, Beguin Y, Kerre T, Poire X, Lewalle P, et al. Chimeric antigen receptor-T-cell therapy for B-cell hematological malignancies: an update of the pivotal clinical trial data. Pharmaceutics 2020;12(2):194.

[115] Gross G, Waks T, Eshhar Z. Expression of immunoglobulin-T-cell receptor chimeric molecules as functional receptors with antibody-type specificity. Proc Natl Acad Sci U S A 1989;86(24):10024–8.

[116] Ren J, Liu X, Fang C, Jiang S, June CH, Zhao Y. Multiplex genome editing to generate universal CAR T cells resistant to PD1 inhibition. Clin Cancer Res 2017;23(9):2255–66.

[117] Griffin GK, Weirather JL, Roemer MGM, Lipschitz M, Kelley A, Chen PH, et al. Spatial signatures identify immune escape via PD-1 as a defining feature of T-cell/histiocyte-rich large B-cell lymphoma. Blood 2021;137 (10):1353–64.

[118] Casey SC, Tong L, Li Y, Do R, Walz S, Fitzgerald KN, et al. MYC regulates the antitumor immune response through CD47 and PD-L1. Science 2016;352(6282):227–31.

[119] Xu-Monette ZY, Zhou J, Young KH. PD-1 expression and clinical PD-1 blockade in B-cell lymphomas. Blood 2018;131(1):68–83.

[120] Merryman RW, Armand P, Wright KT, Rodig SJ. Checkpoint blockade in Hodgkin and non-Hodgkin lymphoma. Blood Adv 2017;1(26):2643–54.

[121] Ansell SM, Minnema MC, Johnson P, Timmerman JM, Armand P, Shipp MA, et al. Nivolumab for relapsed/refractory diffuse large B-cell lymphoma in patients ineligible for or having failed autologous transplantation: a single-arm, phase II study. J Clin Oncol 2019;37(6):481–9.

[122] Ren J, Zhang X, Liu X, Fang C, Jiang S, June CH, et al. A versatile system for rapid multiplex genome-edited CAR T cell generation. Oncotarget 2017;8(10):17002–11.

[123] Upadhyay R, Boiarsky JA, Pantsulaia G, Svensson-Arvelund J, Lin MJ, Wroblewska A, et al. A critical role for Fas-mediated off-target tumor killing in T-cell immunotherapy. Cancer Discov 2021;11(3):599–613.

[124] Junttila MR, de Sauvage FJ. Influence of tumour micro-environment heterogeneity on therapeutic response. Nature 2013;501(7467):346–54.

[125] Casey SC, Amedei A, Aquilano K, Azmi AS, Benencia F, Bhakta D, et al. Cancer prevention and therapy through the modulation of the tumor microenvironment. Semin Cancer Biol 2015;35(Suppl):S199–223.

[126] Hui L, Chen Y. Tumor microenvironment: sanctuary of the devil. Cancer Lett 2015;368(1):7–13.

[127] Wu T, Dai Y. Tumor microenvironment and therapeutic response. Cancer Lett 2017;387:61–8.

[128] Meads MB, Gatenby RA, Dalton WS. Environment-mediated drug resistance: a major contributor to minimal residual disease. Nat Rev Cancer 2009;9(9):665–74.

[129] Ogata A, Chauhan D, Teoh G, Treon SP, Urashima M, Schlossman RL, et al. IL-6 triggers cell growth via the Ras-dependent mitogen-activated protein kinase cascade. J Immunol 1997;159(5):2212–21.

[130] Podar K, Tai YT, Davies FE, Lentzsch S, Sattler M, Hideshima T, et al. Vascular endothelial growth factor triggers signaling cascades mediating multiple myeloma cell growth and migration. Blood 2001;98(2):428–35.

[131] Qiang YW, Kopantzev E, Rudikoff S. Insulinlike growth factor-I signaling in multiple myeloma: downstream elements, functional correlates, and pathway cross-talk. Blood 2002;99(11):4138–46.

[132] Kotlov N, Bagaev A, Revuelta MV, Phillip JM, Cacciapuoti MT, Antysheva Z, et al. Clinical and biological subtypes of B-cell lymphoma revealed by microenvironmental signatures. Cancer Discov 2021;11 (6):1468–89.

[133] Lykken JM, Horikawa M, Minard-Colin V, Kamata M, Miyagaki T, Poe JC, et al. Galectin-1 drives lymphoma CD20 immunotherapy resistance: validation of a preclinical system to identify resistance mechanisms. Blood 2016;127(15):1886–95.

[134] Miller JC, Holmes MC, Wang J, Guschin DY, Lee YL, Rupniewski I, et al. An improved zinc-finger nuclease architecture for highly specific genome editing. Nat Biotechnol 2007;25(7):778–85.

[135] Wood AJ, Lo TW, Zeitler B, Pickle CS, Ralston EJ, Lee AH, et al. Targeted genome editing across species using ZFNs and TALENs. Science 2011;333(6040):307.

[136] Zhang F, Cong L, Lodato S, Kosuri S, Church GM, Arlotta P. Efficient construction of sequence-specific TAL effectors for modulating mammalian transcription. Nat Biotechnol 2011;29(2):149–53.
[137] Workman RE, Pammi T, Nguyen BTK, Graeff LW, Smith E, Sebald SM, et al. A natural single-guide RNA repurposes Cas9 to autoregulate CRISPR-Cas expression. Cell 2021;184(3):675–88. e619.
[138] Pickar-Oliver A, Gersbach CA. The next generation of CRISPR-Cas technologies and applications. Nat Rev Mol Cell Biol 2019;20(8):490–507.

CHAPTER

4

Non-Hodgkin lymphoma treated with anti-CD20 antibody-based immunochemotherapy

Michele Clerico, Simone Ragaini, and Federica Cavallo

Division of Hematology, Department of Molecular Biotechnology and Health Sciences, University of Torino, A.O.U. Città della Salute e della Scienza di Torino, Turin, Italy

Abstract

The CD20 gene encodes a protein expressed on the membrane of B cells: it appears on the surface of normal and malignant B lymphocytes during the pre-B-cell stage. Due to this expression, it has become an interesting target for therapy in CD20-positive B-cell malignancies. Since the introduction of the first-in-class anti-CD20 monoclonal antibody (mAb) rituximab, targeted anti-CD20 mAbs therapy has become the mainstay in the treatment of non-Hodgkin lymphoma (NHL), and rituximab-based therapies are among the most commonly used treatments. Moreover, rituximab paved the way for other engineered antibodies, namely obinutuzumab and ofatumumab. Lately, the recent introduction of CD20xCD3 bispecific antibodies (BsAbs), an innovative immunotherapeutic approach that redirects endogenous CD3-positive T-cells to recognize CD20-positive tumor cells, has shown very promising efficacy in lymphoma treatment. Similarly, although historically anti-CD19 oriented, chimeric antigen receptor (CAR)-T cell therapy has also been introduced as a novel anti-CD20 therapy. Since the introduction of mAbs, several mechanisms have been identified as potentially involved in anti-CD20 resistance, including antibody-dependent cell-mediated cytotoxicity (ADCC), complement-dependent cytotoxicity (CDC), loss of CD20, and induction of apoptosis. More recent studies suggest that tumor microenvironment could also be implicated. This chapter discusses the clinical applications of the three main anti-CD20 mAbs (rituximab, obinutuzumab, and ofatumumab) nowadays and briefly touches on the current experience with anti-CD20xCD3 BsAbs. Subsequently, known mechanisms of resistance to anti-CD20 therapy will be described, concluding with some considerations on future perspectives.

Abbreviations

ACVBP doxorubicin cyclophosphamide vindesine bleomycin and prednisone
ADCC antibody-dependent cell-mediated cytotoxicity
ALL acute lymphoblastic leukemia

https://doi.org/10.1016/B978-0-443-19200-5.00022-1

ASCT autologous stem cell transplantation
BCL2 B-cell lymphoma 2
BLyS B lymphocyte stimulator
B-NHL B-cell non-Hodgkin lymphoma
BsAb bispecific antibody
CAR-T cell chimeric antigen receptor T cell
CDC complement-dependent cytotoxicity
CHOP cyclophosphamide, doxorubicin, vincristine, and prednisone
CLL chronic lymphocytic leukemia
CMR complete metabolic response
CR complete remission
CRS cytokine release syndrome
CVP cyclophosphamide, vincristine, and prednisone
DHAP dexamethasone, cytosine arabinoside, and cisplatin
DLBCL diffuse large B-cell lymphoma
DoR duration of response
EFS event-free survival
EU European Union
Fc fragment crystallizable region
FcRs Fc receptors
FDA Food and Drug Administration
FFS failure-free survival
FL follicular lymphoma
HCL hairy cell leukemia
HLA human leukocyte antigen
ICE ifosfamide, carboplatin, and etoposide
IL interleukin
KIRs killer cell immunoglobulin-like receptors
mAb monoclonal antibody
MAC membrane attack complex
MBL mannose-binding lectin
MCL mantle cell lymphoma
MCP mitoxantrone, chlorambucil, and prednisone
mCRPs membrane-bound complement regulatory proteins
MDSCs myeloid-derived suppressor cells
MZLs marginal zone lymphomas
ORR overall response rate
PFS progression-free survival
PI3Ki phosphatidylinositol-3 kinase inhibitor
POD24 progression of disease within 2 years
PTLDs posttransplant lymphoproliferative disorders
R/R relapse/refractory
TAMs tumor-associated macrophages
TME tumor microenvironment
TNF tumor necrosis factor
Treg tumoral regulatory lymphocytes
TTP time to progression
VIM etoposide, ifosfamide, and methotrexate
WM Waldenström macroglobulinemia

Conflict of interest

No potential conflicts of interest were disclosed.

Introduction

The CD20 gene is placed on chromosome 11, it corresponds to a 33–37 kDa nonglycosylated protein belonging to the membrane-spanning 4-domain family A (MS4A) protein family [1]. It appears on B cells during the pre-B-cell stage, and it is expressed on the surface of normal and malignant B lymphocytes, whereas its expression is lost in terminally differentiated plasmablasts and plasma cells [1,2]. The exact biologic function of CD20 is unknown, but it has been suggested to be involved in B-cell receptor activation, proliferation, and calcium transport [3]. In B-cell malignancies, CD20 expression level generally depends on the specific neoplasm, with the lowest CD20 expression in chronic lymphocytic leukemia (CLL) and the highest CD20 cell-surface expression on diffuse large B-cell lymphoma (DLBCL) and hairy cell leukemia (HCL) [4]. The high levels of expression of CD20 on malignant B cells make it an interesting therapeutic target [3,5].

Since the introduction of the first-in-class targeted therapy with the recombinant chimeric murine/human type I anti-CD20 monoclonal antibody (mAb) rituximab in the 1990s [6–8], the outcome for patients with CD20-positive B-cell malignancies significantly improved. Therefore, anti-CD20 mAbs are nowadays considered the mainstay in the treatment of B-cell non-Hodgkin lymphoma (B-NHL) and rituximab-based therapies are still among the most commonly used treatments in this setting [9–11]. Moreover, the introduction of rituximab paved the way for newly engineered anti-CD20 mAbs, namely obinutuzumab and ofatumumab [12]. In fact, despite its efficacy, rituximab is not effective for all patients and some of them have shown signs of resistance to therapy [2]. Thus, anti-CD20 mAbs with enhanced or novel effector mechanisms were developed to improve efficacy in rituximab-refractory patients.

Based on their mechanisms of action, anti-CD20 mAbs are grouped into type I or type II. Type I mAbs, including rituximab and ofatumumab, translocate CD20 into lipid rafts and activate lytic complement and antibody-dependent cell-mediated cytotoxicity (ADCC). Conversely, type II mAbs induce programmed cell death and ADCC (Fig. 1) [13,14].

Obinutuzumab, a type II humanized glycoengineered anti-CD20 antibody, was designed to overcome the potential mechanisms of resistance to rituximab. Despite a superior activity of obinutuzumab when compared to rituximab demonstrated in progression-free survival (PFS) in untreated follicular lymphoma (FL) [15], results were not replicated in patients with untreated DLBCL [16,17].

Other CD20 mAbs include ofatumumab and ublituximab. No data are available demonstrating a superior efficacy of ofatumumab vs rituximab and this molecule has been withdrawn from the market in the European Union (EU) for commercial reasons [18]. Ublituximab is a chimeric, glycoengineered antibody that showed efficacy in indolent B-cell lymphomas in association with umbralisib, a phosphatidylinositol-3 kinase inhibitor (PI3Ki) [19,20]. In this case, the company withdrew the drug combination due to an increasing imbalance in survival in favor of the control arm in a phase 3 trial [21].

CD20 has been targeted also by radioimmunotherapy. Consolidation therapy with ibritumomab tiuxetan, a CD20 mAb, attached to the radioactive element yttrium-90 (^{90}Y), has shown a PFS prolongation after chemotherapy in FL. However, its benefit seems to be inferior in comparison to rituximab maintenance for 2 years [22,23]. On the other side, consolidation with iodine-131 [^{131}I] tositumomab radioimmunotherapy showed an improved PFS but no difference in overall survival (OS) and an increased cumulative risk of myeloid malignancies in comparison to rituximab with chemotherapy [24].

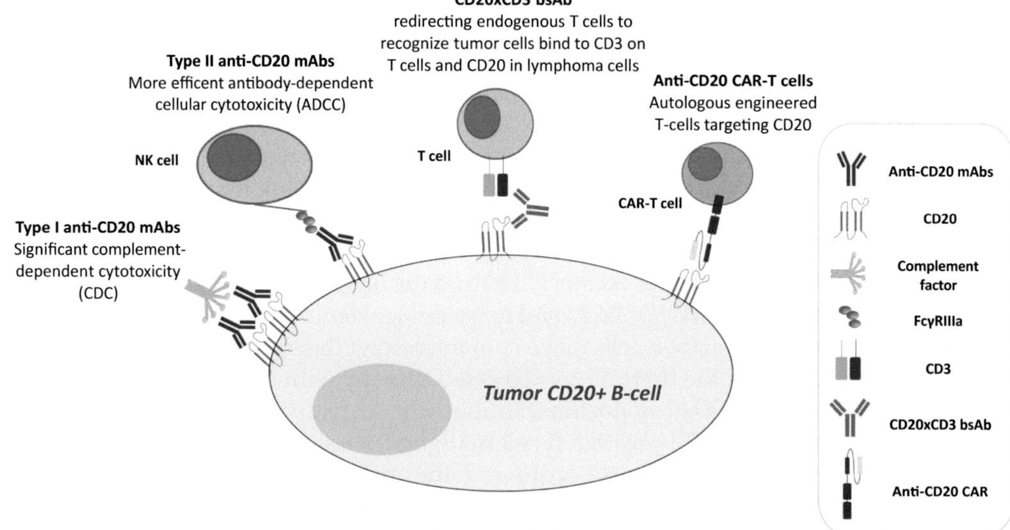

FIG. 1 Overview of anti-CD20 therapies. Mechanisms of action of anti-CD20 therapies: (1) type I anti-CD20 monoclonal antibodies with significant complement-dependent cytotoxicity (CDC); (2) type II anti-CD20 monoclonal antibodies with enhanced antibody-dependent cellular cytotoxicity (ADCC); (3) CD20xCD3 bispecific antibodies redirecting endogenous T-cells to recognize tumor cells by binding to CD3 on T-cells and CD20 in lymphoma cells; and (4) anti-CD20 CAR-T cells consisting of autologous engineered T-cells targeting the CD20 antigen.

An innovative approach to anti-CD20 therapy is represented by the recent introduction of bispecific antibodies (BsAb), redirecting endogenous T-cells to recognize tumor cells. Such molecules concomitantly bind to CD3 on T-cells and CD20 in lymphoma cells [25]. CD20xCD3 IgG-like BsAbs including mosunetuzumab, glofitamab, and epcoritamab showed favorable efficacy and safety profiles in patients with diverse relapse/refractory (R/R) B-NHL [26]. Moreover, in recent years, chimeric antigen receptor (CAR)-T cell therapy has been introduced for lymphomas. It consists of genetically engineered T-cells developed to target receptor proteins expressed on tumor cells. Although anti-CD19 CAR-T cells are the most widely used, CD20 CAR-T cells have been used in patients with advanced B-cell lymphomas and have achieved promising results [27–29].

In this chapter, we will discuss the main clinical application of the three main anti-CD20 mAbs nowadays (namely rituximab, obinutuzumab, and ofatumumab), both as used as single agents and in association with chemotherapy in the two principal lymphoma subtypes (FL and DLBCL). We will then briefly list the current experience with anti-CD20xCD3 BsAbs and conclude with some known mechanisms of resistance to anti-CD20 from a biological point of view.

Clinical experience

Rituximab

The approval of the anti-CD20 antibody rituximab by the Food and Drug Administration (FDA) in 1997 was a conceptual breakthrough in the treatment of B-cell malignancies [12].

Rituximab improved PFS and OS rates when added to chemotherapy in FL and DLBCL, paving the way for mAbs in cancer treatment [8,30]. Actual indications of rituximab include most indolent and aggressive B-cell lymphomas, both in association with chemotherapy and as a single agent. Additionally, rituximab maintenance therapy has been introduced for some lymphoma types [31].

Follicular lymphoma

A pivotal phase 2 trial of rituximab monotherapy in 166 patients with R/R low-grade NHL allowed the initial regulatory approval. The overall response rate (ORR) was 48% with a 6% of complete remission (CR), and the median time to progression (TTP) was 13.0 months [32]. After the initial use of rituximab as 4 weekly doses at 375 mg/m^2 in previously treated patients [33–36], substantial clinical benefit has been reported in FL patients thanks to its incorporation into induction chemotherapy regimens, both in the first-line setting and in R/R patients [37–47]. A variety of chemotherapy regimens were combined with rituximab therapy in these trials, including cyclophosphamide, doxorubicin, vincristine, and prednisone (CHOP), bendamustine, cyclophosphamide, vincristine, and prednisone (CVP), and mitoxantrone, chlorambucil, and prednisone (MCP) regimens. Particularly, four prospective first-line trials, two salvage trials, and a systematic meta-analysis confirmed an improved ORR, PFS, and OS by adding rituximab to chemotherapy [38–40,45]. On the basis of the strong evidence provided by these studies, rituximab plus chemotherapy has been adopted worldwide as the standard of care for the first-line treatment of patients with FL [11]. Moreover, rituximab maintenance every 2 months for 2 years improves PFS, although no impact on OS has been demonstrated [48–50], while a shorter maintenance period results in an inferior benefit [51].

In the relapse setting, rituximab should be added to a noncross-resistant regimen if the previous antibody-containing scheme achieved >6–12-month duration of remission. Rituximab maintenance every 3 months for up to 2 years significantly prolongs PFS and OS in relapsed disease, even after antibody-containing salvage [52]. Finally, in relapsed FL, rituximab in association with lenalidomide has shown to be superior to rituximab monotherapy in terms of response rates and PFS with a trend toward improved OS [53].

Diffuse large B-cell lymphoma

The first study to demonstrate the feasibility and safety of rituximab associated with CHOP as first-line treatment in patients with aggressive NHL (67% with DLBCL) was a phase 2 trial, published in 2001. An ORR of 94% with 61% of CR was demonstrated [54]. A significant advantage both in terms of PFS and OS was subsequently confirmed in a large randomized phase 3 trial [55]. Similar results were published in elderly patients, establishing R-CHOP as the standard of care also in this population [56,57]. However, rituximab maintenance therapy after rituximab-based immunochemotherapy did not show a clinical advantage in terms of event-free survival (EFS), failure-free survival (FFS), and OS [57,58].

Rituximab was evaluated in combination with a variety of salvage chemotherapy regimens for relapse/refractory DLBCL patients, including ifosfamide, carboplatin, and etoposide (ICE), dexamethasone, cytosine arabinoside, and cisplatin (DHAP), and etoposide, ifosfamide, and methotrexate (VIM) regimens [59]. Neither association offered any benefit over other rituximab-based regimens given before or after autologous stem cell transplantation studies [60]. A potential benefit from the addition of rituximab to chemotherapy when compared with historical data was shown [59,61]. Based on these data, rituximab is currently approved worldwide for previously untreated DLBCL in combination with CHOP or other anthracycline-based chemotherapy and in combination with salvage chemotherapy for R/R disease [10].

Other lymphomas

Encouraging results of rituximab use have also been reported in most aggressive and indolent CD20-positive B-cell lymphomas. It has been shown to improve OS in MCL patients, both in the first-line setting (added to induction chemotherapy) and as maintenance [62–65]. The efficacy of rituximab has also been shown in marginal zone lymphomas (MZLs), as a single agent [66–69] and in combination with chemotherapy [70,71]. In highly aggressive lymphoid malignancies, namely Burkitt lymphoma (BL), a significant improvement in EFS was demonstrated [72]. Finally, other B-cell malignancies in which rituximab treatment has been associated with positive outcomes include Waldenström macroglobulinemia (WM) and posttransplant lymphoproliferative disorders (PTLDs) [73–76].

Obinutuzumab

Follicular lymphoma

The efficacy and safety of obinutuzumab with chemotherapy (CHOP, CVP, or bendamustine) plus obinutuzumab maintenance in previously untreated advanced-stage FL patients was compared with the corresponding rituximab-based regimen in the phase 3 GALLIUM study [15]. After a median follow-up of 34.5 months, a significantly lower risk of progression, relapse, or death with obinutuzumab compared to rituximab was demonstrated (estimated 3-year rate PFS, 80.0% vs 73.3%). However, OS was similar in the two arms (94.0% vs 92.1%) [15]. From a safety point of view, high-grade adverse events (AEs) and serious AEs were seen more frequently with obinutuzumab-based therapy, but deaths were similar in the two groups [15]. An updated analysis of the trial, with a median follow-up of almost 5 years, confirmed the improvements in outcomes and in safety seen with obinutuzumab-chemotherapy, but OS remained immature (there were too few events and data may be confounded by the effect of subsequent lines of treatment) [77]. Moreover, early disease progression (within 24 months) was found to be less frequent with obinutuzumab-based therapy than with rituximab-based therapy, with a 46% average risk reduction [78]. Finally, a higher minimal residual disease (MRD)-negativity rate at the end of induction was observed in the obinutuzumab arm (92.6% vs 85.2%), while most MRD-negative patients remained negative during maintenance, with no difference between treatment arms in MRD relapse rates [79].

In the R/R disease, the phase 2 GAUSS study showed no significant PFS difference between obinutuzumab and rituximab monotherapy and a comparable safety profile [80]. Moreover, the phase 3 GADOLIN study demonstrated a PFS advantage of adding obinutuzumab to bendamustine, followed by 2 years of obinutuzumab maintenance, confirming its utility in patients no longer responding to rituximab [81]. Subsequently, an updated analysis of the trial showed a benefit also in terms of OS [82]. In this trial, MRD-negativity at the end of induction (EOI) was associated with improved PFS and OS [83].

Based on these data, obinutuzumab is currently approved by the FDA and European Medicines Agency (EMA) for previously untreated and for R/R advanced FL in combination with chemotherapy [84].

Moreover, good clinical activity has been reported with obinutuzumab plus lenalidomide [85]. The phase II GALEN trial enrolled a total of 89 patients with relapsed/refractory FL and received obinutuzumab-lenalidomide as induction therapy, followed by maintenance therapy. The ORR rate at EOI was 79%, with 38% CR [86]. The same combination has been investigated in a phase 2 study, with previously untreated advanced FL requiring systemic therapy: the ORR was 92% with 47% of CR [87]. Similarly, in a further study of untreated advanced FL with high tumor burden, the 2-year PFS rate was 96%, with an OR rate of 98%. Finally, a phase 1b/2 trial demonstrated promising response rates with polatuzumab vedotin plus obinutuzumab-lenalidomide in patients with R/R FL [88].

Diffuse large B-cell lymphoma

The phase 3 GOYA study compared obinutuzumab-CHOP with rituximab-CHOP in patients with previously untreated advanced DLBCL: PFS and OS were similar between arms [16]. The updated analysis of the trial, with a median follow-up of 47.7 months, confirmed this data, showing no difference from the primary analysis and no significant difference between treatment arms for 5-year OS [89]. Of note, preplanned subgroup analysis of outcome by cell-of-origin showed a trend toward a greater benefit with obinutuzumab in the germinal center of B-cell disease [16].

Obinutuzumab in previously untreated DLBCL has also been tested in the phase 3 GAINED trial, combined with four cycles of intensified (every 14 days) induction chemotherapy with CHOP or doxorubicin, cyclophosphamide, vindesine, bleomycin, and prednisone (ACVBP). After interim analysis with a median follow-up of 25.2 months and enrollment of 670 patients, there was no significant difference between the two arms in the primary end point of 2-year EFS or any of the secondary end points, including PFS. There were 250 and 205 serious AEs, and 10 and one fatal AEs, in the obinutuzumab and rituximab arms, respectively. In conclusion, obinutuzumab did not provide any efficacy advantage over rituximab and was associated with more toxicity [90]. Finally, a phase 2 trial investigating obinutuzumab-miniCHOP in older unfit patients with DLBCL was interrupted due to the very low probability of improving the historical data results of rituximab-miniCHOP [91].

Other lymphomas

The GALLIUM trial enrolled a subset of 195 patients with MZLs (66 nodal; 61 extranodal; 68 splenic). It showed no PFS difference for obinutuzumab plus chemotherapy, while there were higher frequencies of AEs in the obinutuzumab arm vs the rituximab arm [92]. However, it should be noted that at baseline extranodal involvement, bulky disease, and B-symptoms were more common in patients treated with obinutuzumab plus chemotherapy [85,92]. Regarding MCL, the activity of obinutuzumab associated with lenalidomide was observed in 13 patients with R/R disease enrolled in the phase 2 GALEN trial previously described [93]. A further phase 2 trial, LYMA-101, is investigating obinutuzumab plus DHAP followed by autologous stem cell transplantation (ASCT) plus obinutuzumab maintenance: 75% of 73 patients with available data achieved MRD-negativity after induction, and, after 1 year, PFS and OS were 93.4% and 96%, respectively [94]. Promising efficacy and safety have also been reported in both R/R and previously untreated MCL in phase 1–2 OAsIs trial, evaluating the combination therapy of obinutuzumab with Bruton's tyrosine kinase inhibitor (BTKi) ibrutinib and the selective inhibitor of the antiapoptotic protein B-cell lymphoma 2 (anti-BCL-2) venetoclax [95].

Ofatumumab

Good tolerability and modest activity (22% ORR) of ofatumumab as monotherapy in a heavily pretreated rituximab-refractory population affected by FL was shown in a phase 3 study [37]. The further phase 3 HOMER study evaluated the efficacy and safety of ofatumumab vs rituximab in patients with indolent B-NHL (98% of FL). Although patients had relapsed following treatment with a rituximab-containing regimen, all of them were sensitive to rituximab. No clinical advantage over rituximab was shown and the study was halted for futility at a planned interim analysis [96]. In DLBCL, ofatumumab was compared with rituximab plus DHAP as salvage therapy in the ORCHARRD study. Patients responding after two treatment cycles received high-dose chemotherapy and ASCT after their third cycle. This trial failed to find any difference in efficacy or safety between ofatumumab and rituximab [97].

Anti-CD20xCD3 bispecific antibodies

Although several studies combining BsAbs with cytotoxic chemotherapy were commenced and some promising results have begun to emerge [26], we here focus on the main single agents' clinical experience currently obtained.

Mosunetuzumab

The first anti-CD20xCD3 BsAb to be evaluated in patients with R/R B-NHL in clinical practice was mosunetuzumab. The first-in-human trial (which enrolled both indolent and aggressive NHL) showed an ORR of 35%, CR of 19%, with a median duration of response (DoR), and PFS of 7.6 and 1.4 months respectively in patients with aggressive disease. On the other side, patients with indolent NHL (among one-third of FL) had an ORR of 66%, with CR of 48% and DoR and PFS of 16.8 and 11.8 months respectively. Responses were consistent across risk groups, including patients previously exposed to CAR-T cell therapy (10% of patients) [98]. An extended follow-up of 18.3 months of the 90 subjects with R/R FL treated showed an ORR of 80% and a CR of 60%, with median DOR and PFS of 22.8 and 17.9 months, respectively [99]. Responses were consistent also in patients older than 65 years, those refractory to anti-CD20 mAbs and alkylating agents, and those with progression of disease within 2 years (POD24) [100]. These data led to the approval of mosunetuzumab for patients with R/R FL after ≥2 prior lines of therapy by EMA [101]. Of note, a phase 1 trial investigated the use of mosunetuzumab in previously untreated elderly unfit patients with DLBCL: the best ORR of 68% with 42% CR was shown [102].

Glofitamab

The phase 1 study of glofitamab enrolled 171 patients with CD20-positive B-NHL. Patients previously exposed to a median of three prior lines of therapy received a single 1000 mg dose of pretreatment obinutuzumab [in order to mitigate cytokine release syndrome (CRS)] followed by the BsAb intravenously. At doses ≥10 mg the ORR among patients with aggressive NHL was 61% with 49% CR, while in 44 patients with FL, ORR reached 70% with a 48% CR rate [103]. In a separate analysis of patients with R/R FL treated with step-up dosing glofitamab with or without concomitant obinutuzumab, similar complete metabolic responses were observed regardless of obinutuzumab administration, including patients with POD24 [58% and 70% of complete metabolic response (CMR) respectively] [104]. Results of the phase 2 trial were recently published: after a median follow-up of 12.6 months, 52% of patients had an objective response, with 39% of CR, with similar rates of CR observed in the 52 subjects previously exposed to CAR-T cell therapy (35%) and in the 102 who were not (42%). The median time to a CR was 42 days, and the majority of CR were ongoing at 12 months (78%). Median DoR was 18.4 months and 12-month PFS was 37%. Overall, the median PFS was 4.9 months and the estimated 12-month OS among all patients was 50% (median OS was 11.5 months) [105]. Finally, in a preliminary report on 21 patients with R/R MCL, an 81% ORR and 67% CR were observed with glofitamab, regardless of prior BTKi therapy [106].

Epcoritamab

Subcutaneous infusion of epcoritamab was tested in a phase 1/2 trial in 73 subjects with R/R B-NHL. Among 22 patients with DLBCL, the ORR was 68% and the CR rate was 45%, while 90% of patients with FL (nine out of the 10 enrolled) achieved a response, including 50% of CR. Efficacy was noted also in four patients with MCL. The median time to response and to CR were 1.4 and 2.7 months, respectively. The estimated probability of DLBCL responders maintaining remission for at least 6 months was 75% at a median follow-up of 9.2 months [107]. Data from the phase 2 study were recently published. At a median follow-up of 10.7 months, among 157 enrolled patients with R/R DLBCL (38.9% previously exposed to CAR-T cell therapy), the ORR was 63.1% and CR was 38.9%. The median DoR was 12 months, and it was not reached among complete responders. These results were similar across key prespecified subgroups [108].

Odronextamab

A phase 1 trial tested odronextamab in 145 patients with R/R B-NHL. In patients with DLBCL, responses were similar for those who had previously received CAR-T cell therapy (41% of the 82 DLBCL enrolled): ORR was 33% and 39%, respectively; with a CR rate of 24% in both groups. Among patients with FL, ORR was 78% and 63% had a CR. The promising activity was shown in also in MCL and MZL [109].

Safety of BsAbs

The safety profile of BsAbs has been rather consistent across trials, and most AEs have been manageable, with rare treatment interruptions or discontinuation. Toxicities are mainly related to T-cell overactivation. Among these, CRS was the most frequent, occurring in 15%–80% of patients depending on the agent, route of administration, and dosing schedule [26]. However, no fatalities related to CRS have been reported to date across CD20xCD3 BsAb trials. Neurological toxicities with the use of BsAb have also been observed. BsAb is not expected to cross the blood-brain barrier, and virtually no information is available on the presence of activated T-cells or inflammatory cytokines in the CSF of these patients.

Accordingly, neurological AEs in BsAb clinical trials have been rare, generally mild, and self-resolving within hours of their onset. It should be noted that long-term BsAbs safety data are not yet available, and potential AEs related to delayed B-cell recovery will need to be clarified [26].

Anti-CD20 resistance

Several mechanisms have been identified as potentially involved in rituximab resistance, including ADCC, complement-dependent cytotoxicity (CDC), loss of CD20, and induction of apoptosis. Moreover, tumor microenvironment (TME) could also be implicated in anti-CD20 resistance (Fig. 2) [2,110]. Details on these mechanisms are listed below.

Resistance to CDC

Tumor cells have the ability of complement blocking via membrane complement-regulatory proteins. In particular, CDC can be triggered as a cytotoxic mechanism by binding the Fc portion of IgG antibodies to C1q and then to serum protein, leading to its activation. Activation of complement is mediated via the classical pathway, the lectin pathway, or the alternative pathway. Classical pathway activation occurs when C1 (C1q in complex with the serine proteases C1r and C1s) interacts with the Fc region of IgG or IgM antibodies

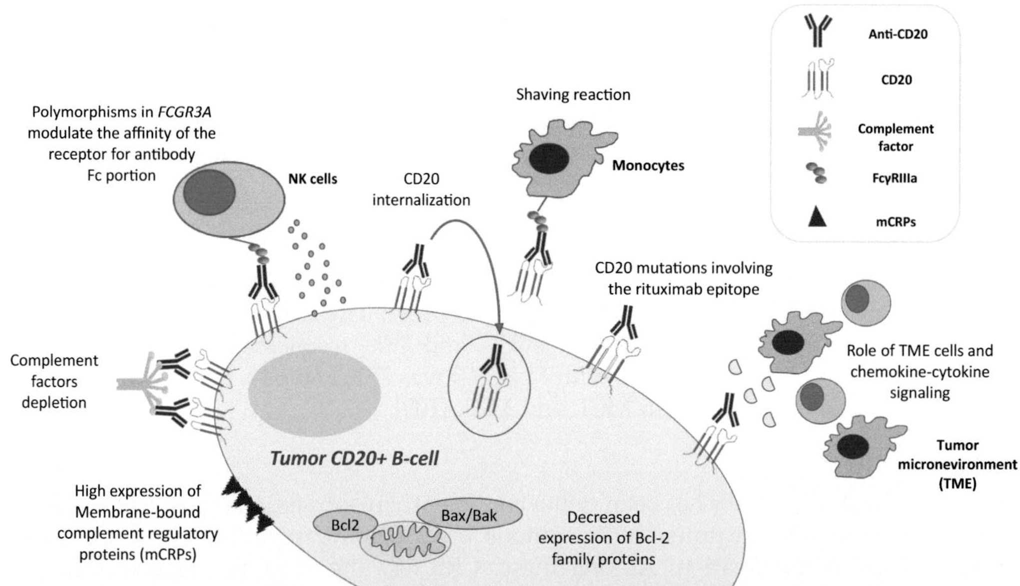

FIG. 2 Summary of mechanisms of resistance to anti-CD20 monoclonal antibodies. Mechanisms of resistance to anti-CD20 mAbs: (1) inhibition of complement-dependent cytotoxicity (CDC) through complement factors depletion; (2) negative regulation of antibody-dependent cell-mediated cytotoxicity (ADCC) by FCGR3A polymorphisms; (3) loss of CD20 antigen through CD20 internalization and "shaving reaction"; (4) CD20 mutations involving rituximab epitote; and (5) role of tumor microenvironment (TME) and chemokine-cytokine signaling.

attached to antigenic surfaces. In the lectin pathway, mannose-binding lectin (MBL) and MBL-associated protease bind to mannose and fucose residues on the surface of pathogens triggering the complement cascade. The alternative pathway is induced by C3 hydrolysis, either spontaneously at a low rate or enhanced by the interaction of C3 with the pathogen's cell surfaces. As a result, the formation of C3 and C5 convertases mediated by the three different pathways leads to the (1) opsonization of the target surface by C3b, (2) anaphylatoxins C3a and C5a release for recruitment of effector cells, and (3) formation of the terminal membrane attack complex (MAC). All these processes are negatively regulated by several membrane-bound complement-regulatory proteins (mCRPs) in order to prevent the overactivation of the complement system [111,112]. The idea that complement depletion contributes to rituximab resistance was suggested by Di Gaetano et al. demonstrating that rituximab therapeutic activity was abolished in knockout animals lacking C1q [113]. Moreover, Klepfish et al. [114] showed a rapid and dramatic clinical and laboratory response to a standard dose of rituximab by adding fresh frozen plasma in previously rituximab-resistant CLL patients. Despite uncontrolled, these results support the hypothesis of complement depletion effect on rituximab resistance in CLL patients. Another mechanism of rituximab resistance linked to CDC might be associated with mCRPs including CD46, CD55, and CD59. In fact, mCRPs which negatively regulate complement activity, are expressed by cancer cells [115]. Some rituximab-resistant cell lines have been reported to express high levels of mCRP [116], possibly as a consequence of selective pressure from repeated exposure to rituximab. If mCRP is blocked by antibodies such as anti-CD55 and anti-CD59 antibodies, the lysis mediated by rituximab is increased in MCL and CLL cells [117]. However, mCRPs have an important regulatory role in protecting normal cells from runaway complement-mediated cytotoxicity, which may restrict the clinical application of mCRP blockade [118].

Resistance to ADCC

ADCC is mediated by the binding of the fragment crystallizable region (Fc) of the antibody bound to the target cell to the Fc receptor (FcRs) of different effector cells such as natural killer (NK) cells, granulocytes, and macrophages, triggering immune cell activation and death of the target cell [118]. Rituximab induces ADCC in lymphoma cell lines when peripheral blood mononuclear cells were used as effector cells [119]. Based on the ADCC mechanism, the impact on B-cell depletion is mediated by rituximab [17,120]. Moreover, NK cells coexpress a wide array of other receptors with activating or inhibitory functions that can influence their ability to elicit ADCC. Inhibitory killer cell immunoglobulin-like receptors (KIRs) interact with public epitopes on human leukocyte antigen (HLA) and are involved in the natural regulation of NK cells. Based on this hypothesis, Terszowski et al. demonstrated that KIR/HLA interactions strongly and selectively inhibit rituximab-induced in vitro ADCC [17,121].

Resistance to apoptosis

Since the binding of rituximab to CD20 independently triggers tumor cell apoptosis, impaired apoptotic signaling pathways could result in resistance to rituximab. Indeed, rituximab-resistant cell lines were shown to demonstrate apoptosis resistance and to have no sensitivity to different cytotoxic chemotherapeutic agents as well as rituximab. In fact, as Olejniczak et al. demonstrated that malignant B cells resistant to multiple chemotherapeutic agents have significantly decreased expression of the Bcl-2 family proteins (Bax, Bak, and Bcl-2) and do not undergo rituximab- or chemotherapy-induced apoptosis [122]. Moreover, hyperactivation of the NF-κB pathway in rituximab-resistant cell lines leads to antiapoptotic proteins overexpression of the BCL-2 family. Resensitization of these clones to rituximab was also possible in vitro by exposing them to inhibitors of these survival pathways [118].

Loss of CD20 antigen

Mutations of the CD20 epitope do not seem to be a relevant mechanism of resistance to rituximab. As Johnson et al. demonstrated, CD20 mutations involving the rituximab epitope were detected in only 1/264 (0.4%) of the diagnostic biopsies and 1/15 (6%) of the biopsies taken at relapse in patients with DLBCL [123]. Conversely, reductions in the density of CD20 expression can occur in CLL and MCL cells after exposure to the antibody. As Beers et al. showed, CLL and MCL cases reduce CD20 expression quite rapidly, whereas FL and DLBCL samples demonstrate significantly lower internalization, corresponding to their greater sensitivity to rituximab [17,124]. Decreased expression of CD20 may also result from trogocytosis, occurring when after immunological synapse is formed, the antibody-CD20 complex is removed and internalized (along with a portion of membrane) by the effector cell instead of being phagocytized, leaving the targeted malignant B cell intact and alive [17,125,126]. This has also been referred to as a "shaving reaction" and serves to modify the efficacy of therapeutic mAbs, modifying both the immune response and inherent B cell function since rituximab/CD20 complexes are removed from the B-cell surface by monocytes [127].

Tumor microenvironment

TME could play a significant role in rituximab resistance. In fact, the mechanisms of B-cell depletion mediated by rituximab could be influenced by TME [128]. This hypothesis is supported by Gong et al. who showed signals from the tumor necrosis factor (TNF) family/B lymphocyte stimulator (BLyS) survival factor, involved in the survival and maturation of marginal zone B cells, integrin-regulated homeostasis, and circulatory dynamics of B cells shape cells sensitivity to anti-CD20 mAbs [129]. Moreover, a recent study showed that the efficacy of front-line anti-CD20 mAbs in FL could be influenced by TMEs since specific immune signatures involving chemokine-cytokine signaling, T-regulatory cells (Tregs), NK cell activity, and interleukin (IL)-17 signaling could define FL patient subsets obtaining maximal benefit from upfront anti-CD20 immunotherapy predicting FL outcome [130].

New approaches of B-cell-directed therapy: Beyond rituximab

Type II anti-CD20 antibodies

The development of anti-CD20 mAbs with enhanced or novel effector mechanisms partly shows improved activity in rituximab-refractory cases [131]. In fact, CDC induction by obinutuzumab is up to 100-fold less than with the type I anti-CD20 mAb rituximab [132], resulting in an increased capacity to bind and activate NK cells in the presence of complement when compared to rituximab [133,134]. In addition, type II anti-CD20 antibodies result in reduced FcγRIIb-induced CD20 internalization, which has been associated with reduced rituximab efficacy [135].

CD20xCD3 bispecific antibodies

As far as bispecific antibodies are concerned, potential mechanisms of resistance may be associated with the loss of CD20 antigen and tumor microenvironment dysfunction [26]. As previously said, loss of the CD20 antigen is known to have a role in anti-CD20 monoclonal antibody therapy resistance. Although higher baseline CD20 expression was not clearly associated with the achievement of response after CD20xCD3 BsAb therapy [136,137], a loss of CD20 was observed in patients with progressive or recurrent disease and in some cases was associated with CD20 gene mutations [138]. However, since CD20 expression is maintained even in patients with progressive disease, alternative mechanisms may be implied in acquired CD20xCD3 BsAb resistance [139]. A second mechanism of resistance to BsAb depends on TME. In fact, activation of regulatory or suppressive T-cells and, conversely, tumor-resident T cells lack of activation within the lymphoma microenvironment may favor resistance [137]. Moreover, chronic TCR triggering promotes a dysfunctional T-cell phenotype known as T-cell "exhaustion," which is associated with blunted antitumor activity [137]. Finally, the lymphoma microenvironment contains several elements, such as tumor-associated macrophages (TAMs), cancer-associated fibroblasts (CAFs), and myeloid-derived suppressor cells (MDSCs), all of which can promote immunosuppression. Whether and how these cells directly limit BsAbs activity remains to be determined [26].

Anti-CD20 CAR-Ts

To date, most of the knowledge about resistance to CAR-T therapy is focused on anti-CD19 CAR-T cells, as they are the most commonly used CAR-T cells in acute lymphoblastic leukemia (ALL) and B-cell lymphomas. Speculatively, at least some of the mechanisms involved in anti-CD19 CAR-T resistance may also underlie anti-CD20 CAR-T one. So far, the known mechanisms of resistance to anti-CD19 CAR-T therapy include (1) loss of antigen expression, (2) T-cell exhaustion, and (3) the immunosuppression played by TME cells [140].

Loss of antigen expression on tumor cells may occur as a result of tumor heterogeneity. It consists of a tumor-intrinsic mechanism by which ALL and lymphoma cells acquire an advantageous phenotype to survive and proliferate under the immunological pressure of CAR-T cells surveillance. Loss of antigen expression can result in the inability of CAR-T cells to recognize and kill tumor cells, leading to treatment failure [141].

The second mechanism refers to T-cell exhaustion [142]. This is a state of T-cell dysfunction resulting from chronic antigen exposure. For this reason, the phenotype of T-cells used to manufacture CAR-T cells might impact treatment outcomes. The exhausted phenotype may depend on the presence of inhibitory receptors, such as PD-1, Tim-3, and LAG-3, that are upregulated on CAR-T cells following antigen recognition [143]. This can result in the inability of CAR-T cells to proliferate and produce effector cytokines, leading to reduced CAR-T cell function.

Lastly, the TME might affect the efficacy of CAR-T therapy. In fact, the complex cross talk of tumor cells, intratumoral Tregs, TAMs, MDSCs, hypoxia, and inhibitory cytokines, such as TGF-β and IL-10, can inhibit the function of CAR-T cells. Furthermore, the physical barrier created by the extracellular matrix can prevent CAR-T cells from accessing tumor cells, limiting their ability to kill tumor cells [140,141]. Although mechanisms of anti-CD20 CAR-Ts have not yet been clarified, it is conceivable that anti-CD20 antigen loss or reduction might lead to CD20 CAR-T cell treatment resistance. Probably, the efficacy of CD20 CAR-T might be influenced by effector and Tregs or other cells including CAFs, TMAs, and MDSCs. In fact, it is plausible that TME heterogeneity might modulate CAR-T therapy efficacy [144]. An understanding of the mechanisms involved in CAR-T resistance will be crucial to improve the outcome of CAR-T therapy in lymphomas.

Conclusions and future perspectives

Since the breakthrough of rituximab, anti-CD20-directed immunotherapy has changed the prognosis of B-NHLs, paving a new targeted approach to the treatment of these diseases. Moreover, the recent development and approval of more sophisticated therapies, namely CAR-T cells and BsAbs, have broadened the horizons of immunotherapy. In the coming years, efforts will be made in order to (1) better identify clinical features and predictive biomarkers of resistance to guide physicians in treating patients and (2) choose the best combination with chemotherapy and cytotoxic agents, as well as better define the optimal indication line for anti-CD20 immunotherapies. Well-designed clinical trial together with translational research will allow the advancement of knowledge in the treatment of lymphomas.

References

[1] Tedder TF, et al. Structure of the gene encoding the human B lymphocyte differentiation antigen CD20 (B1). J Immunol 1989;142(7):2560–8.
[2] Seyfizadeh N, et al. A molecular perspective on rituximab: a monoclonal antibody for B cell non Hodgkin lymphoma and other affections. Crit Rev Oncol Hematol 2016;97:275–90.
[3] Polyak MJ, et al. CD20 homo-oligomers physically associate with the B cell antigen receptor. Dissociation upon receptor engagement and recruitment of phosphoproteins and calmodulin-binding proteins. J Biol Chem 2008;283(27):18545–52.
[4] Olejniczak SH, et al. A quantitative exploration of surface antigen expression in common B-cell malignancies using flow cytometry. Immunol Investig 2006;35(1):93–114.
[5] Horna P, et al. Comparative assessment of surface CD19 and CD20 expression on B-cell lymphomas from clinical biopsies: implications for targeted therapies. Blood 2019;134(Suppl_1):5345.
[6] Maloney DG, et al. IDEC-C2B8 (Rituximab) anti-CD20 monoclonal antibody therapy in patients with relapsed low-grade non-Hodgkin's lymphoma. Blood 1997;90(6):2188–95.
[7] McLaughlin P, et al. Rituximab chimeric anti-CD20 monoclonal antibody therapy for relapsed indolent lymphoma: half of patients respond to a four-dose treatment program. J Clin Oncol 1998;16(8):2825–33.
[8] Salles G, et al. Rituximab in B-cell hematologic malignancies: a review of 20 years of clinical experience. Adv Ther 2017;34(10):2232–73.
[9] Ghielmini M, et al. ESMO Guidelines consensus conference on malignant lymphoma 2011 part 1: diffuse large B-cell lymphoma (DLBCL), follicular lymphoma (FL) and chronic lymphocytic leukemia (CLL). Ann Oncol 2013;24(3):561–76.
[10] Tilly H, et al. Diffuse large B-cell lymphoma (DLBCL): ESMO Clinical Practice Guidelines for diagnosis, treatment and follow-up. Ann Oncol 2015;26(Suppl 5):v116–25.

[11] Dreyling M, et al. Newly diagnosed and relapsed follicular lymphoma: ESMO Clinical Practice Guidelines for diagnosis, treatment and follow-up. Ann Oncol 2021;32(3):298–308.
[12] Pavlasova G, Mraz M. The regulation and function of CD20: an "enigma" of B-cell biology and targeted therapy. Haematologica 2020;105(6):1494–506.
[13] Cragg MS, et al. Complement-mediated lysis by anti-CD20 mAb correlates with segregation into lipid rafts. Blood 2003;101(3):1045–52.
[14] Meyer S, et al. New insights in Type I and II CD20 antibody mechanisms-of-action with a panel of novel CD20 antibodies. Br J Haematol 2018;180(6):808–20.
[15] Marcus R, et al. Obinutuzumab for the first-line treatment of follicular lymphoma. N Engl J Med 2017;377 (14):1331–44.
[16] Vitolo U, et al. Obinutuzumab or rituximab plus cyclophosphamide, doxorubicin, vincristine, and prednisone in previously untreated diffuse large B-cell lymphoma. J Clin Oncol 2017;35(31):3529–37.
[17] Freeman CL, Sehn LH. A tale of two antibodies: obinutuzumab versus rituximab. Br J Haematol 2018;182(1):29–45.
[18] European Medicines Agency. Arzerra; 2019. May 5.
[19] Lunning M, et al. Ublituximab and umbralisib in relapsed/refractory B-cell non-Hodgkin lymphoma and chronic lymphocytic leukemia. Blood 2019;134(21):1811–20.
[20] Chavez JC, et al. The combination of umbralisib plus ublituximab is active in patients with relapsed or refractory marginal zone lymphoma (MZL): results from the phase 2 global Unity-NHL trial. Blood 2021;138(Suppl 1):45.
[21] TG Therapeutics. TG therapeutics announces voluntary withdrawal of the BLA/sNDA for U2 to treat patients with CLL and SLL; 2022. April 15.
[22] Lopez-Guillermo A, et al. A randomized phase II study comparing consolidation with a single dose of 90y ibritumomab tiuxetan (Zevalin®) (Z) vs. maintenance with rituximab (R) for two years in patients with newly diagnosed follicular lymphoma (FL) responding to R-CHOP. Preliminary results at 36 months from randomization. Blood 2013;122(21):369.
[23] Morschhauser F, et al. 90Yttrium-ibritumomab tiuxetan consolidation of first remission in advanced-stage follicular non-Hodgkin lymphoma: updated results after a median follow-up of 7.3 years from the International, Randomized, Phase III First-Line Indolent Trial. J Clin Oncol 2013;31(16):1977–83.
[24] Shadman M, et al. Continued excellent outcomes in previously untreated patients with follicular lymphoma after treatment with CHOP plus rituximab or CHOP plus 131I-Tositumomab: long-term follow-up of phase III randomized study SWOG-S0016. J Clin Oncol 2018;36(7):697–703.
[25] Sun LL, et al. Anti-CD20/CD3 T cell-dependent bispecific antibody for the treatment of B cell malignancies. Sci Transl Med 2015;7(287), 287ra70.
[26] Falchi L, Vardhana SA, Salles GA. Bispecific antibodies for the treatment of B-cell lymphoma: promises, unknowns, and opportunities. Blood 2023;141(5):467–80.
[27] Till BG, et al. CD20-specific adoptive immunotherapy for lymphoma using a chimeric antigen receptor with both CD28 and 4-1BB domains: pilot clinical trial results. Blood 2012;119(17):3940–50.
[28] Tang X, et al. T cells expressing a LMP1-specific chimeric antigen receptor mediate antitumor effects against LMP1-positive nasopharyngeal carcinoma cells in vitro and in vivo. J Biomed Res 2014;28(6):468–75.
[29] Liang A, et al. Safety and efficacy of a novel anti-CD20 chimeric antigen receptor (CAR)-T cell therapy in relapsed/refractory (r/r) B-cell non-Hodgkin lymphoma (B-NHL) patients after failing CD19 CAR-T therapy. J Clin Oncol 2021;39(15_Suppl):2508.
[30] Klein C, Jamois C, Nielsen T. Anti-CD20 treatment for B-cell malignancies: current status and future directions. Expert Opin Biol Ther 2021;21(2):161–81.
[31] European Medicines Agency. MabThera; 2022. August 31.
[32] Davis TA, et al. Single-agent monoclonal antibody efficacy in bulky non-Hodgkin's lymphoma: results of a phase II trial of rituximab. J Clin Oncol 1999;17(6):1851–7.
[33] Piro LD, et al. Extended Rituximab (anti-CD20 monoclonal antibody) therapy for relapsed or refractory low-grade or follicular non-Hodgkin's lymphoma. Ann Oncol 1999;10(6):655–61.
[34] Feuring-Buske M, et al. IDEC-C2B8 (Rituximab) anti-CD20 antibody treatment in relapsed advanced-stage follicular lymphomas: results of a phase-II study of the German Low-Grade Lymphoma Study Group. Ann Hematol 2000;79(9):493–500.
[35] Foran JM, et al. A UK multicentre phase II study of rituximab (chimaeric anti-CD20 monoclonal antibody) in patients with follicular lymphoma, with PCR monitoring of molecular response. Br J Haematol 2000;109(1):81–8.
[36] Colombat P, et al. Rituximab induction immunotherapy for first-line low-tumor-burden follicular lymphoma: survival analyses with 7-year follow-up. Ann Oncol 2012;23(9):2380–5.

[37] Czuczman MS, et al. Prolonged clinical and molecular remission in patients with low-grade or follicular non-Hodgkin's lymphoma treated with rituximab plus CHOP chemotherapy: 9-year follow-up. J Clin Oncol 2004;22 (23):4711–6.

[38] Hiddemann W, et al. Frontline therapy with rituximab added to the combination of cyclophosphamide, doxorubicin, vincristine, and prednisone (CHOP) significantly improves the outcome for patients with advanced-stage follicular lymphoma compared with therapy with CHOP alone: results of a prospective randomized study of the German Low-Grade Lymphoma Study Group. Blood 2005;106(12):3725–32.

[39] Marcus R, et al. CVP chemotherapy plus rituximab compared with CVP as first-line treatment for advanced follicular lymphoma. Blood 2005;105(4):1417–23.

[40] Herold M, et al. Rituximab added to first-line mitoxantrone, chlorambucil, and prednisolone chemotherapy followed by interferon maintenance prolongs survival in patients with advanced follicular lymphoma: an East German Study Group Hematology and Oncology Study. J Clin Oncol 2007;25(15):1986–92.

[41] van Oers MH, et al. Rituximab maintenance improves clinical outcome of relapsed/resistant follicular non-Hodgkin lymphoma in patients both with and without rituximab during induction: results of a prospective randomized phase 3 intergroup trial. Blood 2006;108(10):3295–301.

[42] Marcus R, et al. Phase III study of R-CVP compared with cyclophosphamide, vincristine, and prednisone alone in patients with previously untreated advanced follicular lymphoma. J Clin Oncol 2008;26(28):4579–86.

[43] Salles G, et al. Rituximab combined with chemotherapy and interferon in follicular lymphoma patients: results of the GELA-GOELAMS FL2000 study. Blood 2008;112(13):4824–31.

[44] Hochster H, et al. Maintenance Rituximab after cyclophosphamide, vincristine, and prednisone prolongs progression-free survival in advanced indolent lymphoma: results of the randomized phase III ECOG1496 Study. J Clin Oncol 2009;27(10):1607–14.

[45] Bachy E, et al. Long-term follow up of the FL2000 study comparing CHVP-interferon to CHVP-interferon plus rituximab in follicular lymphoma. Haematologica 2013;98(7):1107–14.

[46] Federico M, et al. R-CVP versus R-CHOP versus R-FM for the initial treatment of patients with advanced-stage follicular lymphoma: results of the FOLL05 trial conducted by the Fondazione Italiana Linfomi. J Clin Oncol 2013;31(12):1506–13.

[47] Rummel MJ, et al. Bendamustine plus rituximab versus CHOP plus rituximab as first-line treatment for patients with indolent and mantle-cell lymphomas: an open-label, multicentre, randomised, phase 3 non-inferiority trial. Lancet 2013;381(9873):1203–10.

[48] Hoster E, et al. Rituximab maintenance versus observation after immunochemotherapy (R-CHOP, R-MCP, R-FCM) in previously untreated follicular lymphoma: a randomised trial of GLSG and OSHO. Hematol Oncol 2017;35(S2):32.

[49] Rummel MJ, et al. Four versus two years of Rituximab maintenance (R-maintenance) following Bendamustine plus Rituximab (B-R): initial results of a prospective, randomized multicenter phase 3 study in first-line follicular lymphoma (the StiL NHL7-2008 MAINTAIN study). Blood 2017;130:483.

[50] Bachy E, et al. Sustained progression-free survival benefit of rituximab maintenance in patients with follicular lymphoma: long-term results of the PRIMA study. J Clin Oncol 2019;37(31):2815–24.

[51] Martinelli G, et al. Long-term follow-up of patients with follicular lymphoma receiving single-agent rituximab at two different schedules in trial SAKK 35/98. J Clin Oncol 2010;28(29):4480–4.

[52] Vidal L, et al. Rituximab maintenance for the treatment of patients with follicular lymphoma: an updated systematic review and meta-analysis of randomized trials. J Natl Cancer Inst 2011;103(23):1799–806.

[53] Leonard JP, et al. AUGMENT: a phase III study of lenalidomide plus rituximab versus placebo plus rituximab in relapsed or refractory indolent lymphoma. J Clin Oncol 2019;37(14):1188–99.

[54] Vose JM, et al. Phase II study of rituximab in combination with CHOP chemotherapy in patients with previously untreated, aggressive non-Hodgkin's lymphoma. J Clin Oncol 2001;19(2):389–97.

[55] Pfreundschuh M, et al. CHOP-like chemotherapy plus rituximab versus CHOP-like chemotherapy alone in young patients with good-prognosis diffuse large-B-cell lymphoma: a randomised controlled trial by the MabThera International Trial (MInT) Group. Lancet Oncol 2006;7(5):379–91.

[56] Coiffier B, et al. CHOP chemotherapy plus rituximab compared with CHOP alone in elderly patients with diffuse large-B-cell lymphoma. N Engl J Med 2002;346(4):235–42.

[57] Habermann TM, et al. Rituximab-CHOP versus CHOP alone or with maintenance rituximab in older patients with diffuse large B-cell lymphoma. J Clin Oncol 2006;24(19):3121–7.

[58] Jaeger U, et al. Rituximab maintenance for patients with aggressive B-cell lymphoma in first remission: results of the randomized NHL13 trial. Haematologica 2015;100(7):955–63.

[59] Kewalramani T, et al. Rituximab and ICE as second-line therapy before autologous stem cell transplantation for relapsed or primary refractory diffuse large B-cell lymphoma. Blood 2004;103(10):3684–8.
[60] Gisselbrecht C, et al. Salvage regimens with autologous transplantation for relapsed large B-cell lymphoma in the rituximab era. J Clin Oncol 2010;28(27):4184–90.
[61] Jermann M, et al. Rituximab-EPOCH, an effective salvage therapy for relapsed, refractory or transformed B-cell lymphomas: results of a phase II study. Ann Oncol 2004;15(3):511–6.
[62] Griffiths R, et al. Addition of rituximab to chemotherapy alone as first-line therapy improves overall survival in elderly patients with mantle cell lymphoma. Blood 2011;118(18):4808–16.
[63] Kluin-Nelemans HC, et al. Treatment of older patients with mantle-cell lymphoma. N Engl J Med 2012;367 (6):520–31.
[64] Le Gouill S, et al. Rituximab after autologous stem-cell transplantation in mantle-cell lymphoma. N Engl J Med 2017;377(13):1250–60.
[65] Dreyling M, et al. Newly diagnosed and relapsed mantle cell lymphoma: ESMO Clinical Practice Guidelines for diagnosis, treatment and follow-up. Ann Oncol 2017;28(Suppl_4):iv62–71.
[66] Tsimberidou AM, et al. Outcomes in patients with splenic marginal zone lymphoma and marginal zone lymphoma treated with rituximab with or without chemotherapy or chemotherapy alone. Cancer 2006;107(1):125–35.
[67] Williams ME, et al. Rituximab extended schedule or retreatment trial for low tumour burden non-follicular indolent B-cell non-Hodgkin lymphomas: Eastern Cooperative Oncology Group Protocol E4402. Br J Haematol 2016;173(6):867–75.
[68] Kalpadakis C, et al. Treatment of splenic marginal zone lymphoma with rituximab monotherapy: progress report and comparison with splenectomy. Oncologist 2013;18(2):190–7.
[69] Kalpadakis C, et al. Rituximab monotherapy in splenic marginal zone lymphoma: prolonged responses and potential benefit from maintenance. Blood 2018;132(6):666–70.
[70] Zucca E, et al. Final results of the IELSG-19 randomized trial of mucosa-associated lymphoid tissue lymphoma: improved event-free and progression-free survival with rituximab plus chlorambucil versus either chlorambucil or rituximab monotherapy. J Clin Oncol 2017;35(17):1905–12.
[71] Zucca E, et al. Marginal zone lymphomas: ESMO Clinical Practice Guidelines for diagnosis, treatment and follow-up. Ann Oncol 2020;31(1):17–29.
[72] Ribrag V, et al. Rituximab and dose-dense chemotherapy for adults with Burkitt's lymphoma: a randomised, controlled, open-label, phase 3 trial. Lancet 2016;387(10036):2402–11.
[73] Gavriatopoulou M, et al. BDR in newly diagnosed patients with WM: final analysis of a phase 2 study after a minimum follow-up of 6 years. Blood 2017;129(4):456–9.
[74] Kastritis E, et al. Waldenström's macroglobulinaemia: ESMO Clinical Practice Guidelines for diagnosis, treatment and follow-up. Ann Oncol 2019;30(5):860–2.
[75] Trappe RU, et al. Response to rituximab induction is a predictive marker in B-cell post-transplant lymphoproliferative disorder and allows successful stratification into rituximab or R-CHOP consolidation in an international, prospective, multicenter phase II trial. J Clin Oncol 2017;35(5):536–43.
[76] Zimmermann H, et al. Modified risk-stratified sequential treatment (subcutaneous rituximab with or without chemotherapy) in B-cell post-transplant lymphoproliferative disorder (PTLD) after solid organ transplantation (SOT): the prospective multicentre phase II PTLD-2 trial. Leukemia 2022;36(10):2468–78.
[77] Hiddemann W, et al. Immunochemotherapy with obinutuzumab or rituximab for previously untreated follicular lymphoma in the GALLIUM study: influence of chemotherapy on efficacy and safety. J Clin Oncol 2018;36 (23):2395–404.
[78] Seymour JF, et al. Association of early disease progression and very poor survival in the GALLIUM study in follicular lymphoma: benefit of obinutuzumab in reducing the rate of early progression. Haematologica 2019;104(6):1202–8.
[79] Pott C, et al. Minimal residual disease response at end of induction and during maintenance correlates with updated outcome in the phase III GALLIUM study of obinutuzumab- or rituximab-based immunochemotherapy in previously untreated follicular lymphoma patients. Blood 2018;132(Suppl 1):396.
[80] Sehn LH, et al. Randomized phase II trial comparing obinutuzumab (GA101) with rituximab in patients with relapsed CD20+ indolent B-cell non-Hodgkin lymphoma: final analysis of the GAUSS study. J Clin Oncol 2015;33(30):3467–74.
[81] Sehn LH, et al. Obinutuzumab plus bendamustine versus bendamustine monotherapy in patients with rituximab-refractory indolent non-Hodgkin lymphoma (GADOLIN): a randomised, controlled, open-label, multicentre, phase 3 trial. Lancet Oncol 2016;17(8):1081–93.

[82] Cheson BD, et al. Overall survival benefit in patients with rituximab-refractory indolent non-Hodgkin lymphoma who received obinutuzumab plus bendamustine induction and obinutuzumab maintenance in the GADOLIN study. J Clin Oncol 2018;36(22):2259–66.
[83] Pott C, et al. MRD response in relapsed/refractory FL after obinutuzumab plus bendamustine or bendamustine alone in the GADOLIN trial. Leukemia 2020;34(2):522–32.
[84] European Medicines Agency. Gazyvaro; 2015. June 19.
[85] Davies A, et al. Obinutuzumab in the treatment of B-cell malignancies: a comprehensive review. Future Oncol 2022;18(26):2943–66.
[86] Morschhauser F, et al. Obinutuzumab combined with lenalidomide for relapsed or refractory follicular B-cell lymphoma (GALEN): a multicentre, single-arm, phase 2 study. Lancet Haematol 2019;6(8):e429–37.
[87] Bachy E, et al. Obinutuzumab plus lenalidomide in advanced, previously untreated follicular lymphoma in need of systemic therapy: a LYSA study. Blood 2022;139(15):2338–46.
[88] Nastoupil LJ, et al. Results of a phase II study of obinutuzumab in combination with lenalidomide in previously untreated, high tumor burden follicular lymphoma (FL). Blood 2019;134(Suppl_1):125.
[89] Sehn LH, et al. A randomized, open-label, phase III study of obinutuzumab or rituximab plus CHOP in patients with previously untreated diffuse large B-cell lymphoma: final analysis of GOYA. J Hematol Oncol 2020;13(1):71.
[90] Le Gouill S, et al. Obinutuzumab vs rituximab for advanced DLBCL: a PET-guided and randomized phase 3 study by LYSA. Blood 2021;137(17):2307–20.
[91] Merli F, et al. Obinutuzumab and miniCHOP for unfit patients with diffuse large B-cell lymphoma. A phase II study by Fondazione Italiana Linfomi. J Geriatr Oncol 2020;11(1):37–40.
[92] Herold M, et al. Immunochemotherapy with obinutuzumab or rituximab in a subset of patients in the randomised GALLIUM trial with previously untreated marginal zone lymphoma (MZL). Hematol Oncol 2017;35(S2):146–7.
[93] Houot R, et al. Obinutuzumab plus Lenalidomide (GALEN) for the treatment of relapse/refractory aggressive lymphoma: a phase II LYSA study. Leukemia 2019;33(3):776–80.
[94] Le Gouill S, et al. Molecular response after obinutuzumab plus high-dose cytarabine induction for transplant-eligible patients with untreated mantle cell lymphoma (LyMa-101): a phase 2 trial of the LYSA group. Lancet Haematol 2020;7(11):e798–807.
[95] Le Gouill S, et al. Ibrutinib, obinutuzumab, and venetoclax in relapsed and untreated patients with mantle cell lymphoma: a phase 1/2 trial. Blood 2021;137(7):877–87.
[96] Maloney DG, et al. A phase 3 randomized study (HOMER) of ofatumumab vs rituximab in iNHL relapsed after rituximab-containing therapy. Blood Adv 2020;4(16):3886–93.
[97] van Imhoff GW, et al. Ofatumumab versus rituximab salvage chemoimmunotherapy in relapsed or refractory diffuse large B-cell lymphoma: the ORCHARRD study. J Clin Oncol 2017;35(5):544–51.
[98] Budde LE, et al. Single-agent mosunetuzumab shows durable complete responses in patients with relapsed or refractory B-cell lymphomas: phase I dose-escalation study. J Clin Oncol 2022;40(5):481–91.
[99] Budde LE, et al. Safety and efficacy of mosunetuzumab, a bispecific antibody, in patients with relapsed or refractory follicular lymphoma: a single-arm, multicentre, phase 2 study. Lancet Oncol 2022;23(8):1055–65.
[100] Budde LE, et al. Mosunetuzumab monotherapy is an effective and well-tolerated treatment option for patients with relapsed/refractory (R/R) follicular lymphoma (FL) who have received ≥2 prior lines of therapy: pivotal results from a phase I/II study. Blood 2021;138(Suppl 1):127.
[101] European Medicines Agency. Lunsumio; 2022. June 23.
[102] Olszewski AJ, et al. Single-agent mosunetuzumab is a promising safe and efficacious chemotherapy-free regimen for elderly/unfit patients with previously untreated diffuse large B-cell lymphoma. Blood 2020;136:43–5.
[103] Hutchings M, et al. Glofitamab, a novel, bivalent CD20-targeting T-cell–engaging bispecific antibody, induces durable complete remissions in relapsed or refractory B-cell lymphoma: a phase I trial. J Clin Oncol 2021;39 (18):1959–70.
[104] Morschhauser F, et al. Glofitamab as monotherapy and in combination with obinutuzumab induces high complete response rates in patients (pts) with multiple relapsed or refractory (R/R) follicular lymphoma (FL). Blood 2021;138:128.
[105] Dickinson MJ, et al. Glofitamab for relapsed or refractory diffuse large B-cell lymphoma. N Engl J Med 2022;387 (24):2220–31.
[106] Phillips T, et al. Glofitamab step-up dosing induces high response rates in patients (pts) with relapsed or refractory (R/R) mantle cell lymphoma (MCL), most of whom had failed prior Bruton's tyrosine kinase inhibitor (BTKi) therapy. Blood 2021;138(Suppl 1):130.

[107] Hutchings M, et al. Dose escalation of subcutaneous epcoritamab in patients with relapsed or refractory B-cell non-Hodgkin lymphoma: an open-label, phase 1/2 study. Lancet 2021;398(10306):1157–69.

[108] Thieblemont C, et al. Epcoritamab, a novel, subcutaneous CD3xCD20 bispecific T-cell-engaging antibody, in relapsed or refractory large B-cell lymphoma: dose expansion in a phase I/II trial. J Clin Oncol 2022;, Jco2201725.

[109] Bannerji R, et al. Odronextamab, a human CD20×CD3 bispecific antibody in patients with CD20-positive B-cell malignancies (ELM-1): results from the relapsed or refractory non-Hodgkin lymphoma cohort in a single-arm, multicentre, phase 1 trial. Lancet Haematol 2022;9(5):e327–39.

[110] Pérez-Callejo D, et al. Action and resistance of monoclonal CD20 antibodies therapy in B-cell non-Hodgkin lymphomas. Cancer Treat Rev 2015;41(8):680–9.

[111] Melis JP, et al. Complement in therapy and disease: regulating the complement system with antibody-based therapeutics. Mol Immunol 2015;67(2 Pt A):117–30.

[112] Zhou X, Hu W, Qin X. The role of complement in the mechanism of action of rituximab for B-cell lymphoma: implications for therapy. Oncologist 2008;13(9):954–66.

[113] Di Gaetano N, et al. Complement activation determines the therapeutic activity of rituximab in vivo. J Immunol 2003;171(3):1581–7.

[114] Klepfish A, Gilles L, Ioannis K, Rachmilewitz EA, Schacner A. Enhancing the action of rituximab in chronic lymphocytic leukemia by adding fresh frozen plasma: complement/rituximab interactions & clinical results in refractory CLL. Ann NYAcad Sci 2009;1173:865–73. https://doi.org/10.1111/j.1749-6632.2009.04803.x.

[115] Geller A, Yan J. The role of membrane bound complement regulatory proteins in tumor development and cancer immunotherapy. Front Immunol 2019;10:1074.

[116] Takei K, et al. Analysis of changes in CD20, CD55, and CD59 expression on established rituximab-resistant B-lymphoma cell lines. Leuk Res 2006;30(5):625–31.

[117] Golay J, et al. CD20 levels determine the in vitro susceptibility to rituximab and complement of B-cell chronic lymphocytic leukemia: further regulation by CD55 and CD59. Blood 2001;98(12):3383–9.

[118] Rezvani AR, Maloney DG. Rituximab resistance. Best Pract Res Clin Haematol 2011;24(2):203–16.

[119] Flieger D, et al. Mechanism of cytotoxicity induced by chimeric mouse human monoclonal antibody IDEC-C2B8 in CD20-expressing lymphoma cell lines. Cell Immunol 2000;204(1):55–63.

[120] Weng WK, Levy R. Two immunoglobulin G fragment C receptor polymorphisms independently predict response to rituximab in patients with follicular lymphoma. J Clin Oncol 2003;21(21):3940–7.

[121] Terszowski G, Klein C, Stern M. KIR/HLA interactions negatively affect rituximab- but not GA101 (obinutuzumab)-induced antibody-dependent cellular cytotoxicity. J Immunol 2014;192(12):5618–24.

[122] Olejniczak SH, et al. Acquired resistance to rituximab is associated with chemotherapy resistance resulting from decreased Bax and Bak expression. Clin Cancer Res 2008;14(5):1550–60.

[123] Johnson NA, et al. CD20 mutations involving the rituximab epitope are rare in diffuse large B-cell lymphomas and are not a significant cause of R-CHOP failure. Haematologica 2009;94(3):423–7.

[124] Beers SA, et al. Antigenic modulation limits the efficacy of anti-CD20 antibodies: implications for antibody selection. Blood 2010;115(25):5191–201.

[125] Valgardsdottir R, et al. Human neutrophils mediate trogocytosis rather than phagocytosis of CLL B cells opsonized with anti-CD20 antibodies. Blood 2017;129(19):2636–44.

[126] Miyake K, Karasuyama H. The role of trogocytosis in the modulation of immune cell functions. Cells 2021;10 (5):1255. https://doi.org/10.3390/cells10051255.

[127] Beum PV, et al. The shaving reaction: rituximab/CD20 complexes are removed from mantle cell lymphoma and chronic lymphocytic leukemia cells by THP-1 monocytes. J Immunol 2006;176(4):2600–9.

[128] Weiner GJ. Rituximab: mechanism of action. Semin Hematol 2010;47(2):115–23.

[129] Gong Q, et al. Importance of cellular microenvironment and circulatory dynamics in B cell immunotherapy. J Immunol 2005;174(2):817–26.

[130] Derenzini E, et al. Follicular lymphoma microenvironment signatures define patients subsets obtaining long term clinical benefit after single-agent first-line anti-CD20 immunotherapy. Blood 2021;138:3500.

[131] Illidge T, et al. Obinutuzumab in hematologic malignancies: lessons learned to date. Cancer Treat Rev 2015;41 (9):784–92.

[132] Herter S, et al. Preclinical activity of the type II CD20 antibody GA101 (obinutuzumab) compared with rituximab and ofatumumab in vitro and in xenograft models. Mol Cancer Ther 2013;12(10):2031–42.

[133] Wang SY, et al. NK-cell activation and antibody-dependent cellular cytotoxicity induced by rituximab-coated target cells is inhibited by the C3b component of complement. Blood 2008;111(3):1456–63.

[134] Kern DJ, et al. GA101 induces NK-cell activation and antibody-dependent cellular cytotoxicity more effectively than rituximab when complement is present. Leuk Lymphoma 2013;54(11):2500–5.
[135] Lim SH, et al. Fc gamma receptor IIb on target B cells promotes rituximab internalization and reduces clinical efficacy. Blood 2011;118(9):2530–40.
[136] Carlo-Stella C, et al. Glofitamab step-up dosing: updated efficacy data show high complete response rates in heavily pretreated relapsed/refractory (R/R) non-Hodgkin lymphoma (NHL) patients. Hematol Oncol 2021;39(S2).
[137] Piccione EC, et al. P1210: immune correlates of response to glofitamab: biomarker findings from a pivotal phase II expansion study in patients with relapsed or refractory (R/R) diffuse large B-cell lymphoma (DLBCL). HemaSphere 2022;6(Suppl):1096–7.
[138] Brouwer-Visser J, et al. Baseline biomarkers of T-cell function correlate with clinical responses to odronextamab (REGN1979), and loss of CD20 target antigen expression identified as a mechanism of treatment resistance. Blood 2020;136:10–1.
[139] Schuster SJ, et al. Characterization of CD20 expression loss as a mechanism of resistance to mosunetuzumab in patients with relapsed/refractory B-cell non-Hodgkin lymphomas. J Clin Oncol 2022;40(16_Suppl):7526.
[140] Ghilardi G, et al. CAR-T TREK through the lymphoma universe, to boldly go where no other therapy has gone before. Br J Haematol 2021;193(3):449–65.
[141] Sterner RC, Sterner RM. CAR-T cell therapy: current limitations and potential strategies. Blood Cancer J 2021;11 (4):69.
[142] Gumber D, Wang LD. Improving CAR-T immunotherapy: overcoming the challenges of T cell exhaustion. EBioMedicine 2022;77, 103941.
[143] Scholler N, et al. Tumor immune contexture is a determinant of anti-CD19 CAR T cell efficacy in large B cell lymphoma. Nat Med 2022;28(9):1872–82.
[144] Tan Su Yin E, Hu YX, Huang H. The breakthrough and the future: CD20 chimeric antigen receptor T-cell therapy for hematologic malignancies. ImmunoMedicine 2022;2(1), e1039.

CHAPTER

5

Targeted therapies for follicular lymphoma

Radhika Takiar[a] *and Tycel J. Phillips*[b]

[a]Division of Hematology and Oncology, Department of Internal Medicine, University of Michigan, Ann Arbor, MI, United States [b]Division of Lymphoma, Department of Hematology & Hematopoietic Cell Transplantation, City of Hope, Duarte, CA, United States

Abstract

Follicular lymphoma (FL) is not only the second most common lymphoma within the United States and Western Europe, but also the most common indolent non-Hodgkin's lymphoma (NHL) overall. Treatment for FL patients is variable and includes observation, radiation, or systemic therapy. As is the case with other NHL, the introduction of anti-CD20 antibodies such as rituximab to chemotherapy significantly improved patient outcomes. Although a minority, some FL patients relapse early within 24 months (POD24) of receipt of chemoimmunotherapy (CIT) or have refractory disease and tend to have worse outcomes compared to those who relapse later. The advent of several novel targeted therapies is expanding our treatment armamentarium and thus far has demonstrated reasonable efficacy with manageable toxicities. Unlike traditional cytotoxic chemotherapy, targeted therapies have different mechanisms of action that target tumor-specific mutations, B-cell survival pathways or utilize the immune system. This chapter highlights the targeted therapy options for relapsed/refractory FL that are approved or actively being investigated.

Abbreviations

ADC antibody-drug conjugate
ADCC antibody-dependent cellular cytotoxicity
AE adverse events
ASCT autologous stem cell transplantation
ASH American Society of Hematology
BR bendamustine and rituximab
BTK Bruton tyrosine kinase
CAR-T chimeric antigen receptor T cell
CI confidence interval
CIT chemoimmunotherapy
CK casein kinase
CR complete response

https://doi.org/10.1016/B978-0-443-19200-5.00021-X

CRS	cytokine release syndrome
DLBCL	diffuse large B-cell lymphoma
DOR	duration of response
EFS	event-free survival
EZH2	enhancer of zeste homolog 2
FFP	freedom from progression
FL	follicular lymphoma
GELF	Groupe d'Etude des Lymphomes Folliculaires
GY	gray
HPF	high-power field
HR	hazard ratio
ICANS	immune effector cell-associated neurotoxicity syndrome
ILROG	International Lymphoma Radiation Oncology Group
IMID	immunomodulatory
IV	intravenous
NHL	non-Hodgkin lymphoma
NK	natural killer
O	obinutuzumab
ORR	overall response rate
OS	overall survival
PD	progressive disease
PFS	progression-free survival
PI3K	phosphatidylinositol 3'kinase
POD24	progression of disease within 24 months
PR	partial response
R/R	relapsed/refractory
R2	rituximab and lenalidomide
R-CHOP	rituximab, cyclophosphamide, doxorubicin, vincristine, and prednisone
R-CVP	rituximab, cyclophosphamide, vincristine, prednisone
RT	radiation therapy
WT	wild type
ZO	zanubrutinib and obinutuzumab

Conflict of interest

No potential conflicts of interest were disclosed.

Introduction

Follicular lymphoma (FL) is the most common indolent lymphoma in the United States and Western Europe and is the second most common lymphoma overall [1]. The incidence of FL is 2.6 per 100,000 men and women per year based on age-adjusted cases between 2015 and 2019. The median age of diagnosis is 64 years according to the most recent SEER data [2]. FL has a variable presentation and long disease course due to its indolent, incurable nature. Typical sites of involvement include lymph nodes, though FL may also involve the spleen, bone marrow, GI tract, and peripheral blood. The majority of patients have stage III or IV disease at diagnosis [3].

Grading of FL is dependent on the number of centroblasts per high-power field (hpf): grade 1 (5/hpf), grade 2 (6–15/hpf), grade 3A (> 15/hpf, centrocytes present), and grade 3B (>15/hpf, solid sheets of centroblasts) [4]. Those with grade 3B FL are treated similarly to diffuse large B cell lymphoma (DLBCL). Typically for grade 1–3A FL, the preferred treatment is observation until there is an indication that warrants treatment. The rationale for this approach derives from the fact that earlier treatment has not shown an overall survival or cause-specific survival advantage when compared to observation alone in asymptomatic patients [5]. The Groupe d'Etude des Lymphomes Folliculaires (GELF) criteria are often used to determine indications for treatment and comprise of the following: a nodal/extranodal, etc. [6,7].

Although FL remains incurable due to both early and late relapses, there has been an improvement in outcomes over time during the rituximab era with 10-year overall survival (OS) of approximately 80% [8]. The backbone of the limited stage (Ann Arbor stage I or II) disease is radiation therapy (RT), as this has shown long-term disease control rates >90% with 10-year OS of 58%–86% along with 10-year progression-free survival (PFS) being 40%–59% [9–14]. A retrospective collaborative study led by the International Lymphoma Radiation Oncology Group (ILROG) was performed for stage I–II FL (grade 1–3A) patients who received ≥24 Gray (Gy) RT [9]. At a median follow-up of 52 months, 5-year freedom from progression (FFP) and OS were 68.9% and 96%, respectively. Based on the aforementioned data, there is likely a proportion of limited-stage FL patients who are cured with radiation alone. More recent data have suggested improvement in FFP with the addition of rituximab to RT but this has not translated to an OS benefit [15].

Initial management of advanced stage (III–IV) FL depends on patient and disease characteristics and must be individualized. For patients who are asymptomatic with a low burden of disease, observation is an option. Prospective randomized trials in the pre-rituximab era have not demonstrated an OS advantage with immediate treatment as opposed to watchful waiting among advanced-stage or asymptomatic FL patients [5,16]. Studies from the rituximab era have demonstrated that immediate treatment with rituximab may prolong the time to initiation of new therapy and prolong PFS; however, this has not translated to an OS advantage [17–19].

For patients with advanced stage FL who warrant treatment, various options exist, including bendamustine and rituximab (BR), lenalidomide and rituximab (R2), and rituximab, cyclophosphamide, doxorubicin, vincristine, and prednisone (R-CHOP) based on results from the StiL NHL1 [20,21], RELEVANCE [22], and BRIGHT [23,24] studies as outlined in Table 1. Although PFS was improved with BR over R-CHOP in the StiL trial (69.5 vs 31.2 months, HR 0.58), there was no difference in OS [20,21]. Often, the choice of initial

TABLE 1 Frontline chemoimmunotherapy for FL.

Trial	Regimen	FL patients (N)	Median follow-up (mo)	OS	*P* value
StiL NHL1	BR vs R-CHOP	279	113	10Y: 71% (BR) vs 66%	
BRIGHT	BR vs R-CHOP/R-CVP	314	65	5Y: 82% (BR) vs 85%	0.5461
RELEVANCE	R2 vs R-CHOP vs R-CVP vs BR	1030	38	3Y: 94% vs 94%	

regimen depends on patient factors since BR has a more favorable toxicity profile with lower rates of neutropenia, infections, and neuropathy compared to other CIT regimens such as R-CHOP or R-CVP. Maintenance therapy with rituximab for 2 years has demonstrated a durable PFS advantage (median PFS 10.5 years with rituximab vs 4.1 years with observation, $P < .001$); however, this has not led to a difference in OS [25,26].

CIT has remained the standard frontline option for patients with advanced-stage FL. Given its incurable nature, FL can have early or late relapses. Those with early relapses, which account for 20% of patients, are defined as "progression of disease within 24 months of diagnosis" (POD24). Two poor prognostic indicators in FL are POD24 or failure to achieve event-free survival (EFS) within 12 months after initial CIT. Data from the National LymphoCare Study has demonstrated that 5-year OS was 50% among the POD24 group as compared to 90% among those without early POD [27–29]. Several novel targeted therapies are actively being investigated within FL patients which will hopefully change the landscape for those with POD24 and even those with late relapses.

Lenalidomide

Lenalidomide is an oral immunomodulatory (IMiD) drug which binds to the cereblon E3 ubiquitin ligase complex resulting in rapid ubiquitination and degradation of the transcription factors, Ikaros and Aiolos, leading to anti-lymphoma effects [30]. Although this is one of the main mechanisms, others have been reported such as IMiD-mediated immune modulation that enhances rituximab effects via natural killer (NK)-cell expansion and antibody-dependent cellular cytotoxicity (ADCC) [31]. Not only is synergy between anti-CD20 directed therapy and lenalidomide seen in vitro, this has been validated in several early phase trials with the combination of Obinutuzumab or rituximab with lenalidomide in both FL and in other indolent non-Hodgkin's lymphomas (NHL) [32–34].

The study that led to the approval of R2 for the second-line and beyond was the AUGMENT trial [35]. Patients with marginal zone lymphoma (MZL) or FL who had received at least 1 prior line of therapy were eligible and randomized in a 1:1 fashion to either R2 or placebo with rituximab. Lenalidomide was dosed at 20 mg daily (10 mg daily for creatinine clearance 30–59 mL/min) on days 1–21 of 28-day cycles. Rituximab was given at 375 mg/m^2 weekly for cycle 1 and then only given on day 1 for the remainder of the cycles (2–5). Treatment was given for 12 cycles or until relapse, progressive disease (PD), or unacceptable toxicity. The primary endpoint was PFS. This phase III multicenter, double-blind study enrolled a total of 358 patients of whom 82% (295 patients) had FL with an even distribution across both arms. At a median follow-up of 28.3 months, PFS was markedly improved with R2 vs R + placebo at 39.4 vs 14.1 months, respectively (HR 0.46, 95% CI 0.34–0.62, $P < .001$).

Additionally, treatment with R2 led to improvement in the overall response rate (ORR) and complete response (CR) as compared to R + placebo, 78% vs 53% and 34% vs 18%, respectively. Although the trial was not powered to detect OS differences, patients with FL seemed to have better OS outcomes with R2 compared to R+ placebo (HR 0.45; 95% CI 0.22–0.92, $P = .02$). In regard to adverse events (AE), infections, neutropenia, and cutaneous reactions were more prevalent among R2 as compared to R + placebo. Five-year follow-up results presented as an abstract at the American Society of Hematology (ASH) 2022 meeting demonstrate ongoing superior efficacy of R2 over R+placebo for both PFS (27.6 vs 14.3 months, $P < .0001$) and OS [36] with similar safety results. A summary of targeted therapy options for relapsed/refractory (R/R) FL is outlined in Table 2.

As previously discussed, R2 has also been evaluated in untreated FL patients [22,33,45,46]. The most robust data in this setting comes from the RELEVANCE trial which was a multicenter, international phase 3 superiority trial comparing R2 to rituximab with

TABLE 2 Targeted therapy for relapsed FL.

Trial	Regimen	FL patients (N)	Median follow-up (mo)	PFS
AUGMENT	R2 vs R+placebo	295	28.3	39.4 mo vs 14.1 mo *P* value <0.001
DELTA	Idelalisib	72	9.7	11 mo
DYNAMO	Duvelisib	83	32.1	9.5 mo
CHRONOS-1	Copanlisib	104	31.5	12.5 mo
UNITY-NHL	Umbralisib	117	27.5	10.6 mo
TIDAL	Zandelisib	121	9.4	Pending
DAWN	Ibrutinib	110	27.7	4.6 mo
Bartlett et al. [37]	Ibrutinib	40	25.5	14 mo
Fowler et al. [38]	Acalabrutinib ±R	27	7.6	Pending
Phillips et al. [39]	Zanubrutinib	33	33.9	10.4 mo
Tam et al. [40]	Zanubrutinib + Obinutuzumab	36	20	25 mo
ROSEWOOD	Zanubrutinib ± Obinutuzumab	217	12.5	27.4 mo (ZO) vs 11.2 mo (O) *P* value: 0.004
Davids et al. [41]	Venetoclax	29		11 mo
CONTRALTO	Venetoclax + R Venetoclax + BR BR alone	163	18	
Morschhauser et al. [42]	Tazemetostat	99	22 (mutant) 35.9 (WT)	13.8 mo (mutant) 11.1 mo (WT)
ROMULUS	R-polatuzumab R-pinatuzumab	20 21	Not estimable	15.3 mo (R-pola) 12.7 mo (R-pina)
Diefenbach et al. [43]	Polatuzumab-vedotin + Obinutuzumab + lenalidomide	56	43.5	NR
Bannerji et al. [44]	Polatuzumab vedotin + Obinutuzumab + venetoclax	74	14.4	12 mo PFS: 73% mPFS NR

NR, *not reached.*

chemotherapy [22]. Patients were randomized to R2 which entailed lenalidomide 20 mg daily on days 2–22 of 28-day cycles for 6–12 total cycles based on confirmation of a CR (or dose reduced to 10 mg daily for creatinine clearance 30–59 mL/min) along with weekly rituximab 375 mg/m^2 for cycle 1 followed by rituximab on day 1 for the remaining cycles (2–6). Those in the rituximab-chemotherapy group received the investigator's choice of R-CHOP, BR, or R-CVP. All patients received maintenance monotherapy with rituximab for 12 cycles. Results are as outlined in Table 1. The primary endpoint of CR at 120 weeks was similar across both groups: 48% with R2 vs 53% with rituximab-chemotherapy ($P = .13$). Patients who received rituximab chemotherapy had higher rates of grade 3–4 neutropenia and febrile neutropenia; meanwhile, those in the R2 group had higher grade 3–4 cutaneous reactions. At 72 months of follow-up, PFS and OS remain similar across both groups without new safety signals, thus providing a chemotherapy-free alternative for untreated FL patients [47].

PI3K inhibitors

Another class of drugs that has been studied extensively within FL are the phosphatidylinositol 3′ kinase (PI3K) inhibitors. PI3K is a kinase that has a catalytic subunit with four different isoforms (alpha, beta, gamma, delta) and when activated, leads to downstream B cell receptor pathway activity leading to cell proliferation and survival. PI3K gamma and delta are expressed in hematopoietic cells and thus play more of a role in B-cell survival [48]. Currently, there is only one PI3K inhibitor, copanlisib, that remains FDA-approved at the moment, as the others were withdrawn based on various factors.

One of the first PI3K inhibitors to be studied in relapsed FL was idelalisib, an orally available, highly selective inhibitor of the delta isoform. A phase Ib study of idelalisib in relapsed indolent NHL established the phase II dose and demonstrated reasonable efficacy [49]. Based on these results, idelalisib was evaluated in an open-label, phase II trial (DELTA study) of 125 patients with relapsed indolent NHL at a dose of 150 mg twice daily until PD or intolerance [50]. This was a heavily pretreated population with a median of four prior lines of therapy. FL patients accounted for 58% of the study population and among these patients, ORR was 54% with 8% CR. The median follow-up was limited to 9.7 months with the median PFS across all patients being 11 months. The most common grade 3 or higher AEs were neutropenia (27%), elevations in serum alanine or aspartate aminotransferase (13%), diarrhea (13%), pneumonia (7%), and dyspnea (3%). Although idelalisib was initially approved for relapsed FL, it was later withdrawn in 2022 due to failure to complete the required phase III confirmatory study.

Another oral PI3K inhibitor that was evaluated in relapsed FL was duvelisib, which inhibits both the gamma and delta isoforms [51]. The DYNAMO study, a single-arm phase II, open-label trial, evaluated the efficacy and safety of duvelisib at 25 mg twice daily among R/R indolent NHL patients [52]. Of a total of 129 patients, 64% had FL. Median prior lines of therapy was three with the majority of patients being refractory to rituximab-based regimens. After a median follow-up of 32 months, the ORR (assessed by the independent review committee) among FL patients was 43% with only 1 patient attaining CR. The median PFS across the cohort was 9.5 months with median DOR being 10 months. The most frequent grade 3 or higher AEs were neutropenia (24.8%), diarrhea (14.7%), anemia (14.7%), colitis (7.8%), and pneumonitis (4.7%). A total of 17 patients died and 5 of these were considered treatment related. Although initially approved, duvelisib was also withdrawn from the market for relapsed FL due to failure to complete the required confirmatory study.

Currently, the only approved PI3K inhibitor is copanlisib which is an intravenous (IV) formulation that is a pan-class PI3K inhibitor but has more pronounced activity against the alpha and delta isoforms [53]. FDA approval for copanlisib was based on the CHRONOS-1 study which was a phase II, open-label trial for heavily pretreated R/R indolent NHL patients [54,55]. Patients were given copanlisib at 60 mg IV for 3 weeks on and 1 week off until PD or unacceptable toxicity. Of 142 patients, 73% had FL, and long-term outcomes among this cohort were notable for ORR 59% and CR 20%. Similar to prior PI3K inhibitor studies, this was also a heavily pretreated population with patients having received a median of three prior lines of therapy. The most common grade 3 AE were hyperglycemia (33%) and hypertension (24%) and for grade 4, neutropenia (15%) and hyperglycemia (7%). The incidence of class-specific AEs seems to be lower with copanlisib as compared to duvelisib and idelalisib which may be due to the intermittent dosing schedule. Additionally, hyperglycemia and hypertension seemed to be transient and would resolve during the off week of therapy. At the moment, copanlisib remains an option for R/R FL patients after at least two prior lines of therapy.

Umbralisib, an inhibitor of PI3K delta isoform and casein kinase-1 (CK1) epsilon, is another PI3K inhibitor that has been studied in the relapsed setting. This dual inhibition still allows for inhibition of the AKT pathway in B lymphoma cells; however, activity against CK1 epsilon disables WNT signaling which ultimately prevents detrimental effects to T regulatory cells' immunosuppressive activities, thereby leading to less immune-related toxicities [56]. UNITY-NHL was a phase IIb open-label study evaluating the efficacy and safety of umbralisib in R/R NHL [57]. Umbralisib was given orally at 800 mg daily until PD or unacceptable toxicity after FL patients had relapsed on at least two or more prior lines of therapy. Of a total of 208 patients, FL accounted for 56% and among this group, the ORR was 45.3% with a CR of 5%. There was a low incidence of umbralisib-related discontinuations (15%) and no deaths from AEs. However, after results from the UNITY-CLL trial were presented, umbralisib's approval was withdrawn for FL. Similar to the other withdrawals, this was related to several factors. During the COVID era, it was noted that the agents were linked to an increased risk of death by the FDA [58]; this in turn had an impact on the need for confirmatory studies to gain formal approval, which the companies behind the agents did not believe was possible with the current environment and requirements mandated by the FDA for approval. Zandelisib was also a PI3K delta inhibitor being evaluated in a phase II trial (TIDAL) which demonstrated an ORR of 78% with a CR of 35% [59]. Although zandelisib initially received fast-track designation, due to the aforementioned issues, development of this drug was halted outside of Japan in 2022.

BTK inhibitors

Bruton tyrosine kinase (BTK) is an essential part of the B-cell signaling cascade which ultimately leads to B-cell proliferation and survival [60]. There are several BTK inhibitors that have been evaluated among indolent NHL patients, notably ibrutinib, acalabrutinib, and zanubrutinib. These are orally bioavailable agents that irreversibly inhibit BTK via covalent binding to a cysteine residue (C481) within the ATP-binding pocket of BTK [61,62].

The first-in-class BTK inhibitor, ibrutinib, was evaluated as monotherapy for R/R FL in the DAWN study, an open-label, phase II trial [63]. FL patients who had relapsed or were refractory to two or more prior lines of therapy (including an anti-CD20 monoclonal antibody along with chemotherapy) received ibrutinib at 560 mg daily until PD or toxicity. The study enrolled 110 patients and at 28 months of follow-up, the ORR was 21% (95% CI, 13.7%–29.7%), which did not meet its primary endpoint, with a CR of 11%. Despite the lower than expected ORR, patients who responded seemed to have durable responses as the median DOR was 19 months. The rate of treatment discontinuation due to AE was low (6%) with the most common serious AEs being pneumonia, pleural effusion, atrial fibrillation, and diarrhea. Another phase II consortium study to evaluate ibrutinib monotherapy enrolled 40 patients with R/R FL after at least one prior line of therapy [37]. The ORR was 38% with a CR of 13% and a median DOR of 14 months. Sensitivity to rituximab was predictive of a higher response rate to therapy compared to those who were rituximab refractory (52.6% vs 16.7%, respectively, $P = .04$).

To further expand upon ibrutinib-based therapy, a phase II trial explored the combination of ibrutinib with rituximab in treatment-naïve FL patients [64,65]. In arm 1 of the study (main study), ibrutinib was given at 560 mg daily continuously until PD or unacceptable toxicity, and rituximab 375 mg/m^2 was given upfront weekly for 4 total doses. As demonstrated in Table 3, the median follow-up was 34 months with an ORR of 85%, a CR of 40%, and a median PFS of 42 months. As compared to historical outcomes with single-agent rituximab in the frontline setting (ORR 47%–58%) [66,67], the combination of ibrutinib and rituximab had a more favorable ORR. The PERSPECTIVE trial, a phase III, multicenter, double-blind placebo-controlled trial comparing ibrutinib in combination with rituximab vs placebo for treatment-naïve FL patients, is actively enrolling to determine whether there is a difference in PFS between the 2 groups (NCT02947347) [68]. SELENE is an example of another active phase III, randomized, double-blind, placebo-controlled trial comparing BR or R-CHOP with ibrutinib vs placebo in previously treated FL patients (NCT01974440) [69].

Acalabrutinib and zanubrutinib are highly selective second-generation BTK inhibitors, with less inhibition of off-target tyrosine kinases, thereby have fewer toxicities [61]. A phase Ib trial of acalabrutinib with or without rituximab was performed among treatment-naïve and R/R FL patients [38]. Rituximab was given (375 mg/m^2) weekly for cycle 1 and then given on day 1 of 28 day cycles for cycles 2–6 and acalabrutinib was administered at 100 mg daily until PD or intolerance. Among patients who received acalabrutinib with rituximab, the ORR was 92% and 39% with a CR of 31% and 8% in treatment-naïve and R/R patients, respectively. Median DOR and PFS have not yet been reached. This again demonstrates a trend toward the added benefit of rituximab to BTK inhibitors in the untreated setting.

TABLE 3 Frontline targeted therapy for FL.

Trial	Regimen	FL patients (N)	Median follow-up (mo)	PFS
Fowler et al. [64,65]	Ibrutinib + rituximab	60	34	41.9 mo
Fowler et al. [38]	Acalabrutinib ± R	13	22	Pending

Results from a multicenter single-arm phase I/II study of zanubrutinib in R/R FL (after at least 1 prior line of therapy) and MZL were recently reported [39]. Zanubrutinib was dosed at 320 mg once daily with the option to switch to 160 mg twice daily until PD or unacceptable toxicity. At a median follow-up of 34 months, ORR and CR rates among the FL cohort were 36.4% and 18.2%, respectively. Treatment was relatively well tolerated with bleeding in 55% of patients but only 1 patient with major hemorrhage, no atrial fibrillation/flutter, and ≥grade 3 infections accounting for 30%, none of which were opportunistic. Incidence of grade ≥3 neutropenia was seen in 18% of FL patients but without higher rates of febrile neutropenia or sepsis.

Zanubrutinib has previously demonstrated safety in combination with obinutuzumab (ZO) [40]. This led to the ROSEWOOD trial which is a phase 2 randomized study to assess the efficacy and safety of ZO compared to obinutuzumab (O) alone in R/R FL patients [70]. Patients who had progressed after at least two prior lines of therapy were randomized in a 2:1 fashion to ZO vs O alone. Obinutuzumab was given weekly for cycle 1 and then administered on day 1 of subsequent cycles (2–6) and then every 8 weeks until a maximum of 20 doses and zanubrutinib was administered at 160 mg twice daily continuously. This trial did allow for a crossover for those who progressed on obinutuzumab alone. At a median follow-up of 12.5 months, the study met its primary endpoint which demonstrated improved ORR among ZO compared to O at 68.3% vs 45.8% ($P = .0017$). Other outcomes such as a CR, an 18-month DOR, and a median PFS also favored ZO over O. Grade 3 or higher AEs with an incidence of >5% were neutropenia (22%) and thrombocytopenia (14%) in the ZO group, and major bleeding was low at 1.4%. Overall, ZO seemed to have favorable responses with a tolerable toxicity profile, and longer-term follow-up will be necessary to better understand whether these responses remain durable, but the combination is being further explored in a phase III trial vs R2 (MAHOGANY, NCT05100862).

BCL-2 inhibitor

The hallmark genetic alteration in FL is translocation t(14;18) which translocates the BCL-2 oncogene at chromosome 18q21.33 to an immunoglobulin heavy chain and thereby leads to overexpression of BCL-2 (anti-apoptotic protein) [71,72]. Despite being a selective oral inhibitor of BCL-2 (BH-3 mimetic), venetoclax response rates in FL have been modest at best. A phase I study evaluated the safety and efficacy of venetoclax when administered to R/R NHL patients [41]. A total of 106 patients were enrolled, 29 of whom had FL with an ORR of 38%, a CR of 14%, and a median PFS of 11 months. The most common grade 3–4 toxicities were cytopenias in 10%–15% of patients. Within the FL cohort, higher doses of venetoclax (1200 mg) led to a higher ORR (44%).

Furthermore, combinations with venetoclax have also been explored in R/R FL patients, specifically in the CONTRALTO trial [73]. The study enrolled 163 patients who were divided into three arms: (A) venetoclax and rituximab, (B) venetoclax and BR, and (C) BR alone. The primary endpoint was to evaluate the efficacy of venetoclax and BR compared to BR or venetoclax and rituximab. ORR was similar in arms B and C at 84%, but lower with arm A at 35%. Fewer patients (61%) in arm B received ≥90% of the planned dose compared to the other groups which was likely a result of AE-related treatment discontinuation. Incidence of grade 3–4 AE was highest in arm B (94%) as compared to 50%–60% in the other groups. This study suggests potential synergistic effects when venetoclax is combined with rituximab, though the combination of venetoclax to BR has similar efficacy to BR alone but significantly worse toxicity.

Several ongoing trials are investigating combinations with venetoclax in treatment-naïve FL patients, such as lenalidomide with venetoclax and obinutuzumab (LEVERAGE, NCT03980171) and PrECOG 0403 (venetoclax with obinutuzumab and bendamustine) [74].

EZH2 inhibitor

A histone methyltransferase, an enhancer of zeste homolog 2 (EZH2), is an epigenetic regulator that is important in cell cycle progression, autophagy, and apoptosis and promotes DNA damage repair [75–77]. Gain of function mutations in EZH2 lead to increased H3K27 trimethylation which ultimately leads to silencing of genes required for cell cycle regulation, and these mutations can be seen in approximately 25%–30% of FL patients.

Tazemetostat is an oral small-molecule inhibitor of EZH2 that has been investigated in NHL. A phase I study evaluated the safety and maximum tolerated dose of tazemetostat among R/R NHL patients and advanced solid tumors [78]. Tazemetostat was found to have a favorable safety profile with recommended phase II dosing at 800mg twice daily. ORR among R/R NHL patients was 38%. Subsequently, an international phase II trial was performed to evaluate the ORR of tazemetostat among R/R FL patients after at least two prior lines of systemic therapy [42]. Patients were further characterized based on the EZH2 mutational status: mutant (44 patients) vs wild type (WT) (54 patients). Tazemetostat was administered at 800mg twice daily in continuous 28-day cycles until PD or unacceptable toxicity for up to 2years. Median prior lines of therapy were 2–3 across both cohorts. The primary endpoints of ORR in the EZH2 mutant and WT cohorts were 69% (95% CI 53–82) and 35% (95% CI 23–49), respectively. Additionally, among patients who were considered "double refractory," meaning they had relapsed on rituximab and chemotherapy induction within 6months, ORR was still 20%–30%. The median PFS was 13.8months among the EZH2 mutant patients vs 11.1months in the WT cohort. A significant difference was only noted in those with an EZH2 mutation who had POD24 vs WT POD24 patients, thus suggesting that the EZH2 mutational status may play a role with POD24 patients. Based on these results, the EZH2 mutation is not warranted for most patients being treated with tazemetostat. Overall, treatment was well tolerated as there were only 8 patients who experienced ≥grade 3 AE, all of which were cytopenias. Based on these results, tazemetostat was FDA approved for FL patients (irrespective of the EZH2 mutation status) after at least 2 prior systemic therapies.

Patients who received 2years of therapy on the aforementioned phase II trial were eligible to continue treatment in a rollover study: TruST (NCT02875548) which is to evaluate the long-term safety profile along with OS and time to treatment failure. Furthermore, combinations with tazemetostat are being actively investigated, such as in the SYMPHONY-1 phase Ib/III trial combining tazemetostat with lenalidomide and rituximab among patients with R/R FL after at least 1 prior line of therapy (NCT04224493). Results from the phase Ib study were presented at ASH in 2022 with the recommended phase III dosing of tazemetostat being 800mg twice daily. The most common grade 3–4 AE was neutropenia (34%). Among 41 patients, the ORR was 98% with 51% attaining a CR and among POD24 patients (n = 11), the ORR was 100% [79].

Antibody-drug conjugates

An antibody-drug conjugate (ADC), a targeted monoclonal antibody that is conjugated to a cytotoxic agent with a protease-cleavable linker, is becoming available for various types of NHL. These agents bind to the specific target antigen, get internalized, and upon cleavage of the linker within the endosome/lysosome, the cytotoxic agent gets released intracellularly. Polatuzumab vedotin and pinatuzumab vedotin are ADC bound to a microtubule inhibitor (monomethyl auristatin E) that targets CD79b and CD22, respectively [80,81]. The ROMULUS study was a phase II trial performed to evaluate the safety and tolerability of rituximab with polatuzumab vedotin or pinatuzumab vedotin among both relapsed DLBCL and FL patients [82]. FL patients were stratified by rituximab refractory (no response or relapse in less than 6months from last rituximab treatment) or relapsed disease (relapse >6months after rituximab therapy). Rituximab was given with polatuzumab or pinatuzumab at 2.4mg/kg every 3weeks until PD or intolerance. A total of 41 FL patients were assessed with approximately half receiving each therapy. The ORR was 70% in the rituximab-polatuzumab group with 45% (9 patients) attaining a CR. The median PFS within the R-polatuzumab group was 15.3months with the median OS not reached. The most common AE was peripheral neuropathy with an incidence of 65% in the polatuzumab arm. Due to 8% of patients having grade 3–4 peripheral sensory neuropathy, it was recommended to dose reduce polatuzumab vedotin to 1.8mg/kg with a maximum of 6–8cycles of therapy.

Furthermore, polatuzumab vedotin has been studied in combination with BR vs BR alone and demonstrated a similar rate of PET-CR between the groups (69% with pola-BR vs 63% BR) and a median PFS of 17 vs 17.3months [83]. More recently, several studies have been evaluating combination therapy with polatuzumab vedotin. A phase Ib/II trial evaluated the safety and efficacy of polatuzumab vedotin with obinutuzumab and lenalidomide for R/R patients after at least 1 line of prior therapy [43]. Patients were given six 28-day cycles followed by maintenance obinutuzumab and lenalidomide (24months) for the responders or those with stable disease. At the end of induction, the ORR was 76% with a CR of 61%. Although the response rates were favorable, there was a fair amount of grade 3–4 toxicity (86%) with the most common grade 3–4 AE being cytopenias and infections. Another ongoing study evaluated the combination of polatuzumab vedotin with Obinutuzumab and venetoclax for 6cycles among R/R FL patients followed by maintenance Obinutuzumab and venetoclax for 8months [44]. After a median follow-up of 14.4months, the 12-month PFS was 73% with the median PFS not reached. At the end of induction, the ORR was 78% with a CR of 57%. Toxicity rates remained high with grade 3–4 AE among 73% of patients, most of which included neutropenia, thrombocytopenia, and infections. Longer follow-up will be necessary in these studies to gain a better understanding of PFS benefits and long-term toxicities.

Loncastuximab tesirine is another ADC but targets CD19 and has a pyrrolobenzodiazepine dimer as the payload [84]. The safety and efficacy of loncastuximab tesirine have been studied in a phase I dose-escalation and dose-expansion study of R/R NHL patients [85,86]. The majority of patients enrolled had DLBCL with a smaller proportion having FL (8%). The ORR among FL patients was 79% with a CR of 64% (nine patients). The median PFS could not be determined with the FL arm and the median OS was not reached. The main toxicities were neutropenia, fatigue, edema, and transaminitis.

Bispecific antibody

Within several hematologic malignancies, a treatment that has demonstrated efficacy in the relapsed/refractory setting and has the potential to be "off the shelf" and easy to administer is a bispecific antibody. Generally speaking, bispecific antibodies are polypeptides that have effector-binding arms that bind to CD3 on T cells and can be directed against epitopes on the surface of tumor cells [87]. In the case of lymphoma, bispecific antibodies become the intermediary between malignant B-cells and effector T-cells which ultimately allows for T-cell-mediated cytotoxicity. Several types of bispecific antibodies have been studied within FL and in December 2022, mosunetuzumab was FDA approved for R/R FL after two or more prior lines of systemic therapy. A summary of the bispecific antibodies is outlined in Table 4.

Mosunetuzumab is a humanized Ig-1 antibody with two antigen-binding Fab arms that target CD3 on T cells and CD20 on malignant B cells with a linked Fc fragment [93]. It was initially studied in a phase I trial of 62 R/R FL patients who had received at least two prior lines of therapy and were given step-up dosing on days 1 and 8 with a target dose on day 15 for cycle 1 and then was given at full dose for subsequent 21–day cycles [88]. This was a heavily pretreated population with a median of three prior lines of therapy and approximately 48% had POD24. Results from the step-up dosing group presented at the ASH Meeting in 2020 demonstrated an ORR of 68% with 50% attaining a CR. Even among patients with double refractory disease, POD24, or prior chimeric antigen receptor T-cell (CAR-T) therapy, the ORR ranged between 50% and 78%. The median DOR was 20.4 months with a median PFS of 11.8 months. There was a small incidence of cytokine release syndrome (CRS) at 23% with the majority being grade 1–2 and neurologic AE at 45% but all being grade 1–2.

Promising results for mosunetuzumab as outlined above led to a phase II international study evaluating mosunetuzumab among FL patients who had relapsed/refractory disease after at least two or more prior lines of therapy [89,94]. After step-up dosing, intravenous mosunetuzumab was given every 21 days and if patients attained a CR after cycle 8, treatment was discontinued; however, if they had a partial response (PR) or stable disease, treatment

TABLE 4 Bispecific antibodies for FL.

Trial	Regimen	FL patients (N)	ORR/CR (%)	Any grade CRS (%)	Any grade neurotoxicity (%)
Assouline et al. [88]	Mosunetuzumab	62	68/50	23	45
Bartlett et al. [89]	Mosunetuzumab	90	78/60	44	
ELM-2	Odronextamab	85	81/75	51	3
Morschhauser et al. [90]	Glofitamab monotherapy	53	81/70	66	0
Hutchings et al. [91,92]	Epcoritamab	12	90/50	59 (Overall)	6 (Overall)

was continued for up to 17 cycles. At a median follow-up of 18 months, 90 patients were enrolled with 53% having POD24. The median number of cycles was 8 and the ORR was 72%. The study met its primary endpoint which was a higher rate of CR (60%) compared to historical control with copanlisib (14%). The most common AE was CRS which occurred in 44% of patients though majority were grade 1–2 and occurred only with cycle 1. The most frequent grade 3–4 AEs included neutropenia (27%), hypophosphatemia (17%), hyperglycemia (8%), and anemia (8%). Updated analysis was presented at the ASH 2022 meeting which demonstrated durable responses at the 27-month follow-up without new serious or fatal toxicities [89]. Due to high rates of durable responses with a fixed duration of therapy in a heavily pretreated population, the FDA approved mosunetuzumab in December 2022. There are several active trials investigating the safety and efficacy of mosunetuzumab when given as a combination therapy in FL.

Another bispecific antibody that has been investigated in R/R FL is odronextamab (REGN1979) which is a hinge-stabilized CD20 × CD3 bispecific antibody, which is fully human with a common light chain purified by protein A chromatography [95]. In a phase I multicenter study, odronextamab was given weekly for 12 doses followed by every 2 weeks until PD or AE among R/R NHL patients (145) of whom 40 patients had FL [96,97]. Among the FL cohort, patients who received a dose of 5 mg or higher had an ORR of 91% with a CR of 72% and the median PFS was 17 months. A prespecified analysis of the FL cohort from the ELM-2 study reported efficacy results for 85 R/R FL patients with a median follow-up of 17 months [98]. Patients were given intravenous odronextamab in 21-day cycles with step-up dosing within cycle 1 followed by a full dose at 80 mg weekly until the end of cycle 4 and maintenance dosing at 160 mg every 2 weeks until PD or toxicity. ORR assessed by the independent central review was 81% with a CR rate of 75%. These responses were durable with the median duration of CR being 18 months and a median PFS of 20 months. Although the incidence of any grade CRS was 51%, after implementing the 0.7/4/20 step-up regimen, there was no subsequent grade 2 or higher CRS.

Glofitamab is an intravenous bispecific antibody that has a 2:1 configuration with two CD20 binding domains and one CD3 binding domain and due to this bivalent CD20 binding, it was found to have higher potency than other bispecific antibodies in preclinical studies [99]. A study done by Morschhauser et al. [90] evaluated glofitamab as monotherapy and in combination with Obinutuzumab among R/R FL patients. Among the monotherapy cohort, ORR and CR were 81% and 70%, respectively. In the combination cohort (19 patients), the ORR was 100% with a CR of 74%. The incidence of CRS was 66%–79%, though only 1 patient across both groups had grade 3 CRS. Additionally, the use of glofitamab as monotherapy or in combinaion led to a reasonable ORR ranging from 43% to 70% among the high-risk subgroups (double-refractory, POD24, PI3K inhibitor refractory).

Epcoritamab (GEN3013) is a subcutaneous formulation of a bispecific antibody derived from a humanized mouse antihuman CD3 monoclonal antibody and a human anti-CD20 monoclonal antibody [100]. Unlike the aforementioned bispecific antibodies, epcoritamab cannot induce T-cell cytotoxicity through Fc-mediated effector functions due to the silencing of the Fc region by 3-point mutations. This modification along with subcutaneous administration demonstrated delayed and lower peak cytokine levels which thereby could potentially reduce CRS severity. In a phase I/II open-label dose escalation trial, epcoritamab was assessed among R/R NHL patients of whom there were 12 FL patients [91,92]. Patients were given epcoritamab weekly for cycles 1–2, every 2 weeks for cycles 3–6, and then every 4 weeks thereafter in 28-day cycles. Compared to prior bispecific antibody studies, these patients were heavily pretreated with a median of 4.5 prior lines of therapy. Among patients who received 0.76–48 mg dosing, the ORR was 90% with 50% (five patients) achieving a CR. The incidence of CRS across all patients was 59%, though this was only grade 1–2. Injection site reactions were common at 47% though predominantly grade 1. Neurologic toxicity was reported in four patients, although only two of them were grade 3 or higher. Results from this trial suggested that subcutaneous epcoritamab was not only efficacious but had limited severity of CRS. Combinations with epcoritamab are actively being investigated such as epcoritamab with R2 [101].

Chimeric antigen receptor T-cell therapy

Autologous anti-CD19 CAR-T is a type of cellular therapy that requires a harvest of autologous T cells which are then expanded ex vivo and transfected with lenti- or retroviral vectors containing RNA that encodes chimeric antigen receptors to recognize CD19 on malignant B cells [102].

ZUMA-5 was a single-arm, multicenter phase II trial performed to evaluate the ORR of axicabtagene ciloleucel (Yescarta) given to patients with R/R indolent NHL (FL and marginal zone lymphoma) after they had progressed on two or more prior lines of therapy [103]. A total of 148 patients were enrolled of whom 84% had FL. At a median follow-up of 17.5 months, ORR and CR among the FL cohort were 94% and 79%, respectively. These responses were durable since 74% of FL who attained a CR maintained remission at the time of data cutoff. The rates of CRS were high at 78% within the FL cohort; however, only 6% had grade 3 or higher CRS. The overall incidence of grade 3–4 neurologic toxicity was seen in 15% of the FL cohort. Additionally, there was 1 treatment-related death for a patient with multisystem organ failure.

Tisagenlecleucel (Kymriah) is another type of anti-CD-19 directed CAR-T but has a different costimulatory domain (4-1BB) compared to Yescarta (CD28). ELARA was a phase II multicenter trial with a primary endpoint of CR among R/R FL patients who progressed after two or more prior lines of therapy or autologous stem cell transplantation (ASCT) [104]. Of 98 patients who were enrolled, 97 received tisagenlecleucel. Baseline characteristics were notable for a median of four prior lines of therapy, POD24 accounting for 63% of patients, and 68% who were double refractory. At a median follow-up of 17 months, the CR rate was 69% with an ORR of 86%. The median DOR, PFS, and OS have not yet been reached and a longer-term follow-up will be necessary. Within 8 weeks of infusion, CRS occurred in 49% of patients, all of which were grade 1–2, and immune effector cell-associated neurotoxicity syndromes (ICANS) were seen in 4% of patients.

Unlike the bispecific antibodies, CAR-T therapy is a one-time treatment that may be easier for certain patients; however, it is restricted to larger academic centers and does have a higher incidence overall of CRS and ICANS.

Conclusions

FL remains the most common indolent B-cell lymphoma and although incurable at this time, given the relapsing/remitting nature, patients are often living for an extended period of time. One of the main challenges in this disease is among patients with early progression (POD24), as their overall survival is inferior to those without POD24. To address this patient population and others with multiple relapses, several novel targeted therapies are actively being investigated. These have ranged from therapies that target FL-specific mutations (venetoclax, tazemetostat), survival pathways (BTK inhibitors and PI3K inhibitors), B cell targeted therapy (ADC), or immunomodulatory agents (lenalidomide, bispecific antibodies, CAR-T). Several of these agents have demonstrated durable responses with minimal toxicity in the relapsed setting, which has led to clinical studies evaluating their efficacy and safety when given in combination. Longer-term follow-up will be necessary to ensure the durability of response without added toxicity before these agents get approved for frontline use. Hopefully, in the future, there will be a better way to identify patients who warrant chemotherapy-free regimens with the goal of prolonging progression-free survival and maintaining quality of life in FL patients (Fig. 1).

Future perspectives

Although treatment options available for relapsed/refractory FL have increased over time, the challenge that lies ahead is to determine the optimal sequencing of these therapies in the

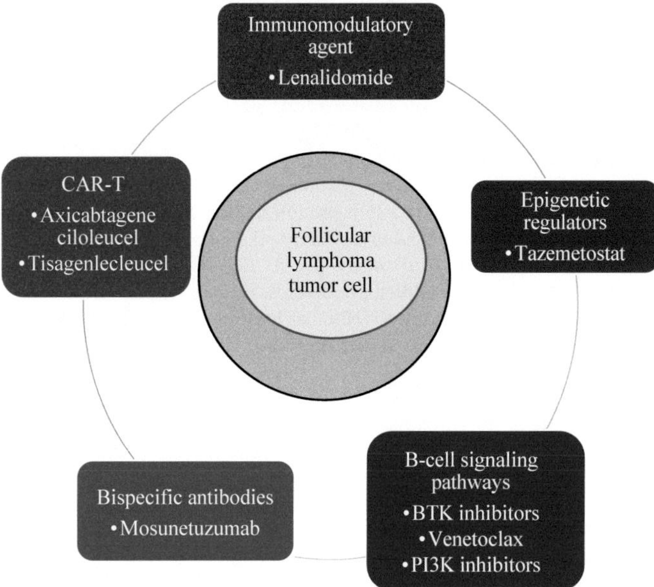

FIG. 1 Classes of approved novel targeted therapy options in follicular lymphoma.

absence of robust comparative studies. At the moment, the decision for the next line of therapy is dependent on patient characteristics (comorbidities, fitness, age), social factors (financial, transportation/distance to an institution with CAR-T or bispecific antibodies), and disease characteristics (e.g., POD24 vs late relapses). At the time of diagnosis, various prognostic and risk stratification tools exist, such as the Follicular Lymphoma International Prognostic Index [105]; however, besides POD24, there is a lack of similar prognostic tools at the time of relapse. Therefore, future investigation with correlative studies analyzing biomarkers pre- and posttreatment may be necessary to help us better understand trends of tumor biology and thereby create treatment algorithms for R/R FL patients.

Acknowledgments

None to report.

References

[1] Teras LR, DeSantis CE, Cerhan JR, Morton LM, Jemal A, Flowers CR. 2016 US lymphoid malignancy statistics by World Health Organization subtypes. CA Cancer J Clin 2016;66(6):443–59. [Internet]; [cited 2023 Feb 24]. Available from: https://pubmed.ncbi.nlm.nih.gov/27618563/.

[2] Follicular lymphoma—cancer stat facts. [Internet]; [cited 2023 Feb 24]. Available from: https://seer.cancer.gov/statfacts/html/follicular.html.

[3] Swerdlow SH, Campo E, Harris NL, Jaffe ES, Pileri SA, Thiele J. WHO classification of tumours of haematopoietic and lymphoid tissues. Geneva: WHO Press; 2017. 176–8, 171–5, 168–70, 150–1 p.

[4] Swerdlow SH, Campo E, Pileri SA, Lee Harris N, Stein H, Siebert R, et al. The 2016 revision of the World Health Organization classification of lymphoid neoplasms. Blood 2016;127(20):2375–90. [Internet]; [cited 2022 Apr 6]. Available from: https://ashpublications.org/blood/article/127/20/2375/35286/The-2016-revision-of-the-World-Health-Organization.

[5] Ardeshna KM, Smith P, Norton A, Hancock BW, Hoskin PJ, MacLennan KA, et al. Long-term effect of a watch and wait policy versus immediate systemic treatment for asymptomatic advanced-stage non-Hodgkin lymphoma: a randomised controlled trial. Lancet 2003;362(9383):516–22. [Internet]; [cited 2023 Feb 24]. Available from: https://pubmed.ncbi.nlm.nih.gov/12932382/.

[6] Brice P, Bastion Y, Lepage E, Brousse N, Haïoun C, Moreau P, et al. Comparison in low-tumor-burden follicular lymphomas between an initial no-treatment policy, prednimustine, or interferon alfa: a randomized study from the Groupe d'Etude des Lymphomes Folliculaires. Groupe d'Etude des Lymphomes de l'Adulte. J Clin Oncol 2016;15(3):1110–7. https://doi-org.proxy.lib.umich.edu/101200/JCO19971531110.

[7] Solal-Céligny P, Lepage E, Brousse N, Tendler CL, Brice P, Haïoun C, et al. Doxorubicin-containing regimen with or without interferon alfa-2b for advanced follicular lymphomas: final analysis of survival and toxicity in the Groupe d'Etude des Lymphomes Folliculaires 86 trial. J Clin Oncol 2016;16(7):2332–8. https://doi.org/10.1200/JCO19981672332.

[8] Sarkozy C, Maurer MJ, Link BK, Ghesquieres H, Nicolas E, Thompson CA, et al. Cause of death in follicular lymphoma in the first decade of the rituximab era: a pooled analysis of French and US cohorts. J Clin Oncol 2019;37(2):144–52. [Internet]; [cited 2023 Mar 10]. Available from: https://pubmed.ncbi.nlm.nih.gov/30481079/.

[9] Brady JL, Binkley MS, Hajj C, Chelius M, Chau K, Balogh A, et al. Definitive radiotherapy for localized follicular lymphoma staged by 18F-FDG PET-CT: a collaborative study by ILROG. Blood 2019;133(3):237–45. [Internet]; [cited 2023 Mar 10]. Available from: https://pubmed.ncbi.nlm.nih.gov/30446493/.

[10] Vaughan Hudson B, Vaughan Hudson G, MacLennan KA, Anderson L, Linch DC. Clinical stage 1 non-Hodgkin's lymphoma: long-term follow-up of patients treated by the British National Lymphoma Investigation with radiotherapy alone as initial therapy. Br J Cancer 1994;69(6):1088–93. [Internet]; [cited 2023 Mar 10]. Available from: https://pubmed.ncbi.nlm.nih.gov/8198975/.

[11] Kamath SS, Marcus RB, Lynch JW, Mendenhall NP. The impact of radiotherapy dose and other treatment-related and clinical factors on in-field control in stage I and II non-Hodgkin's lymphoma. Int J Radiat Oncol Biol Phys 1999;44(3):563–8. [Internet]; [cited 2023 Mar 10]. Available from: https://pubmed.ncbi.nlm.nih.gov/10348285/.

[12] Mac Manus MP, Hoppe RT. Is radiotherapy curative for stage I and II low-grade follicular lymphoma? Results of a long-term follow-up study of patients treated at Stanford University. J Clin Oncol 1996;14(4):1282–90. [Internet]; [cited 2023 Mar 10]. Available from: https://pubmed.ncbi.nlm.nih.gov/8648385/.

[13] Wilder RB, Jones D, Tucker SL, Fuller LM, Ha CS, McLaughlin P, et al. Long-term results with radiotherapy for stage I-II follicular lymphomas. Int J Radiat Oncol Biol Phys 2001;51(5):1219–27. [Internet]; [cited 2023 Mar 10]. Available from: https://pubmed.ncbi.nlm.nih.gov/11728680/.

[14] Campbell BA, Voss N, Woods R, Gascoyne RD, Morris J, Pickles T, et al. Long-term outcomes for patients with limited stage follicular lymphoma: involved regional radiotherapy versus involved node radiotherapy. Cancer 2010;116(16):3797–806. [Internet]; [cited 2023 Mar 10]. Available from: https://pubmed.ncbi.nlm.nih.gov/20564082/.

[15] Ruella M, Filippi AR, Bruna R, Di Russo A, Magni M, Caracciolo D, et al. Addition of rituximab to involved-field radiation therapy prolongs progression-free survival in stage I-II follicular lymphoma: results of a multicenter study. Int J Radiat Oncol Biol Phys 2016;94(4):783–91. [Internet]; [cited 2023 Apr 26]. Available from: https://pubmed.ncbi.nlm.nih.gov/26972651/.

[16] Brice P, Bastion Y, Lepage E, Brousse N, Haïoun C, Moreau P, et al. Comparison in low-tumor-burden follicular lymphomas between an initial no-treatment policy, prednimustine, or interferon alfa: a randomized study from the Groupe d'Etude des Lymphomes Folliculaires. Groupe d'Etude des Lymphomes de l'Adulte. J Clin Oncol 1997;15(3):1110–7. [Internet]; [cited 2023 Mar 10]. Available from: https://pubmed.ncbi.nlm.nih.gov/9060552/.

[17] Solal-Celigny P, Bellei M, Marcheselli L, Pesce EA, Pileri S, McLaughlin P, et al. Watchful waiting in low-tumor burden follicular lymphoma in the rituximab era: results of an F2-study database. J Clin Oncol 2012;30(31):3848–53. [Internet]; [cited 2023 Mar 10]. Available from: https://pubmed.ncbi.nlm.nih.gov/23008294/.

[18] Ardeshna KM, Qian W, Smith P, Braganca N, Lowry L, Patrick P, et al. Rituximab versus a watch-and-wait approach in patients with advanced-stage, asymptomatic, non-bulky follicular lymphoma: an open-label randomised phase 3 trial. Lancet Oncol 2014;15(4):424–35. [Internet]; [cited 2023 Mar 10]. Available from: https://pubmed.ncbi.nlm.nih.gov/24602760/.

[19] Nastoupil LJ, Sinha R, Byrtek M, Ziemiecki R, Zhou X, Taylor M, et al. Outcomes following watchful waiting for stage II-IV follicular lymphoma patients in the modern era. Br J Haematol 2016;172(5):724–34. [Internet]; [cited 2023 Mar 10]. Available from: https://pubmed.ncbi.nlm.nih.gov/26729445/.

[20] Rummel MJ, Niederle N, Maschmeyer G, Banat GA, Von Grünhagen U, Losem C, et al. Bendamustine plus rituximab versus CHOP plus rituximab as first-line treatment for patients with indolent and mantle-cell lymphomas: an open-label, multicentre, randomised, phase 3 non-inferiority trial. Lancet 2013;381(9873):1203–10. [Internet]; [cited 2022 Apr 25]. Available from: https://pubmed.ncbi.nlm.nih.gov/23433739/.

[21] Rummel MJ, Maschmeyer G, Ganser A, Heider A, von Gruenhagen U, Losem C, et al. Bendamustine plus rituximab (B-R) versus CHOP plus rituximab (CHOP-R) as first-line treatment in patients with indolent lymphomas: nine-year updated results from the StiL NHL1 study. J Clin Oncol 2017;35(15 Suppl):7501. https://doi.org/10.1200/JCO20173515_suppl7501.

[22] Morschhauser F, Fowler NH, Feugier P, Bouabdallah R, Tilly H, Palomba ML, et al. Rituximab plus lenalidomide in advanced untreated follicular lymphoma. N Engl J Med 2018;379(10):934–47. [Internet]; [cited 2023 Mar 11]. Available from: https://www.nejm.org/doi/full/10.1056/NEJMoa1805104.

[23] Flinn IW, Van Der Jagt R, Kahl BS, Wood P, Hawkins TE, MacDonald D, et al. Randomized trial of bendamustine-rituximab or R-CHOP/R-CVP in first-line treatment of indolent NHL or MCL: the BRIGHT study. Blood 2014;123(19):2944–52. [Internet]; [cited 2022 Aug 8]. Available from: https://pubmed.ncbi.nlm.nih.gov/24591201/.

[24] Flinn IW, Van Der Jagt R, Kahl B, Wood P, Hawkins T, MacDonald D, et al. First-line treatment of patients with indolent non-Hodgkin lymphoma or mantle-cell lymphoma with bendamustine plus rituximab versus R-CHOP or R-CVP: results of the BRIGHT 5-year follow-up study. J Clin Oncol 2019;37(12):984–91. [Internet]; [cited 2022 Apr 25]. Available from: https://pubmed.ncbi.nlm.nih.gov/30811293/.

[25] Salles G, Seymour JF, Offner F, López-Guillermo A, Belada D, Xerri L, et al. Rituximab maintenance for 2 years in patients with high tumour burden follicular lymphoma responding to rituximab plus chemotherapy (PRIMA): a phase 3, randomised controlled trial. Lancet 2011;377(9759):42–51. [Internet]; [cited 2023 Mar 11]. Available from: https://pubmed.ncbi.nlm.nih.gov/21176949/.

[26] Bachy E, Seymour JF, Feugier P, Offner F, López-Guillermo A, Belada D, et al. Sustained progression-free survival benefit of rituximab maintenance in patients with follicular lymphoma: long-term results of the PRIMA study. J Clin Oncol 2019;37(31):2815–24. [Internet]; [cited 2023 Mar 11]. Available from: https://pubmed.ncbi.nlm.nih.gov/31339826/.

[27] Casulo C, Byrtek M, Dawson KL, Zhou X, Farber CM, Flowers CR, et al. Early relapse of follicular lymphoma after rituximab plus cyclophosphamide, doxorubicin, vincristine, and prednisone defines patients at high risk for death: an analysis from the national LymphoCare study. J Clin Oncol 2015;33(23):2516. [Internet]; [cited 2023 Mar 11]. Available from: /pmc/articles/PMC4879714/.

[28] Maurer MJ, Bachy E, Ghesquières H, Ansell SM, Nowakowski GS, Thompson CA, et al. Early event status informs subsequent outcome in newly diagnosed follicular lymphoma. Am J Hematol 2016;91(11):1096–101. [Internet]; [cited 2023 Mar 11]. Available from: https://pubmed.ncbi.nlm.nih.gov/27465588/.

[29] Casulo C, Dixon JG, Le-Rademacher J, Hoster E, Hochster HS, Hiddemann W, et al. Validation of POD24 as a robust early clinical end point of poor survival in FL from 5225 patients on 13 clinical trials. Blood 2022;139(11):1684–93. [Internet]; [cited 2023 Mar 11]. Available from: https://pubmed.ncbi.nlm.nih.gov/34614146/.

[30] Gandhi AK, Kang J, Havens CG, Conklin T, Ning Y, Wu L, et al. Immunomodulatory agents lenalidomide and pomalidomide co-stimulate T cells by inducing degradation of T cell repressors Ikaros and Aiolos via modulation of the E3 ubiquitin ligase complex CRL4CRBN. Br J Haematol 2014;164(1):811. [Internet]; [cited 2022 Aug 9]. Available from: /pmc/articles/PMC4232904/.

[31] Wu L, Adams M, Carter T, Chen R, Muller G, Stirling D, et al. Lenalidomide enhances natural killer cell and monocyte-mediated antibody-dependent cellular cytotoxicity of rituximab-treated CD20+ tumor cells. Clin Cancer Res 2008;14(14):4650–7. [Internet]; [cited 2022 Aug 9]. Available from: https://pubmed.ncbi.nlm.nih.gov/18628480/.

[32] Bachy E, Houot R, Feugier P, Bouabdallah K, Bouabdallah R, Virelizier EN, et al. Obinutuzumab plus lenalidomide in advanced, previously untreated follicular lymphoma in need of systemic therapy: a LYSA study. Blood 2022;139(15):2338–46. [Internet]; [cited 2023 Mar 15]. Available from: https://pubmed.ncbi.nlm.nih.gov/34936697/.

[33] Fowler NH, Davis RE, Rawal S, Nastoupil L, Hagemeister FB, McLaughlin P, et al. Safety and activity of lenalidomide and rituximab in untreated indolent lymphoma: an open-label, phase 2 trial. Lancet Oncol 2014;15(12):1311–8. [Internet]; Nov 1 [cited 2023 Mar 15]. Available from: https://pubmed.ncbi.nlm.nih.gov/25439689/.

[34] Morschhauser F, Salles G, Le Gouill S, Tilly H, Thieblemont C, Bouabdallah K, et al. An open-label phase 1b study of obinutuzumab plus lenalidomide in relapsed/refractory follicular B-cell lymphoma. Blood 2018;132(14):1486–94. [Internet]; [cited 2023 Mar 15]. Available from: https://pubmed.ncbi.nlm.nih.gov/30068505/.

[35] Leonard JP, Trneny M, Izutsu K, Fowler NH, Hong X, Zhu J, et al. AUGMENT: a phase III study of lenalidomide plus rituximab versus placebo plus rituximab in relapsed or refractory indolent lymphoma. J Clin Oncol 2019;37(14):1188–99.

[36] Leonard JP, Trneny M, Offner F, Mayer J, Zhang H, Nowakowski GS, et al. Five-year results and overall survival update from the phase 3 randomized study augment: lenalidomide plus rituximab (R2) vs rituximab plus placebo in patients with relapsed/refractory indolent non-Hodgkin lymphoma. Blood 2022;140(Supplement 1):561–3.

[37] Bartlett NL, Costello BA, LaPlant BR, Ansell SM, Kuruvilla JG, Reeder CB, et al. Single-agent ibrutinib in relapsed or refractory follicular lymphoma: a phase 2 consortium trial. Blood 2018;131(2):182–90. [Internet]; [cited 2023 Apr 3]. Available from: https://ashpublications.org/blood/article/131/2/182/37018/Single-agent-ibrutinib-in-relapsed-or-refractory.

[38] Fowler NH, Coleman M, Stevens DA, Smith SM, Venugopal P, Martin P, et al. Acalabrutinib alone or in combination with rituximab (R) in follicular lymphoma (FL). 2018;36(15 Suppl):7549. https://doi.org/10.1200/JCO20183615_suppl7549.

[39] Phillips T, Chan H, Tam CS, Tedeschi A, Johnston P, Oh SY, et al. Zanubrutinib monotherapy in relapsed/refractory indolent non-Hodgkin lymphoma. Blood Adv 2022;6(11):3472–9. [Internet]; [cited 2023 Apr 3]. Available from: https://ashpublications.org/bloodadvances/article/6/11/3472/484634/Zanubrutinib-monotherapy-in-relapsed-refractory.

[40] Tam CS, Quach H, Nicol A, Badoux X, Rose H, Miles Prince H, et al. Zanubrutinib (BGB-3111) plus obinutuzumab in patients with chronic lymphocytic leukemia and follicular lymphoma. Blood Adv 2020;4(19):4802–11. [Internet]; [cited 2023 Apr 3]. Available from: https://ashpublications.org/bloodadvances/article/4/19/4802/464076/Zanubrutinib-BGB-3111-plus-obinutuzumab-in.

[41] Davids MS, Roberts AW, Seymour JF, Pagel JM, Kahl BS, Wierda WG, et al. Phase I first-in-human study of Venetoclax in patients with relapsed or refractory non-Hodgkin lymphoma. J Clin Oncol 2017;35(8):826–33. [Internet]; [cited 2022 Aug 9]. Available from: https://pubmed.ncbi.nlm.nih.gov/28095146/.
[42] Morschhauser F, Tilly H, Chaidos A, McKay P, Phillips T, Assouline S, et al. Tazemetostat for patients with relapsed or refractory follicular lymphoma: an open-label, single-arm, multicentre, phase 2 trial. Lancet Oncol 2020;21(11):1433–42. [Internet]; [cited 2023 Apr 11]. Available from: https://pubmed.ncbi.nlm.nih.gov/33035457/.
[43] Diefenbach CS, Kahl BS, Banerjee L, McMillan AK, Miall F, Briones J, et al. A phase Ib/II study of polatuzumab vedotin plus obinutuzumab and lenalidomide in patients with relapsed/refractory follicular lymphoma: final analysis and progression-free survival update. Blood 2022;140(Suppl. 1):2286–8. [Internet]; [cited 2023 Apr 18]. Available from: https://ashpublications.org/blood/article/140/Supplement 1/2286/490640/A-Phase-Ib-II-Study-of-Polatuzumab-Vedotin-Plus.
[44] Bannerji R, Yuen S, Phillips TJ, Arthur C, Isufi I, Marlton P, et al. Polatuzumab vedotin + obinutuzumab + venetoclax in patients with relapsed/refractory (R/R) follicular lymphoma (FL): primary analysis of a phase 1b/2 trial. J Clin Oncol 2021;39(15 Suppl):7534.
[45] Zucca E, Rondeau S, Vanazzi A, Østenstad B, Mey UJM, Rauch D, et al. Short regimen of rituximab plus lenalidomide in follicular lymphoma patients in need of first-line therapy. Blood 2019;134(4):353–62. [Internet]; [cited 2023 Apr 1]. Available from: https://pubmed.ncbi.nlm.nih.gov/31101627/.
[46] Martin P, Jung SH, Pitcher B, Bartlett NL, Blum KA, Shea T, et al. A phase II trial of lenalidomide plus rituximab in previously untreated follicular non-Hodgkin's lymphoma (NHL): CALGB 50803 (Alliance). Ann Oncol 2017;28 (11):2806–12. [Internet]; [cited 2023 Apr 1]. Available from: https://pubmed.ncbi.nlm.nih.gov/28945884/.
[47] Morschhauser F, Nastoupil L, Feugier P, De Colella JMS, Tilly H, Palomba ML, et al. Six-year results from RELEVANCE: lenalidomide plus rituximab (R2) versus rituximab-chemotherapy followed by rituximab maintenance in untreated advanced follicular lymphoma. J Clin Oncol 2022;3239–45 [Lippincott Williams and Wilkins].
[48] Vanhaesebroeck B, Guillermet-Guibert J, Graupera M, Bilanges B. The emerging mechanisms of isoform-specific PI3K signalling. Nat Rev Mol Cell Biol 2010;11:329–41. [Internet]; Nature Publishing Group [cited 2023 Apr 1]. Available from: https://www.nature.com/articles/nrm2882.
[49] Flinn IW, Kahl BS, Leonard JP, Furman RR, Brown JR, Byrd JC, et al. Idelalisib, a selective inhibitor of phosphatidylinositol 3-kinase-δ, as therapy for previously treated indolent non-Hodgkin lymphoma. Blood 2014;123(22):3406–13. [Internet]; [cited 2023 Apr 1]. Available from: https://pubmed.ncbi.nlm.nih.gov/24615776/.
[50] Gopal AK, Kahl BS, de Vos S, Wagner-Johnston ND, Schuster SJ, Jurczak WJ, et al. PI3Kδ inhibition by Idelalisib in patients with relapsed indolent lymphoma. N Engl J Med 2014;370(11):1008–18. [Internet]; [cited 2023 Apr 1]. Available from: /pmc/articles/PMC4039496/.
[51] Flinn IW, O'Brien S, Kahl B, Patel M, Oki Y, Foss FF, et al. Duvelisib, a novel oral dual inhibitor of PI3K-d,g, is clinically active in advanced hematologic malignancies. Blood 2018;131(8):877–87. [Internet]; [cited 2023 Apr 1]. Available from: https://pubmed.ncbi.nlm.nih.gov/29191916/.
[52] Flinn IW, Miller CB, Ardeshna KM, Tetreault S, Assouline SE, Mayer J, et al. DYNAMO: a phase II study of duvelisib (IPI-145) in patients with refractory indolent non-hodgkin lymphoma. J Clin Oncol 2019;912–22. [Internet]; [cited 2023 Apr 1]. Available from: https://pubmed.ncbi.nlm.nih.gov/30742566/.
[53] Liu N, Rowley BR, Bull CO, Schneider C, Haegebarth A, Schatz CA, et al. BAY 80-6946 is a highly selective intravenous PI3K inhibitor with potent p110α and p110δ activities in tumor cell lines and xenograft models. Mol Cancer Ther 2013;12(11):2319–30. [Internet]; [cited 2023 Apr 2]. Available from: https://pubmed.ncbi.nlm.nih.gov/24170767/.
[54] Dreyling M, Panayiotidis P, Egyed M, Follows G, Mollica L, Nagler A, et al. Efficacy of copanlisib monotherapy in patients with relapsed or refractory marginal zone lymphoma: subset analysis from the CHRONOS-1 trial. Blood 2017;130(Suppl. 1):4053. [Internet]; [cited 2023 Apr 2]. Available from: https://ashpublications.org/blood/article/130/Supplement 1/4053/72576/Efficacy-of-Copanlisib-Monotherapy-in-Patients.
[55] Dreyling M, Santoro A, Mollica L, Leppä S, Follows G, Lenz G, et al. Long-term safety and efficacy of the PI3K inhibitor copanlisib in patients with relapsed or refractory indolent lymphoma: 2-year follow-up of the CHRONOS-1 study. Am J Hematol 2020;95(4):362–71. [Internet]; [cited 2023 Apr 2]. Available from: https://pubmed.ncbi.nlm.nih.gov/31868245/.

[56] Maharaj K, Powers JJ, Achille A, Mediavilla-Varela M, Gamal W, Burger KL, et al. The dual PI3Kδ/CK1ε inhibitor umbralisib exhibits unique immunomodulatory effects on CLL T cells. Blood Adv 2020;4(13):3072–84. [Internet]; [cited 2023 Apr 2]. Available from: https://pubmed.ncbi.nlm.nih.gov/32634240/.

[57] Fowler NH, Samaniego F, Jurczak W, Ghosh N, Derenzini E, Reeves JA, et al. Umbralisib, a dual PI3Kδ/CK1ε inhibitor in patients with relapsed or refractory indolent lymphoma. J Clin Oncol 2021;39(15):1609–18.

[58] Gribben J. Umbralisib plus ublituximab (U2) is superior to obinutuzumab plus chlorambucil (O+Chl) in patients with treatment naïve (TN) and relapsed/refractory (R/R) chronic lymphocytic leukemia (CLL): results from the phase 3 unity-CLL study. ASH; 2020.

[59] Zelenetz AD, Jurczak W, Ribrag V, Linton K, Collins GP, López-Jiménez J, et al. Efficacy and safety of zandelisib administered by intermittent dosing (ID) in patients with relapsed or refractory (R/R) follicular lymphoma (FL): primary analysis of the global phase 2 study TIDAL. J Clin Oncol 2022;40(16 Suppl):7511. https://doi.org/10.1200/JCO20224016_suppl7511.

[60] Valla K, Flowers CR, Koff JL. Targeting the B cell receptor pathway in non-Hodgkin lymphoma. Expert Opin Investig Drugs 2018;27(6):513–22. [Internet]; [cited 2023 Apr 3]. Available from: https://pubmed.ncbi.nlm.nih.gov/29855199/.

[61] Shirley M. Bruton tyrosine kinase inhibitors in B-cell malignancies: their use and differential features. Target Oncol 2022;17(1):69–84. [Internet]; [cited 2023 Apr 3]. Available from: https://link.springer.com/article/10.1007/s11523-021-00857-8.

[62] Honigberg LA, Smith AM, Sirisawad M, Verner E, Loury D, Chang B, et al. The Bruton tyrosine kinase inhibitor PCI-32765 blocks B-cell activation and is efficacious in models of autoimmune disease and B-cell malignancy. Proc Natl Acad Sci USA 2010;107(29):13075–80. [Internet]; [cited 2023 Apr 3]. Available from: https://pubmed.ncbi.nlm.nih.gov/20615965/.

[63] Gopal AK, Schuster SJ, Fowler NH, Trotman J, Hess G, Hou JZ, et al. Ibrutinib as treatment for patients with relapsed/refractory follicular lymphoma: results from the open-label, multicenter, phase II DAWN study. J Clin Oncol 2018;36(23):2405–12.

[64] Fowler N, Nastoupil L, de Vos S, Knapp M, Flinn IW, Chen R, et al. Ibrutinib plus rituximab in treatment-naive patients with follicular lymphoma: results from a multicenter, phase 2 study. Blood 2015;126(23):470. [Internet]; [cited 2023 Apr 3]. Available from: https://ashpublications.org/blood/article/126/23/470/93337/Ibrutinib-Plus-Rituximab-in-Treatment-Naive.

[65] Fowler NH, Nastoupil L, De Vos S, Knapp M, Flinn IW, Chen R, et al. The combination of ibrutinib and rituximab demonstrates activity in first-line follicular lymphoma. Br J Haematol 2020;189(4):650–60. [Internet]; [cited 2023 Apr 3]. Available from: https://pubmed.ncbi.nlm.nih.gov/32180219/.

[66] Hainsworth JD, Litchy S, Burris HA, Scullin DC, Corso SW, Yardley DA, et al. Rituximab as first-line and maintenance therapy for patients with indolent non-Hodgkin's lymphoma. J Clin Oncol 2002;20(20):4261–7. [Internet]; [cited 2023 Apr 3]. Available from: https://pubmed.ncbi.nlm.nih.gov/12377971/.

[67] Freedman A, Neelapu SS, Nichols C, Robertson MJ, Djulbegovic B, Winter JN, et al. Placebo-controlled phase III trial of patient-specific immunotherapy with mitumprotimut-T and granulocyte-macrophage colony-stimulating factor after rituximab in patients with follicular lymphoma. J Clin Oncol 2009;27(18):3036–43. [Internet]; [cited 2023 Apr 3]. Available from: https://pubmed.ncbi.nlm.nih.gov/19414675/.

[68] Rule S, Flinn IW, Fowler N, Chen R, Kwei L, Beaupre DM, et al. Phase 3 study of ibrutinib in combination with rituximab versus placebo in combination with rituximab in patients with treatment-naïve follicular lymphoma (perspective). Hematol Oncol 2017;35:427–8. [Internet]; [cited 2023 Apr 3]. Available from: https://onlinelibrary.wiley.com/doi/full/10.1002/hon.2440_12.

[69] Fowler NH, Hiddemann W, Leonard J, Larsen JS, Rose E, Zhuang SH, et al. A phase III study of ibrutinib in combination with either bendamustine and rituximab (BR) or rituximab, cyclophosphamide, doxorubicin, vincristine, and prednisone (R-CHOP) in patients with previously treated follicular lymphoma or marginal zone lymphoma. J Clin Oncol 2015;33(15 Suppl), TPS8601. https://doi.org/10.1200/jco20153315_suppl.tps8601.

[70] Zinzani PL, Mayer J, Auer R, Bijou F, de Oliveira AC, Flowers C, et al. Zanubrutinib plus obinutuzumab (ZO) versus obinutuzumab (O) monotherapy in patients (pts) with relapsed or refractory (R/R) follicular lymphoma (FL): primary analysis of the phase 2 randomized ROSEWOOD trial. J Clin Oncol 2022;40(16 Suppl):7510. https://doi.org/10.1200/JCO20224016_suppl7510.

[71] Adams CM, Clark-Garvey S, Porcu P, Eischen CM. Targeting the Bcl-2 family in B cell lymphoma. Front Oncol 2019;8(January). [Internet]; [cited 2023 Apr 3]. Available from: https://pubmed.ncbi.nlm.nih.gov/30671383/.

[72] Bakhshi A, Wright JJ, Graninger W, Seto M, Owens J, Cossman J, et al. Mechanism of the t(14;18) chromosomal translocation: structural analysis of both derivative 14 and 18 reciprocal partners. Proc Natl Acad Sci USA 1987;84(8):2396. [Internet]; [cited 2023 Apr 3]. Available from: /pmc/articles/PMC304658/?report=abstract.

[73] Zinzani PL, Flinn IW, Yuen SLS, Topp MS, Rusconi C, Fleury I, et al. Venetoclax-rituximab with or without bendamustine vs bendamustine-rituximab in relapsed/refractory follicular lymphoma. Blood 2020;136 (23):2628–37. [Internet]; [cited 2023 Apr 3]. Available from: https://pubmed.ncbi.nlm.nih.gov/32785666/.

[74] Portell CA, Jegede O, Wagner-Johnston ND, Nowakowski GS, Fletcher CD, Cohen JB, et al. Phase II study of venetoclax in combination with obinutuzumab and bendamustine in patients with high tumor burden follicular lymphoma as front line therapy (PrECOG 0403). Blood 2021;138(Supplement 1):814.

[75] Bödör C, Grossmann V, Popov N, Okosun J, O'Riain C, Tan K, et al. EZH2 mutations are frequent and represent an early event in follicular lymphoma. Blood 2013;122(18):3165. [Internet]; [cited 2023 Apr 11]. Available from: /pmc/articles/PMC3814734/.

[76] Duan R, Du W, Guo W. EZH2: a novel target for cancer treatment. J Hematol Oncol 2020;13(1):1–12. [Internet]; [cited 2023 Apr 11]. Available from: https://jhoonline.biomedcentral.com/articles/10.1186/s13045-020-00937-8.

[77] Devan J, Janikova A, Mraz M. New concepts in follicular lymphoma biology: from BCL2 to epigenetic regulators and non-coding RNAs. Semin Oncol 2018;45(5–6):291–302.

[78] Italiano A, Soria JC, Toulmonde M, Michot JM, Lucchesi C, Varga A, et al. Tazemetostat, an EZH2 inhibitor, in relapsed or refractory B-cell non-Hodgkin lymphoma and advanced solid tumours: a first-in-human, open-label, phase 1 study. Lancet Oncol 2018;19(5):649–59. [Internet]; [cited 2023 Apr 11]. Available from: https://pubmed.ncbi.nlm.nih.gov/29650362/.

[79] Batlevi CL, Salles G, Park SI, Phillips TJ, Amengual JE, Andorsky D, et al. Tazemetostat in combination with lenalidomide and rituximab in patients with relapsed/refractory follicular lymphoma: phase 1b results of symphony-1. Blood 2022;140(Suppl. 1):2296–8.

[80] Dornan D, Bennett F, Chen Y, Dennis M, Eaton D, Elkins K, et al. Therapeutic potential of an anti-CD79b antibody-drug conjugate, anti-CD79b-vc-MMAE, for the treatment of non-Hodgkin lymphoma. Blood 2009;114(13):2721–9. [Internet]; [cited 2023 Apr 18]. Available from: https://pubmed.ncbi.nlm.nih.gov/19633198/.

[81] Li D, Poon KA, Yu SF, Dere R, Go MA, Lau J, et al. DCDT2980S, an anti-CD22-monomethyl auristatin E antibody-drug conjugate, is a potential treatment for non-hodgkin lymphoma. Mol Cancer Ther 2013;12 (7):1255–65. [Internet]; [cited 2023 Apr 18]. Available from: https://pubmed.ncbi.nlm.nih.gov/23598530/.

[82] Morschhauser F, Flinn IW, Advani R, Sehn LH, Diefenbach C, Kolibaba K, et al. Polatuzumab vedotin or pinatuzumab vedotin plus rituximab in patients with relapsed or refractory non-Hodgkin lymphoma: final results from a phase 2 randomised study (ROMULUS). Lancet Haematol 2019;6(5):e254–65. [Internet]; [cited 2023 Apr 18]. Available from: https://pubmed.ncbi.nlm.nih.gov/30935953/.

[83] Sehn LH, Kamdar M, Herrera AF, McMillan A, Flowers C, Kim WS, et al. Randomized phase 2 trial of polatuzumab vedotin (pola) with bendamustine and rituximab (BR) in relapsed/refractory (r/r) FL and DLBCL. J Clin Oncol 2018;36(15 Suppl):7507.

[84] Zammarchi F, Corbett S, Adams L, Tyrer PC, Kiakos K, Janghra N, et al. ADCT-402, a PBD dimer-containing antibody drug conjugate targeting CD19-expressing malignancies. Blood 2018;1094–105. [Internet]; American Society of Hematology [cited 2023 Apr 18]. Available from: https://ashpublications.org/blood/article/131/10/1094/36428/ADCT-402-a-PBD-dimer-containing-antibody-drug.

[85] Hamadani M, Radford J, Carlo-Stella C, Caimi PF, Reid E, O'Connor OA, et al. Final results of a phase 1 study of loncastuximab tesirine in relapsed/refractory B-cell non-Hodgkin lymphoma. Blood 2021;137(19):2634–45. Available from: https://ashpublications.org/blood/article/137/19/2634/474210/Final-results-of-a-phase-1-study-of-loncastuximab.

[86] Kahl BS, Hamadani M, Radford J, Carlo-Stella C, Caimi P, Reid E, et al. A phase I study of ADCT-402 (loncastuximab tesirine), a novel pyrrolobenzodiazepine-based antibody–drug conjugate, in relapsed/refractory B-cell non-Hodgkin lymphoma. Clin Cancer Res 2019;25(23):6986–94. Available from: https://pubmed.ncbi.nlm.nih.gov/31685491/.

[87] Choi BD, Cai M, Bigner DD, Mehta AI, Kuan CT, Sampson JH. Bispecific antibodies engage T cells for antitumor immunotherapy. Expert Opin Biol Ther 2011;11:843–53. [Internet]; [cited 2023 Apr 18]. Available from: https://pubmed.ncbi.nlm.nih.gov/21449821/.

[88] Assouline SE, Kim WS, Sehn LH, Schuster SJ, Cheah CY, Nastoupil LJ, et al. Mosunetuzumab shows promising efficacy in patients with multiply relapsed follicular lymphoma: updated clinical experience from a phase I dose-escalation trial. Blood 2020;136(Suppl. 1):42–4. [Internet]; [cited 2023 Apr 21]. Available from: https://ashpublications.org/blood/article/136/Supplement 1/42/470472/Mosunetuzumab-Shows-Promising-Efficacy-in-Patients.

[89] Bartlett NL, Sehn LH, Matasar MJ, Schuster SJ, Assouline S, Giri P, et al. Mosunetuzumab monotherapy demonstrates durable efficacy with a manageable safety profile in patients with relapsed/refractory follicular lymphoma who received ≥2 prior therapies: updated results from a pivotal phase II study. Blood 2022;140(Suppl. 1):1467–70. Available from: https://ashpublications.org/blood/article/140/Supplement 1/1467/487300/Mosunetuzumab-Monotherapy-Demonstrates-Durable.

[90] Morschhauser F, Carlo-Stella C, Dickinson M, Phillips T, Houot R, Offner F, et al. Glofitamab as monotherapy and in combination with obinutuzumab induces high complete response rates in patients (pts) with multiple relapsed or refractory (R/R) follicular lymphoma (FL). Blood 2021;138(Suppl. 1):128. [Internet]; [cited 2023 Apr 22]. Available from: https://ashpublications.org/blood/article/138/Supplement 1/128/478030/Glofitamab-As-Monotherapy-and-in-Combination-with.

[91] Hutchings M, Mous R, Clausen MR, Johnson P, Linton KM, Chamuleau MED, et al. Subcutaneous epcoritamab induces complete responses with an encouraging safety profile across relapsed/refractory B-cell non-Hodgkin lymphoma subtypes, including patients with prior CAR-T therapy: updated dose escalation data. Blood 2020;136(Suppl. 1):45–6. [Internet]; [cited 2023 Apr 22]. Available from: https://ashpublications.org/blood/article/136/Supplement 1/45/470017/Subcutaneous-Epcoritamab-Induces-Complete.

[92] Hutchings M, Mous R, Clausen MR, Johnson P, Linton KM, Chamuleau MED, et al. Dose escalation of subcutaneous epcoritamab in patients with relapsed or refractory B-cell non-Hodgkin lymphoma: an open-label, phase 1/2 study. Lancet 2021;398(10306):1157–69. [Internet]; [cited 2023 Apr 22]. Available from: http://www.thelancet.com/article/S0140673621008898/fulltext.

[93] Sun LL, Ellerman D, Mathieu M, Hristopoulos M, Chen X, Li Y, et al. Anti-CD20/CD3 T cell-dependent bispecific antibody for the treatment of B cell malignancies. Sci Transl Med 2015;7(287). [Internet]; [cited 2023 Apr 21]. Available from: https://www.science.org/doi/10.1126/scitranslmed.aaa4802.

[94] Budde LE, Sehn LH, Matasar M, Schuster SJ, Assouline S, Giri P, et al. Safety and efficacy of mosunetuzumab, a bispecific antibody, in patients with relapsed or refractory follicular lymphoma: a single-arm, multicentre, phase 2 study. Lancet Oncol 2022;23(8):1055–65. Available from: http://www.thelancet.com/article/S1470204522003357/fulltext.

[95] Smith EJ, Olson K, Haber LJ, Varghese B, Duramad P, Tustian AD, et al. A novel, native-format bispecific antibody triggering T-cell killing of B-cells is robustly active in mouse tumor models and cynomolgus monkeys. Sci Rep 2015;5:17943. [Internet]; [cited 2023 Apr 22]. Available from: www.nature.com/scientificreports.

[96] Bannerji R, Allan JN, Arnason JE, Brown JR, Advani R, Ansell SM, et al. Odronextamab (REGN1979), a human CD20 x CD3 bispecific antibody, induces durable, complete responses in patients with highly refractory B-cell non-Hodgkin lymphoma, including patients refractory to CAR T therapy. Blood 2020;136(Suppl. 1):42–3. [Internet]; [cited 2023 Apr 22]. Available from: https://ashpublications.org/blood/article/136/Supplement 1/42/470008/Odronextamab-REGN1979-a-Human-CD20-x-CD3.

[97] Bannerji R, Arnason JE, Advani RH, Brown JR, Allan JN, Ansell SM, et al. Odronextamab, a human CD20×CD3 bispecific antibody in patients with CD20-positive B-cell malignancies (ELM-1): results from the relapsed or refractory non-Hodgkin lymphoma cohort in a single-arm, multicentre, phase 1 trial. Lancet Haematol 2022;9(5):e327–39. [Internet]; [cited 2023 Apr 22]. Available from: https://pubmed.ncbi.nlm.nih.gov/35366963/.

[98] Kim TM, Taszner M, Cho S-G, Novelli S, Le Gouill S, Poon ML, et al. Odronextamab in patients with relapsed/refractory (R/R) follicular lymphoma (FL) grade 1-3a: results from a prespecified analysis of the pivotal phase II study ELM-2. Blood 2022;140(Suppl. 1):2280–2. [Internet]; [cited 2023 Apr 22]. Available from: https://ashpublications.org/blood/article/140/Supplement 1/2280/490642/Odronextamab-in-Patients-with-Relapsed-Refractory.

[99] Bacac M, Colombetti S, Herter S, Sam J, Perro M, Chen S, et al. CD20-TCB with obinutuzumab pretreatment as next-generation treatment of hematologic malignancies. Clin Cancer Res 2018;24(19):4785–97. [Internet]; [cited 2023 Apr 22]. Available from: https://pubmed.ncbi.nlm.nih.gov/29716920/.

[100] Engelberts PJ, Hiemstra IH, de Jong B, Schuurhuis DH, Meesters J, Beltran Hernandez I, et al. DuoBody-CD3xCD20 induces potent T-cell-mediated killing of malignant B cells in preclinical models and provides opportunities for subcutaneous dosing. EBioMedicine 2020;52. [Internet]; [cited 2023 Apr 22]. Available from: https://pubmed.ncbi.nlm.nih.gov/31981978/.

[101] Falchi L, Leppä S, Wahlin BE, Nijland M, Christensen JH, De Vos S, et al. Subcutaneous epcoritamab with rituximab + lenalidomide (R 2) in patients (pts) with relapsed or refractory (R/R) follicular lymphoma (FL): update from phase 1/2 trial. J Clin Oncol 2022;40(16 Suppl):7524.

[102] Ramos CA, Heslop HE, Brenner MK. CAR-T cell therapy for lymphoma. Annu Rev Med 2016;67:165–83. [Internet]; [cited 2023 Apr 22]. Available from: https://pubmed.ncbi.nlm.nih.gov/26332003/.

[103] Jacobson CA, Chavez JC, Sehgal AR, William BM, Munoz J, Salles G, et al. Axicabtagene ciloleucel in relapsed or refractory indolent non-Hodgkin lymphoma (ZUMA-5): a single-arm, multicentre, phase 2 trial. Lancet Oncol 2022;23(1):91–103. [Internet]; [cited 2023 Apr 22]. Available from: https://pubmed.ncbi.nlm.nih.gov/34895487/.

[104] Fowler NH, Dickinson M, Dreyling M, Martinez-Lopez J, Kolstad A, Butler J, et al. Tisagenlecleucel in adult relapsed or refractory follicular lymphoma: the phase 2 ELARA trial. Nat Med 2022;28(2):325–32. [Internet]; [cited 2023 Apr 22]. Available from: https://www.nature.com/articles/s41591-021-01622-0.

[105] Solal-Céligny P, Roy P, Colombat P, White J, Armitage JO, Arranz-Saez R, et al. Follicular lymphoma international prognostic index. Blood 2004;104(5):1258–65. [Internet]; [cited 2023 May 3]. Available from: https://pubmed.ncbi.nlm.nih.gov/15126323/.

CHAPTER

6

Treatment of relapsed follicular lymphoma

Silvia Montoto

Department of Haemato-Oncology, St Bartholomew's Hospital, Barts Health NHS Trust, London, United Kingdom

Abstract

Follicular lymphoma (FL) is the second most frequent subtype of non-Hodgkin's lymphoma, and, as the most common indolent lymphoma, it represents the paradigm of indolent lymphomas. It is characterized by a typical pattern of responses followed by relapses or progressions, and although the outcome of patients with FL has significantly improved in the last decades (principally thanks to the introduction of anti-CD20 monoclonal antibodies), this is a disease that is still considered incurable in 2022 (at least with conventional chemotherapy). Thus, the expectation when treating patients with FL is that they will relapse, so thinking ahead of future treatment options is generally recommended. The knowledge on the biology of FL has significantly increased in the last years and this has led to the introduction of multiple new targeted drugs, expanding the number of treatment options. However, patients with FL are often asymptomatic, even at relapse, so preserving and optimizing a good quality of life by not overtreating patients is of utmost importance. In contrast, there are subsets of patients with a distinctly worse prognosis, such as those who experience an early relapse or those with histological transformation, and, if fit for it, they should be treated more intensively.

Abbreviations

CAR-T Chimeric antigen receptor T-cells
CR complete response
CT cellular therapy
DLBCL diffuse large B-cell lymphoma
EBMT European Society for Blood and Marrow Transplantation
EFS event-free survival
FL follicular lymphoma
HDT-ASCR high-dose therapy with autologous stem cell rescue
MoAb monoclonal antibodies
NCLS National LymphoCare Study
ORR overall response rate
OS overall survival

https://doi.org/10.1016/B978-0-443-19200-5.00007-5

PFS progression-free survival
POD24 progression of disease at 24 months
RT radiotherapy
SCT stem cell therapy
tFL transformed follicular lymphoma

Conflict of interest

No potential conflicts of interest were disclosed.

Background

The natural history and the clinical course of patients with follicular lymphoma (FL) are typically characterized by a pattern of continuous relapses. Although, especially with modern treatments, the overall response rate (ORR) and the complete response (CR) rate are, in general, quite high even at relapse, the ORR/CR rates tend to decrease with each relapse, as does the response duration (RD) and, more importantly, the overall survival (OS). This characteristic pattern, which was first described by Johnson et al. in 1995 [1], has also been confirmed in the rituximab era in a different series [2–4]. Thus, the ORR and CR rates decrease from 97% and 73% in the first line to 69% and 42% in the third line, with a median RD not reached in the first line and of around 2 years after the third line (Table 1). FL is therefore still considered incurable (with conventional treatment). In spite of this, patients with FL can still enjoy a prolonged survival. In contrast to the old report from Stanford (which became a classic and an almost mandatory citation in any study or presentation in FL) that demonstrated that the outcome of patients with FL had not improved over a period longer than 30 years [5], several published series in the current century have shown that the outcome of patients diagnosed with FL in more recent years has significantly improved [6–9] with a median OS at diagnosis of 15–20 years.

In addition, there is a subgroup of patients (those who remain free of events at 12–24 months) with a life expectancy that approaches that of an age- and gender-matched population [10]. At the other extreme of the spectrum, though, there is a group of patients (around 20% of patients diagnosed with FL) with a significantly worse prognosis than the remainder, as demonstrated by Casulo et al. in a classic study [11]. In this paper on the National LymphoCare Study (NLCS), the authors showed that patients with FL treated with immune-chemotherapy who progress in the first 24 months after diagnosis (what has been known as POD24—progression of disease at 24 months—since this paper) have a 5-year OS significantly lower than that of the remainder. The same concept—the adverse impact on the outcome of a short RD [12]—has been confirmed in other studies using different

TABLE 1 ORR, CR rate, EFS/PFS, and OS according to the number of treatment lines.

	ORR (%)	CRR (%)	EFS/PFS (median, months)	OS (median, months)
First line	71–97	38–73	18/127	NR-182
Second line	59–80	30–51	13/29	91–150
Third line	66–69	37–42	12/24	458–134

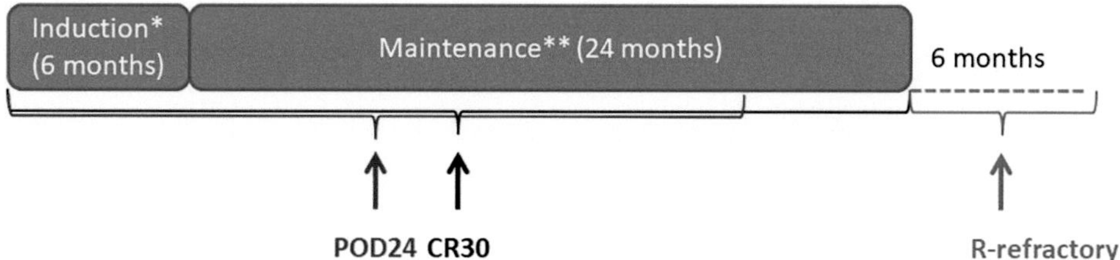

FIG. 1 Outcome measures of response duration.

outcome measures. Thus, the Follicular Lymphoma Analysis of Surrogate Hypothesis (FLASH) group analyzed the data of 3837 patients with FL included in first-line prospective trials, and demonstrated that the CR rate at 30 months after starting induction therapy (CR30) correlated with progression-free survival (PFS) and could be used as a surrogate end point [13]. Along the same lines, refractoriness to rituximab, which is defined as progression during treatment with rituximab or relapse within 6 months after the last dose, is a common outcome measure used in clinical trials to identify patients with a poor prognosis (Fig. 1). Finally, although the majority of the patients can enjoy a relatively long survival, even at relapse, there is another group of patients with a distinctive poor outcome: those who experience histological transformation. Histological transformation was considered in the past as a universal event characteristic of the clinical course of patients with FL: all patients with FL would experience it if they lived long enough. Series with a long follow-up show that the risk significantly decreases after 16–18 years, suggesting that a subgroup of patients with FL will never present with histological transformation [14]. Furthermore, there is a suggestion that the risk of histological transformation has decreased in the rituximab era and that maybe the outcome of patients who experience this event has improved (Table 2). However, the outcome of patients who relapse with transformed FL (tFL) after first-line therapy is significantly worse than that of patients who present with FL at relapse, even in the rituximab era, as shown by the Aristotle study and others [15,16]. In summary, notwithstanding the unquestionable

TABLE 2 Risk and outcome of histological transformation (HT).

Series (year)	*N*	Median follow-up	Actuarial risk	OS after HT
Montoto (2007)	325	15 years	At 10 years: **28%**	Median: 1.2 years
Al-Tourah (2008)	600	7.5 years	At 5 years: **20%**	Median: 1.7 years
Link (2013)	631	5 years	At 5 years: **11%**	At 5 years: 48%; median: 4 years
Sarkozy (2016)	1018	73 months	At 6 years: **4%**	Median: 3.8 years
Alonso (2017)	1734	6 years	At 10 years: **8%**	At 5 years: 26%
Federico (2018)	8116	87 months	At 10 years: **8%**	At 5 years: 43%

TABLE 3 Objectives of treatment in patients with follicular lymphoma.

	Symptomatic improvement	Response rate	Prolonged response	Reduced morbility	Reduced mortality
Expectant management	0	+	0/+	++++	++++
Rituximab	++/+++	++/+++	+	+++	++++
Combination chemotherapy	+++	+++	++	++	+++
Rituximab + PQT	+++	+++	+++	++	+++
Targeted drugs	+++	++/+++	++	++	+++
AutoSCT	+++	+++	+++/++++	++/+++	++
AlloSCT	+++	+++	+++/++++	0/+	+

positive impact that the introduction of rituximab has had on the outcome of patients with FL, the main cause of death in patients with FL in the rituximab era remains the lymphoma itself, including the treatment for the lymphoma [17].

Overview of treatment at relapse: Objectives of treatment

When deciding the best treatment option for a patient with relapsed FL, one has to be guided (the same as at diagnosis) by the objective of the treatment we are aiming at (Table 3). Expectant management, even at relapse, can be appropriate in asymptomatic patients. There are multiple randomized studies demonstrating that expectant management in patients newly diagnosed with FL does not have a negative impact on OS [18,19]. Similar data does not exist at relapse but retrospective data supports the appropriateness of this strategy in the right population [20,21]. Thus, expectant management might be a reasonable option in asymptomatic patients, especially in those in whom the progression or relapse has been detected as an incidental finding investigating other problems. The obvious exceptions would be those with a short duration of response after the previous treatment (as per any of the outcome measures previously discussed), or those with histological transformation. In elderly or frail patients or for those multiply treated, local radiotherapy (RT) can be an option to treat a specific area that is causing symptoms, even if there is a systemic disease. Likewise, when palliation (i.e., symptomatic improvement) is the objective, rituximab monotherapy can be an excellent option in elderly, frail, or multiply treated patients. In earlier relapses, when the objective is not only to achieve a response but to achieve a durable response, the options are chemotherapy (either in combination or monotherapy) or targeted agents, often in combination with anti-CD20 monoclonal antibodies (MoAb) (or other MoAb, if available).

The management of patients with FL has traditionally been guided by a series of principles that have almost become dogma. One example of this is the notion that patients should not be treated with the same agents or the same regimens that they have previously received. This principle does not apply to MoAb, given the fact that their mechanisms of resistance are different than those in conventional chemotherapy drugs, as reviewed in another chapter. The NLCS analyzed the treatment patterns of patients with FL both at initial treatment and at subsequent relapses and showed that 77% of the patients received rituximab as part of their initial therapy and more than half the patients also received rituximab either in monotherapy or in combination in their fifth line of treatment [2]. Actually, there is evidence that patients treated with single-agent rituximab can be successfully re-treated with single-agent rituximab at relapse. Davis et al. reported a phase II trial studying the efficacy of single-agent rituximab in patients with relapsed lymphoma previously treated with rituximab, either as a single agent or in combination [22]. Fifty-eight patients were included and achieved an ORR of 40% with an estimated median RD of 18 months. Similarly, the RESORT study compared the standard induction treatment for patients with previously untreated low-tumor burden FL (single-agent rituximab, four weekly doses) followed by maintenance rituximab, with the same induction treatment (four doses of single-agent rituximab) followed by re-treatment with single-agent rituximab (four weekly doses) at relapse and subsequent relapses [23]. The authors demonstrated the possibility of achieving meaningful responses with re-treatment with rituximab. The ORR after induction therapy was 71% for the whole series, whereas it was 61% for 56 patients in the re-treatment arm that received a first re-treatment and 67% in 12 patients who received a second re-treatment. Although the setting of the trial is very different from the situation of patients who have experienced multiple relapses and were previously treated with immune-chemotherapy, this study supports as a proof of concept the feasibility of rituximab re-treatment, provided there has been a reasonably long duration of the previous response. Along these lines, the GAUSS trial demonstrated that patients with relapsed FL previously treated with rituximab could be re-treated at relapse with rituximab followed by maintenance achieving a 2-year PFS of 50%, provided they had achieved a long RD after the previous treatment with rituximab [24]. In contrast, for patients who have received rituximab as part of the initial therapy and present with disease progression during treatment or within 6 months of the last dose, there is the possibility of re-treatment with another anti-CD20 MoAb: obinutuzumab. Obinutuzumab is a glycoengineered type II anti-CD20 MoAb that, in combination with bendamustine, resulted in a significantly longer PFS than bendamustine monotherapy in patients with rituximab-refractory disease in the GADOLIN study [25]. Although the study was criticized for the weakness of the nonexperimental arm, it led to the license of obinutuzumab in the rituximab-refractory setting.

The other piece of perceived wisdom in the management of patients with FL is that, when deciding the best treatment option for a given patient (either at diagnosis or at relapse), one should be thinking in advance on how this is going to impact on future treatment lines. The typical example of this concept was the recommendation to avoid drugs that could impair stem cell collection (i.e., fludarabine) in patients who might be candidates for high-dose therapy with autologous stem cell rescue (HDT-ASCR), but this has probably become less of an issue since the advent of plerixafor. What might become relevant in the future is the potential impact of previous treatment with bi-specifics on the possibility to proceed to chimeric antigen receptor T-cells (CAR-T) therapy and vice versa. As mentioned previously and reviewed in the previous chapter, there is a plethora of new targeted drugs that are under investigation, and some of them, not many, are approved for routine use in patients with relapsed or refractory FL. The results obtained with many of them are very promising but none of them have provided a significantly long duration of the response and they should be considered either as a palliative treatment (to achieve a response that provides symptomatic improvement and lasts as long as possible) or as a bridge to a more definitive treatment, such as stem cell therapy (SCT) or cellular therapy (CT) in patients fit for these strategies. Of the potential drugs, families, or pathways of greatest interest, lenalidomide is the one that is closer to routine use, with the FDA granting approval for the combination of lenalidomide and rituximab in patients with previously treated FL. BCL-2 antagonists, such as venetoclax, and EZH2 inhibitors, such as tazemetostat, have a very strong biological rationale behind them, but some of the published results, especially in monotherapy, are slightly disappointing and they are currently being investigated in combination with other drugs. Needless to say, clinical trials should always be considered, if available, for patients with multiply relapsed lymphoma.

Although prognostic scores such as the FLIPI (FL International Prognostic Index) are useful to risk-stratify patients at relapse, the same as at diagnosis [26], unfortunately, there are no agreed guidelines on how to use them to select the best treatment at the time of progression. In addition, prognostic scores add limited value in patients with a short duration of response to the last treatment, given the poor outcome of this population.

Treatment in challenging situations: POD24

The fact that patients with a short duration of the response achieved with the previous treatment have a poor prognosis is neither surprising nor new [12]. However, it was the classic NLCS study published by Casulo et al. [11] that defined what has become a common outcome measure in many trials in FL: POD24 (progression of disease at 24 months). In this prospective study, the authors included 2655 patients with FL and selected among them 588 treated with first-line immune-chemotherapy, specifically with R-CHOP. One hundred ten patients presented with disease progression within the first 24 months after the diagnosis and had a 5-year OS of 50%, significantly lower than the OS for the remainder (5-year OS: 70%). Other studies have shown similar results. Thus, Maurer et al. published combined data from Lyon and Iowa-Mayo and showed that patients who remain free of events 12 months after diagnosis have an OS that approaches that of a gender- and age-matched population, whereas patients with an event-free survival (EFS) of 12 months or less had a significant loss of life expectancy when compared to a gender- and age-matched population [10]. The poor outcome of patients with a short RD has been demonstrated not only after conventional therapy but also with more intensive treatments. The Lymphoma Working Party (LWP) of the European Society for Blood and Marrow Transplantation (EBMT) published the long-term follow-up of the Lym1 trial and demonstrated that patients with POD24 after HDT-ASCR had a 10-year OS of 60%, and this was significantly shorter than the 10-year OS of 85% for those who did not progress in the 2 years after HDT-ASCR [27]. With regard to the best treatment for patients who experienced POD24 or EFS12 (or similar), there is no standard approach, but the general consensus is that, if they are fit, they should be treated "aggressively" with salvage chemotherapy followed by consolidation of the response with HDT-ASCR. The NLCS group and the Centre for International Blood and Marrow Transplant Research (CIBMTR) analyzed the outcome of patients who presented with POD24 according to the treatment they received. Patients who received HDT-ASCR in the first year after POD24 had a 5-year OS of 73%, in comparison with a 5-year OS of 60% for patients who did not have HDT-ASCR, and this was statistically significant when adjusted for other variables [28]. Similarly, the German Low Grade Lymphoma Study Group analyzed the role of HDT-ASCR in patients with

POD24 in a study including 162 patients treated in 2 prospective trials who were eligible for HDT-ASCR but had not received HDT-ASCR before POD24. Patients who received HDT-ASCR had a 5-year PFS of 51% with a 5-year OS of 77%, and these figures were similar to those of patients who had not presented with POD24, suggesting that HDT-ASCR could abrogate the negative impact of an early progression after immune-chemotherapy [29]. Recently, the advent of CAR-T therapy has offered hope of better treatment and has widened, where available, the therapeutic options for this population. The ELARA trial was a phase II study that analyzed the role of Tisagenlecleucel in patients with relapsed or refractory FL and recruited 98 patients, including 63% of them with POD24 after the first anti-CD20 treatment and 23% with a relapse in less than 6 months after the previous treatment. The CR rate in the group of patients who had POD24 was 59% [30]. Similarly, ZUMA-5, a phase II study of Axicabtagene ciloleucel in patients with relapsed or refractory indolent lymphoma, included 124 patients with FL, of whom 55% had POD24 after the first treatment with anti-CD20. The CR rate in this high-risk group of patients was 72%, with an estimated duration of response at 18 months of 60% [31]. Although these results can still be considered preliminary, they suggest that CAR-T might be an efficacious treatment option in selected cases.

Treatment in challenging situations: Histological transformation

Histological transformation to an aggressive lymphoma is a well-recognized characteristic event in the natural history and the clinical course of patients with indolent lymphoma. The paradigm, and the most frequent and studied example, is the transformation of an FL to a diffuse large B-cell lymphoma (DLBCL). Old necropsy studies demonstrated a high proportion of cases with a histological transformation not diagnosed or suspected in life, and this was interpreted as the evidence that all patients with FL would eventually present with this event if they lived long enough [32]. Some more recent studies with a long follow-up have shown that the risk of histological transformation is not uniform along follow-up, but it plateaus after some years, supporting the idea that not all patients with FL are destined to present with histological transformation [14,33]. Although comparison of the risk of histological transformation across different studies is hampered by the heterogeneity among them in terms of the definition and criteria of transformation, and the length of follow-up, some studies performed in the rituximab era support the notion that the risk of histological transformation has decreased in more recent times [15,16,33,34]. Moreover, there is some suggestion that the higher the exposure to rituximab, the lesser the risk. Thus, in the Aristotle study, patients who received rituximab both as part of the induction regimen and as maintenance had a significantly lower risk of histological transformation than patients who received rituximab only with the induction therapy, but no maintenance; similarly, patients who received rituximab as part of the induction regimen (but no maintenance) had a lower risk of histological transformation than the group of patients who did not receive rituximab as part of the initial therapy [16]. Finally, there is also a strong hint toward a better outcome for patients who present with histological transformation in more recent years, with the reported median OS approaching 4 years, in comparison with a median OS of around 1 year in the prerituximab era (Table 2). Nevertheless, histological transformation remains an event associated with a poor prognosis in the immune-chemotherapy era and patients with transformed FL (tFL) have a worse outcome than those who relapse with persistent FL [15,16]. The recommended standard strategy for patients with histological transformation is to treat them for DLBCL, based on the fact that the transformed lymphoma behaves clinically and biologically as DLBCL. In this regard, Link et al. demonstrated that patients who received R-CHOP (rituximab, cyclophosphamide, doxorubicin, vincristine, and prednisolone) at the time of histological transformation had a better outcome than those who had been treated with R-CHOP prior to this event, and their OS was similar to that of patients newly diagnosed with DLBCL treated with R-CHOP [33]. The beneficial effect of treatment with R-CHOP was also reported by the Spanish GELTAMO (Grupo Español de Linfoma y Transplante Autólogo de Médula Ósea) [34]. Moreover, a Danish population-based study showed that treatment-naïve patients who received R-CHOP for tFL had an excellent outcome, regardless of whether the response was consolidated or not with HDT-ASCR, suggesting that previously untreated patients who are treated with R-CHOP for histological transformation might not need consolidation with HDT-ASCR [35]. Thus, same as for patients with de novo DLBCL, an immune-chemotherapy regimen containing anthracycline is the best treatment option. However, in contrast with the management of patients with de novo DLBCL, many patients with FL have already received anthracyclines before being diagnosed with histological transformation. Thus, in the American LymphoCare Study analyzing the management of newly diagnosed patients with FL, more than half the patients received immune-chemotherapy as initial therapy and R-CHOP was the most frequently used regimen [36]. Similarly, in a German survey on the management of patients with indolent lymphoma, R-CHOP was used as initial therapy in 67% of the patients who received immune-chemotherapy [37]. In these circumstances, the most frequently used strategy at the time of histological transformation (for those patients who are fit for it) is to administer salvage therapy with a second-line immune-chemotherapy regimen (i.e., R-ICE—rituximab, etoposide, ifosfamide, and carboplatin, R-DHAP—rituximab, dexamethasone, cytarabine, and cisplatine, R-ESHAP—rituximab, etoposide, cytarabine, and cisplatine—to name a few) followed by HDT-ASCR, as per the treatment of relapsed DLBCL. In this sense, there is no evidence that any second-line regimen is better than another, as demonstrated by the CORAL study [38], and the recommendation is to use always the same regimen as second-line treatment to become familiar with its toxicity and with the practicalities associated with its administration. With regard to the efficacy of HDT-ASCR in patients with tFL, the "evidence" comes mostly from retrospective studies showing that patients who are fit enough and achieve a response good enough to proceed to HDT-ASCR have a better outcome than those who do not receive HDT-ASCR. Thus, Sarkozy and colleagues analyzed the risk and impact of histological transformation in patients included in the PRIMA study and demonstrated that those who relapsed with tFL and had HDT-ASCR had a significantly better OS than patients with histological transformation who did not receive HDT-ASCR; in contrast, patients who relapsed with persistent FL had a similar OS regardless of whether they had HDT-ASCR or not at relapse [15]. Similarly, the Spanish GELTAMO showed that consolidation of the response with HDT-ASCR was associated with a better OS, even after adjusting for other variables in multivariate analysis [34]. There are no randomized studies to back this strategy, but it is widely used based on extrapolation from the closest entity (DLBCL at relapse, previously treated with immune-chemotherapy containing anthracycline) for which, in most circumstances, this would be the standard treatment. However, the advent of CAR-T therapy might be challenging this strategy in the future. Uncharacteristically, several prospective trials of CAR-T in patients either with DLBCL [39–41] or in patients with FL [42] allowed the inclusion of patients with transformed lymphoma. Thus, Hirayama et al. reported on a small phase I/II study including patients with FL and with tFL. Among 21 patients, 13 had tFL. This group of patients had a CR rate lower than the rest (46% vs 88%) but with a median RD of 10 months, which is remarkable in this population [42]. The prospective clinical trials for DLBCL JULIET, TRASCEND, and ZUMA-1 allowed the recruitment of patients with histological transformation and included 16%–22% of patients with transformed lymphoma. The TRASCEND study reported the results of this subgroup of patients separately and showed an ORR of 84% with a CR rate of 63%, and a duration of response and PFS longer than for other subtypes [41]. Finally, two studies, BELINDA and ZUMA-7, compared the efficacy of CAR-T and standard of care (that is, salvage therapy followed by HDT-ASCR) in patients with aggressive lymphoma in a randomized fashion [43,44]. These studies allowed the inclusion of patients with transformed lymphoma and they constituted 13%–17% of the study population. Whereas in the BELINDA study there were no statistically significant differences in outcome according to the treatment arm [43], the ZUMA-7 trial showed that patients randomized to the CAR-T arm had a significantly better outcome, with a median EFS of 8 months for patients who received CAR-T, in comparison with 2 months for patients assigned to the standard of care arm [44]. These differences were also observed in the group of patients with histological transformation, who presented an objective response rate of 89%, whereas it was 56% in the HDT-ASCR group. Thus, if these trials resulted in a change in the paradigm of treatment of relapsed DLBCL, the same should be applied to the management of patients with histological transformation, following the maxima of treating patients with transformed lymphoma as patients with DLBCL.

The role of maintenance rituximab for patients with tFL has not been explored in this specific setting, as these patients are often excluded from prospective trials. However, the role of maintenance rituximab has been studied in patients with DLBCL after induction with or without rituximab, showing that maintenance did not add any benefit in patients treated with R-CHOP [45]. Likewise, two randomized trials demonstrated that maintenance rituximab did not improve the outcome after HDT-ASCR [46,47]. No randomized trials have thus shown any evidence that rituximab maintenance results in an improved outcome in patients with DLBCL. A retrospective study from the British Columbia Cancer Agency (BCCA) tried to clarify the role of maintenance in patients with what has been called "histological transformation at diagnosis" (also known as composite or discordant lymphoma, when evidence of high-grade and low-grade lymphoma is found in the same biopsy sample or in different samples at the same time, respectively). Maintenance rituximab after initial therapy with R-CHOP in patients with histological transformation at diagnosis was physician dependent, so the authors took advantage of this to analyze the impact of rituximab maintenance on outcome, but did not find any differences in PFS according to whether patients had received rituximab maintenance or not [48].

The management of patients with tFL is further complicated by the fact that many patients have received several lines of treatment at the time of histological transformation, which limits even more the treatment options. In addition, many patients are also too frail to be considered for salvage therapy and HDT-ASCR. In these cases, the management will be dictated by the age and comorbidities of the patient, by the number and types of previous lines of treatment, and again by the objective of the treatment. In relatively fit patients, the objective should be to achieve a response as long as possible. Ideally, these patients should be included in clinical trials. However, many clinical trials for patients with relapsed or refractory DLBCL exclude patients with histological transformation. In this sense, the combination of rituximab, polatuzumab (a conjugated anti-CD79b MoAb), and bendamustine has produced excellent results in patients with relapsed or refractory DLBCL [49]. Unfortunately, patients with histological transformation were not allowed in this study, but a couple of "real-world" studies have analyzed the efficacy of polatuzumab combinations in patients with DLBCL and have included some patients with transformed lymphoma [50,51]. Although the number of patients with tFL included is small, combinations of polatuzumab can be considered in patients with histological transformation. For frailer patients, overt palliation with gentle chemotherapy, with the aim of controlling symptoms, with a good quality of life, and spending most of the time out of hospital should be the choice.

Consolidation of the response: Maintenance

The beneficial impact on the outcome of maintenance rituximab has been known for long. Several randomized trials [52–55] demonstrated that maintenance rituximab at relapse results in a significantly better PFS than observation (regardless of whether patients had received rituximab or not as part of the induction treatment), and in some of the studies, an advantage in terms of OS was also reported. The latter was confirmed in two metaanalyses of randomized trials [56,57]. However, these studies predated the PRIMA trial [58] that established immune-chemotherapy followed by rituximab maintenance as the standard first-line therapy for patients with advanced stage FL who need therapy; hence, the information on the effect of repeated rituximab maintenance at relapse in patients who have already received maintenance as part of the initial therapy is limited. Unfortunately, no data on maintenance at relapse was available in the report on the long-term follow-up of the PRIMA study [59]. There is anecdotal data suggesting that repeated maintenance at relapse is an option that is considered at recurrence. Thus, in the German survey reporting on treatment patterns at first line and at relapse [37], the authors documented that 12% of the patients received maintenance at first line, whereas this figure increased to 17% and 16% at the first and second relapses, respectively.

Consolidation of the response: Stem cell transplantation (SCT) and cellular therapy (CT)

The role of stem cell transplantation (SCT) in general and, more specifically, of HDT-ASCR has always been the object of passionate controversy among experts in the management of patients with FL and the futileness of HDT-ASCR following the advent of rituximab and, more recently, of novel targeted drugs has been declared by many experts. The reality is that, even if the number of patients referred for SCT has decreased over time (Fig. 2), it still represents two-thirds of the numbers referred for SCT at its peak, with a predictable increase in the number of patients referred for CT. In spite of the lack of randomized trials providing strong evidence in favor of or against this strategy, FL specialists have very strong opinions. In this sense, it is noticeable that in a disease characterized by a long survival even in the

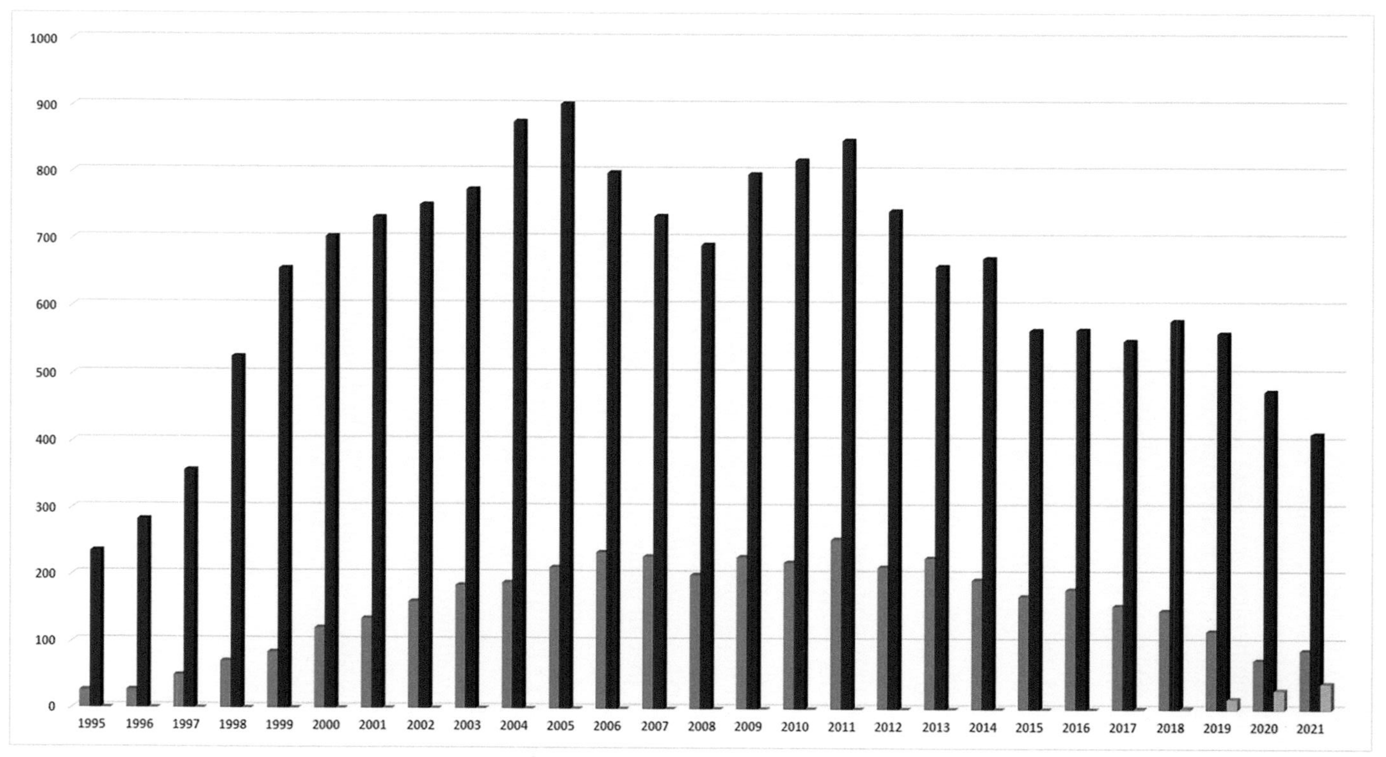

FIG. 2 Evolution of the number of patients receiving stem cell transplant (SCT) or cell therapy (CT) for follicular lymphoma over time. *Data from the European Society for Blood and Marrow Transplantation (EBMT) registry.*

absence of cure, more randomized trials comparing conventional chemotherapy with HDT-ASCR have been performed in the first-line setting than at relapse [60–63]. Randomized trials in the first line have shown similar results: several of them showed an advantage of HDT-ASCR in terms of PFS or EFS but there were no differences in OS, as patients who progressed in the chemotherapy arm were rescued with HDT-ASCR at relapse, abrogating the survival advantage. In contrast, only one randomized trial compared conventional chemotherapy with HDT-ASCR in the relapse setting [64]. The CUP trial randomized patients with relapsed FL to receive conventional chemotherapy or an unpurged HDT-ASCR or a purged HDT-ASCR. This trial has been criticized for many reasons, including the fact that it was performed in the prerituximab era but nonetheless demonstrated that patients assigned to the HDT-ASCR arms had a significant advantage both in terms of PFS and OS over those assigned to the chemotherapy only arm. The main objections to HDT-ASCR from its opponents are twofold. The first one is the increased risk of secondary malignancies, specifically of secondary myelodysplastic syndromes (sMDS) and secondary acute myeloid leukemia (sAML), and the second one is the lack of curative potential. With regard to the increased risk of sMDS/SAML, this was initially reported by the groups of St Bartholomew's Hospital in London, United Kingdom, and the Dana Farber Cancer Institute (DFCI) in Boston, United States [65,66], in patients receiving conditioning regimens including total-body irradiation (TBI). However, a study of the LWP-EBMT demonstrated that the risk of sMDS/SAML was strongly associated with the use of TBI as part of the conditioning regimen, and it was significantly lower in patients who received a chemotherapy-only conditioning regimen [67]. With regard to the concerns regarding the possible lack of a curative potential, this was based on studies on HDT-ASCR with a short follow-up that showed a continuous drop in the PFS curve, supporting that all patients who received HDT-ASCR would eventually relapse. However, the previously mentioned LWP-EBMT study with a median follow-up of 10 years showed that after 7–8 years of follow-up, a *flattening* of the PFS curve could be observed, suggesting that actually a group of patients with FL could enjoy a considerably long remission and be considered cured with HDT-ASCR [67]. Subsequently, other studies with a long follow-up [66,68,69] have shown similar results, supporting the fact that a proportion of patients with FL (probably around 30%–40%) can be cured with HDT-ASCR. Of note, data from the rituximab era, such as the Lym1 LWP-EBMT trial, also supports this statement [27].

Not surprisingly, finding a clear role for allogeneic SCT in patients with FL is even more controversial. Traditionally, the considerably high mortality and morbidity associated with an allogeneic transplant resulted in this option being reserved for fit, relatively young patients who relapsed after HDT-ASCR. The advent of reduced-intensity conditioning regimens (RIC) expanded the population of patients who could benefit and were referred for an allogeneic transplant, but still mostly in the setting of a second SCT in patients who had relapsed after HDT-ASCR. The LWP-EBMT analyzed the outcome of patients who received an RIC-allogeneic transplant for relapsed FL after HDT-ASCR and included 183 patients. The 5-year PFS and OS were 48% and 51%, respectively, but of note, the median duration of the response after RIC-allogeneic transplant was 43 months, whereas it was 14 months after the previous HDT-ASCR [70]. The assumption of the lack of a curative potential for HDT-ACSR led to some authors considering the role of allogeneic transplant as the first SCT, testing the hypothesis that allogeneic transplant could be curative for patients with FL. Notably, the Blood and

TABLE 4 Clinical trials of CAR-T therapy in patients with follicular lymphoma.

Series (year)	Phase	*N*	Median follow-up	ORR/CR	PFS
Hirayama (2019)	I/II	8[a]/21	NR	NR/88%	NR
Fowler (2021)	II	97[b]/119	16 months	86/69%	66% (at 12 months)
Jacobson (2022)	II	124[c]/153	17 months	94/79%	65% (at 18 months)

[a] *FL; NR: not reported.*
[b] *Patients infused.*
[c] *Patients with FL, infused.*

Marrow Transplant Clinical Trials Network (BMT CTN) designed and opened a prospective randomized clinical trial analyzing the efficacy of RIC-allogeneic transplant versus HDT-ASCR for patients with relapsed FL, but unfortunately, this trial had to close prematurely due to lack of recruitment [71]. We are thus left with retrospective registry studies trying to answer this question. Data from the LWP-EBMT including 726 patients receiving HDT-ASCR and 149 patients receiving RIC-allogeneic transplant for relapsed FL showed that patients who received an RIC-allogeneic transplant had a significantly higher nonrelapse mortality (NRM), but a lower risk of relapse, and this resulted in the lack of statistically significant differences either in PFS or OS according to the type of transplant, even after adjusting for other variables on the multivariate analysis [72]. The interpretation of the current evidence (or lack of) has led the EBMT to recommend HDT-ASCR as a standard option in patients with chemosensitive disease on second or subsequent CR, whereas a matched sibling or unrelated donor allogeneic SCT is recommended as a standard option in patients who relapse after HDT-ASCR [73].

As mentioned previously, the novelty in the field is the advent of CT in the form of CAR-T therapy. Although the development of this strategy for patients with FL is clearly behind that for patients with DLBCL, several phase I and phase II studies have shown their efficacy and potential (Table 4). Hirayama and colleagues published a small phase I/II study that included 21 patients with FL (including 13 with transformed lymphoma) and reported an impressive CR rate of 88% for patients with nontransformed FL [42]. In this heavily pretreated population (almost 40% of them had relapsed after HDT-ASCR), no relapses were observed after 16 months. A larger phase II study, the ELARA trial, also showed very promising results [30]. Ninety-eight patients with relapsed/refractory FL (patients with histological transformation were excluded) were included. This was a high-risk population: almost 60% of the patients had high-risk FLIPI at the time of being included in the study, almost 90% were refractory to anti-CD20 therapy, and around one-third of patients had previously failed after HDT-ASCR. In spite of this, the CR rate was almost 70% with an estimated 12-month PFS of 67%. Along the same lines, the ZUMA-5 trial analyzed the efficacy of CAR-T in patients with relapsed/refractory indolent lymphoma. Jacobson and colleagues reported on the subgroup of 124 patients with FL [31]. Once again, this was a high-risk, heavily pretreated population: almost two-thirds of the patients had received three or more lines of therapy, including HDT-ASCR in one-third, and 68% were refractory to the last treatment. The authors demonstrated a very high CR rate (79%) with an estimated PFS at 18 months of 73%. Of note, in this study, 13 patients who relapsed after CAR-T (including 11 patients with FL) were retreated with CAR-T, with a CR rate of 77% and ongoing responses in almost half the patients after 11 months of follow-up. The results of these studies have led the US Food and Drug Administration (FDA) and the European Commission (EC) to approve CAR-T therapy for patients with relapsed/refractory FL.

Conclusions and future perspective

Some of the first considerations to take into account when discussing management options with a patient with relapsed FL are whether the patient needs treatment, what the objective of the treatment is, and what the patient's preferences are, which are all interconnected questions. With regard to the decision to treat or not, the aggressiveness of the disease at relapse will determine whether expectant management is an appropriate option or not. Thus, histological transformation to an aggressive lymphoma or relapse after a short duration of the response to the last treatment requires treatment in the majority of the cases (the exception being very frail patients). In patients with a less aggressive relapse, the choices can vary from simple options such as expectant management, local RT, or single-agent rituximab to the most sophisticated, demanding, and potentially toxic options such as CAR-T therapy, depending on the age, comorbidities, and performance status of the patient and on the number, type, and length of the response to the previous treatments. The possibility of including patients in a prospective clinical trial should always be considered, if available, provided this suits the objectives of the treatment and the preferences of the patient. It is essential to have a frank conversation with the patient and clearly state that even if a clinical trial might be the best option in a given situation, there is always more uncertainty about the potential benefit for the patient (and also about the possible side effects) as they are, by definition, testing drugs that are still experimental. This shouldn't discourage patients to be included in clinical trials if they have realistic expectations. At the end of the day, the outcome of patients with FL has considerably improved in the last decades, which would not have been possible without clinical research including prospective clinical trials. Thus, the future is promising. The advent of CAR-T therapy is opening new options for subgroups of patients with high-risk disease and, although not completely incorporated in the routine algorithm of patients with FL yet, it is foreseeable that in the next years, the role of CAR-T therapy in the management of patients with FL and the best candidates and timing will be delineated.

References

[1] Johnson PW, Rohatiner AZ, Whelan JS, Price CG, Love S, Lim J, et al. Patterns of survival in patients with recurrent follicular lymphoma: a 20-year study from a single center. J Clin Oncol 1995;13(1):140–7.

[2] Link BK, Day BM, Zhou X, Zelenetz AD, Dawson KL, Cerhan JR, et al. Second-line and subsequent therapy and outcomes for follicular lymphoma in the United States: data from the observational national LymphoCare study. Br J Haematol 2019;184(4):660–3.

[3] Rivas-Delgado A, Magnano L, Moreno-Velazquez M, Garcia O, Nadeu F, Mozas P, et al. Response duration and survival shorten after each relapse in patients with follicular lymphoma treated in the rituximab era. Br J Haematol 2019;184(5):753–9.

[4] Salles G, Schuster SJ, Fischer L, Kuruvilla J, Patten PEM, von Tresckow B, et al. A retrospective cohort study of treatment outcomes of adult patients with relapsed or refractory follicular lymphoma (ReCORD-FL). Hema 2022;6(7), e745.

[5] Horning SJ. Natural history of and therapy for the indolent non-Hodgkin's lymphomas. Semin Oncol 1993;20(5 Suppl 5):75–88.

[6] Swenson WT, Wooldridge JE, Lynch CF, Forman-Hoffman VL, Chrischilles E, Link BK. Improved survival of follicular lymphoma patients in the United States. J Clin Oncol 2005;23(22):5019–26.

[7] Fisher RI, LeBlanc M, Press OW, Maloney DG, Unger JM, Miller TP. New treatment options have changed the survival of patients with follicular lymphoma. J Clin Oncol 2005;23(33):8447–52.

[8] Liu Q, Fayad L, Cabanillas F, Hagemeister FB, Ayers GD, Hess M, et al. Improvement of overall and failure-free survival in stage IV follicular lymphoma: 25 years of treatment experience at the University of Texas M.D. Anderson Cancer center. J Clin Oncol 2006;24(10):1582–9.

[9] Mozas P, Nadeu F, Rivas-Delgado A, Rivero A, Garrote M, Balague O, et al. Patterns of change in treatment, response, and outcome in patients with follicular lymphoma over the last four decades: a single-center experience. Blood Cancer J 2020;10(3):31.

[10] Maurer MJ, Bachy E, Ghesquieres H, Ansell SM, Nowakowski GS, Thompson CA, et al. Early event status informs subsequent outcome in newly diagnosed follicular lymphoma. Am J Hematol 2016;91(11):1096–101.

[11] Casulo C, Byrtek M, Dawson KL, Zhou X, Farber CM, Flowers CR, et al. Early relapse of follicular lymphoma after rituximab plus cyclophosphamide, doxorubicin, vincristine, and prednisone defines patients at high risk for death: an analysis from the national LymphoCare study. J Clin Oncol 2015;33(23):2516–22.

[12] Montoto S, Lopez-Guillermo A, Ferrer A, Camos M, Alvarez-Larran A, Bosch F, et al. Survival after progression in patients with follicular lymphoma: analysis of prognostic factors. Ann Oncol 2002;13(4):523–30.

[13] Shi Q, Flowers CR, Hiddemann W, Marcus R, Herold M, Hagenbeek A, et al. Thirty-month complete response as a surrogate end point in first-line follicular lymphoma therapy: an individual patient-level analysis of multiple randomized trials. J Clin Oncol 2017;35(5):552–60.

[14] Montoto S, Davies AJ, Matthews J, Calaminici M, Norton AJ, Amess J, et al. Risk and clinical implications of transformation of follicular lymphoma to diffuse large B-cell lymphoma. J Clin Oncol 2007;25(17):2426–33.

[15] Sarkozy C, Trneny M, Xerri L, Wickham N, Feugier P, Leppa S, et al. Risk factors and outcomes for patients with follicular lymphoma who had histologic transformation after response to first-line Immunochemotherapy in the PRIMA trial. J Clin Oncol 2016;34(22):2575–82.

[16] Federico M, Caballero Barrigon MD, Marcheselli L, Tarantino V, Manni M, Sarkozy C, et al. Rituximab and the risk of transformation of follicular lymphoma: a retrospective pooled analysis. Lancet Haematol 2018;5(8):e359–67.

[17] Sarkozy C, Maurer MJ, Link BK, Ghesquieres H, Nicolas E, Thompson CA, et al. Cause of death in follicular lymphoma in the first decade of the rituximab era: a pooled analysis of French and US cohorts. J Clin Oncol 2019;37(2):144–52.

[18] Ardeshna KM, Smith P, Norton A, Hancock BW, Hoskin PJ, MacLennan KA, et al. Long-term effect of a watch and wait policy versus immediate systemic treatment for asymptomatic advanced-stage non-Hodgkin lymphoma: a randomised controlled trial. Lancet 2003;362(9383):516–22.

[19] Ardeshna KM, Qian W, Smith P, Braganca N, Lowry L, Patrick P, et al. Rituximab versus a watch-and-wait approach in patients with advanced-stage, asymptomatic, non-bulky follicular lymphoma: an open-label randomised phase 3 trial. Lancet Oncol 2014;15(4):424–35.

[20] Nastoupil LJ, Sinha R, Byrtek M, Ziemiecki R, Zhou X, Taylor M, et al. Outcomes following watchful waiting for stage II-IV follicular lymphoma patients in the modern era. Br J Haematol 2016;172(5):724–34.

[21] Arushi K, Mwangi R, Ansell SM, Habermann TM, Cerhan JR, Strouse C, et al. Patterns of therapy initiation during the first decade for patients with follicular lymphoma who were observed at diagnosis in the rituximab era. Blood Cancer J 2021;11(7):133.

[22] Davis TA, Grillo-Lopez AJ, White CA, McLaughlin P, Czuczman MS, Link BK, et al. Rituximab anti-CD20 monoclonal antibody therapy in non-Hodgkin's lymphoma: safety and efficacy of re-treatment. J Clin Oncol 2000;18 (17):3135–43.

[23] Kahl BS, Hong F, Williams ME, Gascoyne RD, Wagner LI, Krauss JC, et al. Rituximab extended schedule or re-treatment trial for low-tumor burden follicular lymphoma: eastern cooperative oncology group protocol e4402. J Clin Oncol 2014;32(28):3096–102.
[24] Sehn LH, Goy A, Offner FC, Martinelli G, Caballero MD, Gadeberg O, et al. Randomized phase II trial comparing Obinutuzumab (GA101) with rituximab in patients with relapsed CD20+ indolent B-cell non-Hodgkin lymphoma: final analysis of the GAUSS study. J Clin Oncol 2015;33(30):3467–74.
[25] Sehn LH, Chua N, Mayer J, Dueck G, Trneny M, Bouabdallah K, et al. Obinutuzumab plus bendamustine versus bendamustine monotherapy in patients with rituximab-refractory indolent non-Hodgkin lymphoma (GADOLIN): a randomised, controlled, open-label, multicentre, phase 3 trial. Lancet Oncol 2016;17(8):1081–93.
[26] Montoto S, Lopez-Guillermo A, Altes A, Perea G, Ferrer A, Camos M, et al. Predictive value of follicular lymphoma international prognostic index (FLIPI) in patients with follicular lymphoma at first progression. Ann Oncol 2004;15(10):1484–9.
[27] Pettengell R, Uddin R, Boumendil A, Johnson R, Metzner B, Martin A, et al. Durable benefit of rituximab maintenance post-autograft in patients with relapsed follicular lymphoma: 12-year follow-up of the EBMT lymphoma working party Lym1 trial. Bone Marrow Transplant 2021;56(6):1413–21.
[28] Casulo C, Friedberg JW, Ahn KW, Flowers C, DiGilio A, Smith SM, et al. Autologous transplantation in follicular lymphoma with early therapy failure: a national LymphoCare study and center for International Blood and Marrow Transplant Research Analysis. Biol Blood Marrow Transplant 2018;24(6):1163–71.
[29] Jurinovic V, Metzner B, Pfreundschuh M, Schmitz N, Wandt H, Keller U, et al. Autologous stem cell transplantation for patients with early progression of follicular lymphoma: a follow-up study of 2 randomized trials from the German low grade lymphoma study group. Biol Blood Marrow Transplant 2018;24(6):1172–9.
[30] Fowler NH, Dickinson M, Dreyling M, Martinez-Lopez J, Kolstad A, Butler J, et al. Tisagenlecleucel in adult relapsed or refractory follicular lymphoma: the phase 2 ELARA trial. Nat Med 2022;28(2):325–32.
[31] Jacobson CA, Chavez JC, Sehgal AR, William BM, Munoz J, Salles G, et al. Axicabtagene ciloleucel in relapsed or refractory indolent non-Hodgkin lymphoma (ZUMA-5): a single-arm, multicentre, phase 2 trial. Lancet Oncol 2022;23(1):91–103.
[32] Garvin AJ, Simon RM, Osborne CK, Merrill J, Young RC, Berard CW. An autopsy study of histologic progression in non-Hodgkin's lymphomas. 192 cases from the National Cancer Institute. Cancer 1983;52(3):393–8.
[33] Link BK, Maurer MJ, Nowakowski GS, Ansell SM, Macon WR, Syrbu SI, et al. Rates and outcomes of follicular lymphoma transformation in the immunochemotherapy era: a report from the University of Iowa/MayoClinic specialized program of research excellence molecular epidemiology resource. J Clin Oncol 2013;31(26):3272–8.
[34] Alonso-Alvarez S, Magnano L, Alcoceba M, Andrade-Campos M, Espinosa-Lara N, Rodriguez G, et al. Risk of, and survival following, histological transformation in follicular lymphoma in the rituximab era. A retrospective multicentre study by the Spanish GELTAMO group. Br J Haematol 2017;178(5):699–708.
[35] Madsen C, Pedersen MB, Vase MO, Bendix K, Moller MB, Johansen P, et al. Outcome determinants for transformed indolent lymphomas treated with or without autologous stem-cell transplantation. Ann Oncol 2015;26(2):393–9.
[36] Friedberg JW, Taylor MD, Cerhan JR, Flowers CR, Dillon H, Farber CM, et al. Follicular lymphoma in the United States: first report of the national LymphoCare study. J Clin Oncol 2009;27(8):1202–8.
[37] Schmidt C, Fetscher S, Gorg C, Kornek P, Nusch A, Kegel T, et al. Treatment of indolent lymphoma in Germany - results of a representative population-based survey. Clin Lymphoma Myeloma Leuk 2011;11(2):204–11.
[38] Gisselbrecht C, Glass B, Mounier N, Singh Gill D, Linch DC, Trneny M, et al. Salvage regimens with autologous transplantation for relapsed large B-cell lymphoma in the rituximab era. J Clin Oncol 2010;28(27):4184–90.
[39] Schuster SJ, Svoboda J, Chong EA, Nasta SD, Mato AR, Anak O, et al. Chimeric antigen receptor T cells in refractory B-cell lymphomas. N Engl J Med 2017;377(26):2545–54.
[40] Neelapu SS, Locke FL, Bartlett NL, Lekakis LJ, Miklos DB, Jacobson CA, et al. Axicabtagene Ciloleucel CAR T-cell therapy in refractory large B-cell lymphoma. N Engl J Med 2017;377(26):2531–44.
[41] Abramson JS, Palomba ML, Gordon LI, Lunning MA, Wang M, Arnason J, et al. Lisocabtagene maraleucel for patients with relapsed or refractory large B-cell lymphomas (TRANSCEND NHL 001): a multicentre seamless design study. Lancet 2020;396(10254):839–52.
[42] Hirayama AV, Gauthier J, Hay KA, Voutsinas JM, Wu Q, Pender BS, et al. High rate of durable complete remission in follicular lymphoma after CD19 CAR-T cell immunotherapy. Blood 2019;134(7):636–40.

[43] Bishop MR, Dickinson M, Purtill D, Barba P, Santoro A, Hamad N, et al. Second-line Tisagenlecleucel or standard Care in Aggressive B-cell lymphoma. N Engl J Med 2022;386(7):629–39.
[44] Locke FL, Miklos DB, Jacobson CA, Perales MA, Kersten MJ, Oluwole OO, et al. Axicabtagene Ciloleucel as second-line therapy for large B-cell lymphoma. N Engl J Med 2022;386(7):640–54.
[45] Habermann TM, Weller EA, Morrison VA, Gascoyne RD, Cassileth PA, Cohn JB, et al. Rituximab-CHOP versus CHOP alone or with maintenance rituximab in older patients with diffuse large B-cell lymphoma. J Clin Oncol 2006;24(19):3121–7.
[46] Haioun C, Mounier N, Emile JF, Ranta D, Coiffier B, Tilly H, et al. Rituximab versus observation after high-dose consolidative first-line chemotherapy with autologous stem-cell transplantation in patients with poor-risk diffuse large B-cell lymphoma. Ann Oncol 2009;20(12):1985–92.
[47] Gisselbrecht C, Schmitz N, Mounier N, Singh Gill D, Linch DC, Trneny M, et al. Rituximab maintenance therapy after autologous stem-cell transplantation in patients with relapsed CD20(+) diffuse large B-cell lymphoma: final analysis of the collaborative trial in relapsed aggressive lymphoma. J Clin Oncol 2012;30(36):4462–9.
[48] Kansara R, Connors JM, Savage KJ, Gerrie AS, Scott DW, Slack GW, et al. Maintenance rituximab following induction R-CHOP chemotherapy in patients with composite or discordant, indolent and aggressive, B-cell non-Hodgkin lymphomas. Haematologica 2016;101(10):e411–4.
[49] Sehn LH, Herrera AF, Flowers CR, Kamdar MK, McMillan A, Hertzberg M, et al. Polatuzumab Vedotin in relapsed or refractory diffuse large B-cell lymphoma. J Clin Oncol 2020;38(2):155–65.
[50] Segman Y, Ribakovsky E, Avigdor A, Goldhecht Y, Vainstein V, Goldschmidt N, et al. Outcome of relapsed/refractory diffuse large B-cell lymphoma patients treated with polatuzumab vedotin-based therapy: real-life experience. Leuk Lymphoma 2021;62(1):118–24.
[51] Wang YW, Tsai XC, Hou HA, Tien FM, Liu JH, Chou WC, et al. Polatuzumab vedotin-based salvage immunochemotherapy as third-line or beyond treatment for patients with diffuse large B-cell lymphoma: a real-world experience. Ann Hematol 2022;101(2):349–58.
[52] Ghielmini M, Schmitz SF, Cogliatti SB, Pichert G, Hummerjohann J, Waltzer U, et al. Prolonged treatment with rituximab in patients with follicular lymphoma significantly increases event-free survival and response duration compared with the standard weekly x 4 schedule. Blood 2004;103(12):4416–23.
[53] Forstpointner R, Unterhalt M, Dreyling M, Bock HP, Repp R, Wandt H, et al. Maintenance therapy with rituximab leads to a significant prolongation of response duration after salvage therapy with a combination of rituximab, fludarabine, cyclophosphamide, and mitoxantrone (R-FCM) in patients with recurring and refractory follicular and mantle cell lymphomas: results of a prospective randomized study of the German low grade lymphoma study group (GLSG). Blood 2006;108(13):4003–8.
[54] van Oers MH, Klasa R, Marcus RE, Wolf M, Kimby E, Gascoyne RD, et al. Rituximab maintenance improves clinical outcome of relapsed/resistant follicular non-Hodgkin lymphoma in patients both with and without rituximab during induction: results of a prospective randomized phase 3 intergroup trial. Blood 2006;108 (10):3295–301.
[55] Pettengell R, Schmitz N, Gisselbrecht C, Smith G, Patton WN, Metzner B, et al. Rituximab purging and/or maintenance in patients undergoing autologous transplantation for relapsed follicular lymphoma: a prospective randomized trial from the lymphoma working party of the European group for blood and marrow transplantation. J Clin Oncol 2013;31(13):1624–30.
[56] Vidal L, Gafter-Gvili A, Salles G, Dreyling MH, Ghielmini M, Hsu Schmitz SF, et al. Rituximab maintenance for the treatment of patients with follicular lymphoma: an updated systematic review and meta-analysis of randomized trials. J Natl Cancer Inst 2011;103(23):1799–806.
[57] Vidal L, Gafter-Gvili A, Salles G, Bousseta S, Oberman B, Rubin C, et al. Rituximab maintenance improves overall survival of patients with follicular lymphoma-individual patient data meta-analysis. Eur J Cancer 2017;76:216–25.
[58] Salles G, Seymour JF, Offner F, Lopez-Guillermo A, Belada D, Xerri L, et al. Rituximab maintenance for 2 years in patients with high tumour burden follicular lymphoma responding to rituximab plus chemotherapy (PRIMA): a phase 3, randomised controlled trial. Lancet 2011;377(9759):42–51.
[59] Bachy E, Seymour JF, Feugier P, Offner F, Lopez-Guillermo A, Belada D, et al. Sustained progression-free survival benefit of rituximab maintenance in patients with follicular lymphoma: long-term results of the PRIMA study. J Clin Oncol 2019;37(31):2815–24.

[60] Lenz G, Dreyling M, Schiegnitz E, Forstpointner R, Wandt H, Freund M, et al. Myeloablative radiochemotherapy followed by autologous stem cell transplantation in first remission prolongs progression-free survival in follicular lymphoma: results of a prospective, randomized trial of the German low-grade lymphoma study group. Blood 2004;104(9):2667–74.

[61] Deconinck E, Foussard C, Milpied N, Bertrand P, Michenet P, Cornillet-LeFebvre P, et al. High-dose therapy followed by autologous purged stem-cell transplantation and doxorubicin-based chemotherapy in patients with advanced follicular lymphoma: a randomized multicenter study by GOELAMS. Blood 2005;105 (10):3817–23.

[62] Sebban C, Mounier N, Brousse N, Belanger C, Brice P, Haioun C, et al. Standard chemotherapy with interferon compared with CHOP followed by high-dose therapy with autologous stem cell transplantation in untreated patients with advanced follicular lymphoma: the GELF-94 randomized study from the Groupe d'Etude des Lymphomes de l'Adulte (GELA). Blood 2006;108(8):2540–4.

[63] Ladetto M, De Marco F, Benedetti F, Vitolo U, Patti C, Rambaldi A, et al. Prospective, multicenter randomized GITMO/IIL trial comparing intensive (R-HDS) versus conventional (CHOP-R) chemoimmunotherapy in high-risk follicular lymphoma at diagnosis: the superior disease control of R-HDS does not translate into an overall survival advantage. Blood 2008;111(8):4004–13.

[64] Schouten HC, Qian W, Kvaloy S, Porcellini A, Hagberg H, Johnson HE, et al. High-dose therapy improves progression-free survival and survival in relapsed follicular non-Hodgkin's lymphoma: results from the randomized European CUP trial. J Clin Oncol 2003;21(21):3918–27.

[65] Apostolidis J, Gupta RK, Grenzelias D, Johnson PW, Pappa VI, Summers KE, et al. High-dose therapy with autologous bone marrow support as consolidation of remission in follicular lymphoma: long-term clinical and molecular follow-up. J Clin Oncol 2000;18(3):527–36.

[66] Rohatiner AZ, Nadler L, Davies AJ, Apostolidis J, Neuberg D, Matthews J, et al. Myeloablative therapy with autologous bone marrow transplantation for follicular lymphoma at the time of second or subsequent remission: long-term follow-up. J Clin Oncol 2007;25(18):2554–9.

[67] Montoto S, Canals C, Rohatiner AZ, Taghipour G, Sureda A, Schmitz N, et al. Long-term follow-up of high-dose treatment with autologous haematopoietic progenitor cell support in 693 patients with follicular lymphoma: an EBMT registry study. Leukemia 2007;21(11):2324–31.

[68] Kornacker M, Stumm J, Pott C, Dietrich S, Sussmilch S, Hensel M, et al. Characteristics of relapse after autologous stem-cell transplantation for follicular lymphoma: a long-term follow-up. Ann Oncol 2009;20(4):722–8.

[69] Metzner B, Pott C, Muller TH, Casper J, Kimmich C, Petershofen EK, et al. Long-term outcome in patients with follicular lymphoma following high-dose therapy and autologous stem cell transplantation. Eur J Haematol 2021;107(5):543–52.

[70] Robinson SP, Boumendil A, Finel H, Schouten H, Ehninger G, Maertens J, et al. Reduced intensity allogeneic stem cell transplantation for follicular lymphoma relapsing after an autologous transplant achieves durable long term disease control. An analysis from the Lymphoma Working Party Of the EBMT. Ann Oncol 2016;27:1088–94.

[71] Tomblyn MR, Ewell M, Bredeson C, Kahl BS, Goodman SA, Horowitz MM, et al. Autologous versus reduced-intensity allogeneic hematopoietic cell transplantation for patients with chemosensitive follicular non-Hodgkin lymphoma beyond first complete response or first partial response. Biol Blood Marrow Transplant 2011;17 (7):1051–7.

[72] Robinson SP, Canals C, Luang JJ, Tilly H, Crawley C, Cahn JY, et al. The outcome of reduced intensity allogeneic stem cell transplantation and autologous stem cell transplantation when performed as a first transplant strategy in relapsed follicular lymphoma: an analysis from the lymphoma working party of the EBMT. Bone Marrow Transplant 2013;48(11):1409–14.

[73] Snowden JA, Sanchez-Ortega I, Corbacioglu S, Basak GW, Chabannon C, de la Camara R, et al. Indications for haematopoietic cell transplantation for haematological diseases, solid tumours and immune disorders: current practice in Europe, 2022. Bone Marrow Transplant 2022;57(8):1217–39.

CHAPTER

7

New monoclonal antibodies for the treatment of acute lymphoblastic leukemia

Mark Gurney and Mark R. Litzow

Division of Hematology, Department of Internal Medicine, Mayo Clinic, Rochester, MN, United States

Abstract

While the majority of pediatric acute lymphoblastic leukemia (ALL) patients can be cured with combination chemotherapy, novel immunotherapies have provided new treatment options for those with relapsed or refractory disease. In adults, ALL remains challenging to treat, with incremental advances delivered by optimization of cytotoxic chemotherapy regimens and supportive care, integration of tyrosine kinase inhibitor therapies for BCR-ABL-positive disease, and the development of novel immunotherapies. Rituximab, in combination with established chemotherapy regimens, reduces relapse in 30%–50% of patients who have CD20-positive disease. In the past decade, antibody-drug conjugates, bispecific antibodies (immune cell engagers), and CAR-T cell therapies utilizing monoclonal antibody (mAb) technology have entered clinical practice, initially presenting important treatment options for patients with relapsed or refractory disease. Beyond this, a variety of antibody-derived therapies are being investigated, including for the treatment of T-cell ALL, a subtype of the disease for which it has been more challenging to identify a suitable tumor-associated antigen. These new generations of ALL immunotherapies possess both common and distinct mechanisms of resistance that investigational therapies aim to overcome. In this chapter, we review the landscape of licensed and investigational mAb-derived therapies for ALL.

Abbreviations

ADC antibody-drug conjugate
ADCC antibody-dependent cellular cytotoxicity
ALL acute lymphoblastic leukemia
AML acute myeloid leukemia
BiTE bispecific T-cell engager
CAR chimeric antigen receptor
CDC complement-dependent cytotoxicity

https://doi.org/10.1016/B978-0-443-19200-5.00003-8

CNS central nervous system
CR complete remission
CRh complete remission with partial hematologic recovery
FDA US Food and Drug Administration
GO gemtuzumab ozogamicin
IO inotuzumab ozogamicin
ITT intention to treat
mAB monoclonal antibody
MHC major histocompatibility complex
MRD measurable residual disease
NHL non-Hodgkin lymphoma
OS overall survival
PFS progression-free survival
Ph Philadelphia chromosome
RCT randomized clinical trial
scFv single-chain variable fragment
SOS sinusoidal obstruction syndrome
TCR T-cell receptor
TKI tyrosine kinase inhibitor

Conflict of interest

No potential conflicts of interest were disclosed.

Introduction

Acute lymphoblastic leukemia (ALL) is a malignant disease arising from precursor B- or T-lineage lymphoid cells which proliferate and accumulate in the bone marrow, blood, and extramedullary sites leading to a range of clinical manifestations [1]. ALL incidence is biphasic, predominating in childhood where it is the most common malignancy [2]. In this age group, the disease can be cured in up to 90% of patients with effective yet burdensome combination cytotoxic chemotherapy-based regimens [3]. A second, smaller peak in incidence occurs in older age. Adult ALL is more challenging to treat, reflecting both disease biology and the ability of patients to tolerate cytotoxic chemotherapies, culminating in higher rates of disease relapse and treatment-related mortality.

Optimal ALL treatment integrates prognostic information, available therapies, and associated risks of short- and long-term adverse effects. Modern prognostication considers clinical, genetic, and disease response-related factors. Age over 35 and white cell count greater than $30 \times 10^9/L$ (B-lineage) or $100 \times 10^9/L$ (T-lineage) at presentation were independently associated with adverse prognosis in a large cohort of adult patients [4]. The prevalence of t(9;22) with the formation of the Philadelphia chromosome (Ph) and BCR-ABL fusion protein, traditionally considered a high cytogenetic risk abnormality prior to the era of BCR-ABL directed tyrosine kinase inhibitors (TKI), increases with age. Cytogenetic markers of adverse risk in Ph-negative ALL include hypodiploidy (<44 chromosomes), *KMT2A* rearrangement, and complex karyotype [5]. Ph-like ALL, a high-risk subgroup of B-lineage ALL with heterogeneous genetic alterations resulting in the activation of cytokine receptor genes and kinase signaling pathways, is also more frequent in adolescent and adult groups [6]. These biological measures of prognosis were largely defined in an era prior to the availability of novel immunotherapies. Direct measures of treatment response can have a dominant prognostic impact.

This has been shown by the achievement of morphologic complete remission (CR) after induction therapy, and subsequently refined through more sensitive measurable residual disease (MRD) assays capable of detecting submicroscopic levels of disease [4,7–9]. Achievement of MRD negativity during therapy is associated with a reduced but not absent risk of future relapse, an occurrence that is challenging to treat.

Standard therapy of ALL varies across age groups. The chemotherapeutic backbone for ALL remains combinations including corticosteroids, anthracyclines, vincristine, methotrexate, and peg-asparaginase, along with prophylaxis directed at the eradication of subclinical CNS disease. Optimized pediatric regimens employ higher exposure to nonmyelosuppressive components vincristine, corticosteroids, and peg-asparaginase to limit long-term toxicities of an efficacious therapy [3,5]. Therapy is divided into induction, consolidation, delayed intensification, and maintenance phases, and can last for up to 3 years in total. Regimens developed for adults have historically included higher exposures to myelosuppressive anthracyclines and alkylators, with the omission of peg-asparaginase due to increased toxicities [10,11]. For adolescent and young adult patients, commonly defined as ages 15–39, the adoption of pediatric-inspired regimens has improved outcomes, albeit with higher rates of toxicity relative to pediatric cases [12,13]. Reflecting the higher relapse risk, consolidation with allogeneic stem cell transplantation (allo-SCT) is more frequently pursued in adult ALL, although it may not be required for patients achieving sustained MRD negativity.

Both molecularly targeted therapies and immunotherapies have revolutionized modern ALL therapy, particularly for adult ALL where cytotoxic therapies alone are less likely to be successful [5]. Tyrosine kinase inhibitors have improved outcomes in Ph-positive disease and have allowed for reduced exposure to cytotoxic chemotherapies [14,15]. Monoclonal antibodies (mAb) applied directly or engineered to deliver a toxic payload in the form of an antibody-drug conjugate (ADC), or to redirect the cytotoxic potential of T-cells (bispecific antibodies and CAR-T cells), are now fundamental to the management of adult B-ALL and the basis of several licensed therapies. Despite the great successes that these recent developments represent, investigational antibody-based therapies seek to optimize the application of this technology and overcome novel mechanisms of resistance.

Central to the rapid introduction of diverse antibody-derived therapies in ALL, relative to other hematological malignancies, is the spectrum of tumor-associated antigens encountered in this disease. 75% of ALL cases are derived from B-cell precursors, with almost ubiquitous expression of the B-cell antigens CD19 and CD22. CD20, present in a subset of cases, is a valuable, but not as widely applicable, target [16]. Crucially, the expression of each of these antigens in healthy tissues is limited to B cells, with on-target, off-tumor toxicities restricted to B-cell aplasia and antibody deficiency (hypogammaglobulinemia), usually a tolerable adverse effect. Contrast this antigenic landscape to acute myeloid leukemia (AML), the predominant acute leukemia of adults, where considerable phenotypic heterogeneity within and between patients is encountered, and putative immunotherapeutic antigens frequently overlap with healthy myeloid progenitor populations with significant clinical consequences [17]. Thus, it is evident why B-ALL and other lymphoid malignancies have been a proving ground for antibody-based immunotherapy. Up to 25% of adult ALL cases are of T-cell lineage, with a distinct immunophenotype. This subtype of the disease harbors a dismal prognosis at relapse; however, antibody-based immunotherapy development has been limited to date by the absence of an ideal tumor antigen, although experimental approaches are attempting to address this area of need. We will first consider the regulatory approved antibody-derived therapies

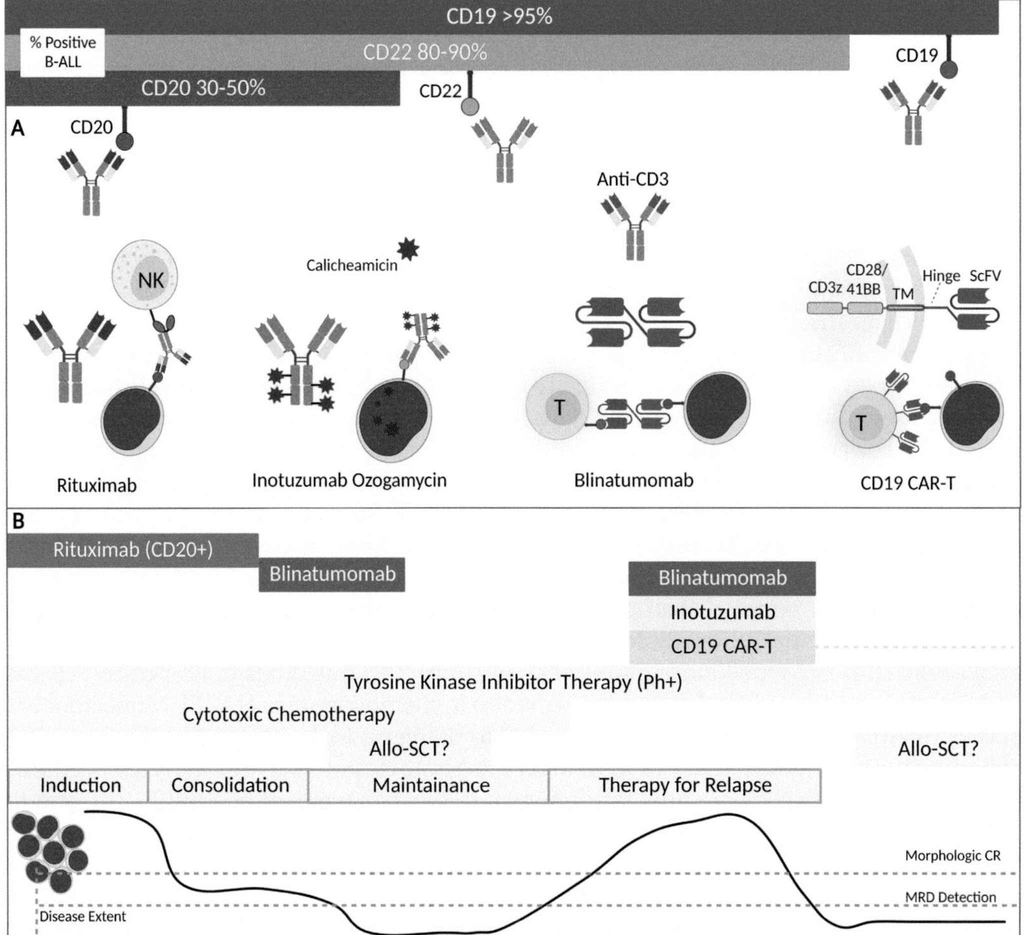

FIG. 1 (A) An overview of regulatory approved antibody-derived therapies for B-ALL and their associated antigens. (B) Schematic outlining the integration of regulatory approved antibody-derived therapies into B-ALL treatment protocols.

for B-ALL by tumor-associated antigen (summarized in Fig. 1), then consider shared and common resistance mechanisms, before exploring experimental approaches in development for B- and T-ALL.

Approved antibody-based therapies for B-ALL

CD20 and rituximab

Defining the role of rituximab treatment in B-ALL has been complex relative to mature B-cell malignancies. Absent on nonmalignant early B-cell precursor cells, only 30%–50% of

B-ALL cases express CD20 in >20% of cells, at diagnosis [18,19]. This contrasts with the almost universal expression of CD20 in adult B-cell-derived non-Hodgkin's lymphoma, where the benefits of rituximab are well established [20]. Intuitively, preclinical data suggested rituximab monotherapy would have limited clinical efficacy [21]. CD20 expression is, however, considered negatively prognostic in B-ALL and has been associated with an increased risk of relapse [19,22]. Thus, the addition of rituximab to combination chemotherapy regimens warranted investigation. Rituximab in combination with hyper-CVAD for adult B-ALL was initially shown to improve survival relative to historical controls for patients <60 years of age [23]. This was followed by a large multicenter, phase III randomized controlled trial (RCT) reported by the GRAAL group (GRAALL-2005), evaluating the addition of 16–18 rituximab doses (375 mg/m^2) across the first year of combination chemotherapy for patients 18–60 years of age with CD20+ (≥20% expression), Ph-negative B-ALL [18]. The addition of rituximab led to similar rates of CR post induction but a significant improvement in 2-year event-free survival (EFS) (65% vs 52%), primarily through a reduction in relapse rates (18% vs 32%), without an increase in serious adverse event rates. Interestingly, rates of severe allergic events attributable to asparaginase therapy were significantly lower in the rituximab group, suggesting that altered tolerance or clearance of asparaginase could have contributed to the benefits observed.

Other insightful studies highlighted the complexity of CD20 expression in ALL and posed the important question as to whether diagnostic phenotyping was sufficient to identify all patients likely to benefit from the addition of rituximab. CD20 is upregulated during induction chemotherapy, by corticosteroid treatment, and is prevalent in residual disease detected by multiparameter flow cytometry [24]. The Phase III UKALLXIV trial aimed to define if rituximab administration was beneficial irrespective of CD20 status and Ph status, recruiting patients between ages 25 and 65 [25]. Rituximab administration was restricted to 4 doses during induction only. The primary outcome of the study, 3-year EFS, favored the rituximab arm, but did not achieve statistical significance (43.7% vs 51.4%, $P=.14$). Analysis restricted to a subgroup of patients with cryopreserved cells also failed to detect an association between CD20 expression level and rituximab effect, suggesting that duration of exposure rather than CD20 expression levels may explain the discordant outcomes of the UKALLXIV trial versus GRAALL-2005 [26].

Recently, a phase II study incorporated both bortezomib and rituximab in B-ALL, with a backbone of a pediatric-inspired chemotherapy regimen for adolescents and young adults. Bortezomib has been shown to have synergism with both chemotherapy in B-ALL and rituximab in B-cell lymphomas—with the regimen reported by Jain et al. resulting in high rates of measurable residual disease (MRD)-negative CR compared to a historical cohort [27]. Further investigation is needed to confirm the potential benefit of this combination. Despite the remaining uncertainty as to the optimal threshold of CD20 expression, timing, and duration of therapy, rituximab is considered a standard of care component of first-line therapy in CD20+ Ph-negative B-ALL, with available evidence supporting administration beyond just induction therapy alone. The availability of other therapeutic targets in B-ALL, which have been potently targeted as monotherapies, may leave some of these questions unanswered.

CD19 and blinatumomab

The transmembrane glycoprotein CD19 (a member of the Ig superfamily) acts as a coreceptor of the B-cell receptor complex and is expressed on B-cells from the pre-B cell stage, peaking in mature B lymphocytes. CD19 is also widely expressed on neoplastic B-cells, and with universal expression in B-ALL, it has long been identified as a promising immunotherapeutic target, strengthened by a biological association with B-ALL cell self-renewal [28]. Monoclonal antibodies targeting CD19 have been evaluated in B-ALL, including the high-affinity Fc-modified, humanized tafasitamab—however, responses have been modest when compared to approaches that redirect T-cell cytotoxicity to CD19-targeting, via antibody technology [29].

Blinatumomab (*B lin*eage-specific *a*nti*tum*or *mo*use monoclonal *a*nti*b*ody) is a pioneering bispecific T-cell engager (BiTE), generated using a single-chain bivalent diabody approach from recombinant scFvs, producing a molecule that binds both CD19 and the CD3 component of the TCR complex, at one-third the size of a regular antibody, and suitable for clinical scale manufacture [30]. Blinatumomab brings benign and malignant CD19-expressing cells and T-cells into proximity and triggers cytotoxic reactions from unstimulated T-cells resulting in the release of perforin and granzyme-containing cytotoxic molecules. Blinatumomab activation is independent of TCR-MHC interactions, but mimics TCR-induced activation, leading to the proliferation and production of cytolytic proteins and inflammatory cytokines (IL-2, IL-6, IL-10, IL-4, IFN-γ, TNF-α). This T-cell activation is responsible for the adverse effect profile, which includes cytokine release syndrome (CRS) and neurotoxicity. Blinatumomab is highly potent, at least in part, due to the induction of serial killing by T-cells [31,32]. Rapidly cleared from circulation, with an elimination half-life of 1–2h, successful clinical implementation of blinatumomab has required delivery by a continuous infusion pump, over 28-day cycles separated by 14-day treatment-free intervals. The development of drug-neutralizing antibodies is rare, with an incidence of <1% [33].

Although also active in the relapsed/refractory setting, the efficacy of blinatumomab in deepening responses to standard therapies has rapidly made it a valuable therapeutic option. Blinatumomab was the first bispecific antibody to be FDA approved, with current indications in the treatment of relapsed/refractory B-ALL, or MRD-positive B-ALL in adults. An initial phase I/II study established the safety benefits of a ramp-up dosing strategy in relapsed/refractory disease [34]. In a subsequent phase II open-label study, blinatumomab (9μg/day for the first 7days and 28μg/day thereafter) resulted in a CR/CRh rate of 43%, a median OS of 6.1months, and grade 3 or worse neurotoxicity rate of 13% in Ph-negative, relapsed/refractory B-ALL. Responses, of which 82% were MRD-negative, were associated with a lower baseline blast count [35]. This dosing strategy informed the phase III TOWER study, in which 405 patients with relapsed/ refractory Ph-negative B-ALL were randomized to blinatumomab (up to 5 cycles and included maintenance cycles every 12weeks for 1year) or combination chemotherapy [36]. Blinatumomab resulted in higher CR rates (34% vs 16%), higher MRD negativity in responders (76% vs 48%), and improved OS (7.7 vs 4months) (Fig. 2A). Long-term follow-up from phase II studies has demonstrated a plateau effect beyond 2years, with 17% of patients surviving 3years or more, including 8/259 patients without subsequent allo-SCT or relapse. Similar efficacy has been demonstrated in the setting of relapsed/refractory Ph-positive B-ALL (including patients with prior second-generation

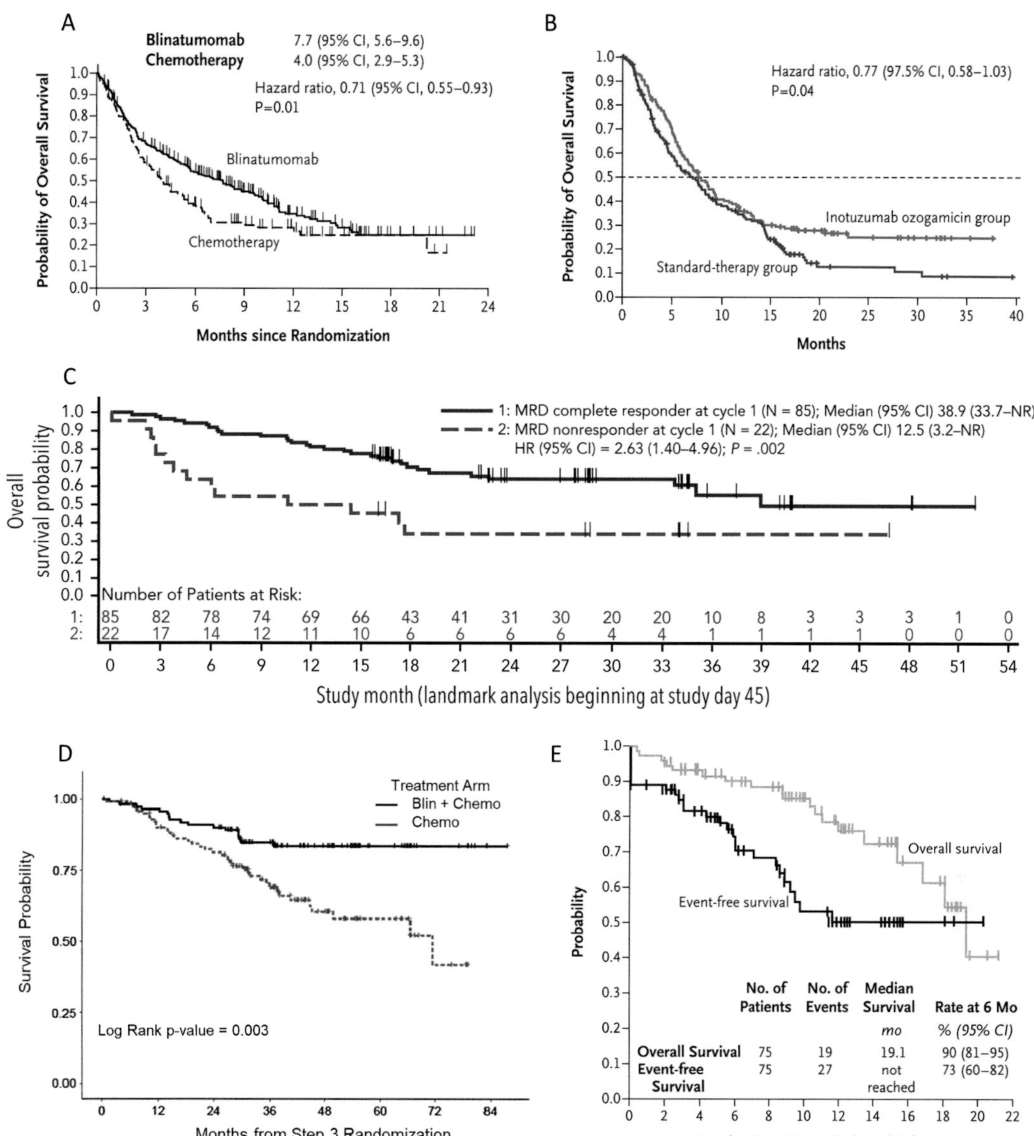

FIG. 2 Selected survival curves from antibody-based ALL therapy trials. (A) TOWER trial, (B) INO-VATE trial, (C) BLAST trial, (D) ECOG-ACRIN E1910, and (E) ELIANA trial.

TKI therapy) in the phase II ALCANTARA trial, the basis for FDA approval to include Ph-positive disease. With long-term follow-up, 5/45 (11%, 31% of CR/CRh responders) patients remained in MRD-negative CR, 4/5 without allo-SCT, and 3/5 with additional TKI therapy over follow-up periods of 12–23 months [37]. In each of the trials discussed above, responses occurred after the first cycle in almost all cases. Together, these studies established blinatumomab monotherapy as an active option in relapsed/refractory B-ALL. Long-term remissions generally required consolidation allo-SCT for the 30–40% of patients with deep responses, although rare long-term remissions without allo-SCT highlight the promise of this therapeutic approach.

Blinatumomab consolidation has also been shown to improve the depth of response for B-ALL in remission. This is best characterized for patients in morphological CR, but with detectable MRD, where highly sensitive molecular or flow cytometry-based techniques detect submicroscopic levels of disease—highly predictive of future relapse in the absence of further therapy [38]. After a smaller phase II study indicated high rates of conversion from MRD-positive to MRD-negative remission, the larger phase II BLAST trial was conducted [39]. In 116 patients with persistent MRD positivity, or MRD relapse after initial chemotherapy (defined as positive $>10^{-3}$), 78% achieved an MRD response (defined as negative or positive $<10^{-4}$) after blinatumomab. The median OS for the whole cohort was 36.5 months, with MRD responders showing clear OS benefit (38.9 vs 12.5 months) (Fig. 2C). Of 36 patients who underwent no further consolidation therapy, 9 (25%) remained in remission at a median follow-up of 24 months, versus 36/73 (49%) for those undergoing allo-SCT—suggesting that allo-SCT was beneficial but may not be required for long-term disease control in all cases. Higher rates of NRM following allo-SCT were observed, resulting in no clear survival difference between the allo-SCT and no further therapy groups for patients undergoing transplant in the first CR, although the study was not designed to address this question [40]. As with relapsed/refractory disease, the rate of grade 3/4 neurotoxicity was 13%, and 98% of those achieving MRD-negative remission did so after one cycle. Intriguingly, the benefit of blinatumomab consolidation has now been extended to patients with residual disease below the threshold of sensitivity of current MRD techniques. The first report from the ECOG-ACRIN E1910 randomized clinical trial indicates a survival benefit of the addition of blinatumomab to consolidation chemotherapy for MRD-negative patients (median OS not reached vs 71.4 months) (Fig. 2D) [41]. Reflecting the lower-risk nature of the cohort, these benefits occurred despite only 20% of patients in each arm receiving allo-SCT.

The efficacy of blinatumomab consolidation is increasingly being investigated to reduce the reliance on more toxic or prolonged components of ALL therapy. A prominent example of this approach is the modification of the standard of care adult combination chemotherapy regimen hyper-CVAD (± rituximab) to include 4 cycles of blinatumomab in place of cycles 5–8 of chemotherapy. Furthermore, with this design, the duration of the maintenance phase (POMP interspersed with three consolidation cycles of blinatumomab) was reduced to 18 months from 2 years. Updated results of this ongoing trial (NCT01371630), conducted in patients aged 14–59 with Ph-negative B-ALL, indicated that 26/27 (96%) achieved MRD-negative remission, with 1 year RFS of 76% comparing favorably to standard induction approaches [42]. This study would later be modified to include inotuzumab ozogamicin (IO) and will be discussed further. Another example of the potential value of integrating blinatumomab consolidation into therapy is in the setting of ALL occurring in persons with Down syndrome—a patient subgroup at a particularly high risk of adverse effects from anthracyclines and methotrexate leading to excess treatment-related mortality, and with an elevated relapse risk. The COG AALL1731 (NCT03914625) study is investigating a less myelosuppressive chemotherapeutic regimen but introducing 3 cycles of blinatumomab consolidation with the aim of reducing treatment-related toxicities.

For Ph-positive B-ALL, second-generation TKIs have shown superior efficacy as monotherapy over imatinib, frequently achieving CR, although often with residual MRD-positive disease. Chemotherapy-based consolidation regimens have generally been applied with the goal of deepening remission, although they can be associated with high rates of adverse effects in combination with TKIs [14]. Blinatumomab has been effectively applied in this scenario. The addition of 2–5 cycles of blinatumomab consolidation for patients achieving CR to an induction regimen of corticosteroid and dasatanib in Ph-positive B-ALL was shown to effectively increase MRD negativity rates from 29% to 52% (by ITT analysis) after 2 cycles in the GIMEMA LAL2116 study [43]. Further follow-up has demonstrated long-term disease-free survival of 71% at 3 years, presenting a paradigm shift toward cytotoxic chemotherapy-free treatment of Ph-positive ALL [44]. Given the expanding indications for blinatumomab in B-ALL, a successful transition to subcutaneous administration would simplify administration, and is the basis of an ongoing phase I clinical trial (NCT04521231) [45].

CD22 and inotuzumab ozogamicin

Inotuzumab ozogamicin (IO) is the first approved therapy to target the B-cell antigen CD22 (Siglec 2). CD22 expression is restricted to developing and mature B-cells. CD22 is a cell surface receptor that, upon binding to sialic acid-containing glycan molecules, transmits an inhibitory stimulus that dampens B-cell activation. The specific sialic acid which CD22 recognizes (α2,6Sia) is widely expressed in immune cells, allowing CD22 to contribute to a complex signaling network that modulates B-cell activation [46]. Ligation of CD22 by therapeutic mAbs can modulate this signaling, in addition to inducing antibody-dependent cellular cytotoxicity (ADCC). Additionally, rapid endocytosis of CD22 upon antibody binding defines an immunotherapeutic target particularly suited to targeting with an ADC molecule. CD22 is expressed in over 90% of B-ALL cases, and although there is some heterogeneity, in 80% of cases over half of the blast population is positive [46,47]. Initial attempts at therapeutic CD22 targeting focused on B-cell NHL. The humanized anti-CD22 antibody, epratuzumab, was evaluated in clinical trials, demonstrating modest efficacy [48]. Epratuzumab was subsequently trialed in combination with cytotoxic chemotherapy regimens for relapsed/refractory B-ALL in children and adults, although again efficacy was modest and responses short-lived [49,50]. Epratuzumab has largely been superseded by IO for malignant indications.

Inotuzumab ozogamyicin (IO) consists of a high-affinity, humanized, anti-CD22 antibody conjugated to a chemically stable disulfide derivative of calicheamicin (a potent DNA binding cytotoxic), via an acid-labile linkage molecule [51,52]. Antibody conjugation for targeted delivery has allowed the low therapeutic index of calicheamicin to be overcome for clinical application. Inotuzumab ozogamicin was developed using a similar structure to gemtuzumab ozogamicin (GO), an approved CD33 targeted ADC which provides incremental benefits for lower-risk AML subtypes in combination with cytotoxic chemotherapy [53]. Upon ligand binding, the ADC is rapidly endocytosed, and the calicheamicin derivative is cleaved in the acid environment of the lysosome. Inotuzumab ozogamicin was developed with all B-cell malignancies in mind, and dose-finding studies were conducted in the setting of B-NHL; however, it has proven of greatest utility to date in the management of B-ALL. This may be best explained by the inherent sensitivity of B-ALL cells to calicheamicin relative to B-NHL (and AML) [52,54–56].

A phase I clinical trial showed promising efficacy at a dose of 1.8 mg/m^2 IO every 3–4 weeks in relapsed/refractory adult B-ALL, but a high rate of hepatic toxicities including sinusoidal obstruction syndrome (SOS), especially for patients proceeding to allo-SCT [57]. Subsequently, the dosing regimen was modified to weekly doses of 0.8, 0.5, and 0.5 mg/m^2, achieving similar response rates, and lower rates of hepatic adverse effects [58]. This approach is also supported by a systems pharmacology model which indicates split dosing provides improved overall leukemic suppression by reducing the contribution of regrowth between doses [56]. The randomized phase 3 INO-VATE study confirmed the benefit of IO over salvage chemotherapy in patients with relapsed/refractory B-ALL. Inotuzumab resulted in higher rates of CR (81% vs 29%), higher rates of MRD negativity in those achieving CR (78% vs 28%), higher progression-free survival (PFS) (5.0 vs 1.8 months), and an OS benefit versus salvage chemotherapy (Fig. 2B). Despite these high initial response rates, the duration of response is generally short-lived, and allo-SCT appears to be essential to durable disease control [59]. In the INO-VATE study, 11% of patients receiving IO developed hepatic SOS, with the incidence again being highest for patients proceeding to allo-SCT (21%). Dual alkylator conditioning and elevated pretransplant bilirubin were associated with subsequent SOS [60]. The other main adverse effect attributable to IO was cytopenia, although the rate of platelet transfusion and febrile neutropenia was lower than with salvage chemotherapy. Unlike blinatumomab, the burden of bone marrow blasts prior to treatment was not associated with an inferior response rate. Furthermore, similar IO response rates were seen in older patients, a group that received less benefit from standard cytotoxic therapies. 13% of patients had Ph-positive disease, although the net benefit of IO relative to chemotherapy appeared to be lower, partly due to increased chemotherapy responses. FDA approval of IO for relapsed/refractory B-ALL was granted in 2018. In practice, to mitigate the risk of SOS, pretransplant exposure is limited to 2 cycles where feasible, and conditioning regimens are adjusted to avoid dual alkylator exposure. Recently, IO has been successfully trialed in pediatric populations in the relapsed/refractory setting—again showing up to 80% CR, and manageable levels of SOS using the same licensed adult dose [61,62]. Further improvements in the relapsed/refractory setting may also be achieved by a combination of IO with Mini-Hyper-CVD discussed below [63].

An ongoing phase II study is investigating the role of lower dose IO for MRD clearance in B-ALL, with an early report showing success in 67% of cases, irrespective of Ph status [64]. 14 of 18 patients remained in MRD-negative CR after a median follow-up period of 18 months with five receiving consolidation allo-SCT and one episode of SOS occurring. Further reports from this and related studies may go on to define IO as a viable consolidation strategy. The impressive activity of IO at relapse has also led to its investigation in combination therapies during frontline induction treatment. In particular, the addition of IO to frontline therapy for older patients, typically considered less likely to be fit for consolidative allo-SCT, has provided an important proving ground. The addition of IO to backbone chemotherapy consisting of lower doses of cytotoxic agents and omission of anthracycline exposure (derived from the Hyper-CVAD regimen), known as Mini-Hyper-CVD, resulted in a durable ORR of 35 months in patients >60 years [65]. Lower rates of SOS (8%) were seen in this setting, in keeping with the expected lower rates of allo-SCT. This regimen has later been adapted to include fractionated dosing of IO to further reduce SOS incidence and integration of consolidation/ maintenance with blinatumomab. This approach produced impressive remission rates in newly diagnosed patients over 60 years of age relative to historical controls treated with Hyper-CVAD [66]. Updated results have indicated 80% rates of MRD-negative responses and a 5-year survival rate of 46% [67]. A notable rate of 39% of deaths in remission and an 11% rate of therapy-related myeloid neoplasm was also reported in this older cohort. High-risk cytogenetic features and age predicted inferior responses to this regimen. The ongoing phase II GMALL-Initial1 (NCT03460522) trial is also examining the use of up-front IO for patients over the age of 55 with Ph-negative B-ALL [68]. In this regimen, IO and dexamethasone are the only systemic therapies delivered during cycle 1, with cycles 2 and 3 of induction comprising IO, intermediate dose methotrexate, cytarabine, and dexamethasone, before conventional combination chemotherapy consolidation and maintenance. 74% of patients achieved MRD-negative remission post the 3 induction cycles. One case of SOS was encountered, and a promising EFS of 73% at 2 years was recently reported. These studies argue for the investigation of up-front IO-containing regimens in future RCTs.

Antibody technology and CAR-T cell therapies

Antibody technology remains fundamental to the realization of CAR-T cell therapy, a genome-edited adoptive cell transfer immunotherapy pioneered in pediatric B-ALL, now being widely applied in the treatment of B-cell malignancies [69]. Current commercial CAR-T cell products are manufactured from autologous T-cells collected by apheresis. The T-cells are then activated and genetically engineered (most commonly using retroviral vectors) to express a synthetic receptor comprising an antigen recognition domain, a hinge domain, a transmembrane domain, and two distinct intracellular T-cell stimulatory domains (Fig. 1A). The antigen recognition domain of licensed CAR-T products is a single-chain variable fragment (scFv) sequence derived from a mAb. The CAR-T cells are subsequently expanded, cryopreserved, and reinfused after lymphodepleting chemotherapy, which supports CAR-T cell expansion and persistence in vivo. Upon contact with a cell expressing the targeted antigen, clustering of CAR molecules at the T-cell surface instigates an activating signal, leading to T-cell activation (independent of HLA/TCR interactions) and a cytotoxic response. The integration of a costimulatory signaling domain in addition to CD3ζ also supports CAR-T cell expansion and persistence, shown to be crucial to clinical effectiveness [70]. CAR-T cells targeting CD19 have proven highly effective in treating relapsed/refractory B-ALL.

While the products vary in characteristics including costimulatory domains, T-cell composition, and gene vectors—with implications for their clinical behavior, all FDA-approved CD19 CAR-T cell products incorporate an scFv derived from a murine CD19 antibody (FMC63) which recognizes a distinct CD19 epitope to blinatumomab. Two CD19 CAR-T products are approved for the treatment of relapsed/refractory B-ALL. Tisagenleleucel (CTL019) was approved for pediatric and young adult patients (up to the age of 25 years) with CD19+ relapsed/refractory B-ALL in 2017 based on the results of a phase II ELIANA study in which 81% of patients achieved MRD-negative remission, and the 12-month event-free survival was 73% (Fig. 2E) [71]. In 2021, brexucabtagene autoleucel (KTE-X19) was approved for adults of all ages with CD19+ relapsed/refractory B-ALL, based on the phase I/II ZUMA-3 trial which demonstrated a 69% rate of MRD-negative CR, and median RFS of 11.6 months [72]. In all, 45% of the patients in the study had previously been treated with blinatumomab, while 18% proceeded to allo-SCT post-CAR-T cell therapy. CAR-T cell therapies have been associated with key adverse effects including CRS and neurotoxicity syndrome. These are generally manageable and reversible, using the anti-IL6 mAb tocilizumab and corticosteroids, respectively, but mandate close monitoring in the weeks after infusion. Grade 3 or greater CRS has an incidence of 20%–30% and grade 3 or greater neurotoxicity was observed in 13% of cases for tisagenleleucel and 25% for brexucabtagene autoleucel during B-ALL treatment. CD19 CAR-T cell therapies are thus a vital option for the management of relapsed disease, although the complexity entailed in apheresis and manufacture and the associated cost remain important practical limitations relative to the alternative antibody-based approaches discussed previously.

Mechanisms of resistance to licensed antibody therapies

The disparate successful implementations of antibody-based therapies for B-ALL are associated with shared and distinct mechanisms of resistance. Mechanistic and clinical observations are expanding our understanding of resistance and informing the design and implementation of novel therapies for both B-ALL and other diseases. Resistance mechanisms to antibody-based therapies will be considered based on whether they reflect alterations to the target antigen or epitope and are summarized in Fig. 3.

Antigen alterations as a mechanism of resistance

Downregulation or alteration of a target antigen under the selective pressure of an antigen-specific immunotherapy is a universal mechanism of resistance that is highly relevant in B-ALL. As CD20 is not universally expressed in B-ALL, and a threshold of 20% positive cells is considered defining for positivity, antigen-negative populations are universal, and preclinical data confirmed rituximab monotherapy would not be capable of elimination of all B-ALL cells [21]. The upregulation of CD20 in MRD populations, and the reduced relapse rates described in clinical trials support the concept that rituximab aids in the elimination of an important CD20-positive chemotherapy-resistant population. Given that CD20 expression in MRD populations is also not universal, antigen-negative populations may drive relapse, supported by data from the pre-rituximab era demonstrating that B-ALL frequently loses CD20 expression at relapse [16,73]. Data specific to the resistance of MRD populations to rituximab in B-ALL is lacking; however, reduced expression of CD20, or structural changes in CD20 encountered in other B-cell malignancies, and discussed elsewhere in this book, may also be applicable in this scenario.

Reflecting the greater baseline expression of CD19 and CD22 in B-ALL and the greater efficacy of monotherapy approaches targeting these antigens, modifications of target antigen expression have been more readily examined as mechanisms of relapse. Intuitively for a target that is not ubiquitously expressed, the extent and homogeneity of CD22 expression have been associated with outcomes during IO therapy [74]. In patients who relapsed post-IO

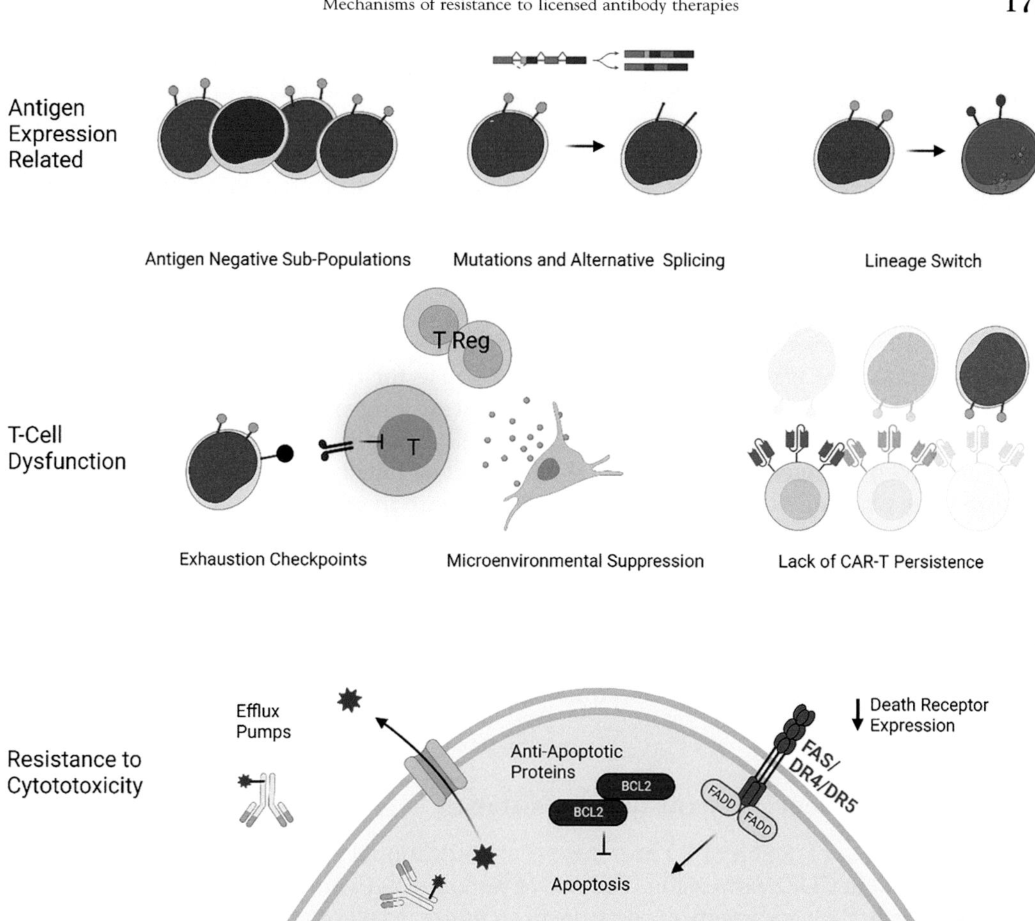

FIG. 3 Mechanisms of relapse to antibody-based immunotherapies for ALL.

therapy, reduced, but not absent, CD22 expression was the predominant phenotypic change specific to IO versus chemotherapy alone [75]. Complete loss of CD22 at relapse post-IO has also been reported [76]. Subgroup analysis of the INO-VATE trial found t(4;11) cases (*KMT2A* rearrangement) were the only group associated with lower response rates to IO. Although this group contained few patients, lineage switch, which is associated with *KMT2A*r, has been described as a mechanism of relapse post IO in t(4;11) ALL [77]. Recently, alternative splicing of CD22, including omission of exon 2, which results in failure of protein production, has been described as a mechanism of resistance post-IO. This alternatively spliced isoform is frequently detectable at diagnosis—laying the foundation for antigen escape relapse [78].

Although considered to be almost universally expressed, dim expression of CD19 is not uncommon, and putative CD19-negative cells have been detected at B-ALL diagnosis [79]. Despite this, these pretreatment factors do not appear to predict responses as CAR-T cells detect very low levels of CD19 [80]. The potential for activated CAR-T cells to stimulate bystander T-cells, including endogenous tumor-specific T-cells, to eliminate CD19-negative populations is under investigation [81]. CD19 antigen escape is best defined in the context of CAR-T cell therapy where potent elimination of CD19-positive cells is often sustained over time, even up to a decade after infusion [82]. CD19-negative relapses comprise 41% of post-CAR-T relapses, with 50% being CD19-positive, and the remainder being predominantly lineage switch (also causing CD19 loss, and predominantly associated with KMT2Ar disease) [83]. A detailed investigation of post-CAR-T B-ALL relapse samples detected mutations in CD19 exons 2–5, and associated high rates of loss of heterozygosity, resulting in loss of CD19 surface expression at relapse [84]. As with CD22, alternative splice variants have also been implicated in resistance to CD19 CAR-T, leading to the loss of the epitope recognized by FMC63 located in exon 2 [85,86]. Unintentional editing of a single leukemic B-cell during CAR-T manufacture was traced to subsequent relapse for one case, via cloaking of CD19 by concurrent CAR and CD19 expression—a rare but striking example of antigen modulation [87]. Given that all current licensed CD19 CAR-T cell therapies share the FMC63 scFv, resistance induced by antigen escape is expected to be a class effect, although novel CD19 CAR-T cell products utilizing scFv's to other CD19 epitopes are in late-stage development [88].

Blinatumomab therapy has also been associated with alterations in CD19 expression, but true CD19-negative relapses appear to be less common (10%–20%), which may reflect the time-limited period of CD19 targeting relative to CAR-T therapy [89,90]. Although blinatumomab recognizes a separate epitope, prior blinatumomab therapy is associated with increased rates of dim CD19 expression, increases in antigen escape relapse, and lower rates of MRD-negative remission post subsequent CAR-T cell therapy [80,91].

Antigen-independent mechanisms of resistance

The mechanism of action of IO presents several additional pathways to resistance not inherently related to CD22 expression. The rate of tumor growth and the efflux of calicheamicin associated with P-glycoprotein expression in malignant cells have been shown to have a greater effect than CD22 expression level on outcomes, based on models which integrated preclinical biomeasures, pharmacokinetic and pharmacodynamic data [56,92]. Preclinical data in which GO was shown to have activity in CD33-negative B-ALL, due to passive exposure to calicheamicin, could contribute to this effect [56]. Furthermore, as calicheamicin has been associated with the induction of apoptosis via a mitochondrial pathway in B-ALL blast cells, expression of BCL-2 family antiapoptotic proteins could lead to IO resistance. This provides a rationale for future combinations with targeted inhibitors of antiapoptotic proteins, including venetoclax, for which preclinical synergy with IO has been described and is the basis of an active clinical trial (NCT05016947) [93]. Intriguingly, IO may sensitize malignant B-cells to rituximab by modulating CD55, an inhibitor of complement-dependent cytotoxicity [94].

The reliance of blinatumomab on cytotoxic T cells allows for T-cell suppressive factors to modulate responses. Cytotoxic T-cell expansion occurs in response to blinatumomab and appears to contribute to clinical response. Expansion of regulatory T-cells (CD4/CD25/FOXp3-positive), also via direct blinatumomab activation, and detectable in peripheral blood during treatment, dampens cytotoxic T-cell proliferation and correlates with nonresponse to blinatumomab [95]. Depletion of regulatory T-cells restored cytotoxic T-cell proliferation in vitro. Expression of PD-L1 on B-ALL blasts, interacting with T-cell checkpoint receptor

PD-1, has also been implicated in modulating responses to blinatumomab [96]. PD-1 inhibition with pembrolizumab has been shown to improve blinatumomab responses in preclinical B-ALL models, laying the foundations for clinical trials investigating checkpoint inhibitor combinations with blinatumomab (NCT03160079) [97].

Over half of the disease relapses post CD19 CAR-T cell therapy retain CD19 expression, implicating other mechanisms of resistance. Loss of CAR-T cell persistence, heralded by B-cell recovery, is a frequent contributing factor to CD19+ relapses [98]. The adaptation of CAR constructs to remove murine elements and reduce immunogenicity may improve persistence and is a promising approach under evaluation [91]. Hypermethylation of death-inducing receptors seen in high-risk B-ALL subtypes may impair T-cell and CAR-T cell killing reliant on the death ligand TRAIL [99]. Microenvironmental factors have come into focus for their role in inducing CAR-T cell resistance. Both cell contact-mediated and cytokine-based mechanisms have been implicated—with myeloid-derived suppressor cells, fibroblasts, and IL-4 mediated suppression being important contributors [100].

The future of licensed antibody-based immunotherapies in ALL

In summary, rituximab provides an incremental but potentially important benefit for those with CD20+ B-ALL. Blinatumomab presents a valuable consolidation strategy in eradicating residual disease post combination-chemotherapy or TKI-induced remission (for Ph-positive disease). Inotuzumab ozogamicin is a useful bridging therapy to induce remission prior to allo-SCT in relapsed disease and is a promising addition to frontline regimens for older patients. CAR-T cell therapies have revolutionized the therapeutic landscape for patients with relapsed disease. Ongoing investigations will likely increase the reliance upon these existing antibody-derived therapies in the up-front management of ALL.

Investigational therapies

Novel approaches to existing immunotherapeutic targets for B-ALL

Alternative CD20 antibodies approved for other indications have also been considered in the management of B-ALL. The human anti-CD20 antibody, ofatumumab, has been safely combined with hyper-CVAD-based therapy in B-ALL, with a 4-year OS of 68% in a study that included patients with all levels of CD20 expression [101]. Preclinical data has confirmed that the enhanced ADCC induced by obinutuzumab is relevant to B-ALL targeting [102]. No direct clinical comparisons to rituximab in B-ALL are available. No clinical data yet exists for the application of bispecific engagers targeting CD20 in B-ALL, including glofitamab (CD20-CD3) which has recently shown impressive activity in relapsed/refractory DLBCL [103]. The relatively homogenous expression of CD19 and CD22 and the success of agents targeting these antigens have led to an understandable focus on the development of novel approaches to ALL.

Loncastuximab tesirine (ADCT-402) is a CD19-targeted ADC which utilizes SG3199 (a PBD-dimer-containing toxin). The phase I dose escalation study was terminated early for slow accrual; however, 3/35 patients treated achieved a CR [104]. Loncastuximab has been approved for relapsed/refractory large B-cell lymphoma. A clinical trial investigating a novel

CD19-CD3 bispecific antibody GNR-084 is currently registered as having commenced (NCT04601584). The availability of licensed, potent CD19-directed therapies sets a high bar for novel bispecific and ADC approaches—CD19 ADCs coltuximab ravansine and denintuzumab mafodotin showed modest activity in early phase trials but were not pursued for further development in B-ALL [105,106].

While IO is being evaluated as an up-front therapy, novel CD22-directed therapies are also under investigation. ADCT-602 is a humanized CD22-directed ADC, also conjugated to SG3199, with preclinical activity confirmed and currently being evaluated in a phase I/II clinical trial in relapsed/refractory B-ALL (NCT03698552). In a recent interim report from the dose-finding portion of this study, performed in a high-risk patient cohort, four patients, including 2/6 patients at the highest dose level trialed, achieved MRD-negative remission, and successful bridging to allo-SCT was reported [107]. MRD-negative remissions were also noted in patients who had received prior IO therapy (>3 months prior). A final administration schedule of weekly dosing has been chosen for the phase II portion of the study based on pharmacokinetic data. Myelosuppression appears to be the main dose-limiting toxicity, with no patients suffering SOS to date. This next phase is eagerly awaited, with the potential to provide an alternative CD22-directed ADC, without the associated risk of SOS—particularly relevant for patients likely to require allo-SCT.

The efficacy of CAR-T cell therapies targeting CD19 for B-cell malignancies, coupled with well-defined limitations, and rapidly deciphered mechanisms of relapse has triggered an explosion in research activity in immune cell therapies. The most common targets under investigation remain B-cell directed [108]. Although a detailed discussion is beyond the scope of this chapter, investigational CAR-T cell therapies aim to improve upon licensed therapies. To overcome antigen-escape mediated relapses, dual-targeted or tandem CAR-T cells targeting both CD19 and CD22 simultaneously have been investigated in several configurations, although the ideal approach and comparative efficacy of these have yet to be clarified [109]. A variety of alterations to CAR design, including both the antibody-derived scFv and stimulatory domains, allow for the fine-tuning of T-cell activation and the associated in vivo behavior of the product [110,111]. Multiplex-edited CAR-T cells can be armored to secrete cytokines or prevent inhibition from microenvironmental signals [112]. Gene editing, or the use of CAR-NK cells, is allowing allogeneic products to be developed—potentially overcoming key logistical limitations and reducing associated cost and delay to treatment availability [113,114]. Several allogeneic approaches are in the advanced stages of clinical evaluation. The allogeneic CD19-directed CAR-T product "UCART19," manufactured using the TALEN genome editing technology, incorporates the knockout of the TRAC gene (encoding for the TCR) and CD52 gene (permitting alemtuzumab lymphodepletion, required for UCART19 expansion), and introduces a CD20 mimic molecule providing a rituximab triggered safety switch. UCART19 has been evaluated in a dose-escalation phase I trial (NCT02746952) [115]. An ORR of 48% and median relapse-free survival of 7.4 months were observed in adults with relapsed/refractory B-ALL, using a multiple dosing strategy to overcome a lack of UCART19 persistence. Importantly, UCART19 was associated with a similar adverse effect profile as established autologous products. PBCAR0191 is another CD19-directed allogeneic CAR-T product incorporating TRAC knockout under clinical evaluation in B-NHL and B-ALL [116]. An intensified lymphodepletion regimen was again required to achieve robust expansion. 4/5 patients with B-ALL treated to date achieved CR, including a patient previously treated with an autologous CAR-T product. The durability of allogeneic CAR-T cell persistence and the resultant clinical responses is an important question that will be answered by larger studies in the future. Taken together, there are a multitude of promising avenues which may form the basis of future CAR-T therapies for B-ALL.

Novel immunotherapeutic targets in B-ALL

Additional targets for antibody-based therapies are also being considered. CD123 (interleukin-3 receptor alpha) is an investigational immunotherapeutic target that may be relevant to both AML and ALL and is being targeted by ADCs, bispecifics, and CAR-T cells. CD123 expression in ALL is heterogeneous, more frequently expressed in B-lineage than T-lineage cases, with 49% of pediatric B-ALL cases showing >50% expression. Flotetuzumab is a CD3-CD123 bispecific molecule, with a human IgG1 Fc domain linker, which has shown promising activity in AML and is being evaluated in a clinical trial for ALL (NCT04681105) [117]. An alternative bispecific antibody approach (XmAb14045) has also been reported, with an ORR of 15% in a phase I trial conducted in CD123-positive malignancies (NCT02730312) [118]. Only one B-ALL case was included in this initial report—and ongoing work is focused on its role in AML (NCT05285813). SAR443579 is a trispecific NK cell engager molecule with antibody binding sites for NKp46 and CD16a on NK cells and CD123 for B-ALL specificity. The planned phase I clinical trial (NCT05086315) includes patients with AML, MDS, and B-ALL [119]. NK cell engagers have varied designs but have potential advantages over T-cell-dependent approaches, including a lower rate of CRS associated with NK cell activation. CD25 (IL-2 receptor alpha chain) is expressed in the majority of Ph-positive BCP-ALL cases but is generally absent in Ph-negative disease [120]. An SG3199-based ADC targeting CD25 has also been examined in a phase I clinical trial, but to date the cohort reported contained AML cases only [121].

Antibody technology is also being applied to modulate the tumor microenvironment, with the aim of indirectly enhancing the efficacy of T-cell redirecting therapies. Antibodies that inhibit immune checkpoint receptor-ligand interactions, including PD1-PDL1 (pembrolizumab, nivolumab), and CTLA4-CD80 (ipilimumab) are being combined with blinatumomab and CAR-T cells to overcome the inhibitory contribution of these pathways [122]. These agents are well established in the management of several solid tumors.

Antibody approaches to T-ALL

The success of antibody-based therapies for B-ALL is dependent on the availability of multiple immunotherapeutic cell surface targets which are restricted to the B-cell compartment. B-cell aplasia and hypogammaglobulinemia are predictable but generally manageable consequences of B-cell targeting. ALL with T-lineage antigen expression (25% of cases) presents a greater challenge. Complete aplasia of T-cells based on targeting of T-lineage antigens has a profoundly immunosuppressive effect, with T-cell depleting agents established in the management of autoimmune conditions, and in solid organ transplantation conditioning. Expression of T-cell antigens also complicates CAR-T manufacture—due to the risk of recognition of antigens on nearby T-cells, leading to fratricide. Novel approaches to T-ALL immunotherapy are seeking to overcome these challenges.

Several CAR-T cell approaches to T-ALL have now reached early-phase clinical trials. CD7 has emerged as a promising target, with a phase I study of a CD7 CAR-T product, resulting in a 90% CR rate among patients with relapsed/refractory T-ALL [123]. The approach taken by Pan et al. in manufacturing the product from donor cells for patients post-allo-SCT and incorporating a CD7 binding/endoplasmic reticulum retention domain allowed for the long-term persistence of CAR-T cells and minimized fratricide. Interestingly, recovery of CD7-negative nonmalignant T-cell and NK cell populations was observed, which may abrogate some of the infective risks of T-cell depletion increasing the viability of this target. CD7 targeting in T-ALL has also been reported using the first example of a base-edited allogeneic CAR-T product to be applied clinically—with emerging clinical reports indicating meaningful responses [113].

CD38 is an established and valuable immunotherapeutic antigen in multiple myeloma—enabled by consistent high-level CD38 expression on malignant plasma cells. CD38 is expressed in other hematological malignancies to varying degrees—including AML and T-ALL. The preclinical activity of daratumumab in targeting T-ALL blasts has been reported, and the utility of daratumumab in a clinical setting is now being evaluated [124,125]. In a retrospective review of compassionate access daratumumab use for patients with relapsed/refractory T-ALL, a low single agent response rate was noted (20%)—although these responses were associated with lower disease burden (e.g., MRD positivity) [126]. Building upon this, daratumumab use has been reported in a small case series to achieve MRD eradication after salvage therapy in post-allo-SCT relapsed T-ALL, with notable successes characterized by long-term responses [127]. Interestingly, the benefits, particularly in a post-allo-SCT setting, may be partially related to immunomodulatory effects including depletion of regulatory T cells [128]. These reports have led to a clinical trial in the setting of MRD-positive-T-ALL through the Eastern Cooperative Oncology Group-American College of Radiology Imaging Network (ECOG-ACRIN) (NCT05289687). Recently, the phase 2 DELPHINUS study examined daratumumab in combination with a reinduction backbone of (VPLD) for pediatric and young adult patients with relapsed T-ALL. The CR rate of 54% was improved relative to historical controls (29%) [129]. Based on these promising results, CD38-directed therapies in development for multiple myeloma, including bispecific antibodies, CAR-T and CAR-NK cell therapies, may also find a future role in the management of T-ALL.

The murine anti-CD3ε mAb OKT3 (muromonab) was the first FDA-approved mAb and was clinically applied in the treatment of solid organ transplant rejection. Although efficacious, it was associated with considerable toxicities, including CRS. The medullary subtype of T-ALL expresses CD3 (20% of adults and 50% of pediatric T-ALL), and the potential to treat with anti-CD3 antibodies has long been recognized [130]. Notably, engagement of CD3 leads to an activation program in malignant T-lineage blast cells which can trigger apoptosis, resembling the negative selection process that eliminates autoreactive T cells receiving strong TCR-mediated activating signals during thymic development, and a mechanism independent of ADCC or CDC [131]. Derivatives of OKT3, engineered for reduced Fc receptor interactions but retaining the core agonistic properties, have proven successful immune modulators to delay the onset of symptoms in patients developing type 1 diabetes, with a considerably safer clinical profile relative to OKT3 [132]. Preclinical studies indicate retained activity in inducing apoptosis of CD3+ T-ALL blasts, although chemotherapy combinations will likely be required to overcome the outgrowth of preexisting antigen-negative subsets [133]. Although sensitive to activation-induced apoptosis, whether there is a therapeutic window to achieve clinically relevant ALL targeting, without significant impairment of T-cell immunity, is a key question for clinical application.

Finally, novel approaches to CAR and target design may result in CAR-T cell products applicable to all hematologic malignancies, for example, epitope editing of CD45 in HSCs is being developed to circumvent on-target off-tumor activity that would otherwise lead to hematopoietic aplasia when targeting the pan-hematopoietic cancer antigen CD45 [134].

In summary, new approaches to well-established targets, repurposing of antibody therapies initially applied in other diseases, and cutting-edge multiplex gene-editing technologies are providing hope for the successful integration of antibody-based therapies to T-ALL in the near future. The landscape of licensed and selected investigational antibody-based therapies for ALL is summarized in Table 1.

TABLE 1 Selected antibody and antibody-derived therapies in adult ALL.

Cell type	Agent	Target(s)	Class	Trial reference
B	***LICENSED***			
	Rituximab	CD20	Chimeric mAB	NCT00327678
	Inotuzumab ozogamicin	CD22	ADC (Calicheamicin)	NCT01564784
	Blinatumomab	CD19 × CD3	BiTE	NCT01466179
	Brexucabtagene Autoleucel	CD19	CAR-T	NCT02614066
	Tisagenlecleucel	CD19	CAR-T	NCT02435849
	INVESTIGATIONAL			
	B-Cell-Directed CAR-T	CD19, CD22, CD38	CAR-T	Multiple products
	Ofatumumab	CD20	Human mAb	NCT01363128
	Loncatuximab Tesirine	CD19	ADC (PBD-Dimer)	NCT02669264
	ADCT-602	CD22	ADC (PBD-Dimer)	NCT03698552
	Zilovertamab Vedotin	ROR1	ADC (MMAE)	NCT03833180
	Pembrolizumab (+Blina)	PD-1	Humanized mAb	NCT03512405
	Nivolumab (+Blina)	PD-1	Human mAb	NCT04546399
	Ipilimumab (+Nivo + Blina)	CTLA-4	Human mAb	NCT02879695
	GNR-084	CD19 × CD3	BiTE	NCT04601584
	ADCT-301	CD25	ADC (PBD-Dimer)	

Continued

TABLE 1 Selected antibody and antibody-derived therapies in adult ALL—cont'd

Cell type	Agent	Target(s)	Class	Trial reference
B or T	Flotetuzumab	CD123 × CD3	BiTE	NCT04681105
	IMGN632	CD123	ADC (IGN)	NCT03386513
	SAR443579	CD123 × CD16a × NKp46	Trispecific NK Engager	NCT05086315
	Daratumumab	CD38	Human mAb	NCT03384654
T	T-Lineage-Directed CAR-T	CD7, CD5, CD38, CD123	CAR-T	Multiple products
	Teplizumab	CD3ε	Antibody (non-Fc)	

ROR1, *receptor tyrosine kinase-like orphan receptor 1;* BiTE, *bispecific T-cell engager;* MMAE, *monomethyl auristatin E;* IGN, *indolinobenzodiazepine pseudodimers;* Blina, *blinatumomab.*

Conclusions

Currently, licensed antibody-based therapies occupy complementary roles in the management of B-ALL. These developments have revolutionized the management of B-ALL, although truly curative therapy remains elusive in many cases. Rational integration of licensed immunotherapies to frontline regimens, an evolving understanding of their distinct mechanisms of resistance, and ongoing efforts to apply these principles to novel immunotherapeutic targets seem likely to define the next key developments in this field. For T-ALL, an effective immunotherapeutic approach has remained elusive, but a variety of promising approaches are in development.

Acknowledgment

Figs. 1 and 3 are original and were created with biorender.com.

References

[1] Arber DA, Orazi A, Hasserjian R, Thiele J, Borowitz MJ, le Beau MM, et al. The 2016 revision to the World Health Organization classification of myeloid neoplasms and acute leukemia. Blood 2016;127:2391–405. https://doi.org/10.1182/BLOOD-2016-03-643544.

[2] Siegel RL, Miller KD, Jemal A. Cancer statistics, 2020. CA Cancer J Clin 2020;70:7–30. https://doi.org/10.3322/CAAC.21590.

[3] Inaba H, Mullighan CG. Pediatric acute lymphoblastic leukemia. Haematologica 2020;105:2524–39. https://doi.org/10.3324/HAEMATOL.2020.247031.

[4] Rowe JM, Buck G, Burnett AK, Chopra R, Wiernik PH, Richards SM, et al. Induction therapy for adults with acute lymphoblastic leukemia: results of more than 1500 patients from the international ALL trial: MRC UKALL XII/ECOG E2993. Blood 2005;106:3760–7. https://doi.org/10.1182/BLOOD-2005-04-1623.

[5] Brown PA, Shah B, Advani A, Aoun P, Boyer MW, Burke PW, et al. Acute lymphoblastic leukemia, version 2.2021, NCCN clinical practice guidelines in oncology. J Natl Compr Cancer Netw 2021;19:1079–109. https://doi.org/10.6004/JNCCN.2021.0042.

[6] Roberts KG, Gu Z, Payne-Turner D, McCastlain K, Harvey RC, Chen IM, et al. High frequency and poor outcome of Philadelphia chromosome-like acute lymphoblastic leukemia in adults. J Clin Oncol 2017;35:394–401. https://doi.org/10.1200/JCO.2016.69.0073.

[7] Ribera JM, Oriol A, Morgades M, Montesinos P, Sarrà J, González-Campos J, et al. Treatment of high-risk Philadelphia chromosome-negative acute lymphoblastic leukemia in adolescents and adults according to early cytologic response and minimal residual disease after consolidation assessed by flow cytometry: final results of the PETHEMA ALL-AR-03 trial. J Clin Oncol 2014;32:1595–604. https://doi.org/10.1200/JCO.2013.52.2425.

[8] Brüggemann M, Raff T, Flohr T, Gökbuget N, Nakao M, Droese J, et al. Clinical significance of minimal residual disease quantification in adult patients with standard-risk acute lymphoblastic leukemia. Blood 2006;107:1116–23. https://doi.org/10.1182/BLOOD-2005-07-2708.

[9] Short NJ, Kantarjian H, Ravandi F, Konopleva M, Jain N, Kanagal-Shamanna R, et al. High-sensitivity next-generation sequencing MRD assessment in ALL identifies patients at very low risk of relapse. Blood Adv 2022;6:4006–14. https://doi.org/10.1182/BLOODADVANCES.2022007378.

[10] Patel B, Kirkwood AA, Dey A, Marks DI, McMillan AK, Menne TF, et al. Pegylated-asparaginase during induction therapy for adult acute lymphoblastic leukaemia: toxicity data from the UKALL14 trial. Leukemia 2017;31:58–64. https://doi.org/10.1038/LEU.2016.219.

[11] Kantarjian HM, O'Brien S, Smith TL, Cortes J, Giles FJ, Beran M, et al. Results of treatment with hyper-CVAD, a dose-intensive regimen, in adult acute lymphocytic leukemia. J Clin Oncol 2000;18:547–61. https://doi.org/10.1200/jco.2000.18.3.547.

[12] Dhédin N, Huynh A, Maury S, Tabrizi R, Beldjord K, Asnafi V, et al. Role of allogeneic stem cell transplantation in adult patients with Ph-negative acute lymphoblastic leukemia. Blood 2015;125:2486–96. https://doi.org/10.1182/BLOOD-2014-09-599894.

[13] Huguet F, Leguay T, Raffoux E, Thomas X, Beldjord K, Delabesse E, et al. Pediatric-inspired therapy in adults with Philadelphia chromosome-negative acute lymphoblastic leukemia: the GRAALL-2003 study. J Clin Oncol 2009;27:911–8. https://doi.org/10.1200/JCO.2008.18.6916.

[14] Foà R, Chiaretti S. Philadelphia chromosome–positive acute lymphoblastic leukemia. N Engl J Med 2022;386:2399–411. https://doi.org/10.1056/NEJMRA2113347/SUPPL_FILE/NEJMRA2113347_DISCLOSURES.PDF.

[15] Martinelli G, Papayannidis C, Piciocchi A, Robustelli V, Soverini S, Terragna C, et al. INCB84344-201: ponatinib and steroids in frontline therapy for unfit patients with Ph+ acute lymphoblastic leukemia. Blood Adv 2022;6:1742–53. https://doi.org/10.1182/BLOODADVANCES.2021004821.

[16] Borowitz MJ, Pullen DJ, Winick N, Martin PL, Bowman WP, Camitta B. Comparison of diagnostic and relapse flow cytometry phenotypes in childhood acute lymphoblastic leukemia: implications for residual disease detection: a report from the children's oncology group. Cytometry B Clin Cytom 2005;68B:18–24. https://doi.org/10.1002/CYTO.B.20071.

[17] Haubner S, Perna F, Köhnke T, Schmidt C, Berman S, Augsberger C, et al. Coexpression profile of leukemic stem cell markers for combinatorial targeted therapy in AML. Leukemia 2019;33:64–74. https://doi.org/10.1038/s41375-018-0180-3.

[18] Maury S, Chevret S, Thomas X, Heim D, Leguay T, Huguet F, et al. Rituximab in B-lineage adult acute lymphoblastic leukemia. N Engl J Med 2016;375:1044–53. https://doi.org/10.1056/NEJMOA1605085/SUPPL_FILE/NEJMOA1605085_DISCLOSURES.PDF.

[19] Thomas DA, O'Brien S, Jorgensen JL, Cortes J, Faderl S, Garcia-Manero G, et al. Prognostic significance of CD20 expression in adults with de novo precursor B-lineage acute lymphoblastic leukemia. Blood 2009;113:6330. https://doi.org/10.1182/BLOOD-2008-04-151860.

[20] Coiffier B, Lepage E, Brière J, Herbrecht R, Tilly H, Bouabdallah R, et al. CHOP chemotherapy plus rituximab compared with CHOP alone in elderly patients with diffuse large-B-cell lymphoma. N Engl J Med 2002;346:235–42. https://doi.org/10.1056/NEJMOA011795.

[21] Nijmeijer B, van Schie MLJ, Willemze R, Falkenburg JHF. Rituximab and Alemtuzumab in combination, but not alone, induce complete remissions in a preclinical animal model of primary human ALL: rationale for combination treatment. Blood 2007;110:2833. https://doi.org/10.1182/BLOOD.V110.11.2833.2833.

[22] Zhou J, Wang J, Liu H, Zheng HF, Ma L, Wang PF, et al. CD20 expression in adult patients with B-lineage acute lymphoblastic leukemia and its prognostic significance. Zhongguo Shi Yan Xue Ye Xue Za Zhi 2015;23:619–22. https://doi.org/10.7534/J.ISSN.1009-2137.2015.03.003.

[23] Thomas DA, O'Brien S, Faderl S, G arcia-Manero G, Ferrajoli A, Wierda W, et al. Chemoimmunotherapy with a modified hyper-CVAD and rituximab regimen improves outcome in de novo Philadelphia chromosome-negative precursor B-lineage acute lymphoblastic leukemia. J Clin Oncol 2010;28:3880–9. https://doi.org/10.1200/JCO.2009.26.9456.

[24] Dworzak MN, Schumich A, Printz D, Pötschger U, Husak Z, Attarbaschi A, et al. CD20 up-regulation in pediatric B-cell precursor acute lymphoblastic leukemia during induction treatment: setting the stage for anti-CD20 directed immunotherapy. Blood 2008;112:3982–8. https://doi.org/10.1182/BLOOD-2008-06-164129.
[25] Marks DI, Kirkwood AA, Rowntree CJ, Aguiar M, Bailey KE, Beaton B, et al. Addition of four doses of rituximab to standard induction chemotherapy in adult patients with precursor B-cell acute lymphoblastic leukaemia (UKALL14): a phase 3, multicentre, randomised controlled trial. Lancet Haematol 2022;9:e262–75. https://doi.org/10.1016/S2352-3026(22)00038-2.
[26] O'Dwyer KM. Rituximab in B-ALL: how much and for whom? Hematologist 2022;19. https://doi.org/10.1182/HEM.V19.4.2022414.
[27] Jain H, Sengar M, Goli VB, Thorat J, Tembhare P, Shetty D, et al. Bortezomib and rituximab in de novo adolescent/adult CD20-positive, Ph-negative pre-B-cell acute lymphoblastic leukemia. Blood Adv 2021;5:3436–44. https://doi.org/10.1182/BLOODADVANCES.2020003368.
[28] Kong Y, Yoshida S, Saito Y, Doi T, Nagatoshi Y, Fukata M, et al. CD34+CD38+CD19+ as well as CD34+CD38-CD19+ cells are leukemia-initiating cells with self-renewal capacity in human B-precursor ALL. Leukemia 2008;22:1207–13. https://doi.org/10.1038/LEU.2008.83.
[29] Klisovic RB, Leung WH, Brugger W, Dirnberger-Hertweck M, Winderlich M, Ambarkhane SV, et al. A phase 2a, single-arm, open-label study of tafasitamab, a humanized, Fc-modified, anti-CD19 antibody, in patients with relapsed/refractory B-precursor cell acute lymphoblastic leukemia. Cancer 2021;127:4190. https://doi.org/10.1002/CNCR.33796.
[30] Nagorsen D, Kufer P, Baeuerle PA, Bargou R. Blinatumomab: a historical perspective. Pharmacol Ther 2012;136:334–42. https://doi.org/10.1016/J.PHARMTHERA.2012.07.013.
[31] Hoffmann P, Hofmeister R, Brischwein K, Brandl C, Crommer S, Bargou R, et al. Serial killing of tumor cells by cytotoxic T cells redirected with a CD19-/CD3-bispecific single-chain antibody construct. Int J Cancer 2005;115:98–104. https://doi.org/10.1002/IJC.20908.
[32] Bargou R, Leo E, Zugmaier G, Klinger M, Goebeler M, Knop S, et al. Tumor regression in cancer patients by very low doses of a T cell-engaging antibody. Science 2008;321:974–7. https://doi.org/10.1126/SCIENCE.1158545.
[33] Zhu M, Wu B, Brandl C, Johnson J, Wolf A, Chow A, et al. Blinatumomab, a bispecific T-cell engager (BiTE(®)) for CD-19 targeted cancer immunotherapy: clinical pharmacology and its implications. Clin Pharmacokinet 2016;55:1271–88. https://doi.org/10.1007/S40262-016-0405-4.
[34] Topp MS, Gökbuget N, Zugmaier G, Klappers P, Stelljes M, Neumann S, et al. Phase II trial of the anti-CD19 bispecific T cell-engager blinatumomab shows hematologic and molecular remissions in patients with relapsed or refractory B-precursor acute lymphoblastic leukemia. J Clin Oncol 2014;32:4134–40. https://doi.org/10.1200/JCO.2014.56.3247.
[35] Topp MS, Gökbuget N, Stein AS, Zugmaier G, O'Brien S, Bargou RC, et al. Safety and activity of blinatumomab for adult patients with relapsed or refractory B-precursor acute lymphoblastic leukaemia: a multicentre, single-arm, phase 2 study. Lancet Oncol 2015;16:57–66. https://doi.org/10.1016/S1470-2045(14)71170-2.
[36] Kantarjian H, Stein A, Gökbuget N, Fielding AK, Schuh AC, Ribera J-M, et al. Blinatumomab versus chemotherapy for advanced acute lymphoblastic leukemia. N Engl J Med 2017;376:836–47. https://doi.org/10.1056/NEJMOA1609783/SUPPL_FILE/NEJMOA1609783_DISCLOSURES.PDF.
[37] Martinelli G, Boissel N, Chevallier P, Ottmann O, Gökbuget N, Rambaldi A, et al. Long-term follow-up of blinatumomab in patients with relapsed/refractory Philadelphia chromosome-positive B-cell precursor acute lymphoblastic leukaemia: final analysis of ALCANTARA study. Eur J Cancer 2021;146:107–14. https://doi.org/10.1016/J.EJCA.2020.12.022.
[38] Berry DA, Zhou S, Higley H, Mukundan L, Fu S, Reaman GH, et al. Association of minimal residual disease with clinical outcome in pediatric and adult acute lymphoblastic leukemia: a meta-analysis. JAMA Oncol 2017;3. https://doi.org/10.1001/JAMAONCOL.2017.0580.
[39] Goekbuget N, Dombret H, Bonifacio M, Reichle A, Graux C, Havelange V, et al. BLAST: a confirmatory, single-arm, phase 2 study of blinatumomab, a bispecific T-cell engager (BiTE®) antibody construct, in patients with minimal residual disease B-precursor acute lymphoblastic leukemia (ALL). Blood 2014;124:379. https://doi.org/10.1182/BLOOD.V124.21.379.379.
[40] Gökbuget N, Dombret H, Bonifacio M, Reichle A, Graux C, Faul C, et al. Blinatumomab for minimal residual disease in adults with B-cell precursor acute lymphoblastic leukemia. Blood 2018;131:1522–31. https://doi.org/10.1182/BLOOD-2017-08-798322.
[41] Litzow MR, Sun Z, Paietta E, Mattison RJ, Lazarus HM, Rowe JM, et al. Consolidation therapy with blinatumomab improves overall survival in newly diagnosed adult patients with B-lineage acute lymphoblastic

leukemia in measurable residual disease negative remission: results from the ECOG-ACRIN E1910 randomized phase III National Cooperative Clinical Trials Network Trial. Blood 2022;140. https://doi.org/10.1182/BLOOD-2022-171751. LBA-1.

[42] Short NJ, Kantarjian HM, Ravandi F, Yilmaz M, Kadia TM, Thompson PA, et al. A phase II study of hyper-CVAD with sequential blinatumomab (Blina), with or without inotuzumab ozogamicin (INO), in adults with newly diagnosed B-cell acute lymphoblastic leukemia (ALL). J Clin Oncol 2022;40:7034. https://doi.org/10.1200/JCO.2022.40.16_SUPPL.7034.

[43] Foà R, Bassan R, Vitale A, Elia L, Piciocchi A, Puzzolo M-C, et al. Dasatinib–blinatumomab for Ph-positive acute lymphoblastic leukemia in adults. N Engl J Med 2020;383:1613–23. https://doi.org/10.1056/NEJMOA2016272/SUPPL_FILE/NEJMOA2016272_DATA-SHARING.PDF.

[44] Chiaretti S, Bassan R, Vitale A, Elia L, Piciocchi A, Viero P, et al. P353: forty months update of the Gimema LAL2116 (D-ALBA) protocol and ancillary LAL2217 study for newly diagnosed adult PH+ all. In: European Hematology Association Annual Congress, vol. 6. Ovid Technologies (Wolters Kluwer Health); 2022. https://doi.org/10.1097/01.HS9.0000844300.04335.AF.

[45] Martínez Sánchez P, Zugmaier G, Gordon P, Jabbour E, Rifón Roca JJ, Schwartz S, et al. Safety and pharmacokinetics of subcutaneous blinatumomab (SC blinatumomab) for the treatment of adults with relapsed or refractory B cell precursor acute lymphoblastic leukemia (R/R B-ALL); results from a phase 1b study. Blood 2022;140:6122–4. https://doi.org/10.1182/BLOOD-2022-157117.

[46] Lanza F, Maffini E, Rondoni M, Massari E, Faini AC, Malavasi F. CD22 expression in B-cell acute lymphoblastic leukemia: biological significance and implications for inotuzumab therapy in adults. Cancers 2020;12. https://doi.org/10.3390/CANCERS12020303.

[47] Raponi S, Stefania De Propris M, Intoppa S, Laura Milani M, Vitale A, Elia L, et al. Flow cytometric study of potential target antigens (CD19, CD20, CD22, CD33) for antibody-based immunotherapy in acute lymphoblastic leukemia: analysis of 552 cases. Leuk Lymphoma 2011;52:1098–107. https://doi.org/10.3109/10428194.2011.559668.

[48] Leonard JP, Coleman M, Ketas JC, Chadburn A, Furman R, Schuster MW, et al. Epratuzumab, a humanized anti-CD22 antibody, in aggressive non-Hodgkin's lymphoma: phase I/II clinical trial results. Clin Cancer Res 2004;10:5327–34. https://doi.org/10.1158/1078-0432.CCR-04-0294.

[49] Raetz EA, Cairo MS, Borowitz MJ, Blaney SM, Krailo MD, Leil TA, et al. Chemoimmunotherapy reinduction with epratuzumab in children with acute lymphoblastic leukemia in marrow relapse: a children's oncology group pilot study. J Clin Oncol 2008;26:3756. https://doi.org/10.1200/JCO.2007.15.3528.

[50] Chevallier P, Huguet F, Raffoux E, Etienne A, Leguay T, Isnard F, et al. Vincristine, dexamethasone and epratuzumab for older relapsed/refractory CD22+ B-acute lymphoblastic leukemia patients: a phase II study. Haematologica 2015;100:e128–31. https://doi.org/10.3324/HAEMATOL.2014.120220.

[51] Hamann PR, Hinman LM, Hollander I, Beyer CF, Lindh D, Holcomb R, et al. Gemtuzumab ozogamicin, a potent and selective anti-CD33 antibody–calicheamicin conjugate for treatment of acute myeloid leukemia. Bioconjug Chem 2001;13:47–58. https://doi.org/10.1021/BC010021Y.

[52] Wynne J, Wright D, Stock W. Inotuzumab: from preclinical development to success in B-cell acute lymphoblastic leukemia. Blood Adv 2019;3:96–104. https://doi.org/10.1182/BLOODADVANCES.2018026211.

[53] Baron J, Wang ES. Gemtuzumab ozogamicin for the treatment of acute myeloid leukemia. Expert Rev Clin Pharmacol 2018;11:549–59. https://doi.org/10.1080/17512433.2018.1478725.

[54] DiJoseph JF, Armellino DC, Boghaert ER, Khandke K, Dougher MM, Sridharan L, et al. Antibody-targeted chemotherapy with CMC-544: a CD22-targeted immunoconjugate of calicheamicin for the treatment of B-lymphoid malignancies. Blood 2004;103:1807–14. https://doi.org/10.1182/BLOOD-2003-07-2466.

[55] Zwaan CM, Reinhardt D, Jürgens H, Huismans DR, Hählen K, Smith OP, et al. Gemtuzumab ozogamicin in pediatric CD33-positive acute lymphoblastic leukemia: first clinical experiences and relation with cellular sensitivity to single agent calicheamicin. Leukemia 2003;17:468–70. https://doi.org/10.1038/SJ.LEU.2402749.

[56] Betts AM, Haddish-Berhane N, Tolsma J, Jasper P, King LE, Sun Y, et al. Preclinical to clinical translation of antibody-drug conjugates using PK/PD modeling: a retrospective analysis of inotuzumab ozogamicin. AAPS J 2016;18:1101–16. https://doi.org/10.1208/S12248-016-9929-7.

[57] Kantarjian H, Thomas D, Jorgensen J, Jabbour E, Kebriaei P, Rytting M, et al. Inotuzumab ozogamicin, an anti-CD22-calecheamicin conjugate, for refractory and relapsed acute lymphocytic leukaemia: a phase 2 study. Lancet Oncol 2012;13:403–11. https://doi.org/10.1016/S1470-2045(11)70386-2.

[58] Kantarjian H, Thomas D, Jorgensen J, Kebriaei P, Jabbour E, Rytting M, et al. Results of inotuzumab ozogamicin, a CD22 monoclonal antibody, in refractory and relapsed acute lymphocytic leukemia. Cancer 2013;119:2728–36. https://doi.org/10.1002/CNCR.28136.

[59] Kantarjian HM, DeAngelo DJ, Stelljes M, Martinelli G, Liedtke M, Stock W, et al. Inotuzumab ozogamicin versus standard therapy for acute lymphoblastic leukemia. N Engl J Med 2016;375:740–53. https://doi.org/10.1056/NEJMOA1509277/SUPPL_FILE/NEJMOA1509277_DISCLOSURES.PDF.
[60] Kantarjian HM, DeAngelo DJ, Advani AS, Stelljes M, Kebriaei P, Cassaday RD, et al. Hepatic adverse event profile of inotuzumab ozogamicin in adult patients with relapsed or refractory acute lymphoblastic leukaemia: results from the open-label, randomised, phase 3 INO-VATE study. Lancet Haematol 2017;4:e387–98. https://doi.org/10.1016/S2352-3026(17)30103-5.
[61] Brivio E, Locatelli F, Lopez-Yurda M, Malone A, Díaz-de-Heredia C, Bielorai B, et al. A phase 1 study of inotuzumab ozogamicin in pediatric relapsed/refractory acute lymphoblastic leukemia (ITCC-059 study). Blood 2021;137:1582–90. https://doi.org/10.1182/BLOOD.2020007848.
[62] O'Brien MM, Ji L, Shah NN, Rheingold SR, Bhojwani D, Yuan CM, et al. Phase II trial of inotuzumab ozogamicin in children and adolescents with relapsed or refractory B-cell acute lymphoblastic leukemia: children's oncology group protocol AALL1621. J Clin Oncol 2022;40:956–67. https://doi.org/10.1200/JCO.21.01693.
[63] Jabbour E, Sasaki K, Short NJ, Ravandi F, Huang X, Khoury JD, et al. Long-term follow-up of salvage therapy using a combination of inotuzumab ozogamicin and mini–hyper-CVD with or without blinatumomab in relapsed/refractory Philadelphia chromosome–negative acute lymphoblastic leukemia. Cancer 2021;127:2025–38. https://doi.org/10.1002/CNCR.33469.
[64] Senapati J, Short N, Alvarado Y, Burger JA, Jain N, Konopleva M, et al. A phase II study of inotuzumab ozogamicin for the treatment of measurable residual disease-positive B-cell acute lymphoblastic leukemia. Blood 2022;140:3253–5. https://doi.org/10.1182/BLOOD-2022-170667.
[65] Kantarjian H, Ravandi F, Short NJ, Huang X, Jain N, Sasaki K, et al. Inotuzumab ozogamicin in combination with low-intensity chemotherapy for older patients with Philadelphia chromosome-negative acute lymphoblastic leukaemia: a single-arm, phase 2 study. Lancet Oncol 2018;19:240–8. https://doi.org/10.1016/S1470-2045(18)30011-1.
[66] Jabbour EJ, Sasaki K, Ravandi F, Short NJ, Garcia-Manero G, Daver N, et al. Inotuzumab ozogamicin in combination with low-intensity chemotherapy (mini-HCVD) with or without blinatumomab versus standard intensive chemotherapy (HCVAD) as frontline therapy for older patients with Philadelphia chromosome-negative acute lymphoblastic leukemia: a propensity score analysis. Cancer 2019;125:2579–86. https://doi.org/10.1002/CNCR.32139.
[67] Macaron W, Kantarjian HM, Short NJ, Ravandi F, Jain N, Kadia TM, et al. Updated results from a phase II study of mini-hyper-CVD (mini-HCVD) plus inotuzumab ozogamicin (INO), with or without blinatumomab (Blina), in older adults with newly diagnosed Philadelphia chromosome (Ph)-negative B-cell acute lymphoblastic leukemia (ALL). J Clin Oncol 2022;40:7011. https://doi.org/10.1200/JCO.2022.40.16_SUPPL.7011.
[68] Stelljes M, Alakel N, Wäsch R, Scholl S, Nachtkamp K, Rank A, et al. Inotuzumab ozogamicin induction followed by standard chemotherapy yields high remission rates and promising survival in older (>55 years) patients with de novo B-lymphoblastic leukemia (GMALL-initial1 trial). Blood 2022;140(Suppl. 1):510–2. https://doi.org/10.1182/BLOOD-2022-162235.
[69] June CH, Sadelain M. Chimeric antigen receptor. Therapy 2018;379:64–73. https://doi.org/10.1056/NEJMRA1706169.
[70] Savoldo B, Ramos CA, Liu E, Mims MP, Keating MJ, Carrum G, et al. CD28 costimulation improves expansion and persistence of chimeric antigen receptor-modified T cells in lymphoma patients. J Clin Invest 2011;121:1822–6. https://doi.org/10.1172/JCI46110.
[71] Maude SL, Laetsch TW, Buechner J, Rives S, Boyer M, Bittencourt H, et al. Tisagenlecleucel in children and young adults with B-cell lymphoblastic leukemia. N Engl J Med 2018;378:439–48. https://doi.org/10.1056/NEJMoa1709866.
[72] Shah BD, Ghobadi A, Oluwole OO, Logan A, Boissel N, Cassaday RD, et al. Phase 2 results of the ZUMA-3 study evaluating KTE-X19, an anti-CD19 chimeric antigen receptor (CAR) T-cell therapy, in adult patients (pts) with relapsed/refractory B-cell acute lymphoblastic leukemia (R/R B-ALL). J Clin Oncol 2021;39:7002. https://doi.org/10.1200/JCO.2021.39.15_SUPPL.7002.
[73] Chen W, Karandikar NJ, McKenna RW, Kroft SH. Stability of leukemia-associated immunophenotypes in precursor B-lymphoblastic leukemia/lymphoma: a single institution experience. Am J Clin Pathol 2007;127:39–46. https://doi.org/10.1309/7R6MU7R9YWJBY5V4.
[74] Shah NN, O'Brien MM, Yuan C, Ji L, Xu X, Rheingold SR, et al. Evaluation of CD22 modulation as a mechanism of resistance to inotuzumab ozogamicin (InO): results from central CD22 testing on the Children's oncology group (COG) phase II trial of INO in children and young adults with CD22+ B-acute lymphoblastic leukemia (B-ALL). J Clin Oncol 2020;38:10519. https://doi.org/10.1200/JCO.2020.38.15_SUPPL.10519.

[75] Kantarjian HM, Stock W, Cassaday RD, DeAngelo DJ, Jabbour EJ, O'Brien SM, et al. Comparison of CD22 expression between baseline, end of treatment, and relapse among patients treated with inotuzumab ozogamicin who responded and subsequently relapsed in two clinical trials. Blood 2018;132:2699. https://doi.org/10.1182/BLOOD-2018-99-110826.

[76] Reinert J, Beitzen-Heineke A, Wethmar K, Stelljes M, Fiedler W, Schwartz S. Loss of CD22 expression and expansion of a CD22dim subpopulation in adults with relapsed/refractory B-lymphoblastic leukaemia after treatment with inotuzumab-ozogamicin. Ann Hematol 2021;100:2727–32. https://doi.org/10.1007/S00277-021-04601-0/FIGURES/3.

[77] Hergott CB, Kim AS, Wadleigh M, Lindsley RC. Resistance to inotuzumab ozogamicin in a B-ALL patient with TET2 and DNMT3A mutations and myeloid lineage switch. Blood 2018;132:2818. https://doi.org/10.1182/BLOOD-2018-99-119207.

[78] Zheng S, Gillespie E, Naqvi AS, Hayer KE, Ang Z, Torres-Diz M, et al. Modulation of CD22 protein expression in childhood leukemia by pervasive splicing aberrations: implications for CD22-directed immunotherapies. Blood Cancer Discov 2022;3:103–15. https://doi.org/10.1158/2643-3230.BCD-21-0087.

[79] Rosenthal J, Naqvi AS, Luo M, Wertheim G, Paessler M, Thomas-Tikhonenko A, et al. Heterogeneity of surface CD19 and CD22 expression in B lymphoblastic leukemia. Am J Hematol 2018;93:E352–5. https://doi.org/10.1002/AJH.25235.

[80] Pillai V, Muralidharan K, Meng W, Bagashev A, Oldridge DA, Rosenthal J, et al. CAR T-cell therapy is effective for CD19-dim B-lymphoblastic leukemia but is impacted by prior blinatumomab therapy. Blood Adv 2019;3:3539–49. https://doi.org/10.1182/BLOODADVANCES.2019000692.

[81] Gerdemann U, Kaminski J, Fleming RA, Tkachev V, Alvarez Calderon F, McGuckin C, et al. CAR-T cell infusion results in activation of CD160+/NKG2D+/CCL5+ non-CAR CD8+ cytotoxic "bystander" T cells in both non-human primates (NHP) and patients receiving B-cell-directed CAR-Ts. Blood 2022;140:1167–8. https://doi.org/10.1182/BLOOD-2022-169435.

[82] Melenhorst JJ, Chen GM, Wang M, Porter DL, Chen C, Collins MKA, et al. Decade-long leukaemia remissions with persistence of CD4+ CAR T cells. Nature 2022;602(7897):503–9. https://doi.org/10.1038/s41586-021-04390-6.

[83] Lamble A, Myers RM, Taraseviciute A, John S, Yates B, Steinberg SM, et al. Preinfusion factors impacting relapse immunophenotype following CD19 CAR T cells. Blood Adv 2022. https://doi.org/10.1182/BLOODADVANCES.2022007423.

[84] Orlando EJ, Han X, Tribouley C, Wood PA, Leary RJ, Riester M, et al. Genetic mechanisms of target antigen loss in CAR19 therapy of acute lymphoblastic leukemia. Nat Med 2018;24(10):1504–6. https://doi.org/10.1038/s41591-018-0146-z.

[85] Sotillo E, Barrett DM, Black KL, Bagashev A, Oldridge D, Wu G, et al. Convergence of acquired mutations and alternative splicing of CD19 enables resistance to CART-19 immunotherapy. Cancer Discov 2015;5:1282–95. https://doi.org/10.1158/2159-8290.CD-15-1020.

[86] Fischer J, Paret C, El Malki K, Alt F, Wingerter A, Neu MA, et al. CD19 isoforms enabling resistance to CART-19 immunotherapy are expressed in B-ALL patients at initial diagnosis. J Immunother 2017;40:187–95. https://doi.org/10.1097/CJI.0000000000000169.

[87] Ruella M, Xu J, Barrett DM, Fraietta JA, Reich TJ, Ambrose DE, et al. Induction of resistance to chimeric antigen receptor T cell therapy by transduction of a single leukemic B cell. Nat Med 2018;24:1499–503. https://doi.org/10.1038/S41591-018-0201-9.

[88] Wang Y, Chen X, Wei S, Mi Y, Shi L, Wang Y, et al. CNCT19 for treatment of patients with relapsed refractory B-cell acute lymphoblastic leukemia (r/r B-cell ALL) in children and adults. Blood 2021;138:2811. https://doi.org/10.1182/BLOOD-2021-145272.

[89] Braig F, Brandt A, Goebeler M, Tony HP, Kurze AK, Nollau P, et al. Resistance to anti-CD19/CD3 BiTE in acute lymphoblastic leukemia may be mediated by disrupted CD19 membrane trafficking. Blood 2017;129:100–4. https://doi.org/10.1182/BLOOD-2016-05-718395.

[90] Mejstríková E, Hrusak O, Borowitz MJ, Whitlock JA, Brethon B, Trippett TM, et al. CD19-negative relapse of pediatric B-cell precursor acute lymphoblastic leukemia following blinatumomab treatment. Blood. Cancer J 2017;7. https://doi.org/10.1038/S41408-017-0023-X.

[91] Myers RM, Li Y, Leahy AB, Barrett DM, Teachey DT, Callahan C, et al. Humanized CD19-targeted chimeric antigen receptor (CAR) T cells in CAR-naive and CAR-exposed children and young adults with relapsed or refractory acute lymphoblastic leukemia. J Clin Oncol 2021;39:3044–55. https://doi.org/10.1200/JCO.20.03458.

[92] Takeshita A, Shinjo K, Yamakage N, Ono T, Hirano I, Matsui H, et al. CMC-544 (inotuzumab ozogamicin) shows less effect on multidrug resistant cells: analyses in cell lines and cells from patients with B-cell chronic lymphocytic leukaemia and lymphoma. Br J Haematol 2009;146:34–43. https://doi.org/10.1111/J.1365-2141.2009.07701.X.

[93] Kirchhoff H, Karsli U, Schoenherr C, Battmer K, Erschow S, Talbot SR, et al. Venetoclax and dexamethasone synergize with inotuzumab ozogamicin-induced DNA damage signaling in B-lineage ALL. Blood 2021;137:2657–61. https://doi.org/10.1182/BLOOD.2020008544.

[94] Takeshita A, Yamakage N, Shinjo K, Ono T, Hirano I, Nakamura S, et al. CMC-544 (inotuzumab ozogamicin), an anti-CD22 immuno-conjugate of calicheamicin, alters the levels of target molecules of malignant B-cells. Leukemia 2009;23:1329–36. https://doi.org/10.1038/LEU.2009.77.

[95] Duell J, Dittrich M, Bedke T, Mueller T, Eisele F, Rosenwald A, et al. Frequency of regulatory T cells determines the outcome of the T-cell-engaging antibody blinatumomab in patients with B-precursor ALL. Leukemia 2017;31:2181–90. https://doi.org/10.1038/LEU.2017.41.

[96] Feucht J, Kayser S, Gorodezki D, Hamieh M, Döring M, Blaeschke F, et al. T-cell responses against CD19+ pediatric acute lymphoblastic leukemia mediated by bispecific T-cell engager (BiTE) are regulated contrarily by PD-L1 and CD80/CD86 on leukemic blasts. Oncotarget 2016;7:76902–19. https://doi.org/10.18632/ONCOTARGET.12357.

[97] Wunderlich M, Manning N, Sexton C, O'Brien E, Byerly L, Stillwell C, et al. PD-1 inhibition enhances blinatumomab response in a UCB/PDX model of relapsed pediatric B-cell acute lymphoblastic leukemia. Front Oncol 2021;11:1137. https://doi.org/10.3389/FONC.2021.642466/BIBTEX.

[98] Turtle CJ, Hanafi LA, Berger C, Gooley TA, Cherian S, Hudecek M, et al. CD19 CAR-T cells of defined CD4+: CD8+ composition in adult B cell ALL patients. J Clin Investig 2016;126:2123–38. https://doi.org/10.1172/JCI85309.

[99] Watanabe A, Miyake K, Akahane K, Goi K, Kagami K, Yagita H, et al. Epigenetic modification of death receptor genes for TRAIL and TRAIL resistance in childhood B-cell precursor acute lymphoblastic leukemia. Genes (Basel) 2021;12. https://doi.org/10.3390/GENES12060864/S1.

[100] Kankeu Fonkoua LA, Sirpilla O, Sakemura R, Siegler EL, Kenderian SS. CAR T cell therapy and the tumor microenvironment: current challenges and opportunities. Mol Ther Oncolytics 2022;25:69–77. https://doi.org/10.1016/J.OMTO.2022.03.009.

[101] Jabbour E, Richard-Carpentier G, Sasaki Y, Konopleva M, Patel K, Roberts K, et al. Hyper-CVAD regimen in combination with ofatumumab as frontline therapy for adults with Philadelphia chromosome-negative B-cell acute lymphoblastic leukaemia: a single-arm, phase 2 trial. Lancet Haematol 2020;7:e523–33. https://doi.org/10.1016/S2352-3026(20)30144-7.

[102] Awasthi A, Ayello J, Van de Ven C, Elmacken M, Sabulski A, Barth MJ, et al. Obinutuzumab (GA101) compared to rituximab significantly enhances cell death and antibody-dependent cytotoxicity and improves overall survival against CD20(+) rituximab-sensitive/-resistant Burkitt lymphoma (BL) and precursor B-acute lymphoblastic leukaemia (pre-B-ALL): potential targeted therapy in patients with poor risk CD20(+) BL and pre-B-ALL. Br J Haematol 2015;171:763–75. https://doi.org/10.1111/BJH.13764.

[103] Dickinson M, Carlo-Stella C, Morschhauser F, Bachy E, Corradini P, Iacoboni G, et al. Glofitamab in patients with relapsed/refractory (R/R) diffuse large B-cell lymphoma (DLBCL) and $\geq$ 2 prior therapies: pivotal phase II expansion results. J Clin Oncol 2022;40:7500. https://doi.org/10.1200/JCO.2022.40.16_SUPPL.7500.

[104] Jain N, Stock W, Zeidan A, Atallah E, McCloskey J, Heffner L, et al. Loncastuximab tesirine, an anti-CD19 antibody-drug conjugate, in relapsed/refractory B-cell acute lymphoblastic leukemia. Blood Adv 2020;4:449–57. https://doi.org/10.1182/BLOODADVANCES.2019000767.

[105] Guerra VA, Jabbour EJ, Ravandi F, Kantarjian H, Short NJ. Novel monoclonal antibody-based treatment strategies in adults with acute lymphoblastic leukemia. Ther Adv Hematol 2019;10:1–17. https://doi.org/10.1177/2040620719849496.

[106] Fathi AT, Borate U, DeAngelo DJ, O'Brien MM, Trippett T, Shah BD, et al. A phase 1 study of denintuzumab mafodotin (SGN-CD19A) in adults with relapsed or refractory B-lineage acute leukemia (B-ALL) and highly aggressive lymphoma. Blood 2015;126:1328. https://doi.org/10.1182/BLOOD.V126.23.1328.1328.

[107] Jain N, Jabbour E, Aldoss I, Konopleva M, Short N, Stein AS, et al. Adct-602, a CD22 targeting antibody drug conjugate bound to PBD toxin in adult patients with relapsed or refractory B-cell acute lymphoblastic leukemia: a phase 1 trial. Blood 2022;140:521–2. https://doi.org/10.1182/BLOOD-2022-170730.

[108] MacKay M, Afshinnekoo E, Rub J, Hassan C, Khunte M, Baskaran N, et al. The therapeutic landscape for cells engineered with chimeric antigen receptors. Nat Biotechnol 2020;38:233–44. https://doi.org/10.1038/s41587-019-0329-2.

[109] Cordoba S, Onuoha S, Thomas S, Pignataro DS, Hough R, Ghorashian S, et al. CAR T cells with dual targeting of CD19 and CD22 in pediatric and young adult patients with relapsed or refractory B cell acute lymphoblastic leukemia: a phase 1 trial. Nat Med 2021;27:1797–805. https://doi.org/10.1038/s41591-021-01497-1.

[110] Roddie C, Dias J, O'Reilly M, Mitsikakou M, Charalambous E, Green L, et al. P1459: safety and efficacy findings of AUTO1, a fast-off rate CD19 car, in relapsed/refractory B-cell non-Hodgkin's lymphoma (B-NHL), and chronic lymphocytic leukemia (CLL)/small lymphocytic lymphoma (SLL). Hemasphere 2022;6:1341–2. https://doi.org/10.1097/01.HS9.0000848692.42285.0C.

[111] Drent E, Themeli M, Poels R, de Jong-Korlaar R, Yuan H, de Bruijn J, et al. A rational strategy for reducing on-target off-tumor effects of CD38-chimeric antigen receptors by affinity optimization. Mol Ther 2017;25:1946–58. https://doi.org/10.1016/j.ymthe.2017.04.024.

[112] Hawkins ER, D'souza RR, Klampatsa A. Armored CAR T-cells: the next chapter in T-cell cancer immunotherapy. Biol Theory 2021;15:95. https://doi.org/10.2147/BTT.S291768.

[113] Georgiadis C, Rasaiyaah J, Gkazi SA, Preece R, Etuk A, Christi A, et al. Base-edited CAR T cells for combinational therapy against T cell malignancies. Leukemia 2021;35:3466–81. https://doi.org/10.1038/S41375-021-01282-6.

[114] Liu E, Marin D, Banerjee P, MacApinlac HA, Thompson P, Basar R, et al. Use of CAR-transduced natural killer cells in CD19-positive lymphoid tumors. N Engl J Med 2020;382:545–53. https://doi.org/10.1056/NEJMoa1910607.

[115] Benjamin R, Jain N, Maus MV, Boissel N, Graham C, Jozwik A, et al. UCART19, a first-in-class allogeneic anti-CD19 chimeric antigen receptor T-cell therapy for adults with relapsed or refractory B-cell acute lymphoblastic leukaemia (CALM): a phase 1, dose-escalation trial. Lancet Haematol 2022;9:e833–43. https://doi.org/10.1016/S2352-3026(22)00245-9.

[116] Shah BD, Jacobson C, Solomon SR, Jain N, Johnson MC, Vainorius M, et al. Allogeneic CAR-T PBCAR0191 with intensified lymphodepletion is highly active in patients with relapsed/refractory B-cell malignancies. Blood 2021;138:302. https://doi.org/10.1182/BLOOD-2021-150609.

[117] Uy GL, Aldoss I, Foster MC, Sayre PH, Wieduwilt MJ, Advani AS, et al. Flotetuzumab as salvage immunotherapy for refractory acute myeloid leukemia. Blood 2021;137:751–62. https://doi.org/10.1182/BLOOD.2020007732.

[118] Ravandi F, Bashey A, Foran JM, Stock W, Mawad R, Blum W, et al. Complete responses in relapsed/refractory acute myeloid leukemia (AML) patients on a weekly dosing schedule of XmAb14045, a CD123 x CD3 T cell-engaging bispecific antibody: initial results of a phase 1 study. Blood 2018;132:763. https://doi.org/10.1182/BLOOD-2018-99-119786.

[119] Stein AS, Bajel A, Fleming S, Jongen-Lavrencic M, Garciaz S, Maiti A, et al. An open-label, first-in-human, dose-escalation study of SAR443579 administered as single agent by intravenous infusion in patients with relapsed or refractory acute myeloid leukemia (R/R AML), B-cell acute lymphoblastic leukemia (B-ALL) or high-risk myelodysplasia (HR-MDS). Blood 2022;140:7476–7. https://doi.org/10.1182/BLOOD-2022-166000.

[120] Chen P, Chu A, Zia H, Koduru P, Collins R, Winick N, et al. CD25 expression in B lymphoblastic leukemia/lymphoma predicts t(9;22)(q34;q11)/Philadelphia chromosome translocation (Ph) and is associated with residual disease in Ph-negative patients. Am J Clin Pathol 2016;146:632–8. https://doi.org/10.1093/AJCP/AQW178.

[121] Goldberg AD, Tallman MS, Solh MM, Ungar D, Rizzieri DA, Walter RB, et al. Results from an ongoing phase 1 study indicate ACDT-301 (Camidanlumab Tesirine) is well-tolerated in patients with relapsed or refractory CD25-positive acute leukemia. Blood 2017;130:2662. https://doi.org/10.1182/BLOOD.V130.SUPPL_1.2662.2662.

[122] Sandhu KS, Huynh-Tran Q, Cooper EE, Zhang J, Palmer J, Tsai N-C, et al. ALL-440: promising safety and efficacy results from an ongoing phase 1/2 study of pembrolizumab in combination with blinatumomab in patients (pts) with relapsed or refractory (R/R) acute lymphoblastic leukemia (ALL). Clin Lymphoma Myeloma Leuk 2021;21:S276. https://doi.org/10.1016/S2152-2650(21)01666-9.

[123] Pan J, Tan Y, Wang G, Deng B, Ling Z, Song W, et al. Donor-derived CD7 chimeric antigen receptor T cells for T-cell acute lymphoblastic leukemia: first-in-human, phase I trial. J Clin Oncol 2021;39:3340–51. https://doi.org/10.1200/JCO.21.00389.

[124] Naik J, Themeli M, de Jong-Korlaar R, Ruiter RWJ, Poddighe PJ, Yuan H, et al. CD38 as a therapeutic target for adult acute myeloid leukemia and T-cell acute lymphoblastic leukemia. Haematologica 2019;104:e100–3. https://doi.org/10.3324/HAEMATOL.2018.192757.

[125] Bride KL, Vincent TL, Im SY, Aplenc R, Barrett DM, Carroll WL, et al. Preclinical efficacy of daratumumab in T-cell acute lymphoblastic leukemia. Blood 2018;131:995. https://doi.org/10.1182/BLOOD-2017-07-794214.

[126] Cerrano M, Bonifacio M, Olivi M, Curti A, Malagola M, Dargenio M, et al. Daratumumab with or without chemotherapy in relapsed and refractory acute lymphoblastic leukemia. A retrospective observational campus ALL study. Haematologica 2022;107:996–9. https://doi.org/10.3324/HAEMATOL.2021.279851.

[127] Ofran Y, Ringelstein-Harlev S, Slouzkey I, Zuckerman T, Yehudai-Ofir D, Henig I, et al. Daratumumab for eradication of minimal residual disease in high-risk advanced relapse of T-cell/CD19/CD22-negative acute lymphoblastic leukemia. Leukemia 2020;34:293–5. https://doi.org/10.1038/S41375-019-0548-Z.
[128] Cerrano M, Castella B, Lia G, Olivi M, Faraci DG, Butera S, et al. Immunomodulatory and clinical effects of daratumumab in T-cell acute lymphoblastic leukaemia. Br J Haematol 2020;191:e28–32. https://doi.org/10.1111/BJH.16960.
[129] Hogan LE, Bhatla T, Teachey DT, Sirvent FJB, Moppett J, Puyó PV, et al. Efficacy and safety of daratumumab (DARA) in pediatric and young adult patients (pts) with relapsed/refractory T-cell acute lymphoblastic leukemia (ALL) or lymphoblastic lymphoma (LL): results from the phase 2 DELPHINUS study. J Clin Oncol 2022;40:10001. https://doi.org/10.1200/JCO.2022.40.16_SUPPL.10001.
[130] Gramatzki M, Burger R, Strobel G, Trautmann U, Bartram CR, Helm G, et al. Therapy with OKT3 monoclonal antibody in refractory T cell acute lymphoblastic leukemia induces interleukin-2 responsiveness. Leukemia 1995;9:382–90.
[131] Trinquand A, Dos Santos NR, Quang CT, Rocchetti F, Zaniboni B, Belhocine M, et al. Triggering the TCR developmental checkpoint activates a therapeutically targetable tumor suppressive pathway in T-cell leukemia. Cancer Discov 2016;6:973–85. https://doi.org/10.1158/2159-8290.CD-15-0675.
[132] Herold KC, Bundy BN, Long SA, Bluestone JA, DiMeglio LA, Dufort MJ, et al. An anti-CD3 antibody, Teplizumab, in relatives at risk for type 1 diabetes. N Engl J Med 2019;381:603–13. https://doi.org/10.1056/NEJMOA1902226.
[133] Quang CT, Zaniboni B, Humeau R, Lengliné E, Dourthe ME, Ganesan R, et al. Preclinical efficacy of humanized, non-FcγR-binding anti-CD3 antibodies in T-cell acute lymphoblastic leukemia. Blood 2020;136:1298–302. https://doi.org/10.1182/BLOOD.2019003801.
[134] Wellhausen N, Rennels AK, Lesch S, Agarwal S, Charria B, Choi G, et al. Epitope editing in hematopoietic cells enables CD45-directed immune therapy. Blood 2022;140:862–4. https://doi.org/10.1182/BLOOD-2022-158684.

CHAPTER

8

Clinical relevance and therapeutic implications of CD20 expression in Hodgkin's lymphoma

Marcelo Antônio Oliveira Santos Veloso[a,b,c] *and Rafael Pinheiro dos Santos*[c]

[a]Hospital Alfa, Division for Internal Medicine, Recife, Brazil [b]Department of Therapeutic Innovation, Federal University of Pernambuco, Center for Biosciences, Recife, Brazil [c]Mauricio de Nassau University, School of Medicine, Recife, Brazil

Abstract

Hodgkin's lymphoma (HL) is a lymphoid neoplasm characterized by malignant cells known as Hodgkin and Reed-Sternberg (HRS) cells immersed in a microenvironment composed of a mixture of reactive cells. Some membrane markers, such as CD30 and CD15, are present in HRS cells. The expression of other cluster differentiation markers in some HL subtypes has gained the scientific community's attention as possible therapeutic targets. One of these markers is CD20, a phosphoprotein usually found in cell lines derived from B lymphocytes. To date, the role of CD20 expression remains controversial. Studies conducted in different clinical settings presented conflicting results, suggesting either improvement or worsening of clinical outcomes. A strong association between HL and Epstein-Barr virus (EBV) infection is well established and seems related to survival mechanisms and disease progression in infected patients and carriers of this malignancy. Furthermore, not only is EBV infection considered a mechanism of disease progression, but also the reactive microenvironment plays a major role in HL progression. Recently, special attention has been given to cell surface markers as a potential target for innovative and specific therapies. The discovery and development of monoclonal antibodies (mAb) resulted in the development of anti-CD20 targeting therapies. Despite promising results identified in patients with non-HL, and in vivo and in vitro models for HL, the anti-CD20 therapy efficacy in HL remained unproved. In addition, there is little clarity on their resistance mechanisms. Therefore, even though it is a promising therapy, there is still much controversy regarding the clinical significance of both the expression of the CD20 marker and its anti-CD20 therapy.

https://doi.org/10.1016/B978-0-443-19200-5.00008-7

Abbreviations

ABVD	doxorubicin, bleomycin, vinblastine, dacarbazine
ADCC	antibody-dependent cellular cytotoxicity
BEACOPP	bleomycin, etoposide, doxorubicin, cyclophosphamide, vincristine, procarbazine, and prednisone
CD	cluster of differentiation
CDC	complement-dependent cytotoxicity
cHL	classic Hodgkin lymphoma
DHAP	dexamethasone, cytarabine and cisplatin
EBV	Epstein-Bar virus
EORTC	European Organization for the Research and Treatment of Cancer
ESR	erythrocyte sedimentation rate
Fc	fragment crystallizable
FcγR	fragment crystallizable gamma receptor
FFS	free-failure survival
HL	Hodgkin lymphoma
HRS	Hodgkin and Reed-Stemberg cells
ICE	ifosfamide, carboplatin and etoposide
LDCHL	lymphocyte-depleted classic Hodgkin lymphoma
LP	lymphocyte-predominant cells
LRCHL	lymphocyte-rich classic Hodgkin lymphoma
mAb	monoclonal antibodies
MAC	membrane attack complex
MCCHL	mixed-cellularity classic Hodgkin lymphoma
NLPHL	nodular lymphocyte-predominant Hodgkin lymphoma
OS	overall survival
PFS	progression-free survival
RR	relative risk
TME	tumor microenvironment

Conflict of interest

No potential conflicts of interest were disclosed.

Introduction

Hodgkin's lymphoma (HL) is a malignant lymphoid neoplasm that occurs in young adults and elderly individuals [1]. The diagnosis of HL is defined in terms of morphological characteristics and immunophenotyping. The immunophenotype of Hodgkin and Reed-Sternberg (HRS) cells is typically characterized by a cluster of differentiation (CD) 30 and CD15 positivity in most cases. The expression of surface antigens of B cells is generally absent; however, studies have shown that CD19, CD20, and CD79a are expressed in a subset of patients, and their clinical significance is still uncertain [2,3].

The CD20 antigen is a transmembrane of highly hydrophobic glycosylated phosphoprotein widely expressed during B-lymphocyte ontogeny. It is thought to be responsible for B-cell activation and differentiation [4]. In lymphocyte-predominant HL and some presentations of classic HL (cHL), the expression of CD20 antigen corroborates the hypothesis that HRS cells derive from germinal-center B cells [5].

After the development of anti-CD20 target therapies, the discovery of CD20 expression in a subset of patients with cHL led the medical community toward several studies about the role of CD20 expression in HL and its potential as a target for chemotherapy. However, decades after these discoveries, both questions appear to remain unsolved.

Etiopathogenesis of classical Hodgkin's lymphoma (cHL) and the role of the CD20 marker

The constitutive analysis demonstrates that HL occurs due to dysplastic cells derived from B lymphocytes, known as HRS cells. Tumor cells are distinct between the two main presentations of HL: HRS cells in classic HL (cHL) and lymphocyte-predominant (LP) cells in the nodular lymphocyte-predominant HL (NLPHL) [1,6]. The tumoral cells are part of an environment surrounded mainly by a rich mixture of mature nonneoplastic inflammatory immune effector cells [1,7,8] such as macrophages, B and T cells, eosinophils, fibroblasts, mast cells, plasma cells, and other cells [9–11].

Peripheral lymphadenopathy is the main clinical presentation of HL, especially in the cervical region. Other organs, such as the liver, lungs, and bone marrow, may be affected in a frequency varying according to each HL subtype. About 40% of patients may present constitutional symptoms (also referred to as B-symptoms), characterized by fever, drenching night sweats, and significant body weight loss [1,6].

The cHL subtype is the most common, which comprises about 90% of cases. Furthermore, cHL can be further subdivided into four more histologically distinct subtypes: nodular sclerosis cHL (NSCHL), lymphocyte-rich cHL (LRCHL), mixed cellularity cHL (MCCHL), and lymphocyte-depleted cHL (LDCHL) [1]. Each histological subdivision presents unique and important immunophenotypic features concerning diagnosis, staging, treatment, and prognosis. Some of these immunophenotypic characteristics can be observed in Table 1.

TABLE 1 Immunophenotypic characteristics in Hodgkin lymphomas—biomarkers.

	Biomarkers		
Subtypes	**CD30**	**CD15 (%)**	**CD20 (%)**
NSCHL	Positive	Positive in ~80	Positive in ~20
MCCHL	Positive	Positive in ~80	Positive in ~20
LDCHL	Positive	Positive in ~80	Positive in ~20
LRCHL	Positive	Positive in ~80	Positive in ~20
NLPHL	Negative	Negative	Positive

Adapted from Swerdlow S, Campo E, Harris N, Jaffe E, Pileri S, Stein H, et al. WHO classification of tumours of haematopoietic and lymphoid tissues. 4th ed. World Health Organization; 2017 and Schmid C, Pan L, Diss T, Isaacson PG. Expression of B-cell antigens by Hodgkin's and Reed-Sternberg cells. Am J Pathol 1991;139(4):701–7.

Epstein-Barr virus (EBV) infection and HL

The EBV infection has been pointed out as a major risk factor for the development of HL. This association is true for all HL subtypes, especially in the MCCHL and LDCHL subtypes, with a lower prevalence in the NLPHL. It is hypothesized that the virus appears to represent a genetic and environmental trigger, contributing to the development of cHL. The prevalence of EBV-associated classical Hodgkin lymphoma (cHL) appears to be elevated in populations characterized by HIV infection, immunodeficiency conditions, and low resource settings [1]. Regarding its mechanism of action, it is well known that EBV can make use of some intracellular machinery aimed at reducing the effective immune response and thereby favoring the survival and progression of malignant HRS cells infected by the pathogen. In addition, dysregulation of CD8+ cytotoxicity related to polymorphisms observed in human leukocyte antigen I and other molecular alterations seems to contribute to tumoral cells' survival [12].

Classical Hodgkin's lymphoma (cHL)

cHL derives primarily from B cells, presenting as a monoclonal lymphoid neoplasm. Among all four subtypes, nodular sclerosis HL stands out with presentation in about 70% of patients, followed by MCCHL [1,7]. Interestingly, MCCHL is more characteristic of patients with HIV infection and living in resource-poor areas. EBV may be one of the explanatory factors of this association [7]. More frequently, cHL tends to manifest in male individuals [1].

In terms of the immunophenotypic profile of cHL, CD15 and CD30 expression is well established in HRS cells, as well as other antigens such as the PAX5 protein and the IRF4/MUM1 transcription factor. The expression of CD20 antigen is described in up to 40% of cases, mostly in the NLPHL subtype [1].

Pathophysiology

For a comprehensive understanding of the pathophysiology involved in HL, one must consider the mechanisms developed by HRS cells, since they play an important role and function to escape the immune system. The microenvironment in which they are inserted can also facilitate their survival and trigger immunomodulatory reactions that favor neoplastic growth.

The role of the tumor microenvironment (TME) and its interactions

To maintain their stability, malignant cells use molecular pathways to communicate with other cells in the surrounding reactive microenvironment through surface receptors. This interaction contributes to the maintenance of their proliferative and antiapoptotic state.

This assumption suggests that cytokines and chemokines are responsible for clinical and histopathological changes associated with cHL. These mediators are produced not only by HRS cells but also by the reactive infiltrate around them [13].

Some studies have revealed that several cytokines and chemokines found in the tumor microenvironment (TME) are responsible for sustaining the inflammatory conditions that drive tumor progression. These cytokines and chemokines are only part of the complex network of pathways that facilitate tumor progression. Transcription factors, intracellular signals, regulators of apoptosis, and surface receptors are some of the other pathways that are also involved. It is believed that these pathways work in concert to promote tumor growth and metastasis. Furthermore, many of these pathways are also involved in other biological processes, such as cell adhesion, motility, and angiogenesis, making them important targets for therapeutic intervention [14].

An in-depth analysis of the microenvironment revealed that CD4+ T cells were the most abundant in the infiltrate [13]. T helper 1 (TH1) cells are essential in the production of cytokines and assist macrophages activation [11]. Macrophages have a central role in tumoral growth since they contribute to immune suppression in certain tumors such as lymphomas and abet cell migration [15]. Consequently, the growth and proliferation of HRS cells are favored [11].

Additionally, activation of crucial signaling pathways, such as nuclear factor kappa B and the Janus kinase-signal transducer, and activator of transcription signaling function as part of this entire apparatus to maintain tumor cells active and resistant. These modifications are mainly due to structural and quantitative genetic changes, such as increased pathway gene expression, chromosomal gains, and mutations that cause tumor suppressor genes to become inactive [11].

Malignant cells, in addition to using their own immune system evasion mechanisms, use the surrounding microenvironment to help them spread. Because of the pathology's progression and significant clinical and histopathological alterations, the physiological mechanisms that act in an uncoordinated manner favor the malignancy of the lymphoma and its cells.

According to studies conducted in vitro and in vivo, some pathways, including complement-dependent cytotoxicity (CDC), direct antitumor effects, and antibody-dependent cellular cytotoxicity (ADCC), are known to partially explain rituximab's effects [16–20]. These mechanisms focus on the elimination of CD20-expressing cells and are summarized in Table 2 and Fig. 1.

TABLE 2 Main described mechanisms of action.

Mechanism	Cellular and molecular features
ADCC	Binding of the antibody to specific cell receptors. Effector immune cell recruitment. Release of cytotoxic substances and phagocytosis
CDC	Antibody binding. Activation of complement by specific ligand. Proteolytic cascade, MAC, and elimination of target cells
Direct cell death	Sensitization to cytotoxic drugs. Blockage of survival pathways. Apoptosis induction

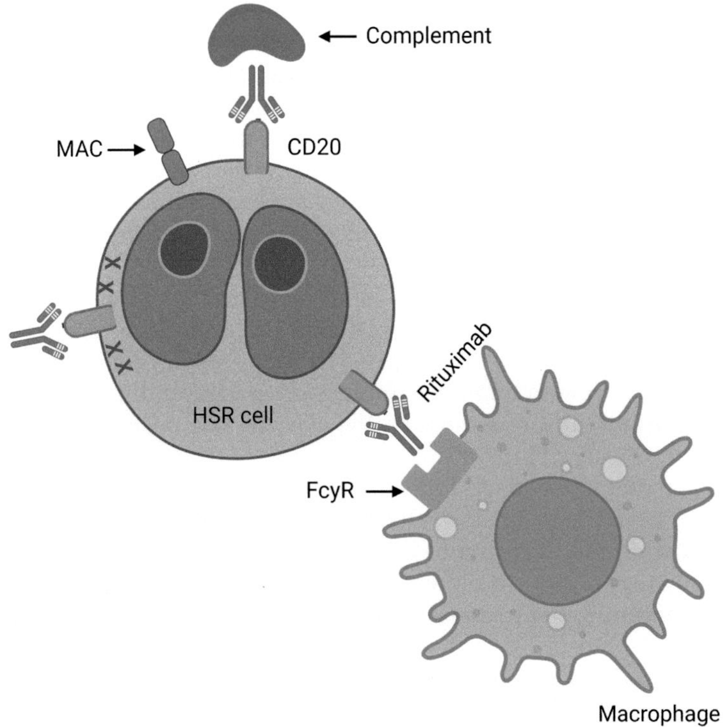

FIG. 1 Proposed anti-CD20 therapy mechanisms of action in HL. *HSR*, Hodgkin and Reed-Stemberg cells; *MAC*, complement membrane attack complex; *FcγR*, Fc gamma receptor.

Antibody-dependent cellular cytotoxicity (ADCC)

The cellular receptors for the fragment crystallizable (Fc) portion of antibodies, specifically the gamma receptor (FcγR), are how ADCC, a crucial mechanism for eliminating harmful pathogens, especially intracellular ones, works [20]. The binding of the antibody to the marked cells is where it all begins. The recruitment of innate immune effector cells, which must express FcγRs, is thus started by these antibodies. Consequently, there is a signaling trigger that prompts the cell to initiate the process of phagocytosis and depositing cytotoxic agents [21].

It is important to be aware that FcγRs can be either activating or inhibitory receptors. FcγRIa, FcγIIa, and FcγIIIa are among the activating ones. FcγRIIb is the sole example of an inhibitory receptor [22]. Genetic changes associated with receptors are directly correlated with clinical responses. The affinity of these connections between receptors and effector cells, such as natural killer (NK) cells and phagocytic cells like monocytes and macrophages, for instance, can be directly influenced by polymorphisms [20].

Through the recognition of opsonized tumor cells, NK cells can identify IgG1 or IgG3 antibodies. Granzymes and perforins are then released, which induces cell lysis. Furthermore, it is hypothesized that this interaction with FcγRs may trigger the expression of the Fas ligand, leading to the apoptosis of tumor cells. In addition to ADCC, other cellular immune system-related mechanisms, especially those involving monocytes and macrophages, can still destroy tumor cells. Those immune cells perform their functions by phagocytosing antibody-coated tumor cells [17].

Complement-dependent cytotoxicity (CDC)

Antibody binding triggers the complement system's traditional route. The complement's C1q subunit recognizes the Fc portion of the IgG, which activates the proteolytic cascade and triggers the formation of the membrane attack complex (MAC), which is responsible for destroying the target cell [20]. The primary mechanism of action of rituximab in vivo seems to be CDC [23,24], due to the decrease in complement components or because of the effects associated with other mechanisms of action [20,25,26].

However, nucleated cells typically have some proteins that seem to be resistant to the complement system's effects and thus interfere with the entire cascade, thereby rendering them immune to the CDC attack. Among these, the proteins CD55, CD46, and CD59 deserve special attention [17]. Thus, further research is necessary to establish the CDC's true efficacy as a mediator of the response to rituximab treatment because its role in some studies still appears to be debatable.

Induction of direct cell death

Some mechanisms to explain direct cell death regulation have been proposed based on a few clinical studies, though they are not yet fully understood. One of these mechanisms is the direct induction of cell death by rituximab through the sensitization of tumor cells to cytotoxic drugs [27–34]. Furthermore, mAb binding results in partial blockades of some survival signaling pathways [20].

In vitro studies suggest that the binding of the anti-CD20 antibody is connected to the growth inhibition and apoptosis of malignant B cells regardless of the CDC, ADCC, and Fc pathways [34,35]. Direct binding to CD20 can inhibit DNA synthesis, halt the cell cycle, relocate phosphatidylserine to the outer membrane, induce apoptosis, activate the serine/threonine protein tyrosine kinases, and initiate caspases, among several other effects [17].

Impact of the CD20+ expression on the evolution and prognosis of HL

The CD20 antigen is a transmembrane protein, which acts as a calcium channel, detectable on the surface of mature normal and neoplastic B cells. Its importance is demonstrated by the biological functions dependent on events that occur at the molecular level, such as cellular growth, intracellular differentiation, and cell-cycle progression of B lymphocytes [36–38].

As previously stated, the expression of B-Cell surface antigens in HRS cells is well documented. Regarding CD20 antigen, the prevalence of its positivity in cHL varies between 13.9% and 38.1% [39–47]. Despite the prevalence, the role of CD20 expression in HL has been a subject of medical interest in the past few years; however, it remains controversial.

In terms of clinical features, the CD20-positive expression appears to be more frequent in older patients (≥45 years) [39,42,48], cases of EBV infection-related HL [39,40], mixed cellularity [19,20,28], and LRCHL subtypes [39,48].

Some authors have proposed that the CD20 expression in HL represents a prognostic factor, either impacting the outcome positively or negatively. On the other hand, other studies suggest that CD20 expression poses no prognostic significance at all.

A Brazilian study with 97 subjects found that CD20 expression was independently associated with poor prognosis and cHL relapse [46]. A similar result was described by Qin et al. in a study with 263 cHL patients, demonstrating that CD20-positive individuals were associated with reduced progression-free survival (PFS) (79.7% vs. 90.6%), but not overall survival (OS) [39]. The analysis of the HL microenvironment suggests that in cHL, patients with less than 10.5 CD20-positive HRS cells in 10 high-power fields were associated with better prognosis [41].

The favorable impact of CD20 expression may indicate that normal B cells are contributing to antitumor response or represent malignant cell precursors that are more responsive to treatment, in the context of a complex role for normal B cells in cHL, including interactions with host immunity, therapeutic late effects, late relapse, salvage, and overall host fitness [10].

In Japan, a study with 389 individuals with cHL, CD20-positive cases showed a higher association with EBV. However, multivariate analysis identified EBV-positivity (but not CD20-positivity) as a poor prognostic factor for OS [40]. The CD20 expression in HRS cells in cHL seems to be closely related to EBV infection, which is a well-known factor associated with unfavorable prognosis in HL. It is therefore plausible that the expression of CD20 may represent a confounding variable in some studies, in which the effect of EBV infection may have been the cause of the impaired prognosis [39].

Other studies found that CD20 expression is associated with a positive prognostic factor. A study analyzing dispersed cell immunophenotype has found that a high CD20 dispersed cells count was an independent prognostic factor of improved PFS (relative risk [RR] 0.46), suggesting that the microenvironment CD20+ cells play a favorable prognostic role in cHL [48]. Curiously, Tzankov et al. have remarked that the expression of CD20 was an independent positive prognostic factor for free-failure survival (FFS) in patients with cHL, from 1974 to 1980, but not in the period between 1981 and 1999, due to improved treatment modalities [43].

In addition, several studies failed to associate the CD20 expression with a significative prognostic role. In a cohort with 310 patients with cHL, Abuelgasim et al. found that neither CD20 expression nor rituximab use significantly impacted outcomes [47]. In line with the above, Fu et al. described that the expression of CD20 was not an independent prognostic factor for FFS and OS [42].

Some evidence suggests that the expression of CD20 correlated inversely with CD15 [45]. The role of CD15 expression in HL per se is also controversial as a prognostic factor. A variety of studies demonstrated no association between CD15 expression and HL outcomes [49]; however, Venkataraman et al. described a more aggressive clinical course for CD15+ NLPHL [50]. In this scenario, the CD20 expression would also be an intermediate marker for the CD15 expression.

Standard approach for HL treatment

The treatment strategy should consider the patient's characteristics and disease stage. Disease staging is based on classifications including Lugano, Ann Arbor, and Cotswolds, as well as their modifications [51–53].

There are four classifications (I–IV) based on the affected sites:

- Stage I refers to the involvement of a single lymph node region (I) or a single local extralymphatic organ or site (IE).
- Stage II involves two or more lymph node regions on the same side of the diaphragm (II) or one or more lymph node regions with extralymphatic extension (IIE).
- Stage III requires lymph node involvement on both sides of the diaphragm or local extralymphatic extension (IIIE).
- Stage IV is characterized by the widespread involvement of one or more extralymphatic organs or sites.

For stratification purposes, Stages I and II are considered early/limited, while Stages III and IV are considered advanced. Additional variables, such as "A" if systemic B symptoms are absent, or "B" if such symptoms are present, can be added to the staging description. "E" stands for extranodal extension. Furthermore, the extent of Bulky disease must be reported [7].

Early-stage disease (Stages I and II) is further classified into favorable and unfavorable categories by research groups specializing in the subject, such as the European Organization for the Research and Treatment of Cancer (EORTC), which defines an unfavorable prognosis as the presence of one or more of the following risk factors: erythrocyte sedimentation rate (ESR) >50 mm/h and no B symptoms or ESR >30 mm/h in those with B symptoms; age ≥ 50 years; mediastinal thoracic ratio >0.35; and more than three involved lymph node sites [54]. The National Comprehensive Cancer Network considers the following unfavorable risk factors: largest tumor diameter >10 cm; >3 involved lymph node sites; ESR 50 mm/h; B symptoms and mediastinal mass ratio >0.33 [55]. A favorable prognosis is the absence of any unfavorable items.

As the preferred combination chemotherapy regimen, ABVD (adriamycin/doxorubicin, bleomycin, vinblastine, and dacarbazine) or BEACOPP (bleomycin, etoposide, doxorubicin, cyclophosphamide, vincristine, procarbazine, and prednisone) along with involved site radiation therapy is considered the gold standard treatment for HL [7]. The following distinct regimens are employed to administer combinations of chemotherapy and radiotherapy:

Two-stage approach:

- Limited stage: Chemotherapy (2–3 cycles) + involved site radiation therapy.
- Advanced stage: Chemotherapy (6 cycles). If still positive → Involve site radiation therapy.

Three-stage approach:

- Favorable limited stage: Chemotherapy (2 cycles) + involved site radiation therapy.
- Unfavorable limited stage: Chemotherapy (4 cycles) + involved site radiation therapy.
- Advanced stage: Chemotherapy (6 cycles). If still positive → Involve site radiation therapy.

To those refractory or recurrent cases:

- Fit: High-dose chemotherapy and autologous stem cell transplant.
- Elderly: Second-line chemotherapy, such as ifosfamide, carboplatin, and etoposide (ICE) and dexamethasone, cytarabine, and cisplatin (DHAP) [56,57].

Clinical efficacy of anti-CD20 therapy on HL

Monoclonal antibodies (mAb) rituximab and obinutuzumab are the most used anti-CD20 therapies. The efficacy of anti-CD20 mAb chemotherapy in the treatment of non-Hodgkin's tumors with high CD20 antigen expression is well established.

Proposed mechanisms of action of anti-CD20 therapy

The importance of benign reactive B cells in the microenvironment surrounding malignant cells underlies the mechanisms of action of anti-CD20 drugs. The expression of the CD20 marker is crucially important when discussing the therapeutic mechanisms, particularly because the mAb currently in use, particularly rituximab, uses this cellular component as a target.

Rituximab functions through binding mechanisms, with a particular affinity for the CD20 marker on the B lymphocyte transmembrane protein. With the exception of some of their lineages, such as stem cells, pro-B cells, and plasma cells, B cells typically express this protein, which is also present in the majority of cancerous B cells [16,58]. The rationale for using rituximab in other hematologic diseases, such as Hodgkin's lymphoma, is based on its mechanism of action and off-label clinical experience [16,59].

CD20, uncertainties, and the rationale for using monoclonal antibodies

Some concerns about the potential effects of chemotherapy on the natural history of HL emerged with the appearance of clinical evidence suggesting that CD20 expression might be associated with a poor prognosis. Some assumptions could justify rituximab use in cHL. The first is that HRS cells rarely express CD20; thus, the removal of CD20-positive reactive B cells supporting HRS cells is believed to deprive malignant cells of survival signals, and the removal of reactive B cells may also potentially increase host immune response against HRS cells [60].

Only a small number of trials examined the effects of adding anti-CD20 therapy to conventional HL chemotherapy because of the uncertainties surrounding the significance of CD20 expression over the HL prognosis. In 2004, a pilot study suggested that rituximab therapy in patients with recurrent cHL could change serum Interleukin 6 cytokine levels, improve B symptoms, and possibly lead to clinical remissions [61]. However, no concrete results were assessed. Some small studies have suggested that rituximab therapy improved the 5-year PFS in patients with newly diagnosed or relapsed Nodular lymphocyte-predominant HL [62,63].

The most important research on anti-CD20 mAb is a multicenter, open-label, randomized phase 2 study by Strati et al., which compared rituximab with the standard chemotherapy regimen of ABVD to ABVD alone in 56 patients with advanced stage cHL and found no difference in OS [64].

Immunogenicity, safety, and resistance mechanism to anti-CD20 antibodies

The first anti-CD20 mAb to be approved for the treatment of non-HL was rituximab in 1997. It has significantly improved survival rates with tolerable toxicity. At present, there is a dearth of information regarding resistance to anti-CD20 therapy, primarily due to the absence of standardized anti-CD20 chemotherapy regimens for Hodgkin lymphoma (HL). The limited availability of substantial clinical trials assessing the effectiveness of anti-CD20 treatment for HL, coupled with uncertainties surrounding the prognostic value of CD20 expression, contributes to the lack of data on anti-CD20 resistance.

In non-HL, despite the initial success of rituximab, many patients have failed to respond and relapsed after first-line treatment. Numerous theories have been put forth to explain how anti-CD20 therapy works, but the precise mechanism is still unknown [65,66]. Rituximab acts in part by docking the Fc receptors on immune effector cells, inducing cytotoxicity by ADCC, CDC, and, rarely, inducing apoptosis [67].

Predicting the relative importance of potential anti-CD20 resistance mechanisms is challenging. The high immunogenicity of this chimeric mAb, whose binding regions derive from murine antihuman CD20, is one of those proposed mechanisms [66]. Resistance to ADCC and CDC, Fc-receptor polymorphisms, downregulation or loss of CD20 expression, altered antibody pharmacokinetics, and altered molecular signaling pathways via CD20 are some additional postulated mechanisms [67].

To overcome resistance and enhance antitumor activities, new generations of anti-CD20 mAb were developed. Second- and third-generation anti-CD20 mAb is a group of fully humanized IgG1 antibodies including ofatumumab, veltuzumab, ocrelizumab, obinutuzumab, ocaratuzumab, and PRO131921 [61].

Regardless of the rationale for developing next-generation fully humanized mAb, clinical data have shown that those new mAb have a similar efficacy and incidence of adverse events as rituximab [65].

Future perspectives

Anti-CD20 chemotherapy has become a mainstream treatment for many B-cell disorders. In non-HL, anti-CD20 mAb use has been successful when combined with conventional therapy (chemo or radio).

However, many questions remain regarding the mechanisms of action and resistance, efficacy differences between different generations of mAb, and its clinical utility alone. These unresolved questions, controversies about CD20 expression significance, and rituximab questionable efficacy for HL have threatened the clinical interest in anti-CD20 mAb as adjuvant therapy for HL.

Notwithstanding these dilemmas, a variety of new anti-CD20 mAb are being developed and will soon be used in clinical practice. How these various generations of anti-CD20 mAb compare clinically is currently unclear. Research breakthroughs in this area may revive interest in anti-CD20 therapy for HL among the medical community.

Conclusions

Despite the recognized expression of CD20 in a subset of patients with cHL, after some decades of efforts, the role of CD20 expression in HL, prognostic significance, and its potential as a target for chemotherapy remain controversial topics. The current evidence failed to associate the CD20 expression with a significative prognostic role or demonstrate concrete benefits of anti-CD20 therapy in HL patients.

Acknowledgment

A special thanks to Lucas Reibenspies, MSc, for kindly designing and providing the figure in this chapter.

References

[1] Swerdlow S, Campo E, Harris N, Jaffe E, Pileri S, Stein H, et al. WHO classification of tumours of haematopoietic and lymphoid tissues. 4th ed. World Health Organization; 2017.
[2] Schmid C, Pan L, Diss T, Isaacson PG. Expression of B-cell antigens by Hodgkin's and Reed-Sternberg cells. Am J Pathol 1991;139(4):701–7.
[3] Zukerberg LR, Collins AB, Ferry JA, Harris NL. Coexpression of CD15 and CD20 by Reed-Sternberg cells in Hodgkin's disease. Am J Pathol 1991;139(3):475–83.
[4] Tedder TF, Streuli M, Schlossman SF, Saito H. Isolation and structure of a cDNA encoding the B1 (CD20) cell-surface antigen of human B lymphocytes. Proc Natl Acad Sci U S A 1988;85(1):208–12.
[5] Santos MAO, Lima MM. CD20 role in pathophysiology of Hodgkin's disease. Rev Assoc Medica Bras 1992 2017;63(9):810–3.
[6] Küppers R, Engert A, Hansmann ML. Hodgkin lymphoma. J Clin Invest 2012;122(10):3439–47.
[7] Connors JM, Cozen W, Steidl C, Carbone A, Hoppe RT, Flechtner HH, et al. Hodgkin lymphoma. Nat Rev Dis Primer 2020;6(1):61.
[8] Ansell SM. Hodgkin lymphoma: diagnosis and treatment. Mayo Clin Proc 2015;90(11):1574–83.
[9] Rengstl B, Newrzela S, Heinrich T, Weiser C, Thalheimer FB, Schmid F, et al. Incomplete cytokinesis and re-fusion of small mononucleated Hodgkin cells lead to giant multinucleated Reed-Sternberg cells. Proc Natl Acad Sci U S A 2013;110(51):20729–34.
[10] Greaves P, Clear A, Coutinho R, Wilson A, Matthews J, Owen A, et al. Expression of FOXP3, CD68, and CD20 at diagnosis in the microenvironment of classical Hodgkin lymphoma is predictive of outcome. J Clin Oncol Off J Am Soc Clin Oncol 2013;31(2):256–62.
[11] Steidl C, Connors JM, Gascoyne RD. Molecular pathogenesis of Hodgkin's lymphoma: increasing evidence of the importance of the microenvironment. J Clin Oncol Off J Am Soc Clin Oncol 2011;29(14):1812–26.
[12] Jona A, Szodoray P, Illés A. Immunologic pathomechanism of Hodgkin's lymphoma. Exp Hematol 2013;41 (12):995–1004.
[13] Skinnider BF, Mak TW. The role of cytokines in classical Hodgkin lymphoma. Blood 2002;99(12):4283–97.
[14] Khan G. Epstein-Barr virus, cytokines, and inflammation: a cocktail for the pathogenesis of Hodgkin's lymphoma? Exp Hematol 2006;34(4):399–406.
[15] Qian BZ, Pollard JW. Macrophage diversity enhances tumor progression and metastasis. Cell 2010;141(1):39–51.

[16] Salles G, Barrett M, Foà R, Maurer J, O'Brien S, Valente N, et al. Rituximab in B-cell hematologic malignancies: a review of 20 years of clinical experience. Adv Ther 2017;34(10):2232–73.
[17] Maloney DG, Smith B, Rose A. Rituximab: mechanism of action and resistance. Semin Oncol 2002;29 (1 Suppl 2):2–9.
[18] Weiner GJ. Rituximab: mechanism of action. Semin Hematol 2010;47(2):115–23.
[19] Boross P, Leusen JHW. Mechanisms of action of CD20 antibodies. Am J Cancer Res 2012;2(6):676–90.
[20] Abulayha A, Bredan A, El Enshasy H, Daniels I. Rituximab: modes of action, remaining dispute and future perspective. Future Oncol Lond Engl 2014;10(15):2481–92.
[21] Nimmerjahn F, Ravetch JV. Antibodies, Fc receptors and cancer. Curr Opin Immunol 2007;19(2):239–45.
[22] Ravetch JV, Lanier LL. Immune inhibitory receptors. Science 2000;290(5489):84–9.
[23] Manches O, Lui G, Chaperot L, Gressin R, Molens JP, Jacob MC, et al. In vitro mechanisms of action of rituximab on primary non-Hodgkin lymphomas. Blood 2003;101(3):949–54.
[24] Harjunpää A, Junnikkala S, Meri S. Rituximab (anti-CD20) therapy of B-cell lymphomas: direct complement killing is superior to cellular effector mechanisms. Scand J Immunol 2000;51(6):634–41.
[25] Kennedy AD, Beum PV, Solga MD, DiLillo DJ, Lindorfer MA, Hess CE, et al. Rituximab infusion promotes rapid complement depletion and acute CD20 loss in chronic lymphocytic leukemia. J Immunol Baltim Md 1950 2004;172(5):3280–8.
[26] van der Kolk LE, Grillo-López AJ, Baars JW, Hack CE, van Oers MH. Complement activation plays a key role in the side-effects of rituximab treatment. Br J Haematol 2001;115(4):807–11.
[27] Alas S, Emmanouilides C, Bonavida B. Inhibition of interleukin 10 by rituximab results in down-regulation of bcl-2 and sensitization of B-cell non-Hodgkin's lymphoma to apoptosis. Clin Cancer Res Off J Am Assoc Cancer Res 2001;7(3):709–23.
[28] Byrd JC, Kitada S, Flinn IW, Aron JL, Pearson M, Lucas D, et al. The mechanism of tumor cell clearance by rituximab in vivo in patients with B-cell chronic lymphocytic leukemia: evidence of caspase activation and apoptosis induction. Blood 2002;99(3):1038–43.
[29] Ghetie MA, Bright H, Vitetta ES. Homodimers but not monomers of Rituxan (chimeric anti-CD20) induce apoptosis in human B-lymphoma cells and synergize with a chemotherapeutic agent and an immunotoxin. Blood 2001;97(5):1392–8.
[30] Hofmeister JK, Cooney D, Coggeshall KM. Clustered CD20 induced apoptosis: src-family kinase, the proximal regulator of tyrosine phosphorylation, calcium influx, and caspase 3-dependent apoptosis. Blood Cells Mol Dis 2000;26(2):133–43.
[31] Jazirehi AR, Huerta-Yepez S, Cheng G, Bonavida B. Rituximab (chimeric anti-CD20 monoclonal antibody) inhibits the constitutive nuclear factor-{kappa}B signaling pathway in non-Hodgkin's lymphoma B-cell lines: role in sensitization to chemotherapeutic drug-induced apoptosis. Cancer Res 2005;65(1):264–76.
[32] Mathas S, Rickers A, Bommert K, Dörken B, Mapara MY. Anti-CD20- and B-cell receptor-mediated apoptosis: evidence for shared intracellular signaling pathways. Cancer Res 2000;60(24):7170–6.
[33] Pedersen IM, Buhl AM, Klausen P, Geisler CH, Jurlander J. The chimeric anti-CD20 antibody rituximab induces apoptosis in B-cell chronic lymphocytic leukemia cells through a p38 mitogen activated protein-kinase-dependent mechanism. Blood 2002;99(4):1314–9.
[34] Shan D, Ledbetter JA, Press OW. Signaling events involved in anti-CD20-induced apoptosis of malignant human B cells. Cancer Immunol Immunother CII 2000;48(12):673–83.
[35] Shan D, Ledbetter JA, Press OW. Apoptosis of malignant human B cells by ligation of CD20 with monoclonal antibodies. Blood 1998;91(5):1644–52.
[36] Einfeld DA, Brown JP, Valentine MA, Clark EA, Ledbetter JA. Molecular cloning of the human B cell CD20 receptor predicts a hydrophobic protein with multiple transmembrane domains. EMBO J 1988;7(3):711–7.
[37] Tedder TF, Engel P. CD20: a regulator of cell-cycle progression of B lymphocytes. Immunol Today 1994;15 (9):450–4.
[38] Tedder TF, Klejman G, Schlossman SF, Saito H. Structure of the gene encoding the human B lymphocyte differentiation antigen CD20 (B1). J Immunol Baltim Md 1950 1989;142(7):2560–8.
[39] Qin Y, Kang SY, He XH, Zhou SY, Liu P, Yang JL, et al. Clinical features and prognosis of CD20-positive classical Hodgkin lymphoma. Zhonghua Yi Xue Za Zhi 2016;96(28):2224–8.

[40] Elsayed AA, Asano N, Ohshima K, Izutsu K, Kinoshita T, Nakamura S. Prognostic significance of CD20 expression and Epstein-Barr virus (EBV) association in classical Hodgkin lymphoma in Japan: a clinicopathologic study. Pathol Int 2014;64(7):336–45.
[41] Lacet DFR, Oliveira CC. Patients with classical Hodgkin lymphoma with less than 10.5 CD20-positive Reed-Sternberg cells in 10 high-power fields have better prognosis. Indian J Hematol Blood Transfus Off J Indian Soc Hematol Blood Transfus 2022;38(3):596–600.
[42] Fu XH, Wang SS, Huang Y, Xiao J, Zhai LZ, Xia ZJ, et al. Prognostic significance of CD20 expression in Hodgkin and Reed-Sternberg cells of classical Hodgkin's lymphoma. Ai Zheng Aizheng Chin J Cancer 2008;27(11):1197–203.
[43] Tzankov A, Krugmann J, Fend F, Fischhofer M, Greil R, Dirnhofer S. Prognostic significance of CD20 expression in classical Hodgkin lymphoma: a clinicopathological study of 119 cases. Clin Cancer Res Off J Am Assoc Cancer Res 2003;9(4):1381–6.
[44] Rygoł B, Krzemień S, Pajak J, Konicki P, Kowal E, Spychałowicz W, et al. CD20 antigen of Hodgkin and Reed-Sternberg cells as possible prognostic factor in patients with Hodgkin's lymphoma—preliminary reports. Pol Arch Med Wewn 2006;116(3):838–44.
[45] Tzankov A, Zimpfer A, Pehrs AC, Lugli A, Went P, Maurer R, et al. Expression of B-cell markers in classical Hodgkin lymphoma: a tissue microarray analysis of 330 cases. Mod Pathol 2003;16(11):1141–7.
[46] Giesta RP, Rocha Filho FD, Ferreira FVA, Quixadá ATS, Heukelbach J, Giesta MAG. Influência do CD 20 na refratariedade do linfoma de Hodgkin clássico ao tratamento inicial com o esquema ABVD, no Ceará, Brasil. J Bras Patol E Med Lab 2009;45:247–52.
[47] Abuelgasim KA, Shammari RA, Alshieban S, Alahmari B, Alzahrani M, Alhejazi A, et al. Impact of cluster of differentiation 20 expression and rituximab therapy in classical Hodgkin lymphoma: real world experience. Leuk Res Rep 2021;15, 100240.
[48] Panico L, Tenneriello V, Ronconi F, Lepore M, Cantore N, Dell'Angelo AC, et al. High CD20+ background cells predict a favorable outcome in classical Hodgkin lymphoma and antagonize CD68+ macrophages. Leuk Lymphoma 2015;56(6):1636–42.
[49] Zafar H, Riaz S, Badar F. Clinical impact of immunophenotype-CD15/CD30 on outcome of Hodgkin lympoma. Blood 2014;124(21):2952.
[50] Venkataraman G, Raffeld M, Pittaluga S, Jaffe ES. CD15-expressing nodular lymphocyte-predominant Hodgkin lymphoma. Histopathology 2011;58(5):803–5.
[51] Cheson BD, Fisher RI, Barrington SF, Cavalli F, Schwartz LH, Zucca E, et al. Recommendations for initial evaluation, staging, and response assessment of Hodgkin and non-Hodgkin lymphoma: the Lugano classification. J Clin Oncol Off J Am Soc Clin Oncol 2014;32(27):3059–68.
[52] Carbone PP, Kaplan HS, Musshoff K, Smithers DW, Tubiana M. Report of the committee on Hodgkin's disease staging classification. Cancer Res 1971;31(11):1860–1.
[53] Lister TA, Crowther D, Sutcliffe SB, Glatstein E, Canellos GP, Young RC, et al. Report of a committee convened to discuss the evaluation and staging of patients with Hodgkin's disease: Cotswolds meeting. J Clin Oncol Off J Am Soc Clin Oncol 1989;7(11):1630–6.
[54] Eichenauer DA, Aleman BMP, André M, Federico M, Hutchings M, Illidge T, et al. Hodgkin lymphoma: ESMO Clinical Practice Guidelines for diagnosis, treatment and follow-up. Ann Oncol Off J Eur Soc Med Oncol 2018;29 (Suppl 4):iv19–29.
[55] Hoppe RT, Advani RH, Ai WZ, Ambinder RF, Armand P, Bello CM, et al. Hodgkin lymphoma, version 2.2020, NCCN Clinical Practice Guidelines in Oncology. J Natl Compr Canc Netw 2020;18(6):755–81.
[56] Moskowitz CH, Nimer SD, Zelenetz AD, Trippett T, Hedrick EE, Filippa DA, et al. A 2-step comprehensive high-dose chemoradiotherapy second-line program for relapsed and refractory Hodgkin disease: analysis by intent to treat and development of a prognostic model. Blood 2001;97(3):616–23.
[57] Josting A, Rudolph C, Reiser M, Mapara M, Sieber M, Kirchner HH, et al. Time-intensified dexamethasone/cisplatin/cytarabine: an effective salvage therapy with low toxicity in patients with relapsed and refractory Hodgkin's disease. Ann Oncol Off J Eur Soc Med Oncol 2002;13(10):1628–35.
[58] Banchereau J, Rousset F. Human B lymphocytes: phenotype, proliferation, and differentiation. Adv Immunol 1992;52:125–262.

[59] Dreyling M, Campo E, Hermine O, Jerkeman M, Le Gouill S, Rule S, et al. Newly diagnosed and relapsed mantle cell lymphoma: ESMO Clinical Practice Guidelines for diagnosis, treatment and follow-up. Ann Oncol Off J Eur Soc. Med Oncol 2017;28(Suppl_4):iv62–71.

[60] Oki Y, Younes A. Does rituximab have a place in treating classic Hodgkin lymphoma? Curr Hematol Malig Rep 2010;5(3):135–9.

[61] Younes A, Romaguera J, Hagemeister F, McLaughlin P, Rodriguez MA, Fiumara P, et al. A pilot study of rituximab in patients with recurrent, classic Hodgkin disease. Cancer 2003;98(2):310–4.

[62] Advani R, Horning S, Hoppe R, Daadi S, Allen J, Natkunam Y, et al. Mature results of a Phase II study of rituximab therapy for nodular lymphocyte—predominant Hodgkin. Lymphoma 2014;32(9):912–9218.

[63] Schulz H, Rehwald U, Morschhauser F, Elter T, Driessen C, Rüdiger T, et al. Rituximab in relapsed lymphocyte-predominant Hodgkin lymphoma: long-term results of a phase 2 trial by the German Hodgkin Lymphoma Study Group (GHSG). Blood 2008;111(1):109–11.

[64] Strati P, Fanale MA, Oki Y, Turturro F, Fayad LE, Bartlett NL, et al. ABVD plus rituximab versus ABVD alone for advanced stage, high-risk classical Hodgkin lymphoma: a randomized phase 2 study. Haematologica 2019;104 (2):e65–7.

[65] Luo C, Wu G, Huang X, Ma Y, Zhang Y, Song Q, et al. Efficacy and safety of new anti-CD20 monoclonal antibodies versus rituximab for induction therapy of CD20+ B-cell non-Hodgkin lymphomas: a systematic review and meta-analysis. Sci Rep 2021;11(1):3255.

[66] Smith MR. Rituximab (monoclonal anti-CD20 antibody): mechanisms of action and resistance. Oncogene 2003;22 (47):7359–68.

[67] Vega GG, Franco-Cea LA, Huerta-Yepez S, Mayani H, Morrison SL, Bonavida B, et al. Overcoming rituximab drug-resistance by the genetically engineered anti-CD20-hIFN-α fusion protein: direct cytotoxicity and synergy with chemotherapy. Int J Oncol 2015;47(5):1735–48.

PART II

Resistance and affinity determination of anti-CD20 antibodies

CHAPTER

9

Therapeutic options for rituximab-resistant patients

Jing Wang[a,*], *Ran Qin*[a,*], *Yanling Jin*[a], *Bili Xia*[a], *and Jianqing Xu*[a,b]

[a]Shanghai Public Health Clinical Center, Fudan University, Shanghai, China [b]Zhongshan Hospital and Institutes of Biomedical Science, Fudan University, Shanghai, China

Abstract

Even though rituximab-based chemo-immunotherapy has prolonged the disease progression-free survival and overall survival time of patients with B-cell malignancies, such as follicular lymphoma, diffuse large B-cell lymphoma, chronic lymphocytic leukemia, and mantle cell lymphoma, a proportion of relapsed/refractory patients with rituximab resistance face limited therapeutic choices and exhibit poor prognosis. Extensive endeavor has been pursued to improve rituximab-based therapy and develop novel agents and strategies. High-dose chemotherapy followed by autologous stem cell transplantation (ASCT) is regarded as the second-line therapy for patients failing chemotherapy, while rituximab resistance is proved as a poor prognostic factor. The introduction of radio-immunotherapies not only improves the clinical activity of rituximab-based immunotherapy when used as monotherapy, but also brings more patients with rituximab resistance fit for ASCT when applied as a conditioning regimen. Strategies aiming to reinvigorate rituximab have been developed based on the increasing primary study on the mechanisms of the activity of rituximab, including improved Fc with higher affinity to the Fcγ receptors and strengthened activity of immune effector cells. Several more anti-CD20 antibodies besides rituximab have been developed and approved as potential choices for the clinical treatment of patients failing rituximab. Besides, small molecule agents targeting the activation and survival signaling pathways of B cells, such as the well-known inhibitors of Bruton's tyrosine kinase, phosphoinositide 3-kinase, have been approved based on their noticeable clinical response in clinical trials. The consolidation of small molecule agents with rituximab was proved to overcome the rituximab resistance, making them potent therapeutic candidates. In addition, the development of new targets for monoclonal antibodies, bispecific antibodies, and chimerical receptor T cells are also strategies to replenish the therapeutic arsenals and bring benefits for patients resistant to rituximab.

*Co-first authors.

https://doi.org/10.1016/B978-0-443-19200-5.00014-2

Abbreviations

ADC	antibody-drug conjugates
ADCC	antibody-dependent cellular cytotoxicity
ADP	antibody-dependent cellular phagocytosis
ASCT	autologous stem cell transplant
BCL-2	B-cell leukemia/lymphoma-2
BCR	B-cell receptor
BiTE	bispecific T-cell engager
BTK	Bruton's tyrosine kinase
CAR-T cells	chimeric antigen receptor T cells
CDC	complement-dependent cytotoxicity
CLL	chronic lymphocytic leukemia
CR	complete response
DCD	direct cell death
DLBCL	diffuse large B-cell lymphoma
FcγR	Fc gamma receptor
FDA	Food and Drug Administration
FL	follicular lymphoma
HDT	high-dose chemotherapy
Ig	immunoglobulin
KIR	killer cell Ig-like receptor
mAb	monoclonal antibody
MCL	mantle cell lymphoma
NHL	non-Hodgkin lymphoma
NK cells	natural killer cells
OR	overall response
ORR	overall response rate
OS	overall survival
PFS	progression-free survival
PI3K	phosphoinositide 3-kinase
PKCβ	protein kinase C-β
RIT	radio-immunotherapy
R/R	relapsed and refractory
SYK	spleen tyrosine kinase
WW	watchful waiting

Conflict of interest

No potential conflicts of interest were disclosed.

Introduction

CD20, also called B1, was identified as the specific antigen expressed on B cells of all stages, from pre-B cells to the mature plasma cells and on most B-cell malignancies, but not on hematopoietic progenitors, which renders it an ideal target for monoclonal antibody (mAb) used in the clinical treatment of B-cell malignancies [1,2]. Based on the extensive studies on the expression and roles of CD20, an anti-CD20 mAb was developed in 1979 [3,4] and first approved by the US Food and Drug Administration (FDA) for the treatment of relapsed and refractory (R/R) non-Hodgkin lymphoma (NHL) in 1997. Rituximab, a human/murine chimeric mAb targeting CD20, is a milestone therapeutic agent for patients with B-cell hematologic malignancies and has been used alone or in combination with other chemotherapies for

20 years [5,6]. With proven safety and efficacy in a long history of clinical use, rituximab has become a standard component of clinical care against CD20-expressing lymphoid malignancies, including indolent and aggressive forms of B-cell NHLs, such as follicular lymphoma (FL), diffuse large B-cell lymphoma (DLBCL), chronic lymphocytic leukemia (CLL), and mantle cell lymphoma (MCL), leading to prolonged time to disease progression and extended overall survival (OS) of patients [7].

Rituximab is a chimeric glycosylated immunoglobulin (Ig) G1-κ mAb composed of murine light- and heavy-chain variable region sequences, and human IgG1 constant region sequences [1]. Mechanisms underlying the elimination of target cells by rituximab include four pathways: antibody-dependent cellular cytotoxicity (ADCC), antibody-dependent cellular phagocytosis (ADP), complement-dependent cytotoxicity (CDC), and direct antitumor effects via either apoptosis or other cell death pathways [7–12].

Even though rituximab has brought about a dramatic revolution to the clinical treatment and OS for patients with CD20+ malignancies, CD20-expressing lymphoid malignancies are still uncurable. Responses to rituximab are not universal, and resistance can develop. Rituximab resistance is generally accepted as a lack of response or overt progression during, or within 6 months of completion of a rituximab-containing regimen [13]. In patients with FL treated in the modern era with immunochemotherapy, rituximab resistance (based on the above definition) was found in 16.7% of patients [14], and the incidence of rituximab resistance in treatment-naïve indolent NHL was 30%–60%, even though the combination approach would reduce the incidence to a lower grade [15]. Despite 20 years of clinical research, rituximab resistance remains a considerable challenge in treating B-cell malignancies. Further studies are urgently needed to develop better strategies to improve the prognosis of aggressive and hard-to-treat rituximab-resistant B-cell malignancies.

Herein, we conduct a summarized review of the strategies to overcome rituximab resistance in preclinical and clinical research. A summary of mechanisms underlying rituximab resistance is also included to guide the rational design of novel therapeutic regimens.

Mechanisms of rituximab resistance

Similar to the other kinds of therapeutic mAbs, ADCC, ADP, and CDC are regarded as the main pathways underlying the mechanisms of the antitumor effect of rituximab due to the effective interaction of the human IgG1 isotype with the human Fc gamma receptor (FcγR) and complement components [16,17]. Based on this, rituximab relies largely on the host to maximally evoke its cytotoxicity. Besides, direct cell death (DCD) induced by rituximab is an additional mechanism inhibiting survival signals and inducing apoptosis confirmed by recent research [18]. Thus, mechanisms of rituximab resistance include both host- or tumor-related signaling (Fig. 1).

Host-related mechanisms of rituximab resistance could be mainly summarized into two aspects: (1) reduced ADCC and ADP activity (Fig. 1A). ADCC occurs as a result of interaction between the Fc portion of rituximab coating the CD20 antigen on tumor cells and membrane-bound FcγRs expressed on the surface of effector cells, such as natural killer (NK) cells, granulocytes, and macrophages [19], triggering phagocytosis and releasing cytotoxic substances [20]. It was revealed that deficiency of FcγRs and blocking Fc receptors reduced the response to rituximab treatments [21]. A genomic polymorphism in FcγRIIIa corresponding

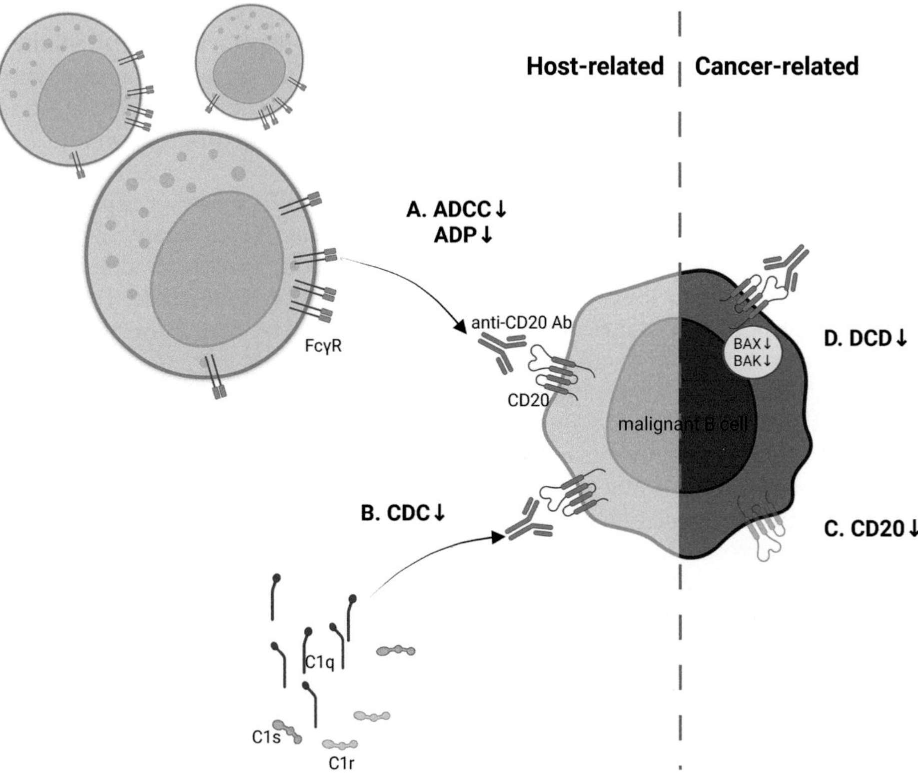

FIG. 1 Mechanisms of rituximab resistance including host-related (A and B) and cancer-related factors (C and D). ADCC, antibody-dependent cellular cytotoxicity; ADP, antibody-dependent cellular phagocytosis; CDC, complement-dependent cytotoxicity; FcγR: Fc-γ receptor; DCD, direct cell death.

to either valine (V) or phenylalanine (F) at position 158 greatly influenced their affinity to IgG1. Patients with homozygous FcγRIIIa-158V/V were declared to show the progression of disease after rituximab treatment, whereas their counterparts with homozygous FcγRIIIa-158F/F achieved prolonged progression-free survival (PFS) [8,22]. Furthermore, FcγRIIb was indicated as the only known inhibitory receptor acting to counterbalance the activator receptors [20]. Genetically modified mice lacking FcγRIIb demonstrated a better tumoral control [21]. Hence, the genetical polymorphism of the active and inhibitory receptors tones the strength of antibody-induced tumor phagocytosis and lysis. Besides, factors influencing the activation and expansion of NK cells were demonstrated to interfere with the response to rituximab, such as cytokines [23,24] and interaction of inhibitory killer cell Ig-like receptors (KIRs) [25]. Additionally, administration of rituximab enhances the degranulation and cytotoxicity of NK cells. Prolonged activation rendered the desensitization of activated receptors and the defects in the cytotoxic potential of NK cells, as declared in a population of CLL patients [26]. (2) Reduced CDC effect (Fig. 1B). The complement is rapidly depleted after treatment with rituximab [27,28]. Blocking either CD59 or CD55, complement regulatory proteins expressed on the membrane enhanced rituximab-related CDC activity [29,30].

Tumor-related mechanisms of rituximab resistance were reported to include factors as follows: (1) Low density of membrane-bound CD20 on tumor cells (Fig. 1C). The expression of CD20 varied among different B-cell neoplasms. The density of CD20 was found to be lower in CLL and MCL than in the other B-cell lymphomas, which was one of the explanations for the poor responses to rituximab monotherapy [13,31–33]. Additionally, the expression of CD20 was not uniform among tumor cells in the entities. Tumor cells with a low density of membrane-bound CD20 would get priority gradually along with the depletion of those with high density caused by the treatment of rituximab. (2) Decreased BAX and BAK have been declared in cell lines exposed to rituximab repeatedly as one of the acquired mechanisms of resistance to caspase-dependent apoptosis [34] (Fig. 1D).

Besides, Elias et al. have reported decreased expression of CD20 caused by trogocytosis (also called "shaving reaction") occurred as opsonized CD20-coated tumor cells by rituximab encounter FcγR-bearing effector cells [35]. As a type I mAb, the binding of rituximab redistributes CD20 into the lipid rafts [36–39]. The immunological synapses formed by redistributed rituximab-coated CD20 were removed or internalized instead of phagocytes leaving the opsonized B cells intact [13,40–42].

Therapeutic options after rituximab resistance

High-dose chemotherapy (HDT) and radio-immunotherapy (RIT) followed by autologous stem cell transplant (ASCT)

For R/R NHL patients, a salvage chemotherapy and HDT followed by ASCT could be curative and are the standard of care in the rituximab era [43–45]. The standard HDT is the combination of carmustine (1,3-bis(2-chloroethyl)-1-nitrosourea), etoposide, cytarabine, and melphalan (BEAM) [45]. The Collaborative Trial in Relapsed Aggressive Lymphoma (CORAL) study reported that only 63% of enrolled patients responded to the HDT and only 51% proceeded to ASCT, with the 3-year PFS and OS rate rendered to 31% and 50%, respectively [45,46]. This study demonstrated that prior rituximab therapy, relapse within 12 months of diagnosis, and second age-adjusted international prognostic index (sIPI) of more than 1, as prognostic factors for poor survival [46]. Modified approaches under investigation aiming to increase the clinical response of HDT consolidated with ASCT focus on better chemotherapy reagents, which could induce a larger proportion of patients to proceed to ASCT and better conditioning regimens for ASCT and the maintenance treatment after that, including RIT used before ASCT in order to improve ASCT outcome [45] (Fig. 2A). RIT is a targeted therapy using the parent mAb conjugated with a radioisotope to realize focused radiation to the antigen-positive tissue. The malignant cells could be killed by the combined effect of the antibody and/or the ionizing radiation, which is able to kill the adjacent tumor cells not binding to the mAb by crossfire radiation without depending on the immune effector cells in the host [45,47]. Yttrium-90 ibritumomab tiuxetan (Zevalin) and iodine-131 tositumomab (Bexxar) are two radioimmunoconjugates in clinical use approved by the FDA [47].

Several studies have evaluated the efficacy of a standard dose of RIT with BEAM as a conditioning regimen for ASCT. Zevalin, in combination with BEAM (namely Z-BEAM), prior to ASCT, was assessed in a clinical trial enrolling 63 patients with transformed NHL inducing a

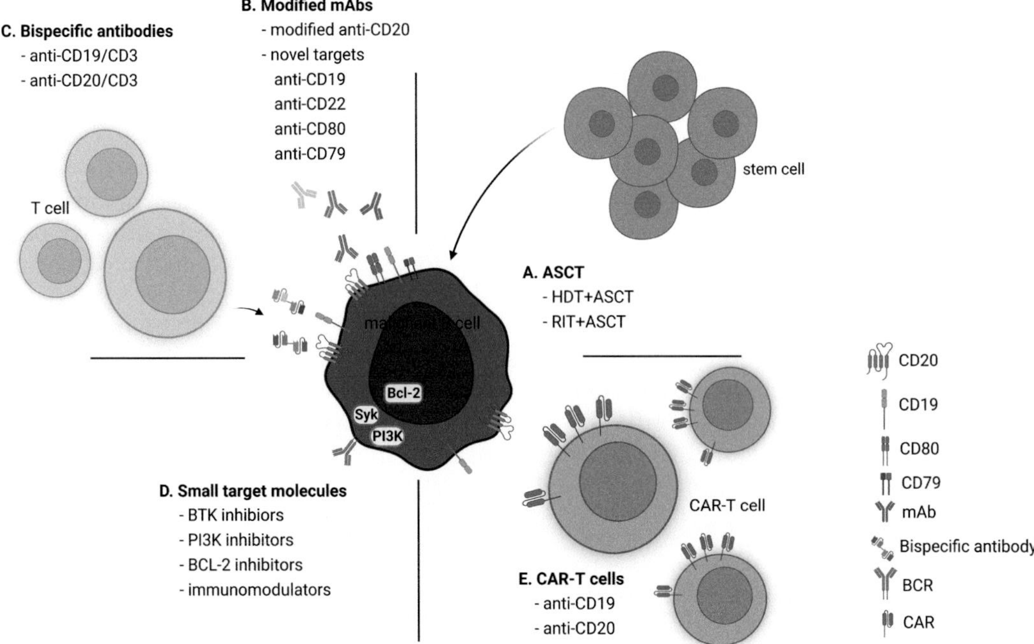

FIG. 2 Potential strategies under investigation for patients resistant to rituximab. (A) Autologous stem cell transplant (ASCT). (B) Modified mAbs. (C) Small target molecules. (D) Bispecific antibodies. (E) CAR-T cells. HDT, high-dose chemotherapy; RIT, radio-immunotherapy; BCR, B-cell receptor; CAR-T, chimerical receptor T cells.

2-year OS rate approaching 90% [48]. In another study, the standard dose of Bexxar consolidated with high-dose BEAM (namely B-BEAM) followed by ASCT was applied in 20 patients with R/R DLBCL, resulting in an impressive result of 80% OR rate with 78% CR as the best performance. The median 5-year OS rate and PFS rate were 72% and 70%, respectively [49]. However, the clinical trial comparing rituximab-BEAM with B-BEAM prior to ASCT in 234 chemotherapy-sensitive relapsed DLBCL patients reported the inferior 2-year PFS rate (47.9% vs. 48.6%) and OS rate (61% vs. 65.5%) for the RIT group compared to rituximab group, respectively [50], which introduced the uncertainty of the superiority of RIT to rituximab to be clarified.

In addition, a myeloablative dose of RIT, alone or in consolidation with other chemotherapy, as a preparative regimen prior to ASCT in patients with high-risk NHL has been confirmed to induce prolonged remissions even in elderly patients in clinical studies without causing additional toxicity [47,51–54]. Notably, high dose of Bexxar was reported to produce promising results even in patients not eligible for transplantation [55], making it profitable for RIT used alone, especially for patients not eligible for ASCT.

Patients with primary refractory disease, PET-positive disease after salvage therapy, early relapsing disease, and MYC-rearranged lymphoma have little chance for durable complete remission with ASCT [56], for whom alternative therapeutic choices are urgently needed.

Type II anti-CD20 mAbs

Anti-CD20 mAbs have been classified into types I and II according to their ability to redistribute CD20 into the lipid rafts and the mechanistic pathways of their actions [36–38]. Rituximab is a type I anti-CD20 mAb relocalizing CD20 into the lipid rafts in the opsonized cells and appears to evoke minimal DCD but significant CDC and ADCC [35,57,58]. The impact of the CDC on the action of rituximab in deleting B-cell tumors has been controversial with potential flaws inducing "shaving reactions." With the convincing success of immunotherapy with rituximab in the clinical treatment of B-cell malignancies, the pursuit of modified reagents with higher affinity to CD20, reduced immunogenicity, and improved ADCC and CDC is intense [57,59], among which some type II anti-CD20 mAbs have been proved to deliver improved efficacy in the patients resistant to rituximab-based immunotherapy in clinical trials, such as tositumomab and obinutuzumab (also known as GA101) (Fig. 2B).

Tositumomab

As a type II mAb, interactions of tositumomab with CD20 do not induce translocation of CD20 to the lipid raft in the opsonized cells, thus showing low action in evoking CDC [60]. It has been demonstrated that rituximab is at least 25 times more active in inducing CDC than tositumomab [37,38,61]. Conjugation of tositumomab to a radionuclide iodine 131, known as ^{131}I tositumomab, was proposed to enhance the irradiation of lymphoma cells by direct cellular binding and impact of the radionuclide [62]. The safety and efficacy of ^{131}I tositumomab were evaluated in a phase II multicenter study of 47 patients in which overall response (OR) rates and complete response (CR) rates were reported inspiringly as 57% and 32%, respectively [63]. Another pivotal clinical trial in a cohort of 60 patients with low-grade and transformed lymphoma, who have failed the previous integrated chemo-immunotherapies, reported a significantly better clinical response with the OR of 65% [64]. The most common adverse event reported was hematologic toxicity, which recovered about 10 weeks later [64–66]. Notably, the safety and clinical response of tositumomab in the treatment of patients resistant to rituximab was confirmed in a clinical trial reported in 2005 [62]. The OR rate and CR rate were reported as 65% and 385, respectively. The median PFS for all enrolled patients was 10.4 months and 24.5 months for responders. Patients with follicular grade 1 or 2 histology and tumor dimer $\leq$7 cm achieved very high OR and CR, with 86% and 57%, respectively, and 48% PFS at 3 years, which showed significantly greater efficacy of tositumomab in the treatment of B-cell lymphoma progressive after rituximab [62]. Anti-CD20 RIT has shown inspiring potential in the clinical treatment of patients with rituximab resistance.

Obinutuzumab

Obinutuzumab is another new-generation humanized type II anti-CD20 antibody that is engineered with higher affinity to CD20 by distinct variable and glycol-engineered Fc regions compared with rituximab [58]. Reduced fucosylation of its Fc region optimized the binding of obinutuzumab to FcγR and, therefore, improved the activity of antibody-dependent cytotoxicity [58,67]. Relative to rituximab, obinutuzumab was demonstrated to perform increased direct and immune effector cell-mediated cytotoxicity in cell lines ex vivo, and superior antitumor activity in human lymphoma xenograft models resulting in complete tumor regression, and increased OS and prominent B-cell depletion in lymphoid tissue in nonhuman primates

[58]. Notably, the well-known multicenter phase III GADOLIN trial in the patient cohort with rituximab-refractory indolent NHL demonstrated the efficacy of obinutuzumab (GA101; G) and bendamustine (B) treatment. Enrolled patients received G 1000 mg (days 1, 8, and 15, cycle 1; day 1, cycles 2–6) plus B 90mg/m^2/d (days 1 and 2, all cycles) (named G-B therapy) or B 120mg/m^2/d monotherapy. Patients, who did not experience disease progression with G-B, received G maintenance (1000mg every 2 months) for up to 2 years [68,69]. G-B therapy was verified to contribute to the prolonged PFS (25.8 months) vs B monotherapy (14.1 months) [68]. OS was also prolonged [68]. Besides, PFS and OS benefits were similar in patients with FL, with a reduction in the risk of death of 33% in iNHL patients and 42% in FL patients [68]. Along with the clinical benefits, the adverse events observed in the G-B and B monotherapy arms were comparable, most commonly neutropenia (G-B 34.8%; B 27.1%), thrombocytopenia (10.8% and 15.8%), anemia (7.4% and 10.8%) and infusion-related reactions (9.3% and 3.4%) [68,69]. The notably prolonged OS, PFS, and comparable side events in rituximab-refractory iNHL patients provided the rationale for the preferred option of G-B therapy in the treatment of these patients.

Solutions to enhance the ADCC effect of anti-CD20 antibodies

Because rituximab relies on the host effectors to a significant grade to perform its maximum B-cell depletion activity, strategies engineered to enhance the affinity of the Fc receptor and the antitumor function of immune effector cells are extensively pursued currently.

Second-generation and third-generation anti-CD20 antibodies

Humanized modification based on rituximab was applied in the second generation of anti-CD20 antibodies to overcome the side effects as a chimeric mAB and to increase affinity for FcγR, among which ocrelizumab was demonstrated with an OR rate of 36% in FL patients refractory/resistant to prior rituximab therapy in a phase I/II clinical trial [70,71]. Third-generation anti-CD20 antibodies were characterized by increased affinity to CD20 and enhanced Fc-FcγR III interaction [72,73]. In addition to the well-known obinutuzumab, which was discussed above, ocaratuzumab (also known as AME-133v) and Pro131921 also induced encouragingly improved clinical efficacy in phase I/II clinical trials enrolling patients with rituximab resistance [74,75].

Strategies to enhance the antitumor functions of immune effector cells

Many efforts have been taken to segment the antitumor responses of immune effector cells in the host. Pathologically complete remission of a patient with R/R DLBCL and HIV infection was reported under the combined treatment of the expanded heterologous iNKT cells and anti-CD20 antibody in our previous work [76]. We modified the anti-CD20 antibody on the Fc with A330L/I332E to introduce better ADCC activity [77,78], while leaving the same Fab. Expanded heterologous iNKT cells were haploidentical from their biological mother, which were applied to provide potent immune effector cells instead malfunctional cells of their own [76]. The dosage of modified anti-CD20 mAb was limited to 10 mg per infusion mixed with iNKT cells prior to infusion, which was far less than that in mAb monotherapy

[76]. The decreased dosage contributed to the mild side effects observed in this patient, with no hematologic toxicity recorded. The patient was confirmed to achieve pathological complete regression 4 weeks after the sixth course. Durable control of the disease has lasted till now with no lesions on CT scanning, leading the PSF to 41 months by November 2022. It deserved further study on the reinvigoration of anti-CD20 antibody by the combination of immune effector cells. Additionally, supplementation with ALT-803 (an agonist of IL-5) and vitamin D3 was reported to significantly increase ADCC against B-cell lymphoma in vivo and deserves extensive investigations [79–81].

Novel targets for mAbs

The merit of searching for novel targets for the candidate mAb against B-cell malignancies was pursued for the clinical treatment of patients resistant to rituximab. These novel targets include CD19, CD22, CD80, CD30, CD52, CD40, CD79b, and CD38, and more are under development [70,82–84] (Fig. 2B). A humanized anti-CD19 mAb tafasitamab (MOR208) has been evaluated in patients with NHL and failed the rituximab-based therapy in a phase II clinical trial, which reported the OR rate as 29% [85]. Tafasitamab was exposed to resister recently in combination with lenalidomide and antibody-drug conjugates (ADCs), i.e., loncastuximab tesirisine-lpyl and an anti-CD79b ADC-polatuzumab vedotin [86]. A series of conjugated forms of anti-CD20 antibody, such as 90Y-epratuzumab and inotuzumab ozogamicin conjugated to 90Y and calicheamicin, respectively, have shown promising results in the clinical treatment of B-cell malignancies in clinical trials [70,87]. Besides, the anti-CD80 mAb (galiximab), anti-CD30 mAb (Brentuximab Vedotin), anti-CD52 mAb (Alemtuzumab), anti-CD40 mAb (SGN-40 and HCD122), and anti-CD79b mAb (Polatuzumab) have been evaluated in clinical trials in patients positively expressed targets accordingly [70]. The efficacy for tumor-control of an anti-CD38 mAB, Daratumumab, was demonstrated in a patient-derived xenograft model of CD20-negative, CD38-positive DLBCL derived from a patient with rituximab-refractory DLBCL, which suggested a potential clinical usage of daratumumab alone or in combination with salvage chemotherapy [70,82].

Bispecific antibodies

A bispecific antibody, which was also named bispecific T-cell engager (BiTE), was designed to bridge the immune effector cells in close proximity to malignant cells resulting in cell-mediated cytotoxicity [88] (Fig. 2C). Blinatumomab, a bispecific antibody with specificity to CD19 on tumor cells and CD3 on T cells, has been approved by the FDA for the treatment of R/R B-cell precursor acute lymphoblastic leukemia and demonstrated modest activity in R/R B-cell NHL. A clinical study in patients with DLBCL under treatment with blinatumomab reported an OR rate of 43% and a CR rate of 19% with a median PFS of 3.7 months [89]. Besides, several bispecific CD3 and CD20 antibodies are under investigation in B-NHL, including mosunetuzumab, GEN3013, REGN1979, and RO7082859 [88]. Whether bispecific antibodies will induce durable remissions remains uncertain and merits long-term study and follow-up.

Small molecules

Chronic activation and dysregulated B-cell-receptor (BCR) signals have fundamentally contributed to B-cell tumor survival and lymphomagenesis [90–93]. BCR activation initiates downstream signaling mainly via the pathways including spleen tyrosine kinase (SYK), Bruton's tyrosine kinase (BTK), phosphoinositide 3-kinase (PI3K), and protein kinase C-β (PKCβ) [94,95]. The dysregulated apoptotic activity of B-cell leukemia/lymphoma-2 (BCL-2) leads to the upregulation of pro-apoptotic BCL-2 proteins and cell cycle arrest, which has been reported as a hallmark in the development of some B-cell malignancies, such as MCL [96]. The therapeutic, targeted molecules inhibiting the critical molecules in the signaling pathway of BCR disrupt signals essential for normal and neoplastic B-cell proliferation, maturation, differentiation, apoptosis, and migration [90] (Fig. 2D).

Two BTK inhibitors, ibrutinib and acalabrutinib, have been approved by the FDA for the clinical treatment of R/R MCL. They are proven to bring prolonged PFS to patients, who have received at least one prior therapy in clinical trials and real-life data [97–99]. More importantly, ibrutinib therapy has been demonstrated to be safely and efficiently used in patients with central nervous systems who were reported to achieve poor response to conventional immunochemotherapy with a limited survival of 6 months [100]. However, acalabrutinib was reported to be associated with low discontinuation rates due to adverse events, including bleeding and atrial fibrillation [99]. Zanubrutinib, a novel BTK inhibitor under development, was demonstrated to have less off-target activity and be efficacious against R/R MCL in clinical trials with a favorable safety profile [101].

Four PI3K inhibitors, indelalisib, copanlisib, duvelisib, and umbralisib, have been approved by the FDA for the treatment of multiple-relapsed FL and reported to induce long-term remissions in patients resistant to previous rituximab-based chemo-immunotherapy [88,102–104].

Other target molecules blocking activation and pro-survival signals have been proven to induce benefit to suitable patients and approved by the FDA for clinical treatment, such as proteasome inhibitors (carfilzomib and ixazomib) [105,106], mTOR inhibitors (everolimus and temsirolimus) [107,108], and BCL2 inhibitors (Venetoclax) [109]. Many target molecules and immunomodulators are under development for improved clinical efficacy and safety [90,110].

Chimeric antigen receptor T cells (CAR-T)

Three anti-CD19 CAR-T cell products, namely axicabtagene ciloleucel, tisagenlecleucel, and lisocabtagene maraleucel have been approved by the FDA for the treatment of patients with aggressive B-cell lymphoma, who have relapsed or have refractory disease after at least two previous lines of therapy, based on their inspiringly high CR rates (60%) and durable tumor control in approximately 40% of these difficult-to-treat patients [88,111–113]. However, about 30% of patients do not respond to or quickly relapse after CD19 CAR-T cell therapy [114]. Therefore, other targets were developed for CAR-T cell treatment strategy, among which the safety and efficacy of anti-CD20 CAR-T cell therapy against R/R B-NHL with rituximab resistance have been evaluated in a prospective, single-center phase 1 clinical trial [113] (Fig. 2E). An OR rate of 100% was reported with 80% of patients achieving CR and 20%

experiencing PR [113]. The median follow-up time was 12.4 months, while PFS and OS had not yet reached by the data cutoff day [113]. The data of this clinical trial provide an appealing perspective for further investigation and potential clinical use of anti-CD20 CAR-T cell in the patients with B-cell malignancies previously treated with rituximab [113].

Watchful waiting (WW)

Without enhancement and interference with the immune system and the tumor cells, WW was treatment-free follow-up under frequent assessment of the lesions and body status [115,116]. As one of the standard approaches for newly diagnosed, asymptomatic patients with advanced-stage, low tumor-burden FL [117–120], WW benefits the patients by postponing repeated disease relapse (2–4) and reducing adverse events due to repeated chemotherapy, including infection and the second primary malignancy [121,122]. The impact and feasibility of WW in patients at the first progression have been evaluated in a retrospective study in a cohort of patients in the National Cancer Center Hospital in Japan [115]. A total of 206 FL patients, who experienced the first progression after responding to the initial treatment, among whom 150 (73%) and 29 (14%) underwent chemotherapies with or without rituximab and rituximab monotherapy, were viewed. As many as 132 patients, who experienced the treatment-free follow-up for longer than 3 months after the first progression, were clarified into the WW group.

As reported, 15 patients in the WW group underwent CR during the treatment-free follow-up. The median time from the first-line treatment failure to the second-line treatment failure was significantly different in the WW cohort (72.8 months; 95% CI, 64.6–94.0) compared to the immediate treatment cohort (23.3 months; 95% CI, 13.4–38.8). The cumulative incidence of histological transformation in the WW group after the treatment-free follow-up was comparable with that in the immediate treatment cohort. In a multivariate analysis, rituximab refractory status, progression of disease within 24 months from the induction of first-line therapy, and a high Follicular Lymphoma International Prognostic Index score at diagnosis were significantly related to a shorter time to the next treatment during WW [115].

With extensive analysis, WW was declared as safely and feasibly conducted to postpone subsequent treatment for FL patients with first-line treatment failure without negative impact on the TTF, OS, and histological transformation risk. Suitable time for initiation of the second-line treatment and selection for the optimal candidate with the most potentiality of benefit are needed for further studies.

Combination strategies

Combination strategies are always considered in the clinical care of patients with B-cell malignancies to increase clinical response and maintain durable remission [123]. Even for patients failing rituximab-based chemo-immunotherapies, consolidation of novel, target molecules with rituximab has been proven to exhibit a synergistic effect and bring benefits to remission and survival.

As a widely investigated immunomodulator, lenalidomide, consolidated with rituximab, has been clarified to overcome rituximab resistance in a single-center, phase II clinical trial in patients with indolent B-cell and MCLs [90,124,125]. Forty-three patients, who were previously resistant to rituximab, received 10 mg lenalidomide daily for 8 weeks, and then received 4 weekly doses of 375 mg/m^2 rituximab; lenalidomide was continued during and after rituximab. Response to therapy was assessed after 8 weeks of lenalidomide and 12 weeks after the first dose of rituximab. The overall response rate (ORR) after 8 weeks of lenalidomide was 30.2%, while the ORR increased to 62.8% 12 weeks after the addition of rituximab to lenalidomide. The PFS was 22.2 months [125]. Another phase II trial reported that the combination of ibrutinib with rituximab was active and well tolerated in patients with R/R MCL [126]. According to the promising activity of regiments based on ibrutinib alone and lenalidomide and rituximab in combination in patients with R/R MCL, the PHILEMON phase II study was conducted applying the triplet combination of ibrutinib, lenalidomide, and rituximab. At a median follow-up period of 17.8 months, 38 of all 50 enrolled patients (76%) had an OR, including 28 patients who had CR and 10 who had PR [127].

The addition of venetoclax to the combination of lenalidomide and rituximab induces an ORR of 56% in R/R MCL patients [90,128]. Most combined strategies under investigation in clinical trials are proven to have well-tolerable safety profiles without the aggravated side effects of multiple therapeutic drugs.

Even though a wide therapeutic repertoire is available to the patients and oncologists, the drug efficacy could be limited to the genetic heterogeneity. As previously described, the polymorphism in the *FcgR3A* gene (rs396991 T/G), which results in a change of amino acid F T to V at position 158 of FcγRIIIa, was associated with prolonged PFS and OS to rituximab-based chemotherapy [22]. High GSTP1 and TOPO2α gene expressions were reported to be associated with shorter OS and PFS in patients with DLBCL undergoing a dose-dense R-CHOP (rituximab, cyclophosphamide, doxorubicin, vincristine, prednisone) regimen [129]. Pharmacogenetics is the analysis of therapeutic and adverse responses to drugs based on an individual's genetic background, which is crucial to associate specific genetic changes with drug response data [130]. A few prognosis models integrating the pharmacogenomic gene signatures and the clinical information provide the predictive capability to ascertain the prognosis of patients prior to the treatment of drug candidates, which may achieve better clinical outcomes [131,132].

Conclusions and perspectives

As the first-line therapy, rituximab-based chemo-immunotherapy has revolutionized the clinical treatment of patients with B-cell malignancies. Unfortunately, R/R patients resistant to rituximab exhibit harsh survival expectancy and poor response to many second-line therapies, such as HDT-consolidated ASCT. Nevertheless, the introduction of RIT prior to ASCT notably improves the prognosis and clinical response of R/R patients. Monotherapy of novel agents, such as modified anti-CD20 antibodies and small targeted molecules, exhibit inspiring response in clinical trials, even though further investigations are still needed to develop more durable responses and prolonged survival with tolerable safety profiles. The combinations of novel strategies have been demonstrated to overcome rituximab resistance without aggregation of side effects, which deserve further studies in clinical trials and practice. BiTE and CAR-T, as novel, individual, therapeutic strategies, are extensively studied and have transformed the therapeutic choices for previously treated and newly diagnosed patients, which are warranted further investigations in the therapeutic arsenals of R/R patients. With the bridge of pharmacogenetics, personalized therapeutic strategy according to the individualized gene signature will benefit patients with efficient treatment choices to achieve improved clinical response and prolonged survival.

Acknowledgments

We would like to thank Biorender.com (https://biorender.com/) for supporting figure drafting. The publication license has been obtained.

References

[1] Banchereau J, Rousset F. Human B lymphocytes: phenotype, proliferation, and differentiation. Adv Immunol 1992;52:125–262.
[2] Engelhard M. Anti-CD20 antibody treatment of non-Hodgkin lymphomas. Clin Immunol 2016;172:101–4.
[3] Nadler LM, Ritz J, Hardy R, Pesando JM, Schlossman SF, Stashenko P. A unique cell surface antigen identifying lymphoid malignancies of B cell origin. J Clin Invest 1981;67(1):134–40.
[4] Stashenko P, Nadler LM, Hardy R, Schlossman SF. Characterization of a human B lymphocyte-specific antigen. J Immunol 1980;125(4):1678–85.
[5] Susanibar-Adaniya S, Barta SK. 2021 update on diffuse large B cell lymphoma: a review of current data and potential applications on risk stratification and management. Am J Hematol 2021;96(5):617–29.
[6] China Anti-cancer Association Lymphoma, Chinese Association for Clinical, Medical Oncology Branch of Chinese International, Promotion Association for Healthcare. Clinical practice guideline for lympoma in China (2021 edition). Zhonghua Zhong Liu Za Zhi 2021;43(7):707–35.
[7] Salles G, Barrett M, Foa R, Maurer J, O'Brien S, Valente N, Wenger M, Maloney DG. Rituximab in B-cell hematologic malignancies: a review of 20 years of clinical experience. Adv Ther 2017;34(10):2232–73.
[8] Maloney DG, Smith B, Rose A. Rituximab: mechanism of action and resistance. Semin Oncol 2002;29(1S2):2–9.
[9] Weiner GJ. Rituximab: mechanism of action. Semin Hematol 2010;47(2):115–23.
[10] Cerny T, Borisch B, Introna M, Johnson P, Rose AL. Mechanism of action of rituximab. Anti-Cancer Drugs 2002;13(Suppl 2):S3–10.
[11] Meyer S, Evers M, Jansen JHM, Buijs J, Broek B, Reitsma SE, Moerer P, Amini M, Kretschmer A, Ten Broeke T, den Hartog MT, Rijke M, Klein C, Valerius T, Boross P, Leusen JHW. New insights in Type I and II CD20 antibody mechanisms-of-action with a panel of novel CD20 antibodies. Br J Haematol 2018;180(6):808–20.
[12] Novo M, Santambrogio E, Frascione PMM, Rota-Scalabrini D, Vitolo U. Antibody therapies for large b-cell lymphoma. Biologics 2021;15:153–74.
[13] Freeman CL, Sehn LH. A tale of two antibodies: obinutuzumab versus rituximab. Br J Haematol 2018;182(1): 29–45.
[14] Mozessohn L, Cheung MC, Crump M, Buckstein R, Berinstein N, Imrie K, Kuruvilla J, Piliotis E, Kukreti V. Chemoimmunotherapy resistant follicular lymphoma: predictors of resistance, association with transformation and prognosis. Leuk Lymphoma 2014;55(11):2502–7.
[15] Rezvani AR, Maloney DG. Rituximab resistance. Best Pract Res Clin Haematol 2011;24(2):203–16.
[16] Anderson DR, Grillo-Lopez A, Varns C, Chambers KS, Hanna N. Targeted anti-cancer therapy using rituximab, a chimaeric anti-CD20 antibody (IDEC-C2B8) in the treatment of non-Hodgkin's B-cell lymphoma. Biochem Soc Trans 1997;25(2):705–8.
[17] Abulayha A, Bredan A, El Enshasy H, Daniels I. Rituximab: modes of action, remaining dispute and future perspective. Future Oncol 2014;10(15):2481–92.
[18] Vega MI, Huerta-Yepez S, Martinez-Paniagua M, Martinez-Miguel B, Hernandez-Pando R, Gonzalez-Bonilla CR, Chinn P, Hanna N, Hariharan K, Jazirehi AR, Bonavida B. Rituximab-mediated cell signaling and chemo/immuno-sensitization of drug-resistant B-NHL is independent of its Fc functions. Clin Cancer Res 2009;15 (21):6582–94.

[19] Bowles JA, Wang SY, Link BK, Allan B, Beuerlein G, Campbell MA, Marquis D, Ondek B, Wooldridge JE, Smith BJ, Breitmeyer JB, Weiner GJ. Anti-CD20 monoclonal antibody with enhanced affinity for CD16 activates NK cells at lower concentrations and more effectively than rituximab. Blood 2006;108(8):2648–54.
[20] Davies A, Berge C, Boehnke A, Dadabhoy A, Lugtenburg P, Rule S, Rummel M, McIntyre C, Smith R, Badoux X. Subcutaneous rituximab for the treatment of B-cell hematologic malignancies: a review of the scientific rationale and clinical development. Adv Ther 2017;34(10):2210–31.
[21] Reff ME, Carner K, Chambers KS, Chinn PC, Leonard JE, Raab R, Newman RA, Hanna N, Anderson DR. Depletion of B cells in vivo by a chimeric mouse human monoclonal antibody to CD20. Blood 1994;83(2):435–45.
[22] Musolino A, Naldi N, Bortesi B, Pezzuolo D, Capelletti M, Missale G, Laccabue D, Zerbini A, Camisa R, Bisagni G, Neri TM, Ardizzoni A. Immunoglobulin G fragment C receptor polymorphisms and clinical efficacy of trastuzumab-based therapy in patients with HER-2/neu-positive metastatic breast cancer. J Clin Oncol 2008;26(11):1789–96.
[23] Maloney DG, Liles TM, Czerwinski DK, Waldichuk C, Rosenberg J, Grillo-Lopez A, Levy R. Phase I clinical trial using escalating single-dose infusion of chimeric anti-CD20 monoclonal antibody (IDEC-C2B8) in patients with recurrent B-cell lymphoma. Blood 1994;84(8):2457–66.
[24] Maloney DG, Grillo-Lopez AJ, White CA, Bodkin D, Schilder RJ, Neidhart JA, Janakiraman N, Foon KA, Liles TM, Dallaire BK, Wey K, Royston I, Davis T, Levy R. IDEC-C2B8 (Rituximab) anti-CD20 monoclonal antibody therapy in patients with relapsed low-grade non-Hodgkin's lymphoma. Blood 1997;90(6):2188–95.
[25] Makanga DR, Jullien M, David G, Legrand N, Willem C, Dubreuil L, Walencik A, Touzeau C, Gastinne T, Tessoulin B, Le Gouill S, Mahe B, Gagne K, Chevallier P, Clemenceau B, Retiere C. Low number of KIR ligands in lymphoma patients favors a good rituximab-dependent NK cell response. Oncoimmunology 2021;10 (1):1936392.
[26] Capuano C, Romanelli M, Pighi C, Cimino G, Rago A, Molfetta R, Paolini R, Santoni A, Galandrini R. Anti-CD20 therapy acts via FcgammaRIIIA to diminish responsiveness of human natural killer cells. Cancer Res 2015;75 (19):4097–108.
[27] Kennedy AD, Beum PV, Solga MD, DiLillo DJ, Lindorfer MA, Hess CE, Densmore JJ, Williams ME, Taylor RP. Rituximab infusion promotes rapid complement depletion and acute CD20 loss in chronic lymphocytic leukemia. J Immunol 2004;172(5):3280–8.
[28] van der Kolk LE, Grillo-Lopez AJ, Baars JW, Hack CE, van Oers MH. Complement activation plays a key role in the side-effects of rituximab treatment. Br J Haematol 2001;115(4):807–11.
[29] Macor P, Tripodo C, Zorzet S, Piovan E, Bossi F, Marzari R, Amadori A, Tedesco F. In vivo targeting of human neutralizing antibodies against CD55 and CD59 to lymphoma cells increases the antitumor activity of rituximab. Cancer Res 2007;67(21):10556–63.
[30] Ziller F, Macor P, Bulla R, Sblattero D, Marzari R, Tedesco F. Controlling complement resistance in cancer by using human monoclonal antibodies that neutralize complement-regulatory proteins CD55 and CD59. Eur J Immunol 2005;35(7):2175–83.
[31] Prevodnik VK, Lavrencak J, Horvat M, Novakovic BJ. The predictive significance of CD20 expression in B-cell lymphomas. Diagn Pathol 2011;6:33.
[32] Beers SA, French RR, Chan HT, Lim SH, Jarrett TC, Vidal RM, Wijayaweera SS, Dixon SV, Kim H, Cox KL, Kerr JP, Johnston DA, Johnson PW, Verbeek JS, Glennie MJ, Cragg MS. Antigenic modulation limits the efficacy of anti-CD20 antibodies: implications for antibody selection. Blood 2010;115(25):5191–201.
[33] Hiraga J, Tomita A, Sugimoto T, Shimada K, Ito M, Nakamura S, Kiyoi H, Kinoshita T, Naoe T. Down-regulation of CD20 expression in B-cell lymphoma cells after treatment with rituximab-containing combination chemotherapies: its prevalence and clinical significance. Blood 2009;113(20):4885–93.
[34] Olejniczak SH, Hernandez-Ilizaliturri FJ, Clements JL, Czuczman MS. Acquired resistance to rituximab is associated with chemotherapy resistance resulting from decreased Bax and Bak expression. Clin Cancer Res 2008;14(5):1550–60.
[35] Elias S, Kahlon S, Kotzur R, Kaynan N, Mandelboim O. Obinutuzumab activates FcgammaRI more potently than other anti-CD20 antibodies in chronic lymphocytic leukemia (CLL). Oncoimmunology 2018;7(6), e1428158.
[36] Chan HT, Hughes D, French RR, Tutt AL, Walshe CA, Teeling JL, Glennie MJ, Cragg MS. CD20-induced lymphoma cell death is independent of both caspases and its redistribution into triton X-100 insoluble membrane rafts. Cancer Res 2003;63(17):5480–9.

[37] Cragg MS, Glennie MJ. Antibody specificity controls in vivo effector mechanisms of anti-CD20 reagents. Blood 2004;103(7):2738–43.

[38] Cragg MS, Morgan SM, Chan HT, Morgan BP, Filatov AV, Johnson PW, French RR, Glennie MJ. Complement-mediated lysis by anti-CD20 mAb correlates with segregation into lipid rafts. Blood 2003;101(3):1045–52.

[39] Beers SA, Chan CH, James S, French RR, Attfield KE, Brennan CM, Ahuja A, Shlomchik MJ, Cragg MS, Glennie MJ. Type II (tositumomab) anti-CD20 monoclonal antibody out performs type I (rituximab-like) reagents in B-cell depletion regardless of complement activation. Blood 2008;112(10):4170–7.

[40] Valgardsdottir R, Cattaneo I, Klein C, Introna M, Figliuzzi M, Golay J. Human neutrophils mediate trogocytosis rather than phagocytosis of CLL B cells opsonized with anti-CD20 antibodies. Blood 2017;129(19):2636–44.

[41] Taylor RP, Lindorfer MA. Fcgamma-receptor-mediated trogocytosis impacts mAb-based therapies: historical precedence and recent developments. Blood 2015;125(5):762–6.

[42] Beum PV, Kennedy AD, Williams ME, Lindorfer MA, Taylor RP. The shaving reaction: rituximab/CD20 complexes are removed from mantle cell lymphoma and chronic lymphocytic leukemia cells by THP-1 monocytes. J Immunol 2006;176(4):2600–9.

[43] Schmitz N, Pfistner B, Sextro M, Sieber M, Carella AM, Haenel M, Boissevain F, Zschaber R, Muller P, Kirchner H, Lohri A, Decker S, Koch B, Hasenclever D, Goldstone AH, Diehl V, German Hodgkin's Lymphoma Study, Lymphoma Working Party of the European Group for Blood and Marrow Transplantation. Aggressive conventional chemotherapy compared with high-dose chemotherapy with autologous haemopoietic stem-cell transplantation for relapsed chemosensitive Hodgkin's disease: a randomised trial. Lancet 2002;359(9323):2065–71.

[44] Zahid U, Akbar F, Amaraneni A, Husnain M, Chan O, Riaz IB, McBride A, Iftikhar A, Anwer F. A review of autologous stem cell transplantation in lymphoma. Curr Hematol Malig Rep 2017;12(3):217–26.

[45] Shimoni A, Zwas ST. Radioimmunotherapy and autologous stem-cell transplantation in the treatment of B-cell non-Hodgkin lymphoma. Semin Nucl Med 2016;46(2):119–25.

[46] Gisselbrecht C, Glass B, Mounier N, Singh Gill D, Linch DC, Trneny M, Bosly A, Ketterer N, Shpilberg O, Hagberg H, Ma D, Briere J, Moskowitz CH, Schmitz N. Salvage regimens with autologous transplantation for relapsed large B-cell lymphoma in the rituximab era. J Clin Oncol 2010;28(27):4184–90.

[47] Eskian M, Khorasanizadeh M, Isidori A, Rezaei N. Radioimmunotherapy-based conditioning regimen prior to autologous stem cell transplantation in non-Hodgkin lymphoma. Int J Hematol Oncol 2018;7(1):IJH01.

[48] Mei M, Wondergem MJ, Palmer JM, Shimoni A, Hasenkamp J, Tsai NC, Simpson J, Nademanee A, Raubitschek A, Forman SJ, Krishnan AY. Autologous transplantation for transformed non-Hodgkin lymphoma using an yttrium-90 ibritumomab tiuxetan conditioning regimen. Biol Blood Marrow Transpl 2014;20(12):2072–5.

[49] Vose JM, Bierman PJ, Loberiza FR, Enke C, Hankins J, Bociek RG, Chan WC, Weisenburger DD, Armitage JO. Phase II trial of 131-Iodine tositumomab with high-dose chemotherapy and autologous stem cell transplantation for relapsed diffuse large B cell lymphoma. Biol Blood Marrow Transpl 2013;19(1):123–8.

[50] Vose JM, Carter S, Burns LJ, Ayala E, Press OW, Moskowitz CH, Stadtmauer EA, Mineshi S, Ambinder R, Fenske T, Horowitz M, Fisher R, Tomblyn M. Phase III randomized study of rituximab/carmustine, etoposide, cytarabine, and melphalan (BEAM) compared with iodine-131 tositumomab/BEAM with autologous hematopoietic cell transplantation for relapsed diffuse large B-cell lymphoma: results from the BMT CTN 0401 trial. J Clin Oncol 2013;31(13):1662–8.

[51] Devizzi L, Guidetti A, Tarella C, Magni M, Matteucci P, Seregni E, Chiesa C, Bombardieri E, Di Nicola M, Carlo-Stella C, Gianni AM. High-dose yttrium-90-ibritumomab tiuxetan with tandem stem-cell reinfusion: an outpatient preparative regimen for autologous hematopoietic cell transplantation. J Clin Oncol 2008;26(32):5175–82.

[52] Gopal AK, Rajendran JG, Gooley TA, Pagel JM, Fisher DR, Petersdorf SH, Maloney DG, Eary JF, Appelbaum FR, Press OW. High-dose [131I]tositumomab (anti-CD20) radioimmunotherapy and autologous hematopoietic stem-cell transplantation for adults > or = 60 years old with relapsed or refractory B-cell lymphoma. J Clin Oncol 2007;25(11):1396–402.

[53] Kang BW, Kim WS, Kim C, Jang G, Lee SS, Choi YH, Lee DH, Kim SW, Kim S, Ryu JS, Huh J, Lee JS, Suh C. Yttrium-90-ibritumomab tiuxetan in combination with intravenous busulfan, cyclophosphamide, and etoposide followed by autologous stem cell transplantation in patients with relapsed or refractory B-cell non-Hodgkin's lymphoma. Investig New Drugs 2010;28(4):516–22.

[54] Kruger PC, Cooney JP, Turner JH. Iodine-131 rituximab radioimmunotherapy with BEAM conditioning and autologous stem cell transplant salvage therapy for relapsed/refractory aggressive non-Hodgkin lymphoma. Cancer Biother Radiopharm 2012;27(9):552–60.

[55] Winter JN, Inwards DJ, Spies S, Wiseman G, Patton D, Erwin W, Rademaker AW, Weitner BB, Williams SF, Tallman MS, Micallef I, Mehta J, Singhal S, Evens AM, Zimmer M, Molina A, White CA, Gordon LI. Yttrium-90 ibritumomab tiuxetan doses calculated to deliver up to 15 Gy to critical organs may be safely combined with high-dose BEAM and autologous transplantation in relapsed or refractory B-cell non-Hodgkin's lymphoma. J Clin Oncol 2009;27(10):1653–9.

[56] Hernandez-Ilizaliturri FJ, Deeb G, Zinzani PL, Pileri SA, Malik F, Macon WR, Goy A, Witzig TE, Czuczman MS. Higher response to lenalidomide in relapsed/refractory diffuse large B-cell lymphoma in nongerminal center B-cell-like than in germinal center B-cell-like phenotype. Cancer 2011;117(22):5058–66.

[57] Cartron G, Dacheux L, Salles G, Solal-Celigny P, Bardos P, Colombat P, Watier H. Therapeutic activity of humanized anti-CD20 monoclonal antibody and polymorphism in IgG Fc receptor FcgammaRIIIa gene. Blood 2002;99(3):754–8.

[58] Mossner E, Brunker P, Moser S, Puntener U, Schmidt C, Herter S, Grau R, Gerdes C, Nopora A, van Puijenbroek E, Ferrara C, Sondermann P, Jager C, Strein P, Fertig G, Friess T, Schull C, Bauer S, Dal Porto J, Del Nagro C, Dabbagh K, Dyer MJ, Poppema S, Klein C, Umana P. Increasing the efficacy of CD20 antibody therapy through the engineering of a new type II anti-CD20 antibody with enhanced direct and immune effector cell-mediated B-cell cytotoxicity. Blood 2010;115(22):4393–402.

[59] Glennie MJ, French RR, Cragg MS, Taylor RP. Mechanisms of killing by anti-CD20 monoclonal antibodies. Mol Immunol 2007;44(16):3823–37.

[60] Teeling JL, Mackus WJ, Wiegman LJ, van den Brakel JH, Beers SA, French RR, van Meerten T, Ebeling S, Vink T, Slootstra JW, Parren PW, Glennie MJ, van de Winkel JG. The biological activity of human CD20 monoclonal antibodies is linked to unique epitopes on CD20. J Immunol 2006;177(1):362–71.

[61] Cragg MS, Walshe CA, Ivanov AO, Glennie MJ. The biology of CD20 and its potential as a target for mAb therapy. Curr Dir Autoimmun 2005;8:140–74.

[62] Horning SJ, Younes A, Jain V, Kroll S, Lucas J, Podoloff D, Goris M. Efficacy and safety of tositumomab and iodine-131 tositumomab (Bexxar) in B-cell lymphoma, progressive after rituximab. J Clin Oncol 2005;23(4): 712–9.

[63] Vose JM, Wahl RL, Saleh M, Rohatiner AZ, Knox SJ, Radford JA, Zelenetz AD, Tidmarsh GF, Stagg RJ, Kaminski MS. Multicenter phase II study of iodine-131 tositumomab for chemotherapy-relapsed/refractory low-grade and transformed low-grade B-cell non-Hodgkin's lymphomas. J Clin Oncol 2000;18(6):1316–23.

[64] Kaminski MS, Zelenetz AD, Press OW, Saleh M, Leonard J, Fehrenbacher L, Lister TA, Stagg RJ, Tidmarsh GF, Kroll S, Wahl RL, Knox SJ, Vose JM. Pivotal study of iodine I 131 tositumomab for chemotherapy-refractory low-grade or transformed low-grade B-cell non-Hodgkin's lymphomas. J Clin Oncol 2001;19(19):3918–28.

[65] Kaminski MS, Zasadny KR, Francis IR, Milik AW, Ross CW, Moon SD, Crawford SM, Burgess JM, Petry NA, Butchko GM, et al. Radioimmunotherapy of B-cell lymphoma with [131I]anti-B1 (anti-CD20) antibody. N Engl J Med 1993;329(7):459–65.

[66] Kaminski MS, Estes J, Zasadny KR, Francis IR, Ross CW, Tuck M, Regan D, Fisher S, Gutierrez J, Kroll S, Stagg R, Tidmarsh G, Wahl RL. Radioimmunotherapy with iodine (131)I tositumomab for relapsed or refractory B-cell non-Hodgkin lymphoma: updated results and long-term follow-up of the University of Michigan experience. Blood 2000;96(4):1259–66.

[67] Niederfellner G, Lammens A, Mundigl O, Georges GJ, Schaefer W, Schwaiger M, Franke A, Wiechmann K, Jenewein S, Slootstra JW, Timmerman P, Brannstrom A, Lindstrom F, Mossner E, Umana P, Hopfner KP, Klein C. Epitope characterization and crystal structure of GA101 provide insights into the molecular basis for type I/II distinction of CD20 antibodies. Blood 2011;118(2):358–67.

[68] Cheson BD, Chua N, Mayer J, Dueck G, Trneny M, Bouabdallah K, Fowler N, Delwail V, Press O, Salles G, Gribben JG, Lennard A, Lugtenburg PJ, Fingerle-Rowson G, Mattiello F, Knapp A, Sehn LH. Overall survival benefit in patients with rituximab-refractory indolent non-Hodgkin lymphoma who received obinutuzumab plus bendamustine induction and obinutuzumab maintenance in the GADOLIN study. J Clin Oncol 2018;36 (22):2259–66.

[69] Sehn LH, Chua N, Mayer J, Dueck G, Trneny M, Bouabdallah K, Fowler N, Delwail V, Press O, Salles G, Gribben J, Lennard A, Lugtenburg PJ, Dimier N, Wassner-Fritsch E, Fingerle-Rowson G, Cheson BD. Obinutuzumab plus bendamustine versus bendamustine monotherapy in patients with rituximab-refractory indolent non-Hodgkin lymphoma (GADOLIN): a randomised, controlled, open-label, multicentre, phase 3 trial. Lancet Oncol 2016;17(8):1081–93.

[70] Amhaz G, Bazarbachi A, El-Cheikh J. Immunotherapy in indolent non-Hodgkin's lymphoma. Leuk Res Rep 2022;17, 100325.

[71] Morschhauser F, Marlton P, Vitolo U, Linden O, Seymour JF, Crump M, Coiffier B, Foa R, Wassner E, Burger HU, Brennan B, Mendila M. Results of a phase I/II study of ocrelizumab, a fully humanized anti-CD20 mAb, in patients with relapsed/refractory follicular lymphoma. Ann Oncol 2010;21(9):1870–6.

[72] Forero-Torres A, de Vos S, Pohlman BL, Pashkevich M, Cronier DM, Dang NH, Carpenter SP, Allan BW, Nelson JG, Slapak CA, Smith MR, Link BK, Wooldridge JE, Ganjoo KN. Results of a phase 1 study of AME-133v (LY2469298), an Fc-engineered humanized monoclonal anti-CD20 antibody, in FcgammaRIIIa-genotyped patients with previously treated follicular lymphoma. Clin Cancer Res 2012;18(5):1395–403.

[73] Cang S, Mukhi N, Wang K, Liu D. Novel CD20 monoclonal antibodies for lymphoma therapy. J Hematol Oncol 2012;5:64.

[74] Zucca E, Conconi A, Martinelli G, Bouabdallah R, Tucci A, Vitolo U, Martelli M, Pettengell R, Salles G, Sebban C, Guillermo AL, Pinotti G, Devizzi L, Morschhauser F, Tilly H, Torri V, Hohaus S, Ferreri AJM, Zachee P, Bosly A, Haioun C, Stelitano C, Bellei M, Ponzoni M, Moreau A, Jack A, Campo E, Mazzucchelli L, Cavalli F, Johnson P, Thieblemont C. Final results of the IELSG-19 randomized trial of mucosa-associated lymphoid tissue lymphoma: improved event-free and progression-free survival with rituximab plus chlorambucil versus either chlorambucil or rituximab monotherapy. J Clin Oncol 2017;35(17):1905–12.

[75] Casulo C, Vose JM, Ho WY, Kahl B, Brunvand M, Goy A, Kasamon Y, Cheson B, Friedberg JW. A phase I study of PRO131921, a novel anti-CD20 monoclonal antibody in patients with relapsed/refractory CD20+ indolent NHL: correlation between clinical responses and AUC pharmacokinetics. Clin Immunol 2014;154(1):37–46.

[76] Wang J, Zhang R, Ding X, Jin Y, Qin R, Xia B, Liao Q, Hu H, Song W, Wang Z, Zhang X, Xu J. Pathologically complete remission to combination of invariant NK T cells and anti-CD20 antibody in a refractory HIV+ diffuse large B-cell lymphoma patient. Immunotherapy 2022;14(8):599–607.

[77] DiLillo DJ, Ravetch JV. Differential Fc-receptor engagement drives an anti-tumor vaccinal effect. Cell 2015;161 (5):1035–45.

[78] Horton HM, Bernett MJ, Pong E, Peipp M, Karki S, Chu SY, Richards JO, Vostiar I, Joyce PF, Repp R, Desjarlais JR, Zhukovsky EA. Potent in vitro and in vivo activity of an Fc-engineered anti-CD19 monoclonal antibody against lymphoma and leukemia. Cancer Res 2008;68(19):8049–57.

[79] Rosario M, Liu B, Kong L, Collins LI, Schneider SE, Chen X, Han K, Jeng EK, Rhode PR, Leong JW, Schappe T, Jewell BA, Keppel CR, Shah K, Hess B, Romee R, Piwnica-Worms DR, Cashen AF, Bartlett NL, Wong HC, Fehniger TA. The IL-15-based ALT-803 complex enhances FcgammaRIIIa-triggered NK cell responses and in vivo clearance of B cell lymphomas. Clin Cancer Res 2016;22(3):596–608.

[80] Bittenbring JT, Neumann F, Altmann B, Achenbach M, Reichrath J, Ziepert M, Geisel J, Regitz E, Held G, Pfreundschuh M. Vitamin D deficiency impairs rituximab-mediated cellular cytotoxicity and outcome of patients with diffuse large B-cell lymphoma treated with but not without rituximab. J Clin Oncol 2014;32(29): 3242–8.

[81] Neumann F, Acker F, Schormann C, Pfreundschuh M, Bittenbring JT. Determination of optimum vitamin D3 levels for NK cell-mediated rituximab- and obinutuzumab-dependent cellular cytotoxicity. Cancer Immunol Immunother 2018;67(11):1709–18.

[82] Vockova P, Svaton M, Karolova J, Pokorna E, Vokurka M, Klener P. Anti-CD38 therapy with daratumumab for relapsed/refractory CD20-negative diffuse large B-cell lymphoma. Folia Biol (Praha) 2020;66(1):17–23.

[83] Wang L, Li LR, Young KH. New agents and regimens for diffuse large B cell lymphoma. J Hematol Oncol 2020;13(1):175.

[84] Bhat SA, Czuczman MS. Novel antibodies in the treatment of non-Hodgkin's lymphoma. Neth J Med 2009;67 (8):311–21.

[85] Jurczak W, Zinzani PL, Gaidano G, Goy A, Provencio M, Nagy Z, Robak T, Maddocks K, Buske C, Ambarkhane S, Winderlich M, Dirnberger-Hertweck M, Korolkiewicz R, Blum KA. Phase IIa study of the CD19 antibody MOR208 in patients with relapsed or refractory B-cell non-Hodgkin's lymphoma. Ann Oncol 2018;29 (5):1266–72.

[86] Kusowska A, Kubacz M, Krawczyk M, Slusarczyk A, Winiarska M, Bobrowicz M. Molecular aspects of resistance to immunotherapies-advances in understanding and management of diffuse large B-cell lymphoma. Int J Mol Sci 2022;23(3).

[87] Linden O, Hindorf C, Cavallin-Stahl E, Wegener WA, Goldenberg DM, Horne H, Ohlsson T, Stenberg L, Strand SE, Tennvall J. Dose-fractionated radioimmunotherapy in non-Hodgkin's lymphoma using DOTA-conjugated,

90Y-radiolabeled, humanized anti-CD22 monoclonal antibody, epratuzumab. Clin Cancer Res 2005;11 (14):5215–22.

[88] Abramson JS, Ghosh N, Smith SM. ADCs, BiTEs, CARs, and small molecules: a new era of targeted therapy in non-Hodgkin lymphoma. Am Soc Clin Oncol Educ Book 2020;40:302–13.

[89] Viardot A, Goebeler ME, Hess G, Neumann S, Pfreundschuh M, Adrian N, Zettl F, Libicher M, Sayehli C, Stieglmaier J, Zhang A, Nagorsen D, Bargou RC. Phase 2 study of the bispecific T-cell engager (BiTE) antibody blinatumomab in relapsed/refractory diffuse large B-cell lymphoma. Blood 2016;127(11):1410–6.

[90] Al-Mansour M. Treatment landscape of relapsed/refractory mantle cell lymphoma: an updated review. Clin Lymphoma Myeloma Leuk 2022;22(11):e1019–31.

[91] Hoogeboom R, van Kessel KP, Hochstenbach F, Wormhoudt TA, Reinten RJ, Wagner K, Kater AP, Guikema JE, Bende RJ, van Noesel CJ. A mutated B cell chronic lymphocytic leukemia subset that recognizes and responds to fungi. J Exp Med 2013;210(1):59–70.

[92] Warsame AA, Aasheim HC, Nustad K, Troen G, Tierens A, Wang V, Randen U, Dong HP, Heim S, Brech A, Delabie J. Splenic marginal zone lymphoma with VH1-02 gene rearrangement expresses poly- and self-reactive antibodies with similar reactivity. Blood 2011;118(12):3331–9.

[93] Saba NS, Liu D, Herman SE, Underbayev C, Tian X, Behrend D, Weniger MA, Skarzynski M, Gyamfi J, Fontan L, Melnick A, Grant C, Roschewski M, Navarro A, Bea S, Pittaluga S, Dunleavy K, Wilson WH, Wiestner A. Pathogenic role of B-cell receptor signaling and canonical NF-kappaB activation in mantle cell lymphoma. Blood 2016;128(1):82–92.

[94] Wilson WH, Young RM, Schmitz R, Yang Y, Pittaluga S, Wright G, Lih CJ, Williams PM, Shaffer AL, Gerecitano J, de Vos S, Goy A, Kenkre VP, Barr PM, Blum KA, Shustov A, Advani R, Fowler NH, Vose JM, Elstrom RL, Habermann TM, Barrientos JC, McGreivy J, Fardis M, Chang BY, Clow F, Munneke B, Moussa D, Beaupre DM, Staudt LM. Targeting B cell receptor signaling with ibrutinib in diffuse large B cell lymphoma. Nat Med 2015;21 (8):922–6.

[95] LeBien TW. Fates of human B-cell precursors. Blood 2000;96(1):9–23.

[96] Klanova M, Klener P. BCL-2 proteins in pathogenesis and therapy of B-cell non-Hodgkin lymphomas. Cancers (Basel) 2020;12(4).

[97] Ma J, Lu P, Guo A, Cheng S, Zong H, Martin P, Coleman M, Wang YL. Characterization of ibrutinib-sensitive and -resistant mantle lymphoma cells. Br J Haematol 2014;166(6):849–61.

[98] Hopper M, Gururaja T, Kinoshita T, Dean JP, Hill RJ, Mongan A. Relative selectivity of covalent inhibitors requires assessment of inactivation kinetics and cellular occupancy: a case study of ibrutinib and acalabrutinib. J Pharmacol Exp Ther 2020;372(3):331–8.

[99] Walter HS, Rule SA, Dyer MJ, Karlin L, Jones C, Cazin B, Quittet P, Shah N, Hutchinson CV, Honda H, Duffy K, Birkett J, Jamieson V, Courtenay-Luck N, Yoshizawa T, Sharpe J, Ohno T, Abe S, Nishimura A, Cartron G, Morschhauser F, Fegan C, Salles G. A phase 1 clinical trial of the selective BTK inhibitor ONO/GS-4059 in relapsed and refractory mature B-cell malignancies. Blood 2016;127(4):411–9.

[100] Tucker DL, Naylor G, Kruger A, Hamilton MS, Follows G, Rule SA. Ibrutinib is a safe and effective therapy for systemic mantle cell lymphoma with central nervous system involvement—a multi-centre case series from the United Kingdom. Br J Haematol 2017;178(2):327–9.

[101] Tam CS, Quach H, Nicol A, Badoux X, Rose H, Prince HM, Leahy MF, Eek R, Wickham N, Patil SS, Huang J, Prathikanti R, Cohen A, Elstrom R, Reed W, Schneider J, Flinn IW. Zanubrutinib (BGB-3111) plus obinutuzumab in patients with chronic lymphocytic leukemia and follicular lymphoma. Blood Adv 2020;4 (19):4802–11.

[102] Gopal AK, Kahl BS, de Vos S, Wagner-Johnston ND, Schuster SJ, Jurczak WJ, Flinn IW, Flowers CR, Martin P, Viardot A, Blum KA, Goy AH, Davies AJ, Zinzani PL, Dreyling M, Johnson D, Miller LL, Holes L, Li D, Dansey RD, Godfrey WR, Salles GA. PI3Kdelta inhibition by idelalisib in patients with relapsed indolent lymphoma. N Engl J Med 2014;370(11):1008–18.

[103] Flinn IW, O'Brien S, Kahl B, Patel M, Oki Y, Foss FF, Porcu P, Jones J, Burger JA, Jain N, Kelly VM, Allen K, Douglas M, Sweeney J, Kelly P, Horwitz S. Duvelisib, a novel oral dual inhibitor of PI3K-delta,gamma, is clinically active in advanced hematologic malignancies. Blood 2018;131(8):877–87.

[104] Dreyling M, Santoro A, Mollica L, Leppa S, Follows GA, Lenz G, Kim WS, Nagler A, Panayiotidis P, Demeter J, Ozcan M, Kosinova M, Bouabdallah K, Morschhauser F, Stevens DA, Trevarthen D, Giurescu M, Cupit L, Liu L, Kochert K, Seidel H, Pena C, Yin S, Hiemeyer F, Garcia-Vargas J, Childs BH, Zinzani PL. Phosphatidylinositol 3-kinase inhibition by copanlisib in relapsed or refractory indolent lymphoma. J Clin Oncol 2017;35(35):3898–905.

[105] Kubiczkova L, Pour L, Sedlarikova L, Hajek R, Sevcikova S. Proteasome inhibitors—molecular basis and current perspectives in multiple myeloma. J Cell Mol Med 2014;18(6):947–61.
[106] Nunes AT, Annunziata CM. Proteasome inhibitors: structure and function. Semin Oncol 2017;44(6):377–80.
[107] Zou Z, Tao T, Li H, Zhu X. mTOR signaling pathway and mTOR inhibitors in cancer: progress and challenges. Cell Biosci 2020;10:31.
[108] Buggy JJ, Elias L. Bruton tyrosine kinase (BTK) and its role in B-cell malignancy. Int Rev Immunol 2012;31 (2):119–32.
[109] Juarez-Salcedo LM, Desai V, Dalia S. Venetoclax: evidence to date and clinical potential. Drugs Context 2019;8, 212574.
[110] Zhou K, Zou D, Zhou J, Hu J, Yang H, Zhang H, Ji J, Xu W, Jin J, Lv F, Feng R, Gao S, Zhou D, Tam CS, Simpson D, Wang M, Phillips TJ, Opat S, Huang Z, Lu H, Song Y, Song Y. Zanubrutinib monotherapy in relapsed/refractory mantle cell lymphoma: a pooled analysis of two clinical trials. J Hematol Oncol 2021;14(1):167.
[111] Locke FL, Ghobadi A, Jacobson CA, Miklos DB, Lekakis LJ, Oluwole OO, Lin Y, Braunschweig I, Hill BT, Timmerman JM, Deol A, Reagan PM, Stiff P, Flinn IW, Farooq U, Goy A, McSweeney PA, Munoz J, Siddiqi T, Chavez JC, Herrera AF, Bartlett NL, Wiezorek JS, Navale L, Xue A, Jiang Y, Bot A, Rossi JM, Kim JJ, Go WY, Neelapu SS. Long-term safety and activity of axicabtagene ciloleucel in refractory large B-cell lymphoma (ZUMA-1): a single-arm, multicentre, phase 1–2 trial. Lancet Oncol 2019;20(1):31–42.
[112] Schuster SJ, Bishop MR, Tam CS, Waller EK, Borchmann P, McGuirk JP, Jager U, Jaglowski S, Andreadis C, Westin JR, Fleury I, Bachanova V, Foley SR, Ho PJ, Mielke S, Magenau JM, Holte H, Pantano S, Pacaud LB, Awasthi R, Chu J, Anak O, Salles G, Maziarz RT, Investigators J. Tisagenlecleucel in adult relapsed or refractory diffuse large b-cell lymphoma. N Engl J Med 2019;380(1):45–56.
[113] Cheng Q, Tan J, Liu R, Kang L, Zhang Y, Wang E, Li Y, Zhang J, Xiao H, Xu N, Li M, Yu L, Li X. CD20-specific chimeric antigen receptor-expressing T cells as salvage therapy in rituximab-refractory/relapsed B-cell non-Hodgkin lymphoma. Cytotherapy 2022;24(10):1026–34.
[114] Westin JR, Kersten MJ, Salles G, Abramson JS, Schuster SJ, Locke FL, Andreadis C. Efficacy and safety of CD19-directed CAR-T cell therapies in patients with relapsed/refractory aggressive B-cell lymphomas: observations from the JULIET, ZUMA-1, and TRANSCEND trials. Am J Hematol 2021;96(10):1295–312.
[115] Fujino T, Maruyama D, Maeshima AM, Saito Y, Ida H, Hosoba R, Yuda S, Makita S, Fukuhara S, Munakata W, Suzuki T, Kuroda J, Izutsu K. The outcome of watchful waiting in patients with previously treated follicular lymphoma. Cancer Med 2022;11(10):2106–16.
[116] Dreyling M, Ghielmini M, Rule S, Salles G, Ladetto M, Tonino SH, Herfarth K, Seymour JF, Jerkeman M, ESMO Guidelines Committee. Newly diagnosed and relapsed follicular lymphoma: ESMO Clinical Practice Guidelines for diagnosis, treatment and follow-up. Ann Oncol 2021;32(3):298–308.
[117] Ardeshna KM, Smith P, Norton A, Hancock BW, Hoskin PJ, MacLennan KA, Marcus RE, Jelliffe A, Vaughan G, Hudson DC, Linch I, British National Lymphoma. Long-term effect of a watch and wait policy versus immediate systemic treatment for asymptomatic advanced-stage non-Hodgkin lymphoma: a randomised controlled trial. Lancet 2003;362(9383):516–22.
[118] Solal-Celigny P, Bellei M, Marcheselli L, Pesce EA, Pileri S, McLaughlin P, Luminari S, Pro B, Montoto S, Ferreri AJ, Deconinck E, Milpied N, Gordon LI, Federico M. Watchful waiting in low-tumor burden follicular lymphoma in the rituximab era: results of an F2-study database. J Clin Oncol 2012;30(31):3848–53.
[119] Nastoupil LJ, Sinha R, Byrtek M, Ziemiecki R, Zhou X, Taylor M, Friedberg JW, Link BK, Cerhan JR, Dawson K, Flowers CR. Outcomes following watchful waiting for stage II–IV follicular lymphoma patients in the modern era. Br J Haematol 2016;172(5):724–34.
[120] Yuda S, Maruyama D, Maeshima AM, Makita S, Kitahara H, Miyamoto KI, Fukuhara S, Munakata W, Suzuki T, Kobayashi Y, Tajima K, Taniguchi H, Tobinai K. Influence of the watch and wait strategy on clinical outcomes of patients with follicular lymphoma in the rituximab era. Ann Hematol 2016;95(12):2017–22.
[121] Sarkozy C, Maurer MJ, Link BK, Ghesquieres H, Nicolas E, Thompson CA, Traverse-Glehen A, Feldman AL, Allmer C, Slager SL, Ansell SM, Habermann TM, Bachy E, Cerhan JR, Salles G. Cause of death in follicular lymphoma in the first decade of the rituximab era: a pooled analysis of French and US cohorts. J Clin Oncol 2019;37 (2):144–52.
[122] Morton LM, Curtis RE, Linet MS, Bluhm EC, Tucker MA, Caporaso N, Ries LA, Fraumeni Jr JF. Second malignancy risks after non-Hodgkin's lymphoma and chronic lymphocytic leukemia: differences by lymphoma subtype. J Clin Oncol 2010;28(33):4935–44.

[123] Zou L, Song G, Gu S, Kong L, Sun S, Yang L, Cho WC. Mechanism and treatment of rituximab resistance in diffuse large B cell lymphoma. Curr Cancer Drug Targets 2019;19(9):681–7.

[124] Poletto S, Novo M, Paruzzo L, Frascione PMM, Vitolo U. Treatment strategies for patients with diffuse large B-cell lymphoma. Cancer Treat Rev 2022;110, 102443.

[125] Chong EA, Ahmadi T, Aqui NA, Svoboda J, Nasta SD, Mato AR, Walsh KM, Schuster SJ. Combination of lenalidomide and rituximab overcomes rituximab resistance in patients with indolent B-cell and mantle cell lymphomas. Clin Cancer Res 2015;21(8):1835–42.

[126] Wang ML, Lee H, Chuang H, Wagner-Bartak N, Hagemeister F, Westin J, Fayad L, Samaniego F, Turturro F, Oki Y, Chen W, Badillo M, Nomie K, DeLa Rosa M, Zhao D, Lam L, Addison A, Zhang H, Young KH, Li S, Santos D, Medeiros LJ, Champlin R, Romaguera J, Zhang L. Ibrutinib in combination with rituximab in relapsed or refractory mantle cell lymphoma: a single-centre, open-label, phase 2 trial. Lancet Oncol 2016;17(1):48–56.

[127] Jerkeman M, Eskelund CW, Hutchings M, Raty R, Wader KF, Laurell A, Toldbod H, Pedersen LB, Niemann CU, Dahl C, Kuitunen H, Geisler CH, Gronbaek K, Kolstad A. Ibrutinib, lenalidomide, and rituximab in relapsed or refractory mantle cell lymphoma (PHILEMON): a multicentre, open-label, single-arm, phase 2 trial. Lancet Haematol 2018;5(3):e109–16.

[128] Mats Jerkeman AK, Niemann CU, Groenbaek K, Hutchings M, Pasanen A, Ekberg S, Wader KF, Glimelius I. Venetoclax, lenalidomide and rituximab for patients with relapsed or refractory mantle cell lymphoma—data from the Nordic Lymphoma Group NLG-MCL7 (VALERIA) Phase I Trial: stopping treatment in molecular remission is feasible. Blood 2020;136(1):15.

[129] Nobili S, Napoli C, Puccini B, Landini I, Perrone G, Brugia M, Benelli G, Doria M, Martelli M, Finolezzi E, Di Rocco A, Del Fava E, Rigacci L, Di Lollo S, Bosi A, Mini E. Identification of pharmacogenomic markers of clinical efficacy in a dose-dense therapy regimen (R-CHOP14) in diffuse large B-cell lymphoma. Leuk Lymphoma 2014;55(9):2071–8.

[130] Shek D, Read SA, Ahlenstiel G, Piatkov I. Pharmacogenetics of anticancer monoclonal antibodies. Cancer Drug Resist 2019;2(1):69–81.

[131] Hu J, Xu J, Yu M, Gao Y, Liu R, Zhou H, Zhang W. An integrated prognosis model of pharmacogenomic gene signature and clinical information for diffuse large B-cell lymphoma patients following CHOP-like chemotherapy. J Transl Med 2020;18(1):144.

[132] Boeschen M, Le Duc D, Stiller M, von Laffert M, Schoneberg T, Horn S. Interactive webtool for analyzing drug sensitivity and resistance associated with genetic signatures of cancer cell lines. J Cancer Res Clin Oncol 2022.

CHAPTER

10

Mechanisms of resistance to anti-CD20 antibodies in lymphoid malignancies

Anne Bordron[a], *Marie Morel*[a], *and Cristina Bagacean*[a,b,c]

[a]LBAI, UMR1227, Univ Brest, Inserm, Brest, France [b]Department of Clinical Hematology, University Hospital of Brest, Brest, France [c]UMR 1304, GETBO, Univ Brest, Inserm, Brest, France

Abstract

Monoclonal antibodies (mAb) belong to a fast-growing therapeutic class. The pan B-cell marker CD20 represents one of the most-studied mAb targets. The first mAb to receive approval by the US Food and Drug Administration, in 1997, was the type I anti-CD20 mAb, rituximab. Several mechanisms of action have been reported such as antibody-dependent cellular cytotoxicity, complement-dependent cytotoxicity, and induction of apoptosis. As an important percentage of patients with B-cell lymphoid malignancies are refractory to anti-CD20 mAbs, the concept of anti-CD20 mAb resistance also emerged, and subsequently, several theories on how this resistance could be overcome. In order to enhance anti-CD20 mAb efficacy, type II and III anti-CD20 mAbs have been developed and one of them is currently approved in B-cell lymphoid malignancies, obinutuzumab. This chapter focuses on the lessons learned so far through investigation of the resistance to anti-CD20 mAbs, notably to rituximab and obinutuzumab, the two approved anti-CD20 mAbs in lymphoid malignancies. Also discussed are several mechanisms that could help circumvent resistance to anti-CD20 mAbs.

Abbreviations

ADCC antibody-dependent cell-mediated cytotoxicity
Ag antigen
cCD20 circulating CD20
CDC complement-dependent cytotoxicity
CLL chronic lymphocytic leukemia
DLBCL diffuse large B-cell lymphoma
EMA European Medicines Agency
F phenylalanine
FADD FAS-Associated Death Domain

https://doi.org/10.1016/B978-0-443-19200-5.00013-0

Fc constant fragment
FcR Fc receptors
FcγR Fcγ receptor
FDA US Food and Drug Administration
FL follicular lymphoma
Flt3 FMS proto-oncogene-like tyrosine kinase 3
FOXO1 Forkhead box O1
H histidine
HACA human antichimeric antibodies
HAMA human antimouse antibodies
HDAC histone deacetylases
HLA human leukocyte antigen
IFR8 interferon regulatory factor 8
Ig immunoglobulin
IL-2 interleukin-2
ITAM immunoreceptor tyrosine-based activation motifs
ITIM immunoreceptor tyrosine-based inhibitory motifs
IVIG intravenous immunoglobulin
mAb monoclonal antibody
MCL mantle cell lymphoma
mCRP complement regulatory proteins
MS4A1 membrane spanning 4-domains A1
NHL non-Hodgkin lymphoma
NK natural killer
PU.1 purine-rich box-1
R arginine
TF transcription factors
V valine
YY1 Yin-Yang 1

Conflict of interest

No potential conflicts of interest were disclosed.

Introduction

Over the last two decades, monoclonal antibodies (mAbs) have become a key part of treatment regimens in lymphoid malignancies. The development of anti-CD20 mAbs can be traced back to 1979 when Stashenko et al. identified the CD20 antigen (called B1) [1]. CD20 is a 33–37-kDa nonglycosylated phosphoprotein expressed on the surface of B cells, starting from the pre-B-cell stage, and expression is lost during terminal differentiation into plasma cells [2]. The gene that encodes the CD20 protein is membrane spanning 4-domains A1 (*MS4A1*) and is located on chromosome 11q12 [2]. As the CD20 protein is not expressed on hematopoietic stem cells or plasma cells, it is a good molecular target antigen for the treatment of mature B-cell malignancies: it minimizes the potential of off-target toxicity and retains humoral protection against previously encountered pathogens, while allowing for repopulation of the B-cell compartment after the anti-CD20 treatment is stopped [3,4].

Therefore, in 1994, Reff developed rituximab, an mAb against CD20 [5]. Three years later, it was the first mAb approved to be used for cancer treatment. Since 1997, when rituximab was first approved by the US Food and Drug Administration (FDA) for the treatment of relapsed or refractory non-Hodgkin lymphoma (NHL), it has demonstrated an important clinical activity across the majority of B-cell neoplasms as a single agent, in combination with chemotherapy or in maintenance [6].

Rituximab is a type I genetically engineered chimeric murine/human anti-CD20 mAb consisting of a glycosylated immunoglobulin (Ig) G1 with a human kappa constant region and murine light and heavy chain variable regions [7]. Rituximab engages the constant fragment (Fc) receptors (FcR) on effector cells, facilitates complement-dependent cytotoxicity (CDC), antibody-dependent cell-mediated cytotoxicity (ADCC), and exerts direct antiproliferative and pro-apoptotic effects [8].

Obinutuzumab is a type II antibody derived by the humanization of the parental B-Ly1 mouse antibody and subsequent glycoengineering of the Fc region as well as a modified elbow-hinge amino-acid sequence [9,10]. The modified elbow-hinge amino-acid substitution and the associated conformational changes enhance the direct cell death activity of obinutuzumab compared to rituximab [11]. Through its defucosylation in the Fc portion, obinutuzumab also has an enhanced binding affinity to Fcγ receptor (FcγR) III, resulting in induction of ADCC greater than that of rituximab [9]. In contrast, CDC makes no meaningful contribution to the action of obinutuzumab [12].

As our understanding of anti-CD20 mAbs' mechanisms of action evolved, the concept of anti-CD20 mAb resistance also emerged, and subsequently, several theories emerged on how this resistance could be overcome. Comprehension of the numerous pathways implicated in the anti-CD20 mAb resistance is an important topic, firstly, because of the widespread use of this immunotherapy in lymphoid malignancies and secondly, because of its relevance in optimizing the design of future anti-CD20 mAbs.

In this chapter, we will review the current knowledge of the mechanisms of anti-CD20 mAb resistance and possible approaches in order to limit or circumvent these mechanisms. We will focus on the anti-CD20 mAbs, rituximab, and obinutuzumab, as they are currently approved by FDA and the European Medicines Agency (EMA) for clinical use in lymphoid malignancies.

Factors influencing anti-CD20 mAb activity/resistance

Pharmacokinetics

The first approved schedule for rituximab, 375 mg/m^2 intravenously, weekly for 4 weeks, was established as a result of drug availability rather than dedicated dose-finding studies [6,13,14]. Ever since, different doses and schedules have been assessed [15–19]. However, clinical studies have shown that there is significant interindividual variability in rituximab exposure despite administering it at similar doses in patients (Fig. 1A) [20,21]. It has also been noted that patients with high disease burden, and thus high antigen load, have lower rituximab levels [22–24]. Some studies also reported a dose-response relationship [17,25,26].

Additionally, higher circulating CD20 (cCD20) levels have been inversely correlated with overall survival in chronic lymphocytic leukemia (CLL) [27]. It has been postulated that the efficacy of rituximab in CLL may be impaired due to high levels of cCD20 leading to preferential binding of rituximab with cCD20 with decreased binding to cell surface CD20 [28]. The formation of cCD20/rituximab complexes can lead to enhanced rituximab clearance.

Rituximab increased clearance may also be induced by the development of antibodies against rituximab. MAbs are large antigenic proteins, which can theoretically induce an

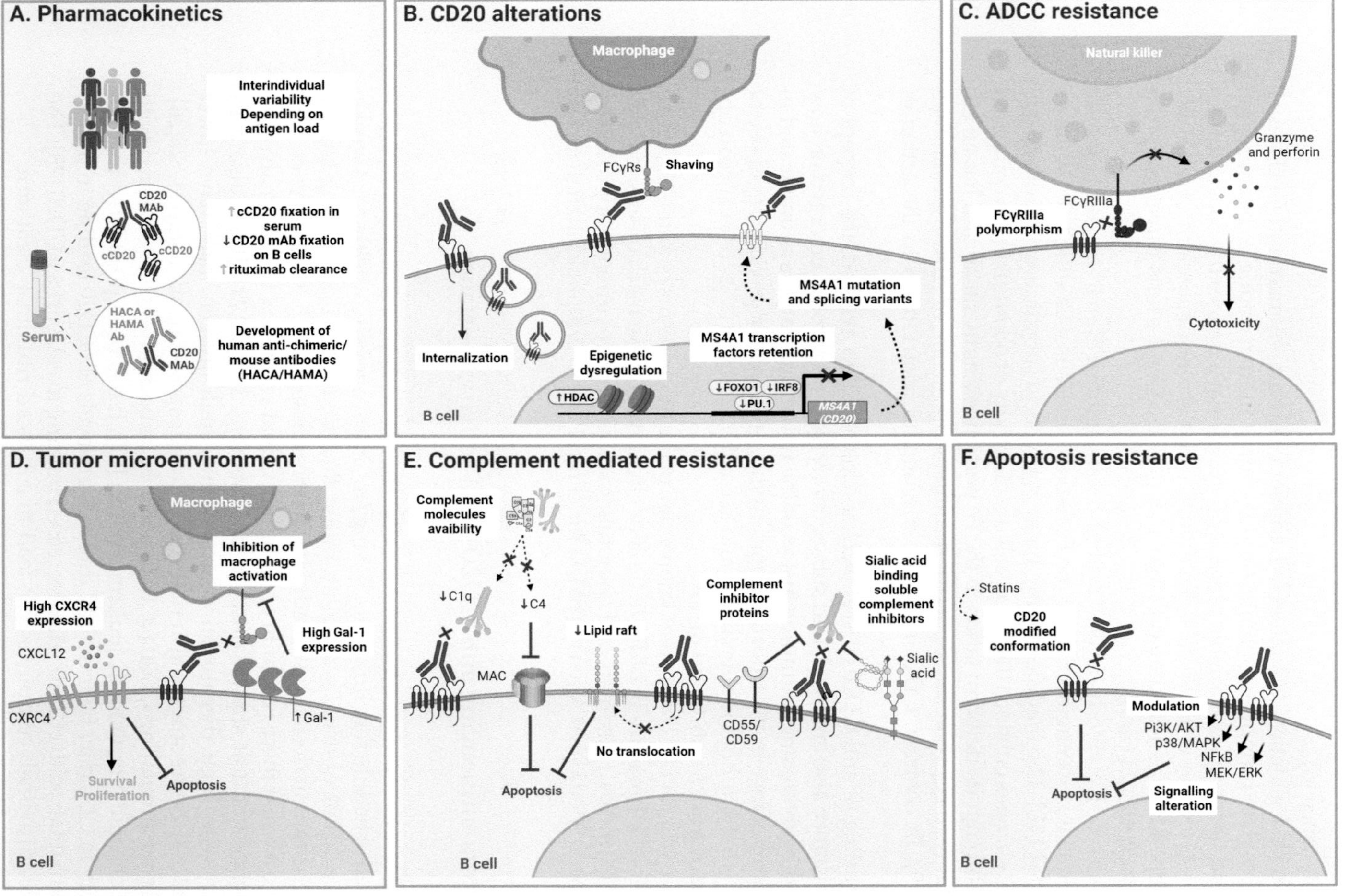

FIG. 1 Factors influencing anti-CD20 monoclonal antibodies' activity and resistance. Schematic representation of factors influencing anti-CD20 monoclonal antibody (mAb) activity and resistance. (A) Pharmacokinetics influences anti-CD20 mAb activity. (B) CD20 alteration induces resistance to anti-CD20 mAb therapy. (C) Antibody-dependent cell-mediated cytotoxicity (ADCC) resistances impair anti-CD20 mAb efficacy. (D) Influence of the tumor microenvironment on anti-CD20 mAb activity. (E) Complement-mediated resistance to anti-CD20 mAb. (F) Apoptosis resistance mechanisms to anti-CD20 mAb. Abbreviations: *CD*, cluster of differentiation; *cCD20*, circulating CD20; *HACA*, human antichimeric antibody; *HAMA*, human antimurine antibody; *FcγR*, constant fragment gamma receptors; *CXCR4*, C-X-C chemokine receptor type 4; *CXCL12*, C-X-C motif chemokine type 12; *Gal-1*, Galectine-1; *MAC*, membrane attack complex.

immune response leading to the formation of anti-antibodies. The development of human antichimeric (HACA) or human antimouse (HAMA) antibodies was evaluated in early trials of rituximab use in patients with B-NHL. However, only one patient developed HACA or HAMA with the rate of HACA formation seeming to be more significant with the use of rituximab for auto-immune diseases such as systemic lupus erythematosus [13,29]. Additionally, as most mAbs in clinical use are now human/humanized, reduced serum levels of antibody anti-mAb formation are unlikely to play a role in resistance.

The selected dose of obinutuzumab for phase III trials was based on the modeling of pooled pharmacokinetic data from patients with relapsed/refractory NHL [6]. As the serum through concentrations generated by the 1600/800 mg doses was similar, with also a comparable toxicity, a fixed dose regimen with a dose of 1000 mg was selected [6]. Although a higher dose of obinutuzumab is administered, compared to rituximab, research data suggested that, for an equal antigenic mass, less obinutuzumab is necessary to induce cytotoxicity, leaving more drug available to bind elsewhere [30]. In a semimechanistic pharmacokinetics/pharmacodynamics model presented recently as a poster, drug removal due to drug-target binding was 4.3-fold lower for obinutuzumab compared to rituximab, the cell-kill coefficient for obinutuzumab was 4.7-fold greater than that for rituximab, and the half-maximal effective concentration of obinutuzumab was 15-fold lower [30]. These data suggest that pharmacokinetics has a less important role in obinutuzumab resistance compared to rituximab.

CD20 alterations

The most studied mechanisms of resistance to anti-CD20 mAbs are alterations in target antigen (Ag) by CD20 "shaving," internalization, mutations, or epigenetic dysregulation (Fig. 1B).

Although there is an important quantity of experimental data concerning each of these mechanisms of resistance to the anti-CD20 mAbs, there is a paucity of published research on the relative contribution of shaving versus internalization to the loss of surface mAb:CD20 or on how the predominant resistance mechanism varies between patients and disease types.

CD20 shaving and internalization

Anti-CD20 mAbs bind to CD20 through their V region and elicit downstream immune effector functions via Fc:FcγR interactions [31]. The contribution to this phenomenon of each type of FcγR-expressing effector cell is still debated. However, a multitude of data supports a role for phagocytic monocytes or macrophages [32–34]. Macrophages may thus be at least partially responsible for the efficacy of anti-CD20 mAbs [35].

Concerning other effector cells such as neutrophils, data are contradictory. Contrary to initial findings [36], it was subsequently shown that neutrophils do not phagocytose CLL B-cell targets opsonized with anti-CD20 antibodies, but rather mediate shaving [37]. Shaving is defined as the elimination of anti-CD20 mAb:Ag complexes from the surface of B cells. For the monocyte/macrophage lineage cells, it has also been reported that they have the ability, via their FcγRs, to mediate the shaving of anti-CD20 mAb:CD20 immune complexes from the surface of B cells in vitro [31,38,39] and in vivo [40]. It has been implied that there is a link between macrophage saturation status and shaving. Initial data suggested that effector mechanisms may be saturated at high burdens of rituximab-opsonized B cells, and as a consequence, opsonized B cells are processed by an alternative pathway, involving removal or shaving of anti-CD20 mAb:CD20 from B cells by monocytes/macrophages [41]. Contrary to these initial observations, it has been later shown that mAb:CD20 shaving is, in fact, limited by macrophage saturation [35]. Macrophage phagocytosis when fully saturated led to a concomitant decrease in shaving and an increase in type I mAb-mediated modulation, suggesting that the two mechanisms of mAb:Ag loss compete. Antigenic modulation has been also proposed as one of the mechanisms of resistance to anti-CD20 mAbs through which B cells internalize CD20 into lysosomes [32].

It has also been shown that more surface rituximab:CD20 complexes were removed by modulation, while shaving removed a substantially greater amount of obinutuzumab: CD20 compared with rituximab:CD20 [35]. This suggests that shaving of mAb:Ag complexes may be a limiting factor to mAbs that are less susceptible to modulation and that glycoengineering could hinder the efficacy of type II anti-CD20 mAb immunotherapy [35].

The level of internalization has also been shown to vary considerably in different lymphoproliferative diseases. Beers et al. showed a higher degree of internalization of CD20 by CLL and mantle cell lymphoma (MCL) cells exposed to rituximab, while follicular lymphoma (FL) was relatively resistant to CD20 internalization, perhaps explaining its greater clinical responsiveness to rituximab [32].

Several strategies have been proposed in order to address the issue of shaving and internalization. Such approaches propose a downmodulation of the shaving reaction based on treatment either with intravenous immunoglobulin (IVIG) or with small molecules that block endocytosis [40,42].

MS4A1 (CD20 gene) mutations, deletions, and aberrant expression of its splicing variants

The first reports of *MS4A1* mutations were published in 2009. Terui et al. identified *MS4A1* C-terminal mutations that were associated with loss of *MS4A1* expression, presumably affecting anti-CD20 mAb binding [43,44]. However, later studies in diffuse large B-cell lymphoma (DLBCL) samples demonstrated that *MS4A1* mutations involving the anti-CD20 binding epitope were present in less than 1% at diagnosis and do not represent a significant cause for resistance to immunochemotherapy [45].

Homozygous deletions of the *MS4A1* gene in CD20-negative relapse of DLBCL have been also reported [46].

Splicing variants of *MS4A1* mRNA have been identified. These variants result in a conformational change of anti-CD20 mAb binding epitope and, therefore, were associated with anti-CD20 mAb resistance [47].

Involvement of transcription factors in **MS4A1** *gene expression*

Different authors have indicated that the amount of CD20 molecules on the surface of the CLL cells is a determinant for the efficiency of anti-CD20 mAbs. Thus, the observations of José Golay in 2001 [48] and repeated in 2022 by Anke Schilhabel [49] indicated that a strong molecular response to ofatumumab (a type I anti-CD20 mAb) appears to be correlated with higher CD20 expression prior to treatment.

Expression of *MS4A1* is achieved thanks to different factors; in particular, transcription factors (TF) (USF, OCT1/2, purine-rich box-1 (PU.1), PiP, ELK1, ETS1, SP1, NFκB, Forkhead box O1 (FOXO1), CREM, and SMAD2/3) (Fig. 2). Among them, PU.1 can be retained. In fact, downregulation of PU.1 on CLL B cells is mediated by an excessive expression of the FMS

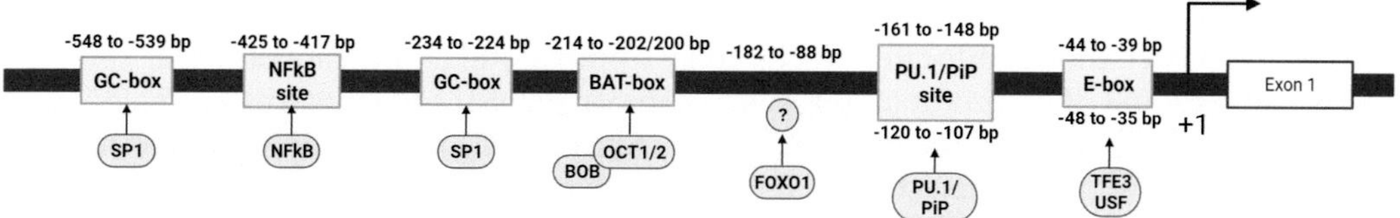

FIG. 2 Transcription factors of *MS4A1 (CD20)* gene. Representation of different transcription factors and binding sites of *MS4A1* gene coding for the CD20 protein.

proto-oncogene-like tyrosine kinase 3 (Flt3) receptor. This abnormality is consistent with the finding of elevated levels of Flt3 ligand in CLL sera. Subsequently, increased Flt3 signaling prevents the expression of PU.1, which downregulates that of *MS4A1*, and accounts for the resistance of CLL B cells to rituximab-induced lysis [50].

A new TF regulates the positive expression of *MS4A1*, the Interferon Regulatory Factor 8 (IFR8). This TF was found to be necessary for efficient *MS4A1* transcription and consequently for efficiency to CD20-targeting immunotherapies [51]. Its precise action on the *MS4A1* gene is not known but IRF8 Knock-Out B-cell lines demonstrated a decrease of the efficacy of ADCC and phagocytosis induced by anti-CD20 mAbs. Reversely, *MS4A1* transcription is negatively regulated by FOXO1 [52]. FOXO1 signaling regulates the abundance of CD20 on the surface of B-NHL cells, thus influencing the response to rituximab-based therapies. Therefore, FOXO1 is important in determining the response of B-cell lymphomas to anti-CD20-based therapies.

Epigenetic dysregulation of CD20

CD20 expression may also be altered via epigenetic regulation. CD20 expression has been reported to be regulated epigenetically both by DNA methyltransferases [53] and by histone deacetylases (HDACs) [54]. Firstly, the nonselective HDAC inhibitors (trichostatin A, valproic acid, romidepsin, and vorinostat) have been explored for their ability to increase *MS4A1* transcription and demonstrated their therapeutic potential in combination with anti-CD20 mAbs [55–57]. More recently, a potent HDAC1 and HDAC3 inhibitor, as well as an HDAC6 inhibitor, have been demonstrated to enhance rituximab activity and improve survival in preclinical trials [58,59].

Resistance to antibody-dependent cell-mediated cytotoxicity (ADCC)

ADCC is one of the most well-characterized mechanisms of action of anti-CD20 mAbs. ADCC is determined by the recognition of the Fc of the mAb by FcγR present on the cells of the innate immune system, mainly natural killer (NK) cells, granulocytes, and macrophages [7,60]. The activating FcγR are FcγRI (CD64), FcγRIIa (CD32A), and FcγRIIIa (CD16), while FcγRIIb (CD32b) has a, primarily, inhibitor effect. These receptors transmit their signals via immunoreceptor tyrosine-based activation motifs (ITAM) or immunoreceptor tyrosine-based inhibitory motifs (ITIM) [61].

Various factors mediate ADCC: the type of effector cell activated, the FcγR, and the antibody type (Fig. 1C).

Effector cell type

ADCC has been mostly allocated to NK cells, from among all the mononuclear cell types [7]. As interleukin-2 (IL-2) promotes NK cell expansion [62–64] and enhances intrinsic NK cell cytotoxicity [64,65], it may enhance ADCC. This concept was previously validated in a pre-clinical mouse model of human B-cell NHL in which the efficacy of rituximab and IL-2 was synergistic compared with either treatment alone [65]. However, these findings did not directly translate into meaningful clinical benefits for patients with rituxumab-refractory NHL in a phase 2 clinical trial [66].

Fcγ receptor polymorphisms

Genetic polymorphisms in the FcγR affect the affinity of effector cells for anti-CD20 mAbs. The most studied polymorphism occurs in FcγRIIIa, with a gene dimorphism encoding a phenylalanine (F) or a valine (V) at position 158 of the protein [7].

A higher in vitro affinity has been shown for the IgG in cells with FcγRIIIa 158V/V compared to those with 158V/F or 158F/F [67]. However, the clinical relevance has been tested in several studies in patients with different subtypes of lymphomas showing variable results, most of them negative [7]. FL was the only type of lymphoproliferative disease in which the FcγRIIIa polymorphism status may be a predictor of survival for patients treated with immunochemotherapy [68]. However, the PRIMA study did not confirm this correlation [69].

No association has been found either between FcγRIIIa polymorphisms and response rates in patients with DLBCL treated with R-CHOP (rituximab-cyclophosphamide, doxorubicin, vincristine, prednisone) [70], MCL treated with rituximab and Hyper-CVAD (cyclophosphamide, vincristine, doxorubicin, and dexamethasone) [71], or in CLL treated with rituximab or alemtuzumab [72].

SNPs affecting rituximab response have also been described in FcγRIIa, with different responses depending on the presence of a histidine (H) or an arginine (R) at position 131, with higher affinity to FcγRIIa 131H/H haplotype [73]. However, clinical studies did not validate any correlation between FcγRIIa polymorphisms and clinical response [69,74].

Antibody type

In order to overcome variability in FcγR-binding affinity, novel mAbs with enhanced Fc receptor affinity were developed, like the third-generation type II, anti-CD20 mAb, obinutuzumab [9,12]. This modification is responsible for the superior ADCC effect of obinutuzumab, as it compensates for inhibitory interactions between NK-cell Fc receptor and class I human leukocyte antigen (HLA), which leads to the recruitment of additional NK cells, the main effectors of ADCC [75].

Tumor microenvironment

Circulating B cells and B cells in the marginal zone of lymph nodes are destroyed by different mechanisms in the human-CD20 transgenic mouse model [76]. This suggests that differences in microenvironment signaling can play a role in mediating anti-CD20 resistance and can partially explain the variation in response rates noted among different CD20-expressing malignancies (Fig. 1D) [77].

CXCR4 expression was associated with poor prognosis in DLBCL patients treated with R-CHOP [78]. Moreover, the CXCR4 antagonist plerixafor enhances the effect of rituximab in DLBCL cell lines [79].

Lymphoma Gal-1expression in the local microenvironment was also identified as a mediator of resistance to CD20 immunotherapy and mAb-dependent phagocytosis by impeding macrophage activation and/or function [80].

The therapeutic function of anti-CD20 mAbs also depends on tumor-specific CD8+ T-cell responses initiated by anti-CD20 through macrophages and dendritic cells. The CTLA-4 blockade can synergize with the anti-CD20 activity and overcome adaptive immune response-related resistance in B-cell lymphoma [81].

Complement-mediated resistance

CDC is a mechanism very used by rituximab and other anti-CD20 mAbs and is mediated by the recruitment and consumption of complement molecules. This concerns among others, the first molecule of the complement namely C1q [82]. So, a nonimmunodeficient mice model generated by stable transduction of the human *CD20* cDNA in the murine lymphoma line EL4 demonstrated that a lack of C1q abolished the protective effect of rituximab (Fig. 1E) [83]. Of note, ofatumumab, another type I anti-CD20 mAb, is able to induce a rapid and important exhaustion of complement C4 levels. In this context, this important complement molecule prevents the action of the anti-CD20 mAb [84]. To remedy this, patients received fresh-frozen plasma, which strongly improved the activity of the anti-CD20 mAb [85,86].

Another mechanism of complement resistance is linked to the lipid and protein composition of the B-cell membrane. Thus, the amount of CD20 at the B-cell surface may be related to other particular structures present on B cells, namely the lipid rafts. Its recruitment into these structures determines its quantity and influences the efficiency of rituximab, as reported in NHL [87]. Concerning proteins, complement regulatory proteins (mCRPs) are implicated [88]. Among these molecules, CD55 and CD59 are frequently involved [89]. Their blockage has been shown to be effective to increase rituximab-induced CDC [90,91].

Finally, aberrant glycosylation can induce resistance to rituximab. It is the case of sialylation. Sialic acid acts frequently via an α2-3 or α2-6 glycosidic linkage to galactose and *N*-acetylgalactosamine. The presence of sialic acids is implicated in the recruitment of soluble complement inhibitors and their removal by neuraminidase increases rituximab-induced CDC [92–94].

Resistance to apoptosis

In addition to CDC and ADCC, anti-CD20 mAbs can directly induce apoptosis. The direct cytotoxicity of rituximab has been shown to be caspase-dependent, acting mainly through activation of the Src family tyrosine kinases (Src TK) of the FAS apoptotic pathway and through inhibition of several antiapoptotic signaling pathways such as NFkB, p38 MAPK, ERK1/2, and AKT (Fig. 1F) [7,95].

Hyper-cross-linking of anti-CD20 mAbs aggregates lipid rafts, transactivating Src TK and initiating downstream signaling resulting in apoptotic response [96]. One mechanism of resistance to this anti-CD20 action has been shown to be generated by statins that can indirectly affect the conformation of CD20 molecules expressed on the surface of B cells, impairing their recognition by mAbs and finally diminishing the antitumor effects of anti-CD20 mAbs [97].

The downstream signals from cell death receptors, such as FAS (CD95) can also induce apoptosis through binding to the FAS ligand (FASL), clustering of receptors, binding their intracellular domains to the FAS-Associated Death Domain (FADD), activating pro-caspase 8 domains, and coactivating several effector caspases [7].

A synergy in the induction of apoptosis between rituximab and the FAS-agonist mAb (CH-11) has been demonstrated [98]. The mechanism underlying the immunosensitization of B-NHL cells by rituximab works via the inhibition of NFkB and is mediated by Yin-Yang 1 (YY1) [99].

Rituximab has also been shown to be able to modulate intracellular signaling pathways NFkB, p38MAPK, MEK/ERK, and PI3K/AKT. Any signaling alteration affecting the apoptotic balance could alter sensitivity to rituximab [98,100–103].

Future perspectives

The important progress outlined above in identifying the mechanisms of resistance to anti-CD20 mAbs permitted the development of second- and third-generation anti-CD20 mAbs. However, there are still important limitations of the anti-CD20 mAb therapy.

The biggest unmet need in NHL treatment remains in DLBCL, but it is unlikely that anti-CD20 mAbs, in combination with standard chemotherapy, will be further investigated in this indication [8]. Emerging therapies in NHL involve notably anti-CD19, but also anti-CD20 CAR-T cells and T-cell-dependent bispecific antibodies. The preliminary results of an ongoing phase 1/2 clinical trial (NCT03277729) of a third-generation CD20 CAR-T cells (MB-106) in patients with relapsed, refractory B-cell NHL and CLL have recently been reported [104,105]. This trial included patients, who had previously received CD19 CAR-T cells. In all, 16 patients had been treated, including 1 patient with CLL. The overall response rate was 94% with 15 of 16 treated patients responding and 10 of 16 patients achieving a complete response (62%). Similarly, the CD20/CD3 bispecific antibody mosenotuzumab clinical activity was explored in the phase I/Ib part of the GO29781 (NCT02500407) trial, where DLBCL, transformed FL, and FL who failed ≥2 lines of therapy were enrolled [106]. Budde et al. recently published the results of the phase II analysis of the GO29781 trial and among the 90 patients enrolled, the overall response rate was 80% and 54 (60%) had a complete response, with a median progression-free survival, which was not reached in the updated analysis [107]. These results are encouraging and we await further follow-up of long-term responses.

Concerning CLL, several recent and ongoing trials are investigating novel, chemotherapy-free combinations of rituximab and obinutuzumab. Both, combinations of anti-CD20 mAbs with venetoclax, an inhibitor of Bcl2, or with the BTK inhibitors ibrutinib and acalabrutinib showed improved outcomes compared to immunochemotherapy [108–110].

Conclusions

Anti-CD20 mAbs have now been used in lymphoid malignancies for more than 20 years. Despite the fact that rituximab was widely used for more than 2 decades, the exact mechanisms of action, as well as the role of each known mechanism in vivo, are not completely known. Rituximab resistance is a common clinical occurrence in lymphoid malignancies, which generated an important research activity. Nonetheless, the mechanisms of resistance remain incompletely defined and there is surprisingly little knowledge of how to approach anti-CD20 rituximab resistance. Deliberately engineered to overcome mechanisms of rituximab resistance, obinutuzumab has demonstrated improved efficacy over rituximab in preclinical analysis. However, despite this significant advantage shown by preclinical analysis, in clinical trials, the benefit was not universal and was limited to CLL and FL. Based on the benefit dependent on histological subtypes, it is tempting to suggest that the advantage of obinutuzumab may be most apparent in the setting of rituximab resistance.

Despite the limitations of anti-CD20 mAbs, a number of promising approaches have been explored to overcome resistance or to enhance their effectiveness. Combinations of anti-CD20 mAbs with agents designed to enhance CD20 expression, to augment complement activity, or increase susceptibility to apoptosis have been investigated. As new inhibitors and antibodies are developed, an improved life expectancy is expected for patients with lymphoid malignancies.

Acknowledgment

The authors thank Thomas Marshall and Mary Elizabeth Marshall Smith for editing the manuscript.

References

[1] Stashenko P, Nadler LM, Hardy R, Schlossman SF. Characterization of a human B lymphocyte-specific antigen. J Immunol 1980;125:1678–85.
[2] Tedder TF, Klejman G, Schlossman SF, Saito H. Structure of the gene encoding the human B lymphocyte differentiation antigen CD20 (B1). J Immunol 1981;142:2560–8.
[3] Cragg MS, Walshe CA, Ivanov AO, Glennie MJ. The biology of CD20 and its potential as a target for mAb therapy. Curr Dir Autoimmun 2005;8:140–74.
[4] Marshall MJE, Stopforth RJ, Cragg MS. Therapeutic antibodies: what have we learnt from targeting CD20 and where are we going? Front Immunol 2017;8:1245.
[5] Reff ME, Carner K, Chambers KS, Chinn PC, Leonard JE, Raab R, Newman RA, Hanna N, Anderson DR. Depletion of B cells in vivo by a chimeric mouse human monoclonal antibody to CD20. Blood 1994;83:435–45.
[6] Freeman CL, Sehn LH. A tale of two antibodies: obinutuzumab versus rituximab. Br J Haematol 2018;182:29–45.
[7] Pérez-Callejo D, González-Rincón J, Sánchez A, Provencio M, Sánchez-Beato M. Action and resistance of monoclonal CD20 antibodies therapy in B-cell non-Hodgkin lymphomas. Cancer Treat Rev 2015;41:680–9.
[8] Klein C, Jamois C, Nielsen T. Anti-CD20 treatment for B-cell malignancies: current status and future directions. Expert Opin Biol Ther 2021;21:161–81.
[9] Mössner E, Brünker P, Moser S, Püntener U, Schmidt C, Herter S, Grau R, Gerdes C, Nopora A, van Puijenbroek E, Ferrara C, Sondermann P, Jäger C, Strein P, Fertig G, Friess T, Schüll C, Bauer S, Dal Porto J, Del Nagro C, Dabbagh K, Dyer MJS, Poppema S, Klein C, Umaña P. Increasing the efficacy of CD20 antibody therapy through the engineering of a new type II anti-CD20 antibody with enhanced direct and immune effector cell-mediated B-cell cytotoxicity. Blood 2010;115:4393–402.
[10] Niederfellner G, Lammens A, Mundigl O, Georges GJ, Schaefer W, Schwaiger M, Franke A, Wiechmann K, Jenewein S, Slootstra JW, Timmerman P, Brännström A, Lindstrom F, Mössner E, Umana P, Hopfner K-P, Klein C. Epitope characterization and crystal structure of GA101 provide insights into the molecular basis for type I/II distinction of CD20 antibodies. Blood 2011;118:358–67.
[11] Cheadle EJ, Sidon L, Dovedi SJ, Melis MHM, Alduaij W, Illidge TM, Honeychurch J. The induction of immunogenic cell death by type II anti-CD20 monoclonal antibodies has mechanistic differences compared with type I rituximab. Br J Haematol 2013;162:842–5.

[12] Herter S, Herting F, Mundigl O, Waldhauer I, Weinzierl T, Fauti T, Muth G, Ziegler-Landesberger D, Van Puijenbroek E, Lang S, Duong MN, Reslan L, Gerdes CA, Friess T, Baer U, Burtscher H, Weidner M, Dumontet C, Umana P, Niederfellner G, Bacac M, Klein C. Preclinical activity of the type II CD20 antibody GA101 (obinutuzumab) compared with rituximab and ofatumumab in vitro and in xenograft models. Mol Cancer Ther 2013;12:2031–42.

[13] McLaughlin P, Grillo-López AJ, Link BK, Levy R, Czuczman MS, Williams ME, Heyman MR, Bence-Bruckler I, White CA, Cabanillas F, Jain V, Ho AD, Lister J, Wey K, Shen D, Dallaire BK. Rituximab chimeric anti-CD20 monoclonal antibody therapy for relapsed indolent lymphoma: half of patients respond to a four-dose treatment program. J Clin Oncol 2023;41:154–62.

[14] Grillo-López AJ. Rituximab: an insider's historical perspective. Semin Oncol 2000;27:9–16.

[15] Coiffier B, Haioun C, Ketterer N, Engert A, Tilly H, Ma D, Johnson P, Lister A, Feuring-Buske M, Radford JA, Capdeville R, Diehl V, Reyes F. Rituximab (anti-CD20 monoclonal antibody) for the treatment of patients with relapsing or refractory aggressive lymphoma: a multicenter phase II study. Blood 1998;92:1927–32.

[16] Byrd JC, Murphy T, Howard RS, Lucas MS, Goodrich A, Park K, Pearson M, Waselenko JK, Ling G, Grever MR, Grillo-Lopez AJ, Rosenberg J, Kunkel L, Flinn IW. Rituximab using a thrice weekly dosing schedule in B-cell chronic lymphocytic leukemia and small lymphocytic lymphoma demonstrates clinical activity and acceptable toxicity. J Clin Oncol 2001;19:2153–64.

[17] O'Brien SM, Kantarjian H, Thomas DA, Giles FG, Freireich EJ, Cortes J, Lerner S, Keating MJ. Rituximab dose-escalation trial in chronic lymphocytic leukemia. J Clin Oncol 2001;19:2165–70.

[18] Salles G, Seymour JF, Offner F, López-Guillermo A, Belada D, Xerri L, Feugier P, Bouabdallah R, Catalano JV, Brice P, Caballero D, Haioun C, Pedersen LM, Delmer A, Simpson D, Leppa S, Soubeyran P, Hagenbeek A, Casasnovas O, Intragumtornchai T, Fermé C, Gomes da Silva M, Sebban C, Lister A, Estell JA, Milone G, Sonet A, Mendila M, Coiffier B, Tilly H. Rituximab maintenance for 2 years in patients with high tumour burden follicular lymphoma responding to rituximab plus chemotherapy (PRIMA): a phase 3, randomised controlled trial. Lancet 2011;9759:42–51.

[19] van Oers MHJ, Van Glabbeke M, Giurgea L, Klasa R, Marcus RE, Wolf M, Kimby E, van Veer M, Vranovsky A, Holte H, Hagenbeek A. Rituximab maintenance treatment of relapsed/resistant follicular non-Hodgkin's lymphoma: long-term outcome of the EORTC 20981 phase III randomized intergroup study. J Clin Oncol 2010;28:2853–8.

[20] Tobinai K, Kobayashi Y, Narabayashi M, Ogura M, Kagami Y, Morishima Y, Ohtsu T, Igarashi T, Sasaki Y, Kinoshita T, Murate T. Feasibility and pharmacokinetic study of a chimeric anti-CD20 monoclonal antibody (IDEC-C2B8, rituximab) in relapsed B-cell lymphoma. Ann Oncol 1998;9:527–34.

[21] Igarashi T, Kobayashi Y, Ogura M, Kinoshita T, Ohtsu T, Sasaki Y, Morishima Y, Murate T, Kasai M, Uike N, Taniwaki M, Kano Y, Ohnishi K, Matsuno Y, Nakamura S, Mori S, Ohashi Y, Tobinai K. IDEC-C2B8 study Group in Japan. Factors affecting toxicity, response and progression-free survival in relapsed patients with indolent B-cell lymphoma and mantle cell lymphoma treated with rituximab: a Japanese phase II study. Ann Oncol 2002;13:928–43.

[22] Jager U, Fridrik M, Zeitlinger M, Heintel D, Hopfinger G, Burgstaller S, Mannhalter C, Oberaigner W, Porpaczy E, Skrabs C, Einberger C, Drach J, Raderer M, Gaiger A, Putman M, Greil R, Arbeitsgemeinschaft Medikamentöse Tumortherapie (AGMT) Investigators. Rituximab serum concentrations during immuno-chemotherapy of follicular lymphoma correlate with patient gender, bone marrow infiltration and clinical response. Haematologica 2012;97:1431–8.

[23] Pfreundschuh M, Müller C, Zeynalova S, Kuhnt E, Wiesen MHJ, Held G, Rixecker T, Poeschel V, Zwick C, Reiser M, Schmitz N, Murawski N. Suboptimal dosing of rituximab in male and female patients with DLBCL. Blood 2014;123:640–6.

[24] Berinstein NL, Grillo-López AJ, White CA, Bence-Bruckler I, Maloney D, Czuczman M, Green D, Rosenberg J, McLaughlin P, Shen D. Association of serum rituximab (IDEC–C2B8) concentration and anti-tumor response in the treatment of recurrent low-grade or follicular non-Hodgkin's lymphoma. Ann Oncol 1998;9:995–1001.

[25] Gibiansky E, Gibiansky L, Chavanne C, Frey N, Jamois C. Population pharmacokinetic and exposure-response analyses of intravenous and subcutaneous rituximab in patients with chronic lymphocytic leukemia. CPT Pharmacometrics Syst Pharmacol 2021;10:914–27.

[26] Keating M, O'Brien S. High-dose rituximab therapy in chronic lymphocytic leukemia. Semin Oncol 2000;27:86–90.

[27] Manshouri T, Do K, Wang X, Giles FJ, O'Brien SM, Saffer H, Thomas D, Jilani I, Kantarjian HM, Keating MJ, Albitar M. Circulating CD20 is detectable in the plasma of patients with chronic lymphocytic leukemia and is of prognostic significance. Blood 2003;101:2507–13.

[28] Keating MJ, O'Brien S, Albitar M. Emerging information on the use of rituximab in chronic lymphocytic leukemia. Semin Oncol 2002;29:70–4.

[29] Looney RJ, Anolik JH, Campbell D, Felgar RE, Young F, Arend LJ, Sloand JA, Rosenblatt J, Sanz I. B cell depletion as a novel treatment for systemic lupus erythematosus: a phase I/II dose-escalation trial of rituximab. Arthritis Rheum 2004;50:2580–9.

[30] Kamisoglu K, Phipps A, Jamois C, Buchheit V, Meneses-Lorente G, Fingerle-Rowson G, Wagg J, Mager DE. Greater efficacy and potency of Obinutuzumab compared with rituximab in chronic lymphocytic leukemia patients confirmed by a semi-mechanistic pharmacokinetic/Pharmacodynamic model. Blood 2017;130:1267.

[31] Beum PV, Peek EM, Lindorfer MA, Beurskens FJ, Engelberts PJ, Parren PWH, van de Winkel JGJ, Taylor RP. Loss of CD20 and bound CD20 antibody from opsonized B cells occurs more rapidly because of trogocytosis mediated by Fc receptor-expressing effector cells than direct internalization by the B cells. J Immunol 2011;187:3438–47.

[32] Beers SA, French RR, Claude Chan HT, Lim SH, Jarrett TC, Mora Vidal R, Wijayaweera SS, Dixon SV, Kim H, Cox KL, Kerr JP, Johnston DA, Johnson PWM, Sjef Verbeek J, Glennie MJ, Cragg MS. Antigenic modulation limits the efficacy of anti-CD20 antibodies: implications for antibody selection. Blood 2010;115:5191–201.

[33] Uchida J, Hamaguchi Y, Oliver JA, Ravetch JV, Poe JC, Haas KM, Tedder TF. The innate mononuclear phagocyte network depletes B lymphocytes through fc receptor–dependent mechanisms during anti-CD20 antibody immunotherapy. J Exp Med 2004;199:1659–69.

[34] Minard-Colin V, Xiu Y, Poe JC, Horikawa M, Magro CM, Hamaguchi Y, Haas KM, Tedder TF. Lymphoma depletion during CD20 immunotherapy in mice is mediated by macrophage FcγRI, FcγRIII, and FcγRIV. Blood 2008;112:1205–13.

[35] Dahal LN, Huang C-Y, Stopforth RJ, Mead A, Chan K, Bowater JX, Taylor MC, Narang P, Claude Chan HT, Kim JH, Vaughan AT, Forconi F, Beers SA. Shaving is an epiphenomenon of type I and II anti-CD20–mediated phagocytosis, whereas antigenic modulation limits type I monoclonal antibody efficacy. J Immunol 2018;201:1211–21.

[36] Golay J, Da Roit F, Bologna L, Ferrara C, Leusen JH, Rambaldi A, Klein C, Introna M. Glycoengineered CD20 antibody obinutuzumab activates neutrophils and mediates phagocytosis through CD16B more efficiently than rituximab. Blood 2013;122:3482–91.

[37] Valgardsdottir R, Cattaneo I, Klein C, Introna M, Figliuzzi M, Golay J. Human neutrophils mediate trogocytosis rather than phagocytosis of CLL B cells opsonized with anti-CD20 antibodies. Blood 2017;129:2636–44.

[38] Beum PV, Kennedy AD, Williams ME, Lindorfer MA, Taylor RP. The shaving reaction: rituximab/CD20 complexes are removed from mantle cell lymphoma and chronic lymphocytic leukemia cells by THP-1 monocytes. J Immunol 2006;176:2600–9.

[39] Beum PV, Lindorfer MA, Taylor RP. Within peripheral blood mononuclear cells, antibody-dependent cellular cytotoxicity of rituximab-opsonized Daudi cells is promoted by NK cells and inhibited by monocytes due to shaving. J Immunol 2008;181:2916–24.

[40] Li Y, Williams ME, Cousar JB, Pawluczkowycz AW, Lindorfer MA, Taylor RP. Rituximab-CD20 complexes are shaved from Z138 mantle cell lymphoma cells in intravenous and subcutaneous SCID mouse models. J Immunol 2007;179:4263–71.

[41] Williams ME, Densmore JJ, Pawluczkowycz AW, Beum PV, Kennedy AD, Lindorfer MA, Hamil SH, Eggleton JC, Taylor RP. Thrice-weekly low-dose rituximab decreases CD20 loss via shaving and promotes enhanced targeting in chronic lymphocytic leukemia. J Immunol 2006;177:7435–43.

[42] Sarkar K, Kruhlak MJ, Erlandsen SL, Shaw S. Selective inhibition by rottlerin of macropinocytosis in monocyte-derived dendritic cells. Immunology 2005.

[43] Terui Y, Mishima Y, Sugimura N, Kojima K, Sakurai T, Mishima Y, Kuniyoshi R, Taniyama A, Yokoyama M, Sakajiri S, Takeuchi K, Watanabe C, Takahashi S, Ito Y, Hatake K. Identification of CD20 C-terminal deletion mutations associated with loss of CD20 expression in non-Hodgkin's lymphoma. Clin Cancer Res 2009;15:2523–30.

[44] Mishima Y, Terui Y, Takeuchi K, Matsumoto-Mishima Y, Matsusaka S, Utsubo-Kuniyoshi R, Hatake K. The identification of irreversible rituximab-resistant lymphoma caused by CD20 gene mutations. Blood Cancer J 2011;1:e15.

[45] Johnson NA, Leach S, Woolcock B, deLeeuw RJ, Bashashati A, Sehn LH, Connors JM, Chhanabhai M, Brooks-Wilson A, Gascoyne RD. CD20 mutations involving the rituximab epitope are rare in diffuse large B-cell lymphomas and are not a significant cause of R-CHOP failure. Haematologica 2009;94:423–7.

[46] Nakamaki T, Fukuchi K, Nakashima H, Ariizumi H, Maeda T, Saito B, Yanagisawa K, Tomoyasu S, Homma M, Shiozawa E, Yamochi-Onizuka T, Ota H. CD20 gene deletion causes a CD20-negative relapse in diffuse large B-cell lymphoma. Eur J Haematol 2012;89:350–5.

[47] Henry C, Deschamps M, Rohrlich P-S, Pallandre J-R, Rémy-Martin J-P, Callanan M, Traverse-Glehen A, Grand Clément C, Garnache-Ottou F, Gressin R, Deconinck E, Salles G, Robinet E, Tiberghien P, Borg C, Ferrand C. Identification of an alternative CD20 transcript variant in B-cell malignancies coding for a novel protein associated to rituximab resistance. Blood 2010;115:2420–9.

[48] Golay J, Lazzari M, Facchinetti V, Bernasconi S, Borleri G, Barbui T, Rambaldi A, Introna M. CD20 levels determine the in vitro susceptibility to rituximab and complement of B-cell chronic lymphocytic leukemia: further regulation by CD55 and CD59. Blood 2001;98:3383–9.

[49] Schilhabel A, Walter PJ, Cramer P, von Tresckow J, Kohlscheen S, Szczepanowski M, Laqua A, Fischer K, Eichhorst B, Böttcher S, Schneider C, Tausch E, Brüggemann M, Kneba M, Hallek M, Ritgen M. CD20 expression as a possible novel prognostic marker in CLL: application of EuroFlow standardization technique and normalization procedures in flow cytometric expression analysis. Cancers (Basel) 2022;14:4917.

[50] Mankaï A, Bordron A, Renaudineau Y, Martins-Carvalho C, Takahashi S, Ghedira I, Berthou C, Youinou P. Purine-rich Box-1–mediated reduced expression of CD20 alters rituximab-induced lysis of chronic lymphocytic leukemia B cells. Cancer Res 2008;68:7512–9.

[51] Grzelak L, Roesch F, Vaysse A, Biton A, Legendre R, Porrot F, Commère P-H, Planchais C, Mouquet H, Vignuzzi M, Bruel T, Schwartz O. IRF8 regulates efficacy of therapeutic anti-CD20 monoclonal antibodies. Eur J Immunol 2022;52:1648–61.

[52] Pyrzynska B, Dwojak M, Zerrouqi A, Morlino G, Zapala P, Miazek N, Zagozdzon A, Bojarczuk K, Bobrowicz M, Siernicka M, Machnicki MM, Gobessi S, Barankiewicz J, Lech-Maranda E, Efremov DG, Juszczynski P, Calado D, Golab J, Winiarska M. FOXO1 promotes resistance of non-Hodgkin lymphomas to anti-CD20-based therapy. OncoImmunology 2018;7, e1423183.

[53] Ushmorov A, Leithäuser F, Sakk O, Weinhaüsel A, Popov SW, Möller P, Wirth T. Epigenetic processes play a major role in B-cell-specific gene silencing in classical Hodgkin lymphoma. Blood 2006;107:2493–500.

[54] Sugimoto T, Tomita A, Hiraga J, Shimada K, Kiyoi H, Kinoshita T, Naoe T. Escape mechanisms from antibody therapy to lymphoma cells: downregulation of CD20 mRNA by recruitment of the HDAC complex and not by DNA methylation. Biochem Biophys Res Commun 2009;390:48–53.

[55] Park J, Thomas S, Munster PN. Epigenetic modulation with histone deacetylase inhibitors in combination with immunotherapy. Epigenomics 2015;7:641–52.

[56] Shimizu R, Kikuchi J, Wada T, Ozawa K, Kano Y, Furukawa Y. HDAC inhibitors augment cytotoxic activity of rituximab by upregulating CD20 expression on lymphoma cells. Leukemia 2010;24:1760–8.

[57] Zhao W-L, Wang L, Liu Y-H, Yan J-S, Leboeuf C, Liu Y-Y, Wu W-L, Janin A, Chen Z, Chen S-J. Combined effects of histone deacetylase inhibitor and rituximab on non-Hodgkin's B-lymphoma cells apoptosis. Exp Hematol 2007;35:1801–11.

[58] Frys S, Simons Z, Hu Q, Barth MJ, Gu JJ, Mavis C, Skitzki J, Song L, Czuczman MS, Hernandez-Ilizaliturri FJ. Entinostat, a novel histone deacetylase inhibitor is active in B-cell lymphoma and enhances the anti-tumour activity of rituximab and chemotherapy agents. Br J Haematol 2015;169:506–19.

[59] Bobrowicz M, Dwojak M, Pyrzynska B, Stachura J, Muchowicz A, Berthel E, Dalla-Venezia N, Kozikowski M, Siernicka M, Miazek N, Zapala P, Domagala A, Bojarczuk K, Malenda A, Barankiewicz J, Graczyk-Jarzynk A, Zagozdzon A, Gabrysiak M, Diaz JJ, Karp M, Lech-Maranda E, Firczuk M, Giannopoulos K, Efremov DG, Laurenti L, Baatout D, Frenzel L, Malinowska A, Slabicki M, Zenz T, Zerrouqi A, Golab J, Winiarska M. HDAC6 inhibition upregulates CD20 levels and increases the efficacy of anti-CD20 monoclonal antibodies. Blood 2017;130:1628–38.

[60] Bagacean C, Zdrenghea M, Tempescul A, Cristea V, Renaudineau Y. Anti-CD20 monoclonal antibodies in chronic lymphocytic leukemia: from uncertainties to promises. Immunotherapy 2016;8:569–81.

[61] Nimmerjahn F, Ravetch JV. Fcgamma receptors: old friends and new family members. Immunity 2005;24:19–28.

[62] Caligiuri MA, Zmuidzinas A, Manley TJ, Levine H, Smith KA, Ritz J. Functional consequences of interleukin 2 receptor expression on resting human lymphocytes. Identification of a novel natural killer cell subset with high affinity receptors. J Exp Med 1990;171:1509–26.

[63] Caligiuri MA, Murray C, Robertson MJ, Wang E, Cochran K, Cameron C, Schow P, Ross ME, Klumpp TR, Soiffer RJ. Selective modulation of human natural killer cells in vivo after prolonged infusion of low dose recombinant interleukin 2. J Clin Invest 1993;91:123–32.

[64] Meropol NJ, Barresi GM, Fehniger TA, Hitt J, Franklin M, Caligiuri MA. Evaluation of natural killer cell expansion and activation in vivo with daily subcutaneous low-dose interleukin-2 plus periodic intermediate-dose pulsing. Cancer Immunol Immunother 1998;46:318–26.

[65] Eisenbeis CF, Grainger A, Fischer B, Baiocchi RA, Carrodeguas L, Roychowdhury S, Chen L, Banks AL, Davis T, Young D, Kelbick N, Stephens J, Byrd JC, Grever MR, Caligiuri MA, Porcu P. Combination immunotherapy of B-cell non-Hodgkin's lymphoma with rituximab and interleukin-2: a preclinical and phase I study. Clin Cancer Res 2004;10:6101–10.

[66] Khan KD, Emmanouilides C, Benson Jr DM, Hurst D, Garcia P, Michelson G, Milan S, Ferketich AK, Piro L, Leonard JP, Porcu P, Eisenbeis CF, Banks AL, Chen L, Byrd JC, Caligiuri MA. A phase 2 study of rituximab in combination with recombinant interleukin-2 for rituximab-refractory indolent non-Hodgkin's lymphoma. Clin Cancer Res 2006;12:7046–53.

[67] Hatjiharissi E, Xu L, Santos DD, Hunter ZR, Ciccarelli BT, Verselis S, Modica M, Cao Y, Manning RJ, Leleu X, Dimmock EA, Kortsaris A, Mitsiades C, Anderson KC, Fox EA, Treon SP. Increased natural killer cell expression of CD16, augmented binding and ADCC activity to rituximab among individuals expressing the fc {gamma}RIIIa-158 V/V and V/F polymorphism. Blood 2007;110:2561–4.

[68] Persky DO, Dornan D, Goldman BH, Braziel RM, Fisher RI, Leblanc M, Maloney DG, Press OW, Miller TP, Rimsza LM. Fc gamma receptor 3a genotype predicts overall survival in follicular lymphoma patients treated on SWOG trials with combined monoclonal antibody plus chemotherapy but not chemotherapy alone. Haematologica 2012;97:937–42.

[69] Ghesquières H, Cartron G, Francis Seymour J, Delfau-Larue MH, Offner F, Soubeyran P, Perrot A, Brice P, Bouabdallah R, Sonet A, Dupuis J, Casasnovas O, Catalano JV, Delmer A, Jardin F, Verney A, Dartigues P, Salles G. Clinical outcome of patients with follicular lymphoma receiving chemoimmunotherapy in the PRIMA study is not affected by FCGR3A and FCGR2A polymorphisms. Blood 2012;120:2650–7.

[70] Fabisiewicz A, Paszkiewicz-Kozik E, Osowiecki M, Walewski J, Siedlecki JA. FcγRIIA and FcγRIIIA polymorphisms do not influence survival and response to rituximab, cyclophosphamide, doxorubicin, vincristine, and prednisone immunochemotherapy in patients with diffuse large B-cell lymphoma. Leuk Lymphoma 2011;52:1604–6.

[71] Galimberti S, Palumbo GA, Caracciolo F, Benedetti E, Pelosini M, Brizzi S, Ciabatti E, Fazzi R, Stelitano C, Quintana G, Conte E, Tibullo D, Di Raimondo F, Petrini M. The efficacy of rituximab plus hyper-CVAD regimen in mantle cell lymphoma is independent of FCgammaRIIIa and FCgammaRIIa polymorphisms. J Chemother 2007;19:315–21.

[72] Lin TS, Flinn IW, Modali R, Lehman TA, Webb J, Waymer S, Moran ME, Lucas MS, Farag SS, Byrd JC. FCGR3A and FCGR2A polymorphisms may not correlate with response to alemtuzumab in chronic lymphocytic leukemia. Blood 2005;105:289–91.

[73] Bruhns P, Iannascoli B, England P, Mancardi DA, Fernandez N, Jorieux S, Daëron M. Specificity and affinity of human Fcgamma receptors and their polymorphic variants for human IgG subclasses. Blood 2009;113:3716–25.

[74] Carlotti E, Palumbo GA, Oldani E, Tibullo D, Salmoiraghi S, Rossi A, Golay J, Pulsoni A, Foà R, Rambaldi A. FcgammaRIIIA and FcgammaRIIA polymorphisms do not predict clinical outcome of follicular non-Hodgkin's lymphoma patients treated with sequential CHOP and rituximab. Haematologica 2007;92:1127–30.

[75] Terszowski G, Klein C, Stern M. KIR/HLA interactions negatively affect rituximab- but not GA101 (obinutuzumab)-induced antibody-dependent cellular cytotoxicity. J Immunol 2014;192:5618–24.

[76] Gong Q, Ou Q, Ye S, Lee WP, Cornelius J, Diehl L, Yu Lin W, Hu Z, Lu Y, Chen Y, Wu Y, Meng YG, Gribling P, Lin Z, Nguyen K, Tran T, Zhang Y, Rosen H, Martin F, Chan AC. Importance of cellular microenvironment and circulatory dynamics in B cell immunotherapy. J Immunol 2005;174:817–26.

[77] Torka P, Barth M, Ferdman R, Hernandez-Ilizaliturri FJ. Mechanisms of resistance to monoclonal antibodies (mAbs) in lymphoid malignancies. Curr Hematol Malig Rep 2019;14:426–38.

[78] Laursen MB, Reinholdt L, Schönherz AA, Due H, Starberg Jespersen D, Grubach L, Schmidt Ettrup M, Røge R, Falgreen S, Sørensen S, Støve Bødker J, Schmitz A, Johnsen HE, Bøgsted M, Dybkær K. High CXCR4 expression impairs rituximab response and the prognosis of R-CHOP-treated diffuse large B-cell lymphoma patients. Oncotarget 2019;10:717–31.

[79] Reinholdt L, Laursen MB, Schmitz A, Bødker JS, Jakobsen LH, Bøgsted M, Johnsen HE, Dybkær K. The CXCR4 antagonist plerixafor enhances the effect of rituximab in diffuse large B-cell lymphoma cell lines. Biomark Res 2016;4:12.

[80] Lykken JM, Horikawa M, Minard-Colin V, Kamata M, Miyagaki T, Poe JC, Tedder TF. Galectin-1 drives lymphoma CD20 immunotherapy resistance: validation of a preclinical system to identify resistance mechanisms. Blood 2016;127:1886–95.
[81] Ren Z, Guo J, Liao J, Luan Y, Liu Z, Sun Z, Liu X, Liang Y, Peng H, Fu YX. CTLA-4 limits anti-CD20-mediated tumor regression. Clin Cancer Res 2017;23:193–203.
[82] Weiner GJ. Rituximab: mechanism of action. Semin Hematol 2010;47:115–23.
[83] Di Gaetano N, Cittera E, Nota R, Vecchi A, Grieco V, Scanziani E, Botto M, Introna M, Golay J. Complement activation determines the therapeutic activity of rituximab in vivo. J Immunol 2003;171:1581–7.
[84] Tempescul A, Bagacean C, Riou C, Bendaoud B, Hillion S, Debant M, Buors C, Berthou C, Renaudineau Y. Ofatumumab capacity to deplete B cells from chronic lymphocytic leukaemia is affected by C4 complement exhaustion. Eur J Haematol 2016;96:229–35.
[85] Middleton O, Cosimo E, Dobbin E, McCaig AM, Clarke C, Brant AM, Leach MT, Michie AM, Wheadon H. Complement deficiencies limit CD20 monoclonal antibody treatment efficacy in CLL. Leukemia 2015;29:107–14.
[86] Klepfish A, Gilles L, Ioannis K, Rachmilewitz EA, Schattner A. Enhancing the action of rituximab in chronic lymphocytic leukemia by adding fresh frozen plasma: complement/rituximab interactions & clinical results in refractory CLL. Ann N Y Acad Sci 2009;1173:865–73.
[87] Meyer zum Büschenfelde C, Feuerstacke Y, Götze KS, Scholze K, Peschel C. GM1 expression of non-Hodgkin's lymphoma determines susceptibility to rituximab treatment. Cancer Res 2008;68:5414–22.
[88] Fishelson Z, Donin N, Zell S, Schultz S, Kirschfink M. Obstacles to cancer immunotherapy: expression of membrane complement regulatory proteins (mCRPs) in tumors. Mol Immunol 2003;40:109–23.
[89] Takei K, Yamazaki T, Sawada U, Ishizuka H, Aizawa S. Analysis of changes in CD20, CD55, and CD59 expression on established rituximab-resistant B-lymphoma cell lines. Leuk Res 2005;30:625–31.
[90] Golay J, Zaffaroni L, Vaccari T, Lazzari M, Borleri GM, Bernasconi S, Tedesco F, Rambaldi A, Introna M. Biologic response of B lymphoma cells to anti-CD20 monoclonal antibody rituximab in vitro: CD55 and CD59 regulate complement-mediated cell lysis. Blood 2000;95:3900–8.
[91] Terui Y, Sakurai T, Mishima Y, Mishima Y, Sugimura N, Sasaoka C, Kojima K, Yokoyama M, Mizunuma N, Takahashi S, Ito Y, Hatake K. Blockade of bulky lymphoma-associated CD55 expression by RNA interference overcomes resistance to complement-dependent cytotoxicity with rituximab. Cancer Sci 2006;97:72–9.
[92] Meri S, Pangburn MK. Discrimination between activators and nonactivators of the alternative pathway of complement: regulation via a sialic acid/polyanion binding site on factor H. Proc Natl Acad Sci U S A 1990;87:3982–6.
[93] Hörl S, Bánki Z, Huber G, Ejaz A, Windisch D, Muellauer B, Willenbacher E, Steurer M, Stoiber H. Reduction of complement factor H binding to CLL cells improves the induction of rituximab-mediated complement-dependent cytotoxicity. Leukemia 2013;27:2200–8.
[94] Winkler MT, Bushey RT, Gottlin EB, Campa MJ, Guadalupe ES, Volkheimer AD, Weinberg JB, Patz Jr EF. Enhanced CDC of B cell chronic lymphocytic leukemia cells mediated by rituximab combined with a novel anti-complement factor H antibody. PLoS One 2017;12, e0179841.
[95] Bonavida B. Postulated mechanisms of resistance of B-cell non-Hodgkin lymphoma to rituximab treatment regimens: strategies to overcome resistance. Semin Oncol 2014;41:667–77.
[96] Deans JP, Li H, Polyak MJ. CD20-mediated apoptosis: signalling through lipid rafts. Immunology 2002;107:176–82.
[97] Winiarska M, Bil J, Wilczek E, Wilczynski GM, Lekka M, Engelberts PJ, Mackus WJM, Gorska E, Bojarski L, Stoklosa T, Nowis D, Kurzaj Z, Makowski M, Glodkowska E, Issat T, Mrowka P, Lasek W, Dabrowska-Iwanicka A, Basak GW, Wasik M, Warzocha K, Sinski M, Gaciong Z, Jakobisiak M, Parren PW, Golab J. Statins impair antitumor effects of rituximab by inducing conformational changes of CD20. PLoS Med 2008;5, e64.
[98] Bonavida B. Rituximab-induced inhibition of antiapoptotic cell survival pathways: implications in chemo/immunoresistance, rituximab unresponsiveness, prognostic and novel therapeutic interventions. Oncogene 2007;26:3629–36.
[99] Vega MI, Jazirehi AR, Huerta-Yepez S, Bonavida B. Rituximab-induced inhibition of YY1 and Bcl-xL expression in Ramos non-Hodgkin's lymphoma cell line via inhibition of NF-kappa B activity: role of YY1 and Bcl-xL in Fas resistance and chemoresistance, respectively. J Immunol 2005;175:2174–83.
[100] Olejniczak SH, Hernandez-Ilizaliturri FJ, Clements JL, Czuczman MS. Acquired resistance to rituximab is associated with chemotherapy resistance resulting from decreased Bax and Bak expression. Clin Cancer Res 2008;14:1550–60.

[101] Vega MI, Martínez-Paniagua M, Huerta-Yepez S, González-Bonilla C, Uematsu N, Bonavida B. Dysregulation of the cell survival/anti-apoptotic NF-kappaB pathway by the novel humanized BM-ca anti-CD20 mAb: implication in chemosensitization. Int J Oncol 2009;35:1289–96.

[102] Alas S, Emmanouilides C, Bonavida B. Inhibition of interleukin 10 by rituximab results in down-regulation of bcl-2 and sensitization of B-cell non-Hodgkin's lymphoma to apoptosis. Clin Cancer Res 2001;7:709–23.

[103] Fresno Vara JA, Casado E, de Castro J, Cejas P, Belda-Iniesta C, González-Barón M. PI3K/Akt signalling pathway and cancer. Cancer Treat Rev 2004;30:193–204.

[104] Shadman M, Yeung CC, Redman M, Lee SY, Lee DH, Ra S, Ujjani CS, Dezube BJ, Poh C, Warren EH, Chapuis AG, Green DJ, Cowan AJ, Cassaday RD, Kiem H-P, Gauthier J, Turtle CJ, Lynch RC, Smith SD, Gopal AK, Maloney DG, Till BG. High efficacy and low toxicity of MB-106, a third generation CD20 targeted CAR-T for treatment of relapsed/refractory B-NHL and CLL. Transplant Cell Ther 2022;28:S182–3.

[105] Coombs CC, Easaw S, Grover NS, O'Brien SM. Cellular therapies in chronic lymphocytic leukemia and Richter's transformation: recent developments in chimeric antigen receptor T-cells, natural killer cells, and allogeneic stem cell transplant. Cancers (Basel) 2023;15:1838.

[106] Budde LE, Assouline S, Sehn LH, Stephen JS, Sung-Soo Y, Dok Hyun Y, Matthew JM, Bosch F, Kim WS, Nastoupil LJ, Flinn IW, Shadman M, Diefenbach C, O'Hear C, Huang H, Kwan A, Li C-C, Piccione EC, Wei MC, Yin S, Bartlett NL. Single-agent mosunetuzumab shows durable complete responses in patients with relapsed or refractory b-cell lymphomas: phase I dose-escalation study. J Clin Oncol 2022;40:481–91.

[107] Budde LE, Sehn LH, Matasar M, et al. Safety and efficacy of mosunetuzumab, a bispecific antibody, in patients with relapsed or refractory follicular lymphoma: a single-arm, multicentre, phase 2 study. Lancet Oncol 2022;23:1055–65.

[108] Fischer K, Al-Sawaf O, Bahlo J, Fink AM, Tandon M, Dixon M, Robrecht S, Warburton S, Humphrey K, Samoylova O, Liberati AM, Pinilla-Ibarz J, Opat S, Sivcheva L, Le Dû K, Fogliatto LM, Niemann CU, Weinkove R, Robinson S, Kipps TJ, Boettcher S, Tausch E, Humerickhouse R, Eichhorst B, Wendtner CM, Langerak AW, Kreuzer KA, Ritgen M, Goede V, Stilgenbauer S, Mobasher M, Hallek M. Venetoclax and Obinutuzumab in patients with CLL and coexisting conditions. N Engl J Med 2019;380:2225–36.

[109] Moreno C, Greil R, Demirkan F, Tedeschi A, Anz B, Larratt L, Simkovic M, Novak J, Strugov V, Gill D, Gribben JG, Kwei K, Dai S, Hsu E, Dean JP, Flinn IW. First-line treatment of chronic lymphocytic leukemia with ibrutinib plus obinutuzumab versus chlorambucil plus obinutuzumab: final analysis of the randomized, phase III iLLUMINATE trial. Haematologica 2022;107:2108–20.

[110] Sharman JP, Egyed M, Jurczak W, Skarbnik A, Pagel JM, Flinn IW, Kamdar M, Munir T, Walewska R, Corbett G, Fogliatto LM, Herishanu Y, Banerji V, Coutre S, Follows G, Walker P, Karlsson K, Ghia P, Janssens A, Cymbalista F, Woyach JA, Ferrant E, Wierda WG, Munugalavadla V, Yu T, Wang MH, Byrd JC. Efficacy and safety in a 4-year follow-up of the ELEVATE-TN study comparing acalabrutinib with or without obinutuzumab versus obinutuzumab plus chlorambucil in treatment-naïve chronic lymphocytic leukemia. Leukemia 2022;36:1171–5.

CHAPTER

11

Kinetic exclusion assay using cellular membranes for affinity determination of anti-CD20 antibody

Madelynn Grier[a], Helen J. McBride[b], Thomas R. Glass[a], and Qing Chen[c]

[a]Sapidyne Instruments Inc., Boise, ID, United States [b]TORL Biotherapeutics, Culver City, CA, United States [c]Amgen Inc., Thousand Oaks, CA, United States

Abstract

CD20 is a small nonglycosylated tetraspanin protein expressed by a majority of B cells. Since the FDA approval of rituximab to treat non-Hodgkin's lymphoma (NHL), anti-CD20 antibodies have played important roles in the treatment of patients with various kinds of lymphoma as well as autoimmune diseases. However, despite the high response observed in the first round of treatment, resistance to anti-CD20 antibodies eventually develops in patients who experience a relapse. Innovative therapies need to be developed to overcome the mechanisms of resistance and to continue the progress in the treatment of lymphoma and autoimmune diseases. This requires researchers to better understand CD20 biology and take the lessons learned from the success and limitations of anti-CD20 monoclonal antibody therapies to develop novel bispecific and cell therapy approaches. Binding affinity is a critical attribute of target engagement that impacts the efficacy of biologics. We explain, in detail, the methods used to determine target binding affinity and focus on the KinExA technology and its best practices in the study of integral membrane proteins. We sincerely hope the methodology described in this chapter contributes to more rapid discovery and development of new biologic therapies that benefit patients.

Abbreviations

ADA antidrug antibodies
ADC antibody drug conjugates
ADCC antibody-dependent cell-mediated cytotoxicity
ADCP antibody-dependent cell-mediated phagocytosis
BsAb bispecific antibodies
CAR-T chimeric antigen receptor T-cell

https://doi.org/10.1016/B978-0-443-19200-5.00005-1

CBP	constant binding partner
CDC	complement-dependent cytotoxicity
CLL	chronic lymphocytic leukemia
DLBCL	diffuse large B-cell lymphoma
FL	follicular lymphoma
GPA	granulomatosis with polyangiitis
HSC	hematopoietic stem cells
IMP	integral membrane protein
IRR	immune-related responses
K_d	dissociation constant
KinExA	kinetic exclusion assay
k_{off}	dissociation rate constant
k_{on}	association rate constant
mAb	monoclonal antibody
MCL	mantle cell lymphoma
MPA	microscopic polyangiitis
MS	multiple sclerosis
NHL	non-Hodgkin's lymphoma
NK	natural killer cells
NSB	nonspecific binding
OS	overall survival
PFS	progression-free survival
PV	pemphigus vulgaris
RA	rheumatoid arthritis
***R*max**	maximum response in SPR
SPR	surface plasmon resonance

Conflict of interest

Thomas and Madelynn are employees of Sapidyne Instruments, the manufacturer of the KinExA technology described in the text. Qing Chen is an employee of Amgen Inc., which is a bio-pharmaceutical company.

Anti-CD20 antibodies and biology

CD20 biology

CD20 is a 33–37 kDa, nonglycosylated tetraspanin protein in the MS4A (membrane-spanning 4-domain family A) family [1,2]. The protein consists of four hydrophobic transmembrane domains with two short extracellular loops [3]. CD20 forms dimeric and homo-tetrameric oligomers and is associated with other cell-surface and cytoplasmic proteins contributing to signal transduction in B cells [4–6]. Even with the intense study since its identification, the biological function of CD20 is still unclear.

CD20 is expressed by a majority of B cells starting from late pre-B lymphocytes and is not expressed by pro-B lymphocytes or B cell precursors. Expression of CD20 is lost in terminally differentiated plasma blasts and plasma cells. The level of CD20 expression is extremely variable across specific B-cell malignancies, with the lowest expression observed in chronic lymphocytic leukemia (CLL), diffuse large B cell lymphoma (DLBCL), and hairy cell leukemia patients [7,8].

CD20 is an ideal target for monoclonal antibody (mAb) therapeutic approaches. A key feature is its expression pattern that allows for the depletion of normal expressing cells being tolerated and restored over time from hematopoietic stem cells (HSCs). CD20 is also expressed at relatively high levels, and its oligomeric organization makes it amenable to the effector function, complement-dependent cytotoxicity (CDC). Additionally, its structure with two short extracellular loops places binding epitopes for anti-CD20 mAbs close to the plasma membrane which is known to support antibody-dependent cell-mediated cytotoxicity (ADCC) and antibody-dependent cell-mediated phagocytosis (ADCP) effector functions [9,10]. Binding to CD20 can also directly induce apoptosis, providing a fourth potential mechanism of action to support tumor cell depletion.

Approved antibodies and indications

Rituximab

Rituximab (marketed as Rituxan and multiple biosimilar versions) is a chimeric mouse/human therapeutic IgG1 monoclonal antibody that is used extensively for the treatment of B-cell malignancies, including B-cell non-Hodgkin's lymphoma (NHL) in combination with chemotherapy and other therapeutic regimens. NHL is the most common adult hematological cancer, accounting for the sixth most common cancer and the ninth leading cause of cancer deaths in the United States [11,12]. Approximately 85% of all NHLs are diagnosed with a B-cell origin, and of those, more than 95% express the CD20 target [13,14].

The challenge for newer agents is to demonstrate superiority over rituximab's impressive standard of care, particularly in the combination setting common in the treatment of hematologic malignancies. Rituximab has demonstrated safety and efficacy in so many diseases that it is affectionately called "Vitamin R" by clinicians [15].

Ofatumumab

Ofatumumab (marketed as Arzerra in oncology indications) is a second-generation, fully human anti-CD20 mAb. Ofatumumab recognizes a complex epitope spread across both the small and large extracellular loops of CD20 and has a significantly slower off-rate, leading to higher CDC activity as compared to rituximab [16,17].

Surprisingly, ofatumumab does not induce direct apoptosis of tumor cells, unlike rituximab. Additionally, there is no trogocytosis or internalization observed upon ofatumumab binding to CD20 [18,19]. It appears the trade-off of CDC for direct apoptosis was not beneficial across oncology indications as the clinical performance of Arzerra in oncology indications has been disappointing outside of CLL [20]. This has led to Novartis discontinuing the marketing of Arzerra outside the United States in favor of ofatumumab's alter-ego Kesimpta for the treatment of MS.

Obinutuzumab

Obinutuzumab (Gazvya) is a humanized, glycoengineered IgG1 monoclonal antibody against CD20. Obinutuzumab recognizes a unique epitope of CD20 and induces higher levels of direct apoptosis with reduced CD20 internalization as compared to rituximab. Additionally, the lack of fucosylation in the Fc region enhances its binding affinity to FcγRs, leading to enhanced ADCC and ADCP as compared to rituximab. There is a trade-off, however, given where obinutuzumab binds, as CDC is reduced up to 100-fold compared to rituximab [21].

Clinically, higher rates of immune-related responses (IRRs) have been reported with obinutuzumab as compared to rituximab. The increased binding of obinutuzumab for FcγRs leads to stronger FcγR activation that is associated with rapid cytokine release. Although obinutuzumab prolongs progression-free survival in NHL as compared to rituximab, there is no significant difference in overall survival (OS). Taken together, this has led to limited uptake of obinutuzumab vs rituximab in clinical practice.

Type I and Type II antibodies

An early observation of anti-CD20 mAbs is that a subset can cause the CD20 protein to redistribute on the surface of B cells, forming lipid rafts [22]. This served as an early way to classify anti-CD20 mAbs into either Type I or Type II [23,24]. Rituximab and ofatumumab are examples of Type I mAbs that bind to CD20 and cause mobilization into lipid rafts. Obinutuzumab in contrast doesn't cause redistribution and is an example of a type II antibody [25].

The formation of CD20-containing lipid rafts has functional implications. Based on structural analyses of type I and type II mAbs in complex with CD20, type I binders allow for additional mAbs to bind to oligomeric CD20 structures [25,26]. In contrast, type II binders appear to bind and span the extracellular loops of CD20, thus preventing additional molecules from binding to the target [27]. All anti-CD20 mAbs used in the clinic to date have been IgG1 antibodies. Although both type I and type II anti-CD20 mAbs can induce ADCC and ADCP effector functions, type I mAbs also exhibit higher CDC based on the clustering of the target protein, while type II mAbs produce higher levels of direct apoptosis [25,28]. The clustering of CD20 within lipid rafts causes an increased rate of CD20 internalization resulting in a reduction in surface CD20 expression, known as antigenic modulation, which is an important mechanism of resistance to anti-CD20 mAb treatment [29]. Type II antibodies such as obinutuzumab do not lead to significant CD20 internalization.

Because of the high frequency of rituximab-resistant B-cell lymphomas, novel biologic therapeutics against the CD20 target are being tested clinically, including chimeric antigen receptor T cells (CAR-Ts), antibody-drug conjugates (ADCs), and bispecific antibodies (BsAb) to improve clinical outcomes. But for these modalities to be successful, the mechanisms of resistance to CD20-targeted antibodies should be understood.

Resistance to anti-CD20 antibodies

Rituximab's clinical performance has revolutionized the treatment of NHL. However, similar to most therapeutic mAbs used in oncology, rituximab's effectiveness wanes over time. Most NHL patients will eventually relapse, and only 40% of patients who initially respond to rituximab subsequently respond with retreatment [30,31]. There are multiple paths to rituximab resistance that impact its key mechanisms of action including insufficient CDC activity due to increased expression of complement regulatory proteins such as CD55, CD59, or factor H [32,33], reduced ADCC in patients expressing the low-affinity polymorphism of FcγRIIIa, 158F, on natural killer (NK) cells [34], exhaustion of effector function components (NK cells, macrophages, or complement) [35,36], a polymorphism in complement component 1q (C1q) (276G) that reduces CDC activity [37], or abnormal composition and distribution of lipid rafts with a concomitant reduction in direct apoptosis [38].

Additionally, trogocytosis, essentially "shaving" CD20 off the cell membrane, can be caused by macrophages that bind to rituximab/CD20 complexes on the cell surface. Instead of phagocytosing the cells, the macrophages nibble the piece of the membrane containing the complexes to sample it for the immune system [35,39]. This results in antigen loss and effectively makes the cancer cells "immune" to anti-CD20 therapy.

However, the most common cause of resistance to anti-CD20 monoclonal antibodies is reduced cell-surface CD20 expression. As previously noted, type I antibodies that induce clustering of CD20 into lipid rafts can also cause increased internalization of the target, but there are upstream mechanisms that reduce CD20 expression including (de)regulation of transcriptional, posttranscriptional, or posttranslational mechanisms that have also been implicated [40]. Many of these resistance mechanisms are inherent in the biology of CD20 and are challenging to overcome, even with new approaches that require reduced target expression for their activity. But other resistance mechanisms, particularly the loss or reduction in effector cells, can be bypassed through bispecific or CAR-T therapies that don't rely on effector function to deliver efficacy.

Other mechanisms of resistance are specific to nononcology indications, such as rheumatoid arthritis (RA), granulomatosis with polyangiitis (GPA), microscopic polyangiitis (MPA), and pemphigus vulgaris (PV), where rituximab is also approved [41]. The primary mechanism of resistance in autoimmune indications is immunogenicity, and the development of neutralizing antidrug antibodies (ADAs). Neutralizing ADAs block the activity of rituximab, reducing its efficacy by lowering the free concentration of the drug. They also have the potential to cause serious adverse events through the formation of immune complexes that can cause secondary inflammation, particularly in the kidney.

Although rituximab has demonstrated clinical efficacy in other autoimmune conditions, such as multiple sclerosis (MS), it is not approved in those indications, although it is commonly used off-label to treat both primary progressive and relapsing-remitting patients. Ocrelizumab, a humanized anti-CD20 antibody is, however, approved for use in both forms of MS [42,43]. Ocrelizumab's development for autoimmune indications was in part due to the high frequency of ADAs and concomitant loss of efficacy observed with rituximab's use in RA patients [44]. Ofatumumab, a fully human monoclonal antibody to CD20 marketed under the brand name Kesimpta, is also approved for MS using a subcutaneous self-injection presentation [45]. These next-generation CD20 antibodies are providing a new level of efficacy in autoimmune conditions, in large part because they avoid the most common resistance mechanism in autoimmune conditions.

Anti-CD20 antibodies and biology summary

As we look to the future of anti-CD20 therapies, it is clear that different mechanisms dominate efficacy in different indications. Attempts to improve the performance of rituximab by enhancing some mechanisms (e.g., ADCC or CDC) at the expense of others have met with limited success. This is likely due to immune effector deficiencies (e.g., NK cells or complement) in some forms of lymphoma such as CLL, limiting the efficacy of monoclonal antibody approaches [46,47]. Of the additional modalities being developed, cell therapies and bispecific antibodies would be expected to be immune to the predominant resistance mechanisms observed in oncology indications as neither approach relies on effector functions. Additionally, such modalities have relatively reduced requirements for target expression to generate efficacy. A key challenge for these modalities is the optimization of affinities between multiple targets required for their mechanisms of action. A prerequisite for such a balancing act is to use the best available binding affinity techniques to achieve a product profile with the best chance of clinical success. The development of mosunetuzumab, a bispecific CD20-directed CD3 T-cell engager, and its recent FDA accelerated approval for the treatment of relapsed or refractory FL, is an excellent example of incorporating lessons learned in bispecific design to create a clinically successful molecule.

An example highlighting the importance of choosing the appropriate method for affinity determination has recently been published for the CD20 target and rituximab [47]. Classical methods using flow cytometry failed to provide an accurate affinity measurement for rituximab, underestimating its affinity by 25-fold, contributing to wasted attempts to improve the affinity of second- and third-generation monoclonal antibodies in the hopes of producing better efficacy. Hopefully, developers of novel anti-CD20 therapies will take the lessons learned from monoclonal antibody therapies to CD20 into account to improve their chances of clinical success.

Binding characterization technologies

Surface plasmon resonance

Surface plasmon resonance (SPR) is an optical technique used for the characterization of molecular interactions. The binding of a free partner in solution to an immobilized partner on a dextrin-coated thin gold film changes the refractive index of the liquid layer contacting the film. This change is exploited in the SPR assay. Polarized light is directed at the gold film to which one binding partner is attached. A solution containing the second binding partner then flows over the film. As the binding of the mobile partner occurs, mass accumulates on the surface of the film. This changes the extinction angle of the light reflecting off of the film. This alteration is monitored as a decrease in the intensity of the reflected light. These alterations are used to measure the association phase of the interactions and subsequently the dissociation phase. These data are used to determine the kinetic rate constants (k_a,k_d) and the maximum response (Rmax). K_d is then calculated as k_d/k_a.

Flow cytometry

A method for the characterization of cell-surface receptors is flow cytometry. These instruments are capable of generating an apparent K_d value for interaction between cells or beads coated with a protein and a binding partner in the solution. In this technique, the cells or beads are kept at a constant concentration (density), and the soluble binding partner is titrated in a dilution series. A constant number of cells are then incubated with the diluted binding partner samples, rinsed, and exposed to a fluorescently labeled secondary antibody unless the binding partner is directly labeled itself. The overall fluorescence intensity in each sample corresponds to the amount of binding partner captured by the cells. Fitting the antibody-target binding isotherm as a function of total antibody concentrations in titration to a nonlinear regression model can produce an apparent K_d value for the interaction.

KinExA

The KinExA instrument works by using a highly sensitive fluorometer that measures the fluorescence output from a capillary flow cell. The flow cell contains a retaining screen that allows for functionalized beads to be held in place while solutions flow over them. Replacement of the solid-phase column occurs automatically after each sample.

An experiment prepared for KinExA consists of a dilution series in which one binding partner is held at a constant concentration in solution, while the other is serially diluted to achieve a range of full to zero inhibition of the constant binding partner. In KinExA parlance, the binding partner kept constant is the constant binding partner (CBP), and the second agent is referred to as the titrant. These terms are generic as they define the role each molecule will play in the experiment. Molecules can switch roles as necessary for convenience and assay optimization. For example, more precious molecules should be used in the role of CBP as this role requires the least material in the assay setup [48,49]. The samples containing both binding partners are incubated and allowed to come to equilibrium. When equilibrium is reached, the samples flow over titrant-coated beads that serve to capture a fraction of the CBP not already bound in solution (Figs. 1 and 2). Contact time with the capture phase is intentionally short, typically around 0.5 s. For nanomolar and tighter binders, this short contact time prevents significant dissociation of CBP-titrant complexes that might otherwise contribute to the captured fraction on the titrant-coated beads. This method, which kinetically excludes

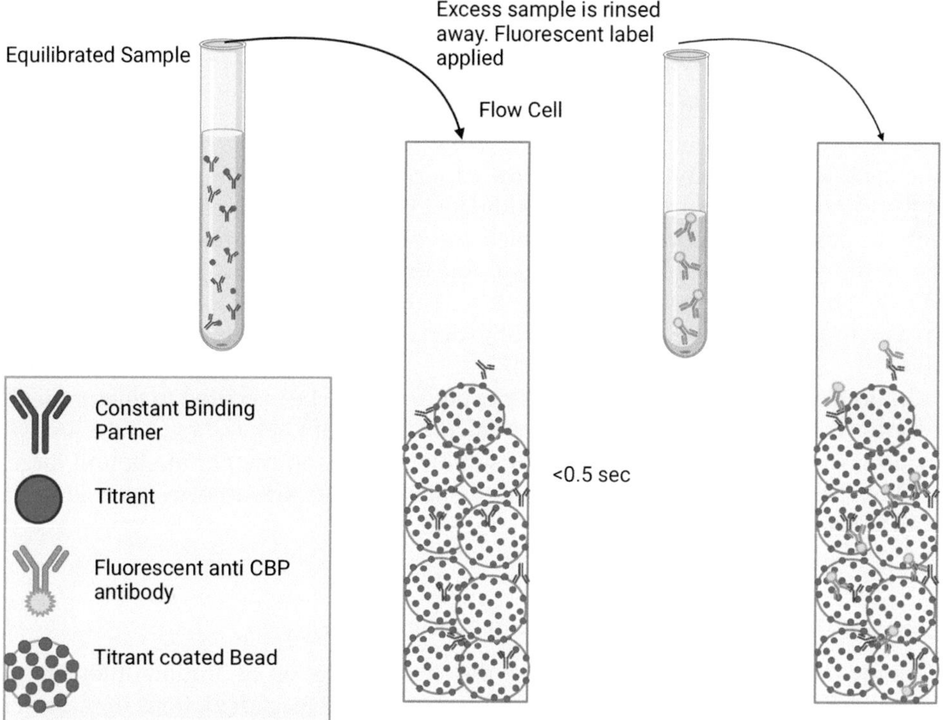

FIG. 1 Forward KinExA assay format. *Created with Biorender.*

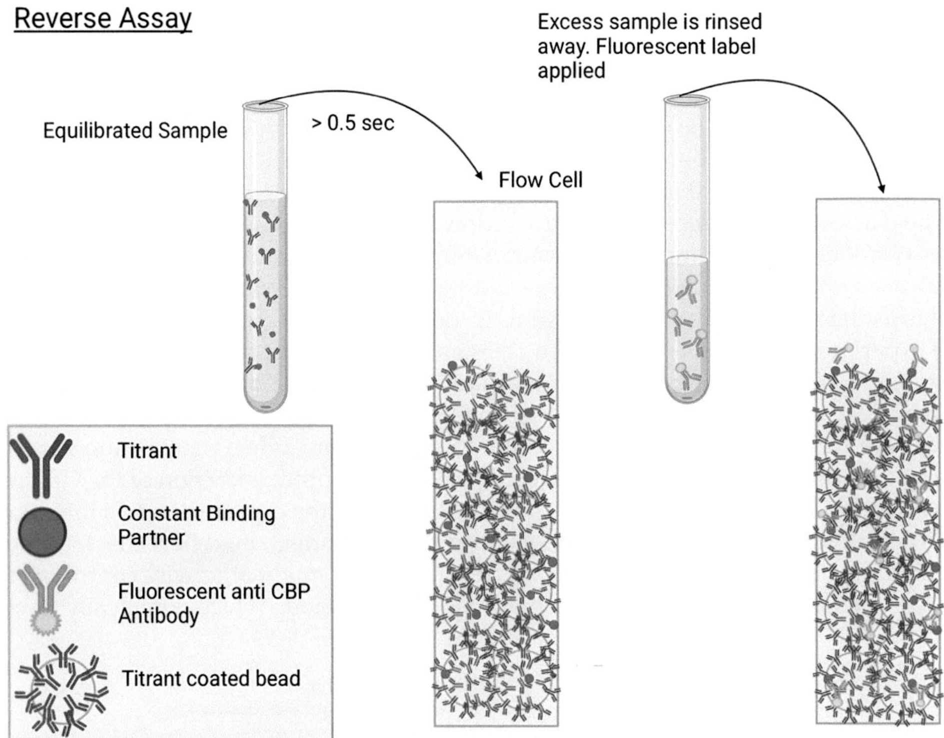

FIG. 2 Reverse KinExA assay formats. *Created with Biorender.*

solution complexes from contributing to the captured CBP, is where the technique gets its name, KinExA being a contraction of the kinetic exclusion assay, see KinExA mode below for more discussion. A fluorescently labeled secondary antibody that binds the CBP then flows over the column. The result is a measurable fluorescence signal proportional to the unbound CBP present in the equilibrated mixture. The titrant-coated beads in this assay serve only as a method of detection and the K_d value derived reflects the unmodified interaction in solution.

In addition to K_d determination, a kinetic experiment can be executed to determine the k_{on} using KinExA. This allows for the k_{off} to be calculated using $k_{off}=K_d*k_{on}$. KinExA assay can also be used to characterize the binding of soluble proteins to membrane-bound targets on intact whole cells [50,51]. For these measurements, the cells are used in the role of titrant, see more below.

Comparison of binding characterization technologies

SPR is the most widely used method for the characterization of binding interactions. An advantage of SPR is that because this method exclusively detects deviations in mass, it eliminates the need to label one of the interacting partners. On the other hand, direct immobilization of one partner to the dextran gold film may alter the conformation of the protein and make it difficult for binding to the protein to be characterized in its native conformation [52]. The kinetic exclusion assay is able to reduce the need for immobilization of one partner to a probe used only to assay the concentration of free CBP in an equilibrated solution. Similarly, the use of a secondary label occurs only after the free fraction has been captured. Neither of these can interfere with the soluble or membrane binding that precedes them resulting in a near-native state characterization. In addition, SPR monitors association and dissociation phases in real time to determine the analyte concentration-dependent on-rates (k_{on}, k_a) and the concentration-independent off-rates (k_{off}, k_d) of interactions. The K_d values are ratios of the off-rates divided by the on-rates [53]. In the case of an interaction with a very slow k_{off}, it takes a long running time in the dissociation phase to observe >5% decrease of the signal, which is required for reliable determination of the off-rates, and subsequently to derive k_{on} and K_d values. KinExA directly measures K_d and k_{on} and from these values calculates the k_{off}. Interactions that have very slow dissociation rates, can easily be measured with KinExA, without having to monitor during what may still be a lengthy incubation time. Additionally, while the kinetic exclusion assay can be adapted for cellular receptors, SPR is not suitable for use with intact cells though there have been reports using detergent-solubilized membranes [54] and membrane mimetics [55,56].

Flow cytometry provides information about the antibody-receptor complex (antibody bound to cells) and the apparent equilibrium dissociation constant (K_d) is elucidated by fitting the antibody-receptor binding isotherm as a function of total antibody concentration to a nonlinear regression model. The CBP in flow cytometry experiments is always the cells and cell-binding ligand, frequently an antibody, is titrated. Ligand depletion [57] limits the practical application of flow cytometry for K_d measurement to roughly nM and weaker binders. Attempts have been made to circumvent this limitation, in particular it is recognized that either low expression levels or low cell densities are conducive to reducing the effect of ligand depletion [58]. Since there is a minimum number of cells required for statistical accuracy (usually a few thousand), the cell density is decreased by increasing the reaction volume which for low pM binders can result in impractically long experiments to achieve a sufficient number of counted cells. On the other hand, low expression levels may lead to problems differentiating between ligand concentrations. Attempts have also been made to account for ligand depletion mathematically [58] though they seem not to be widely adopted. In a KinExA cell or membrane assay the cells, or cell membrane fragments, are titrated and the cell-binding ligand is the CBP. Here, K_d is determined by measuring the free CBP concentration at equilibrium in a series of solutions of varying cell/membrane concentrations. KinExA is not subject to ligand depletion effects and is routinely used for pM and sub-pM binders. The anti-CD20 antibody, rituximab, was initially measured using flow cytometry but when recently investigated using KinExA, a 25-fold tighter binding affinity was measured. The difference is attributed to the well-known sensitivity limitation of flow cytometry in K_d measurement [47].

In comparison with flow cytometry and SPR, the KinExA technology is a superior choice for accurate K_d value determination in terms of its versatility and sensitivity, especially for very strong interactions. However, it is important to consider the pros and cons of each instrument when conducting measurements. While KinExA is undoubtedly more sensitive, it is not high throughput. SPR on the other hand in most cases can complete measurements in a relatively short time frame. The recently developed Biacore 8K+ can process >200 single-cycle kinetics in a day. In the instance that a large antibody library needs to be characterized, the two instruments are often used in tandem to expedite the process of finding the tightest interaction. SPR can be used to quickly weed out the nonbinders, categorize the remaining binders, and then KinExA can be used to accurately measure the tightest interactions.

Important controls for analytical validity in KinExA experiments

KinExA mode

In a kinetic exclusion assay, it is important that the period of time in which each increment of the sample comes into contact with the solid phase be short enough that competition between the solid phase and soluble titrant does not significantly contribute to the measured binding signal. When this condition is met, the experiment is said to be in KinExA mode. In the case of faster on-rates and, especially, binders weaker than nM, significant competition *can* occur between the bound soluble complexes and the solid phase. When the system is not in KinExA mode, the percent free CBP will be artificially increased by the additional CBP captured from the dissociated complex during the sample/beads contact time. When analyzed, this overestimation of the free CBP results in an artifactually weaker K_d value. In order to test for this, we capitalize on the variability in measured percent free CBP as a function of flow rate. Higher flow rates reduce the contact time with the beads and shift the experiment toward the KinExA mode. Simply increasing the flow rate until the percent free stops decreasing yields the KinExA mode flow rate that should be implemented for the system being studied.

Linearity

As previously stated, in KinExA, the signals are generated by flowing soluble CBP across a solid phase with immobilized titrant. The CBP is continuously replenished as the solution proceeds through the flow cell, which keeps it at a constant concentration. The immobilized titrant is finite and thus subject to saturation with CBP for long enough flows or high enough CBP concentrations. This situation results in a hyperbolic binding response as shown by the solid line in Fig. 3. KinExA analysis software operates under the assumption that the measured voltage output is directly proportional to the concentration of unbound CBP binding sites in the solution. This direct proportionality is approximately true for only a range of concentrations. This means there is a workable linear range under which the K_d value determination is not subject to significant error. Defining this workable range can be done with a linearity test. Sapidyne recommends that this test be conducted in the event that the signals produced in preliminary testing do not change proportionally to concentrations of CBP. The linear range test consists of generating a five-point titration curve of the CBP including points at 4, 2, 1, 0.5, and 0 times the desired operating concentration. The KinExA Pro software supplied with KinExA instruments will calculate the hyperbolic concentration of the half-maximum signal. Sapidyne's recommendation is that the CBP concentration be less than or equal to 20% of the concentration of the half-maximum signal. Fig. 2 illustrates the

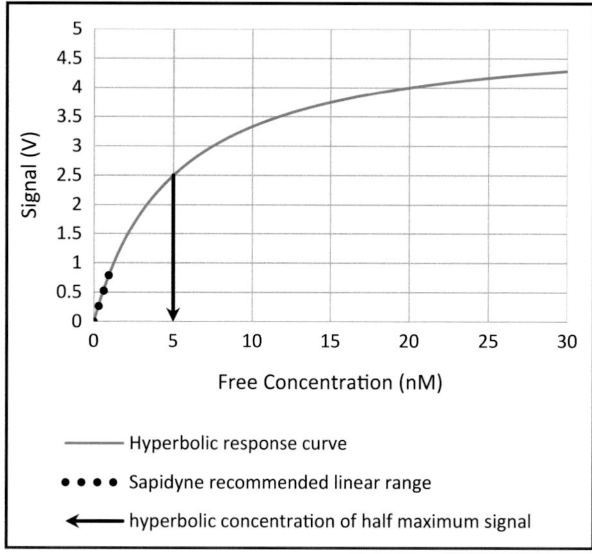

FIG. 3 The maximum recommended CBP concentration for linear operation is 0.2 times the concentration of half-maximum signal.

recommended range. In practice adjusting the CBP concentration and/or sample volume to give a signal less than 2 V nearly always ensures a sufficiently linear response using the supplied red filter set in the instrument.

Capture percentage

The most common measurement conducted on a KinExA instrument is between a bivalent antibody in the role of CBP and a monovalent ligand as the titrant. A potential issue is that a bivalent antibody captured by the solid phase will contribute to the voltage output the same whether its second binding site is occupied by a soluble titrant molecule or not. This could skew the measurement of the unbound fraction of binding sites. However, as has been published previously [59,60], with low capture percentages, as are typical in KinExA experiments, the probability of capture by the solid phase is affected by the number of free binding sites on a multivalent CBP, and a double unbound CBP molecule has approximately twice the chance of capture as a single bound CBP. Thus, with an overall capture percentage of less than 20%, the error produced by valencies over one is insignificant and the signal accurately represents the free binding sites in solution (Fig. 4).

$$\text{Capture fraction} \approx 1 - \sqrt{\text{Double bead packs signal/Normal bead packs signal}} \quad (1)$$

The capture percentage for a specific system can be easily measured. Within the solid-phase column, the signal level decays exponentially with distance from the top of the bead column, and measuring the signal at two different positions in the bead pack directly shows the decay. Two signals are measured keeping all experimental conditions the same except the bead pack height is doubled for one. Eq. (1) is then used to obtain the capture percentage for the system (Eq. (1) taken from Sapidyne Instruments HTG 250 used with permission).

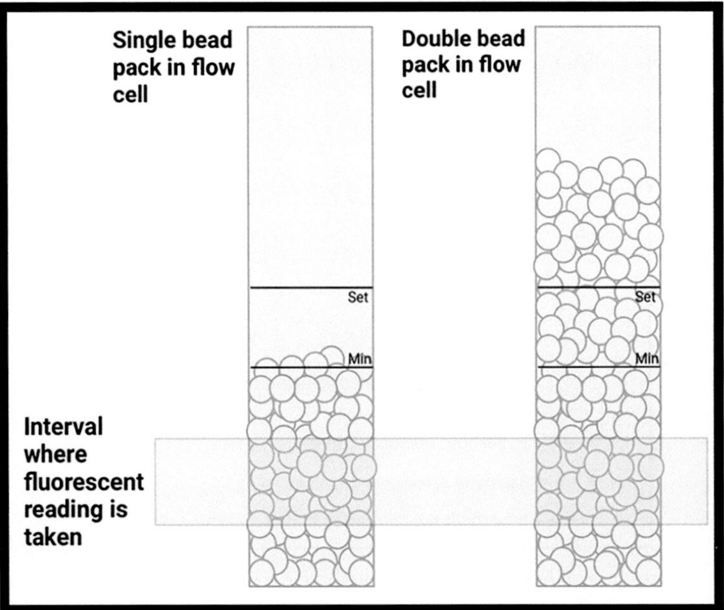

FIG. 4 Single vs double bead pack. *Created with Biorender.*

Analysis of soluble protein targets

When analyzing an experiment with KinExA software, users must report the nominal concentrations (in molar binding sites) of each binding partner and specify whether the CBP or titrant is to be used as the reference concentration, while the other concentration is floated in the analysis. The signals generated from the captured CBP in each sample are recorded as voltages from the fluorimeter. The resulting equilibrium curves (voltage vs titrant concentration) are fit with Eq. (2) by varying the Sig100 (signal from a sample with zero titrant), NSB, K_d, and the floated concentration. A more detailed description of the math behind the KinExA analysis can be found elsewhere [60,61].

$$\text{Signal} = \frac{(\text{Sig100} - \text{NSB})}{[\text{CBP}]}\left[\frac{([\text{CBP}] - [\text{titrant}] - K_d) + \left([\text{Titrant}]t^2 + [\text{CBP}]^2 + K_d^2 - 2([\text{CBP}])([\text{Titrant}]) + 2(K_d)([\text{Titrant}]) + 2(K_d)([\text{CBP}])\right)^{\frac{1}{2}}}{2}\right] + \text{NSB} \quad (2)$$

The reason one concentration is referenced while the other is floated is that the accuracy of K_d value is tied to the accuracy of the reported concentrations of the binding partners. In many

	K_d (pM)	Activity (%)	Residual Error	Factor change in K_d
Titrant Specified	2.47	CBP= 28.6%	1.37%	Assumed Correct
CBP Specified	8.64	Titrant= 350%	1.37%	3.5
Both specified	0.08	Both Assumed 100%	15%	30.8

FIG. 5 K_d error when one or both binding partners are specified for the analysis. ©*Sapidyne Instruments Inc. used by permission.*

cases, the active concentration can differ substantially from the nominal concentration which is usually determined through UV absorbance at 280 nm (A280). In choosing a reference molecule and calculating the other's activity, the accuracy of K_d value becomes tied to the accuracy of only the reference molecules reported concentration instead of the concentration of both binding partners. This can significantly reduce the overall error in the K_d value calculation as seen in Fig. 5. Once the values corresponding to the optimum fit are identified, the activity of the floated concentration is calculated as the optimum concentration divided by the nominal concentration (as reported by the user). For example, if the reported CBP concentration is 100 pM, but the best fit active concentration is 75 pM, the CBP molecule is reported as 75% active. Looking at the reported activity and deciding if it is plausible can help when deciding which molecule to use as the reference. An activity of over 100% is unlikely to be true as this implies that the active binding concentrations exceed the total protein concentration previously measured. In this case, it would be reasonable to switch the reference concentration and reanalyze. Any error in the reference concentration will introduce a proportional error in K_d values.

KinExA best practice calls for at least two curves with differing CBP concentrations to be run and analyzed together using a multicurve analysis tool. An experiment prepared at a CBP concentration at or near K_d value will exhibit K_d-controlled binding, resulting in a shallow curve, whose position and shape are highly sensitive to K_d values. Experiments prepared at sufficiently high concentrations of CBP produce a steep curve in which the shape and position are highly dependent on the active CBP concentration and provide accurate information about the activity of one of the binding partners. Running one of each of these curves will produce optimal data. When analyzing two or more curves together, the spacing between the two curves, with respect to their reported CBP and titrant concentrations, can improve confidence in the K_d value determination and can also give an indication of nonstandard (i.e., not 1 to 1) binding. For example, in the case of cooperativity, the fit discrepancy produced by cooperative binding will be elucidated in a multicurve analysis. Positive cooperative binding causes the data to be steeper, while negative cooperativity results in a flatter curve. When analyzing only a single curve, either can be mistaken for a concentration error which can produce similar results. In Fig. 6, the data from positively cooperative molecules are shown. Here, the data points on the low curve are steeper than the standard binding theory allows, pointing to positive cooperativity. In Fig. 7, the same data are analyzed using KinExA

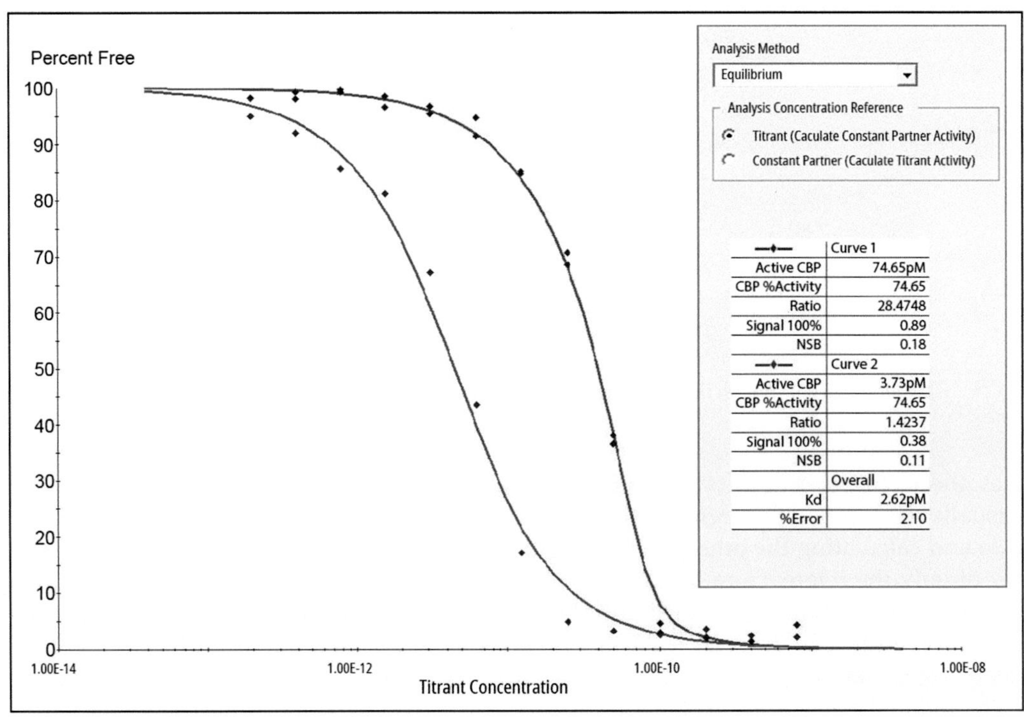

FIG. 6 Data analyzed with noncooperative analysis. ©*Sapidyne Instruments Inc. used by permission.*

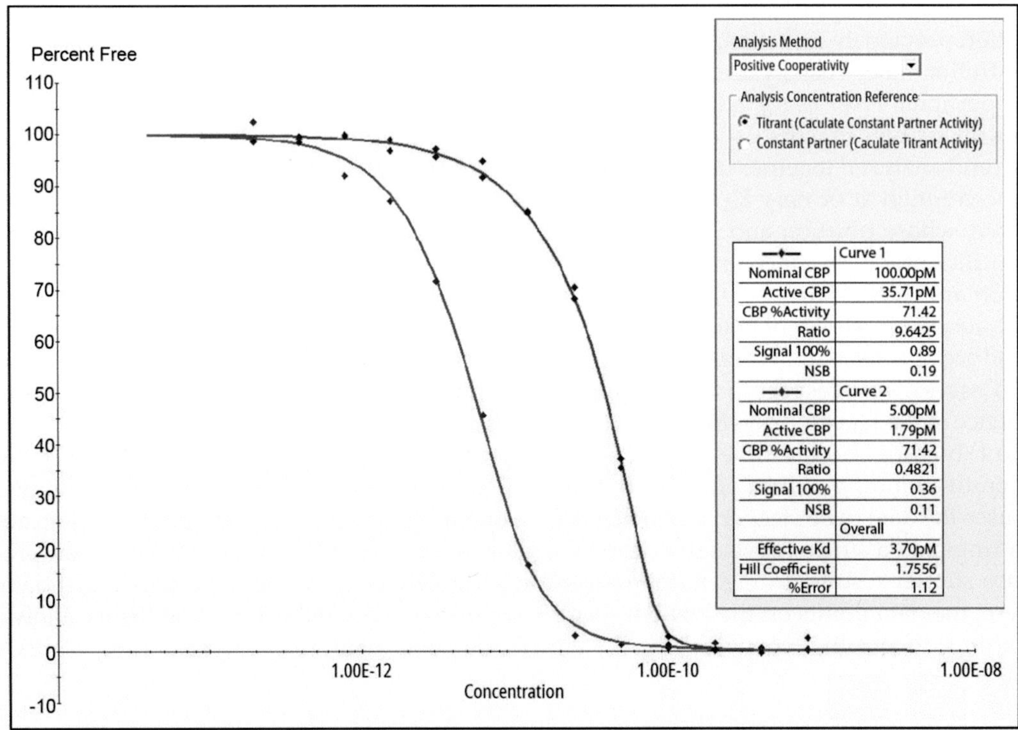

FIG. 7 Same data analyzed using cooperative analysis. ©*Sapidyne Instruments Inc. used by permission.*

cooperativity analysis, which reports a Hill coefficient of 1.7 (strong positive cooperativity), and the theoretical curve and the data points are now in significantly better agreement.

To measure the association rate, solutions containing a constant concentration of each binding partner are mixed at a recorded time and placed on the instrument for sampling. As the reaction approaches equilibrium, the instrument draws samples from the mixed binding partners. Over time, the signal will decrease as the free CBP in the solution is bound by the titrant. When equilibrium is reached, the signal will become constant, and the experiment can be stopped. This directly records the association rate of the binding partners. Using these data with K_d value from equilibrium experiments allows the calculation of the off-rate. In normal use, the KinExA platform routinely measures the equilibrium K_d value, the on-rate value, and the active concentration of either the CBP or titrant molecule relative to the other.

Analysis of integral membrane protein targets

Binding analysis using whole cells and antispecies antibody-coated beads

In addition to measuring soluble protein targets, it is critical to develop robust and reliable methods to study binding kinetics and equilibrium of therapeutic candidates to protein targets resident or associated with the cell membrane. Membrane and whole-cell assay preparation is similar to a soluble measurement but differs in that neither cells nor membrane fragments can pass through the KinExA instrument due to clogging. Because KinExA analysis relies solely on the signal generated from unbound CBP in solution, cells and membrane fragments can be incorporated into the KinExA assay as the titrated partner and then removed from the solution prior to sampling on the instrument. Removal of the cells from the solution is simple. Once the assay has been prepared and the interaction has come to equilibrium, the samples are spun down and the supernatant collected. The pellet contains the cells or membranes along with the bound fraction of the CBP, while the supernatant contains only the free CBP. The supernatant samples can then be run on the KinExA instrument (Fig. 8).

The whole-cell analysis differs from soluble systems in that the samples being run through the instrument no longer contain mixtures of single and double-free CBP but instead contain solely double-free molecules. The whole cell analysis algorithm is modified to account for this difference. Similarly, the KinExA analysis requires that the concentration of at least one binding partner be specified and used as the reference. When the soluble binding partner is used as the reference, the KinExA Pro software will report an expression level (binding epitopes/cell) for the membrane-bound binding partner. If the user has more confidence in the expression level, it can be used as the reference and the activity of the soluble target calculated.

Binding analysis using cell membrane and antispecies antibody-coated beads

In Vaish et al. [47], a modified version of the whole-cell assay analysis was used to determine the K_d value of rituximab. A common issue found with cell measurements is the difference in cell receptor expression after multiple passages. Vaish and coauthors found that after

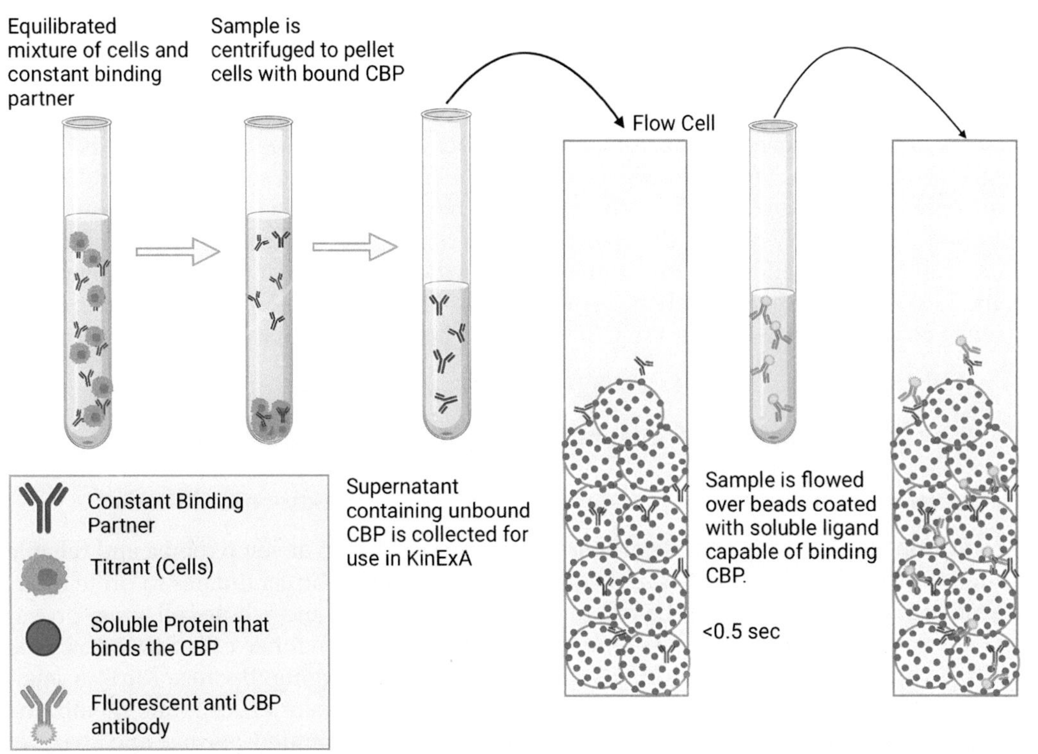

FIG. 8 Whole cell assay technique. Cells are incubated with target, then centrifuged. Supernatant is removed and sampled on KinExA. *Created with BioRender.*

six passages, cell viability remained at 91% but CD20 expression on the WIL-2 cells dropped to 50% [47]. To mitigate this issue, several large-scale cell cultures were prepared, and cell receptor expression levels were determined by flow cytometry. Each culture was frozen at −80 °C and a total of four large culture batches were accumulated. The four cultures were then thawed, combined and processed into a large batch of cellular fragments, which were then aliquoted and frozen at −80 °C. Usage of the same batch of the cell membrane allowed for the standardization of measurement protocols simplifying repeated K_d measurements and comparisons across molecules and across the time span of therapeutic development.

During experiment preparation, automated dilution series of the membranes was performed in a background of the rituximab antibody in the role of CBP. Four different CBP concentrations were used to exploit the advantages of the multicurve analysis. Fig. 9 illustrates major steps to automatically set up the sample preparation, including pipetting antibody solutions with specific concentrations to each well and serial dilution of the membrane in the 24-well deep-well plates. After incubation, the samples were centrifuged to pellet the membranes. The supernatant was then transferred to a 24-well-filtering plate on top of a collection plate that was subsequently centrifuged to collect the filtered solutions [46].

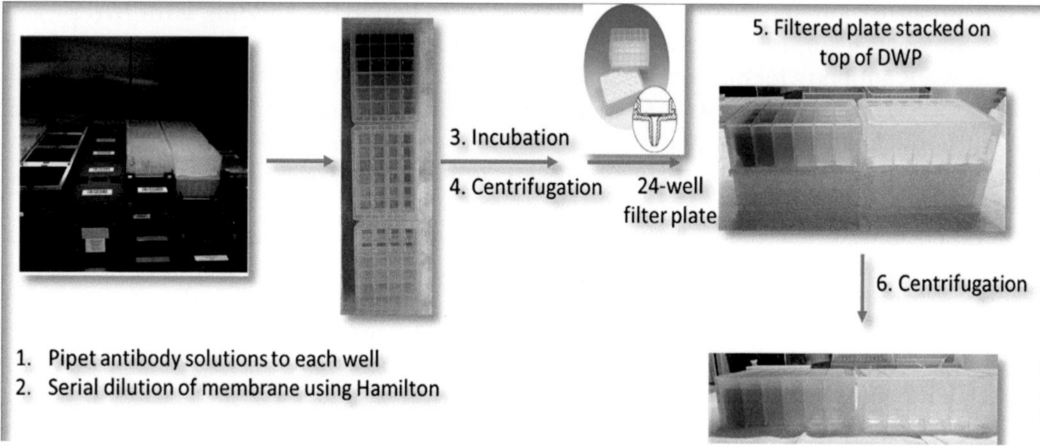

FIG. 9 Model rituximab to CD20 cell membrane experiment preparation using blue dye.

The resulting samples containing the unbound fraction of rituximab could then be used in the KinExA whole-cell analysis with the caveat that the reported expression level is now interpreted as receptors per milligram of the membrane in solution rather than molecules per cell. The binding affinity of rituximab to membrane-bound CD20 was measured as 79 pM (95% CI: 50–115 pM) [47], indicating the strong interaction between rituximab and membrane-bound CD20.

Determination of the free CBP concentration in the binding of soluble and membrane protein targets

The KinExA assay requires accurate determination of free CBP concentration as a percentage of the total CBP in solution. The voltages recorded from the fluorometer are signals generated from the fluorescently labeled secondary antibodies that bind to bead-captured free CBP in each sample. There are several options to capture the free CBP for binding analysis of soluble and integral membrane protein (IMP) targets. Table 1 summarizes several pairs of protein-coupled beads and corresponding fluorescently labeled secondary antibodies used

TABLE 1 Assay format comparison.

	Antigen coupled beads	Antibody coupled beads	Anti-Fc coupled beads
Soluble protein	Xie et al. [51], Rathanaswami et al. [48], and Bee et al. [49]	Rathanaswami et al. [48] and Bee et al. [49]	
Membrane protein	Rathanaswami et al. [50] and Xie et al. [51] (ECD coupling)		Rathanaswami et al. [50] and Vaish et al. [47]
Fluorescently labeled secondary antibody	Antispecies IgG antibody	Antibody to a different epitope on the same antigen	Antispecies IgG antibody

in the literature. Rathanaswami et al. compared three antibodies binding with two protein targets on the cell surface using anti-huFc and TNFa-coupled beads [50]. Xie et al. compared an anti-IGFR antibody for binding with soluble IGFR and IGFR on cell surfaces using soluble IGFR coupled beads [51]. Vaish et al. reported K_d value determination of rituximab for binding with CD20 in the cell membrane using anti-huFc-coupled beads [47]. Rathanaswami et al. and Bee et al. described a comparison of antigen-coupled beads vs antibody-coupled beads in the study of soluble protein interactions [48,49].

In practice, we often consider reagent and sample quality and quantity, as well as operational efficiency when choosing the pair of protein-coupled beads and fluorescently labeled secondary antibodies. This is especially important when determining the K_d values of engineered antibodies with low expression of IMP in the membrane. In a recent study of integral membrane target binding with a peptide-conjugated antibody, we observed a much lower fluorescent signal than the parental antibody using anti-huFc-coupled beads and Alexa 647 labeled anti-huIgG antibody. Knowing the antibody sample has a stronger binding affinity with the protein target than anti-huFc, we attempted to capture the free antibody with the extracellular domain (ECD) of the IMP target and quantify the captured antibody using the same Alexa 647 labeled anti-huIgG antibody. We observed ~3× fluorescent signal increase for the parental antibody and ~10× increase for the peptide-conjugated antibody. The increase in fluorescent signal allowed us to use a smaller volume of samples in incubation with IMP membrane, of which we had a very limited quantity.

Conclusions

While anti-CD20 antibodies have demonstrated success in treating B-cell malignancies, a large percentage of patients develop resistance to these drugs over time. Multiple resistance mechanisms have been identified, including reduced CD20 expression on the cancer cell surface directly reducing the binding of anti-CD20 antibodies. Encouraged by successful cancer treatments using chimeric antigen receptor (CAR) T cells targeting CD19, global clinical trials are in progress for CAR-T therapies targeting CD20 alone or in combination with CD19 and CD22 [62,63]. Biopharmaceutical companies have also engaged in the development of bispecific immunomodulatory molecules to overcome the resistance to anti-CD20 therapy in lymphomas [64]. In addition to the FDA-approved anti-CD20/CD3 bispecific, mosunetuzumab (Roche), other bispecific molecules with different formats are being studied clinically. Genmab and AbbVie have studied epcoritamab in patients with relapsed, progressive, or refractory B-cell lymphoma, Xencor had a trial of plamotamab in NHL patients, Genentech developed glofitamab for patients with relapsed or refractory DLBCL, and Regeneron reported their evaluation of odronextamab in two trials at the American Society of Hematology Annual Meeting 2022.

When considering approaches to overcome rituximab drug resistance, it is critical to obtain the best possible information on the cause of resistance and how the new approach will avoid the pitfalls of previous attempts to improve monoclonal antibody approaches. In the case of membrane proteins such as CD20 and bispecific and CAR-T approaches, we strongly believe the best practice for binding and affinity measurements requires the use of membrane-bound CD20. Even so, binding is only one piece of the puzzle and the goal of improving drug performance is inextricably tied to the goal of better understanding of CD20 biology and the various mechanisms of drugs acting on it.

Binding characterization technology is constantly evolving and improving. With more multispecific molecules generated, we can expect to see continued advancements in the specific measurement and characterization of these molecules both in solution and on cell surfaces. Integration of NanoPen assays [65] in the Beacon Systems (https://www.berkeleylights.com/publications-category/beacon-system/) with machine learning algorithms is one of several promising approaches that will provide new insights in protein/protein interactions in the years to come.

References

[1] Oettgen HC, Bayard PJ, Van Ewijk W, Nadler LM, Terhorst CP. Further biochemical studies of the human B-cell differentiation antigens B1 and B2. Hybridoma 1983;2(1):17–28.

[2] Beers SA, Chan CHT, French RR, Cragg MS, Glennie MJ. CD20 as a target for therapeutic type I and II monoclonal antibodies. Semin Hematol 2010;47(2):107–14.

[3] Eon Kuek L, Leffler M, Mackay GA, Hulett MD. The MS4A family: counting past 1, 2 and 3. Immunol Cell Biol 2016;94(1):11–23.

[4] Tedder TF, Schlossman SF. Phosphorylation of the B1 (CD20) molecule by normal and malignant human B lymphocytes. J Biol Chem 1998;263(20):10009–15.

[5] Bubien JK, Zhou LJ, Bell PD, Frizzell RA, Tedder TF. Transfection of the CD20 cell surface molecule into ectopic cell types generates a Ca^{2+} conductance found constitutively in B lymphocytes. J Cell Biol 1993;121(5):1121–32.

[6] Polyak MJ, Li H, Shariat N, Deans JP. CD20 homo-oligomers physically associate with the B cell antigen receptor. Dissociation upon receptor engagement and recruitment of phosphoproteins and calmodulin-binding proteins. J Biol Chem 2008;283(27):18545–52.

[7] Prevodnik VK, Lavrenčak J, Horvat M, Novakovič BJ. The predictive significance of CD20 expression in B-cell lymphomas. Diagn Pathol 2011;6:33.

[8] Olejniczak SH, Stewart CC, Donohue K, Czuczman MS. A quantitative exploration of surface antigen expression in common B-cell malignancies using flow cytometry. Immunol Investig 2006;35(1):93–114.

[9] Xia MQ, Hale G, Waldmann H. Efficient complement-mediated lysis of cells containing the CAMPATH-1 (CDw52) antigen. Mol Immunol 1993;30(12):1089–96.

[10] Cleary KLS, Chan HTC, James S, Glennie MJ, Cragg MS. Antibody distance from the cell membrane regulates antibody effector mechanisms. J Immunol 2017;198(10):3999–4011.

[11] Siegel RL, Miller KD, Jemal A. Cancer statistics, 2016. CA Cancer J Clin 2016;66(1):7–30.

[12] Dotan E, Aggarwal C, Smith MR. Impact of rituximab (Rituxan) on the treatment of B-cell non-Hodgkin's lymphoma. P T 2010;35(3):148–57.

[13] Cheson BD, Leonard JP. Monoclonal antibody therapy for B-cell non-Hodgkin's lymphoma. N Engl J Med 2008;359(6):613–26.

[14] Armitage JO, Weisenburger DD. New approach to classifying non-Hodgkin's lymphomas: clinical features of the major histologic subtypes. Non-Hodgkin's Lymphoma Classification Project. J Clin Oncol 1998;16 (8):2780–95.

[15] Mo C, Vire B, Wiestner A. Rituximab: therapeutic benefit! Vitamin R? Semin Hematol 2010;47(2):105–6.

[16] Teeling JL, French RR, Cragg MS, van den Brakel J, Pluyter M, Huang H, Chan C, et al. Characterization of new human CD20 monoclonal antibodies with potent cytolytic activity against non-Hodgkin lymphomas. Blood 2004;104(6):1793–800.

[17] Teeling JL, Mackus WJM, Wiegman LJJM, van den Brakel JHN, Beers SA, French RR, van Meerten T, et al. The biological activity of human CD20 monoclonal antibodies is linked to unique epitopes on CD20. J Immunol 2006;177(1):362–71.

[18] Novartis Pharmaceutical Corporation. Arzerra (ofatumumab) [package insert]. U.S. Food and Drug Administration website. Revised 2016. Accessed January 2023.

[19] Robak T, Robak E. New anti-CD20 monoclonal antibodies for the treatment of B-cell lymphoid malignancies. BioDrugs 2011;25(1):13–25.
[20] Alduaij W, Illidge TM. The future of anti-CD20 monoclonal antibodies: are we making progress? Blood 2011;117(11):2993–3001.
[21] Casan JML, Wong J, Northcott MJ, Opat S. Anti-CD20 monoclonal antibodies: reviewing a revolution. Hum Vaccin Immunother 2018;14(12):2820–41.
[22] Deans JP, Robbins SM, Polyak MJ, Savage JA. Rapid redistribution of CD20 to a low density detergent-insoluble membrane compartment. J Biol Chem 1998;273(1):344–8.
[23] Cragg MS, Glennie MJ. Antibody specificity controls in vivo effector mechanisms of anti-CD20 reagents. Blood 2004;103(7):2738–43.
[24] Lim SH, Beers SA, French RR, Johnson PWM, Glennie MJ, Cragg MS. Anti-CD20 monoclonal antibodies: historical and future perspectives. Haematologica 2010;95(1):135–43.
[25] Oldham RJ, Cleary KLS, Cragg MS. CD20 and its antibodies: past, present, and future. Onco Therapeutics 2014;5(1–2):251–2.
[26] Cragg MS, Morgan SM, Chan HTC, Morgan BP, Filatov AV, Johnson PWM, French RR, et al. Complement-mediated lysis by anti-CD20 mAb correlates with segregation into lipid rafts. Blood 2003;101(3):1045–52.
[27] Niederfellner G, Lammens A, Mundigl O, Georges GJ, Schaefer W, Schwaiger M, Franke A, et al. Epitope characterization and crystal structure of GA101 provide insights into the molecular basis for type I/II distinction of CD20 antibodies. Blood 2011;118(2):358–67.
[28] Chan HTC, Hughes D, French RR, Tutt AL, Walshe CA, Teeling JL, Glennie MJ, et al. CD20-induced lymphoma cell death is independent of both caspases and its redistribution into triton X-100 insoluble membrane rafts. Cancer Res 2003;63(17):5480–9.
[29] Beers SA, French RR, Chan HTC, Lim SH, Jarrett TC, Vidal RM, Wijayaweera SS, et al. Antigenic modulation limits the efficacy of anti-CD20 antibodies: implications for antibody selection. Blood 2010;115(25):5191–201.
[30] Li H, Zhang G, Jiang C, Zhang F, Ke C, Zhao H, Sun Y, et al. Suppression of Rituximab-resistant B-cell lymphoma with a novel multi-component anti-CD20 mAb nanocluster. Oncotarget 2015;6(27):24192–204.
[31] Yang J, Kopeček J. Polymeric biomaterials and nanomedicines. J Drug Deliv Sci Technol 2015;30(Pt B):318–30.
[32] Hörl S, Bánki Z, Huber G, Ejaz A, Windisch D, Muellauer B, Willenbacher E, et al. Reduction of complement factor H binding to CLL cells improves the induction of rituximab-mediated complement-dependent cytotoxicity. Leukemia 2013;27(11):2200–8.
[33] Golay J, Lazzari M, Facchinetti V, Bernasconi S, Borleri G, Barbui T, Rambaldi A, et al. CD20 levels determine the in vitro susceptibility to rituximab and complement of B-cell chronic lymphocytic leukemia: further regulation by CD55 and CD59. Blood 2001;98(12):3383–9.
[34] Ahlgrimm M, Pfreundschuh M, Kreuz M, Regitz E, Preuss K-D, Bittenbring J. The impact of Fc-γ receptor polymorphisms in elderly patients with diffuse large B-cell lymphoma treated with CHOP with or without rituximab. Blood 2011;118(17):4657–62.
[35] Kennedy AD, Beum PV, Solga MD, DiLillo DJ, Lindorfer MA, Hess CE, Densmore JJ, et al. Rituximab infusion promotes rapid complement depletion and acute CD20 loss in chronic lymphocytic leukemia. J Immunol 2004;172(5):3280–8.
[36] Capuano C, Romanelli M, Pighi C, Cimino G, Rago A, Molfetta R, Paolini R, et al. Anti-CD20 therapy acts via FcγRIIIA to diminish responsiveness of human natural killer cells. Cancer Res 2015;75(19):4097–108.
[37] Racila E, Link BK, Weng W-K, Witzig TE, Ansell S, Maurer MJ, Huang J, et al. A polymorphism in the complement component C1qA correlates with prolonged response following rituximab therapy of follicular lymphoma. Clin Cancer Res 2008;14(20):6697–703.
[38] Janas E, Priest R, Wilde JI, White JH, Malhotra R. Rituxan (anti-CD20 antibody)-induced translocation of CD20 into lipid rafts is crucial for calcium influx and apoptosis. Clin Exp Immunol 2005;139(3):439–46.
[39] Williams ME, Densmore JJ, Pawluczkowycz AW, Beum PV, Kennedy AD, Lindorfer MA, Hamil SH, et al. Thrice-weekly low-dose rituximab decreases CD20 loss via shaving and promotes enhanced targeting in chronic lymphocytic leukemia. J Immunol 2006;177(10):7435–43.
[40] Tsai P-C, Hernandez-Ilizaliturri FJ, Bangia N, Olejniczak SH, Czuczman MS. Regulation of CD20 in rituximab-resistant cell lines and B-cell non-Hodgkin lymphoma. Clin Cancer Res 2012;18(4):1039–50.
[41] Rituxan [package insert] Genentech. U.S. Food and Drug Administration website. Revised 2021. Accessed January 2023.
[42] Chisari CG, Sgarlata E, Arena S, Toscano S, Luca M, Patti F. Rituximab for the treatment of multiple sclerosis: a review. J Neurol 2022;269(1):159–83.

[43] Brancati S, Gozzo L, Longo L, Vitale DC, Drago F. Rituximab in multiple sclerosis: are we ready for regulatory approval? Front Immunol 2021;12, 661882.

[44] Einarsson JT, Evert M, Geborek P, Saxne T, Lundgren M, Kapetanovic MC. Rituximab in clinical practice: dosage, drug adherence, Ig levels, infections, and drug antibodies. Clin Rheumatol 2017;36(12):2743–50.

[45] Kesimpta [package insert] Novartis Pharmaceutical Corporation. U.S. Food and Drug Administration website. Revised 2020. Accessed January 2023.

[46] Zent CS, Pinney JJ, Chu CC, Elliott MR. Complement activation in the treatment of B-cell malignancies. Antibodies 2020;9(4):68.

[47] Vaish A, Lin JS, McBride HJ, Grandsard PJ, Chen Q. Binding affinity determination of therapeutic antibodies to membrane protein targets: Kinetic Exclusion Assay using cellular membranes for anti-CD20 antibody. Anal Biochem 2020;609, 113974.

[48] Rathanaswami P, Richmond K, Manchulenko K, Foltz IN. Kinetic analysis of unpurified native antigens available in very low quantities and concentrations. Anal Biochem 2011;414(1):7–13.

[49] Bee C, Abdiche YN, Stone DM, Collier S, Lindquist KC, Pinkerton AC, Pons J, et al. Exploring the dynamic range of the kinetic exclusion assay in characterizing antigen-antibody interactions. PLoS One 2012;7(4), e36261.

[50] Rathanaswami P, Babcook J, Gallo M. High-affinity binding measurements of antibodies to cell-surface-expressed antigens. Anal Biochem 2008;373(1):52–60.

[51] Xie L, Mark Jones R, Glass TR, Navoa R, Wang Y, Grace MJ. Measurement of the functional affinity constant of a monoclonal antibody for cell surface receptors using kinetic exclusion fluorescence immunoassay. J Immunol Methods 2005;304(1–2):1–14.

[52] Drake AW, Tang ML, Papalia GA, Landes G, Haak-Frendscho M, Klakamp SL. Biacore surface matrix effects on the binding kinetics and affinity of an antigen/antibody complex. Anal Biochem 2012;429(1):58–69.

[53] Karlsson R. SPR for molecular interaction analysis: a review of emerging application areas. J Mol Recognit 2004;17(3):151–61.

[54] Navratilova I, Dioszegi M, Myszka DG. Analyzing ligand and small molecule binding activity of solubilized GPCRs using biosensor technology. Anal Biochem 2006;355(1):132–9.

[55] Vaish A, Guo S, Murray RM, Grandsard PJ, Chen Q. On-chip membrane protein cell-free expression enables development of a direct binding assay: a curious case of potassium channel KcsA-Kv1.3. Anal Biochem 2018;556:70–7.

[56] Sharma P, Plant M, Lam SK, Chen Q. Kinetic analysis of antibody binding to integral membrane proteins stabilized in SMALPs. BBA Adv 2021;1, 100022.

[57] Hunter SA, Cochran JR. Cell-binding assays for determining the affinity of protein-protein interactions: technologies and considerations. Methods Enzymol 2016;580:21–44.

[58] Stein RA, Wilkinson JC, Guyer CA, Staros JV. An analytical approach to the measurement of equilibrium binding constants: application to EGF binding to EGF receptors in intact cells measured by flow cytometry. Biochemistry 2001;40(20):6142–54.

[59] Glass TR, Winzor DJ. Confirmation of the validity of the current characterization of immunochemical reactions by kinetic exclusion assay. Anal Biochem 2014;456:38–42.

[60] Ohmura N, Lackie SJ, Saiki H. An immunoassay for small analytes with theoretical detection limits. Anal Chem 2001;73(14):3392–9.

[61] Darling RJ, Brault P-A. Kinetic exclusion assay technology: characterization of molecular interactions. Assay Drug Dev Technol 2004;2(6):647–57.

[62] Tan Su Yin E, Xian Hu Y, Huang H. The breakthrough and the future: CD20 chimeric antigen receptor T-cell therapy for hematologic malignancies. Immunomedicine 2022. Published online October 5, 2022.

[63] MedicineUSNLo.ClinicalTrial.govU.S.NationalLibraryofMedicine; https://clinicaltrials.gov/ct2/results?term=CD20%2BCART&Search=Apply&recrs=a&recrs=e&age_v=&gndr=&type=&rslt=.

[64] Castaneda-Puglianini O, Chavez JC. Bispecific antibodies for non-Hodgkin's lymphomas and multiple myeloma. Drugs Context 2021;10. 2021-2-4.

[65] Cho H, Gonzales-Wartz KK, Huang D, Yuan M, Peterson M, Liang J, Beutler N, Torres JL, Cong Y, Postnikova E, Bangaru S, Talana CA, Shi W, Yang ES, Zhang Y, Leung K, Wang L, Peng L, Skinner J, Li S, Wu NC, Liu H, Dacon C, Moyer T, Cohen M, Zhao M, Lee FE-H, Weinberg RS, Douagi I, Gross R, Schmaljohn C, Pegu A, Mascola JR, Holbrook M, Nemazee D, Rogers TF, Ward AB, Wilson IA, Crompton PD, Tan J. Bispecific antibodies targeting distinct regions of the spike protein potently neutralize SARS-CoV-2 variants of concern. Sci Transl Med 2021;13, eabj5413.

PART III

Therapeutic anti-CD20 antibodies against noncancer diseases

CHAPTER

12

Clinical efficacy of anti-CD20 antibodies in autoimmune diseases

Zeineb Zian[a], *Abubakar Umar Anka*[b], *Hamisu Abdullahi*[c], *Emna Bouallegui*[d], *Shayan Maleknia*[e], *and Gholamreza Azizi*[f,g]

[a]Biomedical Genomics and Oncogenetics Research Laboratory, Faculty of Sciences and Techniques of Tangier, Abdelmalek Essaadi University, Tetouan, Morocco [b]Department of Medical Laboratory Science, College of Medical Sciences, Ahmadu Bello University Zaria, Zaria, Nigeria [c]Department of Immunology, School of Medical Laboratory Sciences, Usmanu Danfodiyo University Sokoto, Sokoto, Nigeria [d]Ministry of public health Qatar MOPH, Doha, Qatar [e]Biopharmaceutical Research Center, AryoGen Pharmed Inc., Alborz University of Medical Sciences, Karaj, Iran [f]Non-communicable Diseases Research Center, Alborz University of Medical Sciences, Karaj, Iran [g]Department of Neurology, Thomas Jefferson University, Philadelphia, PA, United States

Abstract

Anti-CD20 monoclonal antibodies such as Rituximab, Ofatumumab, Obinutuzumab, Ocrelizumab, Ublituximab, and Veltuzumab are widely used to treat several disorders including autoimmune diseases. Their role is to achieve B-cell depletion mainly through Fc-dependent effector functions. The main molecular mechanisms considered responsible for CD20+ cell elimination by anti-CD20 monoclonal antibodies are antibody-dependent cellular cytotoxicity (ADCC), antibody-dependent cellular phagocytosis (ADCP), complement-dependent cytotoxicity (CDC), direct anti-B-cell effects through apoptosis or other cell death pathways. Several clinical trials of these agents have been accomplished in different autoimmune diseases such as rheumatoid arthritis, multiple sclerosis, pemphigus vulgaris, systemic sclerosis, and systemic lupus erythematosus. Recently, the efficacy of anti-CD20 monoclonal antibodies in immune deregulation diseases was also reported. As a first-generation anti-CD20 monoclonal antibody which was approved in 1997, rituximab became an extraordinarily secure choice for the control of autoimmune and lymphoproliferative manifestations associated with primary immunodeficiencies in particular immune thrombocytopenic purpura, autoimmune hemolytic anemia, and granulomatous disease in subjects who suffered from common variable immunodeficiency, and autoimmune lymphoproliferative syndrome patients. In total, anti-CD20 monoclonal antibody therapies are generally well tolerated, but some precautions must be taken to ensure their safety. There is some concern about their adverse events, including hypogammaglobulinemia, which increases the risk of infection. Currently, more investigations are ongoing in order to study the long-term safety profile and reduce severe adverse events.

https://doi.org/10.1016/B978-0-443-19200-5.00016-6

Abbreviations

ADCC	antibody-dependent cellular cytotoxicity
ADCP	antibody-dependent cellular phagocytosis
AE	autoimmune encephalitis
AHA	autoimmune hemolytic anemia
ALPS	autoimmune lymphoproliferative syndrome
APC	antigen-presenting cell
CASPR2	contactin-associated protein-like-2
CD	clusters of differentiation
CDC	complement-dependent cytotoxicity
CLL	chronic lymphocytic leukemia
CVID	common variable immunodeficiency
FDA	Food and Drug Administration
GAD65	glutamic acid decarboxylase 65
GPA	granulomatosis with polyangiitis
IgG	immunoglobulin G
ITP	immune thrombocytopenia purpura (ITP)
LGI1	leucine-rich glioma-inactivated-1
mAb	monoclonal antibody
MG	myasthenia gravis
MPA	microscopic polyangiitis
MRI	magnetic resonance imaging
mRSS	modified Rodnan skin-score
MS	multiple sclerosis
NHL	non-Hodgkin lymphoma
NMDAR	NMDA receptor
PCD	programmed cell death
PPMS	primary progressive MS
PV	pemphigus vulgaris
RA	rheumatoid arthritis
RRMS	relapsing-remitting MS
SLEDAI	systemic lupus erythematosus disease activity index
SPMS	secondary progressive MS
SSc	systemic sclerosis
Tfh	T follicular helper

Conflict of interest

No potential conflicts of interest were disclosed.

Introduction

Autoimmune disease (AD) is one of the emerging noncommunicable diseases. Epidemiological studies have estimated that the overall prevalence of ADs is approximately 3%–5% in the general population [1,2] and they represent the 10th most common cause of mortality in developing countries [1,3]. There are many treatment modalities for ADs ranging from traditional disease-modifying antirheumatic drugs and immunosuppressants that exert nonspecific immune suppression to targeted agents such as biologic agents and small molecule inhibitors, including anticytokine therapies, monoclonal antibodies (mAbs), biological inhibitors of T-cell function, and B-cell inhibition, which aim at specific cytokines and intracellular signal pathways [4,5]. An optimal therapy strategy for ADs would fulfill four main criteria: (i) specifically target the pathogenic cells and leave the remainder of the immune system functioning normally, (ii) reestablish immune tolerance that is stable over time without the need for continuous or long-term therapy, (iii) has low toxicity and few adverse effects (AEs), and (iv) is overall cost-effective when compared to alternative approaches [6].

CD20 is present in B cells, a subset of T lymphocytes and follicular dendritic cells [7–9]. The expression of CD20 on B cells occurs concurrently with IgM expression on the surface and influences the conductance of transmembrane calcium, cell cycle progression, and B-cell proliferation and differentiation [10,11]. CD20 is also associated with lipid rafts, but the degree of association is governed by extracellular triggering, which involves CD20 conformational changes and B-cell antigen receptor (BCR) aggregation [12,13]. BCR and CD20 colocalize after receptor ligation and then rapidly separate before the endocytosis of BCR, while CD20 stays on the cell surface.

Anti-CD20 therapy is widely used for the treatment of diseases with an increased expression of CD20 antigen. Anti-CD20 monoclonal antibodies (mAbs) are one of the most successful and effective antibodies used to treat several disorders including autoimmune diseases [14,15]. Their role is to achieve B-cell depletion. Anti-CD20 mAbs were initially developed for the treatment of B-cell proliferative conditions, such as non-Hodgkin's lymphoma (NHL) and chronic lymphocytic leukemia (CLL) [16], and then were used to treat rheumatoid arthritis (RA) as B-lymphocyte depletion would be a safe and effective therapy and lead to clinical benefits [17]. This clear clinical improvement of anti-CD20 mAb therapy in RA patients, particularly those with refractory to other available treatments, has resulted in the expansion of these anti-CD20 mAbs for other autoimmune diseases with both T- and B-cell etiology, such as multiple sclerosis (MS) and systemic lupus erythematosus (SLE).

To date, different anti-CD20 mAbs exist, including Rituximab, Ofatumumab, Obinutuzumab, Ocrelizumab, Ublituximab, and Veltuzumab. Each anti-CD20 mAb is specified with a unique target epitope on the CD20 molecule surface. Rituximab and Obinutuzumab are the most common mAbs used as anti-CD20 agents, which link to CD20 antigen at the plasma membrane and then lead to tumor cell death as a consequence of the activated C1q cascade. Rituximab is well known as the first anti-CD20 mAb associated with therapeutic effects in several diseases and could be used to treat refractory CD20+ B-cell non-Hodgkin's lymphoma and B-cell malignancies. Ocrelizumab is the first approved therapy for primary progressive MS (PPMS) and has also been approved for relapsing-remitting MS (RRMS). Among patients with relapsing MS, ocrelizumab was associated with lower rates of disease activity and progression than IFN beta-1a during 96 weeks [18].

Using new generations of anti-CD20 mAbs that are either humanized or fully human has also been shown to be associated with suitable outcomes in animals and humans [19,20]. They will play crucial roles in the future of treatment for MS and probably other autoimmune diseases. The second generation of anti-CD20 molecules that binds to a different epitope is called Ofatumumab. Ofatumumab is more effective in killing the target cells compared to rituximab [15]. This mAb is approved for the treatment of resistant CLL and is associated with good therapeutic results in the treatment of RA [21]. Four molecular mechanisms are considered responsible for CD20 cell elimination by anti-CD20 mAbs: Antibody-dependent cellular cytotoxicity (ADCC), antibody-dependent cellular phagocytosis (ADCP), complement-dependent cytotoxicity (CDC), and direct antitumor effects through apoptosis or other cell death pathways.

Several clinical trials of these agents have been accomplished in different autoimmune diseases, and more investigations are ongoing in order to study the long-term safety profile and determine severe AEs, although their FDA approval for CLL using obinutuzumab and ofatumumab in autoimmune diseases remains under investigation. Here we provide an update on the latest approved anti-CD20 mAbs and ongoing clinical trials as well as on the impact of side effects on autoimmune diseases, including RA, MS, and SLE.

Cellular and molecular mechanisms of autoimmunity

AD results from failure to sustain tolerance to self-antigens. Many of the ADs involving one or multiple organ systems (polyautoimmunity) afflict 3% or more of people worldwide, mostly women. Predisposing factors for AD include genetic background and environmental factors including infectious pathogens, xenobiotic exposures, and hormonal status. Some common mechanisms for losing self-tolerance include defective immunomodulation by a regulatory T cell (Treg) and CD8 suppressor T cells, reduced deletion or enhanced activation of autoreactive Th cells, aberrant maturation of regulatory B subsets and the pathological expansion of CD21low B cells, dysregulated signaling, antigenic mimicking between self-antigens and foreign molecules, or expression of new epitopes on previously hidden or xenobiotic-modified self-proteins. In general, organ-specific AD has a generally cell-mediated (Th1 or Th17) mechanism, while polyautoimmunity incorporates a robust autoantibody (Th2)-dependent mechanism [22–24]. These lead to disruption of immune tolerance to self-antigens because of the retention of autoreactive lymphocyte clones not correctly undergoing apoptosis. The immune system is composed of many different lymphocytes, including B and CD4 T cells. Autoimmune cellular pathways depend on the action of several cytokines, including B-cell-specific and -independent functions. Innate immune responses also play an important role in the development of autoimmune diseases, such as SLE. Cells of the innate immune system, as the first line of defense, infiltrate the injured tissues and orchestrate the inflammation, dead cell removal, and self and external antigens. Moreover, they directly initiate the adaptive immune responses. The suppression of adaptive immunity is an approach that involves B-cell depletion and drugs used in this perspective include anti-CD20 mAbs.

CD20 expression leads to the proliferation of B cells and subsequent antibody production. Activated B cells express high levels of CD20, which is a common target of autoimmunity [25]. The major circuit of the B-cell sensitivity pathway is regulated by a molecular mechanism known as "CD20" signaling, which has several roles [26]. Understanding better the cellular and molecular mechanisms involved in the autoreactivity process based on B cell and CD20 signaling is essential for providing effective treatments to patients at risk of developing autoimmunity or as part of a diagnostic tool for the early detection of manifestations.

CD20 is a membrane glycoprotein expressed on cells of the hematopoietic system that has been associated with autoimmune diseases such as RA. Autoimmunity development begins when CD20-expressing B cells interact with self-antigens that normally do not elicit an immune response. Many mechanisms are well known to result in CD20 expression and subsequent B-cell activation in autoimmunity development, primarily involving the aberrant presentation of self-antigens by nonself-antigen-presenting cells (APCs). These aberrant APC interactions may cause the development of autoimmune inflammation leading to tissue damage and disease manifestations including chronic inflammatory disorder [27].

T follicular helper (Tfh) cells are an effector CD4+ T-cell subset that helps B cells activate and differentiate to create a protective humoral (antibody-based) response during infection [28]. Tfh cells are so-called because of their potential to aid the recirculating mature B-cell pool, also known as follicular B cells, by migrating between follicles of secondary lymphoid organs (SLO). Tfh cells may come into contact with recirculating follicular B cells along the T-B boundary, in the B-cell follicle, the interfollicular area, and in germinal centers (GC). The initial cognate meeting between primed CXCR5+ CD4+ Tfh cells and B cells with bound antigens occurs at the T-B boundary during responses to protein antigens.

Tfh cells, which express high levels of CXC-chemokine receptor 5 (CXCR5), as well as the surface receptors such as inducible T-cell costimulator (ICOS) and programmed cell death protein 1 (PD1), the transcriptional repressor B-cell lymphoma 6 (BCL-6), and the cytokine interleukin-21 (IL-21), enhance B-cell response in germinal centers, which are required for class transferring recombination and somatic hypermutation to generate high-affinity antibody-making plasma cells and memory B cells. Tfh cells help to eliminate infections by stimulating humoral response, but they are also linked to autoimmunity [29].

The molecular mechanisms of autoimmunity that lead to CD20 expression and B-cell activation are shown to be the processes that involve interaction of B cells with self-antigens or foreign antigens, T cells recognizing such antigens, and an autoreactive T-cell clone having a receptor for such an antigen. It is concluded that there must be a focus on self-/nonself-interactions in the immunological synapse between T cells and B cells during the initiation of AD [30].

The molecular mechanism of CD20 expression and B-cell activation lies in the interaction between Th9 cells, dendritic cells, and natural killer (NK) cells. Antigen-specific activated Th9 cells and de novo B-cell production led to inflammation and immune responses that induce activation of dendritic cells. These cells secrete different soluble factors that can either directly activate innate immune response pathways or generate IL-6 secreted by activated macrophages, which act directly on mast cells to induce the release of myeloperoxidase (MPO) from these cells [31]. This process results in IL-6-mediated activation of antigen-specific CD4 T lymphocytes and upregulation of surface molecules such as the CD40 ligand (CD40L) on circulating monocytes/macrophages that recruit naïve CD4 T lymphocytes to sites of infection. As a result, CD20 expression is rapidly induced following adaptive immune response events [32]. CD20 expression is upregulated on several cell types, including T cells and B cells, but not on resting lymphocytes. CD20 expression was also upregulated by many other stimuli including interferon gamma and IL-2 [10]. CD20 can also be induced by proinflammatory cytokines such as TNF-alpha and IL-1beta, which are essential to control inflammatory diseases.

List of FDA-approved anti-CD20 antibodies, off-label anti-CD20 antibodies, and clinical trials on anti-CD20 antibodies in autoimmune diseases

Rituximab

Rituximab, a chimeric antibody also known as Rituxan or MabThera (manufactured by Biogen and Genentech in the United States and Hoffmann-La Roche in Canada), is a first-generation CD20 mAb and the first anti-CD20 treatment used in MS. This drug was approved in 1997 for the treatment of some cancers and autoimmune disorders and is on the list of essential medicines of the WHO [61]. While rituximab has no Food and Drug Administration (FDA) or European Medicines Agency (EMA) approval to be used in MS, it is often used off-label, especially in resistant cases. A number of rituximab biosimilar compounds are now being investigated [33]. There have been few high-quality studies on its efficacy, even its widespread use in MS. The first phase I clinical trial of rituximab is known as HERMES [34].

While level 1 studies are sparse, a limited number of observational and cohort studies demonstrate that rituximab improves MRI and clinical outcomes in RRMS, PPMS, and SPMS, with lower ARR, T2, and gadolinium-enhancing lesions [35–37,62]. While the data shows that rituximab is likely to be useful, particularly in RRMS, interest in its usage is declining as other treatments such as ocrelizumab and ofatumumab become more widely accessible and have greater therapeutic effectiveness. However, there are now active clinical investigations that may give fresh evidence of the beneficial impact [62].

Rituximab has been shown to limit cell growth as well as produce ADCC, CDC, and direct programmed cell death [40,49]. This mAb is commonly used in lymphoma treatment, either alone or combined with other treatments, for relapsed and refractory lymphomas [63,64]. Rituximab-cyclophosphamide, doxorubicin, vincristine, and prednisone (R-CHOP) chemotherapy is still the standard treatment for newly diagnosed diffuse large B-cell lymphoma (DLBCL). Despite rituximab's unrivaled success, some patients failed to react or, more often, relapsed and became resistant after taking treatment. Rituximab research has taken a major step in understanding the drug's mechanism of action and developing appropriate therapy for patients who have acquired resistance to it. The development of anti-CD20 mAbs remains a prominent priority for scientific and clinical researchers.

Ocrelizumab

Ocrelizumab (also known as Ocrevus and commercialized by Genentech in the United States) is a humanized anti-CD20 mAb (from mice) administered intravenously and links to an epitope that overlaps with that of rituximab. Ocrelizumab is a humanized or totally human mAb with an unaltered Fc domain, with the goal of lowering immunogenicity when compared to the chimeric mAb rituximab. Ocrelizumab (PRO70769, 2H7) is a type I anti-CD20 IgG1 mAb that has been humanized. It differs from rituximab at various amino acid locations within the CDRs of the variable sections of the light and heavy chains. As a result, it displayed a better binding affinity for low-affinity FcRIIIa receptor (CD16) variants [40]. Furthermore, when compared to rituximab, ocrelizumab demonstrated stronger ADCC and reduced CDC activity in lymphoid malignancies. Currently, a phase I/II study in patients with relapsed/refractory follicular lymphoma (FL) has demonstrated that ocrelizumab exhibited superior efficacy and safety for the treatment of these patients after rituximab failed therapy [49,65]. Ocrelizumab, which particularly depletes B cells, was authorized by the FDA in March 2017 for the treatment of MS patients, specifically those with active PPMS [39,66]. After 9 months of the US approval, the EMA clearance introduced a new era of B-cell-targeted MS therapy. The acceptability of anti-CD20 drugs is reflected in Ocrevus's market share, which represented 13.8% of MS pharmaceutical sales a year after introduction [67]. The recommended starting concentration is 300 mg in 250 mL 0.9% NaCl, followed by a second injection after 2 weeks, and then every 6 months of 600 mg in 500 mL 0.9% NaCl [38].

Following its approval by the FDA in March 2017, Genentech undertook a phase IV human clinical trial of Ocrelizumab in young adults to study the side effects of this drug, including a higher risk of cancer or consequences in pregnant women and their newborns [43].

Ofatumumab

Ofatumumab is an anti-CD20, totally human monoclonal IgG1 antibody, which binds strongly to a different membrane epitope to rituximab and ocrelizumab [41,68]. Ofatumumab is the first entirely human type 1 IgG1 kappa (IgG1) mAb. Ofatumumab was approved by the FDA in 2014 for treating CLL, but has been linked to hepatitis B and PML in postmarket studies. Although it has recently been assessed for usage in RRMS, ofatumumab is currently approved for the treatment of Chronic Lymphocytic Leukemia under the trade name Arzerra [41]. In 2015, Novartis obtained the rights from GlaxoSmithKline (GSK) to develop ofatumumab for cancer and autoimmune diseases. Ofatumumab may be injected subcutaneously by patients or healthcare professionals using an auto-injector pen at 4-week intervals. This is an advantage for patients with chronic diseases that require frequent medication administration, as it provides better access to therapy than traditional antibody treatments, which need a day to be set aside in a health institution for the infusion. Although ofatumumab leads to CDC more than ADCC, it has the same mechanisms of cell lysis as ocrelizumab [69]. In addition to its strong efficacy in RA [70] and hematological malignancies [71], the role of ofatumumab has also been evaluated for the treatment of MS.

A small phase 2 double-blind, randomized, placebo-controlled research was conducted on 38 patients with RRMS who were randomly assigned to receive either intravenous ofatumumab or a placebo at 2-week intervals. This study showed that ofatumumab was well tolerated by patients and no decrease in total blood IgG was found [72].

Of all of these new mAbs, ofatumumab is the most advanced in clinical development, with a low off-rate and significant CDC activity [40]. Furthermore, when compared to rituximab, ofatumumab exhibited better complement activation against both rituximab-sensitive and resistant non-Hodgkin's lymphoma cell lines that express increased levels of complement defense proteins and low levels of CD20 antigen that did not succeed in undergoing CDC with rituximab [16]. In addition, in a phase I/II dose escalation study, ofatunumab showed an improved response against relapsed/refractory FL with an overall response rate (ORR) of 43% [58]. In phase I/II trials on lymphoma and leukemia (particularly CLL), higher complement activity was observed without an increase in toxicity [16]. Ofatumumab may lead to higher efficacy when combined with chemotherapy for tumor clearance and this is under investigation in ongoing trials in both FL and DLBCL [40].

Veltuzumab

Veltuzumab (IMMU-106, hA20) is a humanized type I anti-CD20 IgG1 mAb, similar to rituximab, with a single amino acid change (Asp101 instead of Asn101) inside the variable heavy chain, which results in a slower off-rate [49]. Veltuzumab has demonstrated antiproliferative, apoptotic, and ADCC actions in vitro; however, this alteration leads to more robust binding avidities and greater effects on CDC than rituximab [49].

Furthermore, intravenous or subcutaneous injections of relatively low doses demonstrated substantial anti-B-cell lymphoma efficacy in cynomolgus monkeys (*Macaca fascicularis*) and decreased tumor development in mice having human B-cell lymphomas [16]. Furthermore, when administered subcutaneously, veltuzumab produces effective blood transport and is pharmacologically active when compared with other methods.

Obinutuzumab

Obinutuzumab (originally GA101) is a fully humanized, the first FDA- and EMEA-approved recombinant type II anti-CD20 and IgG1 Fc-optimized mAbs. It is currently approved for use in first-line CLL patients in combination with chlorambucil, as well as in combination with bendamustine followed by obinutuzumab monotherapy to treat patients suffering from FL who relapsed or are refractory to a rituximab-containing regimen [44,45]. The creation of obinutuzumab was largely predicated on the assumed role of FcRIIIA-mediated mechanisms in rituximab clinical activity, which was reinforced by the effect of the FcRIIIA-158VF polymorphism in clinical response discovered in several FL investigations [44–46].

Obinutuzumab exhibits lower CDC than rituximab but higher ADCC and phagocytosis, as well as better direct B-cell killing activities [44–46]. Obinutuzumab associated with chemotherapy has been shown to have anticancer activity in patients with CLL [46], in those with previously treated indolent and aggressive non-Hodgkin's lymphoma [44,45], and in those with rituximab-resistant indolent non-Hodgkin's lymphoma [47].

In a GALLIUM trial conducted on patients with previously untreated indolent non-Hodgkin's lymphoma (FL or marginal-zone lymphoma), the effectiveness and safety of induction with obinutuzumab were compared to that with rituximab, each combined with chemotherapy, followed by maintenance therapy with the same mAb [73]. The authors of this GALLIUM study found that obinutuzumab had a longer progression-free survival than rituximab. However, according to the CT-based evaluation, the rate of response was not significantly different. Both of the groups had identical overall survival. The trial revealed that obinutuzumab with chemotherapy had a 34% reduced risk of progression, relapse, or mortality than rituximab with chemotherapy (a significant difference) [73]. The results of this GALLIUM trial revealed that replacing rituximab with obinutuzumab in the context of immunochemotherapy and maintenance treatment resulted in a significantly prolonged progression-free survival in patients with previously untreated FL. Obinutuzumab had a greater prevalence of serious AEs than rituximab [73] (Table 1).

Mechanisms of action of anti-CD20 antibodies and their effects in autoimmune diseases

CD20 is a good target for antibody-mediated therapeutic B-cell reduction because it is expressed at elevated levels in the majority of B-cell malignancies but cannot be internalized

TABLE 1 List of FDA-approved anti-CD20 mAbs in autoimmune diseases.

S/ no	Anti-CD20 antibody	Source	Generation/ year of FDA-approval	FDA-approved indications	Mechanism of action	Off-label indications	Clinical trial	References
1	Rituximab	Chimeric	First/1997	NHL, CLL, RA, GPA, MPA	CDC, ADCC, PCD, ADCP	MS	RRMS, PPMS, and SPMS	[33–38]
2	Ocrelizumab	Humanized IgG1	Second/ 2017	MS; RRMS and PPMS	High ADCC Low CDC	–	–	[7,8,38,39]
3	Y90-Ibritumomab tiuxetan (Zevalin)	Murine IgG1κ	First/2002	NHL	High CDC Low ADCC	–	–	[9,11,12]
4	Reditux	Murine IgG1	First/2007[a]	–	Biosimilar	–	–	[13,40]
5	Ofatumumab	Fully human IgG1κ	Second/ 2009	CLL, MS, and RRMS	High CDC	RA; hematological malignancies	–	[8,41,42]
6	Obinutuzumab	Humanized IgG2κ (glycoengineered Fc portion)	Third/2013	Used intravenously against chronic lymphocytic Leukemia, non-Hodgkin's lymphoma, diffuse large B-cell lymphoma	High PCD and ADCC, Low CDC	–	–	[40,43–48]
7	Veltuzumab	Humanized IgG1κ	Second/ Phase II human trial	Orphan status designation for ITP and pemphigus	High CDC	–	–	[40,49,50]
8	Tositumomab	Murine IgG2aλ	First/2003	NHL	High PCD Low CDC	–	–	[51–55]
9	Ublituximab	Chimeric; IgG1 Glycoengineered	Third/ Phase II human trial	–	High ADCC	–	Chronic lymphocytic leukemia; RRMS (NCT03277261)	[38]
10	Ocaratuzumab	Humanized IgG1 (engineered Fc portion)	Third/ Phase II human trial	–	High ADCC	–	RA, relapsed/ refractory follicular lymphoma	[40,56–60]

[a] *India FDA approved*

ADCC, *antibody-dependent cellular cytotoxicity;* ADCP, *antibody-dependent cellular phagocytosis;* CD, *clusters of differentiation;* CDC, *complement-dependent cytotoxicity;* CLL, *chronic lymphocytic leukemia;* FDA, *Food and Drug Administration;* GPA, *granulomatosis with polyangiitis;* IgG, *immunoglobulin G;* ITP, *immune thrombocytopenia;* MPA, *microscopic polyangiitis;* MS, *multiple sclerosis;* NHL, *non-Hodgkin lymphoma;* PCD, *programmed cell death;* RA, *rheumatoid arthritis;* RRMS, *relapsing remitting MS;* PPMS, *primary progressive MS;* SPMS, *secondary progressive MS.*

or removed from the plasma membrane after mAb therapy. The triggering of BCR initiates a well-defined and complex chain of signaling actions that result in the phosphorylation of adaptor proteins such as CD19, the activation of various kinases such as BTK and AKT, the activation of phospholipase C, the induction of calcium flux, and the activation of mitogen-activated protein (MAP) kinases [42]. Anti-CD20 antibodies exert their effects mainly through mechanisms such as ADCC, ADCP, CDC, and reactive oxygen species (dependent nonapoptotic cell death), pathways using professional cell death machinery including apoptosis, caspase activation, and cytochrome *c* release [48,50] (Fig. 1).

B-cell ADCC, which is the process of killing a target cell via antibodies or complement, is a significant mechanism of anti-CD20 antibody impact in autoimmune disorders. It inhibits protein production by expressing cells and also kills some cells infected with DNA viruses or bacteria. When an antibody establishes a bridge between a target cell with foreign antigens

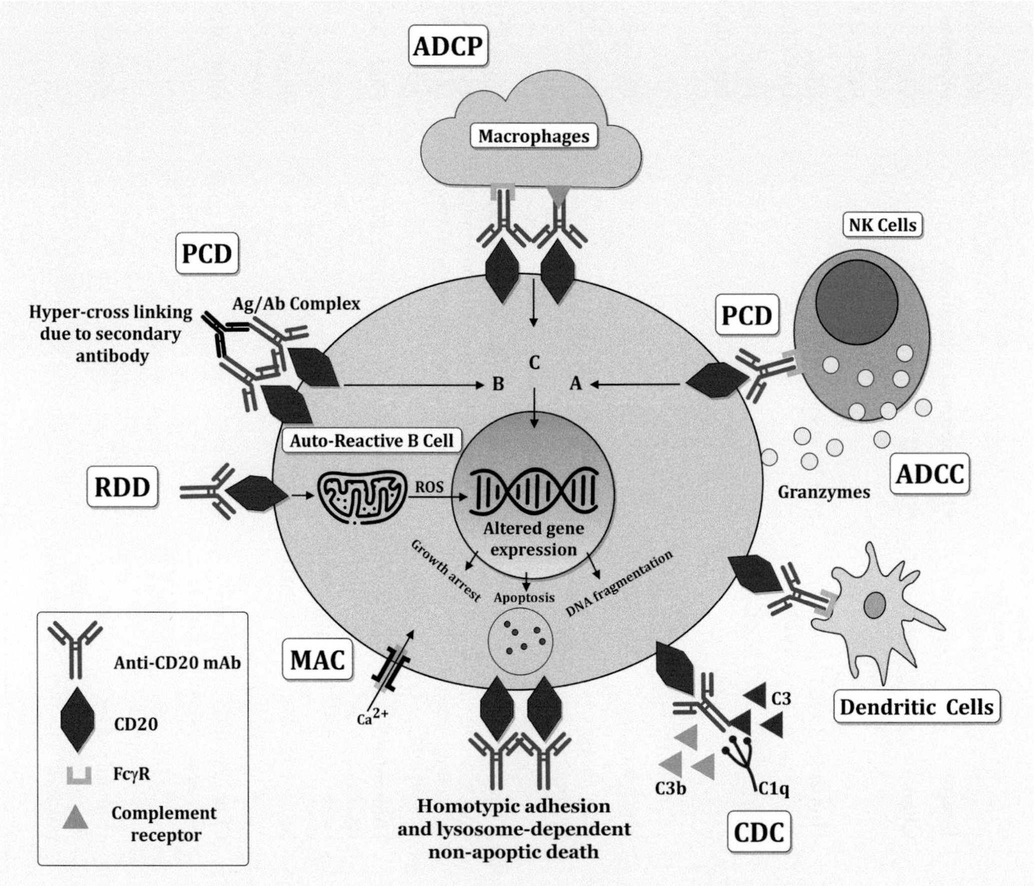

FIG. 1 Schematic illustration of the mechanisms of action of anti-CD20 mAbs.

on its surface and an effector cell, often an NK cell expressing FcRs, ADCC occurs. The cross-linking of the FcRs starts a chain reaction of signals that leads to the release of lytic chemicals from the effector cell, resulting in the lysis of the target cell [51]. ADCC is a cell-mediated immune defense lytic mechanism using autoreactive antibodies as part of the humoral immune response to restrict and regulate infection in which Fc receptor-bearing effector cells of the immune system actively recognize and kill antibody target cells. The presence of an effector cell, which might be any immune cell that can secrete lethal proteins or chemicals, is required for ADCC. NK cells have previously been demonstrated to interact with IgG antibodies. As a result, it is usually assumed that CD56+ and CD3 NK cells catalyze ADCC. However, macrophages, neutrophils, and eosinophils are critical cell types that may cause ADCC [50]. The effects of ADCC can control CD20 antigen-positive B cells and render them nonpermissive for further proliferation and differentiation, thereby preventing morbidity and mortality. Autoantibodies such as anti-CD20 have been shown to preferentially recognize extracellular epitopes of CD20, suggesting that these antibodies may be more effective at binding to CD20 on the surface of activated B cells than they are within B cells themselves. Anti-CD20 interactions with activated lymphocytes also lead to apoptosis, which can block proliferation through degranulation and activation of caspase-1/7 (cellular degradation) pathways, or lyse red blood cells through ADCC activity [52]. The mechanism of B-cell ADCC on CD20 is that, as CD20 is a natural antigen that binds to its receptor CD137, the antibody can bind to it or in some cases inhibit it from binding to CD137. If CD20 is bound by an antibody, the binding leads to covalent modification of its receptor. This triggers signaling pathways that eventually lead to cell death (apoptosis), which plays a role in many autoimmune diseases, including multiple sclerosis and RA. Autoantibodies can also induce apoptosis by interacting with cell death receptors such as FasL. Another way in which ADCC could play a role is by directly disrupting intracellular pathways involved in cell division such as cyclin D1 and CDC functions providing extravasated antigens with high levels of antigen recognition and expansion of B cells that can be used as a target for immune response [53,54].

The mechanism of ADCP can be divided into antibody-dependent, nonimmune phagocytosis, and complement-mediated lysis. an antibody can enter the lysosomes via two pathways: receptor-mediated endocytosis and FcRIII-mediated phagocytosis. The mechanism of ADCP takes place in the fluid phase of blood circulation since antibodies pass through initial lymphatic capillaries by binding to Fc receptors in the reticuloendothelial system, which leads to the recruitment of neutrophils and monocytes/macrophages leading to the release of various cytokines [55]. It has been shown that the interferon regulatory factor 8 (IRF8) gene, which is essential for effective CD20 transcription, reduced the efficacy of ADCC and ADCP induced by anti-CD20 antibodies. A correlation between levels of IRF8 and CD20 RNA or proteins has been shown in normal and malignant B cells. Therefore, IRF8 regulates CD20 expression and controls the depleting capacity of anti-CD20 antibodies [59]. The mechanism of B-cell apoptosis triggered by anti-CD20 antibodies in autoimmune diseases, such as RA and psoriatic arthritis (PsA), has not been fully elucidated. B-cell apoptosis is one of several apoptotic pathways involved in the occurrence and remission of autoimmune diseases. Anti-CD20 antibodies can induce cell death through a caspase-dependent apoptotic signal pathway by activating the Fas receptor on an activated T lymphocyte cell that induces mitochondrial reactive oxygen species generation and caspase cascade activation [31].

Efficacy of anti-CD20 antibodies therapy in autoimmune diseases

Rheumatologic diseases

RA is a chronic autoimmune disease characterized by synovial inflammation leading to damage to cartilage and subchondral bone. Rituximab therapy depletes circulating CD20+ B cells, which remain at low levels for 6–12 months after treatment. Bokarwa et al. have assessed the efficacy of rituximab treatment for 48 RA patients with confirmed erosive disease refractory to combination therapy with disease-modifying antirheumatic drugs (DMARDs) and TNF-α inhibitors. They demonstrated that rituximab efficiently reduced the activity of RA in more than 70% of the patients treated [59]. In addition, rituximab can be used recurrently in the same patient and potentially increase sensitivity to previously ineffective treatment modalities. Based on this study, rituximab therapy was well tolerated by most RA patients, with no allergic reactions, such as rashes or anaphylactic reactions following rituximab infusions. However, one patient complained of nausea just after the administration of this drug. Another AE that occurred after 3 months of rituximab treatment was pneumonia, which required hospitalization for one patient. Although there was no evidence of an AE on the study's outcome, there were two deaths from myocardial infarction, one within 1 month of rituximab treatment and the other 13 months after rituximab treatment [59]. Ocrelizumab has been shown in several clinical trials to limit the spread of joint lesions in RA patients and to induce improvements in all secondary endpoints, including ACR50 response, ACR70 response, and DAS28-ESR clinical remission, resulting in improvements in the signs and symptoms of RA broadly similar to those reported for other biologic agents [60]. A significantly greater ACR20 response was demonstrated at week 24 with Ofatumumab compared to the placebo. Substantially more robust responses were observed in key secondary endpoints such as ACR50, ACR70, change from baseline in DAS28-CRP and DAS28-ESR, EULAR response, physical function (HAQ-DI), and fatigue (FACIT-F). Relative to rituximab, ofatumumab exhibited higher C1q binding and stronger complement-dependent cytotoxicity, even in CLL cells with low levels of CD2032 expression [74].

SLE is an autoimmune disease with a wide range of cell expressions. The activation of the immune system is essentially related to B cells by generating various cytokines and by operating as potent antigen-presenting cells. Autoantibodies production and the development of immune deposits in tissues can account for the pathogenic role of B cells in this disease. One of the most serious complications of SLE that affects the kidneys is Lupus nephritis (LN). Relevant studies assessed the effect of rituximab on SLE, especially LN. Rituximab is the most widely used agent for B-cell depletion therapy in patients with active SLE who do not respond to conventional immunosuppression [75]. Moreover, it shows significant promise in the treatment of LN by decreasing disease activity, with a low incidence of AEs. Upon rituximab treatment, a decline in creatinine and dsDNA antibodies was displayed with an increase in C3 and C4 levels. Rituximab promotes lysis of B cells by complement and Fc receptor-bearing cytotoxic cells and also induces apoptosis [76]. The first published open-label study using rituximab as a B-cell depletion treatment conducted on six female patients with active SLE reported the safety and efficacy of this drug [77]. Disease activity according to BILAG scores [78] and laboratory markers including hemoglobin, erythrocyte sedimentation rate, urine protein: creatinine, and C3 concentrations had markedly improved after 6 months of follow-up. In addition to this drug, many studies investigate the efficacy of Ocrelizumab in patients with LN. These patients had a reduction of 50% in the urinary protein creatinine ratio at 48 weeks compared with placebo-treated patients, but this treatment was associated with serious infections [79]. After ofatumumab-based treatment, a decrease in SLEDAI score and normalization of anti-dsDNA antibodies and C3 were observed. It represents a well tolerated and effective alternative to rituximab for B-cell depletion for the patients who became rituximab resistant [80].

Systemic sclerosis or scleroderma is an immune-mediated rheumatic disease characterized by fibrosis and vascular disease of the skin and internal organs. Although it is rare, scleroderma has a high morbidity and mortality. Further insight into SSc has allowed for improved management of the disease, including enhanced disease streaming and more systematic assessment and follow-up [81]. Rituximab is a safe and effective therapy for the treatment of severe forms of SSc. A significant improvement was observed in the skin condition, with a reduction in modified Rodnan skin-score (mRSS) in most patients and stable pulmonary function rituximab, in its role as a disease modifier providing long-term benefits to this patient population with an early form of the disease [82]. The effectiveness of anti-CD20 mAbs in patients with SSc changes was confirmed after months of follow-up. Previous studies that evaluated the safety of anti-CD20 mAbs therapy in patients suffering from SSc showed that a decrease in myofibroblast score was described in several patients after weeks of anti-CD20 treatment initiation [83,84].

Neurological diseases

MS is an autoimmune and neurologic disease characterized by an accumulation of inflammatory cytokines and cells at the sites of demyelization formation causing a chronic demyelinating disorder [85]. T and B lymphocytes play important roles in the pathogenesis of MS and are potential treatment targets. B-cell-depleting therapies mediated by anti-CD20 antibodies opened up a new and promising path in RRMS and PPMS treatment. However, they cannot be recommended in other forms of MS, such as SPMS, as they have not yet been evaluated. They are considered as a promising alternative or supplement to the existing DMT panel. The available data from clinical trials worldwide confirms the advantages of these drugs on both clinical and imaging assessments of inflammatory activity for patients with RRMS, as well as for those with PPMS in reducing disability accumulation [38,86].

Anti-CD20 treatments were recognized as a very effective and frequently well tolerated treatment for MS patients as they have improved our understanding of MS pathogenesis and evolution, and they have become very important in the therapy of these patients due to their efficacy and satisfactory safety profiles. Early anti-CD20 treatments have been shown to improve MS patient outcomes, including reducing the rate of relapses and minimizing the accrual of disability. Furthermore, these therapies may provide better protection against relapse-associated worsening and progression of disability independent of relapses [87]. Many clinical trials using anti-CD-20 mAbs as a therapeutic agent have been approved and found positive effects in MS. Rituximab, Ocrelizumab, and Ofatumumab are three common therapeutic antibodies used to treat MS disease [38]. Generally, these three anti-CD20 mAbs have shown in clinical trials reduced time to disease evolution and radiographic findings. Rituximab has been widely used in the treatment of RRMS. After treatment with

Rituximab, the inflammatory lesions were reduced within 4 weeks in patients with RRMS, and a rapid and total depletion of peripheral B cells which express CD20 was observed. Rituximab significantly reduces inflammatory activity, Magnetic resonance imaging (MRI) and decreases disease activity. These results observed in patients suffering from MS suggest that rituximab can treat RRMS. Thus, it was found that the efficacy and effectiveness of the treatment were preserved in the larger trials over a longer period of time and that it was possible to maintain the localized efficacy and protection profile in these trials [34]. According to the MRI finding, rituximab provides a reduction of GAD-improving lesions and reduced T2 lesions [35]. Recent studies have shown that Ocrelizumab can be also a treatment option for MS disease. It was proved that Ocrelizumab can also reduce disease activity, Annualized Relapse Rate (ARR), and disability at 12 and 24 weeks. Therefore, PPMS patients showed a reduction in measures of clinical and MRI progression after treatment with this drug. Moreover, this antibody is well tolerated with a high-efficacy disease-modifying therapy (DMT) for RMS and represents a valuable treatment for delaying disease progression in patients with PPMS [88]. A recent review reported that extended interval dosing between rituximab or ocrelizumab infusions in MS has been linked to a low risk of disease activity as it can be performed without lack of efficacy and while improving patient safety [89]. On the other hand, delaying anti-CD20 infusions by 3–6 months increases the chance of having a sufficient humoral response to COVID-19 vaccination in patients with MS [90]. According to the MRI results, Ofatumumab treatment led to a decrease in brain lesion activity in patients with relapsing forms of MS. Ofatumumab-based therapy also causes a decrease in neurofilament light chain levels without change in brain volume [91]. Despite these findings, more research is needed to fully assess the risk-benefit ratio of anti-CD20 treatments and their impact over longer periods of use, particularly when compared to more established traditional treatments [38]. Additional studies on the mechanisms that make B-cell depletion so effective in MS will help to progress and improve our understanding of the pathogenesis of the disease and identify new therapeutic approaches [38]. Future investigations are highly needed to improve anti-CD20 treatment administration regimens by managing dosing, timing, and treatment duration. Postmarketing and observational studies should be performed to spotlight long-term benefits and risks, as well as to better investigate the risk of infections and malignancies, particularly in older MS patients [16,38].

Autoimmune encephalitis (AE) is described as a series of disorders involving antibodies against neuronal synaptic and cell surface antigens. rituximab is the most common second-line immunotherapy, used in nearly half of the patients with AE. Rituximab treatment varied by EA subtype, with the highest rates of rituximab adoption in NMDA receptor (NMDA R)-EA patients and the lowest in glutamic acid decarboxylase 65 (GAD65)-EA patients [92]. All patients were started after previous first-line immunotherapy. Patients with NMDAR-AE and GAD65 disease were slightly more sensitive to rituximab therapy when their disease was more severe. Patients with NMDAR-AEs were treated earlier and were more likely than other AE subgroups to receive short-term rituximab therapy without repeated maintenance reinfusions [93]. The efficacy of early treatment with rituximab in NMDAR, leucine-rich glioma-inactivated-1 (LGI1), and contactin-associated protein-like-2 (CASPR2)-AEs suggests that short-term therapy may be a treatment option. It has been also suggested that patients with long-standing GAD65 disease are less likely to benefit from B-cell depletion than other AE subgroups. However, NMDAR-AE and LGI1-AE patients treated with rituximab had lower recurrence rates compared with untreated patients demonstrating the efficacy of rituximab in preventing relapses. Its efficacy is believed to be superior to that of other regimens [94]. The effectiveness of rituximab in anti-GAD65 encephalitis, for instance, is not nearly as well defined. That is consistent with the globally lower response rate to immunotherapy for this disease compared with encephalitis due to antibodies targeting extracellular neuronal structures. In contrast to rituximab, ocrelizumab showed a decline in CDC and an increase in ADCC activity [95].

Myasthenia gravis (MG) is a classic autoimmune disease caused by specific autoantibodies at the neuromuscular junction. Direct effects of rituximab include CDC and ADCC, and indirect effects involve structural changes, apoptosis, and sensitization of cancer cells to chemotherapy. Rituximab also increases its Treg cells, which favorably affects MG immunity. Other predictors of positive response were young age at onset and mild disease. Rituximab shortens the time to remission and reduces the need for additional immunosuppressive therapy in patients with new-onset MG [96]. Although rituximab may be safe for long-term use in MG, caution should be exercised in its use as this therapy carries a small risk of progressive multifocal leukoencephalopathy [97] Ofatumumab demonstrated maintained remission in a patient with refractory MG [96].

Dermatological diseases

Pemphigus vulgaris (PV) is a severe autoimmune antibody-mediated blistering disease involving the skin and mucous membranes. Rituximab is a valuable drug for pemphigus, although it may delay the response of mucous membranes and skin folds. The most striking finding was the rapid and long-lasting clinical response to rituximab treatment achieved in all PV patients. All patients tolerated treatment with rituximab very well. Side effects such as nausea, facial edema, chills, and precordial pain occurred only during the first or second infusion and were controlled by paracetamol and antihistamines and a slowed infusion rate [98]. Ocrelizumab-based treatment induces a decline in disease activity after 6 completed weeks prompting a second attempt to substitute cyclophosphamide with methotrexate. This latter was causing severe strain and the effectiveness seemed sufficiently similar between the two drugs, so methotrexate was stopped and cyclophosphamide was restarted. Remission was maintained for 5months, until recurrence of extensive vesicles required a second premedicated two-part loading dose of ocrelizumab at month 6 [99] (Table 2).

Efficacy of anti-CD20 antibodies therapy for immune dysregulation disorders

Common variable immunodeficiency (CVID) is well known to be a numerous series of immune deregulation issues in particular to an infectious difficulty of antibody deficiency. It is also characterized by decreased IgG levels, decreased IgA and/or IgM levels, shortage of hemagglutinin, and irrelevant reaction to pneumococcal vaccination [81]. Several researchers added the hit use of rituximab for the treatment of CVID. Rituximab has a long-lasting reaction and it may be taken into consideration with the known second-line therapy, previous to

TABLE 2 Outcomes and side effects of anti-CD20 for autoimmune diseases.

Diseases	Anti-CD20	Outcomes	Side effects	References
SLE	Rituximab	– High rate of clinical response – No major clinical response rate	– Postrituximab relapses – Elevated levels of anti-DNA antibodies – High levels of circulating BAFF	[76]
	Ocrelizumab	– Overall renal response rates – No significant difference compared to the placebo group Does not produce HAC	Serious infections in the subgroup receiving background MMF	[83]
	Obinutuzumab	Induces B cell cytotoxicity more efficient in in vitro whole blood assays in SLE	–	
	Ofatumumab	Decrease in SLEDAI score	–	[42]
MS	Rituximab	Lower disease activity with decreased new GAD-enhancing and T2 lesions volume	Severe or disabling AEs and infusion-associated symptoms expression	[38]
	Ocrelizumab	Reduction in disease activity and disability	Upper respiratory infections and neoplasms	[100]
	Ofatumumab	Decreasing relapse incidence	Mostly mild-to-moderate-severity AEs	
RA	Rituximab	Reduced the activity of RA	Steroid-induced diabetes, osteoporosis, pathologic fracture of bones, and serious infections	[99,101]
	Ocrelizumab	Impede the spread of joint lesions	–	[81]
	Ofatumumab	Greater ACR20 response	Stronger complement-dependent cytotoxicity	[82]

different immunomodulatory therapy [100]. Moreover, previous reports suggested that rituximab is not contraindicated for the treatment of CVID-related thrombocytopenia [102]. It has been proved that rituximab became an extraordinarily powerful and comparatively secure choice for the control of immune thrombocytopenic purpura (ITP) and autoimmune hemolytic anemia (AHA) in subjects who suffered from CVID. After the infusion of rituximab, patients developed a severe infection that occurred while the patients were not receiving Ig replacement therapy. Also, a decrease in gamma globulin levels was observed [103]. Therapy based on anti-CD20 mAbs additionally improved the renovation of adequate hemoglobin, white blood cells, and platelet counts inside the autoimmune lymphoproliferative syndrome (ALPS) patients. Rituximab progressed thrombocytopenia for 14–36 months in 7 of 12 ALPS subjects [104].

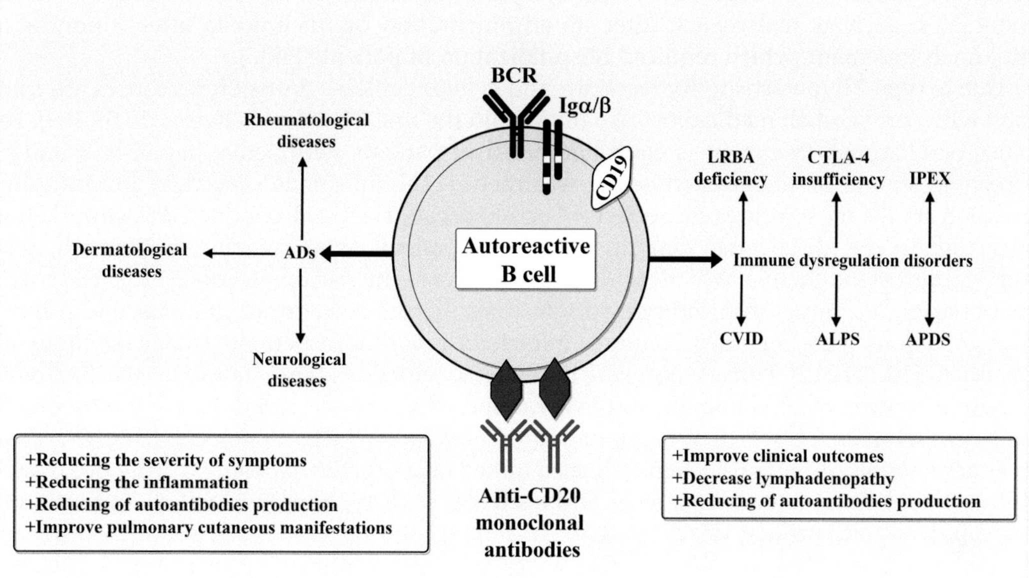

FIG. 2 Efficacy of anti-CD20 monoclonal antibodies therapy in some autoimmune diseases and immune dysregulation disorders.

In a recent study aiming to characterize the responsiveness of patients who suffered from CTLA-4 insufficiency to specific therapies, 123 of 173 CTLA4 mutation carriers were treated for immune complications with abatacept, rituximab, sirolimus, and corticosteroids [105]. These drugs ameliorated disease severity, especially in cases of lymphocytic organ infiltration. The study authors advise treating symptomatic lymphoid infiltrations in CTLA-4 insufficiency with corticosteroids, rituximab, or a combination of both. Although histologic evaluations often exhibit a predominant infiltration of T cells, the B-cell-targeted anti-CD20 therapy with rituximab was clinically very efficient [105]. Moreover, rituximab showed efficiency and safety in ITP [106,107] complicating CVID [103,108], and it should be used in refractory or relapsing cases of any autoimmune cytopenias in the setting of CTLA-4 insufficiency. Rituximab helps to eliminate CD80- and CD86-expressing B cells, which activate effector T cells in the setting of CTLA-4 insufficiency. Fig. 2 summarized the efficacy of anti-CD20 mAbs therapy in autoimmune diseases and immune dysregulation disorders.

Side effects and prerequisites related to anti-CD20 antibodies therapy in autoimmune diseases

While anti-CD20 mAb therapies are generally well tolerated, some precautions must be taken to ensure safety. Rituximab treatment was well tolerated by most RA patients, with no allergic reactions, such as rashes or anaphylactic reactions. However, this drug can cause some AEs, such as nausea just after its administration or pneumonia after 3 months of rituximab treatment, which required hospitalization of patients [59].

Due to type 2 hypersensitivity reactions and cytokine release, infusion responses are common with ocrelizumab medication, usually within the first 24 h after delivery [18,59,109]. Because ocrelizumab treatment is contraindicated in patients with active hepatitis B and C, screening should be undertaken before treatment [110]. Infections caused by immunosuppression are the most serious side effects of ocrelizumab. Tran et al. conducted postmarketing surveillance and discovered that up to 30% of patients who receive ocrelizumab have hypogammaglobulinemia, which significantly increases the risk of infection [110]. Moreover, nasopharyngitis, upper respiratory tract infections, herpes zoster exacerbations, and urinary tract infections were the most common infections reported in patients under ocrelizumab treatment [18,111,112]. Furthermore, the patient's vaccination status should be checked prior to administration of ocrelizumab, and live vaccines should be avoided during the treatment with ocrelizumab. It is worth noting that there is no data on the teratogenicity of ocrelizumab in either animals or humans. Klein et al. also linked ocrelizumab exposure during pregnancy to B-cell depletion in newborns, renal and testicular toxicity, lymphoid follicle formation in bone marrow, and primate death [113]. Accordingly, contraception is advised for women for 6 months following the last infusion. There has also been a higher prevalence of neoplasms, specifically different types of breast cancer, in patients treated with ocrelizumab. However, the mechanical role of antibody exposure has not yet been identified [39,66]. A major safety concern with many MS treatments is the risk of progressive multifocal leukoencephalopathy (PML), which has been linked to some medications used to treat this condition. Although no cases of PML were observed during the clinical trials that led to the drug's approval, few patients have since been reported in postmarketing surveillance. A number of these cases have previously received treatment for MS with other drugs such as standard disease-modifying therapies (DMTs) and natalizumab, making a causal relationship difficult to establish and the risk/benefit of therapy unchanged [114].

Other studies have investigated the safety of ofatumumab and indicated AEs including infection, neutropenia, infusion-related reaction, anemia, thrombocytopenia, cough, and pneumonia [115,116].

The MIRROR study found that AEs of ofatumumab were mild to moderate in severity, without any fatal reactions. Notably, the most serious AEs were mainly infusion reactions, with one case of cytokine-release syndrome occurring after taking the first dose of ofatumumab. Other uncommon AEs that occurred in a single patient included cholelithiasis, hypokalemia, angioedema, and urticaria [68]. No cases of opportunistic infection or incident neoplasm were observed in two phase 2 trials of RRMS, and no immunogenic responses were reported in any of the patients treated with this drug. One case of PML-related death has been reported in a patient who received ofatumumab and had a history of CLL and other comorbid malignant diseases [101].

While anti-CD20 mAbs treatments seem to have a high and strong efficacy and positive safety profiles, there is some concern about AEs when switching to, or from, another therapeutic, such as teriflunomide or interferon-β. Because these therapeutics are still in their infancy in treating MS, the risk profile of transferring to, or from, these treatments is currently unknown [117]. However, when comparing other therapies with anti-CD20 drugs, the efficacy and safety of teriflunomide, interferon-β, or fingolimod are typically inferior, making medication changing possible to be beneficial overall [117]. Close monitoring of patients during the months following therapy switching is highly recommended, until anti-CD20 agents are widely used, to detect any AEs. Additionally, a dosing study of subcutaneous veltuzumab was started in patients suffering from RA. However, the sponsor decided to conclude it and redesign the protocol (NCT01390545) [16]. Finally, the most common AEs of anti-CD20 mAbs are infusion reactions, which are thought to be caused by an excess of CDC [38,118]. It is critical to follow established protocols of safety when administering these agents intravenously, such as premedication with an antihistamine like diphenhydramine and an antipyretic like acetaminophen. Preventive glucocorticoid dosing may also be considered to diminish the risk of serious side effects [38].

Anti-CD20 mAb efficacy seems to be decreased after several months of treatment in clinical trials due to therapeutic resistance. It is unknown what is causing this therapeutic resistance.

Several mechanisms, including direct apoptosis of the targeted B cells, CDC of B cells, and Fc receptor-mediated effector functions, including ADCC and ADCP of B cells, are thought to be responsible for B-cell depletion by anti CD20-targeting mAbs [119]. Different anti-CD20 mAbs favorably use different methods for depleting B cells and modifying CD20 molecules. Type I mAbs induce CD20 to be redistributed into lipid rafts and internalized, but type II mAbs do not seem to cluster CD20 and leave it on the cell surface. Thus, CD20 is compartmentalized into lipid rafts and has strong CDC activity in response to the type I mAbs rituximab, ocaratuzumab, ocrelizumab, ofatumumab, ublituximab, and Veltuzumab [119]. The type II mAbs obinutuzumab, ibritumomab, tiuxetan, and tositumomab, on the other hand, exhibit little to no CD20 clustering and CDC activity and instead cause highly effective B-cell apoptosis, ADCC, and ADCP in their target cells [120–122]. Obinutuzumab was glycoengineered to remove a fucose sugar residue from the Fc region in addition to its type II modality. This modification reduces obinutuzumab affinity for complement and increases it for activating Fc g receptors on NK cells and neutrophils, leading to more effective ADCC of both malignant B cells and B cells from RA and SLE patients than rituximab [123,124].

Notably, type I anti-CD20 mAbs bind twice as many molecules per cell as type II mAbs do, which is probably because these mAbs have different binding mechanisms [125,126]. While type II mAbs interact with CD20 to produce "terminal" complexes that prevent the association of additional type II mAbs and complement components, type I mAbs bind to CD20 to form "seeding" complexes that permit the recruitment of additional IgG or CD20 molecules, favoring effective complement activation [126].

New developments and challenges

During the period of precision medicine, antibody-based therapies are rapidly improved with emerging developments and novel proof-of-concept formats. In this context, antibody-drug conjugates (ADCs), a class of drugs formed by mAbs linked to a small molecule drug with a stable linker, have evolved. Currently, the FDA has approved 10 ADCs, and more than 90 ADCs are still in clinical and preclinical development [127,128].

To date, most of the developed ADCs are to treat cancer, but there is much potential for using ADCs for treating nononcological diseases. In the context of ADs, Yasunaga et al.

demonstrated that inflammation in the mouse autoimmune arthritis model was suppressed to a greater extent using anti-IL-7R ADC (A7R-ADC) conjugated to monomethyl auristatin E. Thus, A7R-ADC could be a new promising alternative to current therapy for this disease [129]. Furthermore, Brentuximab vedotin (BV), ABBV-3373, and DSTA4637S are currently under clinical testing for some ADs, such as systemic sclerosis [130,131].

Similar to the concept of ADCs, antigen-drug conjugates (AgDCs) are developed by combining two therapeutic approaches in order to treat ADs (immunomodulatory agents and antigen-specific immunotherapies). However, AgDCs are assumed to show increased affinity specificity by targeting endogenous autoantibodies or cognate B-cell receptors, thus essentially flipping the mechanism of ADCs [132]. A study by Pickens et al. conducted on a mouse model of MS with which the autoreactive antigen is identified has shown both the efficacy and safety of in vivo AgDC therapy [132]. The results of this study highlight the benefits of codelivery of AgDCs to treat ADs.

Further studies are needed to extend this tempered optimism of ADC to several ADs.

Conclusions

In the last 15 years, B cells have once again been found to be active actors in the autoimmune etiology rather than only bystanders. This has been fueled in part by B-cell depletion treatments' clinical effectiveness (BCDTs). BCDTs, including those targeting CD20, are currently used to treat autoimmune conditions like SLE and MS, despite being initially developed as a method of eradicating malignant B cells. Some unexpected results have come from the use of BCDTs in autoimmune diseases. For instance, even when BCDT successfully manages the condition, it has no effect on antibody levels and antibody-secreting plasma cells, even though these cells are assumed to play a negative pathogenic role in autoimmune disease [133]. Beyond their function in the production of autoantibodies, B cells have been shown by anti-CD20 mAbs to play a significant role in autoimmune disorders. Eventually, more focused B-cell-mediated therapy will be possible with a greater understanding of how B cells contribute to the emergence of specific autoimmune diseases. While the first generation of anti-CD20 mAbs was also beneficial for some autoimmune diseases like RA and RRMS, the most recent generation is showing effectiveness for these conditions and appears to have an elevated safety profile in terms of immunogenicity. Additionally, the most recent versions of ofatumumab offer a technique of subcutaneous administration that is more practical and well tolerated, while ocrelizumab offers the first treatment for PPMS that has been approved by the FDA. The most effective strategy for using anti-CD20 mAbs in the treatment of autoimmune diseases will ultimately depend on several aspects, such as efficacy, safety, tolerability, administration method, accessibility, cost, and patient preference [16].

Since the expiration of the rituximab patent in Europe in February 2013 and the United States in September 2016, the pharmaceutical industry has been enthusiastic about developing a newer generation of anti-CD20 mAbs in these recent years. Thus, since 2015, the FDA has approved four biosimilars (Zarxio, Inflectra, Erelzi, and Amjevita), and biosimilars of rituximab are in the pipeline [134]. This FDA approval of biosimilars of rituximab may drive price competition and lower the cost of rituximab. However, it is uncertain if rituximab or its biosimilars would be a viable option for patients who suffered from MS as the FDA has now approved ocrelizumab for RRMS and PPMS. Even though ofatumumab has not yet been approved to treat autoimmune diseases, still with ongoing trials of subcutaneous ofatumumab in MS and RA, it will probably become a significant actor if approved [16].

References

[1] Eaton WW, Rose NR, Kalaydjian A, Pedersen MG, Mortensen PB. Epidemiology of autoimmune diseases in Denmark. J Autoimmun 2007;29(1):1–9.

[2] Jacobson DL, Gange SJ, Rose NR, Graham NM. Epidemiology and estimated population burden of selected autoimmune diseases in the United States. Clin Immunol Immunopathol 1997;84(3):223–43.

[3] Cooper GS, Bynum MLK, Somers EC. Recent insights in the epidemiology of autoimmune diseases: improved prevalence estimates and understanding of clustering of diseases. J Autoimmun 2009;33(3–4):197–207.

[4] Park Y, Kwok SK. Recent advances in cell therapeutics for systemic autoimmune diseases. Immune Netw 2022;22(1), e10.

[5] Rosato E, Pisarri S, Salsano F. Current strategies for the treatment of autoimmune diseases. J Biol Regul Homeost Agents 2010;24(3):251–9.

[6] Rosenblum MD, Gratz IK, Paw JS, Abbas AK. Treating human autoimmunity: current practice and future prospects. Sci Transl Med 2012;4(125), 125sr1.

[7] Lee KY, Jeon SY, Hong JW, Kim YH, Song KH, Kim KH. CD20 positive T cell lymphoma involvement of skin. Ann Dermatol 2011;23(4):529.

[8] Petrasch S, Brittinger G, Wacker HH, Schmitz J, Kosco-Vilbois M. Follicular dendritic cells in non-Hodgkin's lymphomas. Leuk Lymphoma 1994;15(1–2):33–43.

[9] Nelson BH. CD20 + B cells: the other tumor-infiltrating lymphocytes. J Immunol 2010;185(9):4977–82.

[10] Pavlasova G, Mraz M. The regulation and function of CD20: an "enigma" of B-cell biology and targeted therapy. Haematologica 2020;105(6):1494–506.

[11] Tedder TF, Engel P. CD20: a regulator of cell-cycle progression of B lymphocytes. Immunol Today 1994;15 (9):450–4.

[12] Chen TX, Fan YT, Peng BW. Distinct mechanisms underlying therapeutic potentials of CD20 in neurological and neuromuscular disease. Pharmacol Ther 2022;238, 108180.

[13] Janas E, Priest R, Wilde JI, White JH, Malhotra R. Rituxan (anti-CD20 antibody)-induced translocation of CD20 into lipid rafts is crucial for calcium influx and apoptosis. Clin Exp Immunol 2005;139(3):439–46.

[14] Polyak MJ, Tailor SH, Deans JP. Identification of a cytoplasmic region of CD20 required for its redistribution to a detergent-insoluble membrane compartment. J Immunol 1998;161(7):3242–8.

[15] Teeling JL, Mackus WJM, Wiegman LJJM, van den Brakel JHN, Beers SA, French RR, et al. The biological activity of human CD20 monoclonal antibodies is linked to unique epitopes on CD20. J Immunol 2006;177(1):362–71.

[16] Du FH, Mills EA, Mao-Draayer Y. Next-generation anti-CD20 monoclonal antibodies in autoimmune disease treatment. Auto Immun Highlights 2017;8(1):12.

[17] Edwards JC, Cambridge G. Sustained improvement in rheumatoid arthritis following a protocol designed to deplete B lymphocytes. Rheumatol Oxf Engl 2001;40(2):205–11.

[18] Hauser SL, Bar-Or A, Comi G, Giovannoni G, Hartung HP, Hemmer B, et al. Ocrelizumab versus interferon Beta-1a in relapsing multiple sclerosis. N Engl J Med 2017;376(3):221–34.

[19] Mok CC. Rituximab for the treatment of rheumatoid arthritis: an update. Drug Des Devel Ther 2013;8:87–100.

[20] Coiffier B, Haioun C, Ketterer N, Engert A, Tilly H, Ma D, et al. Rituximab (anti-CD20 monoclonal antibody) for the treatment of patients with relapsing or refractory aggressive lymphoma: a multicenter phase II study. Blood 1998;92(6):1927–32.

[21] Castillo J, Milani C, Mendez-Allwood D. Ofatumumab, a second-generation anti-CD20 monoclonal antibody, for the treatment of lymphoproliferative and autoimmune disorders. Expert Opin Investig Drugs 2009;18 (4):491–500.

[22] Wilbrink R, Spoorenberg A, Arends S, van der Geest KSM, Brouwer E, Bootsma H, et al. CD27-CD38lowCD21low B-cells are increased in axial spondyloarthritis. Front Immunol 2021;12, 686273.

[23] Bolon B. Cellular and molecular mechanisms of autoimmune disease. Toxicol Pathol 2012;40(2):216–29.

[24] Bakhtiar S, Kaffenberger C, Salzmann-Manrique E, Donhauser S, Lueck L, Karaca NE, et al. Regulatory B cells in patients suffering from inborn errors of immunity with severe immune dysregulation. J Autoimmun 2022;132, 102891.
[25] Pateinakis P, Pyrpasopoulou A. CD20+ B cell depletion in systemic autoimmune diseases: common mechanism of inhibition or disease-specific effect on humoral immunity? Biomed Res Int 2014;2014:1–5.
[26] Baker D, Marta M, Pryce G, Giovannoni G, Schmierer K. Memory B cells are major targets for effective immunotherapy in relapsing multiple sclerosis. EBioMedicine 2017;16:41–50.
[27] Hoffman W, Lakkis FG, Chalasani G. B cells, antibodies, and more. Clin J Am Soc Nephrol 2016;11(1):137–54.
[28] Crotty S. T follicular helper cell differentiation, function, and roles in disease. Immunity 2014;41(4):529–42.
[29] Shimoda M, Tran KA, Toda M. Cellular factors. In: Atopic dermatitis : Inside out or outside in [internet]. Elsevier; 2023. p. 134–45. [cité 26 oct 2022]. Disponible sur: https://linkinghub.elsevier.com/retrieve/pii/B9780323847445000140.
[30] Hampe CS. B cells in autoimmune diseases. Scientifica 2012;2012:1–18.
[31] Gan PY, Summers SA, Ooi JD, O'Sullivan KM, Tan DSY, Muljadi RCM, et al. Mast cells contribute to peripheral tolerance and attenuate autoimmune vasculitis. J Am Soc Nephrol 2012;23(12):1955–66.
[32] Blüml S, McKeever K, Ettinger R, Smolen J, Herbst R. B-cell targeted therapeutics in clinical development. Arthritis Res Ther 2013;15(S1):S4.
[33] Greenwald M, Tesser J, Sewell KL. Biosimilars have arrived: rituximab. Art Ther 2018;2018:3762864.
[34] Hauser SL, Waubant E, Arnold DL, Vollmer T, Antel J, Fox RJ, et al. B-cell depletion with rituximab in relapsing-remitting multiple sclerosis. N Engl J Med 2008;358(7):676–88.
[35] de Flon P, Gunnarsson M, Laurell K, Söderström L, Birgander R, Lindqvist T, et al. Reduced inflammation in relapsing-remitting multiple sclerosis after therapy switch to rituximab. Neurology 2016;87(2):141–7.
[36] Naegelin Y, Naegelin P, von Felten S, Lorscheider J, Sonder J, Uitdehaag BMJ, et al. Association of rituximab treatment with disability progression among patients with secondary progressive multiple sclerosis. JAMA Neurol 2019;76(3):274–81.
[37] Linden J, Granåsen G, Salzer J, Svenningsson A, Sundström P. Inflammatory activity and vitamin D levels in an MS population treated with rituximab. Mult Scler J Exp Transl Clin 2019;5(1), 2055217319826598.
[38] Florou D, Katsara M, Feehan J, Dardiotis E, Apostolopoulos V. Anti-CD20 agents for multiple sclerosis: spotlight on ocrelizumab and ofatumumab. Brain Sci 2020;10(10):E758.
[39] Sheridan C. Genentech's Ocrevus heralds new chapter in MS treatment. Nat Biotechnol 2017;35(5):393–4.
[40] Singh V, Gupta D, Almasan A. Development of novel anti-Cd20 monoclonal antibodies and modulation in Cd20 levels on cell surface: looking to improve immunotherapy response. J Cancer Sci Ther 2015;7(11):347–58.
[41] AlDallal SM. Ofatumumab—a valid treatment option for chronic lymphocytic leukemia patients. Ther Clin Risk Manag 2017;13:905–7.
[42] Kozlova V, Ledererova A, Ladungova A, Peschelova H, Janovska P, Slusarczyk A, et al. CD20 is dispensable for B-cell receptor signaling but is required for proper actin polymerization, adhesion and migration of malignant B cells. Komarova Y, éditeur, PLOS ONE 2020;15(3), e0229170.
[43] Food and Drug Administration. BLA Approval Letter. Washington, DC, USA: Department of Health and Human Services; 2017.
[44] GAZYVA (obinutuzumab) Prescribing Information Revised 2013, https://www.accessdata.fda.gov/drugsatfda_docs/label/2013/125486s000lbl.pdf. last accessed October 21, 2022.
[45] GAZYVA (obinutuzumab) Prescribing Information Revised 2016, https://www.accessdata.fda.gov/drugsatfda_docs/label/2016/125486s013lbl.pdf. last accessed October 21, 2022.
[46] Lundin J, Osterborg A. Advances in the use of monoclonal antibodies in the therapy of chronic lymphocytic leukemia. Semin Hematol 2004;41(3):234–45.
[47] Giles FJ, Vose JM, Do KA, Johnson MM, Manshouri T, Bociek G, et al. Circulating CD20 and CD52 in patients with non-Hodgkin's lymphoma or Hodgkin's disease. Br J Haematol 2003;123(5):850–7.
[48] Li L, Yang J, Wang J, Kopeček J. Amplification of CD20 cross-linking in rituximab-resistant B-lymphoma cells enhances apoptosis induction by drug-free macromolecular therapeutics. ACS Nano 2018;12(4):3658–70.
[49] Morschhauser F, Leonard JP, Fayad L, Coiffier B, Petillon MO, Coleman M, et al. Humanized anti-CD20 antibody, veltuzumab, in refractory/recurrent non-Hodgkin's lymphoma: phase I/II results. J Clin Oncol Off J Am Soc Clin Oncol 2009;27(20):3346–53.
[50] Payandeh Z, Bahrami AA, Hoseinpoor R, Mortazavi Y, Rajabibazl M, Rahimpour A, et al. The applications of anti-CD20 antibodies to treat various B cells disorders. Biomed Pharmacother 2019;109:2415–26.

[51] Forthal DN, Finzi A. Antibody-dependent cellular cytotoxicity in HIV infection. AIDS 2018;32(17):2439–51.
[52] Bello C, Sotomayor EM. Monoclonal antibodies for B-cell lymphomas: rituximab and beyond. Hematology 2007;2007(1):233–42.
[53] Kohrt HE, Houot R, Goldstein MJ, Weiskopf K, Alizadeh AA, Brody J, et al. CD137 stimulation enhances the antilymphoma activity of anti-CD20 antibodies. Blood 2011;117(8):2423–32.
[54] Zahavi D, Weiner L. Monoclonal antibodies in cancer therapy. Antibodies 2020;9(3):34.
[55] Herbrand U. Antibody-dependent cellular phagocytosis: the mechanism of action that gets no respect a discussion about improving bioassay reproducibility. BioProcessing 2016;15(1):26–9.
[56] Coiffier B. Rituximab and CHOP-like chemotherapy in good-prognosis diffuse large-B-cell lymphoma. Nat Clin Pract Oncol 2006;3(11):594–5.
[57] Pfreundschuh M, Trümper L, Osterborg A, Pettengell R, Trneny M, Imrie K, et al. CHOP-like chemotherapy plus rituximab versus CHOP-like chemotherapy alone in young patients with good-prognosis diffuse large-B-cell lymphoma: a randomised controlled trial by the MabThera international trial (MInT) group. Lancet Oncol 2006;7(5):379–91.
[58] Coiffier B, Lepage E, Briere J, Herbrecht R, Tilly H, Bouabdallah R, et al. CHOP chemotherapy plus rituximab compared with CHOP alone in elderly patients with diffuse large-B-cell lymphoma. N Engl J Med 2002;346 (4):235–42.
[59] Bokarewa M, Lindholm C, Zendjanchi K, Nadali M, Tarkowski A. Efficacy of anti-CD20 treatment in patients with rheumatoid arthritis resistant to a combination of methotrexate/anti-TNF therapy. Scand J Immunol 2007;66(4):476–83.
[60] Rigby W, Tony HP, Oelke K, Combe B, Laster A, von Muhlen CA, et al. Safety and efficacy of ocrelizumab in patients with rheumatoid arthritis and an inadequate response to methotrexate: results of a forty-eight-week randomized, double-blind, placebo-controlled, parallel-group phase III trial. Arthritis Rheum 2012;64(2):350–9.
[61] World Health Organization.WHO Model List of Essential Medicines (22nd List); 2021. Available online: https://www.who.int/publications/i/item/WHO-MHP-HPS-EML-2021.02 (accessed on 20 October 2022).
[62] Salzer J, Svenningsson R, Alping P, Novakova L, Björck A, Fink K, et al. Rituximab in multiple sclerosis: a retrospective observational study on safety and efficacy. Neurology 2016;87(20):2074–81.
[63] Czuczman MS, Gregory SA. The future of CD20 monoclonal antibody therapy in B-cell malignancies. Leuk Lymphoma 2010;51(6):983–94.
[64] Coiffier B. Rituximab therapy in malignant lymphoma. Oncogene 2007;26(25):3603–13.
[65] Morschhauser F, Marlton P, Vitolo U, Lindén O, Seymour JF, Crump M, et al. Results of a phase I/II study of ocrelizumab, a fully humanized anti-CD20 mAb, in patients with relapsed/refractory follicular lymphoma. Ann Oncol 2010;21(9):1870–6.
[66] Ocrelizumab (Ocrevus) for MS. Med Lett Drugs Ther 2017;59(1523):98–101.
[67] Forbes. How Much Can Roche's Share Price Grow If Ocrevus Doubles Its Share in Multiple Sclerosis Market? 2019. Available online: https://www.forbes.com/sites/greatspeculations/2019/03/13/how-much-canroches-share-price-grow-if-ocrevus-doubles-its-share-in-multiple-sclerosis-market/#25c78a3c4c98 (accessed on 24 October 2022).
[68] Bar-Or A, Grove RA, Austin DJ, Tolson JM, VanMeter SA, Lewis EW, et al. Subcutaneous ofatumumab in patients with relapsing-remitting multiple sclerosis: the MIRROR study. Neurology 2018;90(20):e1805–14.
[69] Babiker HM, Glode AE, Cooke LS, Mahadevan D. Ublituximab for the treatment of CD20 positive B-cell malignancies. Expert Opin Investig Drugs 2018;27(4):407–12.
[70] Østergaard M, Baslund B, Rigby W, Rojkovich B, Jorgensen C, Dawes PT, et al. Ofatumumab, a human anti-CD20 monoclonal antibody, for treatment of rheumatoid arthritis with an inadequate response to one or more disease-modifying antirheumatic drugs: results of a randomized, double-blind, placebo-controlled, phase I/II study. Arthritis Rheum 2010;62(8):2227–38.
[71] Reagan JL, Castillo JJ. Ofatumumab for newly diagnosed and relapsed/refractory chronic lymphocytic leukemia. Expert Rev Anticancer Ther 2011;11(2):151–60.
[72] Sorensen PS, Lisby S, Grove R, Derosier F, Shackelford S, Havrdova E, et al. Safety and efficacy of ofatumumab in relapsing-remitting multiple sclerosis: a phase 2 study. Neurology 2014;82(7):573–81.
[73] Marcus R, Davies A, Ando K, Klapper W, Opat S, Owen C, et al. Obinutuzumab for the first-line treatment of follicular lymphoma. N Engl J Med 2017;377(14):1331–44.
[74] Taylor PC, Uattrocchi E, Mallett S, Kurrasch R, Petersen J, Chang DJ. Ofatumumab, a fully human anti-CD20 monoclonal antibody, in biological-naive, rheumatoid arthritis patients with an inadequate response to methotrexate: a randomised, double-blind, placebo-controlled clinical trial. Ann Rheum Dis 2011;70(12):2119–25.

[75] Shah K, Cragg M, Leandro M, Reddy V. Anti-CD20 monoclonal antibodies in systemic lupus erythematosus. Biologicals 2021;69:1–14.
[76] Al-Omary HL, Alawad ZM, Bernieh B. Anti CD20 monoclonal antibody (rituximab) as a rescue treatment in severe and refractory SLE. Biomed Pharmacol J 2018;11(1):453–62.
[77] Leandro MJ, Edwards JC, Cambridge G, Ehrenstein MR, Isenberg DA. An open study of B lymphocyte depletion in systemic lupus erythematosus. Arthritis Rheum 2002;46(10):2673–7.
[78] Hay EM, Bacon PA, Gordon C, Isenberg DA, Maddison P, Snaith ML, et al. The BILAG index: a reliable and valid instrument for measuring clinical disease activity in systemic lupus erythematosus. Q J Med 1993;86 (7):447–58.
[79] Mysler EF, Spindler AJ, Guzman R, Bijl M, Jayne D, Furie RA, et al. Efficacy and safety of Ocrelizumab in active proliferative lupus nephritis: results from a randomized, double-blind, phase III study: Ocrelizumab in lupus nephritis. Arthritis Rheum 2013;65(9):2368–79.
[80] Masoud S, McAdoo SP, Bedi R, Cairns TD, Lightstone L. Ofatumumab for B cell depletion in patients with systemic lupus erythematosus who are allergic to rituximab. Rheumatol Oxf Engl 2018;57(7):1156–61.
[81] Mogensen TH, Bernth-Jensen JM, Petersen CC, Petersen MS, Nyvold C, Gadegaard KH, et al. Common variable immunodeficiency unmasked by treatment of immune thrombocytopenic purpura with rituximab. BMC Blood Disord 2013;13(1):4.
[82] McQueen FM, Solanki K. Rituximab in diffuse cutaneous systemic sclerosis: should we be using it today? Rheumatology 2015;54(5):757–67.
[83] Lafyatis R, Kissin E, York M, Farina G, Viger K, Fritzler MJ, et al. B cell depletion with rituximab in patients with diffuse cutaneous systemic sclerosis. Arthritis Rheum 2009;60(2):578–83.
[84] Bosello S, De Santis M, Lama G, Spanò C, Angelucci C, Tolusso B, et al. B cell depletion in diffuse progressive systemic sclerosis: safety, skin score modification and IL-6 modulation in an up to thirty-six months follow-up open-label trial. Arthritis Res Ther 2010;12(2):R54.
[85] Goodin DS. The epidemiology of multiple sclerosis. In: Handbook of Clinical Neurology. Elsevier; 2014. p. 231–66. Disponible sur https://linkinghub.elsevier.com/retrieve/pii/B9780444520012000108.
[86] Ontaneda D, Thompson AJ, Fox RJ, Cohen JA. Progressive multiple sclerosis: prospects for disease therapy, repair, and restoration of function. Lancet Lond Engl 2017;389(10076):1357–66.
[87] Bar-Or A, O'Brien SM, Sweeney ML, Fox EJ, Cohen JA. Clinical perspectives on the molecular and pharmacological attributes of anti-CD20 therapies for multiple sclerosis. CNS Drugs 2021;35(9):985–97.
[88] Lamb YN. Ocrelizumab: a review in multiple sclerosis. Drugs 2022;82(3):323–34.
[89] Rolfes L, Meuth SG. Stable multiple sclerosis patients on anti-CD20 therapy should go on extended interval dosing-"yes". Mult Scler J 2022;28(5):691–3.
[90] Disanto G, Sacco R, Bernasconi E, Martinetti G, Keller F, Gobbi C, et al. Association of disease-modifying treatment and anti-CD20 infusion timing with humoral response to 2 SARS-CoV-2 vaccines in patients with multiple sclerosis. JAMA Neurol 2021;78(12):1529.
[91] Kang C, Blair HA. Ofatumumab: a review in relapsing forms of multiple sclerosis. Drugs 2022;82(1):55–62.
[92] Thaler FS, Zimmermann L, Kammermeier S, Strippel C, Ringelstein M, Kraft A, et al. Rituximab treatment and long-term outcome of patients with autoimmune encephalitis: real-world evidence from the GENERATE registry. Neurol Neuroimmunol Neuroinflamm 2021;8(6), e1088.
[93] Nissen MS, Ryding M, Meyer M, Blaabjerg M. Autoimmune encephalitis: current knowledge on subtypes, disease mechanisms and treatment. CNS Neurol Disord Drug Targets 2020;19(8):584–98.
[94] Stasi R. Rituximab in autoimmune hematologic diseases: not just a matter of B cells. Semin Hematol 2010;47 (2):170–9.
[95] Blackburn KM, Denney DA, Hopkins SC, Vernino SA. Low recruitment in a double-blind, placebo-controlled trial of Ocrelizumab for autoimmune encephalitis: a case series and review of lessons learned. Neurol Ther 2022;11(2):893–903.
[96] Menon D, Barnett C, Bril V. Novel treatments in myasthenia gravis. Front Neurol 2020;11:538.
[97] Berger JR, Malik V, Lacey S, Brunetta P, Lehane PB. Progressive multifocal leukoencephalopathy in rituximab-treated rheumatic diseases: a rare event. J Neurovirol 2018;24(3):323–31.
[98] Didona D, Maglie R, Eming R, Hertl M. Pemphigus: current and future therapeutic strategies. Front Immunol 2019;10:1418.

[99] Benesh G, Andriano TM, Cohen SR. Pemphigus vulgaris successfully treated with ocrelizumab following rituximab allergy. JAAD Case Rep 2021;16:12–5.

[100] Walter JE, Farmer JR, Foldvari Z, Torgerson TR, Cooper MA. Mechanism-based strategies for the management of autoimmunity and immune dysregulation in primary immunodeficiencies. J Allergy Clin Immunol Pract 2016;4(6):1089–100.

[101] Avila J, Han J, Zaydan I. Progressive multifocal leukoencephalopathy associated with Ofatumumab presenting as Alexia without agraphia: a case report (P4.319). Neurology 2014;82(10 supplement). Disponible sur: https://n.neurology.org/content/82/10_Supplement/P4.319.

[102] Wakim M, Shah A, Arndt PA, Garratty G, Weinberg K, Hofstra T, et al. Successful anti-CD20 monoclonal antibody treatment of severe autoimmune hemolytic anemia due to warm reactive IgM autoantibody in a child with common variable immunodeficiency. Am J Hematol 2004;76(2):152–5.

[103] Gobert D, Busse JB, Cunningham-Rundles C, Galicier L, Dechartres A, Berezne A, et al. Efficacy and safety of rituximab in common variable immunodeficiency-associated immune cytopenias: a retrospective multicentre study on 33 patients. Br J Haematol 2011;155(4):498–508.

[104] Rao VK, Price S, Perkins K, Aldridge P, Tretler J, Davis J, et al. Use of rituximab for refractory cytopenias associated with autoimmune lymphoproliferative syndrome (ALPS). Pediatr Blood Cancer 2009;52(7):847–52.

[105] Egg D, Rump IC, Mitsuiki N, Rojas-Restrepo J, Maccari ME, Schwab C, et al. Therapeutic options for CTLA-4 insufficiency. J Allergy Clin Immunol 2022;149(2):736–46.

[106] Birgens H, Frederiksen H, Hasselbalch HC, Rasmussen IH, Nielsen OJ, Kjeldsen L, et al. A phase III randomized trial comparing glucocorticoid monotherapy versus glucocorticoid and rituximab in patients with autoimmune haemolytic anaemia. Br J Haematol 2013;163(3):393–9.

[107] Arnold DM, Vrbensky JR, Karim N, Smith JW, Liu Y, Ivetic N, et al. The effect of rituximab on anti-platelet autoantibody levels in patients with immune thrombocytopenia. Br J Haematol 2017;178(2):302–7.

[108] Wang J, Cunningham-Rundles C. Treatment and outcome of autoimmune hematologic disease in common variable immunodeficiency (CVID). J Autoimmun 2005;25(1):57–62.

[109] Auricchio F, Scavone C, Cimmaruta D, Di Mauro G, Capuano A, Sportiello L, et al. Drugs approved for the treatment of multiple sclerosis: review of their safety profile. Expert Opin Drug Saf 2017;16(12):1359–71.

[110] Tran V, Miller P, Olson J, Miller T, Miravalle A. The effect of Ocrelizumab therapy on immunoglobulin levels in patients with multiple sclerosis (P4.2-042). Neurology 2019;92(15 supplement). Disponible sur https://n.neurology.org/content/92/15_Supplement/P4.2-042.

[111] Montalban X, Hauser SL, Kappos L, Arnold DL, Bar-Or A, Comi G, et al. Ocrelizumab versus placebo in primary progressive multiple sclerosis. N Engl J Med 2017;376(3):209–20.

[112] Kappos L, Li D, Calabresi PA, O'Connor P, Bar-Or A, Barkhof F, et al. Ocrelizumab in relapsing-remitting multiple sclerosis: a phase 2, randomised, placebo-controlled, multicentre trial. Lancet Lond Engl 2011;378(9805):1779–87.

[113] Klein C, Lammens A, Schäfer W, Georges G, Schwaiger M, Mössner E, et al. Epitope interactions of monoclonal antibodies targeting CD20 and their relationship to functional properties. MAbs 2013;5(1):22–33.

[114] Clifford D., Gass A., Richert N., Tornatore C., Vermersch P., Hughes R., et al. Cases Reported as Progressive Multifocal Leukoencephalopathy in Ocrelizumab-Treated Patients with Multiple Sclerosis. 2019;1.

[115] Byrd JC, Brown JR, O'Brien S, Barrientos JC, Kay NE, Reddy NM, et al. Ibrutinib versus ofatumumab in previously treated chronic lymphoid leukemia. N Engl J Med 2014;371(3):213–23.

[116] Österborg A, Udvardy M, Zaritskey A, Andersson PO, Grosicki S, Mazur G, et al. Phase III, randomized study of ofatumumab versus physicians' choice of therapy and standard versus extended-length ofatumumab in patients with bulky fludarabine-refractory chronic lymphocytic leukemia. Leuk Lymphoma 2016;57(9):2037–46.

[117] Gross RH, Corboy JR. Monitoring, switching, and stopping multiple sclerosis disease-modifying therapies. Contin Minneap Minn 2019;25(3):715–35.

[118] van der Kolk LE, Grillo-López AJ, Baars JW, Hack CE, van Oers MH. Complement activation plays a key role in the side-effects of rituximab treatment. Br J Haematol 2001;115(4):807–11.

[119] Marshall MJE, Stopforth RJ, Cragg MS. Therapeutic antibodies: what have we learnt from targeting CD20 and where are we going? Front Immunol 2017;8:1245.

[120] Reddy V, Dahal LN, Cragg MS, Leandro M. Optimising B-cell depletion in autoimmune disease: is obinutuzumab the answer? Drug Discov Today 2016;21(8):1330–8.

[121] Mössner E, Brünker P, Moser S, Püntener U, Schmidt C, Herter S, et al. Increasing the efficacy of CD20 antibody therapy through the engineering of a new type II anti-CD20 antibody with enhanced direct and immune effector cell-mediated B-cell cytotoxicity. Blood 2010;115(22):4393–402.
[122] Walshe CA, Beers SA, French RR, Chan CHT, Johnson PW, Packham GK, et al. Induction of cytosolic calcium flux by CD20 is dependent upon B cell antigen receptor signaling. J Biol Chem 2008;283(25):16971–84.
[123] Reddy V, Klein C, Isenberg DA, Glennie MJ, Cambridge G, Cragg MS, et al. Obinutuzumab induces superior B-cell cytotoxicity to rituximab in rheumatoid arthritis and systemic lupus erythematosus patient samples. Rheumatol Oxf Engl 2017;56(7):1227–37.
[124] Tobinai K, Klein C, Oya N, Fingerle-Rowson G. A review of Obinutuzumab (GA101), a novel type II anti-CD20 monoclonal antibody, for the treatment of patients with B-cell malignancies. Adv Ther 2017;34(2):324–56.
[125] Rougé L, Chiang N, Steffek M, Kugel C, Croll TI, Tam C, et al. Structure of CD20 in complex with the therapeutic monoclonal antibody rituximab. Science 2020;367(6483):1224–30.
[126] Kumar A, Planchais C, Fronzes R, Mouquet H, Reyes N. Binding mechanisms of therapeutic antibodies to human CD20. Science 2020;369(6505):793–9.
[127] Theocharopoulos C, Lialios PP, Samarkos M, Gogas H, Ziogas DC. Antibody-drug conjugates: functional principles and applications in oncology and beyond. Vaccine 2021;9(10):1111.
[128] Pettinato MC. Introduction to antibody-drug conjugates. Antibodies 2021;10(4):42.
[129] Yasunaga M, Manabe S, Matsumura Y. Immunoregulation by IL-7R-targeting antibody-drug conjugates: overcoming steroid-resistance in cancer and autoimmune disease. Sci Rep 2017;7(1):10735.
[130] Fernandez-Codina A, Nevskaya T, Pope J. Op0172 Brentuximab Vedontin for skin involvement in refractory diffuse cutaneous systemic sclerosis, interim results of a phase Iib open-label trial. Ann Rheum Dis 2021;80 (Suppl 1):103–4.
[131] Stoffel B, McPherson M, Hernandez A, Goess C, Mathieu S, Waegell W, et al. Pos0365 anti-Tnf glucocorticoid receptor modulator antibody drug conjugate for the treatment of autoimmune diseases. Ann Rheum Dis 2021;80(Suppl 1):412–3.
[132] Pickens CJ, Christopher MA, Leon MA, Pressnall MM, Johnson SN, Thati S, et al. Antigen-drug conjugates as a novel therapeutic class for the treatment of antigen-specific autoimmune disorders. Mol Pharm 2019;16 (6):2452–61.
[133] Dsw L, Ol R, Jl G. B cell depletion therapies in autoimmune disease: advances and mechanistic insights. Nat Rev Drug Discov 2021;20(3). Disponible sur https://pubmed.ncbi.nlm.nih.gov/33324003/.
[134] Panesar K. Biosimilars: current approvals and pipeline agents. US Pharm 2016;41(10):26–9.

CHAPTER

13

B-cell depletion with obinutuzumab for the treatment of proliferative lupus nephritis

Matthew Salvatore Snyder and Richard Furie

Division of Rheumatology, Department of Medicine, Donald and Barbara Zucker School of Medicine at Hofstra/Northwell, Great Neck, NY, United States

Abstract

Lupus nephritis (LN) is the most common and severe manifestation of systemic lupus erythematosus (SLE), affecting more than one-third of patients. LN is also an important contributor to morbidity and mortality in SLE patients. Despite advances in immunosuppressive therapies, outcomes have not significantly improved over the last two decades as only a minority of patients achieve the desired end point of complete renal response in clinical trials, underscoring a major therapeutic unmet need.

Aberrant B-cell function plays an important role in the pathogenesis of SLE, and therefore, therapies targeting their depletion have been investigated for LN treatment. Among these therapies include the anti-CD20 monoclonal antibodies, rituximab and obinutuzumab. Although LUNAR, the phase III, randomized, placebo-controlled trial of rituximab for the treatment of LN failed to meet its primary end point of renal response when compared with placebo, there were signals from the trial and other studies that suggested a potential role for B-cell depletion in LN treatment. Recent data with obinutuzumab demonstrated that it produces more potent and durable B-cell depletion and is clinically superior to rituximab in the treatment of B-cell malignancies. The NOBILITY trial was a phase II, multicenter, randomized, double-blind trial that compared obinutuzumab to placebo in patients with proliferative LN. NOBILITY met its primary end point of complete renal response, suggesting that more profound B-cell depletion enhances outcomes in those with proliferative LN. Obinutuzumab is currently being studied for the treatment of proliferative LN in a global phase III trial (NCT04221477).

Abbreviations

ACE-I angiotensin converting enzyme-inhibitor
ADCC antibody-dependent cell-mediated cytotoxicity
ADCP antibody-dependent cellular phagocytosis
ARB angiotensin receptor blocker

https://doi.org/10.1016/B978-0-443-19200-5.00015-4

AZA azathioprine
BAFF B-cell-activating factor
BILAG British Isles Lupus Assessment Group
C3 complement 3
C4 complement 4
CAR chimeric antigen receptor
CDC complement-dependent cytotoxicity
CRR complete renal response
CYC cyclophosphamide
dsDNA double-stranded DNA
FcγRIIB Fcγ receptor IIB
GC glucocorticoids
HCQ hydroxychloroquine
ISN/RPS International Society of Nephrology/Renal Pathology Society
LN lupus nephritis
MMF mycophenolate mofetil
NR no response
PRR partial renal response
SLE systemic lupus nephritis
UPCR urine protein-to-creatinine ratio

Conflict of interest

RF has received research support and/or research consulting fees from Genentech, Kyverna, GSK, Aurinia Pharmaceuticals, and AstraZeneca.
MS has no potential conflicts of interest to disclose.

Introduction

Lupus nephritis (LN) is the most common and severe manifestation of systemic lupus erythematosus (SLE), affecting about 38% of patients during their lifetimes [1]. It is the result of inflammation within the glomerulus, tubulointerstitial space, and vascular compartments [2]. Patients present in a variety of ways, but the hallmark of lupus glomerulonephritis is proteinuria. While clinicians can only determine whether LN is present, they can generally predict the LN class based on the clinical presentation and laboratory results. However, the gold standard for diagnosis is kidney biopsy. The International Society of Nephrology/Renal Pathology Society (ISN/RPS) classification provides the nephropathologist with a standardized and universal classification scheme [2]. ISN/RPS classification guides the clinician in determining a treatment regimen and prognosis.

Patients with LN tend to be young with a mean age of 35.1 years. Those of Asian, African, or Hispanic race/ethnicity not only more frequently develop LN than Caucasians, but also their disease is more severe [3]. The overall risk of developing end-stage kidney disease (ESKD) within 10 years of LN diagnosis is 10.1% [3]; but, it can be up to fourfold higher among patients with class IV LN [4]. Despite advances with immunosuppressive therapies, the progression to ESKD in LN has not changed over the last two decades [3,4]. LN is associated with a threefold increased risk of death compared to those without LN [3]. In fact, recent data suggest that mortality among those with LN has been on the rise in the United States, especially among those of African ancestry [5]. In LN clinical trials, a minority of patients achieve the desired end point, a complete renal response. Thus, one of the greatest unmet needs of SLE patients is more efficacious and safer therapies for those with LN. Here, we discuss the treatment of proliferative LN and the role of B-cell depletion with obinutuzumab as a potential therapeutic option for proliferative LN.

Treatment of LN

The goal of LN treatment is to prevent nephron loss and protect the kidney from short- and long-term damage [6]. Although treatment of LN was traditionally divided into two phases, induction and maintenance, such nomenclature is being retired by many in the field, who view the treatment as a continuum with modifications made to the dose of medication as opposed to the medication itself [6]. The goal of initial therapy is to achieve a complete renal response (sometimes referred to as remission) within the first year of treatment as several investigators have noted that those patients who have reductions of proteinuria below a urine protein-to-creatinine ratio (UPCR) threshold of 0.7 or 0.8 have lower risks of loss of renal function [7–10]. Immunosuppressive therapy is essential to induce and sustain remission, to reduce the risk of relapse, and to prevent further kidney injury.

LN therapies have included glucocorticoids (GC), immunosuppressive medications, such as azathioprine (AZA), tacrolimus or mycophenolate mofetil (MMF), and cytotoxic agents, such as cyclophosphamide (CYC) [11–14]. Although the LUNAR trial failed to achieve its end point, rituximab remains a choice among clinicians, especially for those patients who do not respond to conventional approaches [15,16]. In 2020 and 2021, belimumab and voclosporin, respectively, were approved by the US FDA [17,18]. Most clinicians rely on MMF for maintenance therapy [19]. These treatments are ideally combined with hydroxychloroquine (HCQ) and renoprotective agents, such as angiotensin-converting enzyme inhibitors (ACE-I) or angiotensin receptor blockers (ARBs) if there are no contraindications [6]. Although these interventions have increased the 5-year overall patient survival to 80%, the rates of complete renal response at 1 year remain unacceptably low (20%–40%), and progression to ESKD is high, thus highlighting the need for novel therapies [3,4,6]. Given the key role of B cells in SLE pathogenesis, B-cell-depleting therapies, such as rituximab, ocrelizumab, and obinutuzumab, have been studied as potential therapies for LN [15,20,21].

There are several professional organizations that have issued proliferative LN treatment guidelines, including the American College of Rheumatology (ACR) in 2012, the Joint European League Against Rheumatism and European Renal Association-European Dialysis and Transplant Association (EULAR/ERA-EDTA) in 2019, and the Kidney Disease: Improving Global Outcomes (KDIGO) in 2021 [22–24]. Although these guidelines can provide a framework for proliferative LN management, the emergence of high-quality randomized control trials and novel therapies has rendered some guidelines obsolete and will likely result in significant changes in management guidelines in the near future. The KDIGO guidelines will be reviewed here as they are the most recently published guidelines [24].

All patients with SLE should be treated with antimalarials unless there are contraindications because they are generally well tolerated and have benefits in lowering SLE and LN flares, increase response rates to therapy, lower cardiovascular and thrombotic events in patients with antiphospholipid antibodies, lower risks for organ damage, improve lipid profiles, and contribute to the preservation of bone mass [24–41]. Initial therapy for proliferative LN (Class III/IV with or without Class V) includes a reduced-dose GC regimen consisting of intravenous pulse methylprednisolone 0.25–0.5 g/day up to 3 days followed by oral prednisolone 0.6–1.0 mg/kg of ideal body weight per day with a gradual GC taper to less than 7.5 mg/day by 3 months [24]. In addition to GCs, initial treatment with low-dose intravenous CYC 500 mg every 2 weeks for 6 doses or oral MMF 2–3 g/day for 6 months is recommended [24]. The combination of the aforementioned therapeutic options is considered the standard of care. The choice of regimen is determined by patient factors (age, ability to tolerate an oral regimen, concern for fertility, comorbidities, previous exposure to proliferative LN treatments, and personal preferences), cost, toxicities, and physician experience. These guidelines did not incorporate data from randomized controlled trials for the treatment of proliferative LN with belimumab (BLISS-LN) or voclosporin (AURORA 1) as add-on therapies to the standard of care regimens, both of which met their primary renal end points [13,18,24]. Therefore, updated guidelines for proliferative LN treatment are needed. A multitarget approach with a combination GC, MMF, and traditional calcineurin inhibitors, specifically tacrolimus, has been shown to be superior to CYC but is not considered first-line in KDIGO recommendations because the use of this multitarget approach was not studied in diverse SLE populations [24,42].

Following initial therapy, KDIGO recommended maintenance therapy with oral MMF 1–2 g/day as first-line therapy [13,24]. Depending on patient factors, especially pregnancy, AZA can be considered instead of MMF [24]. However, if MMF or AZA cannot be tolerated, then tacrolimus, cyclosporine A, or mizoribine can be considered [24].

The role of B-cells in SLE and LN pathogenesis and targets for treatment

B-cells in healthy individuals serve several functions to generate normal immune responses, whereas in SLE subjects, polyclonal B-cell hyperreactivity, disturbances in B-cell maturation and differentiation, lack of B-cell immunoregulatory functions, abnormal cytokine production, and synthesis of autoantibodies, are observed [43–46]. Patients with SLE produce several types of autoantibodies to nuclear complexes, such as antibodies to DNA and other components of the nucleosome [43]. Although the reactivities of these autoantibodies vary between subjects with SLE, they are considered one of the main drivers of inflammation and damage in SLE and LN [43–46].

There are many different approaches that can be taken to target B-cells in SLE and LN [44]. Although general strategies include depleting B-cells or inhibiting their function or interactions with other cell types, the most direct method to neutralize B-cells is to reduce their numbers [44]. B-cell depletion has long been accomplished with antibodies directed against a cell-surface protein, CD20. CD20 is present in most mature B-cell populations but not in plasma cells [44]. CD20 is the target for rituximab, ofatumumab, ocrelizumab, and obinutuzumab [44]. By binding this protein on the B-cell surface, these monoclonal antibodies result in the depletion of circulating B-cell populations through direct cell death, antibody-dependent cytotoxicity, and/or complement-dependent cytotoxicity (CDC) [15,20,21,47,48].

B-cell-depleting therapies for proliferative LN

Rituximab, a chimeric type I monoclonal antibody that selectively binds CD20, was the first B-cell-depleting therapy to be studied for extrarenal SLE and proliferative LN [15,47]. The EXPLORER trial, a randomized, double-blind, multicenter, placebo-controlled phase II/III trial in patients with moderately-to-severely active extrarenal SLE, compared the effects of rituximab and standard of care to placebo plus standard of care. The study failed to meet its primary end point of British Isles Lupus Assessment Group (BILAG) index improvement [47].

In the LUNAR trial, rituximab and MMF were compared to placebo and MMF in patients with proliferative LN [15]. Renal responses in LUNAR were classified as complete renal response (CRR), partial renal response (PRR), or no response (NR) [15]. When compared to placebo, rituximab as an add-on to background therapy did not provide statistically significant benefit ($P = .18$) in overall renal response (CRR and PRR); however, there was numerical superiority among rituximab-treated patients (56.9%) when compared to placebo (45.8%) in overall renal response rates (CRR or PRR). Although there was no benefit of rituximab across secondary end points, several favorable signals emerged from this study. For example, there was a statistically significant decrease in double-stranded DNA (dsDNA) levels and an increase in complement 3 (C3) and complement 4 (C4) levels in rituximab-treated patients compared to placebo [15]. Further, it was observed that there was a statistically higher proportion of rituximab-treated patients with a reduction in proteinuria at week 78 compared to placebo (73.6% vs 56.9%, respectively; $P = .036$). A striking observation was that there were fewer numbers of rituximab-treated patients, who required cyclophosphamide rescue therapy compared to placebo (0/72 vs 8/72, respectively).

Similar to the LUNAR trial, the BELONG trial evaluated ocrelizumab treatment in patients with proliferative LN. Ocrelizumab was associated with a higher rate of serious infections in the subgroup receiving background MMF therapy, resulting in an early termination of the BELONG trial [20]. Analysis of the limited dataset revealed a numerically but not statistically significant increase in renal response rates among those, who received ocrelizumab compared to placebo [20].

Despite the failure of LUNAR and BELONG to attain key clinical primary or secondary outcomes, the community still believed in B-cell depletion for the treatment of LN.

The need for type II B-cell-depleting agents

There were several explanations provided by the authors of LUNAR as to why key primary and secondary clinical outcomes were not met [15]. Among these reasons included: (1) the duration of the study was too short, as evidenced by the attainment of a significant reduction in proteinuria at week 78 in rituximab-treated patients that was not achieved at week 52; (2) the study end point included urinary sediment, a metric notorious for inconsistent results; however, removal of this component in a post hoc analysis did not alter the results in any major way; (3) the study had too small a sample size; with the same effect size and hundreds more patients enrolled, the result may have been statistically significant; (4) more steroids were used in the placebo group; and (5) B-cell depletion may have been inadequate [15].

This final point is supported by subsequent analyses that suggested that the rapidity, depth, and duration of peripheral B-cell depletion were associated with greater renal response rates and that the presence of residual B cells in peripheral blood after rituximab administration has been associated with inferior clinical responses in SLE and LN [49–51]. It has also been observed that there is substantial variability in the degree of B-cell depletion that is observed in SLE patients following rituximab [49–52]. The resistance to B-cell depletion by type I anti-CD20 antibodies in SLE, such as rituximab, may occur through several mechanisms, such as Fcγ receptor IIB (FcγRIIB)-mediated internalization of CD20, ineffective CDC, decreased engagement of effector cells due to natural killer-cell defects or Fc receptor polymorphisms, acquired deficiencies in antibody-dependent cellular phagocytosis (ADCP), and immunogenicity to rituximab, which may be overcome by type II, humanized CD20-depleting agents [51–56].

Obinutuzumab is a novel, type II, humanized anti-CD20 monoclonal antibody that was developed to address the need for therapeutics with greater potency than rituximab [57]. It has a glycoengineered posttranslational Fc region that was developed to increase activity by enhancing binding affinity to the FcγRIII receptor on immune effector cells. It also has a modified elbow-hinge amino acid sequence compared to type I agents that together enhance direct cell death and antibody-dependent, cell-mediated cytotoxicity/phagocytosis (ADCC/ADCP), while decreasing CDC (Figs. 1–3) [56–60]. This differs from rituximab in that rituximab results in B-cell depletion through ADCC and CDC by clustering CD20 within lipid rafts with a small role in its ability to directly cause cell death [56–58,61]. These unique properties of obinutuzumab have translated clinically as its superiority compared to rituximab in both malignancies and autoimmune conditions [21,53,54,60,62,63]. With obinutuzumab resulting in greater B-cell depletion than rituximab in SLE patient samples, greater efficacy in the treatment of murine LN, and superiority to rituximab in the treatment of B-cell malignancies, the NOBILITY trial was designed to assess its performance in the treatment of proliferative LN [21,53,54,63].

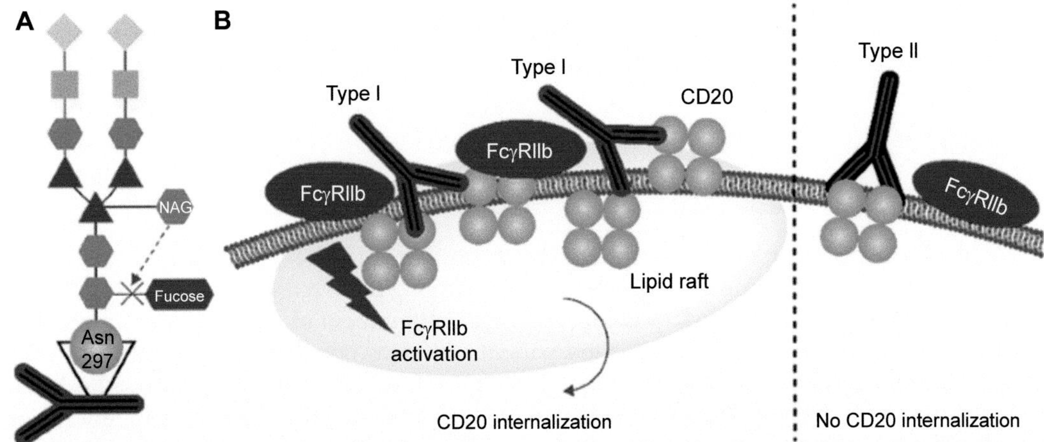

FIG. 1 Structure and binding behavior of obinutuzumab, glycoengineered structure, and type II binding properties of obinutuzumab. (A) Glycoengineering by defucosylation of immunoglobulin G oligosaccharides in the Fc region of obinutuzumab. In Chinese hamster ovary producer cells, *N*-acetylglucosamine (NAG) is assembled into oligosaccharides, which sterically prevents the addition of fucose to the carbohydrate attached to asparagine (Asn) 297 [58]. (B) Hypothetical model of CD20-binding properties of type I and II antibodies. In contrast to intertetrameric CD20 binding of type I antibodies, intratetrameric binding of type II antibodies to CD20 does not lead to FcγRIIb-mediated internalization of CD20 in lipid rafts [58].

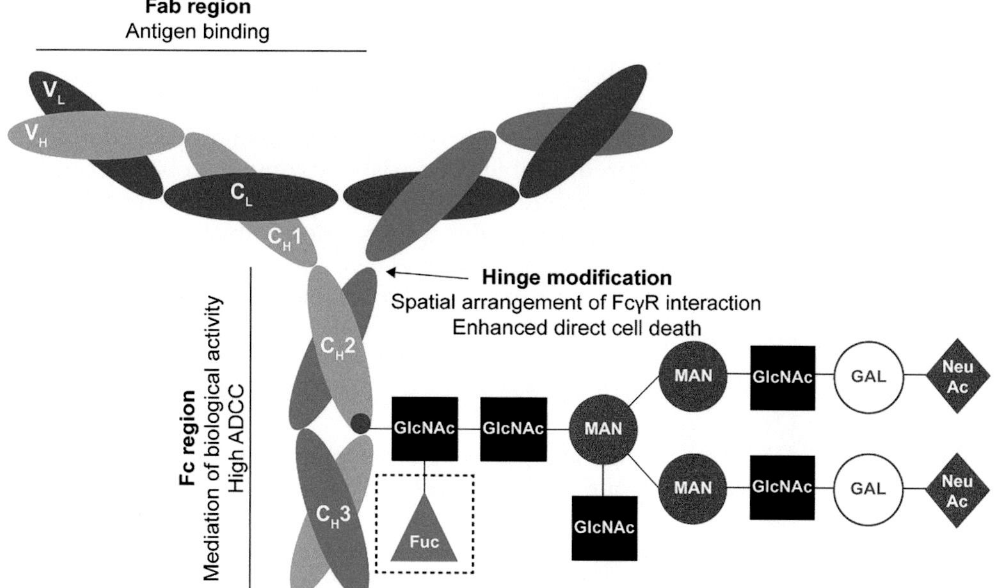

FIG. 2 Structure of obinutuzumab and the Fc-attached glycan tree modified by glycoengineering. The illustration shows the main peptide chains of obinutuzumab that compose the Fab antigen-binding domain (V_H, V_L, C_H1, and C_H) and the Fc domain (C_H2 and C_H3), which interacts with FcγRs. The glycan tree is attached to asparagine 297. The core fucose that is not added to the glycan tree is highlighted with a dashed box [59]. *ADCC*, antibody-dependent cell-mediated cytotoxicity; C_H, constant heavy chain; C_L, constant light chain; *Fuc*, fucose; *Gal*, galactose; *GlcNAc*, *N*-acetylglucosamine; *Man*, mannose; *NeuAc*, *N*-acetylneuraminic acid; V_H, variable heavy chain; V_L, variable light chain [59].

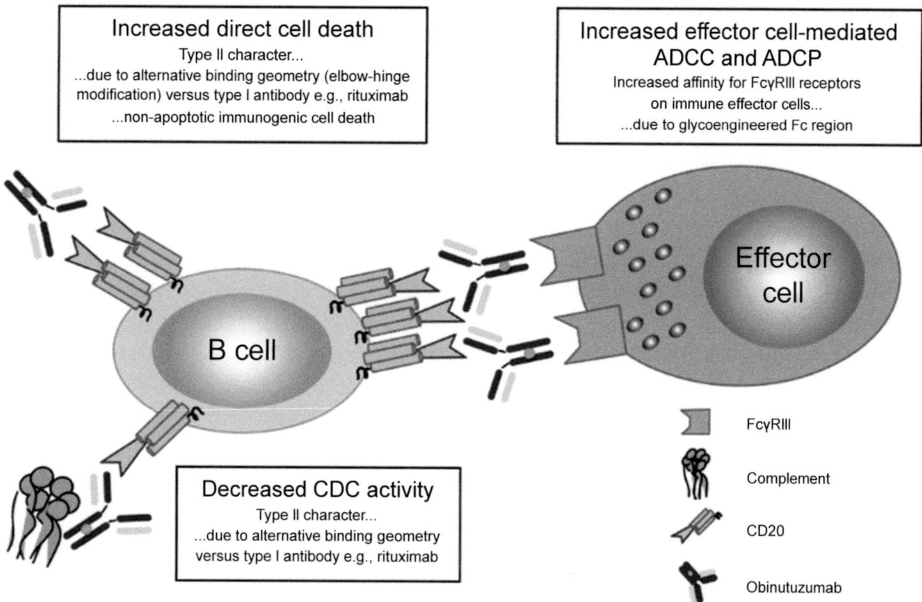

FIG. 3 Putative mechanisms of action of obinutuzumab. Please refer to the text for further information and supporting Refs. [57, 60]. *ADCC*, antibody-dependent cell-mediated cytotoxicity; *ADCP*, antibody-dependent cellular phagocytosis; *CDC*, complement-dependent cytotoxicity [57,60].

Obinutuzumab treatment in proliferative LN

The NOBILITY trial is the only controlled trial to date of obinutuzumab in proliferative LN. It is a phase 2, multicenter, randomized, double-blind trial that compares obinutuzumab to a placebo in patients with proliferative LN treated with MMF and GCs [21]. The main goal of the trial was to test the hypothesis that enhanced B-cell depletion with obinutuzumab would increase the rate of CRR when added to the standard of care compared with the standard of care alone [21]. In contrast to the LUNAR trial, which combined CRR and PRR in the end point, the NOBILITY trial used CRR alone as the primary end point at week 52. CRR required a UPCR of <0.5 without an increase of creatinine >115% of baseline as well as serum creatinine less than or equal to the upper limit of normal and <10 RBC/high power field without red blood cell casts [21].

This trial achieved its primary end point and showed that a significantly greater proportion of patients in the obinutuzumab group [22/63 patients (35%)] achieved CRR than in the placebo group (14/62 patients [23%]) at week 52 with an effect size of 12% ($P=.115$) [21]. Importantly, a higher proportion of obinutuzumab-treated patients (26/63 patients [41%]) achieved a CRR compared with placebo (14/62 patients [23%]) through week 104 with an effect size of 19% ($P=.026$) despite this being 1.5 years after the last obinutuzumab treatment, demonstrating the sustained effect of obinutuzumab and that a prolonged period of time may be needed for healing in proliferative LN patients [21].

Secondary end points from NOBILITY demonstrated that there were greater improvements in anti-dsDNA antibodies, C3, C4, and proteinuria [21]. Importantly, there was also a statistically significant increase in estimated glomerular filtration rate at week 4 and weeks 24 through 104 [adjusted mean difference, 9.7 mL/min/1.73 m^2 (95%CI 1.7–18) vs a reduction from baseline in the placebo group ($P=.017$)] [21]. Furthermore, obinutuzumab resulted in a rapid and potent depletion of B cells with 98% of treated patients having a peripheral $CD19^+$ B-cell count of ≤5 cells/μL by 2 weeks (after one infusion), which was sustained through week 52. Efficacy occurred without an increase in the incidence of serious adverse events, serious infections, or death compared with placebo [21].

The summary of adverse events of obinutuzumab in LN patients through week 104 is summarized in Table 1 [21]. Most patients (58 of 64; 91%) from the NOBILITY trial experienced at least one adverse event in the obinutuzumab group, but this frequency was comparable to the placebo group (54 of 61 patients; 89%) [21]. The most common adverse events in patients treated with obinutuzumab were urinary tract infections and bronchitis. A minority of events were considered to be serious, with 16 of 64 patients (25%) in the obinutuzumab group and 18 of 61 patients (30%) in the placebo group having at least one serious event [21]. There were fewer patients in the obinutuzumab group with serious infections than in the placebo group: five of 64 patients (8%) in the obinutuzumab group and 11 of 61 patients (18%) in the placebo group [21]. Infusion-related reactions occurring within 24 h of the infusions occurred in 10 of 61 patients (16%) in the obinutuzumab group and 6 of 61 patients (10%) in the placebo group [21]. The infusion-related events recorded in these patients most commonly occurred with the first infusion and included headache, nausea, hypertension, and tachycardia. All of the reported infusion-related events resolved with supportive care and none were categorized as serious. One death was reported in the obinutuzumab group, which was due to a gastrointestinal perforation [21]. One patient in the placebo group died of progressive multifocal leukoencephalopathy [21].

TABLE 1 Safety summary for NOBILITY trial through week 104.

	Obinutuzumab $n = 64$	**Placebo** $n = 61$
Any adverse event	58 (91)	54 (89)
Deaths	1 (2)	4 (7)
Serious adverse events	16 (25)	18 (30)
Serious infection adverse events	5 (8)	11 (18)
Infection adverse event	48 (75)	38 (62)
Most common adverse events[a]		
Urinary tract infection	15 (23)	13 (21)
Bronchitis	12 (19)	5 (8)
Herpes zoster	9 (15)	6 (10)
Abdominal pain	7 (11)	3 (5)
Infusion-related reaction	7 (11)	6 (10)
Nausea	6 (9)	3 (5)
Upper respiratory tract infection	6 (9)	5 (8)
Hypertension	6 (9)	3 (5)
Anemia	5 (8)	4 (7)
Nasopharyngitis	5 (8)	6 (10)
Pharyngitis	5 (8)	4 (7)
Arthralgia	5 (8)	4 (7)
Headache	5 (8)	4 (7)
Conjunctivitis	4 (6)	2 (3)
Influenza	4 (6)	2 (3)
Neutropenia	3 (5)	3 (5)
Diarrhea	3 (5)	5 (8)
Peripheral edema	3 (5)	3 (5)
Gastroenteritis	3 (5)	6 (10)
Sinusitis	3 (5)	0
Insomnia	3 (5)	4 (7)
Frequent urination	3 (5)	0
Cough	3 (5)	1 (2)
Infusion-related reaction[b]	10 (16)	6 (10)
Serious infusion-related reaction	0	0
Progressive multifocal leukoencephalopathy	0	1 (2)

[a] *Events that occurred in at least 5% of patients in the obinutuzumab group.*
[b] *Includes all treatment-related adverse events that occurred in the 24 h from the start of blinded obinutuzumab or placebo infusions.*
Data are n *(%) of patients. One patient randomized to placebo inadvertently received obinutuzumab during the first cycle. This patient is included in the obinutuzumab group for safety analyses [21].*

TABLE 2 B-cell depletion to ≤5 cells/μL in NOBILITY and LUNAR.

CD19 measurement	NOBILITY obinutuzumab +MMF ($n = 63$)	LUNAR rituximab + MMF ($n = 72$)
Baseline	0% (0 of 48)	0% (0 of 65)
Week 2	98% (51 of 52)	52% (35 of 67)
Week 4	96% (54 of 56)	74% (49 of 66)
Week 12	96% (52 of 54)	87% (59 of 68)
Week 24	93% (52 of 56)	52% (31 of 60)
Week 52	94% (51 of 54)	48% (30 of 63)

In NOBILITY, obinutuzumab 1000 mg was administered on days 1, 15, 168, and 182. In LUNAR, rituximab 1000 mg was administered on days 1, 15, 168, and 182. Patients in both studies received treatment with MMF, pulse-dose corticosteroids, and a corticosteroid taper [15,21].

Post hoc analysis further separated outcomes at week 76 of the NOBILITY trial in obinutuzumab-treated patients who had sustained depletion of B cells (defined as those who had <0.4 cells/μL at weeks 26 and 52) vs those who did not. At 76 weeks, 50% in the sustained B-cell depletion group achieved CRR compared to 35% in the nonsustained B-cell depletion group. Thus, the CRR effect size was enhanced by 15% for the sustained depleters compared with those who had partial recovery of B cells. This observation highlights the importance that profound and sustained B-cell depletion is needed to optimize renal responses in patients with proliferative LN [21].

Comparison between $CD19^+$ B cell data from the NOBILITY and LUNAR trials demonstrated that treatment with obinutuzumab resulted in quicker, deeper, and more durable peripheral B-cell depletion than with rituximab (Table 2) [15,21]. In obinutuzumab-treated patients, 51 of 54 patients (94%) remained B-cell depleted to a value of ≤5 cells/μL through week 52, whereas fewer than half of patients (30 of 63 [48%]) treated with rituximab remained B-cell depleted to the same value over the same period of time [15,21]. Such a comparison suggests greater B-cell depletion achieved with obinutuzumab resulted in enhanced clinical responses in proliferative LN.

Conclusions

Proliferative LN is a common complication of SLE that introduces significant morbidity and mortality [1,3,4]. Despite advances in immunosuppressive therapies over the last few decades, there are still many patients with LN who do not achieve adequate renal responses [3,4]. B cells play a pivotal role in the pathogenesis of SLE and LN, but previous studies failed to demonstrate the benefit of rituximab over standard of care. Recent data with obinutuzumab suggest that deeper and more durable peripheral B-cell depletion may be necessary to yield significant clinical responses in patients with proliferative LN. Obinutuzumab is currently being studied for the treatment of proliferative LN in a global phase III trial (NCT04221477).

Building on the observations from the NOBILITY trial, other approaches to achieve profound B-cell depletion include antibodies with other specificities. For example, studies are underway in SLE and LN with ianalumab, a monoclonal antibody directed against the B-cell-activating factor (BAFF) receptor. Favorable results have been observed in the treatment of patients with Sjogren's Syndrome with this monoclonal antibody [64]. Pioneered in B-cell-malignancies, bispecific antibodies, such as mosunetuzumab, target both CD3 and CD20 with the intent of activating and directing T-cells to the B-cell target. Chimeric antigen receptor (CAR) T-cell therapy has been successfully evaluated in SLE [65,66]. The future is bright for our patients with SLE and LN as new therapeutic strategies evolve into approved treatments.

References

[1] Rovin BH, Stillman I. Kidney. In: Lahita R, editor. Systemic lupus erythematosus. 5th ed. San Diego, CA, USA: Academic Press; 2011. p. 769–814.

[2] Bajema IM, Wilhelmus S, Alpers CE, Bruijn JA, Colvin RB, Cook HT, D'Agati VD, Ferrario F, Haas M, Jennette JC, Joh K, Nast CC, Noël LH, Rijnink EC, Roberts ISD, Seshan SV, Sethi S, Fogo AB. Revision of the International Society of Nephrology/Renal Pathology Society classification for lupus nephritis: clarification of definitions, and modified National Institutes of Health activity and chronicity indices. Kidney Int 2018;93(4):789–96. https://doi.org/10.1016/j.kint.2017.11.023. Epub 2018 Feb 16 29459092.

[3] Hanly JG, O'Keeffe AG, Su L, Urowitz MB, Romero-Diaz J, Gordon C, Bae SC, Bernatsky S, Clarke AE, Wallace DJ, Merrill JT, Isenberg DA, Rahman A, Ginzler EM, Fortin P, Gladman DD, Sanchez-Guerrero J, Petri M, Bruce IN, Dooley MA, Ramsey-Goldman R, Aranow C, Alarcón GS, Fessler BJ, Steinsson K, Nived O, Sturfelt GK, Manzi S, Khamashta MA, van Vollenhoven RF, Zoma AA, Ramos-Casals M, Ruiz-Irastorza G, Lim SS, Stoll T, Inanc M, Kalunian KC, Kamen DL, Maddison P, Peschken CA, Jacobsen S, Askanase A, Theriault C, Thompson K, Farewell V. The frequency and outcome of lupus nephritis: results from an international inception cohort study. Rheumatology 2016;55(2):252–62. https://doi.org/10.1093/rheumatology/kev311. Epub 2015 Sep 5. PMCID:PMC4939728 26342222.

[4] Tektonidou MG, Dasgupta A, Ward MM. Risk of end-stage renal disease in patients with lupus nephritis, 1971–2015: a systematic review and Bayesian meta-analysis. Arthritis Rheumatol 2016;68:1432–41. https://doi.org/10.1002/art.39594.

[5] Yen E, Rajkumar S, Sharma R, Singh R. Lupus nephritis mortality in the United States, 1999-2019: profound disparities by race/ethnicity and place of residence and a recent worsening trend [abstract]. *Arthritis* Rheumatol 2021;73(Suppl 9). https://acrabstracts.org/abstract/lupus-nephritis-mortality-in-the-united-states-1999-2019-profound-disparities-by-race-ethnicity-and-place-of-residence-and-a-recent-worsening-trend/. [Accessed October 5, 2022].

[6] Tamirou F, Houssiau FA. Management of lupus nephritis. J Clin Med 2021;10(4):670. https://doi.org/10.3390/jcm10040670. 33572385. PMCID: PMC7916202.

[7] Tamirou F, D'Cruz D, Sangle S, Remy P, Vasconcelos C, Fiehn C, Ayala GM, Gilboe IM, Tektonidou M, Blockmans D, et al. Long-term follow-up of the MAINTAIN Nephritis Trial, comparing azathioprine and mycophenolate mofetil as maintenance therapy of lupus nephritis. Ann Rheum Dis 2016;75:526–31. https://doi.org/10.1136/annrheumdis-2014-206897.

[8] Tamirou F, Lauwerys BR, Dall'Era M, Mackay M, Rovin B, Cervera R, Houssiau FA. MAINTAIN nephritis trial investigators A proteinuria cut-off level of 0.7 g/day after 12 months of treatment best predicts long-term renal outcome in lupus nephritis: data from the MAINTAIN Nephritis Trial. Lupus Sci Med 2015;2, e000123. https://doi.org/10.1136/lupus-2015-000123.

[9] Dall'Era M, Cisternas MG, Smilek DE, Straub L, Houssiau FA, Cervera R, Rovin BH, Mackay M. Predictors of long-term renal outcome in lupus nephritis trials: lessons learned from the euro-lupus nephritis cohort. Arthritis Rheumatol 2015;67:1305–13. https://doi.org/10.1002/art.39026.

[10] Ugolini-Lopes MR, Seguro L, Castro M, Daffre D, Lopes AC, Borba EF, Bonfá E. Early proteinuria response: a valid real-life situation predictor of long-term lupus renal outcome in an ethnically diverse group with severe biopsy-proven nephritis? Lupus Sci Med 2017;4, e000213. https://doi.org/10.1136/lupus-2017-000213.

[11] Austin III HA, Klippel JH, Balow JE, le Riche NG, Steinberg AD, Plotz PH, Decker JL. Therapy of lupus nephritis. Controlled trial of prednisone and cytotoxic drugs. N Engl J Med 1986;314:614–9. https://doi.org/10.1056/NEJM198603063141004.

[12] Houssiau FA, Vasconcelos C, D'Cruz D, Sebastiani GD, Garrido EE, Danieli MG, Abramovicz D, Blockmans D, Mathieu A, Direskeneli H, et al. Immunosuppressive therapy in lupus nephritis: the Euro-Lupus Nephritis Trial, a randomized trial of low-dose versus high-dose intravenous cyclophosphamide. Arthritis Rheum 2002;46:2121–31. https://doi.org/10.1002/art.10461.

[13] Appel GB, Contreras G, Dooley MA, Ginzler EM, Isenberg D, Jayne D, Li LS, Mysler E, Sánchez-Guerrero J, Solomons N, et al. Mycophenolate mofetil versus cyclophosphamide for induction treatment of lupus nephritis. J Am Soc Nephrol 2009;20:1103–12. https://doi.org/10.1681/ASN.2008101028.

[14] Liu Z, Zhang H, Liu Z, Xing C, Fu P, Ni Z, Chen J, Lin H, Liu F, He Y, et al. Multitarget therapy for induction treatment of lupus nephritis: a randomized trial. Ann Intern Med 2015;162:18–26. https://doi.org/10.7326/M14-1030.

[15] Rovin BH, Furie R, Latinis K, Looney RJ, Fervenza FC, Sanchez-Guerrero J, Maciuca R, Zhang D, Garg JP, Brunetta P, Appel G, LUNAR Investigator Group. Efficacy and safety of rituximab in patients with active proliferative lupus nephritis: the Lupus Nephritis Assessment with Rituximab study. Arthritis Rheum 2012;64(4):1215–26. https://doi.org/10.1002/art.34359. Epub 2012 Jan 9 22231479.

[16] Fanouriakis A, Kostopoulou M, Alunno A, et al. 2019 update of the EULAR recommendations for the management of systemic lupus erythematosus. Ann Rheum Dis 2019;78:736–45.

[17] Furie R, Rovin BH, Houssiau F, Malvar A, Teng YKO, Contreras G, Amoura Z, Yu X, Mok CC, Santiago MB, Saxena A, Green Y, Ji B, Kleoudis C, Burriss SW, Barnett C, Roth DA. Two-year, randomized, controlled trial of Belimumab in lupus nephritis. N Engl J Med 2020;383(12):1117–28. https://doi.org/10.1056/NEJMoa2001180. 32937045.

[18] Rovin BH, Teng YKO, Ginzler EM, Arriens C, Caster DJ, Romero-Diaz J, Gibson K, Kaplan J, Lisk L, Navarra S, Parikh SV, Randhawa S, Solomons N, Huizinga RB. Efficacy and safety of voclosporin versus placebo for lupus nephritis (AURORA 1): a double-blind, randomised, multicentre, placebo-controlled, phase 3 trial. Lancet 2021;397(10289):2070–80. https://doi.org/10.1016/S0140-6736(21)00578-X. Epub 2021 May 7. Erratum in: Lancet 2021 May 29; 397(10289):2048 33971155.

[19] Dooley MA, Jayne D, Ginzler EM, Isenberg D, Olsen NJ, Wofsy D, Eitner F, Appel GB, Contreras G, Lisk L, et al. Mycophenolate versus azathioprine as maintenance therapy for lupus nephritis. N Engl J Med 2011;365:1886–95. https://doi.org/10.1056/NEJMoa1014460.

[20] Mysler EF, Spindler AJ, Guzman R, Bijl M, Jayne D, Furie RA, Houssiau FA, Drappa J, Close D, Maciuca R, Rao K, Shahdad S, Brunetta P. Efficacy and safety of ocrelizumab in active proliferative lupus nephritis: results from a randomized, double-blind, phase III study. Arthritis Rheum 2013;65:2368–79. https://doi.org/10.1002/art.38037.

[21] Furie RA, Aroca G, Cascino MD, Garg JP, Rovin BH, Alvarez A, Fragoso-Loyo H, Zuta-Santillan E, Schindler T, Brunetta P, Looney CM, Hassan I, Malvar A. B-cell depletion with obinutuzumab for the treatment of proliferative lupus nephritis: a randomised, double-blind, placebo-controlled trial. Ann Rheum Dis 2022;81:100–7.

[22] Hahn BH, McMahon MA, Wilkinson A, Wallace WD, Daikh DI, Fitzgerald JD, Karpouzas GA, Merrill JT, Wallace DJ, Yazdany J, Ramsey-Goldman R, Singh K, Khalighi M, Choi SI, Gogia M, Kafaja S, Kamgar M, Lau C, Martin WJ, Parikh S, Peng J, Rastogi A, Chen W, Grossman JM, American College of Rheumatology. American College of Rheumatology guidelines for screening, treatment, and management of lupus nephritis. Arthritis Care Res 2012;64(6):797–808. https://doi.org/10.1002/acr.21664. 22556106. PMCID: PMC3437757.

[23] Fanouriakis A, Kostopoulou M, Cheema K, et al. 2019 Update of the Joint European League Against Rheumatism and European Renal Association–European Dialysis and Transplant Association (EULAR/ERA–EDTA) recommendations for the management of lupus nephritis. Ann Rheum Dis 2020;79:713–23.

[24] Kidney Disease: Improving Global Outcomes (KDIGO) Glomerular Diseases Work Group. KDIGO 2021 clinical practice guideline for the management of glomerular diseases. Kidney Int 2021;100(4S):S1–S276.

[25] Galindo-Izquierdo M, Rodriguez-Almaraz E, Pego-Reigosa JM, et al. Characterization of patients with lupus nephritis included in a large cohort from the Spanish Society of Rheumatology Registry of Patients with Systemic Lupus Erythematosus (RELESSER). Medicine (Baltimore) 2016;95:e2891.

[26] Pons-Estel GJ, Alarcon GS, Burgos PI, et al. Mestizos with systemic lupus erythematosus develop renal disease early while antimalarials retard its appearance: data from a Latin American cohort. Lupus 2013;22:899–907.

[27] Kasitanon N, Fine DM, Haas M, et al. Hydroxychloroquine use predicts complete renal remission within 12 months among patients treated with mycophenolate mofetil therapy for membranous lupus nephritis. Lupus 2006;15:366–70.

[28] Mejia-Vilet JM, Cordova-Sanchez BM, Uribe-Uribe NO, et al. Immunosuppressive treatment for pure membranous lupus nephropathy in a Hispanic population. Clin Rheumatol 2016;35:2219–27.

[29] Kaiser R, Cleveland CM, Criswell LA. Risk and protective factors for thrombosis in systemic lupus erythematosus: results from a large, multi-ethnic cohort. Ann Rheum Dis 2009;68:238–41.

[30] Petri M. Use of hydroxychloroquine to prevent thrombosis in systemic lupus erythematosus and in antiphospholipid antibody-positive patients. Curr Rheumatol Rep 2011;13:77–80.

[31] Ruiz-Irastorza G, Egurbide MV, Pijoan JI, et al. Effect of antimalarials on thrombosis and survival in patients with systemic lupus erythematosus. Lupus 2006;15:577–83.

[32] Tektonidou MG, Laskari K, Panagiotakos DB, et al. Risk factors for thrombosis and primary thrombosis prevention in patients with systemic lupus erythematosus with or without antiphospholipid antibodies. Arthritis Rheumatol 2009;61:29–36.

[33] Fessler BJ, Alarcon GS, McGwin Jr G, et al. Systemic lupus erythematosus in three ethnic groups: XVI. Association of hydroxychloroquine use with reduced risk of damage accrual. Arthritis Rheumatol 2005;52:1473–80.

[34] Pakchotanon R, Gladman DD, Su J, et al. More consistent antimalarial intake in first 5 years of disease is associated with better prognosis in patients with systemic lupus erythematosus. J Rheumatol 2018;45:90–4.

[35] Pokroy-Shapira E, Gelernter I, Molad Y. Evolution of chronic kidney disease in patients with systemic lupus erythematosus over a long period follow-up: a single-center inception cohort study. Clin Rheumatol 2014;33:649–57.

[36] Pons-Estel GJ, Alarcon GS, McGwin Jr G, et al. Protective effect of hydroxychloroquine on renal damage in patients with lupus nephritis: LXV, data from a multiethnic US cohort. Arthritis Rheumatol 2009;61:830–9.

[37] Shaharir SS, Ghafor AH, Said MS, et al. A descriptive study of the factors associated with damage in Malaysian patients with lupus nephritis. Lupus 2014;23:436–42.

[38] Siso A, Ramos-Casals M, Bove A, et al. Previous antimalarial therapy in patients diagnosed with lupus nephritis: influence on outcomes and survival. Lupus 2008;17:281–8.

[39] Hodis HN, Quismorio Jr FP, Wickham E, et al. The lipid, lipoprotein, and apolipoprotein effects of hydroxychloroquine in patients with systemic lupus erythematosus. J Rheumatol 1993;20:661–5.

[40] Tam LS, Gladman DD, Hallett DC, et al. Effect of antimalarial agents on the fasting lipid profile in systemic lupus erythematosus. J Rheumatol 2000;27:2142–5.

[41] Lakshminarayanan S, Walsh S, Mohanraj M, et al. Factors associated with low bone mineral density in female patients with systemic lupus erythematosus. J Rheumatol 2001;28:102–8.

[42] Liu Z, Zhang H, Liu Z, et al. Multitarget therapy for induction treatment of lupus nephritis. Ann Intern Med 2015;162:18–26.

[43] Dörner T, Giesecke C, Lipsky PE. Mechanisms of B cell autoimmunity in SLE. Arthritis Res Ther 2011;13(5):243. https://doi.org/10.1186/ar3433. Epub 2011 Oct 27 22078750. PMCID: PMC3308063.

[44] Atisha-Fregoso Y, Toz B, Diamond B. Meant to B: B cells as a therapeutic target in systemic lupus erythematosus. J Clin Invest 2021;131(12), e149095. https://doi.org/10.1172/JCI149095.

[45] Bhat P, Radhakrishnan J. B lymphocytes and lupus nephritis: new insights into pathogenesis and targeted therapies. Kidney Int 2008;0085-2538. 73(3):261–8. https://doi.org/10.1038/sj.ki.5002663.

[46] Waldman M, Madaio MP. Pathogenic autoantibodies in lupus nephritis. Lupus 2005;14(1):19–24. https://doi.org/10.1191/0961203305lu2054oa. 15732283.

[47] Merrill JT, Neuwelt CM, Wallace DJ, Shanahan JC, Latinis KM, Oates JC, Utset TO, Gordon C, Isenberg DA, Hsieh HJ, Zhang D, Brunetta PG. Efficacy and safety of rituximab in moderately-to-severely active systemic lupus erythematosus: the randomized, double-blind, phase II/III systemic lupus erythematosus evaluation of rituximab trial. Arthritis Rheum 2010;62(1):222–33. https://doi.org/10.1002/art.27233. 20039413. PMCID: PMC4548300.

[48] Masoud S, McAdoo SP, Bedi R, Cairns TD, Lightstone L. Ofatumumab for B cell depletion in patients with systemic lupus erythematosus who are allergic to rituximab. Rheumatology 2018;57(7):1156–61. https://doi.org/10.1093/rheumatology/key042.

[49] Vital EM, Dass S, Buch MH, et al. B cell biomarkers of rituximab responses in systemic lupus erythematosus. Arthritis Rheum 2011;63:3038–47.

[50] Gomez Mendez LM, Cascino MD, Garg J, et al. Peripheral blood B cell depletion after rituximab and complete response in lupus nephritis. Clin J Am Soc Nephrol 2018;13:1502–9.

[51] Md Yusof MY, Shaw D, El-Sherbiny YM, et al. Predicting and managing primary and secondary non-response to rituximab using B-cell biomarkers in systemic lupus erythematosus. Ann Rheum Dis 2017;76:1829–36.

[52] Anolik JH, Campbell D, Felgar RE, et al. The relationship of Fcgamma RIIIa genotype to degree of B cell depletion by rituximab in the treatment of systemic lupus erythematosus. Arthritis Rheum 2003;48:455–9.

[53] Reddy V, Cambridge G, Isenberg DA, et al. Internalization of rituximab and the efficiency of B cell depletion in rheumatoid arthritis and systemic lupus erythematosus. Arthritis Rheumatol 2015;67:2046–55.

[54] Reddy V, Klein C, Isenberg DA, et al. Obinutuzumab induces superior B-cell cytotoxicity to rituximab in rheumatoid arthritis and systemic lupus erythematosus patient samples. Rheumatology 2017;56:1227–37.

[55] Ahuja A, Teichmann LL, Wang H, et al. An acquired defect in IgG-dependent phagocytosis explains the impairment in antibody-mediated cellular depletion in lupus. J Immunol 2011;187:3888–94.

[56] Mössner E, Brünker P, Moser S, et al. Increasing the efficacy of CD20 antibody therapy through the engineering of a new type II anti-CD20 antibody with enhanced direct and immune effector cell-mediated B-cell cytotoxicity. Blood 2010;115:4393–402.

[57] Tobinai K, Klein C, Oya N, et al. A review of obinutuzumab (GA101), a novel type II anti-CD20 monoclonal antibody, for the treatment of patients with B-cell malignancies. Adv Ther 2017;34:324–56. https://doi.org/10.1007/s12325-016-0451-1.

[58] Goede V, Klein C, Stilgenbauer S. Obinutuzumab (GA101) for the treatment of chronic lymphocytic leukemia and other B-cell non-Hodgkin's lymphomas: a glycoengineered type II CD20 antibody. Oncol Res Treat 2015;38:185–92.

[59] Illidge T, Klein C, Sehn LH, Davies A, Salles G, Cartron G. Obinutuzumab in hematologic malignancies: lessons learned to date. Cancer Treat Rev 2015;41(9):784–92. https://doi.org/10.1016/j.ctrv.2015.07.003. Epub 2015 Jul 14 26190254.

[60] Goede V, Fischer K, Busch R, et al. Obinutuzumab plus chlorambucil in patients with CLL and coexisting conditions. N Engl J Med 2014;370:1101–10.

[61] Alduaij W, Ivanov A, Honeychurch J, Cheadle EJ, Potluri S, Lim SH, Shimada K, Chan CH, Tutt A, Beers SA, Glennie MJ, Cragg MS, Illidge TM. Novel type II anti-CD20 monoclonal antibody (GA101) evokes homotypic adhesion and actin-dependent, lysosome-mediated cell death in B-cell malignancies. Blood 2011;117(17):4519–29. https://doi.org/10.1182/blood-2010-07-296913. Epub 2011 Mar 4 21378274. PMCID: PMC3099571.

[62] Marcus R, Davies A, Ando K, et al. Obinutuzumab for the first-line treatment of follicular lymphoma. N Engl J Med 2017;377:1331–44.

[63] Marinov AD, Wang H, Bastacky SI, et al. The type II anti-CD20 antibody obinutuzumab (GA101) is more effective than rituximab at depleting B cells and treating disease in a murine lupus model. Arthritis Rheumatol 2021;73:826–36.

[64] Bowman SJ, Fox R, Dörner T, Mariette X, Papas A, Grader-Beck T, Fisher BA, Barcelos F, De Vita S, Schulze-Koops H, Moots RJ, Junge G, Woznicki JN, Sopala MA, Luo WL, Hueber W. Safety and efficacy of subcutaneous ianalumab (VAY736) in patients with primary Sjögren's syndrome: a randomised, double-blind, placebo-controlled, phase 2b dose-finding trial. Lancet 2022;399(10320):161–71. https://doi.org/10.1016/S0140-6736(21)02251-0. Epub 2021 Nov 30 34861168.

[65] Mougiakakos D, Krönke G, Völkl S, Kretschmann S, Aigner M, Kharboutli S, Böltz S, Manger B, Mackensen A, Schett G. CD19-targeted CAR T cells in refractory systemic lupus erythematosus. N Engl J Med 2021;385(6):567–9. https://doi.org/10.1056/NEJMc2107725. 34347960.

[66] Mackensen A, Müller F, Mougiakakos D, Böltz S, Wilhelm A, Aigner M, Völkl S, Simon D, Kleyer A, Munoz L, Kretschmann S, Kharboutli S, Gary R, Reimann H, Rösler W, Uderhardt S, Bang H, Herrmann M, Ekici AB, Buettner C, Habenicht KM, Winkler TH, Krönke G, Schett G. Anti-CD19 CAR T cell therapy for refractory systemic lupus erythematosus. Nat Med 2022;28(10):2124–32. https://doi.org/10.1038/s41591-022-02017-5. Epub 2022 Sep 15 36109639.

CHAPTER

14

Anti-CD20 antibodies in glomerular diseases, their resistance and reversal approaches

Lakshmi Kannan

Pikeville Medical Center, Adjunct Clinical Faculty, University of Pikeville Kentucky College of Osteopathic Medicine, Pikeville, KY, United States

Abstract

Anti-CD20 monoclonal antibody-mediated depletion of B cells has contributed to the understanding of the role of B cells in several autoimmune diseases. They were initially developed to treat B cell proliferative disorders, including non-Hodgkin's lymphoma and chronic lymphocytic leukemia. Subsequently, they have been used to treat autoimmune disorders, and for renal disorders, rituximab has emerged as a possible adjunct or alternative treatment option in glomerular diseases based on the rationale that the removal of autoantibody-producing or T cell-activating B cells would lead to clinical improvement.

Rituximab is a chimeric monoclonal antibody and can induce antidrug antibodies, which could neutralize B-cell cytotoxicity and impact clinical outcomes. In such cases, humanized anti-CD20 monoclonal antibodies seem to be a satisfying therapeutic alternative for patients with antirituximab antibodies and resistant or relapsing nephrotic/nephritic syndromes.

Abbreviations

AAV	ANCA-associated vasculitis
ANCA	antineutrophil cytoplasmic antibodies
APC	antigen processing cells
CAMR	chronic antibody mediated rejection
EGPA	eosinophilic granulomatosis with polyangiitis
FDA	Food and Drug Administration
FSGS	focal segmental glomerulosclerosis
GEMRITUX	rituximab for severe membranous nephropathy
GFR	glomerular filtration rate
GPA	granulomatous polyangiitis
HACA	human antichimeric antibodies
HAHA	human-antihuman antibodies

https://doi.org/10.1016/B978-0-443-19200-5.00009-9

HCV	hepatitis C virus
HIV	human immunodeficiency virus
HUS	hemolytic uremic syndrome
ICU	intensive care unit
IL	interleukin
LN	lupus nephritis
LUNAR	Lupus Nephritis Assessment with Rituximab Study
mAb	monoclonal antibody
MAINRITSAN	maintenance of remission using rituximab in systemic ANCA-associated vasculitis.
MCD	minimal change disease
MENTOR	rituximab or cyclosporine in the treatment of membranous nephropathy
MMF	mycophenolate mofetil
MN	membranous nephropathy
MPA	microscopic polyangiitis
NIAT	nonimmunosuppressive antiproteinuric treatment
PLA2R	phospholipase A2 receptor
PTLD	posttransplant lymphoproliferative disorder
RAVE	rituximab versus cyclophosphamide for ANCA-associated vasculitis
RITAZAREM	rituximab versus azathioprine in remission of maintenance
RITUXILUP	trial of rituximab and mycophenolate mofetil without oral steroids for lupus nephritis
RITUXVAS	rituximab versus cyclophosphamide in ANCA-associated renal vasculitis
RTX	rituximab
SLE	systemic lupus erythematosus
SMPDL	3b-sphingomyelin-phosphodiesterase-acid-like-3b
STARMEN	sequential treatment with tacrolimus and rituximab versus alternating corticosteroids and cyclophosphamide in primary membranous nephropathy
STAT	signal transducer and activator of transcription 6
SVV	small vessel vasculitis
TMA	thrombotic microangiopathic hemolytic anemia
TNF	tumor necrosis factor
TTP	thrombotic thrombocytopenic purpura
UCHL1	ubiquitin carboxyl-terminal hydrolase L1

Conflict of interest

No potential conflicts of interest were disclosed.

Introduction

CD20 is a transmembrane calcium channel involved in B-cell activation, proliferation, and differentiation. It is expressed during cell differentiation from pro-B cells to plasma cells and is present on the surface of late pre-B cells through mature memory stages of B cells [1]. Anti-CD20 monoclonal antibodies (mAbs) save early pre-B cells and plasma cells, thus allowing for long-term immune memory retention and B-cell reconstitution after depletion.

Anti-CD20 monoclonal antibodies include the first murine-human chimera, rituximab, and the newer next-generation humanized versions, ocrelizumab, obinutuzumab, and veltuzumab, and the fully human, ofatumumab [2].

Rituximab (RTX) was the first anti-CD20 mAb, introduced in 1997, which has gained FDA approval for the treatment of non-Hodgkin lymphoma, chronic lymphocytic leukemia, rheumatoid arthritis, polyangiitis granulomatosis, microscopic polyangiitis, and various other immune-mediated renal disorders. It is a murine/human unconjugated chimeric monoclonal antibody, consisting of two heavy chains of 451 amino acids and two light chains of 213 amino acids with a molecular weight of 145kD [3]. The half-life is 59.8h (ranging from 11.1 to 104.6h) after the first infusion and 174h (ranging from 26 to 442h) after the fourth infusion [4]. The half-life is increased to 10–14 days in patients with renal disease. RTX persists in circulation for 3–6 months and is not eliminated by conventional hemodialysis [5].

In addition to direct cytotoxic effects (complement- and antibody-dependent), various indirect effects, including modifications of the lipid raft, activation of kinase and caspase, and effects on apoptotic/antiapoptotic molecules, appear to play a crucial role in the observed response to rituximab treatment.

The clinical application of monoclonal antibodies has been challenged by immunogenicity as nonhumanized mAbs can stimulate the production of antibodies to some regions of the mAbs such as the fragment of antigen binding and the fragment of crystallizable and complementarity-determining regions (CDR). The antidrug antibody produced limits the binding of mAb to target antigens and promotes its clearance.

With the emergence of antibodies to mAbs, it is important to understand the immunogenic potential of the biologics, the clinical significance of antidrug antibodies, and ways to counteract the development of resistance.

Lupus nephritis

Systemic lupus erythematosus (SLE) is a chronic inflammatory disease that can affect virtually every organ in the body. When it affects the kidneys, it is referred to as lupus nephritis (LN).

Incidence

SLE patients represent 2% of the hemodialysis population [6]. Approximately 70% of patients with SLE develop kidney damage during their evolution [7]. In autopsies, more than 95% of patients with SLE have lupus nephritis [8].

Pathophysiology

Lupus nephritis remains one of the most serious complications of SLE. B cells are strongly involved in the pathogenesis of SLE and LN.

Role of anti-CD20 mAb

Based on the LUNAR study [9], 144 patients with class III or IV LN were randomized to receive an intravenous infusion of placebo or 1g of RTX at 0, 2, 24, and 26 weeks. All patients received three boluses of 1g methylprednisolone, mycophenolate 1g three times a day and prednisone. At the end of 52 weeks, the incidence of complete or partial response with RTX was higher without statistical significance and there were further reductions in anti-DNA titers and improvements in complement levels [10].

From the RITUXILUP trial with RTX, and mycophenolate mofetil without prednisone, response was obtained in almost 90% of the patients: complete remission in 52% and partial remission in 34% at 37 weeks [11].

ANCA-associated vasculitis

ANCA-associated vasculitis (AAV) is characterized by leucocyte infiltration of blood vessel walls, fibrinoid necrosis, and vascular damage. Granulomatosis with polyangiitis (GPA) and microscopic polyangiitis (MPA) are the major subgroups of AAV.

Incidence

Studies in Europe have reported annual incidence rates of 2.1–14.4, 2.4–10.1, and 0.5–6.8 per million for GPA, MPA, and EGPA, respectively [12]. A recent study from Minnesota, United States, recorded a prevalence of 421 per million [13].

Pathophysiology

AAV is a necrotizing small-vessel vasculitis (SVV) that affects predominantly capillaries, venules, arterioles, and small arteries, and (less often) medium arteries and veins. Myeloperoxidase and proteinase 3 are two major antigens in patients with AAV. The development of a pathogenic immune response to ANCA is a multifactorial process that can include genetic predisposition (e.g., genetically determined specific T-cell receptors and abnormal neutrophil expression of ANCA antigens), environmental adjuvant factors (e.g., silica exposure), an initiating antigen (e.g., ANCA antigen complementary peptide), and failure to suppress the autoimmune response (e.g., ineffective T-cell regulation).

Once pathogenic ANCA is in circulation, they activate neutrophils by reacting with ANCA antigens. ANCA-induced neutrophil activation is facilitated by neutrophil priming, which causes the release and display of ANCA antigens on the surface of neutrophils, where they are available to interact with ANCA. The binding of ANCA-to-ANCA antigens on the surface of neutrophils and in the microenvironment of the inflammation (e.g., on the surface of endothelial cells) activates neutrophils through the binding of Fab to ANCA on neutrophils and, more importantly, through Fc receptor engagement. Activated neutrophils release factors (e.g., properdin) that activate the alternative complement pathway leading to the generation of C5a, which not only activates neutrophils but also recruits more neutrophils to the site of inflammation. Complement activation established an inflammatory amplification loop that causes very destructive, localized necrotizing inflammation. A mild injury may resolve with the remodeling of the vessel to a normal structure. More severe injury persists; more monocytes mature into macrophages, and fibroblasts and myofibroblasts are activated to lay down interstitial collagen, resulting in fibrosis/sclerosis of injured vessels and adjacent tissue.

Role of anti-CD20 mAbs

Corticosteroids have been the mainstay of the induction of remission in AAV. The Rituximab versus Cyclophosphamide Trial for ANCA-Associated Vasculitis (RAVE) successfully reduced prednisone by 5 months. The RAVE trial found that rituximab is not inferior to oral cyclophosphamide for remission induction in 197 patients with newly diagnosed or flaring GPA or MPA [14].

The Rituximab versus Cyclophosphamide in ANCA-Associated Renal Vasculitis (RITUXVAS) trial compared a combination of rituximab with two IV cyclophosphamide doses against IV cyclophosphamide for 3–6 months, followed by azathioprine. As opposed to RAVE, the RITUXVAS trial did include patients with severe renal disease (median eGFR, 18 mL/min per 1.73 m^2). The two groups had similarly high rates of remission induction at 12 months (76% rituximab versus 82% cyclophosphamide) [15].

Maintenance of remission using rituximab in systemic ANCA-associated Vasculitis (MAINRITSAN) trial that compared low-dose rituximab (500 mg on days 0 and 14, and then at months 6, 12, and 18) with azathioprine (until 22 months) after induction with cyclophosphamide [16,17]. Rituximab was superior to azathioprine in maintaining remission at 28 months. Optimal maintenance therapy after rituximab has been evaluated in the rituximab versus azathioprine in remission of maintenance (RITAZAREM) trial, which enrolled patients who achieved remission with rituximab after experiencing a relapse. The patients received 1000 mg of rituximab every 4 months for five doses, or 2 mg/kg per day of azathioprine for 24 months [17].

Membranous nephropathy

Idiopathic membranous nephropathy (MN) is the most common cause of nephrotic syndrome in adults (80%) and the second or third cause of end-stage renal disease [18].

Incidence

MN is the second most-common nephropathy in adults after focal segmental glomerulosclerosis. It commonly occurs above 40 years of age with a peak incidence between 50 and 60 years in the United States. The incidence is 8–10 cases per 1 million people worldwide, and 12 per 1 million people per year in the United States [19].

Pathophysiology

Pathogenetic understanding of MN was achieved during the past decade with the identification of the M-type PLA2R autoantibody in 70%–80% of the patients [20,21]. In another 3%–5% of patients, autoantibodies directed against thrombospondin type-1 domain-containing 7A were identified [22]. It is characterized by a pathological change in the glomerular basement membrane (GBM) caused by the accumulation of immune complexes in the spaces between podocytes and the glomerular basement membrane. These immune complexes consist of intrinsic or exogenous antigens "preplanted" between the podocytes and GBM, circulating antibodies, and membrane attack complex (C5-C9).

Role of anti-CD20 mAbs

In 2001, Remuzzi et al. [22] reported the use of RTX for idiopathic membranous nephropathy. Ruggenenti et al. [19] treated eight patients with IMN and nephrotic syndrome with 4 weekly doses of rituximab (375 mg m^{-2}) and followed them for 1 year. Treatment resulted in a 60% reduction in urinary protein excretion with notably modest side effects and no major adverse events.

Based on a study by Fervenza et al. in 2008 [23], 15 patients were enrolled, out of which seven had failed previous immunosuppressive treatment. They were followed up for 12 months and the mean drop in proteinuria from baseline to 12 months was 6.2 ± 4.8 g or a reduction of 48% ($P = .0003$).

In the GEMRITUX trial in 2017, rituximab combined with a nonimmunosuppressive antiproteinuric treatment (NIAT) was compared with NIAT alone. Rituximab-treated patients received 2 infusions of 375 mg/m^2 on days 1 and 8. In extended follow-up (median follow-up was 17 months), a significant difference was reported, with remission occurring in 64.9% in the NIAT-rituximab group but only 34.2% in the NIAT-alone group, respectively ($P < .01$) [96].

The MENTOR trial [25] compared rituximab with cyclosporine A in the treatment of MN. A total of 60% in the rituximab group achieved complete remission compared to only 20% in the cyclosporine group. Rituximab therapy had both better adherence and, by inducing longer-lasting remission, is overall more cost-effective.

The recently published STARMEN RCT [25] compared a 6-month induction course with tacrolimus (followed by a gradual decrease over another 3 months) in combination with a single dose of rituximab of 1 g at month 6 with cyclical therapy with methylprednisolone and cyclophosphamide over 6 months. At 24 months, cyclical therapy was shown to be superior.

Minimal change disease

Incidence

Minimal change disease (MCD) is the most common cause of idiopathic nephrotic syndrome in childhood, accounting for up to 90% of cases. In adults, it only accounts for 10%–15% of cases of idiopathic nephrotic syndrome [26]. Overall, the long-term prognosis is excellent with remission rates of 75% to 90% and a low risk of end-stage kidney disease (<5%) [27,28].

Pathophysiology

The pathophysiology of MCD is not fully understood, but initial podocyte injury, caused by dysregulation of adaptive immunity, is the crucial first step in pathogenesis. The role of B cells in the pathogenesis of MCD has gained attention due to the successful use of anti-CD20 mAbs in these patients [29]. An IgG antibody directed against Ubiquitin Carboxyl-Terminal

Hydrolase L1 (UCHL1) was shown to cause podocyte detachment and relapse in mice [30]. In murine models, B cells activated locally in the kidney were able to induce glomerular injury and proteinuria by the production of IL-4 [31]. In contrast, IL-4-deficient B cells did not induce proteinuria, whereas overexpression of IL-4 alone was sufficient to cause foot process effacement and proteinuria.

In kidney biopsies of patients with MCD, STAT6 activation induced by IL-4 increased, suggesting IL-4 exposure in these patients. Recently, Shimada et al. postulated a "two hit" theory to describe the pathogenesis of MCD [32]. Accordingly, cytokines (e.g., IL-13), microbial products, or allergens induce a direct stimulation of podocytes leading to the induction of CD80 (also named B7.1) as the initial hit. This causes an alteration of the podocyte structure and increases permeability. Under normal conditions, CD80 expression in podocytes is controlled by regulatory T regulatory (Treg) or the production of cytotoxic T lymphocyte antigen 4 (CTLA-4) and IL-10 by the podocyte itself. Hence, a second hit due to Treg dysregulation or impaired podocyte autoregulation is crucial and leads to sustained podocyte injury and MCD.

Role of anti-CD20 mAbs

Current recommended first-line treatments for MCD and FSGS are limited to a high-dose steroid, cyclophosphamide (CTX), calcineurin inhibitors (CNI), or mycophenolate mofetil (MMF), with steroid therapies being the most conventional [33].

Modifications to T cells were observed in patients enrolled in a multicenter, double-blind, randomized trial that evaluated the efficacy of rituximab compared to a control group in childhood MCD [34]. Rituximab-treated patients had a low relapse rate and were shown to specifically reduce the frequency of CD4+ follicular T cells (TFH cells) that drive naïve and memory B cells to differentiate into antibody-secreting cells [35,36].

Focal segmental glomerulosclerosis

Focal segmental glomerulosclerosis (FSGS) is a histological pattern of glomerular lesions that includes several different clinicopathological diseases that share podocyte injury as a primary pathophysiologic feature.

Incidence

The estimated incidence of FSGS varies from 1.4 to 21 cases per million population. FSGS can occur at any age, occurring in around 7%–10% of children and 20%–30% of adults with nephrotic syndrome. The incidence of FSGS is around 5 times higher in black patients when compared to white patients, with an annual incidence of 24 cases and 5 cases per million population, respectively, in the United States [37,38].

Pathophysiology

Primary FSGS is an immune-mediated podocytopathy with a characteristic focal pattern of glomerulosclerosis with five different histologic variants on light microscopy [39]. Secondary forms of FSGS are a sign of adaptive glomerular changes due to excessive nephron workload and hyperfiltration [40].

The pathophysiology involves podocyte injury and evidence of the presence of one or more circulating permeability factors that alter podocyte integrity, such as the urokinase plasminogen activator receptor [41], corticotrophin-like cytokine factor-1 and anti-CD40 antibodies [42].

Role of anti-CD20 mAbs

Hansrivijit et al. [42] reported that 53.6% of FSGS patients achieved remission with the use of rituximab. The mechanism by which it achieves remission is through B-cell independent mechanisms—it regulates the activity of acid—sphingomyelinase, which is essential for signaling molecules on the podocytes [43,44]. It might cross-react with sphingomyelin-phosphodiesterase-acid-like-3b (SMPDL-3b) [45] and a reduction in SMPDL-3b-positive podocytes was observed in biopsies showing FSGS. Rather than acting on antibody production directly, rituximab might prevent actin cytoskeleton remodeling in the podocytes by preserving sphingolipid-related enzymes and SMPDL-3b and ASMase activity [46,47].

Cryoglobulinemia

Cryoglobulinemia is a systemic vasculitis caused by immune complexes formed by monoclonal IgM rheumatoid factor and polyclonal IgG, which precipitate at temperatures less than 37 degrees and cause small vessel vasculitis.

Incidence

Cryoglobulinemia is a rare disease, and more than 90% of cases are secondary to hepatitis C infection.

Pathophysiology

Cryoglobulins have been identified in several situations, including 15%–20% of HIV-infected individuals, 40%–65% of Hepatitis C-infected patients, and approximately 64% of HIV/hepatitis C coinfected individuals.

Chronic immune stimulation and lymphoproliferation lead to increased production of mono-, oligo-, or polyclonal immunoglobulins, leading to the formation of cryoglobulins.

Role of anti-CD20 mAbs

Several studies have shown that RTX is highly effective for the treatment of HCV-associated mixed cryoglobulinemia.

A multicenter phase II study (EUDRACT) [48] to evaluate the efficacy of low-dose rituximab (250 mg/m^2 given twice a week apart) in patients with mixed cryoglobulinemia associated with HCV refractory showed that low dose is as effective as the higher dose of 375 mg/m^2. The cumulative response rate at month 3 was 81% in this study compared to 86% in patients in other studies using high-dose rituximab.

Thrombotic microangiopathy

Thrombotic microangiopathies (TMAs) are a group of disorders characterized by microangiopathic hemolytic anemia, thrombocytopenia, and microthrombi [49].

Incidence

Thrombotic thrombocytopenic purpura (TTP) and hemolytic uremic syndrome (HUS) are the primary forms of TMA. The incidence of TTP in adults is about 3 per 1,000,000 [50] and the incidence of HUS in children is about 3 per 100,000 [51].

Pathophysiology

TTP is caused by a severe deficiency of the enzyme ADAMTS13 (a disintegrin and metalloproteinase with a type I thrombospondin motif, member 13) due to acquired autoantibodies or genetic mutations. Whereas typical HUS follows a diarrheal illness caused by Shiga toxin-producing *Escherichia coli*, atypical HUS is associated with complement-mediated damage. About 50%–70% of patients with aHUS have genetic mutations in complement regulatory genes [52] and a small subset has autoantibodies against complement Factor H, a major regulator of the alternative complement pathway [53,54].

Role of anti-CD20 mAbs

Plasma exchange and corticosteroids as standard therapy reduce the mortality of TTP by 10%–15% but the recurrence rate is 50%–60%. Rituximab is used in refractory and/or relapsed TTP with a high response [55].

In a phase-II study of RTX in acute TTP [56], 40 patients were treated with RTX (375 mg/m^2 $\times$ 4 dosages) in conjunction with standard therapy (PEX and steroids). In the RTX group, there was a reduction in the number of plasmaphereses, the hospitalization rate in the ICU, and the relapse rate among patients, who received RTX compared to the control group. Therefore, among patients, who receive RTX as soon as possible, the prognosis improves if RTX is administered within 3 days.

In patients with anticomplement factor H antibody, rituximab leads to depletion of peripheral B cells leading to short-lived plasmacytes that secrete antifactor H antibody.

Kidney transplant

Rituximab is not licensed for use in renal transplantation but is used "off-label" in a variety of situations:

1. ABO-incompatible kidney transplantation
   Rituximab is widely used in ABO blood group incompatible transplantation (ABOi). Historically, splenectomy was performed with the quadruple drug immunosuppression for ABOi kidney transplantations. The first use of rituximab to replace splenectomy came from Stockholm in 2003 [56]. A protocol with a 10-day pretransplant conditioning period was used in four patients, starting with a single dose of rituximab (375 mg/m^2), followed by a full dose of tacrolimus, mycophenolate mofetil, and prednisolone, followed by antigen-specific immunoadsorption. The ABO-antibodies were readily removed by the antigen-specific immunoadsorption and were kept at a low level post transplantation by further adsorptions. There were no side effects and all patients have normal renal transplant function [57].
   In another study by Tydén and colleagues [57], one dose of rituximab (375 mg/m^2), was given 10 days prior to transplant to 12 patients, together with other immunosuppressants. Postoperatively, a standard triple-drug immunosuppressive protocol was followed, together with an immunosorbent. In the patient with the longest follow-up (almost 3 years), the CD20-positive cells were not detectable until 12 months after transplantation.
2. Cellular rejection
   The use of rituximab for acute renal allograft rejection was mainly based on case reports and case series. In a randomized controlled trial, Zarkhin et al. [58] reported 1-year outcomes of rituximab versus standard-of-care immunosuppression for biopsy-confirmed acute transplant rejection with B-cell infiltrates, in 20 consecutive recipients (2–23 years). Rituximab was administered intravenously at a standard dose of 375 mg/m^2 per week for four consecutive weeks. Complete tissue B-cell depletion and rapid peripheral B-cell depletion were observed.
3. Chronic antibody-mediated rejection (CAMR)
   There are a few studies on the use of rituximab for CAMR. Fehr et al. [59] treated four patients with CAMR with steroids and rituximab (375 mg/m^2). Six months after treatment with rituximab, GFR was significantly improved (P = .009).
   Rituximab has been used in the treatment of transplant glomerulopathy and in the prevention of CAMR. Loupy et al. [60] found that patients with DSA and negative cytotoxic cross-match, who received rituximab and plasmapheresis in addition to IVIG and ATG, had lower CAMR rates 1 year after transplant than those who did not receive rituximab and plasmapheresis (13.3% compared to 41.3%, P = .03).
4. Posttransplant lymphoproliferative disease
   Besides, posttransplant lymphoproliferative disorder (PTLD) encompasses a heterogeneous group of lymphoproliferative disorders that may occur after the transplantation of solid organs and hematopoietic cells [61,62]. PTLD has been reported in 1% of renal transplant recipients [63]. Rituximab has been demonstrated to be an effective treatment for PTLD [64]. In a retrospective study of eight patients with PTLD, Nieto-Rios et al. [64] concluded that the disorder can be successfully managed, with a reduction in immunosuppression,

the conversion to m-TOR, and rituximab-based schemes. First-line therapy consisted of rituximab administered as a 375mg/m^2 intravenous infusion for 4h, weekly. The overall response rate was 87.5% (62.5% complete response, 25% partial response). Survival was 87.5%, with a median follow-up of 34months.

Resistance to anti-CD20 mAb

The immunogenicity of mABs is one of the major parameters that can restrict their therapeutic and diagnostic applications. It provokes the formation of antidrug antibodies (ADAs). ADAs can affect the pharmacokinetic, efficacy, and toxicity profile of mAbs. As mAbs have evolved from murine to chimeric to humanized and fully human iterations, the frequency of ADAs has reduced but still forms in about 26.3% of patients treated with fully human mAbs. A recent review by van Brummelen that examined data from FDA drug reports showed that ADA formed in 1%–2% of patients treated with rituximab, and 6% of patients receiving obinutuzumab, but no data were available for ofatumumab.

Several factors affect immunogenicity, such as protein structure, doses, treatment program, coprescription of patients, immune status of patients, genetic predisposition, underlying disease, and age and gender of patients. When a target antigen is present on the cell membrane, mAbs bind to the target antigen and quickly internalize along with the target antigen, leading to rapid uptake of mAbs into the cell. The internalized mAb, which then acts as an antigen, is processed and eventually presented to T cells through interaction between the T-cell receptor and the major histocompatibility complex II-antigen complex on antigen-presenting cells (APC), resulting in ADA production through a T-cell-dependent manner (Fig. 1).

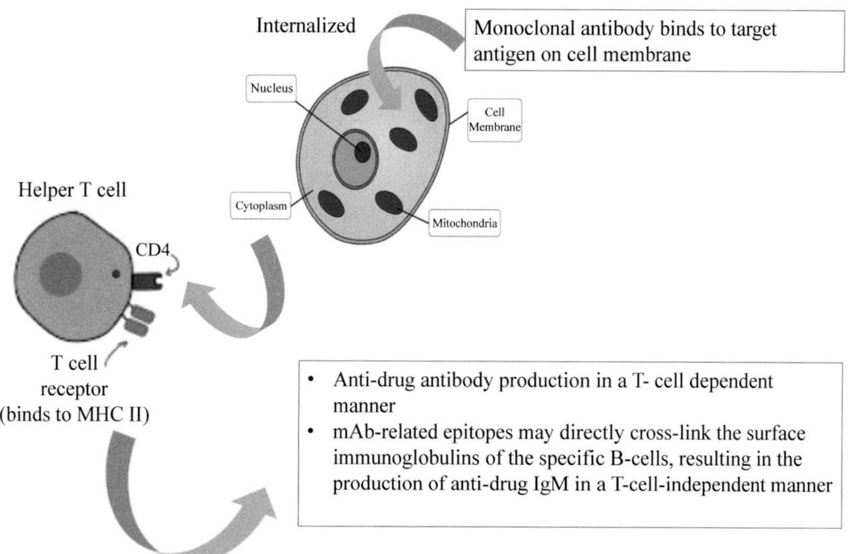

FIG. 1 Mechanism of action of triggering immunogenicity.

Rituximab is a human/murine chimeric mAb that is composed of the human kappa and igG1 constant regions connected to the murine light- and heavy-chain variable parts, respectively.

Human antichimeric antibodies (HACA) against rituximab often develop with treatment due to the chimeric makeup of rituximab. Clinically, the immunogenicity of rituximab is suspected to play a detrimental role in efficacy and tolerability [65,66]. A safety analysis of RA patients treated with rituximab in combination with MTX in clinical trials showed that 11% of patients developed a positive HACA titer at least once during treatment with rituximab. Furthermore, in the HERMES trial, a phase II study of rituximab in relapsing-remitting multiple sclerosis (RRMS), HACA was detected in 24.6% of patients treated with rituximab at week 48; but, there was no association between the presence of HACA and efficacy or adverse effects [67].

Distinctions have been made between nonneutralizing antibodies that do not inhibit the clinical effect of a drug and neutralizing antidrug antibodies. However, the presence of neutralizing antidrug antibodies is not always associated with a decreased therapeutic effect. Pharmacological efficacy depends on the balance between drug concentrations and antidrug-antibodies' levels; in some cases, drug levels are sufficient to induce the therapeutic drug effect. In contrast, nonneutralizing antidrug antibodies link to a portion far from the paratope of the drug molecule and do not neutralize its therapeutic activity (e.g., to the allotope). In such cases, the formation of antibodies is triggered by polymorphisms expressed in the constant portion of the immunoglobulin, which vary between individuals. The biologic effect of nonneutralizing antidrug antibodies is less well understood; but, the formation of immune complexes may accelerate drug clearance by the reticuloendothelial system.

A case study described a young patient with severe, resistant SLE, who initially responded to rituximab; but, eventually, rituximab treatment became inadequate to control her disease, and high levels of antirituximab antibodies were found [68]. She then received veltuzumab for compassionate use and achieved disease remission.

In a study on 15 patients with nephrotic syndrome getting rituximab, HACA was detected in six patients at various time points; but, it was not associated with responders versus nonresponders.

A phase I/II dose-escalation trial of rituximab for SLE patients showed the development of HACA in 6 patients out of 17 at a level > 100 ng/mL [69]. These HACA titers were associated with African American ancestry, reduced B-cell depletion, and lower levels of rituximab at 2 months after initial infusion. ADA development may be a significant determinant of a secondary loss of efficacy at retreatment and may be predictive of the occurrence of infusion reactions.

In MN, although rituximab appeared to be an attractive first-line treatment option, there was a nonresponse rate of approximately 30%–40%. In a study of 42 patients treated with rituximab, two doses of 1 g 2 weeks apart, antirituximab Abs were detectable in 10 patients. Antirituximab Ab neutralized rituximab in the serum in 8 of 10 patients was associated with a higher rate of relapses ($P < .001$) [95]. Three resistant patients were treated with ofatumumab, a fully humanized anti-CD20 antibody, and all achieved remission [70]. Alternative B-cell depleting agents, such as ofatumumab or type II anti-CD20 Ab Obinutuzumab, may prove to be a safe and effective rescue therapy for patients either refractory or sensitized against rituximab; but, the available evidence is limited to single case reports/series [71].

From these case studies, it can be found that the primary reason for the immunogenicity of mAbs lies in the proteinaceous nature of these molecules, their structure, and the posttranslational changes acquired in the production process.

Approaches to reversal

New generations of anti-CD20 mAbs that are either humanized or fully human have been developed to address the issues of immunogenicity (Fig. 2). Humanized versions include ocrelizumab, veltuzumab, and obinutuzumab, while ofatumumab is currently the only fully human-available anti-CD20 mAb.

Obinutuzumab and ofatumumab are directed to a different epitope on CD20 and have a higher affinity for CD20 than rituximab. Obinutuzumab is a humanized type II anti-CD20 monoclonal antibody, and modification of the structure of the glycan tree in the Fc fragment leads to increased affinity to FcgRIII and thus potentiates antibody-dependent cellular cytotoxicity. Ofatumumab is a type I anti-CD20 human antibody and activated complement-dependent cytotoxicity more effectively. Characteristics are shown in Table 1.

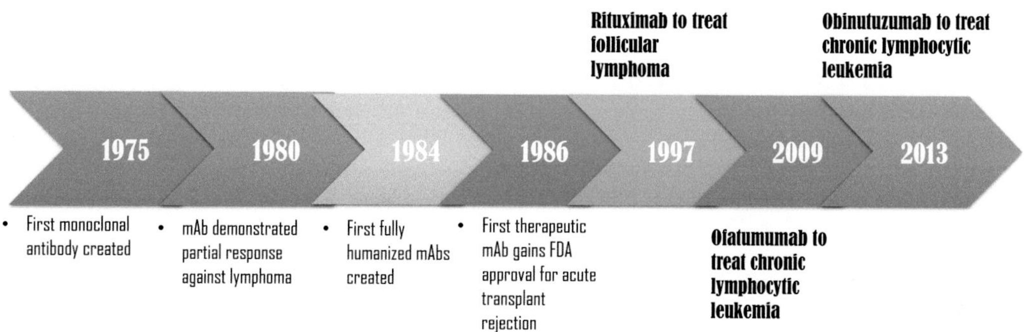

FIG. 2 Timeline of events leading to the development of newer anti-CD20 monoclonal antibodies.

TABLE 1 Characteristics of newer anti-CD20 mAbs.

Format/ generation	Drug	Special features
Humanized/ second	Ocrelizumab	Binds an overlapping epitope region as rituximab. Increased binding affinity. Enhanced ADCC and fewer CDCs compared to rituximab
	Veltuzumab	Complementarity-determining regions are similar to rituximab. Greater binding avidity and effect on CDC than rituximab
	Obinutuzumab	Binds to an epitope on CD20 that partially overlaps that of rituximab. Greater ADCC than rituximab
Fully human/ 2nd	Ofatumumab	Binds to an epitope distinct from that recognized by rituximab, ocrelizumab, veltuzumab, and obinutuzumab. Greater CDC and apoptosis than rituximab

In the 48-week phase II study of ofatumumab in RRMS [72], none of the patients tested positive for human antihuman antibodies (HAHA), while in the phase II study of ocrelizumab in RRMS the incidence of HAHA was similar between the ocrelizumab and placebo groups (2%–3%) [73]. Furthermore, even in cases where HAHA develops, there has not been a consistent association between immunogenicity and lack of efficacy or adverse effects. For example, in a phase I study of veltuzumab in idiopathic thrombocytopenic purpura (ITP), many patients developed immunogenicity to veltuzumab, but still showed clinical improvement [70].

In patients where the "one-size-fits-all" approach is ineffective, precision medicine or the personalized approach considering the characteristics of each patient improves clinical outcomes and minimizes unnecessary adverse events. Genotypic differences relating to monoclonal antibody recognition, metabolism, and disease-related signaling are likely to explain a significant amount of variability seen in their efficacy and toxicity. Although CDC is believed to be the major effector mechanism for rituximab, the anti-CD20 family now includes several agents of different constitutions, each with a distinct ADCC and CDC profile (Table 2). ADCC depends on the binding of the Fc domain to the Ig receptor (FcγR) of effector cells such as natural killer cells (NK), monocytes, macrophages, and dendritic cells [68]. Classes of these receptors include stimulatory (high-affinity FcγRI, and low-affinity FcγRIIA and FcγRIIIA) and inhibitory FcγRs (FcγRIIB) [69]. FcγR binding also facilitates the elimination of immune complexes by myeloid cells; but, this mechanism appears to be less significant for agents with cellular targets such as CD20 [70]. Allelic polymorphisms of genes responsible for such receptors are associated with variability in the binding strength of monoclonal antibodies.

TABLE 2 Case studies showing the use of new-generation anti-CD20 monoclonal antibodies.

Case study/ case series	Drug	Disease condition	Reason for using new anti-CD20 mAbs
Hudson et al. (2022) [74]	Obinutuzumab	Primary membranous nephropathy	Refractory to initial rituximab therapy (patients who did not achieve clinical and/or immunological remission after a first rituximab course)
McAdoo et al. (2016) [75]	Obinutuzumab	Primary membranous nephropathy	Refractory to multiple lines of therapy including rituximab
Basu (2014) [76]	Ofatumumab	ANCA-associated vasculitis	To avoid immunogenic antidrug reactions
Podesta et al. (2020) [69]	Ofatumumab	Nephrotic syndrome	Resistance to rituximab
Sethi et al. (2020) [77]	Ofatumumab	Multirelapsing membranous nephropathy	Rituximab-induced serum sickness

TABLE 2 Case studies showing the use of new-generation anti-CD20 monoclonal antibodies—cont'd

Case study/ case series	Drug	Disease condition	Reason for using new anti-CD20 mAbs
Bonanni et al. (2015) [78]	Obinutuzumab	Membranous nephropathy	Rituximab-refractory patients
Fujinaga et al. (2018) [79]	Ofatumumab	Rituximab-resistant nephrotic syndrome	Allergic to rituximab
Reynolds et al. (2021) [80]	Ofatumumab	Complicated rituximab-resistant nephrotic syndrome	Antirituximab antibodies
Solomon et al. (2019) [81]	Ofatumumab	Recurrent FSGS postkidney transplant	Antirituximab antibodies
Wagner et al. (2018) [82]	Ofatumumab	Recurrent FSGS postkidney transplant	Antirituximab antibodies
Haarhaus et al. (2016) [83]	Ofatumumab	Recurrent FSGS postkidney transplant	Antirituximab antibodies
Masoud et al. (2018) [84]	Ofatumumab	Lupus nephritis	Intolerance to rituximab
Thornton et al. (2015) [85]	Ofatumumab	Lupus nephritis	Intolerance to rituximab
Hassan et al. (2020) [86]	Ofatumumab	Lupus nephritis	Intolerance to rituximab
Lundberg et al. (2017) [87]	Ocrelizumab, obinutuzumab, or ofatumumab	Lupus nephritis	Relapses on rituximab
Schimdt et al. (2021) [88]	Ofatumumab	IgA vasculitis	Allergic reaction to rituximab
Wang et al. (2017) [89]	Ocrelizumab	PLA2R-associated membranous nephropathy	Antirituximab antibodies
Vivarelli et al. (2017) [90]	Ofatumumab	Childhood nephrotic syndrome	Antirituximab antibodies
Bernard et al. (2020) [91]	Ofatumumab	Nephrotic syndrome	Allergic to rituximab
Ural et al. (2022) [92]	Ofatumumab	Nephrotic syndrome postrenal—transplantation in children	Antirituximab antibodies
Ravani et al. (2021) [93]	Ofatumumab	Postrenal transplant FSGS	Resistance to rituximab

Conclusions

Anti-CD20 mAbs have demonstrated that B cells are important players in autoimmune diseases and more understanding of the pathogenesis will allow for the development of more targeted B-cell-mediated therapies. Although next-generation anti-CD20 mAbs have been shown to be more potent than rituximab in vitro, there are no head-to-head trials except for very few (Table 2): a Phase III trial directly comparing the safety profile and tolerability in patients with relapsing-remitting multiple sclerosis on IV rituximab, who switch to IV ocrelizumab versus those who continue on rituximab (NCT02980042) [97]; the NOBILITY trial, a multicentric trial with obinutuzumab, to evaluate the safety and efficacy of the drug in patients with LN (NCT02550652). Preliminary results showed complete remission in 34% of the patients and partial remission in 55% at week 52; the BELONG trial evaluated ocrelizumab in LN and found that 42.7%, 31.5%, and 34.7% of the participants achieved a complete renal response at week 48 with ocrelizumab 400mg, 1000mg, or placebo, respectively (NCT00626197).

Further studies are needed to confirm and to better understand the clinical implications of ADA development, their impact of the safety profile of RTX, and on its efficacy in systemic diseases such as SLE and AAV (Table 3).

TABLE 3 Clinical trials using new generation anti-CD20 monoclonal antibodies.

Clinical trial	Drugs	Disease condition
NCT05376319	Obinutuzumab vs RTX	Anti-PR3 positive ANCA-associated vasculitis
NCT05050214	ORION study-efficacy of obinutuzumab	Primary membranous nephropathy
Ravani et al. (2021) [93]	Ofatumumab with rituximab	Steroid-dependent and calcineurin inhibitor-dependent idiopathic nephrotic syndrome
NCT04983888	Safety and efficacy of obinutuzumab	Primary FSGS in adults
NCT02550652	NOBILITY trial-obinutuzumab	Lupus nephritis
NCT00626197	Ocrelizumab	Lupus nephritis
NCT04221477	REGENCY trial-comparing obinutuzumab + mycophenolate to placebo + mycophenolate	Lupus nephritis
NCT04702256	OBILUP trial-obinutuzumab + mycophenolate to corticosteroids+ mycophenolate	Lupus nephritis
NCT05039619	Pharmacokinetics of obinutuzumab	Lupus nephritis
NCT04629248	Obinutuzumab with tacrolimus	Membranous nephropathy
Mysler et al. (2013) [94]	Efficacy and safety of ocrelizumab	Proliferative lupus nephritis

Acknowledgments

Statement of ethics

The Ethics Committee of the Pikeville Medical Center does not require ethical approval for book chapters.

Funding

None.

Prior presentations

Not applicable.

Data availability statement

All data generated or analyzed are included in this chapter.

References

[1] Cheson BD, Leonard JP. Monoclonal antibody therapy for B-cell non-Hodgkin's lymphoma. N Engl J Med 2008;359:613–26. https://doi.org/10.1056/NEJMra0708875.

[2] Du FH, Mills EA, Mao-Draayer Y. Next-generation anti-CD20 monoclonal antibodies in autoimmune disease treatment. Autoimmun Highlights 2017;8:12. https://doi.org/10.1007/s13317-017-0100-y.

[3] Reff M, Carner K, Chambers K, Chinn P, Leonard J, Raab R, et al. Depletion of B cells in vivo by a chimeric mouse human monoclonal antibody to CD20. Blood 1994;83:435–45. https://doi.org/10.1182/blood.V83.2.435.435.

[4] Kronbichler A, Windpessl M, Pieringer H, Jayne DRW. Rituximab for immunologic renal disease: what the nephrologist needs to know. Autoimmun Rev 2017;16:633–43. https://doi.org/10.1016/j.autrev.2017.04.007.

[5] Vieira CA, Agarwal A, Book BK, Sidner RA, Bearden CM, Gebel HM, et al. Rituximab for reduction of anti-HLA antibodies in patients awaiting renal transplantation: 1. Safety, pharmacodynamics, and pharmacokinetics 1. Transplantation 2004;77:542–8. https://doi.org/10.1097/01.TP.0000112934.12622.2B.

[6] Sabucedo AJ, Contreras G. ESKD, transplantation, and dialysis in lupus nephritis. Semin Nephrol 2015;35:500–8. https://doi.org/10.1016/j.semnephrol.2015.08.011.

[7] Pakozdi A, Pyne D, Sheaff M, Rajakariar R. Utility of a repeat renal biopsy in lupus nephritis: a single centre experience. Nephrol Dial Transplant 2018;33:507–13. https://doi.org/10.1093/ndt/gfx019.

[8] Kon T, Yamaji K, Sugimoto K, Ogasawara M, Kenpe K, Ogasawara H, et al. Investigation of pathological and clinical features of lupus nephritis in 73 autopsied cases with systemic lupus erythematosus. Mod Rheumatol 2010;20:168–77. https://doi.org/10.3109/s10165-009-0260-3.

[9] Rovin BH, Furie R, Latinis K, Looney RJ, Fervenza FC, Sanchez-Guerrero J, et al. Efficacy and safety of rituximab in patients with active proliferative lupus nephritis: the lupus nephritis assessment with rituximab study. Arthritis Rheum 2012;64:1215–26. https://doi.org/10.1002/art.34359.

[10] Gomez Mendez LM, Cascino MD, Garg J, Katsumoto TR, Brakeman P, Dall'Era M, et al. Peripheral blood B cell depletion after rituximab and complete response in lupus nephritis. Clin J Am Soc Nephrol 2018;13:1502–9. https://doi.org/10.2215/CJN.01070118.

[11] Condon MB, Ashby D, Pepper RJ, Cook HT, Levy JB, Griffith M, et al. Prospective observational single-centre cohort study to evaluate the effectiveness of treating lupus nephritis with rituximab and mycophenolate mofetil but no oral steroids. Ann Rheum Dis 2013;72:1280–6. https://doi.org/10.1136/annrheumdis-2012-202844.

[12] Watts RA, Mahr A, Mohammad AJ, Gatenby P, Basu N, Flores-Suárez LF. Classification, epidemiology and clinical subgrouping of antineutrophil cytoplasmic antibody (ANCA)-associated vasculitis. Nephrol Dial Transplant 2015;30:i14–22. https://doi.org/10.1093/ndt/gfv022.

[13] Guillevin L. La granulomatose éosinophilique avec polyangéite (syndrome de Churg et Strauss). Presse Med 2012;41:1004–13. https://doi.org/10.1016/j.lpm.2012.07.008.
[14] Stone JH, Merkel PA, Spiera R, Seo P, Langford CA, Hoffman GS, et al. Rituximab versus cyclophosphamide for ANCA-associated vasculitis. N Engl J Med 2010;363:221–32. https://doi.org/10.1056/NEJMoa0909905.
[15] Jones RB, Cohen Tervaert JW, Hauser T, Luqmani R, Morgan MD, Peh CA, et al. Rituximab versus cyclophosphamide in ANCA-associated renal vasculitis. N Engl J Med 2010;363:211–20. https://doi.org/10.1056/NEJMoa0909169.
[16] Guillevin L, Pagnoux C, Karras A, Khouatra C, Aumaître O, Cohen P, et al. Rituximab versus azathioprine for maintenance in ANCA-associated vasculitis. N Engl J Med 2014;371:1771–80. https://doi.org/10.1056/NEJMoa1404231.
[17] Gopaluni S, Smith RM, Lewin M, McAlear CA, Mynard K, Jones RB, et al. Rituximab versus azathioprine as therapy for maintenance of remission for anti-neutrophil cytoplasm antibody-associated vasculitis (RITAZAREM): study protocol for a randomized controlled trial. Trials 2017;18:112. https://doi.org/10.1186/s13063-017-1857-z.
[18] Couser WG. Primary membranous nephropathy. Clin J Am Soc Nephrol 2017;12:983–97. https://doi.org/10.2215/CJN.11761116.
[19] Ruggenenti P, Debiec H, Ruggiero B, Chianca A, Pellé T, Gaspari F, et al. Anti-phospholipase A_2 receptor antibody titer predicts post-rituximab outcome of membranous nephropathy. J Am Soc Nephrol 2015;26:2545–58. https://doi.org/10.1681/ASN.2014070640.
[20] Beck LH, Bonegio RGB, Lambeau G, Beck DM, Powell DW, Cummins TD, et al. M-type phospholipase A_2 receptor as target antigen in idiopathic membranous nephropathy. N Engl J Med 2009;361:11–21. https://doi.org/10.1056/NEJMoa0810457.
[21] Tomas NM, Beck LH, Meyer-Schwesinger C, Seitz-Polski B, Ma H, Zahner G, et al. Thrombospondin type-1 domain-containing 7A in idiopathic membranous nephropathy. N Engl J Med 2014;371:2277–87. https://doi.org/10.1056/NEJMoa1409354.
[22] Remuzzi G, Chiurchiu C, Abbate M, Brusegan V, Bontempelli M, Ruggenenti P. Rituximab for idiopathic membranous nephropathy. Lancet 2002;360:923–4. https://doi.org/10.1016/S0140-6736(02)11042-7.
[23] Fervenza FC, Cosio FG, Erickson SB, Specks U, Herzenberg AM, Dillon JJ, et al. Rituximab treatment of idiopathic membranous nephropathy. Kidney Int 2008;73:117–25. https://doi.org/10.1038/sj.ki.5002628.
[24] Fervenza FC, Appel GB, Barbour SJ, Rovin BH, Lafayette RA, Aslam N, et al. Rituximab or cyclosporine in the treatment of membranous nephropathy. N Engl J Med 2019;381:36–46. https://doi.org/10.1056/NEJMoa1814427.
[25] Fernández-Juárez G, Rojas-Rivera J, van de Logt A-E, Justino J, Sevillano A, Caravaca-Fontán F, et al. The STARMEN trial indicates that alternating treatment with corticosteroids and cyclophosphamide is superior to sequential treatment with tacrolimus and rituximab in primary membranous nephropathy. Kidney Int 2021;99:986–98. https://doi.org/10.1016/j.kint.2020.10.014.
[26] Vivarelli M, Massella L, Ruggiero B, Emma F. Minimal change disease. Clin J Am Soc Nephrol 2017;12:332–45. https://doi.org/10.2215/CJN.05000516.
[27] Waldman M, Crew RJ, Valeri A, Busch J, Stokes B, Markowitz G, et al. Adult minimal-change disease: clinical characteristics, treatment, and outcomes. Clin J Am Soc Nephrol 2007;2:445–53. https://doi.org/10.2215/CJN.03531006.
[28] Gauckler P, Shin II J, Alberici F, Audard V, Bruchfeld A, Busch M, et al. Rituximab in adult minimal change disease and focal segmental glomerulosclerosis—what is known and what is still unknown? Autoimmun Rev 2020;19, 102671. https://doi.org/10.1016/j.autrev.2020.102671.
[29] Jamin A, Berthelot L, Couderc A, Chemouny JM, Boedec E, Dehoux L, et al. Autoantibodies against podocytic UCHL1 are associated with idiopathic nephrotic syndrome relapses and induce proteinuria in mice. J Autoimmun 2018;89:149–61. https://doi.org/10.1016/j.jaut.2017.12.014.
[30] Kim AHJ, Chung J-J, Akilesh S, Koziell A, Jain S, Hodgin JB, et al. B cell-derived IL-4 acts on podocytes to induce proteinuria and foot process effacement. JCI Insight 2017;2, e81836. https://doi.org/10.1172/jci.insight.81836.
[31] Shimada M, Araya C, Rivard C, Ishimoto T, Johnson RJ, Garin EH. Minimal change disease: a "two-hit" podocyte immune disorder? Pediatr Nephrol 2011;26:645–9. https://doi.org/10.1007/s00467-010-1676-x.
[32] Korbet SM, Whittier WL. Management of adult minimal change disease. Clin J Am Soc Nephrol 2019;14:911–3. https://doi.org/10.2215/CJN.01920219.

[33] Benz K, Büttner M, Dittrich K, Campean V, Dötsch J, Amann K. Characterisation of renal immune cell infiltrates in children with nephrotic syndrome. Pediatr Nephrol 2010;25:1291–8. https://doi.org/10.1007/s00467-010-1507-0.

[34] Boumediene A, Vachin P, Sendeyo K, Oniszczuk J, Zhang S, Henique C, et al. NEPHRUTIX: a randomized, double-blind, placebo vs rituximab-controlled trial assessing T-cell subset changes in minimal change nephrotic syndrome. J Autoimmun 2018;88:91–102. https://doi.org/10.1016/j.jaut.2017.10.006.

[35] Bezombes C, Fournié J-J, Laurent G. Direct effect of rituximab in B-cell-derived lymphoid neoplasias: mechanism, regulation, and perspectives. Mol Cancer Res 2011;9:1435–42. https://doi.org/10.1158/1541-7786.MCR-11-0154.

[36] Kitiyakara C, Kopp JB, Eggers P. Trends in the epidemiology of focal segmental glomerulosclerosis. Semin Nephrol 2003;23:172–82. https://doi.org/10.1053/snep.2003.50025.

[37] Sim JJ, Batech M, Hever A, Harrison TN, Avelar T, Kanter MH, et al. Distribution of biopsy-proven presumed primary glomerulonephropathies in 2000-2011 among a racially and ethnically diverse US population. Am J Kidney Dis 2016;68:533–44. https://doi.org/10.1053/j.ajkd.2016.03.416.

[38] Fogo AB, Lusco MA, Najafian B, Alpers CE. AJKD atlas of renal pathology: focal segmental glomerulosclerosis. Am J Kidney Dis 2015;66:e1–2. https://doi.org/10.1053/j.ajkd.2015.04.007.

[39] Fogo AB. Causes and pathogenesis of focal segmental glomerulosclerosis. Nat Rev Nephrol 2015;11:76–87. https://doi.org/10.1038/nrneph.2014.216.

[40] Kronbichler A, Saleem MA, Meijers B, Shin II J. Soluble urokinase receptors in focal segmental glomerulosclerosis: a review on the scientific point of view. J Immunol Res 2016;2016:1–14. https://doi.org/10.1155/2016/2068691.

[41] Königshausen E, Sellin L. Circulating permeability factors in primary focal segmental glomerulosclerosis: a review of proposed candidates. Biomed Res Int 2016;2016:1–9. https://doi.org/10.1155/2016/3765608.

[42] Hansrivijit P, Cheungpasitporn W, Thongprayoon C, Ghahramani N. Rituximab therapy for focal segmental glomerulosclerosis and minimal change disease in adults: a systematic review and meta-analysis. BMC Nephrol 2020;21:134. https://doi.org/10.1186/s12882-020-01797-7.

[43] Bezombes C. Rituximab antiproliferative effect in B-lymphoma cells is associated with acid-sphingomyelinase activation in raft microdomains. Blood 2004;104:1166–73. https://doi.org/10.1182/blood-2004-01-0277.

[44] Bollinger CR, Teichgräber V, Gulbins E. Ceramide-enriched membrane domains. Biochim Biophys Acta 2005;1746:284–94. https://doi.org/10.1016/j.bbamcr.2005.09.001.

[45] Perosa F, Favoino E, Caragnano MA, Dammacco F. Generation of biologically active linear and cyclic peptides has revealed a unique fine specificity of rituximab and its possible cross-reactivity with acid sphingomyelinase-like phosphodiesterase 3b precursor. Blood 2006;107:1070–7. https://doi.org/10.1182/blood-2005-04-1769.

[46] Fornoni A, Sageshima J, Wei C, Merscher-Gomez S, Aguillon-Prada R, Jauregui AN, et al. Rituximab targets podocytes in recurrent focal segmental glomerulosclerosis. Sci Transl Med 2011;3. https://doi.org/10.1126/scitranslmed.3002231.

[47] Visentini M, Tinelli C, Colantuono S, Monti M, Ludovisi S, Gragnani L, et al. Efficacy of low-dose rituximab for the treatment of mixed cryoglobulinemia vasculitis: phase II clinical trial and systematic review. Autoimmun Rev 2015;14:889–96. https://doi.org/10.1016/j.autrev.2015.05.013.

[48] Tsai H-M. Untying the knot of thrombotic thrombocytopenic purpura and atypical hemolytic uremic syndrome. Am J Med 2013;126:200–9. https://doi.org/10.1016/j.amjmed.2012.09.006.

[49] Deford CC, Reese JA, Schwartz LH, Perdue JJ, Kremer Hovinga JA, Lämmle B, et al. Multiple major morbidities and increased mortality during long-term follow-up after recovery from thrombotic thrombocytopenic purpura. Blood 2013;122:2023–9. https://doi.org/10.1182/blood-2013-04-496752.

[50] Noris M, Remuzzi G. Hemolytic uremic syndrome. J Am Soc Nephrol 2005;16:1035–50. https://doi.org/10.1681/ASN.2004100861.

[51] Legendre CM, Licht C, Muus P, Greenbaum LA, Babu S, Bedrosian C, et al. Terminal complement inhibitor eculizumab in atypical hemolytic–uremic syndrome. N Engl J Med 2013;368:2169–81. https://doi.org/10.1056/NEJMoa1208981.

[52] Moore I, Strain L, Pappworth I, Kavanagh D, Barlow PN, Herbert AP, et al. Association of factor H autoantibodies with deletions of CFHR1, CFHR3, CFHR4, and with mutations in CFH, CFI, CD46, and C3 in patients with atypical hemolytic uremic syndrome. Blood 2010;115:379–87. https://doi.org/10.1182/blood-2009-05-221549.

[53] Caprioli J, Noris M, Brioschi S, Pianetti G, Castelletti F, Bettinaglio P, et al. Genetics of HUS: the impact of MCP, CFH, and IF mutations on clinical presentation, response to treatment, and outcome. Blood 2006;108:1267–79. https://doi.org/10.1182/blood-2005-10-007252.

[54] Scully M, Hunt BJ, Benjamin S, Liesner R, Rose P, Peyvandi F, et al. Guidelines on the diagnosis and management of thrombotic thrombocytopenic purpura and other thrombotic microangiopathies. Br J Haematol 2012;158:323–35. https://doi.org/10.1111/j.1365-2141.2012.09167.x.

[55] Scully M, McDonald V, Cavenagh J, Hunt BJ, Longair I, Cohen H, et al. A phase 2 study of the safety and efficacy of rituximab with plasma exchange in acute acquired thrombotic thrombocytopenic purpura. Blood 2011;118:1746–53. https://doi.org/10.1182/blood-2011-03-341131.

[56] Tydén G, Kumlien G, Fehrman I. Successful ABO-incompatible kidney transplantations without splenectomy using antigen-specific immunoadsorption and rituximab. Transplantation 2003;76:730–1. https://doi.org/10.1097/01.TP.0000078622.43689.D4.

[57] Tydén G, Kumlien G, Genberg H, Sandberg J, Lundgren T, Fehrman I. ABO-incompatible kidney transplantation and rituximab. Transplant Proc 2005;37:3286–7. https://doi.org/10.1016/j.transproceed.2005.09.002.

[58] Zarkhin V, Li L, Kambham N, Sigdel T, Salvatierra O, Sarwal MM. A randomized, prospective trial of rituximab for acute rejection in pediatric renal transplantation. Am J Transplant 2008;8:2607–17. https://doi.org/10.1111/j.1600-6143.2008.02411.x.

[59] Fehr T, Rüsi B, Fischer A, Hopfer H, Wüthrich RP, Gaspert A. Rituximab and intravenous immunoglobulin treatment of chronic antibody-mediated kidney allograft rejection. Transplantation 2009;87:1837–41. https://doi.org/10.1097/TP.0b013e3181a6bac5.

[60] Loupy A, Suberbielle-Boissel C, Zuber J, Anglicheau D, Timsit M-O, Martinez F, et al. Combined posttransplant prophylactic IVIg/anti-CD 20/plasmapheresis in kidney recipients with preformed donor-specific antibodies: a pilot study. Transplantation 2010;89:1403–10. https://doi.org/10.1097/TP.0b013e3181da1cc3.

[61] Cockfield SM. Identifying the patient at risk for post-transplant lymphoproliferative disorder. Transpl Infect Dis 2001;3:70–8. https://doi.org/10.1034/j.1399-3062.2001.003002070.x.

[62] Svoboda J, Kotloff R, Tsai DE. Management of patients with post-transplant lymphoproliferative disorder: the role of rituximab. Transpl Int 2006;19:259–69. https://doi.org/10.1111/j.1432-2277.2006.00284.x.

[63] Evens AM, Roy R, Sterrenberg D, Moll MZ, Chadburn A, Gordon LI. Post-transplantation lymphoproliferative disorders: diagnosis, prognosis, and current approaches to therapy. Curr Oncol Rep 2010;12:383–94. https://doi.org/10.1007/s11912-010-0132-1.

[64] Nieto-Rios JF, de Los G, Ríos SM, Serna-Higuita LM, Ocampo-Kohn C, Aristizabal-Alzate A, Gálvez-Cárdenas KM, et al. Treatment of post-transplantation lymphoproliferative disorders after kidney transplant with rituximab and conversion to m-TOR inhibitor. Colomb Med (Cali) 2016;47:196–202.

[65] van Vollenhoven RF, Emery P, Bingham CO, Keystone EC, Fleischmann R, Furst DE, et al. Longterm safety of patients receiving rituximab in rheumatoid arthritis clinical trials. J Rheumatol 2010;37:558–67. https://doi.org/10.3899/jrheum.090856.

[66] Hauser SL, Waubant E, Arnold DL, Vollmer T, Antel J, Fox RJ, et al. B-cell depletion with rituximab in relapsing–remitting multiple sclerosis. N Engl J Med 2008;358:676–88. https://doi.org/10.1056/NEJMoa0706383.

[67] Tahir H. Humanized anti-CD20 monoclonal antibody in the treatment of severe resistant systemic lupus erythematosus in a patient with antibodies against rituximab. Rheumatology 2005;44:561–2. https://doi.org/10.1093/rheumatology/keh533.

[68] Looney RJ, Anolik JH, Campbell D, Felgar RE, Young F, Arend LJ, et al. B cell depletion as a novel treatment for systemic lupus erythematosus: a phase I/II dose-escalation trial of rituximab. Arthritis Rheum 2004;50:2580–9. https://doi.org/10.1002/art.20430.

[69] Podestà MA, Ruggiero B, Remuzzi G, Ruggenenti P. Ofatumumab for multirelapsing membranous nephropathy complicated by rituximab-induced serum-sickness. BMJ Case Rep 2020;13, e232896. https://doi.org/10.1136/bcr-2019-232896.

[70] Klomjit N, Fervenza FC, Zand L. Successful treatment of patients with refractory PLA2R-associated membranous nephropathy with Obinutuzumab: a report of 3 cases. Am J Kidney Dis 2020;76:883–8. https://doi.org/10.1053/j.ajkd.2020.02.444.

[71] Teisseyre M, Boyer-Suavet S, Crémoni M, Brglez V, Esnault V, Seitz-Polski B. Analysis and management of rituximab resistance in PLA2R1-associated membranous nephropathy. Kidney Int Rep 2021;6:1183–8. https://doi.org/10.1016/j.ekir.2021.01.022.

[72] Kappos L, Li D, Calabresi PA, O'Connor P, Bar-Or A, Barkhof F, et al. Ocrelizumab in relapsing-remitting multiple sclerosis: a phase 2, randomised, placebo-controlled, multicentre trial. Lancet 2011;378:1779–87. https://doi.org/10.1016/S0140-6736(11)61649-8.

[73] Ellebrecht CT, Choi EJ, Allman DM, Tsai DE, Wegener WA, Goldenberg DM, et al. Subcutaneous veltuzumab, a humanized anti-CD20 antibody, in the treatment of refractory pemphigus vulgaris. JAMA Dermatol 2014;150:1331. https://doi.org/10.1001/jamadermatol.2014.1939.

[74] Hudson R, Rawlings C, Mon SY, Jefferis J, John GT. Treatment resistant M-type phospholipase A2 receptor associated membranous nephropathy responds to obinutuzumab: a report of two cases. BMC Nephrol 2022;23:134. https://doi.org/10.1186/s12882-022-02761-3.

[75] McAdoo SP, Bedi R, Tarzi R, Griffith M, Pusey CD, Cairns TD. Ofatumumab for B cell depletion therapy in ANCA-associated vasculitis: a single-centre case series. Rheumatology 2016;55:1437–42. https://doi.org/10.1093/rheumatology/kew199.

[76] Basu B. Ofatumumab for rituximab-resistant nephrotic syndrome. N Engl J Med 2014;370:1268–70. https://doi.org/10.1056/NEJMc1308488.

[77] Sethi S, Kumar S, Lim K, Jordan SC. Obinutuzumab is effective for the treatment of refractory membranous nephropathy. Kidney Int Rep 2020;5:1515–8. https://doi.org/10.1016/j.ekir.2020.06.030.

[78] Bonanni A, Rossi R, Murtas C, Ghiggeri GM. Low-dose ofatumumab for rituximab-resistant nephrotic syndrome. BMJ Case Rep 2015;, bcr2015210208. https://doi.org/10.1136/bcr-2015-210208.

[79] Fujinaga S, Sakuraya K. Single infusion of low-dose ofatumumab in a child with complicated nephrotic syndrome with anti-rituximab antibodies. Pediatr Nephrol 2018;33:527–8. https://doi.org/10.1007/s00467-017-3866-2.

[80] Reynolds BC, Lamb A, Jones CA, Yadav P, Tyerman KS, Geddes CC. UK experience of ofatumumab in recurrence of focal segmental glomerulosclerosis post-kidney transplant. Pediatr Nephrol 2022;37:199–207. https://doi.org/10.1007/s00467-021-05248-9.

[81] Solomon S, Zolotnitskaya A, del Rio M. Ofatumumab in post-transplantation recurrence of focal segmental glomerulosclerosis in a child. Pediatr Transplant 2019;23, e13413. https://doi.org/10.1111/petr.13413.

[82] Kienzl-Wagner K, Rosales A, Scheidl S, Giner T, Bösmüller C, Rudnicki M, et al. Successful management of recurrent focal segmental glomerulosclerosis. Am J Transplant 2018;18:2818–22. https://doi.org/10.1111/ajt.14998.

[83] Haarhaus ML, Svenungsson E, Gunnarsson I. Ofatumumab treatment in lupus nephritis patients. Clin Kidney J 2016;9:552–5. https://doi.org/10.1093/ckj/sfw022.

[84] Masoud S, McAdoo SP, Bedi R, Cairns TD, Lightstone L. Ofatumumab for B cell depletion in patients with systemic lupus erythematosus who are allergic to rituximab. Rheumatology 2018;57:1156–61. https://doi.org/10.1093/rheumatology/key042.

[85] Thornton CC, Ambrose N, Ioannou Y. Ofatumumab: a novel treatment for severe systemic lupus erythematosus. Rheumatology 2015;54:559–60. https://doi.org/10.1093/rheumatology/keu475.

[86] Hassan SU, Md Yusof MY, Emery P, Dass S, Vital EM. Biologic sequencing in systemic lupus erythematosus: after secondary non-response to rituximab, switching to humanised anti-CD20 agent is more effective than belimumab. Front Med (Lausanne) 2020;7. https://doi.org/10.3389/fmed.2020.00498.

[87] Lundberg S, Westergren E, Smolander J, Bruchfeld A. B cell-depleting therapy with rituximab or ofatumumab in immunoglobulin A nephropathy or vasculitis with nephritis. Clin Kidney J 2016;sfw106. https://doi.org/10.1093/ckj/sfw106.

[88] Schmidt T, Schulze M, Harendza S, Hoxha E. Successful treatment of PLA2R1-antibody positive membranous nephropathy with ocrelizumab. J Nephrol 2021;34:603–6. https://doi.org/10.1007/s40620-020-00874-2.

[89] Wang C-S, Liverman RS, Garro R, George RP, Glumova A, Karp A, et al. Ofatumumab for the treatment of childhood nephrotic syndrome. Pediatr Nephrol 2017;32:835–41. https://doi.org/10.1007/s00467-017-3621-8.

[90] Vivarelli M, Colucci M, Bonanni A, Verzani M, Serafinelli J, Emma F, et al. Ofatumumab in two pediatric nephrotic syndrome patients allergic to rituximab. Pediatr Nephrol 2017;32:181–4. https://doi.org/10.1007/s00467-016-3498-y.

[91] Bernard J, Lalieve F, Sarlat J, Perrin J, Dehoux L, Boyer O, et al. Ofatumumab treatment for nephrotic syndrome recurrence after pediatric renal transplantation. Pediatr Nephrol 2020;35:1499–506. https://doi.org/10.1007/s00467-020-04567-7.

[92] Ural Z, Helvacı Ö, Özbaş B, Güz G, Derici Ü. Unexpected late response to ofatumumab in adult post-transplantation recurrent focal segmental glomerulosclerosis. Case Report Transplant Proc 2022;54:1632–5. https://doi.org/10.1016/j.transproceed.2022.04.019.

[93] Ravani P, Colucci M, Bruschi M, Vivarelli M, Cioni M, DiDonato A, et al. Human or chimeric monoclonal anti-CD20 antibodies for children with nephrotic syndrome: a superiority randomized trial. J Am Soc Nephrol 2021;32:2652–63. https://doi.org/10.1681/ASN.2021040561.

[94] Mysler EF, Spindler AJ, Guzman R, Bijl M, Jayne D, Furie RA, et al. Efficacy and safety of ocrelizumab in active proliferative lupus nephritis: results from a randomized, double-blind. Phase III Study Arthritis Rheum 2013;65:2368–79. https://doi.org/10.1002/art.38037.

[95] Boyer-Suavet S, Andreani M, Lateb M, Savenkoff B, Brglez V, Benzaken S, et al. Neutralizing anti-rituximab antibodies and relapse in membranous nephropathy treated with rituximab. Front Immunol 2020;10. https://doi.org/10.3389/fimmu.2019.03069.

[96] Gauckler P, Shin II J, Alberici F, Audard V, Bruchfeld A, Busch M, et al. Rituximab in membranous nephropathy. Kidney Int Rep 2021;6:881–93. https://doi.org/10.1016/j.ekir.2020.12.035.

[97] Sorensen PS, Lisby S, Grove R, Derosier F, Shackelford S, Havrdova E, et al. Safety and efficacy of ofatumumab in relapsing-remitting multiple sclerosis: a phase 2 study. Neurology 2014;82:573–81. https://doi.org/10.1212/WNL.0000000000000125.

CHAPTER

15

Adverse events following rituximab therapy in pemphigus patients

Sahar Dadkhahfar

Skin Research Center, Shahid Beheshti University of Medical Sciences, Tehran, Iran

Abstract

Pemphigus is a group of autoimmune blistering dermatoses characterized by blisters and erosions secondary to circulating autoantibodies that cause the destruction of epidermal cell adhesion. Target antigens are desmogleins 1 and 3, which are transmembrane glycoproteins mediating cell adhesion between keratinocytes. Accordingly, pemphigus has been considered a B-cell-mediated disease; however, a growing body of evidence indicates the role of T cells in this autoimmune disorder. In 2018, rituximab (RTX) was approved by the US FDA for the treatment of moderate-to-severe pemphigus vulgaris in adults.

RTX targets CD20, a transmembrane surface molecule associated with membrane-spanning 4-domain family A (MS4A) proteins. CD20 is expressed by pre-B lymphocytes and B lymphocytes but not plasma cells. It can have a role in many B-cell lineage malignancies and autoimmune disorders via several mechanisms. It has been established that in pemphigus RTX exerts its effect by depletion of B cells and lymphoid resident memory B cells, with a further reduction of circulating pathogenic antidesmoglein autoantibodies. In addition, RTX is believed to modify both humoral and acquired immune responses in pemphigus.

Although extremely effective and relatively safe, RTX therapy in pemphigus patients may be associated with several unfavorable outcomes such as myocardial infarction, ventricular fibrillation, cardiogenic shock, hypoxia, pulmonary infiltrates, acute respiratory distress syndrome and acute kidney failure, and even death. Catastrophic drug reactions, including Stevens-Johnson syndrome/toxic epidermal necrolysis, have infrequently been reported in patients given RTX. Progressive multifocal leukoencephalopathy and hepatitis B virus activation potentially leading to fulminant hepatitis have also been reported.

Dermatologists must be vigilant about these side effects in their daily management of pemphigus patients. This chapter reviews RTX efficacy and complications of RTX treatment in PV and the remedies.

Abbreviations

ASMSG Association of the Scientific Medical Societies in Germany
BAD British Association of Dermatologists
BSD Brazilian Society of Dermatology
DBC Dermatology Branch of China International Exchange and Promotion Association for Medical and Healthcare
EADV European Academy of Dermatology and Venereology

https://doi.org/10.1016/B978-0-443-19200-5.00004-X

IRR	infusion-related reactions
MMF	mycophenolate mofetil
PV	pemphigus vulgaris
RTX	rituximab
US FDA	The US Food and Drug Administration

Conflict of interest

No potential conflicts of interest were disclosed.

Introduction

Pemphigus is an autoimmune bullous disease characterized by mucocutaneous blisters and erosions caused by circulating pathogenic IgG autoantibodies directed against desmogleins found within desmosomes that mediate cell-to-cell adhesion of keratinocytes [1]. Pemphigus vulgaris (PV) is the most common subtype of this group, with an incidence range from 0.5 to 50 per million populations, contingent on geographical region and ethnicity. The mean age of onset is 40–60 years; however, the occurrence of pemphigus in childhood and elderly has been reported [2].

The characteristic lesions of PV are blisters that rupture easily, leaving painful mucocutaneous erosions (Fig. 1) [3]. Disruption of the skin barrier in PV may lead to dehydration, malnutrition and weight loss, and infections; therefore, PV can be considered a potentially life-threatening disorder [3].

Pemphigus is considered an antibody-mediated autoimmune disease. The target antigens are desmogleins 1 and 3 which are desmosomal transmembrane glycoproteins mediating interkeratinocyte adhesion [4,5]. That said, there is strong evidence supporting the role of abnormal T-cell subpopulations in PV. In fact, it has been established that an imbalance of regulatory T cells leads to the unexpected activation of autoreactive CD4+ T cells with subsequent induction of autoantibody formation [6].

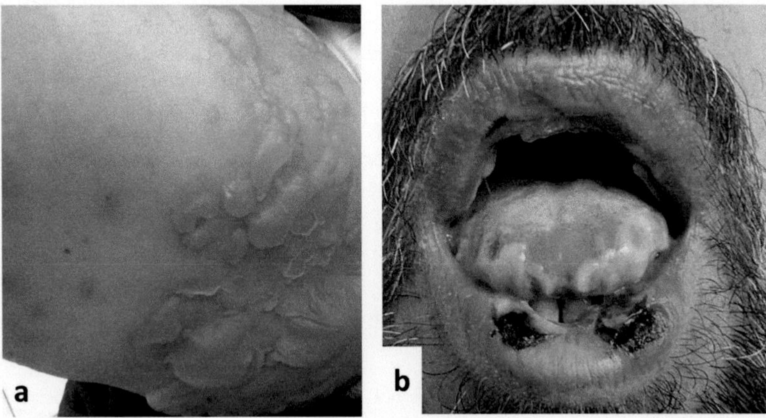

FIG. 1 (A) Multiple blisters in a new PV patient. (B) Painful erosions of PV in the oral mucosa.

For years, systemic corticosteroids have been the mainstay of PV treatment. These agents can control disease within a few weeks. Conventionally, dermatologists would start tapering corticosteroids after the initial disease control over months or years to the minimum dose required for the maintenance of remission [7–9]. Corticosteroids are commonly combined with other immunosuppressive agents such as azathioprine and mycophenolate mofetil (MMF), to reduce their maintenance dosages with the aim of final discontinuation of steroids [1,7–9].

While the advent of systemic steroid therapy considerably improved the prognosis of pemphigus, these groups of diseases can still be life threatening, now mainly due to adverse events resulting from corticosteroid treatment. Severe infection is one of the most important causes of death during PV treatment as the result of an immunocompromised state.

The role of rituximab (RTX) as the first-line therapeutic option for pemphigus has been established during the past decade [10]. RTX depletes B cells after binding to CD20. The US Food and Drug Administration (FDA) approved RTX as a first-line therapy for moderate-to-severe pemphigus in 2018. Recent studies have proven the efficacy and safety of RTX in the treatment of PV and other subtypes of pemphigus; however, there are increasing reports of RTX side effects. Proper management of PV patients requires a thorough understanding of the RTX mechanism of action and its side effects. This chapter embarks on the application of RTX in the management of PV and reviews the current evidence on its side effects.

Diagnosis and treatment of PV

The diagnosis of PV depends on the integration of clinical presentations, histopathology findings, DIF study, and serologic tests (Fig. 2) [11]. After proper diagnosis, the treatment plan needs to be set. Treatment response to PV consists of various phases. The first phase is the consolidation phase when no new lesions appear for at least 2 weeks, and 80% of existing lesions show improvement. In this phase, dermatologists may taper oral corticosteroids.

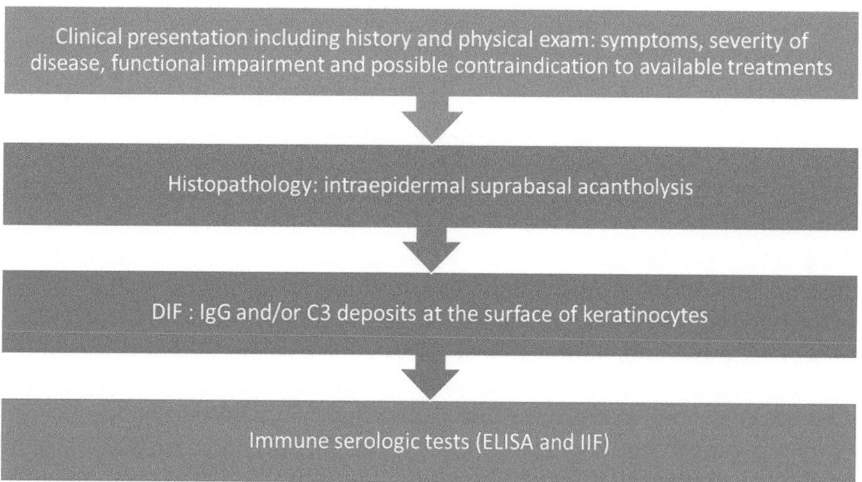

FIG. 2 Clinical approach to the patient with PV. DIF, direct immunofluorescence; IIF, indirect immunofluorescence.

The next phase of the treatment is complete remission, characterized by the nonappearance of new or established lesions in a patient with minimal treatment. Complete remission off therapy is defined as no lesions after discontinuing therapy for at least 2 months. Relapse is characterized by the reappearance of three or more new lesions in a month which do not heal without treatment in 1 week [11,12].

Application of rituximab in pemphigus

Several studies have established the prominent efficacy of RTX in the treatment of PV even before its approval in the United States and Europe in 2018 and 2019, respectively [13].

The initial investigations showed RTX's efficacy in resistant cases of PV to standard immunosuppressive therapies [14,15].

Subsequently, RTX was evaluated as a first-line therapy early in the disease course [15]. Further investigations demonstrated that the first-line administration of RTX allowed rapid tapering of corticosteroid dosages [1,16–18]. The result of such studies led to the conduction of a pivotal RITUX 3 study to investigate RTX for naïve and previously untreated pemphigus patients [10].

RITUX 3 was the prospective, randomized controlled multicenter open-label trial that evaluated RTX as a steroid-sparing, adjuvant, first-line therapy for PV [10]. This study revealed the superiority of RTX plus short-term prednisone to standard-dose prednisone in regard to efficacy and side effects in the treatment of moderate-to-severe PV. Therefore, many dermatologists now consider first line administration of RTX in the treatment of PV patients.

Rituximab dosing in pemphigus

Most authorities and guidelines recommend an RTX induction regimen with two 1 g IV infusions 14 days apart in adjunction with a short course of glucocorticoids [2]. Thereafter, maintenance therapy could be achieved by 500 mg IV infusions at months 12 and 18 followed by every 6 months, if necessary, based on clinical assessment according to the European guidelines. American guidelines recommend 500 mg IV infusions at month 12 and each 6 months afterward or depending on clinical assessment [2]. Management of relapse is based on clinical evaluation. Patients can be treated with a 1 g IV infusion of RTX and/or an increase in oral steroid dosage [2]. Ensuing RTX administration should be considered ≥16 weeks after the earlier infusion [2].

According to the current data, two main RTX regimens can be administrated for pemphigus patients; the lymphoma protocol includes four doses of 375 mg/m^2 infusions every week [19], while the other regimen, which is based on the rheumatoid arthritis protocol, composed of two doses of 1 g intravenous infusions of RTX every 2 weeks [19].

Based on a recent literature review, both protocols are effective in managing refractory PV. Response rate, relapse rate, and serious infections were lower in lymphoma protocol but the mortality rate was higher, and there were some cases of nonresponders [20]. Administration of the RA protocol resulted in a higher response rate with the cost of more relapse rate and number of infections compared to the lymphoma protocol [19]; however, there was a lower mortality rate and no nonresponders in cases who had received RA protocol.

In refractory cases of PV, another protocol is recommended a combination of RTX with intravenous immunoglobulin in selective cases with favorable outcomes. Many authorities believe intravenous immunoglobulin is recommended for those at risk of infections or with extensive disease [21,22].

Contraindications include severe active infections, a history of anaphylaxis or IgE-mediated hypersensitivity to murine proteins of RTX, pregnancy, breastfeeding, severe heart failure, and arrhythmia [21].

Guidelines for pemphigus treatment

Several guidelines are available for the treatment of pemphigus. The most applicable guidelines are the European Academy of Dermatology and Venereology (EADV), the Association of the Scientific Medical Societies in Germany (ASMSG), the Brazilian Society of Dermatology (BSD), the British Association of Dermatologists (BAD), the Dermatology Branch of China International Exchange and Promotion Association for Medical and Healthcare (DBC), and the French Society of Dermatology (FSD) [23]. There is also an international panel of experts in the treatment of pemphigus [11].

EADV is the only guideline recommending RTX as a first-line treatment of mild pemphigus [24]. The preferred protocol is two infusions of 1 g 2 weeks apart rather than four infusions of 375 mg/m^2 1 week apart, according to the DBC and EADV [24,25]. As said by the BAD guidelines, the RA protocol is more cost benefit and preferable [8].

As mentioned above, the use of RTX as part of the maintenance therapy and relapse treatment is considered in some guidelines [11–13]. The EADV recommends an extra cycle of RTX in relapsed cases formerly received RTX, particularly when relapse occurs early between 4 and 6 months during the tapering of oral steroids [9,12,13].

Infusion-related reactions

Adverse events related to the use of RTX include infusion-related reactions (IRRs). IRR usually occurs within 24 h of drug infusion [26]. IRR includes hypersensitivity reactions and cytokine-release syndrome that occur as the result of the pharmacological or biological agent infusion causing the cytokine release. The clinical symptoms of RTX-induced IRR usually occur within a few minutes to 2 h after the initiation of infusion [27] and differ from mild adverse events to life-threatening reactions [28]. The common findings are headache, nausea, tachycardia, hypotension, rash, and shortness of breath. More severe reactions include angioedema, hypoxia, bronchospasm, myocardial infarction, ventricular fibrillation, and cardiovascular collapse [29].

Infectious side effects

The most common and worrisome side effect of RTX therapy in pemphigus remains to be the infectious side effects [30].

RTX administration eliminates the CD20+ B cells without upsetting stem cells or present plasma cells [30]. Following RTX administration the B cells level declines to the minimum for 6–12 months, mitigating the humoral immune reaction against foreign antigens [31].

Additionally, recent evidences show the possible effects of RTX on the T-cell function that predisposes the individuals under treatment to opportunistic infections [32].

According to a recent review of the literature, the most common causative organisms are viral agents and the most serious infections are bacterial. The summarized infectious events and their causative organisms are depicted in Table 1.

Whether RTX therapy is associated with less infectious side effects compared to conventional PV treatment is not yet elucidated. However, dermatologists should be vigilant about the incidence of infectious side effects and consider prompt intervention when necessary [33]. The incidence of unpredicted lethal infections including progressive multifocal leukoencephalopathy is not assessable due to the uncommonness of pemphigus [11].

Cardiovascular side effects

The presence of adherence junctions and intercellular connecting structures are common features of the heart and skin. For that reason, chronic skin diseases may have cardiovascular manifestations [34].

Although there is a risk of cardiovascular collapse and even sudden death during the RTX infusion, particularly with the first infusion, there is a paucity of studies investigating these adverse events in PV [35].

A recent cohort study suggests that patients with PV with previous RTX treatment had less predisposition to hypertension, hyperlipidemia, type 2 diabetes, obesity, myocardial infarction, stroke, and peripheral vascular disease compared with those treated with conventional adjuvant drugs such as azathioprine/MMF [36]. The findings of this study suggest the long-term safety profile of RTX and recommend consideration of RTX in patients with cardiovascular and metabolic risk factors [36].

Another study evaluated the effects of RTX on electrocardiogram (ECG) parameters in 80 patients with PV. According to this study, the mean corrected QT interval, premature atrial contraction, and premature ventricular contraction showed a significant increase after RTX infusion, suggesting potential arrhythmogenic effects of RTX [37]. Further studies are needed to investigate the cardiac side effects of RTX in PV patients.

Skin-related side effects

Similar to any other drug skin is a common target for RTX adverse events are one of the most common adverse events related to RTX treatment in PV.

Pruritus, urticaria, angioedema, blister, skin ulcer, Stevens-Johnson syndrome, and toxic epidermal necrolysis are the most commonly reported cutaneous side effects of RTX [2]. New onset psoriasis and palmoplantar pustulosis are among the cutaneous disorders reported in the setting of RTX treatment [38,39].

With regard to neoplastic disorders, iatrogenic Kaposi's sarcoma has been reported in a case of pemphigus vegetans who were treated with RTX and corticosteroid in the absence

TABLE 1 Summary of the infectious event after treatment with rituximab in pemphigus patients.

Activated infection	Type of pemphigus	Mean infection onset after 1st dose (days)	Causative agent(s)
Sepsis	6 PV/1 PV or PF)	14	*S. aureus, Acinobacter, P. aeruginosa, E. E. faecalis, C. freundii*
Bacteremia	PV	30	*S. aureus*
Pneumonia	PV	94	NM
Brain abscess	PV	5	*Listeria monocytogenes*
Lung abscess	PV	14	Anaerobic bacteria
Perirectal phlegmon and intrapelvic abscesses	PV	168	NM
Nocardiosis	PF	77	*Nocardia farcinica*
Hip arthritis	PV	91	*Pseudomonas aeruginosa*
Herpes zoaster	2 PV/1 PF/2 PV or PF	12	Varicella-zoster virus
Herpes simplex	6 PV/1 PV or PF)	12	Herpes simplex virus
Cytomegalovirus gastritis/ retinitis/cutaneous	PV	470	Cytomegalovirus
COVID-19	PV	7410	SARS-CoV-2
Pneumonia	5 PV/1 PF	150	*Pneumocystis jiroveci*
Tinea pedis	PF	210	NM
Sepsis	3 PV/1 PF/2 PV or PF	780	NM
Pneumonia	5 PV/6 PV or PF	37.5	NM
Skin infection	2 PV/2PF/1 PV or PF	216.25	NM
Musculoskeletal infection	2 PF/1 PV or PF	67	NM
Pyelonephritis	PV or PF	360	NM
Late-onset neutropenia and fever	PV	217	NM
Uncomplicated urinary tract infection	PV or PF	NM	NM
Intracranial septic thrombosis	PV	14	NM
Dental caries	PF	NM	NM

PV, pemphigus vulgaris; PF, pemphigus foliaceus; NM, not mentioned.

of HIV infection [40]. Additionally, there is a report of Bowen disease of the nail unit with concurrent HPV-16 infection in a pemphigus patient after RTX therapy [41]. Interestingly, there is a report of RTX-induced reticulate pigmentation of the face in PV [42].

It is hard to draw a calculation and consider a causal effect for RTX treatment and these cutaneous adverse events in PV patients. However, alteration of the immune system by RTX may result in such diverse adverse events.

Paradoxical worsening

The unexpected (paradoxical) worsening of PV following RTX is rare but real which is compatible with our experience [43]. According to the current evidence, these patients can be properly managed using diverse strategies such as corticosteroids and alternative antibody-removal therapies like plasmapheresis and IVIg [44]. Further studies are necessary to investigate potential (bio)markers to predict possible unexpected worsening of PV patients treated with RTX.

Resistance to RTX

Relapse and resistance

Relapse means recurrence of skin lesions after primary disease control and resistance means absence of clinical response to RTX. Relapse and resistance are common in PV patients. Suggested mechanisms of resistance include the following: (1) memory and germinal B cells may persist in the spleen and lymph nodes; (2) novel lineages of autoreactive B cells may appear after emission from tolerance; (3) longstanding autoreactive plasma cells may continue autoantibody production; (4) autoreactive CD41 TH cells; (5) autoantibodies to RTX may form that interfere with RTX binding; (6) alterations in RTX pharmacokinetics; and (7) biochemical changes to lipid raft signaling.

According to a study by Hammers et al., the persistence of antidesmoglein 3 B-cell clones contributed to RTX resistance in patients with PV. Elimination of the remaining clones with additional doses of RTX or another autoantibody-obliterating agent is, therefore, the goal in treating resistance [45].

Predictors of RTX adverse effects

The current evidence suggests that IRR incidence and severity are related to a cytokine storm occurring as the result of interaction between NK cells and CD20-positive cells [46].

To date, no preclinical models can predict the occurrence of IRR in mice and nonhuman primates. However, a retrospective study has analyzed patients treated with RTX proposing a model for prediction of the incidence of adverse reactions, with a specificity rate of 96% by using a combination of existing splenomegaly, hemoglobin levels, allergy history, and female gender. While this model is simple and practical, it has to be validated prospectively. Furthermore, the validity of these parameters for the prediction of IRR incidence is not clarified [46]. Another study found that a high absolute lymphocyte count can identify patients who do not show any adverse event from rapid RTX infusion with good specificity. Nevertheless, a lack of sensitivity can ensue when screening potential patients for adverse events [47].

Prevention of rituximab-associated side effects

Several recommendations are required to reduce and manage IRR. The first infusion should start with an infusion rate of 50mg per hour with close monitoring every 30min. The rate of infusion can be increased every 30min by 50mg per hour up to a maximum of 400mg per hour.

Premedication with intravenous methylprednisolone 100mg 30min before each infusion decreases the rate and severity of IRRs and is recommended. Premedication with an antipyretic and an antihistamine such as acetaminophen and chlorpheniramine is recommended before each RTX infusion. Prophylaxis for PCP with cotrimoxazole during and after RTX treatment is recommended by some authorities [2].

Similar to other indications, RTX is contraindicated in PV patients with active, severe infections, those in a severely immunocompromised state, and those with severe heart failure or severe, uncontrolled cardiac disease [2].

Prophylactic antiviral therapy is recommended in patients at risk of reactivation of HBV. We recommend consultation with an infectious disease expert for deciding on the antiviral agent. Prophylactic isoniazid 300mg BD is mandatory for those at risk of reactivation of tuberculosis (e.g., positive patients who have positive PPD or QuantiFERON test). The duration for anti-tb prophylaxis is recommended for at least 9 months and the author recommends discontinuation of prophylaxis after consultation with an infectious disease expert [21].

Future perspectives

Anti-CD20 antibodies vary depending on cellular response upon binding and can be categorized as type I (e.g., rituximab, ofatumumab, veltuzumab, and ocrelizumab) or type II (e.g., tositumomab or obinutuzumab/GA101). Further understanding of anti-CD20 epitope binding and signaling has led to the introduction of next-generation mAbs that minimize expense by subcutaneous administration, prevention of relapse and resistance, and attenuation of the adverse effects observed in RTX therapy. Type I mAbs concentrate CD20 into lipid rafts on the plasma membrane, resulting in the clustering of CD20 with further recruitment and activation of complement [44,45]. In contrast, type II mAbs show enhanced adhesion and improved direct induction of cell death compared to type I mAbs, with a minimal complement-dependent cytotoxicity (CDC) response [45]. That said, the new and emerging anti-CD20 antibodies are potentially favorable adjuncts in the treatment of patients with recalcitrant PV.

Veltuzumab is a novel anti-CD20 mAb with a reported efficacy in the treatment of refractory PV patients [45]. This type I, humanized anti-CD20 mAb has framework regions of epratuzumab, a humanized anti-CD22 antibody. Its major superiority over RTX is its subcutaneous route of administration in low doses, making it more applicable and cost benefit for patients [46]. Ofatumumab is a type I, fully human, anti-CD20 monoclonal antibody, which targets an epitope of CD20 different from the RTX binding site and has been proven to be safe and effective for the treatment of lymphoproliferative and other autoimmune disorders [47]. A phase III randomized placebo-controlled trial of subcutaneous ofatumumab in pemphigus was recently terminated in 2018 (NCT01920477), and the results of this study are not published yet.

Acknowledgments

Special thanks to Dr. Yasaman Vali and Dr. Nikoo Mozafari for proof editing the chapter and Dr. Saeid Pourdavoodi for helping with the clinical images.

References

[1] Joly P, et al. A single cycle of rituximab for the treatment of severe pemphigus. N Engl J Med 2007;357(6):545–52.
[2] Frampton JE. Rituximab: a review in pemphigus vulgaris. Am J Clin Dermatol 2020;21(1):149–56.
[3] Kasperkiewicz M, et al. Pemphigus. Nat Rev Dis Primers 2017;3:17026.
[4] Kowalewski C, Hashimoto T, Joly P. Editorial: autoimmune blistering diseases. Front Immunol 2020;11:1614.
[5] Gheisari M, et al. Cutaneous type of pemphigus vulgaris. J Am Acad Dermatol 2020;83(3):919–20.
[6] Sahin I, Isik S. Blindness following cosmetic injections of the face. Plastic Reconstruct Surg 2012;130(5):738e.
[7] Kridin K. Emerging treatment options for the management of pemphigus vulgaris. Ther Clin Risk Manag 2018;14:757–78.
[8] Harman KE, et al. British Association of Dermatologists' guidelines for the management of pemphigus vulgaris 2017. Br J Dermatol 2017;177(5):1170–201.
[9] Hertl M, et al. Pemphigus. S2 Guideline for diagnosis and treatment-guided by the European Dermatology Forum (EDF) in cooperation with the European Academy of Dermatology and Venereology (EADV). J Eur Acad Dermatol Venereol 2015;29(3):405–14.
[10] Joly P, et al. First-line rituximab combined with short-term prednisone versus prednisone alone for the treatment of pemphigus (Ritux 3): a prospective, multicentre, parallel-group, open-label randomised trial. Lancet 2017;389 (10083):2031–40.
[11] Murrell DF, et al. Diagnosis and management of pemphigus: recommendations of an international panel of experts. J Am Acad Dermatol 2020;82(3). 575–585.e1.
[12] Abdollahimajd F, et al. Management of pemphigus in COVID-19 pandemic era; a review article. Arch Acad Emerg Med 2020;8(1), e51.
[13] Cholera M, Chainani-Wu N. Management of pemphigus vulgaris. Adv Ther 2016;33(6):910–58.
[14] Didona D, et al. Pemphigus: current and future therapeutic strategies. Front Immunol 2019;10:1418.
[15] Tavakolpour S, et al. Sixteen-year history of rituximab therapy for 1085 pemphigus vulgaris patients: a systematic review. Int Immunopharmacol 2018;54:131–8.
[16] Ahmed AR, et al. First line treatment of pemphigus vulgaris with a novel protocol in patients with contraindications to systemic corticosteroids and immunosuppressive agents: preliminary retrospective study with a seven year follow-up. Int Immunopharmacol 2016;34:25–31.
[17] Cho YT, et al. First-line combination therapy with rituximab and corticosteroids is effective and safe for pemphigus. Acta Derm Venereol 2014;94(4):472–3.
[18] Lunardon L, et al. Adjuvant rituximab therapy of pemphigus: a single-center experience with 31 patients. Arch Dermatol 2012;148(9):1031–6.
[19] Kasperkiewicz M, Schmidt E. Current treatment of autoimmune blistering diseases. Curr Drug Discov Technol 2009;6(4):270–80.
[20] Zakka LR, Shetty SS, Ahmed AR. Rituximab in the treatment of pemphigus vulgaris. Dermatol Ther (Heidelb) 2012;2(1):17.
[21] Daneshpazhooh M, et al. Iranian guideline for rituximab therapy in pemphigus patients. Dermatol Ther 2019;32 (5), e13016.

[22] Ahmed AR, et al. Treatment of pemphigus vulgaris with rituximab and intravenous immune globulin. N Engl J Med 2006;355(17):1772–9.
[23] Zhao W, et al. Comparison of guidelines for management of pemphigus: a review of systemic corticosteroids, rituximab, and other immunosuppressive therapies. Clin Rev Allergy Immunol 2021;61(3):351–62.
[24] Schmidt E, et al. S2k guidelines for the treatment of pemphigus vulgaris/foliaceus and bullous pemphigoid: 2019 update. JDDG. J Deutsch Dermatol Gesellsch 2020;18(5):516–26.
[25] Zuo Y-G, et al. Chinese expert proposal on the diagnosis and management of pemphigus vulgaris (2020)#. Int J Dermatol Venereol 2020;3(3):148–55.
[26] Doessegger L, Banholzer ML. Clinical development methodology for infusion-related reactions with monoclonal antibodies. Clin Transl Immunol 2015;4(7), e39.
[27] Chung CH. Managing premedications and the risk for reactions to infusional monoclonal antibody therapy. Oncologist 2008;13(6):725–32.
[28] D'Arena G, et al. Adverse drug reactions after intravenous rituximab infusion are more common in hematologic malignancies than in autoimmune disorders and can be predicted by the combination of few clinical and laboratory parameters: results from a retrospective, multicenter study of 374 patients. Leukemia Lymphoma 2017;58(11):2633–41.
[29] Brown BA, Torabi M. Incidence of infusion-associated reactions with rituximab for treating multiple sclerosis: a retrospective analysis of patients treated at a US Centre. Drug Safety 2011;34:117–23.
[30] Shahrigharahkoshan S, et al. A review of reported infectious events following rituximab therapy in pemphigus patients. Dermatol Ther 2022;35(3), e15264.
[31] Schmidt E. Rituximab as first-line treatment of pemphigus. Lancet 2017;389(10083):1956–8.
[32] Sfikakis P, et al. Increased expression of the FoxP3 functional marker of regulatory T cells following B cell depletion with rituximab in patients with lupus nephritis. Clin Immunol 2007;123(1):66–73.
[33] Lima RB, et al. Septic shock in a refractory pemphigus vulgaris patient after rituximab therapy. Dermatol Ther 2021;34(1), e14725.
[34] Shahidi-Dadras M, et al. Cardiac function in pemphigus vulgaris patients before and after steroid pulse therapy. J Dermatol Treat 2021;32(7):855–9.
[35] Yoshida K, et al. Sudden cardiac death in a patient with thrombotic thrombocytopenic purpura: a case report. Hematol Rep 2022;14(2):203–9.
[36] Kridin K, Mruwat N, Ludwig RJ. Association of rituximab with risk of long-term cardiovascular and metabolic outcomes in patients with pemphigus. JAMA Dermatol 2022.
[37] Aidi S, et al. Adverse electrocardiographic effects of rituximab infusion in pemphigus patients. Dermatol Ther 2020;33(6), e14299.
[38] Neema S, et al. Rituximab-induced new onset palmo-plantar pustulosis in patients with pemphigus foliaceus: a rare adverse effect. Dermatol Ther 2022;35(9), e15714.
[39] Charoenpipatsin N, et al. Rituximab-induced psoriasis in a patient with pemphigus foliaceous: a case report and literature review. J Dermatol 2022;49(8):e251–2.
[40] Daflaoui H, et al. Iatrogenic Kaposi's sarcoma induced by rituximab and corticosteroid treatment for pemphigus vegetans in an HIV-negative patient. Indian J Dermatol Venereol Leprol 2022;88(3):409–12.
[41] Wen P, et al. Bowen disease of the nail unit associated with HPV-16 infection in a pemphigus patient following rituximab treatment. Eur J Dermatol 2022;32(2):270–2.
[42] Sanke S, et al. Rituximab induced reticulate pigmentation over face in pemphigus vulgaris. Dermatol Ther 2020;33(4), e13752.
[43] Mokos M, Lakoš Jukić I, Marinović B. Transient worsening of pemphigus vulgaris resembling toxic epidermal necrolysis after the first cycle of rituximab therapy. Dermatol Ther 2022;35(6), e15469.
[44] Mahmoudi H, et al. Unexpected worsening of pemphigus vulgaris after rituximab: a report of three cases. Int Immunopharmacol 2019;71:40–2.
[45] Huang A, Madan RK, Levitt J. Future therapies for pemphigus vulgaris: rituximab and beyond. J Am Acad Dermatol 2016;74(4):746–53.
[46] Paul F, Cartron G. Infusion-related reactions to rituximab: frequency, mechanisms and predictors. Expert Rev Clin Immunol 2019;15(4):383–9.
[47] Lang DS, Fong CC. Prediction of adverse events in patients receiving rapid rituximab infusion: validation of a predictive model. Clin J Oncol Nurs 2014;18(1):89–92.

CHAPTER

16

Immune monitoring of patients treated with anti-CD20 therapeutic monoclonals for autoimmune disorders

Bruno Brando and Arianna Gatti

Hematology Laboratory and Transfusion Center, Western Milan Hospital Consortium, Legnano General Hospital, Legnano, Milano, Italy

Abstract

Immunosuppression has been centered on T cells, due to their role in allo- and autoimmunity. Patients on rituximab for lymphomas improve their concomitant rheumatoid arthritis, highlighting the role of B cells in autoimmunity. B cells differentiate from precursors to antibody-secreting plasma cells. CD20 is expressed from pre-B to mature activated memory B cells. By eliminating CD20+ cells, naïve precursors initially devoid of autoreactivity and long-living plasma cells are spared. Rituximab aims at eliminating the B cell memory of pathogenic IgG autoantibodies, hoping that this has not proceeded to autoreactive CD20− plasma cells.

Rituximab is approved for rheumatoid arthritis, polyangiitis, and pemphigus, but is successfully used in the off-label treatment of almost all autoimmune disorders. Therapeutic antibodies offer the opportunity to monitor their effects on cell targets, the disappearance and reappearance of the relevant cells, and to evidence deviations from the expected patterns. The ISCCA flow protocol has been devised to monitor and optimize the treatment schemes, to identify treatment-resistant patients, to evaluate the B cell repopulation, and to prevent overimmunosuppression. This protocol allows the high-sensitivity analysis of very small B cell subsets during the depletion and repopulation phases. In anti-CD20 treated autoimmune diseases, the early and long-lasting disappearance of B cells, the slow repopulation by naïve CD27− B cells, and the reduced memory of CD27+ IgG+ B cells are indicators of good response. The commitment of IgG-switched memory B cells to plasma cells can be also evaluated. Limitations of the monitoring of the functional B cell subsets in peripheral blood are, however, present and discussed. Despite the high individual and disease-related variability, the ISCCA protocol is of help in the management of anti-CD20 treatments in autoimmune disorders, in case of escape phenomena, disease relapses, and overimmunosuppression.

Abbreviations

ADCC antibody-dependent cell-mediated cytotoxicity
ADCP antibody-dependent cell-mediated phagocytosis

https://doi.org/10.1016/B978-0-443-19200-5.00010-5

BCR	B cell receptor
Breg	B cells with regulatory and immunosuppressive functions
BSA	bovine serum albumin
CDC	complement-dependent cytotoxicity
cy	cytoplasmic prefix (immunoglobulins or antigens)
EMA	European Medicine Agency
Fc-γ	immunoglobulin Fc-gamma receptor type III (CD16)
Ig	immunoglobulin(s)
IL-10	interleukin-10
ISCCA	Italian Society for Clinical Cell Analysis
LLOD	lowest level of detection
LLOQ	lowest level of quantitation
mAb	monoclonal antibody
mFCM	multicolor flow cytometry
NK	natural killer
RA	rheumatoid arthritis
s	cell surface prefix (immunoglobulins or antigens)
SLE	systemic lupus erythematosus

Conflict of interest

Dr. Bruno Brando has received lecture fees from Becton Dickinson Biosciences (United States, Spain, Russia, Italy), Alexion Pharma UK, and Flow Assessment S.r.L Italy.
Dr. Arianna Gatti declares no conflicts of interest.

Introduction

During the past decades, autoimmune disorders have been generally treated with immunosuppressors mostly focused on T cell-mediated response. The concept of the T cell dependence of both adaptive and autoreactive immune reactions was central in classical immunology for many years [1,2]. Therefore, a number of immunosuppressive drugs and therapeutic schedules directed against T cells and their soluble products have been developed and used over the years, along with the almost ubiquitous corticosteroids.

The original aim of regimens focused on T cells was the restoration of self-tolerance or the reset of aggressive auto- and alloimmune responses, which can be sometimes achieved, however, using very intensive therapeutic schemes. Anti-T cell immunosuppressive therapies are basically effective, but for a price, being associated with heavy side effects, frequent overimmunosuppression, opportunistic infections, metabolic disorders, and cancer [3].

Although the role of T cells and their soluble products is clearly demonstrated in autoimmune disorders [2], especially in rheumatoid arthritis (RA) [4] and systemic lupus erythematosus (SLE) [5], the almost incidental evidence that the depletion of B cells can also be effective in such diseases [6,7] has prompted a rethinking of the B cell role in the pathogenesis of auto- and alloimmune reactions [8].

This evidence came from clinical observations in the late 1990s, in which RA patients receiving methotrexate who developed lymphoproliferative disorders were successfully treated with the anti-CD20 monoclonal antibody (mAb) rituximab, showing at the same time a striking improvement of the concomitant RA [7]. This finding has highlighted the role of B cells in autoreactive tissue damage, with the rapid development of new therapeutic regimens focused on B cell response both in adults and children [9,10]. This novel approach aimed at depleting the cell machinery involved in the production of allo- and autoantibodies responsible for the damage of target tissues, and a new therapeutic scenario was opened.

During the last decade, evidence was being accumulated on the rational usage of anti-B cell treatment in both autoimmune disorders and alloimmune responses in solid organ transplantation [11]. Anti-CD20 mAbs are today widely used in almost all autoimmune diseases, although as an "off-label" treatment in the majority of cases.

Functional and phenotypic development of B cells

B cells play a fundamental role in immune response, being the precursors of antibody-producing plasma cells. They also act as antigen-presenting cells to T lymphocytes and secrete a number of cytokines and soluble factors of effector, regulatory, and suppressor types.

B lymphocytes undergo a complex maturation and differentiation pathway that can be easily studied by cell immunophenotyping and multicolor flow cytometry (mFCM) (Fig. 1).

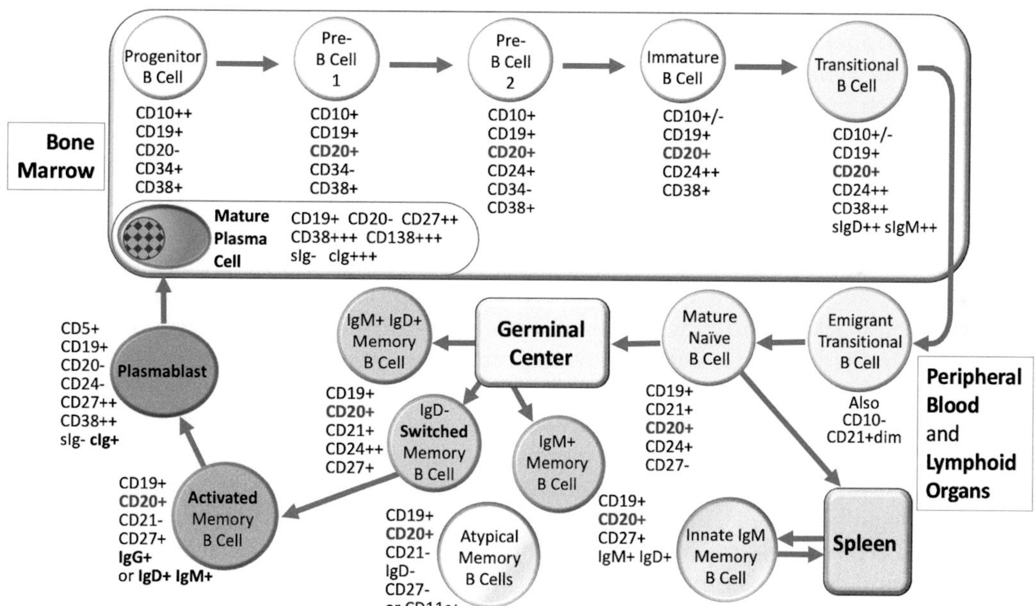

FIG. 1 Schematic representation of the functional and immunophenotypic characterization of the main B cell subsets during their differentiation pathway from bone marrow progenitors to mature plasma cells. The expression of surface CD20 from pre-B stage-1 to activated memory B cells is evidenced in *red*. The germinal center-dependent and -independent maturation paths are depicted, with the spleen playing a role in the generation and remodeling of IgM memory B cells. The generation of some minor atypical subsets is also described in the main text. *Symbols and abbreviations:* + to +++ expression intensity of a cell marker, from low to high; − sign, denotes negative expression; +/− sign, denotes a dim positive or absent marker; *sIg*, cell surface immunoglobulin; *cIg*, intracytoplasmic immunoglobulin.

B Cells stem from CD34+ CD10+ CD38++ CD45^{low} progenitors based in the bone marrow. The maturation process takes place in the bone marrow and is supported by stromal cells and by a series of cytokines and growth factors. Maturing B cells are then released in the bloodstream as CD45+ CD19+ CD10+ CD24^{high} CD38^{high} sIgM++ sIgD+ transitional B cells [12,13]. B cell ontogenesis is characterized by an ordered sequence of appearance and disappearance of surface and intracellular markers during the maturation process [14], including CD19, CD20, CD21, CD22, CD23, CD24, cytoplasmic (cy), and surface (s) immunoglobulins (Ig).

Once in the systemic circulation, recent bone marrow emigrant transitional B cells may undergo various differentiation pathways: they may enter the spleen, where they differentiate into innate sIgM memory B cells, or more classically they interact with the germinal centers, where they develop the antigen experience with the help of T cells. At this stage, variable segments of heavy and light immunoglobulin chains recombine, to favor the deletion of potentially autoreactive cell clones and the induction of self-tolerance [13,15]. The process of self-tolerance or central tolerance includes the elimination by apoptosis of B and T cells endowed with high-affinity receptors to autoantigens. This multistep purging process may, however, be incomplete, letting some autoreactive T and B cells escape into the periphery, whereas in healthy subjects they are normally kept quiescent. Under the influence of genetic and environmental factors, such cells can evade the local mechanisms of control and attack peripheral tissues [2,16].

Antigen-experienced B lymphocytes can remain quiescent until a new antigen exposure occurs, at which point they rapidly differentiate into activated memory cells, acquiring the hallmark CD27 surface antigen and also modifying their sIg expression. CD27 seems to be acquired gradually during this process, and it is possible to dissect functionally CD27^{dim} from CD27^{high} memory B cells [17]. CD27^{dim} B cells are T- and germinal center-independent, more abundant during infancy, and display a less mutated B cell antigen receptor. Conversely, CD27^{high} memory B cells depend on both T cells and germinal centers to survive, prevail in the elderly, and display a more diverse B cell receptor repertoire (Fig. 2). The use of alternative cell markers and other types of subset classification may generate controversial terminology in the literature, with nonoverlapping descriptions of the various functional B cell subpopulations and their phenotypes.

CD27+ memory B cells can be chiefly dissected into mutually exclusive sIgM+ and sIgG+ subsets, while smaller subpopulations expressing sIgD, sIgA, and rarely sIgE can be still detectable. A few memory B lymphocytes may also lack the sIg expression and are classified as "double negative" B cells, endowed with special functions that will be discussed later.

Memory B cells expressing sIgM seem involved in the innate, spleen-dependent first-line defense [18], and can be also split into sIgM+^{dim} and sIgM+^{high} cells, with marked functional and transcriptomic differences (Fig. 2) [19].

Surface IgG+ switched CD27+ memory B cells, by contrast, have undergone the final deterministic commitment to plasma cells. Terminally activated sIgG+ memory B cells lose the CD20 and CD24 antigens, express CD38+^{high} and evolve as plasmablasts that briefly circulate and can be either short-lived or differentiate into long-living CD19+ CD20− CD38+^{high} CD138+^{high} cyIg+^{high} antibody-secreting plasma cells [20], depending on their final location and on the stimuli they receive from the local environment.

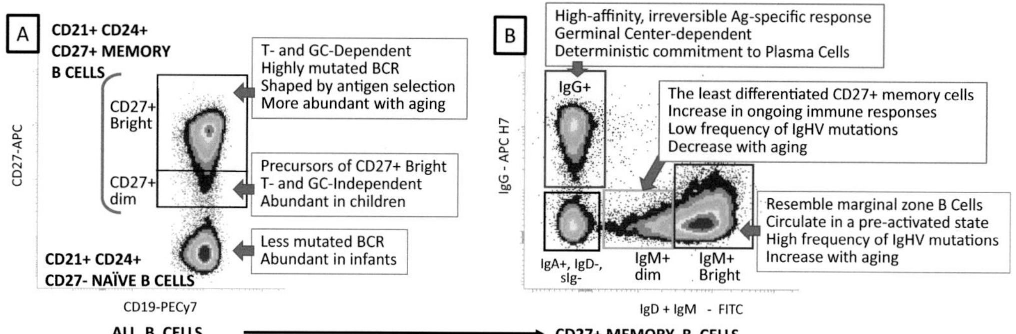

FIG. 2 Multicolor flow cytometric representation of the phenotypic spectrum of the main mature CD19+ CD27+ memory B cell subpopulations, with a short summary of their functional features. Panel (A): Clean CD19+ mature B cells are divided into CD27− naïve and CD27+ memory B cells. B cells dimly expressing the CD27+ evolve into CD27+ bright upon antigen-driven pressure and show a different sIgG/sIgM distribution. No markers are, however, able to dissect precisely CD27+dim from CD27+bright memory B cells. Panel (B): Surface immunoglobulin expression by the whole CD27+ memory B cell population. CD27+ memory B cells expressing sIgM dimly or brightly have differentiated functions and differ transcriptomically by the expression of more than 75 genes and by BAFF receptor density. CD27+ sIgG+ cells represent memory-switched, activated cells committed to plasma cell differentiation. CD27+ memory B cells that are negative for sIgG, sIgD, and sIgM can include sIgA+ B cells, functionally resembling sIgG+ cells, and may also include sIg− elements. *APC/APC-H7*, allophycocyanin fluorescent dye and its -H7 derivative; *FITC*, fluorescein isothiocyanate dye; *PECy7*, phycoerythrin-cyanin 7 dye.

The development of a number of possible variations, including the generation of a variety of autoimmunity-prone B lymphocyte subsets, has, however, been demonstrated, along with the normal maturation pathway. Among CD19+ CD10− CD27− CD21^{low} B cells, both normally reactive and autoimmunity-prone lymphocyte subsets can be identified also in normal subjects [21]. The switch from naïve cells to atypical or "double-negative" sIgD− CD27− memory B cells [22,23], the age-related CD11c+ or ABC cells, playing a role in inflammation and autoimmunity [24,25], have been also characterized. Despite being a minor cell subpopulation, double-negative memory B cells in turn display an amazing functional heterogeneity, as shown by single-cell transcriptomic analysis. In this small subset, several subpopulations with opposite functions and a surprising T cell-independent sIgE+ B cell cluster have been demonstrated [23].

In immunized individuals, even a subset of CD27− sIgM+ B cells that bona fide display the features and the behavior of memory cells has been described [26].

Lastly, upon activation, B cells acquire a strong antigen-presenting function and express CD80 and CD86, which mediate the interaction with T cells via CTLA-4 and CD28 [27].

Of course, not all B cells can potentially exert autoreactive and inflammatory functions. Several B cell subsets, also of the memory type, display immunosuppressive, tolerogenic, and antiinflammatory properties, due to the secretion of Interleukin 10 (IL-10) and other molecules upon stimulation. Such cells are collectively named regulatory B cells (or Breg); they do not display a single specific phenotype, but can be demonstrated among different subsets at various degrees of maturation, differentiation, gene profiling, and immunophenotype [28–32], as briefly summarized in Table 1.

TABLE 1 Some of the best phenotypically and functionally characterized B regulatory (Breg) populations share the production of the immunosuppressive cytokine IL-10.

Subtype of Bregs	Phenotype	Suppressive molecules produced	Functions
Transitional B cells	CD19+ CD24^{high} CD38^{high}	IL-10	Highest producer of IL-10 Inhibit Th1 response Inhibit Th17 differentiation Convert T CD4+ into Tregs
Granzyme B cells	CD19+ CD1d^{high} CD38+ CD147+ sIgM+	IL-10, Granzyme B	Suppress Th17 response Degrade T cell receptor-ζ The TGF-β+ subset suppresses allergy
CD1d+ CD5+ B cells	CD19+ CD1d^{high} CD5+	IL-10	Suppress Th17 response May also produce Granzyme
BR-1 B cells	CD19+ CD25^{high} CD71^{high} CD73− CD274+	IL-10, IgG4	Suppress antigen-specific CD4+ T cells Counteract T cell activation through PD-1 Tolerogenic IgG4 produced by CD27− B cells
CD24^{high} CD27^{high} B10 cells	CD19+ CD25+ CD24^{high} CD27^{high} CD48^{high}	IL-10	Increased in some autoimmune disorders Inhibit TNF-α by antigen-specific CD4+ T cells

Bregs exhibit pleiotropic activities, so overlappings among the various populations are common, both in vivo and in vitro. Other minor Breg subsets have been also described (summarized from Refs. [28–32]).

Immunophenotyping by mFCM is the method of choice to quickly classify and enumerate heterogeneous cell populations, to follow their differentiation steps, and to monitor immunological and cellular therapies [33]. Special flow cytometers are also able to isolate by electronic sorting specific cell subsets to be studied by proteomic, transcriptomic, and other genetic techniques [34].

CD20 as a marker of mature B cells

CD20 is associated with B cell receptor (BCR) in lipid rafts on the cell membrane of mature B cells. During cell activation, it probably acts as a costimulatory molecule, mobilizing calcium ions to propagate intracellularly the signals generated by BCR engagement. Curiously, its specific ligand has not been yet identified, whereas the CD20-knockout animals just show negligible changes [35].

During B lymphocyte maturation, CD20 is expressed from the pre-B stage-1 to the activated memory cell, also known as the marginal zone mature B cell [36]. This very peculiar pattern of expression has been made the basis for the selection of CD20 as the ideal target for B cell-depleting therapies. Eliminating mature CD20-positive cells spares B cell precursors as well as long-living plasma cells. This theoretically ensures the replacement of the killed autoreactive mature memory B cell clones by newly generated antigen-naïve cells, at least initially devoid of autoreactivity. CD20-negative long-living plasma cells are also spared, thus ensuring the maintenance of protective antibodies.

CD20 is expressed at high molecular density on the B cell surface, at about 150,000 copies per cell [37], and the extracellular epitopes recognized by the various anti-CD20 therapeutic mAbs are close to the cell surface [35]. These features greatly facilitate the interaction with complement and the effector cells involved in the killing mechanisms mediated by the anti-CD20 mAbs.

It is also well known that a small subset of peripheral T lymphocytes (from 1% to 6%) dimly express surface CD20. The origin and function of such CD20+ T cells are still not fully elucidated, although an effector role, the production of inflammatory cytokines, and the possible involvement in the pathogenesis of multiple sclerosis have been shown [38].

Mechanism of action of rituximab and other anti-CD20 therapeutic antibodies

Whatever the clinical aim of the B cell-depleting therapies, anti-CD20 mAbs act on cell targets with at least four different mechanisms. The two major mechanisms are complement-dependent cytotoxicity (CDC) and antibody-dependent cell-mediated cytotoxicity (ADCC), the latter exerted by cells endowed by the Fc-γ receptor type 3. More recently, mechanisms of cell killing by antibody-dependent cell-mediated opsonic phagocytosis (ADCP) exerted by neutrophils, monocytes, and macrophages and a mechanism of direct induction of apoptosis have been also demonstrated [39,40].

To accomplish the killing of the target cells, an efficient complement system should be present, and an adequate repertoire of cells expressing the Fc-γ receptors should be available, namely natural killer (NK) lymphocytes, T-NK cells, monocytes, macrophages, and neutrophils.

The Fc-γ receptor type 3, recognized as the CD16 cell surface antigen, is used to accomplish the cell-mediated cytotoxic functions elicited by the binding of anti-CD20 to its cellular targets. A genetic polymorphism of CD16 has been demonstrated, which results in a different receptor expression on the effector cell surface according to its zygosity [41–44]. The V/V homozygous status is found in some 10% of people and is characterized by the highest CD16 cell density and ADCC activity. The heterozygous V/F status is found in about one-third of subjects and is associated with intermediate activity. Homozygous F/F subjects represent about half of the people and have a low CD16 density and a proportionally reduced activity. These differences may at least partly account for the large individual variability of response to anti-CD20 therapies, since the CD16 expression density has been shown to be linearly related to ADCC activity [43]. This important issue can be evaluated by mFCM, studying the CD16 expression on NK cells by cytometric quantitative fluorescence methods [45], preferentially before treatment with anti-CD20 is started.

Today, at least six anti-CD20 therapeutic mAbs have passed a phase-II trial in autoimmune diseases, or have been approved for the treatment of specific autoimmune disorders: Rituximab, Obinutuzumab, Ocrelizumab, Ofatumumab, Ublituximab, and Veltuzumab [40,46,47]. Such molecules are not fully equivalent and have been classified as first, second, and third generation, respectively, according to their partial or full humanization process and to other chemical features. The differences in the primary biochemical structure of the different anti-CD20 mAbs, along with the changes introduced by the technique of glycoengineering, account for a spectrum of behavioral differences, mostly related to variations in the binding affinity of the mAb Fc portion with cell CD16. Anti-CD20 mAbs have different half-lives, different pharmacodynamics in the various autoimmune disorders, exert CDC, ADCC, ADCP, and apoptosis in variable proportions [39], and also recognize different epitopes of the CD20 molecule. As a matter of fact, despite acting on the same cell and on the same molecular target with similar mechanisms of action, the various anti-CD20 therapeutic mAbs must be considered as different drugs.

The pharmacodynamics of the same anti-CD20 mAbs used to treat lymphoproliferative disorders and autoimmune diseases is also remarkably different. In autoimmune diseases, the overall size of the B cell target mass is usually more or less reduced by the concomitant use of corticosteroids and other immunosuppressors. This regularly determines an excess of antibodies that produces a long-lasting B cell depletion over 6–8 months or more after a single therapeutic dose is administered. Conversely, in the majority of full-blown lymphoproliferative diseases, the total cell burden may be sometimes bulky, creating—among several shortcomings—a stoichiometric excess of antigen. This may lead to an underexposure to the drug in certain patients, as pointed out in some studies that have suggested evaluating preliminarily the overall tumor mass in order to administer a proportional anti-CD20 dosage [48,49].

The rationale for B cell depletion treatment in autoimmune disorders

Besides the demonstration of a clear autoantibody-mediated pathogenesis of many autoimmune diseases, ectopic germinal centers rich in B cells can be demonstrated in the synovium of patients with RA. Established peripheral mechanisms of differentiation and activation of CD27+ memory B cells could be also evidenced, perpetuating the local pathological autoimmune reaction [50,51]. The B lymphocyte role as antigen-presenting cells to T lymphocytes should be also taken into account as an additional mechanism that fuels the local inflammatory response.

In autoimmune diseases, the presence of autoreactive antibodies of multiple specificities has long been the indicator of the ongoing immune processes, with various degrees of diagnostic sensitivity and specificity [52,53]. Not only in systemic and organ-specific autoimmune diseases may one detect different types of autoantibodies in serum, but also naturally occurring and tumor-associated autoantibodies can be often demonstrated, with a questionable pathogenic activity [52].

One problem in the clinical practice with autoantibody evaluation is that in most cases they are not correlated with the disease activity grade [54–57]. A few clear-cut examples in which autoantibody levels correlate with disease activity are the anti-PLA2R antibodies in glomerulonephritides [58] and the anti-Aquaporin-4 in the neuromyelitis optica spectrum [59,60].

By depleting CD20+ B cells with rituximab, the hope is that the memory of pathogenic IgG autoantibodies is still confined within antigen-primed CD20+ memory B cells and that such priming has not proceeded to plasmablasts and long-living CD20-negative plasma cells.

Studies from various centers in a spectrum of autoimmune diseases concurred in identifying long-living CD27+ memory B cells as the most critical target for the successful implementation of anti-CD20 therapeutic protocols. Evidences about this issue have been collected in RA [61–63], neuromyelitis optica spectrum [64], myasthenia gravis [65], and multiple sclerosis [66].

After using anti-CD20 mAbs in autoimmune diseases, the repopulation by naïve B cells and a persistently reduced level of memory B cells have been taken as consistent indicators of a favorable response to treatment in a variety of disorders and clinical settings, despite the "off-label" usage of such drugs in most cases. The wider and more convincing evidence has been collected in RA [67,68] and juvenile RA patients [51]. The same findings have been reproducibly verified in primary glomerulonephritides [58,69,70], in multiple sclerosis [66,71] and the neuromyelitis optica complex [42,64], in systemic sclerosis [72,73], in Sjögren's syndrome [74], and also in allogeneic transplantation [11]. More controversial results have, however, been observed in SLE and lupus nephritis [30,75,76], indicating that many other immunological or genetic issues play a role in this multifaceted disease.

Once autoimmune IgG-switched activated memory B cells evolve to CD20-negative plasmablasts and plasma cells [77], anti-CD20 therapeutic antibodies become of no use, generating the clinical picture of an anti-CD20-refractory or resistant disease. In such instances, alternative therapeutic schedules based on proteasome inhibitors like bortezomib or the anti-plasma cell daratumumab (Anti-CD38 mAb), originally indicated for myeloma and plasma cell dyscrasias, have been successfully used [78]. This type of "rescue" treatment has been reported in SLE and lupus nephritis [30], membranous glomerulonephritis [70], ANCA-related nephritis [79], myasthenia gravis [80], immune thrombocytopenia [81], warm antibody autoimmune hemolytic anemia [82], acute and chronic graft-versus-host disease [83], pre- and posttransplantation membranous glomerulonephritis [84], and anti-HLA desensitization for allogeneic transplantation [11].

The repopulation of B cells after anti-CD20 is discontinued occurs very slowly, with B cells remaining undetectable for 6–8 to 10 months or more, with a high interpatient variability. The B cell recovery is similar both in rituximab-naïve subjects and in patients already treated with repeated doses of the drug. Under normal circumstances, multiple rituximab courses do not seem to produce cumulative effects on the B cell recovery capability [85], except for the cases that may develop overimmunosuppression.

Circulating plasmablasts as effectors in autoimmune disorders

Plasmablasts derive from CD27+ Ig-switched activated memory B cells and represent a further step ahead of the B cell commitment to antibody-secreting plasma cells. Plasmablasts are short-lived cycling cells that are expanded during secondary responses and in autoimmunity and are programmed to produce small amounts of high-affinity antibodies [86].

Peripheral blood plasmablasts are detectable in low numbers in the peripheral blood of steady-state healthy subjects (typically <2 cells/μL), express CD19, CD27, CD38^{high}, and heterogeneous CD138, while they are negative for surface Ig, CD20, and CD24 [87], and for that reason, they are resistant to anti-CD20 therapies.

In some studies, the role of circulating plasmablasts as effectors in autoimmune disorders has been highlighted, and their level was taken as an indicator of disease activity or of response to therapy. Earlier studies on rituximab treatment in RA patients considered the persistence of circulating plasmablasts as an indicator of clinical nonresponse and bad outcomes [88,89].

Cloned plasmablasts have been demonstrated to produce antibodies against citrullinated antigens in RA patients [90]. Increased plasmablast levels have been observed in patients with actively untreated minimal change nephrotic syndrome and in IgG4-related disorders [91,92]. Interestingly, increased plasmablast levels have been also detected in patients with active idiopathic pulmonary arterial hypertension associated with antiendothelial antibodies, a disease that has been recently classified as autoimmune pathogenesis [93].

Immune monitoring of anti-CD20 therapies in autoimmune disorders

In autoimmune diseases, treatment monitoring is in most cases based on the patient's clinical response only, since reliable biological indicators are often lacking or are not readily available [53,94]. This empirical, subjective approach seems to be of questionable efficacy, since autoimmune disorders are very severe diseases, lasting many years or lifelong, are treated with heavy multidrug antiinflammatory and immunosuppressive regimens, and tend to recur frequently, with the need for repeated therapeutic courses. Taking advantage of the clear antigen/antibody relationship between rituximab and its cell target, it is therefore important to guide anti-CD20 therapies with a rationale, objective, and sensitive monitoring protocol, as stressed in the more recent literature [36,71,95–97].

Some basic questions must be answered when using immunosuppressors in a patient with an autoimmune disorder: is the targeted immune mechanism adequately suppressed? Is the expected mechanism of action of the drug(s) functioning correctly? Are escape or resistance phenomena detectable, especially during the acute phase treatment? At treatment discontinuation, is the recovery of the immune status oriented to quiescence/tolerance or is it suggesting/threatening disease relapses? How long is it safe to go on with maintenance therapies, to keep the disease under control and avoid overimmunosuppression?

Unfortunately, using conventional immunosuppressive regimens, just a few laboratory tools can be used to partially answer some of these questions, namely the measurement of blood T CD4+, serum immunoglobulin and complement levels, and the few autoantibody titers that may be correlated with disease activity.

The use of therapeutic mAbs acting on circulating cells, by contrast, offers the unique opportunity to identify and enumerate the relevant cell target, to verify its disappearance under treatment, to monitor the quantity and the quality of repopulation of the involved cell subset after mAb discontinuation, and to evaluate the possible additional phenomena, such as target antigen modulation, escape from the expected depletion pattern, and the long-term immunosuppression. All these issues can be easily addressed using mFCM [33,34].

An immune monitoring protocol for patients receiving anti-CD20 therapies for autoimmune disorders should be in place, with the aim of assisting the medical specialists in the safe and rational usage of these potent but delicate drugs. Such testing should be readily available on demand and give an easily interpretable report within a few hours.

A working group of the Italian Society for Clinical Cell Analysis—ISCCA—has devised a practical immune monitoring protocol to identify and enumerate the most mature B cell functional subsets with clinical relevance, using a common benchtop 8-color flow cytometer, an instrument now very popular in many clinical laboratories [96] and fully compliant with the above-described requirements.

The original ISCCA protocol allows the simultaneous identification and enumeration of the lymphocyte subsets with clinical relevance in a single mFCM tube, namely CD3+ T cells, CD4+ and CD8+ T cell subsets, NK cells, B cells, Memory and Naïve B cells, IgM+ and IgG+ switched memory cells, plasmablasts/plasma cells. Moreover, additional B cell subsets not yet validated as clinical indicators, such as CD27+dull/CD27+bright memory B cells, double-negative memory B cells, and IgM+low/IgM+high memory B cells, can be also evaluated.

The originally described reagent cocktail (8-color, 10-markers) has been further implemented with the addition of an anti-sIgD conjugated antibody, to obtain an 11-marker panel, still manageable with an ordinary 3-laser 8-color instrument (see Appendix 1). A more complex configuration of the test including anti-CD21 and anti-CD24 (10-color, 13-markers), to be used on a higher class of instrumentation, has been more recently developed, to encompass all the remaining B cell subsets, including transitional, recent bone marrow emigrants, mature-naïve, activated memory, atypical memory, and other minor phenotypic variants (Fig. 3).

The assay can be accomplished on demand on a fresh 3-mL EDTA blood sample and requires about 75 min of turnaround time. Since a very large dataset of leukocytes must be collected (i.e., millions of CD45+ white cells) to ensure the required high-sensitivity enumeration of the small B cell subsets, a technical procedure of white cell concentration known as "bulk-lysis" must be performed using 1–2 mL of a blood sample, as described in detail [96] and in Appendix 1. This procedure concentrates leukocytes by a factor of 5–10 and eliminates all the interfering cellular and soluble blood components. Since bulk-lysis disrupts the original white cell concentration with red cell lysis and washings, the absolute enumeration of the cell subsets can be accomplished only using a dual platform approach (i.e., multiplying each cell subset percentage by the absolute lymphocyte level), along with a separate instrumental full blood count and electronic differential.

When samples from rituximab-treated patients are analyzed, the B cell compartment can be extremely reduced. The acquisition of at least 1 million CD45+ white cells, the more the better, is therefore required to represent adequately all the relevant B cell subsets. When B cells are at least $\geq$0.5/μL and 200–300 clean B cell events are collected, the B cell subsetting becomes possible and can be clinically meaningful.

This analysis technique, known as high-sensitivity mFCM, ensures reproducibly the lowest level of quantitation (LLOQ) in the range of 0.002% or 0.2–0.3 cells/μL. Using the described technique, the operational definition of cytometric "disappearance" of a given cell subset can

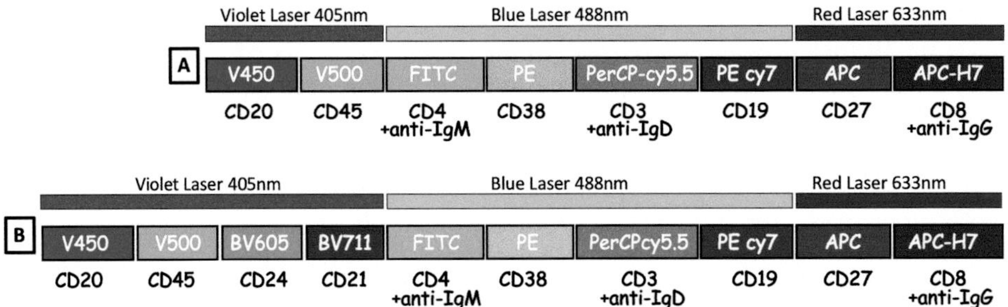

FIG. 3 Marker and fluorochrome composition of the antibody panels for the multicolor flow cytometric analysis of functional B cell subsets. Upper row (A): The ISCCA Protocol panel in its 8-color, 11-markers format including surface IgD. To increase the information with a limited number of fluorescence channels, surface immunoglobulin reagents are conjugated with the same fluorochromes of the mutually exclusive T cell markers, and are subsequently separated by electronic gating, as shown in Fig. 4A. This protocol can be analyzed with an ordinary 8-color instrument equipped with three laser sources, schematized by the horizontal colored bars, indicating the fluorescent dyes that are respectively excited. Lower row (B): The most recent upgrade of the ISCCA Protocol panel, introducing CD21 and CD24 for a more precise and extensive evaluation of transitional, recent bone marrow emigrant B cells, activated memory, and atypical memory B cells. This protocol (10-color, 13-markers), however, requires an instrumentation of higher class to be accomplished. *APC/APC-H7*, allophycocyanin fluorescent dye and its -H7 derivative; *BV605/711*, Brilliant Violet dyes 605 and 711; *FITC*, fluorescein isothiocyanate dye; *PECy7*, phycoerythrin-cyanin 7 dye; *PerCP-cy5.5*, peridinin-chlorophyll protein-cyanin 5.5 dye; *V450/500*, Violet 450 and 500 dyes.

be applied when its level falls below 0.1 cell/μL. The higher level of sensitivity of the present technique is evident, as compared to previous studies [88,89,98,99], thus prompting a reformulation of the cell subset thresholds that may be associated with disease quiescence or relapse.

It should be reminded that the sensitivity level for the detection of rare cells is not a predefined feature of the assay, but it strictly depends on the total amount of "clean" CD45+ white cells acquired, which represent the "denominator" cell reference. The established rules for the flow cytometric rare event analysis must be applied [96]. To give an example, acquiring a cluster of 50 relevant cell events as the LLOQ, when 200,000 CD45 + cells are collected the sensitivity level is 0.025%, while when 1,500,000 events are acquired the assay sensitivity increases to 0.0033%.

The ISCCA Protocol specificity is close to 100%, as limited to the analysis of peripheral B cell subsets. Due to the extensive coverage of all known B cell subsets, this assay can be also applied to the preliminary study of congenital and acquired immunodeficiencies with antibody deficits.

It is well known, however, that the quantity and quality of circulating B cells may not necessarily mirror the immune events taking place in the diseased tissues and organs.

The associated measurement of T cells and T cell subsets in the same tube is necessary to ensure a continuous monitoring also of the T lymphocyte compartment, which may be variably affected by the other administered drugs and by the anti-CD20 mAbs themselves [38,100–102]. Clinical studies reported in the EMA Mabthera product information document [103] and included in some European national guidelines indicate that at least 250 T CD4+ cells/μL should be present in the peripheral blood before a safe anti-CD20 treatment is undertaken for an autoimmune disorder.

Before treatment with anti-CD20 is started, the quasi-quantitative baseline analysis of CD16 density on the NK cell surface can be useful and informative, both to quantify the residual NK cell repertoire surviving the previous immunosuppressive treatments and in the attempt to predict the patient's ADCC activity, as discussed above. This can be accomplished by another simple 3-color analysis including CD45/CD3/CD16, preferably after an adequate washout period from previous immunosuppressive or antiinflammatory treatments.

In Fig. 4A, an example of the mFCM analysis of B cell subsets in a healthy subject using the extended 10-color ISCCA protocol is illustrated, along with the generated results of clinical relevance in percentage (Fig. 4B). Percent values are then reported to lymphocyte and/or B cells per microliter in order to obtain the absolute levels of the populations of interest.

Monitoring the expected peripheral B cell patterns during anti-CD20 treatment

The peripheral blood levels of B lymphocyte subsets in normal steady-state subjects are very variable, with coefficients of variation of measurements approaching 100% [20,104]. Functional B cell subset levels change dynamically with age, during pregnancy [13,17,18], and are also very sensitive to common immune and inflammatory stimuli. This is why it is difficult to establish clear-cut reference values within reasonable ranges of variability. The individual patient's monitoring with serial measurements is therefore the only means to provide an individual picture of the subset ups and downs occurring with time, with disease activity, and in association with the therapeutic anti-CD20 schedule.

Patients with autoimmune disorders, and especially those with rheumatologic diseases, are in most cases treated with complex and sequential immunosuppressive and antiinflammatory regimens and often become considered eligible for rituximab therapy as a second or third treatment line. It is therefore difficult to find those patients with a normal peripheral lymphocyte profile at a baseline check. Recently, the usage of rituximab as the first-line therapy in glomerulonephritides has been taken into account [105].

Total peripheral blood B cell depletion occurs as early as 72 h from the intravenous anti-CD20 administration, and the average rituximab half-life in blood is around 20 days in most cases.

After the first course of rituximab, a second check is advisable after 3 months, when all treated subjects are expected to show virtually undetectable peripheral B cell levels. This early check is of help in identifying patients who may have developed some form of resistance to the drug or who have a recalcitrant, progressive disease. The B cell depletion typically lasts up to 8–10 months after a single dose of rituximab, and sometimes more. The wide disease- and patient-related variability suggests performing repeated checks every 3 months, in order to identify the "early repopulators" and to monitor the quantity and the quality of the recovery of B cells and their functional subsets.

According to anecdotal experience deriving mostly from RA patients, an absolute total B cell level <1 cell/μL indicates an adequate depletion and a satisfactory effect of the anti-CD20 mAb, in most cases suggesting that a further course of rituximab can be postponed. During the repopulation phase, the prevalence of naïve B cells vs memory B cells and the prevalence of sIgM+ memory over sIgG+ memory can be taken as good prognostic indicators. Conversely, the opposite conditions may support the decision to administer additional rituximab doses.

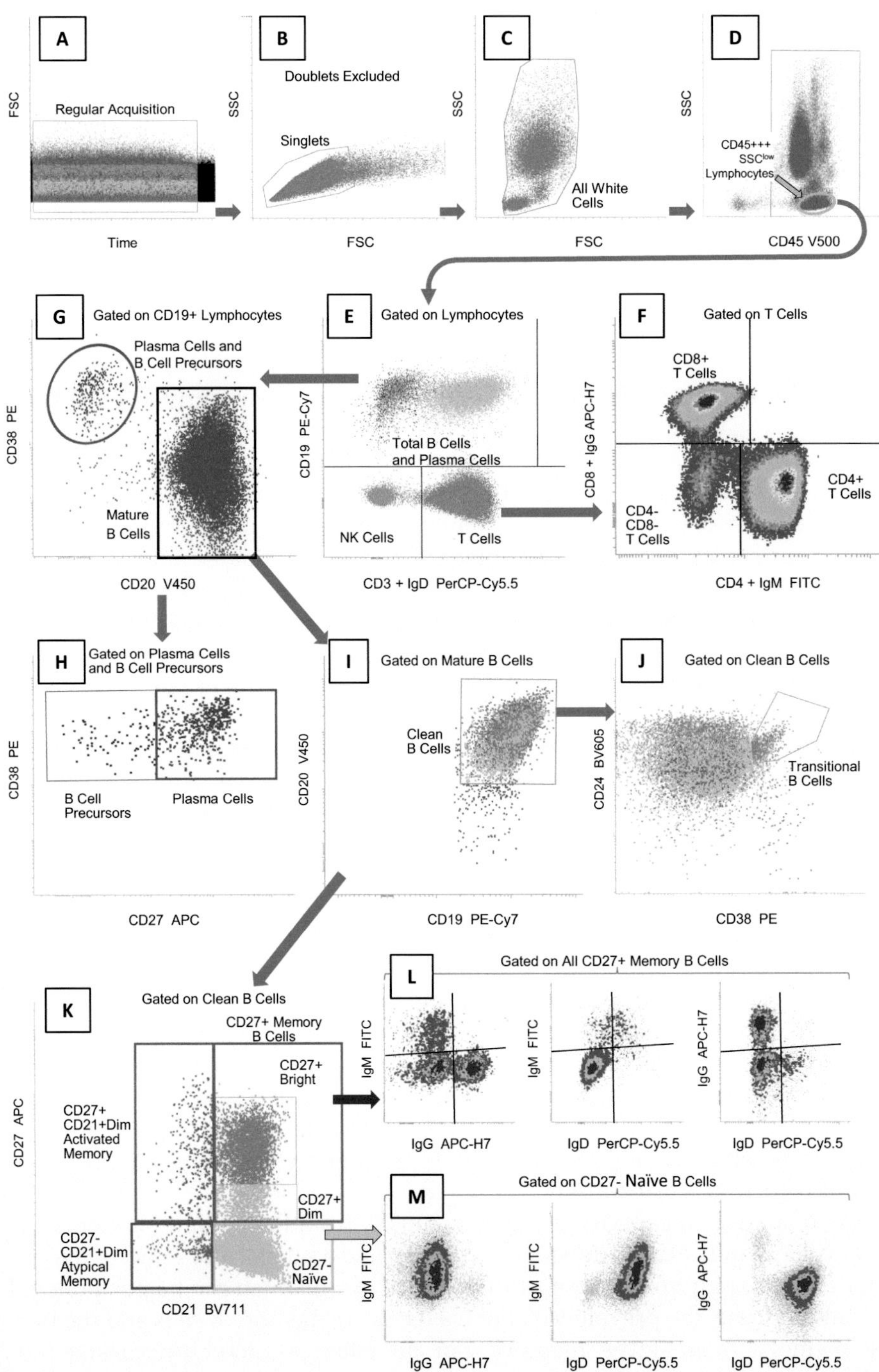

FIG. 4A See figure legend on next page.

FIG. 4A Example of the logical gating sequence to determine the functional B cell subsets, using the extended 10-color ISCCA Protocol in the peripheral blood of a healthy subject. First row (upper) (Panels from A to D): The cell events flowing regularly are accepted, then the cell doublets and aggregates are excluded. White cells are identified through their light scatter features, then lymphocytes are defined as CD45+++/Side Scatter low cells and gated by the *green* elliptical region. Second row: Lymphocytes in panel (E) are divided into the three major populations T, B, and NK cells. The T cells in the lower right quadrant are then dissected into CD4+ and CD8+ subsets in the panel (F). The upper part of the panel (E) contains CD19+ B cells, smeared by the IgD expression (in cyan). CD19+ B cells are then cleaned from precursors and plasma cells by CD20 and CD38 in panel (G). Third row: B cell precursors and plasma cells are differentiated by CD27 and CD38 in panel (H). Mature B cells are defined as CD19+/CD20+ elements and cleaned from nonspecific events in panel (I). Transitional B cells are defined in clean B cells as CD38++/CD24+ elements in panel (J). Fourth row (lower): In panel (K), clean B cells are first divided into CD27+/CD21+ memory and CD27−/CD21+ naïve cells. CD27+dim memory, CD27+/CD21+dim activated memory, and CD27−/CD21+dim atypical memory cells are also defined. The surface Ig expression of all memory B cells is depicted in row (L), where sIgG+ memory cells prevail over sIgM+ cells. Just for comparison, in the lower row (M) the sIg expression by naïve cells is shown, with an almost exclusive coexpression of sIgM and sIgD.

Gate Hierarchy	Event Number	% Of Parent Population
All Events	**2500000**	-
Regular Acquisition	2019756	**80.8%** of All Events
Singlets	1988540	**98.4%** of Regular Events
FSC/SSC White Cells	1884323	**94.7%** of Singlets
CD45+++ Lymphocytes	697248	**37%** of White Cells
T Cells	495018	**71%** of Lymphocytes
CD4+ T Cells	313757	**45%** of Lymphocytes
CD8+ T Cells	153384	**22%** of Lymphocytes
CD4- CD8- T Cells	27866	**4%** of Lymphocytes
NK Cells	83643	**12%** of Lymphocytes
CD19+ Lymphocytes	118516	**17%** of Lymphocytes
Plasma Cells	345	**0.3%** of CD19+ Lympho
B Precursors	91	**0.076%** of CD19+ Lympho
Clean B Cells	117996	**16.9%** of Lymphocytes
Transitional B Cells	476	**0.4%** of Clean B Cells
CD27+ Memory B Cells	49546	**42%** of Clean B Cells
CD27+ Bright	35673	**72%** of Memory B Cells
CD27+ Dim	13870	**28%** of Memory B Cells
CD27- Naive B Cells	63711	**54%** of Clean B Cells
Activated Memory B Cells	3503	**3%** of Clean B Cells
Atypical Memory B Cells	1109	**0.9%** of Clean B Cells
IgD+ Memory B Cells	7926	**16%** of Memory B Cells
IgM+ Memory B Cells	9411	**19%** of Memory B Cells
IgG+ Memory B Cells	28732	**58%** of Memory B Cells

FIG. 4B Results table summarizing the numeric representation of the various subsets, also indicating the percent fraction of the respective parent population, to be included in the report. Each parent population and their subsets are evidenced with a common color background, for the sake of clarity. This result table reports also the levels of the minor B cell subpopulations that are still of investigational interest. Absolute levels of B cell subsets can be calculated from a full blood count using lymphocytes/μL and clean B cells/μL.

The varied rituximab schedules in autoimmune disorders: The risk of overimmunosuppression

Due to its high efficacy and the overall favorable safety profile, rituximab is being administered rather liberally in patients with autoimmune disorders, and in some cases, it is used in long-term schemes, sometimes also as a maintenance therapy [106,107].

The standard rheumatologic dosage is traditionally two 1000 mg doses, 15 days apart, to be repeated in case of clinical relapse. More recently, reduced dosage schemes (i.e., two 500 mg doses, 15 days apart, every 6 months) [108] or even "ultralow" schemes (i.e., 200 mg doses) have been also experimented successfully [109].

Although the experience is still very limited, it seems likely that the timing of immune monitoring checks should be adjusted according to the administered rituximab doses and timing, with predictable dose-dependent changes in cell-level dynamics.

Repeated rituximab courses are being used in the majority of patients with autoimmune disorders, as predefined schemes or following disease relapses. This has proved to be relatively safe, but the serum Ig levels, and especially of IgM, tend to decrease markedly with the number of rituximab courses [110].

The use of repeated standard doses in the long term has raised concern about the possible generation of permanent immunosuppression, with the irreversible disruption of the physiological antibody-producing machinery and an increased risk of infection. The combination of additional immunosuppressors of disease-specific and patient-specific factors may cooperate in generating posttreatment hypogammaglobulinemia, especially if low Ig levels and lymphopenia are already present at treatment start [40,111]. Moderate to marked hypogammaglobulinemia and severe infections can be detected in about 25%–30% of patients, and in some 4% of all cases, the antibody deficiency may become permanent, requiring long-term intravenous Ig replacement therapy [112,113].

In some studies, the use of very prolonged treatments with anti-CD20 has been judged too risky [114], and the resulting dose-dependent increased rate of infection in patients receiving multiple rituximab doses has been highlighted [106,115,116].

During the recent COVID-19 pandemic, concern has been raised on the possibly increased susceptibility to SARS-CoV2 of rheumatological patients on rituximab, and on the efficacy of the newly developed mRNA vaccines in these immunocompromised subjects [117]. Luckily, patients with autoimmune disorders receiving rituximab do not seem to show a clearly increased rate of infection by SARS-CoV2, owing to innate immunity and T CD8+ cells being able to provide an adequate antiviral response [118].

Patients with autoimmune disorders treated with rituximab, however, display a lower or significantly impaired antibody response to COVID-19 infection and to mRNA vaccine, similar to what was observed with conventional influenza and pneumococcal vaccines [119–121]. The partial humoral response could be observed in a fraction of patients in whom an initial B cell repopulation was detectable [122], indicating that vaccinations in patients with autoimmune diseases receiving rituximab should be postponed at least until a meaningful B cell recovery is taking place.

In selected severely symptomatic cases with absent B cells and no antibody response, passive immunization with convalescent plasma or monoclonal antibodies can be considered [117,123]. In such patients, the immune monitoring of functional B cell subsets plays an important role in guiding the appropriate clinical decisions.

Resistance to rituximab and escape phenomena in autoimmune disorders treated with anti-CD20

The advent of murine therapeutic mAbs in the 1980s was characterized by the evidence of an intense antidrug immunization occurring in the majority of treated patients. Both the antimouse Ig isotype and antiidiotype antibodies were commonly detectable, which hampered the mAb efficacy, preventing retreatments and causing side effects during infusion [124]. This prompted efforts to reduce the murine content of therapeutic mAbs, leading to the development with a time of chimeric, humanized, and fully human antibodies [125].

While >80% of patients treated with murine mAbs developed significant reactions and strong immunization, those receiving chimeric, humanized, and human therapeutic antibodies showed just a reduction in the rate and severity of reactions, proving that humanization cannot be assumed per se as the only key to abolishing such drawbacks [125,126].

Lower rates of infusion-related adverse events have been described in RA and SLE patients, as compared to non-Hodgkin's lymphoma patients [127].

The concomitant usage of other immunosuppressants in autoimmune diseases—mainly corticosteroids—and the blocking of the antibody-producing chain induced by anti-CD20 treatments remarkably reduce the rate of anti-mAb immunization, but probably also mask the intrinsic antigenicity of the drugs [125].

The development of neutralizing antichimeric mAb immunization in patients with autoimmune disorders may be detected in 11%–43% of treated subjects [110,128–130], and this has been also associated with infusion-related reactions. Using second- and third-generation anti-CD20 mAbs, this occurrence seems greatly mitigated, although not entirely abolished [131].

As illustrated in greater detail in other parts of this volume, resistance to anti-CD20 treatment in lymphoproliferative diseases is a multifaceted phenomenon, involving not only anti-mAb immunization but also a complex series of molecular events occurring within the cell target [44,132].

In autoimmune disorders, a downregulation of CD20 on the B cell target with the repopulation of CD19+ CD20− modulated B cells can be sometimes detected in individual patients using the ISCCA protocol (data not shown) and taken as a further escape mechanism. An operational disease "resistance" to anti-CD20 treatment can develop whenever the pathogenic autoantibody production consolidates in long-lived plasma cells, as discussed above.

In membranous glomerulonephritis with nephrotic syndrome and severe nonselective proteinuria, the urinary loss of rituximab determines a shorter mAb half-life and a lower exposure to the drug, markedly reducing its effectiveness, unless changes in the therapeutic schedule are made [133,134]. Similarly, anecdotal reports have described an accelerated clearance of therapeutic mAbs in various treated patients undergoing ascites drainage after infusion [135,136].

In most cases of rituximab resistance, immune monitoring can disclose unexpected changes in B cell recovery, such as a faster reconstitution, that may indicate the need for investigating the causes of resistance to treatment, the escape from the expected mechanism of action, and the possible need for changes in the therapeutic schedule, including the switch to different mAbs.

Limitations and open issues in the immune monitoring of autoimmune disorders treated with anti-CD20

Autoimmune diseases generate from a complex interaction of factors, both genetic and environmental. More than 200 autoimmune disease risk loci have been identified so far, which may account for a number of different individual molecular signatures [16,57,137], different configurations of immune mechanisms, and different clinical courses and severity. Thus, it is likely that acting on a single molecular target, as it happens when using anti-CD20 mAbs, could not be enough to fully control complex, multifactorial diseases like autoimmune disorders [30].

The massive B cell depletion exerted by anti-CD20 mAbs is not selective, targeting also the subsets involved in the control of autoimmunity and of the negative regulation of immune response, like Bregs [30]. Although the beneficial role of Bregs in maintaining the tolerance in autoimmunity is well established [31], their fate and dynamic during anti-CD20 therapies are still to be elucidated. The abrupt disappearance of B cells in the local microenvironment of diseased tissues and of secondary lymphoid organs may induce a homeostatic rearrangement also of T cell homing and changes in Tregs, with possible beneficial effects [101].

Despite decades of studies on dozens of autoimmune disease biomarkers [53,68,94], indicators that may provide clear-cut information of clinical relevance on a single-patient basis are unfortunately still lacking. Moreover, in autoimmune disorders, it is still not possible for clinicians to accurately predict prognosis and treatment response at disease onset at an individual patient level [58,138].

Anti-CD20 mAbs are clinically effective also in autoimmune disorders not strictly mediated by autoantibodies, like multiple sclerosis [139], or in other diseases in which T cells play a pivotal role [5,140]. Other still elusive biological and regulatory mechanisms involving different players of the immune response must be therefore involved, which need further investigation.

The very wide individual variability of the peripheral B cell subsets in healthy subjects [104], in rituximab-treated quiescent patients, and throughout the anti-CD20 therapy cycles makes it difficult to establish reliable thresholds or reference values of the various B cell subsets with general applicability, and this is a limitation of the ISCCA Protocol. The accurate monitoring of the individual patients with time is thus the only way that at present allows us to evaluate and interpret the ongoing immune events.

The monitoring of peripheral blood changes induced by anti-CD20 can be taken as a good starting point for the rational usage of rituximab in autoimmune disorders, but probably it cannot be entirely explanatory about what is going on in the damaged target tissues and organs, where resident CD20+ B cells can still survive.

A reliable mFCM B cell functional subsetting, including the surface expression of IgD, IgM, and IgG, can be accomplished only using freshly drawn peripheral blood (i.e., <4h) because the Ig chains on the B cell surface are very labile [96]. This can be another limiting factor, if blood samples have to be referred to distant laboratories.

Due to the lack of formal dose-finding trials in the majority of autoimmune disorders amenable to anti-CD20 therapy, the immune monitoring of B cell functional subsets seems to be a valuable tool to guide physicians beyond the mere clinical response of individual patients, especially in the long-term management of immunosuppressive therapy. The limited and at present not very systematic approach used in RA and glomerulonephritides clearly indicates that it is essential to perform the checks according to an orderly, predefined, and prospective schedule, adjusted according to the timing and dosage of the administered anti-CD20 mAb. If this simple rule is not applied, the informative value provided by immune monitoring may be lost.

Concluding remarks and future perspectives

The ISCCA Protocol provides the most extensive characterization and enumeration of all the functional B cell subsets that can be defined by multicolor immunophenotyping in a single tube. At present, its usage proved valuable in monitoring RA, glomerulonephritides, neuromyelitis optica, and multiple sclerosis. A wider experience in other autoimmune diseases should, however, be gathered by standardized prospective studies, for a better evaluation of its strengths and weaknesses in the various clinical conditions, with the usage of alternative schedules and of other anti-CD20 mAbs.

The more we dig into the complexity of functional B cell subsets, the more "autoimmunity-prone" populations with potential pathogenic roles are discovered, whose precise meaning and clinical importance are still not fully elucidated. Efforts are needed to study more in depth the role in autoimmune diseases of those newly discovered minor and atypical B cell subsets that can be identified and enumerated by the ISCCA Protocol.

The hematology laboratories providing mFCM testings are today kept under great pressure by a number of different medical specialists, who enjoy the good clinical response of patients receiving anti-CD20 therapies for various autoimmune diseases. As a common experience, such colleagues can be often in trouble when a therapeutic decision has to be made, especially after the acute phase treatment has been completed and relapses or complications occur in the middle and long term. Not all medical specialists who have recently included the anti-CD20 mAbs in their therapeutic repertoire are equally familiar with the biological subtleties of B cell pathophysiology.

The medical and laboratory staff, experts on B cell immunology and pharmacokinetics, must therefore establish a close and collaborative contact with them and be of help and advice, always keeping in mind the added value of a collegial supportive role aimed at the benefit of the patients.

Appendix 1

Technical Summary of the 8-Colors 11-Markers ISCCA Protocol (BD FACSCanto II and FACSLyric instruments)

Blood sample: 3 mL of EDTA-anticoagulated blood, to be kept at room temperature <4 h from drawing.

Bulk lysis procedure: Two mL of the blood of rituximab-treated patients (1 mL is enough in treatment-naïve subjects) are admixed with 10 mL of ammonium chloride lysing buffer at pH 7.4 for 10 min. After centrifugation, two washings with 10 mL PBS addition with 0.2% BSA (bovine serum albumin) will follow. The final cell pellet is resuspended with 250 μL PBS-0.2% BSA.

Staining procedure: 100 μL of the well-resuspended sample is incubated with the following mixture of pretitrated monoclonal antibodies, either in dried form (i.e., Becton Dickinson-BD Lyotube) or as liquid add-ons.

Here the 8-color, 11-marker panel using products Becton Dickinson Biosciences (San José, CA, United States) is shown:

- CD20 (clone L27)-V450
- CD45 (clone 2D1)-V500c
- CD4 (clone SK3)-FITC + anti-IgM (clone G20-127)-FITC
- CD38 (clone HB7)-PE
- CD3 (clone SK7)-PerCP Cy5.5 + anti-IgD (clone IA6-2)-PerCP Cy5.5
- CD19 (clone SJ25C1)-PE-Cy7
- CD27 (clone L128)-APC
- CD8 (clone SK1)-APC H7 + anti-IgG (clone G18-145)-APC H7

(**Note**: The extended 10-color 13-marker ISCCA Protocol to be used on the appropriate instrumentation can be accomplished by simply adding pretitrated amounts of CD21 (clone B-ly4)-BV711 and CD24 (clone ML5)-BV605). This option has been validated on a 12-color FACSLyric flow cytometer.

The incubation is performed at room temperature for 20 min, in the dark. After incubation, the sample is washed once with 2 mL of PBS-0.2% BSA and resuspended in 500 μL of PBS-0.2% BSA. The final sample must be protected from light and processed as soon as possible, ideally within 1 h.

Flow cytometric analysis: This procedure has been optimized for the BD FACSCanto II and BD FACSLyric flow cytometers, equipped with Violet (405 nm), Blue (488 nm), and Red (633 nm) lasers and standardized using BD CS&T beads according to the EuroFlow recommendations.

(*Glier H, Novakova M, te Marvelde J*, et al. *Comments on EuroFlow standard operating procedures for instrument setup and compensation for BD FACS canto II, Navios, and BD FACS lyric instruments. Journal of Immunological Methods 2019; 475: 112680*). An application setting must be created—where applicable—defining target fluorescence intensity values, following the manufacturer's instructions.

The samples are acquired at a medium rate, with the aim of collecting at least 1 million clean CD45+ events (the more the better), monitoring continuously the time parameter in order to prevent fluidic perturbations, as illustrated in Fig. 4A.

Even under the worst depletion conditions, if the acquisition allows the capture of 200–300 clean B cell events, the subsetting of the functional B cells is possible and may provide meaningful data for clinical use. The rules for accepting the lowest levels of detection and quantitation (LLOD and LLOQ, respectively) and the operational definition of "B cell disappearance" (if <0.1 B cell/μL) must be always applied, since the ISCCA Protocol is a type of cytometric assay able to perform "rare event analyses."

Suggested timing for samplings and results interpretation:

(1) A baseline check is useful, especially if performed after an adequate washout period from previous treatments. At baseline, the quasi-quantitative evaluation of the CD16 expression on NK cells is also advisable. This can be done using a simple 3-color mixture of CD45-FITC/ CD16-PE/CD3-PerCP, quantitating the CD16-PE density with Quantibrite calibration beads (*Pannu KK, Joe ET, Iyer SB. Performance evaluation of QuantiBRITE phycoerythrin beads. Cytometry 2001; 45: 250–258*).

(2) A second check is recommended at 3 months from the last anti-CD20 MoAb administration of the therapeutic cycle, whatever the anti-CD20 dosage and timing schedule. At this timepoint, all treated patients must show the virtual absence of clean B cells (i.e., <0.1/μL).

If at 3 months the B cell level is >0.3–0.5/μL, an additional check after 1 more month is advisable, in order to identify potential "early repopulators." If at 3 months the B cell level is >1/μL, this finding can be taken as a sign of early repopulation, to be carefully evaluated especially if memory B cells represent the majority of the B cells.

Additional anti-CD20 doses would not be recommended if the B cell level is <1/μL, and this finding may indicate the opportunity of postponing further anti-CD20 doses.

(3) Further checks are recommended at regular intervals (i.e., every 3 months) during the follow-up, and repeated in case of clinically relevant events (i.e., disease relapse, superimposed infections, need of major therapeutic changes). The gradual repopulation of the B cell compartment is usually expected from 8 to 12 months from the last ordinary anti-CD20 dose, taking into account a marked individual variability. Using lower-dose protocols the repopulation may be expected earlier, and this is an issue still to be verified experimentally.

The quality of the B cell repopulation can be of help in defining an immunologically quiescent status (favorable pattern) or a reactive status (unfavorable pattern) often associated with an unstable disease or impending relapse, as summarized in the following table:

Repopulation pattern.	Memory vs naïve B cells	Memory sIgG+ vs sIgM+
Favorable	Memory % < Naïve %	sIgG+ < sIgM+
Unfavorable	Memory % > Naïve %	sIgG+ > sIgM+

In case of severe hypogammaglobulinemia or serum IgG deficit, testing can be used to identify the persistence of B cell depletion or the lack of memory B cells.

References

[1] Janossy G, Panayi G, Duke O, Bofill M, Poulter LW, Goldstein G. Rheumatoid arthritis: a disease of T lymphocyte-macrophage immunoregulation. Lancet 1981;2(8251):839–42.

[2] Chatenoud L. Progress towards the clinical use of CD3 monoclonal antibodies in the treatment of autoimmunity. Curr Opin Organ Transplant 2009;14:351–6.

[3] Ruiz R, Kirk AD. Long-term toxicity of immunosuppressive therapy. In: Transplantation of the liver. Elsevier; 2015. p. 1354–63. https://doi.org/10.1016/B978-1-4557-0268-8.00097-X.

[4] Cope AP, Schulze-Koops H, Aringer M. The central role of T cells in rheumatoid arthritis. Clin Exp Rheumatol 2007;25(5 Suppl 46):S4–11.

[5] Suárez-Fueyo A, Bradley SJ, Tsokos GC. T cells in systemic lupus erythematosus. Curr Opin Immunol 2016;43:32–8.

[6] Edwards JCW, Cambridge G. Sustained improvement in rheumatoid arthritis following a protocol designed to deplete B lymphocytes. Rheumatology (Oxford) 2001;40:205–11.

[7] Stewart M, Malkovska V, Krishnan J, Lessin L, Barth W. Lymphoma in a patient with rheumatoid arthritis receiving methotrexate treatment: successful treatment with rituximab. Ann Rheum Dis 2001;60:892–3.

[8] Leandro MJ, Edwards JCW, Cambridge G. Clinical outcome in 22 patients with rheumatoid arthritis treated with B lymphocyte depletion. Ann Rheum Dis 2002;61:883–8.

[9] Kaegi C, Wuest B, Schreiner J, Steiner UC, Vultaggio A, Matucci A, Crowley C, Boyman O. Systematic review of safety and efficacy of rituximab in treating immune-mediated disorders. Front Immunol 2019;10:1990. https://doi.org/10.3389/fimmu.2019.01990.

[10] Wilkinson MGL, Rosser EC. B cells as a therapeutic target in paediatric rheumatic disease. Front Immunol 2019;10:214. https://doi.org/10.3389/fimmu.2019.00214.

[11] Beausang JF, Fan HC, Sit R, Hutchins MU, Jirage K, Curtis R, Hutchins E, Quake SR, Yabu JM. B cell repertoires in HLA-sensitized kidney transplant candidates undergoing desensitization therapy. J Transl Med 2017;15:9. https://doi.org/10.1186/s12967-017-1118-7.

[12] Capolunghi F, Cascioli S, Giorda E, Rosado MM, Plebani A, Auriti C, Seganti G, Zuntini R, Ferrari S, Cagliuso M, Quinti I, Carsetti R. CpG drives human transitional B cells to terminal differentiation and production of natural antibodies. J Immunol 2008;180:800–8.

[13] Carsetti R, Terreri S, Conti MG, Fernandez Salinas A, Corrente F, Capponi C, Albano C, Piano Mortari E. Comprehensive phenotyping of human peripheral blood B lymphocytes in healthy conditions. Cytometry A 2022;101(2):131–9.

[14] Bendall SC, Davis KL, David Amir E-A, Tadmor MD, Simonds EF, Chen TJ, Shenfeld DK, Nolan GP, Pe'er D. Single-cell trajectory detection uncovers progression and regulatory coordination in human B cell development. Cell 2014;157(3):714–25.

[15] Nemazee D. Mechanisms of central tolerance for B cells. Nat Rev Immunol 2017;17(5):281–94.

[16] Harley ITW, Allison K, Scofield RH. Polygenic autoimmune disease risk alleles impacting B cell tolerance act in concert across shared molecular networks in mouse and in humans. Front Immunol 2022;13, 953439. https://doi.org/10.3389/fimmu.2022.953439.

[17] Grimsholm O, Piano Mortari E, Davydov AN, Shugay M, Obraztsova AS, Bocci C, Marasco E, Marcellini V, Aranburu A, Farroni C, Silvestris DA, Cristofoletti C, Giorda E, Scarsella M, Cascioli S, Barresi S, Lougaris V, Plebani A, Cancrini C, Finocchi A, Moschese V, Valentini D, Vallone C, Signore F, de Vincentiis G, Zaffina S, Russo G, Gallo A, Locatelli F, Tozzi AE, Tartaglia M, Chudakov DM, Carsetti R. The interplay between CD27 ^{dull} and CD27 ^{bright} B cells ensures the flexibility, stability and resilience of human B cell memory. Cell Rep 2020;30(9):2963–77. e6 https://doi.org/10.1016/j.celrep.2020.02.022.

[18] Aranburu A, Piano Mortari E, Baban A, Giorda E, Cascioli S, Marcellini V, Scarsella M, Ceccarelli S, Corbelli S, Cantarutti N, De Vito R, Inserra A, Nicolosi L, Lanfranchi A, Porta F, Cancrini C, Finocchi A, Carsetti R. Human B-cell memory is shaped by age- and tissue-specific T-independent and GC-dependent events. Eur J Immunol 2017;47(2):327–44.

[19] Bautista D, Vásquez C, Ayala-Ramírez P, Téllez-Sosa J, Godoy-Lozano E, Martínez-Barnetche J, Franco M, Angel J. Differential expression of IgM and IgD discriminates two subpopulations of human circulating IgM+ IgD + CD27+ B cells that differ phenotypically, functionally and genetically. Front Immunol 2020;11:736. https://doi.org/10.3389/fimmu.2020.00736.

[20] Perez-Andres M, Paiva B, Nieto WG, Caraux A, Schmitz A, Almeida J, Vogt Jr RF, Marti GE, Rawstron AC, Van Zelm MC, Van Dongen JJ, Johnsen HE, Klein B, Orfao A. Human peripheral blood B-cell compartments: a crossroad in B-cell traffic. Cytometry B Clin Cytom 2010;78(Suppl 1):S47–60.

[21] Wilfong EM, Vowell KN, Crofford LJ, Kendall PL. Multiparameter analysis of human B lymphocytes identifies heterogeneous $CD19^{+}CD21^{lo}$ subsets. Cytometry A 2022. https://doi.org/10.1002/cyto.a.24699. Epub ahead of print.

[22] Frasca D, Diaz A, Romero M, Blomberg BB. Phenotypic and functional characterization of double negative B cells in the blood of individuals with obesity. Front Immunol 2021;12, 616650. https://doi.org/10.3389/fimmu.2021.616650.

[23] Stewart A, Ng JC-F, Wallis G, Tsioligka V, Fraternali F, Dunn-Walters DK. Single-cell transcriptomic analyses define distinct peripheral B cell subsets and discrete development pathways. Front Immunol 2021;12, 602539. https://doi.org/10.3389/fimmu.2021.602539.
[24] Zhang W, Zhang H, Liu S, Xia F, Kang Z, Zhang Y, Liu Y, Xiao H, Chen L, Huang C, Shen N, Xu H, Li F. Excessive CD11c+ Tbet+ B cells promote aberrant T_{FH} differentiation and affinity-based germinal center selection in lupus. Proc Natl Acad Sci U S A 2019;116(37):18550–60.
[25] Sachinidis A, Xanthopoulos K, Garyfallos A. Age-associated B cells (ABCs) in the prognosis, diagnosis and therapy of systemic lupus erythematosus (SLE). Mediterr J Rheumatol 2020;31(3):311–8.
[26] Della Valle L, Dohmen SE, Verhagen OJHM, Berkowska MA, Vidarsson G, van der Schoot CE. The majority of human memory B cells recognizing RhD and tetanus resides in IgM+ B cells. J Immunol 2014;193:1071–9.
[27] Lorenzetti R, Janowska I, Smulski CR, Frede N, Henneberger N, Walter L, Schleyer MT, Hüppe JM, Staniek J, Salzer U, Venhoff A, Troilo A, Voll RE, Venhoff N, Thiel J, Rizzi M. Abatacept modulates CD80 and CD86 expression and memory formation in human B-cells. J Autoimmun 2019;101:145–52.
[28] van de Veen W, Stanic B, Yaman G, Wawrzyniak M, Söllner S, Akdis DG, Rückert B, Akdis CA, Akdis M. IgG4 production is confined to human IL-10-producing regulatory B cells that suppress antigen-specific immune responses. J Allergy Clin Immunol 2013;131(4):1204–12.
[29] Mauri C, Menon M. The expanding family of regulatory B cells. Int Immunol 2015;27(10):479–86.
[30] Cassia M, Alberici F, Gallieni M, Jayne D. Lupus nephritis and B-cell targeting therapy. Expert Rev Clin Immunol 2017;13:951–62.
[31] Jansen K, Cevhertas L, Ma S, Satitsuksanoa P, Akdis M, van de Veen W. Regulatory B cells, A to Z. Allergy 2021;76(9):2699–715.
[32] Yang SY, Long J, Huang MX, Luo PY, Bian ZH, Xu YF, Wang CB, Yang SH, Li L, Selmi C, Gershwin ME, Zhao ZB, Lian ZX. Characterization of organ-specific regulatory B cells using single-cell RNA sequencing. Front Immunol 2021;12, 711980. https://doi.org/10.3389/fimmu.2021.711980.
[33] Campbell JDM, Fraser AR. Flow cytometric assays for identity, safety and potency of cellular therapies. Cytometry B Clin Cytom 2018;94B:725–35.
[34] Cossarizza A, Chang HD, Radbruch A, Abrignani S, Addo R, Akdis M, Andrä I, Andreata F, Annunziato F, Arranz E, Bacher P, et al. Guidelines for the use of flow cytometry and cell sorting in immunological studies (third edition). Eur J Immunol 2021;51:2708–3145.
[35] Beers SA, Chan CHT, French RR, Cragg MS, Glennie MJ. CD20 as a target for therapeutic type I and II monoclonal antibodies. Semin Hematol 2010;47:107–14.
[36] Brando B, Gatti A, Lurati AM, Faggioli PML. Monitoring anti-B cell immunotherapies in autoimmune diseases: go with the flow. A position paper of the Italian society for clinical cell analysis (ISCCA). Beyond Rheumatol 2019;1(2):52–62. e263 https://doi.org/10.4081/br.2019.26.
[37] Bikoue A, George F, Poncelet P, Mutin M, Janossy G, Sampol J. Quantitative analysis of leukocyte membrane antigen expression: normal adult values. Cytometry 1996;26:137–47.
[38] Lee AYS. CD20+ T cells: an emerging T cell subset in human pathology. Inflamm Res 2022. https://doi.org/10.1007/s00011-022-01622-x.
[39] Bologna L, Gotti E, Manganini M, Rambaldi A, Intermesoli T, Introna M, Golay J. Mechanism of action of type II, glycoengineered, anti-CD20 monoclonal antibody GA101 in B-chronic lymphocytic leukemia whole blood assays in comparison with rituximab and alemtuzumab. J Immunol 2011;186:3762–9.
[40] Sacco KA, Abraham RS. Consequences of B-cell-depleting therapy: hypogammaglobulinemia and impaired B-cell reconstitution. Immunotherapy 2018;10:713–28.
[41] Moraru M, Black LE, Muntasell A, Portero F, López-Botet M, Reyburn HT, Pandey JP, Vilches C. NK cell and Ig interplay in defense against herpes simplex virus type 1: epistatic interaction of CD16A and IgG1 allotypes of variable affinities modulates antibody-dependent cellular cytotoxicity and susceptibility to clinical reactivation. J Immunol 2015;195(4):1676–84.
[42] Kim SH, Jeong IH, Hyun JW, Joung A, Jo HJ, Hwang SH, Yun S, Joo J, Kim HJ. Treatment outcomes with rituximab in 100 patients with neuromyelitis optica: influence of FCGR3A polymorphisms on the therapeutic response to rituximab. JAMA Neurol 2015;72(9):989–95.
[43] Oboshi W, Watanabe T, Matsuyama Y, Kobara A, Yukimasa N, Ueno I, Aki K, Tada T, Hosoi E. The influence of NK cell-mediated ADCC: structure and expression of the CD16 molecule differ among FcγRIIIa-V158F genotypes in healthy Japanese subjects. Hum Immunol 2016;77(2):165–71.

[44] Kusowska A, Kubacz M, Krawczyk M, Slusarczyk A, Winiarska M, Bobrowicz M. Molecular aspects of resistance to immunotherapies. Advances in understanding and management of diffuse large B-cell lymphoma. Int J Mol Sci 2022;23(3):1501. https://doi.org/10.3390/ijms23031501.

[45] Mizrahi O, Ish Shalom E, Baniyash M, Klieger Y. Quantitative flow cytometry: concerns and recommendations in clinic and research. Cytometry B Clin Cytom 2018;94(2):211–8.

[46] Krajnc N, Bsteh G, Berger T, Mares J, Hartung HP. Monoclonal antibodies in the treatment of relapsing multiple sclerosis: an overview with emphasis on pregnancy, vaccination and risk management. Neurotherapeutics 2022;19(3):753–73.

[47] Kaegi C, Wuest B, Crowley C, Boyman O. Systematic review of safety and efficacy of second- and third-generation CD20-targeting biologics in treating immune-mediated disorders. Front Immunol 2022;12, 788830. https://doi.org/10.3389/fimmu.2021.788830.

[48] Tout M, Casasnovas O, Meignan M, Lamy T, Morschhauser F, Salles G, Gyan E, Haioun C, Mercier M, Feugier P, Boussetta S, Paintaud G, Ternant D, Cartron G. Rituximab exposure is influenced by baseline metabolic tumor volume and predicts outcome of DLBCL patients: a Lymphoma Study Association report. Blood 2017;129(19):2616–23.

[49] Cottereau AS, Nioche C, Dirand AS, Clerc J, Morschhauser F, Casasnovas O, Meignan M, Buvat I. ^{18}F-FDG PET dissemination features in diffuse large B-cell lymphoma are predictive of outcome. J Nucl Med 2020;61(1):40–5.

[50] Teng YK, Levarht EW, Toes RE, Huizinga TW, van Laar JM. Residual inflammation after rituximab treatment is associated with sustained synovial plasma cell infiltration and enhanced B cell repopulation. Ann Rheum Dis 2009;68(6):1011–6.

[51] Marasco E, Aquilani A, Cascioli S, Moneta GM, Caiello I, Farroni C, Giorda E, D'Oria V, Pires Marafon D, Magni-Manzoni S, Carsetti R, De Benedetti F. Switched memory B cells are increased in oligoarticular and polyarticular juvenile idiopathic arthritis and their change over time is related to response to tumor necrosis factor inhibitors. Arthritis Rheum 2018;70(4):606–15.

[52] Lleo A, Invernizzi P, Gao B, Podda M, Gershwin ME. Definition of human autoimmunity. Autoantibodies versus autoimmune disease. Autoimmun Rev 2010;9:A259–66.

[53] Sheldon J. Developments in laboratory testing for autoimmune diseases. Clin Chem Lab Med 2018;56(6):865–8.

[54] Cambridge G, Leandro MJ, Lahey LJ, Fairhead T, Robinson WH, Sokolove J. B cell depletion with rituximab in patients with rheumatoid arthritis: multiplex bead array reveals the kinetics of IgG and IgA antibodies to citrullinated antigens. J Autoimmun 2016;70:22–30.

[55] Hassan RI, Gaffo AL. Rituximab in ANCA-associated vasculitis. Curr Rheumatol Rep 2017;19:6.

[56] Baglaenko Y, Chang NH, Johnson SR, Hafiz W, Manion K, Ferri D, Noamani B, Bonilla D, Rusta-Sellehy S, Lisnevskaia L, Silverman E, Bookman A, Landolt-Marticorena C, Wither J. The presence of anti-nuclear antibodies alone is associated with changes in B cell activation and T follicular helper cells similar to those in systemic autoimmune rheumatic disease. Arthritis Res Ther 2018;20:264.

[57] Barturen G, Beretta L, Cervera R, Van Vollenhoven R, Alarcón-Riquelme ME. Moving towards a molecular taxonomy of autoimmune rheumatic diseases. Nat Rev Rheumatol 2018;14(2):75–93.

[58] Del Vecchio L, Allinovi M, Rocco P, Brando B. Rituximab therapy for adults with nephrotic syndromes: standard schedules or B cell-targeted therapy? J Clin Med 2021;10(24):5847.

[59] Kim SH, Kim W, Li XF, Jung IJ, Kim HJ. Repeated treatment with rituximab based on the assessment of peripheral circulating memory B cells in patients with relapsing neuromyelitis optica over 2 years. Arch Neurol 2011;68(11):1412–20.

[60] Wingerchuk DM, Lucchinetti CF. Neuromyelitis optica spectrum disorder. N Engl J Med 2022;387:631–9.

[61] Nakou M, Katsikas G, Sidiropoulos P, Bertsias G, Papadimitraki E, Raptopoulou A, Koutala H, Papadaki HA, Kritikos H, Boumpas DT. Rituximab therapy reduces activated B cells in both the peripheral blood and bone marrow of patients with rheumatoid arthritis: depletion of memory B cells correlates with clinical response. Arthritis Res Ther 2009;11:R131. https://doi.org/10.1186/ar2798.

[62] Sellam J, Rouanet S, Hendel-Chavez H, Miceli-Richard C, Combe B, Sibilia J, Le Loët X, Tebib J, Jourdan R, Dougados M, Taoufik Y, Mariette X. CCL19, a B cell chemokine, is related to the decrease of blood memory B cells and predicts the clinical response to rituximab in patients with rheumatoid arthritis. Arthritis Rheum 2013;65:2253–61.

[63] Pelzek AJ, Grönwall C, Rosenthal P, Greenberg JD, McGeachy M, Moreland L, Rigby WFC, Silverman GJ. Disease associated anti-citrullinated protein memory B cells in rheumatoid arthritis persist in clinical remission. Arthritis Rheum 2017;69(6):1176–86.

[64] Lebrun C, Cohen M, Rosenthal-Allieri MA, Bresch S, Benzaken S, Marignier R, Seitz-Polski B, Ticchioni M. Only follow-up of memory B cells helps monitor rituximab administration to patients with neuromyelitis optica spectrum disorders. Neurol Ther 2018;7:373–83.

[65] Ruetsch-Chelli C, Bresch S, Seitz-Polski B, Rosenthal A, Desnuelle C, Cohen M, Brglez V, Ticchioni M, Lebrun-Frenay C. Memory B cells predict relapse in rituximab-treated myasthenia gravis. Neurotherapeutics 2021;18 (2):938–48.

[66] Baker D, Marta M, Pryce G, Giovannoni G, Schmierer K. Memory B cells are major targets for effective immunotherapy in relapsing multiple sclerosis. EBioMedicine 2017;16:41–50.

[67] Roll P, Dörner T, Tony HP. Anti-CD20 therapy in patients with rheumatoid arthritis: predictors of response and B cell subset regeneration after repeated treatment. Arthritis Rheum 2008;58(6):1566–75.

[68] Becerra E, De La Torre I, Leandro MJ, Cambridge G. B cell phenotypes in patients with rheumatoid arthritis relapsing after rituximab: expression of B cell-activating factor-binding receptors on B cell subsets. Clin Exp Immunol 2017;190(3):372–83.

[69] Leibler C, Moktefi A, Matignon M, Debiais-Delpech C, Oniszczuk J, Sahali D, Cohen JL, Grimbert P, Audard V. Rituximab and fibrillary glomerulonephritis: interest of B cell reconstitution monitoring. J Clin Med 2018;7 (11):430. https://doi.org/10.3390/jcm7110430.

[70] Bomback AS, Fervenza FC. Membranous nephropathy: approaches to treatment. Am J Nephrol 2018;47(Suppl 1):30–42. https://doi.org/10.1159/000481635.

[71] Novi G, Bovis F, Fabbri S, Tazza F, Gazzola P, Maietta I, Currò D, Bruschi N, Roccatagliata L, Boffa G, Lapucci C, Pesce G, Cellerino M, Solaro C, Laroni A, Capello E, Mancardi G, Sormani M, Inglese M, Uccelli A. Tailoring B cell depletion therapy in MS according to memory B cell monitoring. Neurol Neuroimmunol Neuroinflamm 2020;7(5), e845. https://doi.org/10.1212/NXI.0000000000000845.

[72] Gernert M, Tony HP, Schwaneck EC, Gadeholt O, Schmalzing M. Autologous hematopoietic stem cell transplantation in systemic sclerosis induces long-lasting changes in B cell homeostasis toward an anti-inflammatory B cell cytokine pattern. Arthritis Res Ther 2019;21(1):106. https://doi.org/10.1186/s13075-019-1889-8.

[73] Elhai M, Boubaya M, Distler O, Smith V, Matucci-Cerinic M, Alegre Sancho JJ, Truchetet ME, Braun-Moscovici Y, Iannone F, Novikov PI, Lescoat A, et al. Outcomes of patients with systemic sclerosis treated with rituximab in contemporary practice: a prospective cohort study. Ann Rheum Dis 2019;78(7):979–87.

[74] Mariette X, Criswell LA. Primary Sjögren's syndrome. N Engl J Med 2018;379(1):97. https://doi.org/10.1056/NEJMc1804598.

[75] Reddy V, Jayne D, Close D, Isenberg D. B-cell depletion in SLE: clinical and trial experience with rituximab and ocrelizumab and implications for study design. Arthritis Res Ther 2013;15(Suppl 1):S2. https://doi.org/10.1186/ar3910.

[76] Yo JH, Barbour TD, Nicholls K. Management of refractory lupus nephritis: challenges and solutions. Open Access Rheumatol 2019;11:179–88. https://doi.org/10.2147/OARRR.S166303.

[77] Khodadadi L, Cheng Q, Radbruch A, Hiepe F. The maintenance of memory plasma cells. Front Immunol 2019;10:721. https://doi.org/10.3389/fimmu.2019.00721.

[78] Hiepe F, Dörner T, Hauser AE, Hoyer BF, Mei H, Radbruch A. Long-lived autoreactive plasma cells drive persistent autoimmune inflammation. Nat Rev Rheumatol 2011;7:170–8.

[79] Bontscho J, Schreiber A, Manz RA, Schneider W, Luft FC, Kettritz R. Myeloperoxidase-specific plasma cell depletion by bortezomib protects from anti-neutrophil cytoplasmic autoantibodies-induced glomerulonephritis. J Am Soc Nephrol 2011;22(2):336–48.

[80] Beecher G, Putko BN, Wagner AN, Siddiqi ZA. Therapies directed against B-cells and downstream effectors in generalized autoimmune myasthenia gravis: current status. Drugs 2019;79:353–64.

[81] Li G, Wang S, Li N, Liu Y, Feng Q, Zuo X, Li X, Hou Y, Shao L, Ma C, Gao C, Hou M, Peng J. Proteasome inhibition with Bortezomib induces apoptosis of long-lived plasma cells in steroid-resistant or relapsed immune thrombocytopaenia. Thromb Haemost 2018;118(10):1752–64.

[82] Pasquale R, Giannotta JA, Barcellini W, Fattizzo B. Bortezomib in autoimmune hemolytic anemia and beyond. Ther Adv Hematol 2021;12:1–19.

[83] Zeiser R, Sarantopoulos S, Blazar BR. B-cell targeting in chronic graft-versus-host disease. Blood 2018;131 (13):1399–405.

[84] Barbari A. Pre- and posttransplant refractory idiopathic membranous glomerulonephritis: the forgotten potential culprit. Exp Clin Transplant 2017;5:483–9.

[85] López J, Merino L, Piris L, Herrera FS, Llorente I, Humbría A, Ortiz AM, Velasco T, García-Vicuña R, Castañeda S, González Álvaro I, Muñoz-Calleja C. Rituximab induces a lasting, non-cumulative remodelling of the B-cell compartment. Clin Exp Rheumatol 2019;37(4):615–22.
[86] Tellier J, Nutt SL. Plasma cells: the programming of an antibody-secreting machine. Eur J Immunol 2019;49:30–7.
[87] Flores-Montero J, de Tute R, Paiva B, Perez JJ, Boettcher S, Wind H, Sanoja L, Puig L, Lecrevisse Q, Vidriales MB, van Dongen JJM, Orfao A. Immunophenotype of normal vs. myeloma plasma cells: toward antibody panel specifications for MRD detection in multiple myeloma. Cytometry B Clin Cytom 2016;90B:61–72.
[88] Dass S, Rawstron AC, Vital EM, Henshaw K, McGonagle D, Emery P. Highly sensitive B cell analysis predicts response to rituximab therapy in rheumatoid arthritis. Arthritis Rheum 2008;58:2993–9.
[89] Vital EM, Dass S, Rawstron AC, Buch MH, Goëb V, Henshaw K, Ponchel F, Emery P. Management of nonresponse to rituximab in rheumatoid arthritis. Arthritis Rheum 2010;62(5):1273–9.
[90] Li S, Yu Y, Yue Y, Liao H, Xie W, Thai J, Mikuls TR, Thiele GM, Duryee MJ, Sayles H, Payne JB, Klassen LW, O'Dell JR, Zhang Z, Su K. Autoantibodies from single circulating plasmablasts react with citrullinated antigens and *Porphyromonas gingivalis* in rheumatoid arthritis. Arthritis Rheum 2016;68(3):614–26.
[91] Oniszczuk J, Beldi-Ferchiou A, Audureau E, Azzaoui I, Molinier-Frenkel V, Frontera V, Karras A, Moktefi A, Pillebout E, Zaidan M, El Karoui K, Delfau-Larue MH, Hénique C, Ollero M, Sahali D, Mahévas M, Audard V. Circulating plasmablasts and high level of BAFF are hallmarks of minimal change nephrotic syndrome in adults. Nephrol Dial Transplant 2021;36:609–17.
[92] Lin W, Zhang P, Chen H, Chen Y, Yang H, Zheng W, Zhang X, Zhang F, Zhang W, Lipsky PE. Circulating plasmablasts/plasma cells: a potential biomarker for IgG4-related disease. Arthritis Res Ther 2017;19:25. https://doi.org/10.1186/s13075-017-1231-2.
[93] Blum LK, Cao RRL, Sweatt AJ, Bill M, Lahey LJ, Hsi AC, Lee CS, Kongpachith S, Ju CH, Mao R, Wong HH, Nicolls MR, Zamanian RT, Robinson WH. Circulating plasmablasts are elevated and produce pathogenic anti-endothelial cell autoantibodies in idiopathic pulmonary arterial hypertension. Eur J Immunol 2018;48 (5):874–84.
[94] Robinson WH, Mao R. Biomarkers to guide clinical therapeutics in rheumatology? Curr Opin Rheumatol 2016;28(2):168–75.
[95] van Dam LS, Oskam JM, Kamerling SWA, Arends EJ, Bredewold OW, Berkowska MA, van Dongen JJM, Rabelink TJ, van Kooten C, Teng YKO. Highly sensitive flow cytometric detection of residual B-cells after rituximab in anti-neutrophil cytoplasmic antibodies-associated vasculitis patients. Front Immunol 2020;11, 566732. https://doi.org/10.3389/fimmu.2020.566732.
[96] Gatti A, Buccisano F, Scupoli MT, Brando B. The ISCCA flow protocol for the monitoring of anti-CD20 therapies in autoimmune disorders. Cytometry B Clin Cytom 2021;100(2):194–205.
[97] Singh N, Handa S, Mahajan R, Sachdeva N, De D. Comparison of the efficacy and cost-effectiveness of an immunologically targeted low-dose rituximab protocol with the conventional rheumatoid arthritis protocol in severe pemphigus. Clin Exp Dermatol 2022;47(8):1508–16.
[98] Möller B, Aeberli D, Eggli S, Fuhrer M, Vajtai I, Vögelin E, Ziswiler HR, Dahinden CA, Villiger PM. Class-switched B cells display response to therapeutic B-cell depletion in rheumatoid arthritis. Arthritis Res Ther 2009;11(3):R62. https://doi.org/10.1186/ar2686.
[99] Kim SH, Hyun JW, Kim HJ. Individualized B cell-targeting therapy for neuromyelitis optica spectrum disorder. Neurochem Int 2019;130, 104347. https://doi.org/10.1016/j.neuint.2018.11.022.
[100] Lavielle M, Mulleman D, Goupille P, Bahuaud C, Sung HC, Watier H, Thibault G. Repeated decrease of CD4+ T-cell counts in patients with rheumatoid arthritis over multiple cycles of rituximab treatment. Arthritis Res Ther 2016;18(1):253. https://doi.org/10.1186/s13075-016-1152-5.
[101] Sentís A, Diekmann F, Llobell A, de Moner N, Espinosa G, Yagüe J, Campistol JM, Mirapeix E, Juan M. Kinetic analysis of changes in T- and B-lymphocytes after anti-CD20 treatment in renal pathology. Immunobiology 2017;222(4):620–30.
[102] Capasso N, Nozzolillo A, Scalia G, Lanzillo R, Carotenuto A, De Angelis M, Petruzzo M, Saccà F, Russo CV, Brescia Morra V, Moccia M. Ocrelizumab depletes T-lymphocytes more than rituximab in multiple sclerosis. Mult Scler Relat Disord 2021;49, 102802. https://doi.org/10.1016/j.msard.2021.102802.
[103] European Medicine Agency. Mabthera®. ANNEX I—summary of product characteristics; Last updated 22/03/2023. p. 47. Available from: https://www.ema.europa.eu/en/documents/product-information/mabthera-epar-product-information_en.pdf. [Accessed 1 November 2022].

[104] Carrion C, Guérin E, Gachard N, le Guyader A, Giraut S, Feuillard J. Adult bone marrow three-dimensional phenotypic landscape of B-cell differentiation. Cytometry B Clin Cytom 2019;96(1):30–8.

[105] Rovin BH, Adler SG, Barratt J, Bridoux F, Burdge KA, Chan TM, Cook HT, Fervenza FC, Gibson KL, Glassock RJ, Jayne DRW, Jha V, et al. Executive summary of the KDIGO 2021 Guideline for the management of glomerular diseases. Kidney Int 2021;100(4):753–79.

[106] Vikse J, Jonsdottir K, Kvaløy JT, Wildhagen K, Omdal R. Tolerability and safety of long-term rituximab treatment in systemic inflammatory and autoimmune diseases. Rheumatol Int 2019;39:1083–90.

[107] Charles P, Perrodeau É, Samson M, Bonnotte B, Néel A, Agard C, Huart A, Karras A, Lifermann F, Godmer P, Cohen P, et al. Long-term rituximab use to maintain remission of antineutrophil cytoplasmic antibody-associated vasculitis: a randomized trial. Ann Intern Med 2020;173(3):179–87.

[108] Bertsias A, Avgoustidis N, Papalopoulos I, Repa A, Kougkas N, Kalogiannaki E, Bertsias G, Flouri I, Sidiropoulos P. Rheumatoid arthritis patients initiating rituximab with low number of previous bDMARDs failures may effectively reduce rituximab dose and experience fewer serious adverse events than patients on full dose: a 5-year cohort study. Arthritis Res Ther 2022;24(1):132. https://doi.org/10.1186/s13075-022-02826-6.

[109] den Broeder AA, Verhoef LM, Fransen J, Thurlings R, van den Bemt BJF, Teerenstra S, Boers N, den Broeder N, van den Hoogen FHJ. Ultra-low dose of rituximab in rheumatoid arthritis: study protocol for a randomised controlled trial. Trials 2017;18(1):403. https://doi.org/10.1186/s13063-017-2134-x.

[110] van Vollenhoven RF, Emery P, Bingham 3rd CO, Keystone EC, Fleischmann R, Furst DE, Macey K, Sweetser M, Kelman A, Rao R. Longterm safety of patients receiving rituximab in rheumatoid arthritis clinical trials. J Rheumatol 2010;37(3):558–67.

[111] Patel SY, Carbone J, Jolles S. The expanding field of secondary antibody deficiency: causes, diagnosis, and management. Front Immunol 2019;10:33. https://doi.org/10.3389/fimmu.2019.00033.

[112] Roberts DM, Jones RB, Smith RM, Alberici F, Kumaratne DS, Burns S, Jayne DR. Rituximab-associated hypogammaglobulinemia: incidence, predictors and outcomes in patients with multi-system autoimmune disease. J Autoimmun 2015;57:60–5.

[113] Barmettler S, Ong MS, Farmer JR, Choi H, Walter J. Association of immunoglobulin levels, infectious risk, and mortality with rituximab and hypogammaglobulinemia. JAMA Netw Open 2018;1(7), e184169. https://doi.org/10.1001/jamanetworkopen.2018.4169.

[114] Zecca C, Gobbi C. Long-term treatment with anti-CD20 monoclonal antibodies is untenable because of risk: YES. Mult Scler 2022;28(8):1173–5.

[115] Luna G, Alping P, Burman J, Fink K, Fogdell-Hahn A, Gunnarsson M, Hillert J, Langer-Gould A, Lycke J, Nilsson P, Salzer J, et al. Infection risks among patients with multiple sclerosis treated with Fingolimod, Natalizumab, Rituximab, and injectable therapies. JAMA Neurol 2020;77(2):184–91.

[116] Opdam MAA, de Leijer JH, den Broeder N, Thurlings RM, van der Weele W, Nurmohamed MT, Kok MR, van Bon L, Ten Cate DF, Verhoef LM, den Broeder AA. Rituximab dose-dependent infection risk in rheumatoid arthritis is not mediated through circulating immunoglobulins, neutrophils or B-cells. Rheumatology (Oxford) 2022;, keac318. https://doi.org/10.1093/rheumatology/keac318.

[117] Furlan A, Forner G, Cipriani L, Vian E, Rigoli R, Gherlinzoni F, Scotton P. COVID-19 in B cell-depleted patients after rituximab: a diagnostic and therapeutic challenge. Front Immunol 2021;12, 763412. https://doi.org/10.3389/fimmu.2021.763412.

[118] Baker D, Roberts CAK, Pryce G, Kang AS, Marta M, Reyes S, Schmierer K, Giovannoni G, Amor S. COVID-19 vaccine-readiness for anti-CD20-depleting therapy in autoimmune diseases. Clin Exp Immunol 2020;202(2):149–61.

[119] Boyarsky BJ, Ruddy JA, Connolly CM, Ou MT, Werbel WA, Garonzik-Wang JM, Segev DL, Paik JJ. Antibody response to a single dose of SARS-CoV-2 mRNA vaccine in patients with rheumatic and musculoskeletal diseases. Ann Rheum Dis 2021;80(8):1098–9.

[120] Troldborg A, Thomsen MK, Bartels LE, Andersen JB, Vils SR, Mistegaard CE, Johannsen AD, Hermansen MF, Mikkelsen S, Erikstrup C, Hauge EM, Ammitzbøll C. Time since Rituximab treatment is essential for developing a humoral response to COVID-19 mRNA vaccines in patients with rheumatic diseases. J Rheumatol 2022;49(6):644–9.

[121] Bellinvia A, Aprea MG, Portaccio E, Pastò L, Razzolini L, Fonderico M, Addazio I, Betti M, Amato MP. Hypogammaglobulinemia is associated with reduced antibody response after anti-SARS-CoV-2 vaccination in MS patients treated with anti-CD20 therapies. Neurol Sci 2022;43(10):5783–94.
[122] Bonelli MM, Mrak D, Perkmann T, Haslacher H, Aletaha D. SARS-CoV-2 vaccination in rituximab-treated patients: evidence for impaired humoral but inducible cellular immune response. Ann Rheum Dis 2021;80:1355–6.
[123] Colombo D, Gatti A, Alabardi P, Bompane D, Bonardi G, Mumoli N, Faggioli P, Clerici P, Brando B, Mazzone A. COVID-19-associated pneumonia in a B-cell-depleted patient with non-Hodgkin lymphoma: recovery with hyperimmune plasma. J Hematol 2022;11(2):77–80.
[124] Chatenoud L, Jonker M, Villemain F, Goldstein G, Bach JF. The human immune response to the OKT3 monoclonal antibody is oligoclonal. Science 1986;232(4756):1406–8.
[125] Hwang WY, Foote J. Immunogenicity of engineered antibodies. Methods 2005;36(1):3–10. https://doi.org/10.1016/j.ymeth.2005.01.001.
[126] Isaacs JD, Watts RA, Hazleman BL, Hale G, Keogan MT, Cobbold SP, Waldmann H. Humanised monoclonal antibody therapy for rheumatoid arthritis. Lancet 1992;340(8822):748–52.
[127] Gilaberte Reyzabal S, Isenberg D. Differences in the development of adverse infusion reactions to Rituximab in patients with systemic lupus erythematosus, rheumatoid arthritis and non-Hodgkin's lymphoma—enigma variations. Front Med 2022;9, 882891. https://doi.org/10.3389/fmed.2022.882891.
[128] Wincup C, Menon M, Smith E, Schwartz A, Isenberg D, Jury EC, Mauri C, ABIRISK Consortium. Presence of anti-rituximab antibodies predicts infusion-related reactions in patients with systemic lupus erythematosus. Ann Rheum Dis 2019;78(8):1140–2.
[129] Boyer-Suavet S, Andreani M, Lateb M, Savenkoff B, Brglez V, Benzaken S, Bernard G, Nachman PH, Esnault V, Seitz-Polski B. Neutralizing anti-rituximab antibodies and relapse in membranous nephropathy treated with rituximab. Front Immunol 2020;10:3069. https://doi.org/10.3389/fimmu.2019.03069.
[130] Teisseyre M, Boyer-Suavet S, Crémoni M, Brglez V, Esnault V, Seitz-Polski B. Analysis and management of rituximab resistance in PLA2R1-associated membranous nephropathy. Kidney Int Rep 2021;6(4):1183–8.
[131] Du FH, Mills EA, Mao-Draayer Y. Next-generation anti-CD20 monoclonal antibodies in autoimmune disease treatment. Autoimmun Highlights 2017;8(1):12. https://doi.org/10.1007/s13317-017-0100-y.
[132] Berendsen MR, Stevens WBC, van den Brand M, van Krieken JH, Scheijen B. Molecular genetics of relapsed diffuse large B-cell lymphoma: insight into mechanisms of therapy resistance. Cancers 2020;12(12):3553. https://doi.org/10.3390/cancers12123553.
[133] Fervenza FC, Abraham RS, Erickson SB, Irazabal MV, Eirin A, Specks U, Nachman PH, Bergstralh EJ, Leung N, Cosio FG, Hogan MC, Dillon JJ, Hickson LJ, Li X, Cattran DC, Mayo Nephrology Collaborative Group. Rituximab therapy in idiopathic membranous nephropathy: a 2-year study. Clin J Am Soc Nephrol 2010;5(12):2188–98.
[134] Fogueri U, Cheungapasitporn W, Bourne D, Fervenza FC, Joy MS. Rituximab exhibits altered pharmacokinetics in patients with membranous nephropathy. Ann Pharmacother 2019;53(4):357–63.
[135] Kovarik J, Breidenbach T, Gerbeau C, Korn A, Schmidt AG, Nashan B. Disposition and immunodynamics of basiliximab in liver allograft recipients. Clin Pharmacol Ther 1998;64(1):66–72.
[136] Kaneko T, Doki K, Yamada T, Yamamoto Y, Moriwaki T, Suzuki Y, Homma M. Distribution of therapeutic monoclonal antibodies into ascites in advanced gastric cancer patients with peritoneal metastasis: case reports and literature review. Cancer Chemother Pharmacol 2022. https://doi.org/10.1007/s00280-022-04479-3.
[137] Wampler Muskardin TL, Paredes JL, Appenzeller S, Niewold TB. Lessons from precision medicine in rheumatology. Mult Scler 2020;26(5):533–9.
[138] Freeman L, Longbrake EE, Coyle PK, Hendin B, Vollmer T. High-efficacy therapies for treatment-naïve individuals with relapsing-remitting multiple sclerosis. CNS Drugs 2022;36(12):1285–99.
[139] Chisari CG, Sgarlata E, Arena S, Toscano S, Luca M, Patti F. Rituximab for the treatment of multiple sclerosis: a review. J Neurol 2022;269(1):159–83.
[140] Boldison J, Da Rosa LC, Wong FS. Regulatory B cells in type 1 diabetes. Methods Mol Biol 2021;2270:419–35.

CHAPTER

17

Clinical efficacy of anti-CD20 antibodies in neurological and neuromuscular diseases

Yuan-teng Fan[a,*], *Tao-xiang Chen*[b,*], *Yu-min Liu*[a], *and Bi-wen Peng*[c]

[a]Department of Neurology, Zhongnan Hospital, Wuhan University, Wuhan, China [b]Department of Physiology, School of Basic Medical Sciences, Wuhan University, Wuhan, China [c]Department of Physiology, Hubei Provincial Key Laboratory of Developmentally Originated Disease, School of Basic Medical Sciences, Wuhan University, Wuhan, China

Abstract

Cluster of differentiation 20 (CD20) is an integral membrane protein expressed mainly on different developmental stages of B lymphocytes and rarely on T lymphocytes, and it functions as a link to the B cell antigen receptor (BCR) and immune microenvironment via regulating calcium ion influx, and cell cycle progression and interaction between isotypic BCRs and their coreceptors. Diverse therapeutic monoclonal antibodies (mAbs) targeting CD20 are generated and grouped into two types based on the ability to redistribute CD20 into lipid rafts, which results in huge differences in response. Currently, multiple anti-CD20 mAbs have been approved as drugs for neurological and neuromuscular diseases with promising clinical efficacy. This chapter aims to summarize the potential mechanisms, development, and current evidence for anti-CD20 therapy in neurological and neuromuscular diseases.

Abbreviations

AChR	acetylcholine receptor
ADCC	antibody-dependent cell-mediated cytotoxicity
AE	autoimmune encephalitis
BBB	blood-brain barrier
BCR	B cell antigen receptor

*Co-first authors.

https://doi.org/10.1016/B978-0-443-19200-5.00012-9

CD20	cluster of differentiation 20
CDC	complement-dependent cytotoxicity
CIDP	chronic inflammatory demyelinating polyradiculoneuropathy
CNS	central nervous system
CSF	cerebrospinal fluid
DM	dermatomyositis
DMT	disease-modifying therapy
IBM	inclusion body myositis
IIMs	idiopathic inflammatory myopathies
IL	interleukin
IMNM	immune-mediated necrotizing myopathy
IRRs	infusion-related reactions
mAbs	monoclonal antibodies
MAC	membrane attack complex
MG	myasthenia gravis
MS	multiple sclerosis
MS4A	membrane-spanning 4 domain family A
MuSK	muscle-specific kinase
NK	natural killer
NMOSD	neuromyelitis optica spectrum disorder
OBZ	obinutuzumab
OCR	ocrelizumab
OFA	ofatumumab
PCs	plasma cells
PMN-MDSCs	polymorphonuclear myeloid-derived suppressor cells
PPMS	primary progressive MS
RMS	relapsing MS
RRMS	relapsing-remitting MS
RTX	rituximab
SPMS	secondary progressive MS
Ub	ublituximab

Conflict of interest

No potential conflicts of interest were disclosed.

Introduction

Cluster of differentiation 20 (CD20) is an integral membrane protein that is expressed mainly on B lymphocytes and rarely on T lymphocytes. MS4A1, the gene encoding for CD20, belongs to a protein family of membrane-spanning 4 domain family A (MS4A), which includes 18 members. The MS4A gene cluster is mainly located on chromosome 11q12 in humans (chromosome 19 in mice). The CD20 protein consists of four transmembrane helices (TMs), one intracellular loop, and two extracellular loops (ECLs), with both cytoplasmic N- and C-termini [1]. The ECL connecting TM3 and TM4 is larger than the other one and contains a disulfide bond between C167 and C183 residues inside its domain [2]. CD20 is a nonglycosylated phosphoprotein with three isoforms (33, 35, and 37 kDa) for differential phosphorylation on different serine and threonine residues in its cytoplasmic domain [3,4]. CD20 phosphorylation is increased in proliferating malignant B lymphocytes compared with resting B lymphocytes, and this elevated expression permits the binding of a monoclonal antibody (mAb) that targets CD20 to initiate tumor lymphocyte deletion.

Rituximab (RTX) was the first mAb targeting CD20, and since its approval for the treatment of CD20$^+$ non-Hodgkin lymphoma (NHL) in 1997, more anti-CD20 mAbs have been developed and applied for the treatment of most B cell lymphomas [5]. Moreover, RTX has shown significant clinical efficacy for the majority of autoimmune diseases, such as rheumatoid arthritis and multiple sclerosis (MS) [6]. To date, endogenous CD20 ligands have not been found and the precise physiological function and regulation of CD20 have not been clarified. However, the clinical efficacy and plausible prognosis of these different anti-CD20 mAbs provide insights into the function of CD20 in the pathogenesis of B cell lymphoma and most autoimmune diseases in the nervous and neuromuscular systems. Meanwhile, the adverse events of monoclonal antibody therapy also highlight the dual role of CD20$^+$ lymphocytes in immunopathogenesis [7].

Accumulating evidence supports CD20 as an immunotherapy target to affect membrane organization, thus profoundly altering the fate of B lymphocytes [5,8] and also the quantity and activity of some T lymphocytes [9–11]. Here, we will focus on the physiological and pathophysiological roles of CD20 and the outcomes of anti-CD20 therapy in neurological and neuromuscular diseases.

Physiological and pathophysiological roles of CD20$^+$ lymphocytes

CD20 expression profile and its regulation

On B lymphocytes, CD20 is expressed in both the antigen-independent developmental phase in the bone marrow and the antigen-dependent differentiation phase in secondary lymphoid organs or tissues. CD20 presents on more mature B-lineage cells in the four stages of bone marrow B-lymphocyte development, starting from late pre-B lymphocytes and progressively strengthening on immature B lymphocytes and naïve B lymphocytes (mature B lymphocytes) [12]. After exiting the bone marrow, mature B lymphocytes reside in the peripheral lymphoid organs. In response to antigen stimulation, mature B lymphocytes with sustained CD20 expression are activated and become effector cells. In addition to being expressed on normal B lymphocytes from peripheral blood and lymphoid organs, more CD20 is present on the surface of activated B lymphocytes [4,13], and it is also observed on the surface of memory B lymphocytes and even on plasmablasts, although its expression is lost in antibody-producing plasma cells (PCs).

CD20 was also reported to be present at a very low level on a subset of T lymphocytes in peripheral blood from healthy human blood [14] and in the thymus, bone marrow, secondary lymphoid organs, and cerebrospinal fluid (CSF) from MS patients [15]. This subpopulation of CD20$^+$ T lymphocytes was more likely to be $\gamma\delta$ T cell antigen-receptor positive, CD8$^+$, and CD45RO$^+$, and developed later in life [16].

The MS4A1 gene consists of eight exons, and multiple transcription factors have been identified to interact with its upstream promoter elements such as the "PU.1/PiP" binding site and the BAT box to elaborately regulate CD20 expression [5]. The "PU.1/PiP" binding element is occupied only in CD20$^+$ B lymphocytes and NHL B lymphocytes while the

PU.1/Pip complex is absent from CD20$^-$ B cell lines, suggesting the "PU.1/PiP" binding element is critical for CD20 expression [17]. The BAT box can be efficiently transactivated by OCT binding, which is essential for promoting CD20 expression in pre-B lymphocytes and for constitutive CD20 expression in mature B lymphocytes [18]. Increased PU.1 and OCT2 may promote transcriptional CD20 activation in NHL and primary CLL B lymphocytes [19].

Possible physiological roles of CD20$^+$ lymphocytes

CD20$^+$ lymphocytes have been proved to be involved in humoral immunity mediated by antibodies, antigen presentation to T lymphocytes [20], and production of various cytokines and chemokines that play a role in immune regulation [21]. CD20 protein functions as a link to the B cell antigen receptor (BCR) signal and immune microenvironment by promoting calcium ion transport, regulating the cell cycle progression, and harmonizing the interaction between isotypic BCR and its coreceptor.

As a tetraspanin, the CD20 protein has been considered a Ca^{2+} channel in homodimeric or homotetrameric CD20 oligomers or a component of store-operated Ca^{2+} channels involved in B cell activation [22–24]. Nevertheless, the loss of CD20 expression on B lymphocytes weakens anti-IgM- or anti-CD19-induced cytosolic Ca^{2+} enhancement [25] while CD20$^+$ lymphocytes lacking BCR cannot induce Ca^{2+} entry following CD20 ligation [24,26], suggesting that CD20 functions as a regulator to mediate BCR-activated Ca^{2+} influx. Stronger evidence from the cryo-EM structural analysis of CD20 shows that CD20 surface molecules form a compact, double-square-barrel dimer that acts as a regulator, but not an ion channel [27].

CD20 has been shown to act as a regulator of the cell-cycle progression of B lymphocytes [28]. B lymphocytes transduced with CD20-lentiviral vectors entered the G1b phase of the cell cycle perhaps by regulating the BCR-induced intracellular Ca^{2+} concentration while nontransduced B lymphocytes remained in the G0 phase [29].

Functional BCR is required for the development of humoral immunity, while CD20 that is physically coupled to BCR and other surface molecules or cytoplasmic proteins, such as major histocompatibility complex class II (MHCII), CD40 molecules, and tyrosine kinases, is involved in signal transduction [24]. The high-resolution proximity ligation assay shows that CD20 and the coreceptor CD19 are in close proximity with IgD-BCR on resting B lymphocytes and with IgM-BCR on activated B lymphocytes, and loss of CD20 expression increases the proximity of IgM-BCR/CD19, thus leading to transient B cell activation followed by CD22, CD81, and CD40 internalization, which suggests CD20 as a nanoscale receptor organizer of BCR/CD19 signaling [8,30].

Immunopathology of CD20$^+$ lymphocytes

CD20$^+$ lymphocytes exert pathogenic roles through both antibody-dependent and antibody-independent pathways in the majority of autoimmune disorders [31,32].

Although CD20 is not present on PCs, it is still involved in the antibody-dependent immunopathology of B lymphocytes by affecting the evolution of PC from its precursor plasmablast. The anti-CD20 treatment targeting plasmablasts results in a marked decrease in the short-lived PC population. At the early stage of peripheral blood B-lymphocyte culture, the addition of CD20 antibody remarkably decreased pokeweed mitogen-induced IgM and

IgG production [33]. CD20 deficiency at the mature B lymphocyte stage could generate a transcriptional switch and metabolic reprogramming to promote the differentiation of long-lived PCs, implying that the timely removal of CD20 surface molecules might create an appropriate milieu for the development of PCs [8].

Activated CD20$^+$ B lymphocytes can present specific antigens to T lymphocytes in association with MHC molecules in the presence of various costimulatory factors, thus promoting T-cell activation and differentiation and producing a variety of cytokines and chemokines to regulate the maturation and migration of other immune effectors. CD20$^+$ B lymphocyte-induced effectors include T helper (Th) 1 cells, Th 17 cells, CD8$^+$ T cells, and myeloid cells, and these peripheral immune cells interact with the central nervous system (CNS) resident cells, secreting a range of proinflammatory mediators to induce inflammation within the CNS parenchyma and promoting neuronal demyelination in MS [34]. The anti-CD20-mediated B lymphocyte removal has been demonstrated to efficiently inhibit inflammatory pathogenesis and limit new disease activity [35]. In addition, compared with CD20$^-$ T lymphocytes, CD20$^+$ T lymphocytes more frequently produce interleukin (IL)-4, IL-17, interferon-γ, and tumor necrosis factor-α in MS [16]. These pieces of evidence disclose that CD20$^+$ lymphocytes can play a pathogenic role in antibody-independent pathways.

Perspectives on the development of anti-CD20 mAbs

Two types of anti-CD20 mAbs were developed successively to suppress tumor progression and inflammatory response in CD20$^+$ tumors and some autoimmune disorders. Type I anti-CD20 mAbs include RTX, ocrelizumab (OCR), ofatumumab (OFA), and ublituximab (Ub), preferentially targeting CD20 in the compartmentation of lipid rafts. Type II anti-CD20 mAbs, typified by obinutuzumab (OBZ), mainly target CD20 in nonlipid rafts [36].

Anti-CD20 mAbs delete CD20$^+$ target cells mainly by inducing (i) antibody-dependent cell-mediated cytotoxicity (ADCC) by linking the Fc domain of mAb to the Fcγ receptor (FcγR) on effector cells, (ii) complement-dependent cytotoxicity (CDC) by activating the complement C1q to form a membrane attack complex (MAC), (iii) apoptosis in the mitochondrial caspase pathway [37], and (iv) direct death in the noncaspase pathway. Although all of the anti-CD20 mAbs target identical antigens, they have their own biased binding epitopes of the CD20 molecule and different mechanisms of action and efficacy. Some of these drugs have been approved by the Food and Drug Administration (FDA) and European Medicines Agency (EMA) for use in certain autoimmune diseases of the nervous system, while others are still in clinical trials (Fig. 1).

RTX is a chimeric mAb-bearing murine antigen-binding domain linked to human IgG1 constant domains. Full-length RTX cross-links CD20 dimers into higher order circular assemblies, in which RTX homotypic Fab-Fab interactions enrich Fc domains to form an Fc hexamer platform for binding to complements [27,38]. Thus, RTX is highly efficient in CD20$^+$ B-lymphocyte depletion by CDCs. RTX-coated CD20$^+$ cells could also be deleted via ADCC pathways due to the linking of FcγRIII on natural killer (NK) cells with its Fc domain. In addition, RTX induces apoptosis, even in the absence of cross-linking with FcR [39]. The efficacy of RTX in peripheral blood CD20$^+$ cell removal has been confirmed in multiple autoimmune disorders of the nervous system. However, its B-lymphocyte clearance efficacy is not appreciated in the CNS and CSF due to the weak CNS permeability of RTX [40] and local

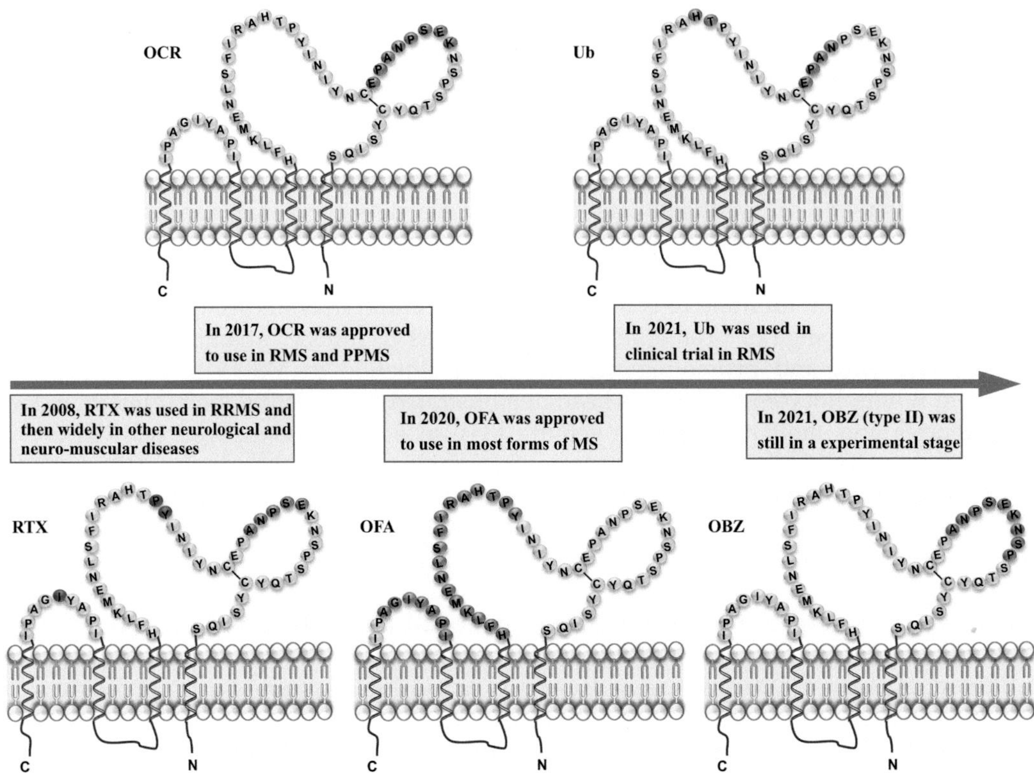

FIG. 1 The epitopes of CD20 and the evolution of anti-CD20 mAbs in neurological and neuromuscular diseases. The primary and second epitopes are colored *orange* and *pink*, respectively.

complement shortage [41]. Immune complexes formed by RTX and CD20 in lipid rafts may cross-link with FcγRIIb, thus leading to CD20 internalization from the surface of B lymphocytes and reduced clinical efficacy [42].

OCR is a recombinant humanized IgG1 derived from 2H7 and plays a greater role in the depletion of $CD20^+$ B lymphocytes via ADCC based on its higher affinity for FcγRIII receptors on NK cells but lower CDC than RTX [43]. OCR is the first anti-CD20 mAb to be approved by the FDA and EMA for relapsing MS (RMS) and primary progressive MS (PPMS) therapy [44,45]. Data from clinical trials identified the roles of OCR in the depletion of B lymphocytes and inhibition of disability progression [46–49].

OFA is an anti-CD20 IgG1κ and a fully human anti-CD20 mAb derived from 2F2 that exhibits a greater potency in recruiting complement and a slower off-rate than RTX, thus exerting a higher CDC efficacy [50]. Moreover, OFA presents appreciable cell lysis, even at a level of 4500 CD20 molecules/cell, while RTX activity is observed at a level of at least 30,000 CD20 molecules/cell [51]. As a fully human anti-CD20 mAb, OFA is safer because of its weaker immunogenicity, and it has been approved for the treatment of most forms of MS by the FDA and EMA in tandem [44].

Similar to RTX, Ub derived from the rat cell line YB2/0 also belongs to the type I chimeric anti-CD20 IgG1 mAb. Glycoengineering of the Fc domain of the anti-CD20 mAb improves its affinity to FcγRIII, thus inducing stronger ADCC [52]. Glycol-engineered Ub activates NK cells more efficiently at lower concentrations than RTX [53–55].

OBZ is a Fc-engineered humanized IgG1 anti-CD20 mAb [56]. Its glycol-engineered Fc domain is responsible for its higher affinity to FcγRIII on effector cells, such as NK cells and macrophages, and thus its stronger ADCC potency [57]. The potency of OBZ binding to CD20 on cells is about half of that for RTX. Compared with RTX, OBZ binding to CD20 mainly occurs in other regions of B lymphocytes instead of in lipid rafts and induces homotypic cell aggregation. OBZ shows a superior ability to induce direct cell death rather than classic apoptosis. Even in the absence of complement and immune effector cells, OBZ-induced cell death can be observed in normal human B lymphocytes [58]. In addition, OBZ shows very weak potency for complement recruitment, which is independent of CD20 levels on cells [59]. CD20 complexes with divalent Fabs fragments from RTX and OFA promote the oligomerization of IgG Fc domains for C1q recruitment, whereas CD20 complexes with monovalent binding to Fabs from OBZ lack Fc oligomerization and are unable to concatenate with additional molecules [38]. OBZ treatment depletes B lymphocytes in the blood, spleen, and brain in a MS animal model [60].

Clinic implications of CD20 as a therapeutic target in neurological and neuromuscular diseases

CD20 in autoimmune diseases in the CNS

Immunotherapy is the major treatment for autoimmune diseases. In the acute process, most patients are treated with high-dose glucocorticoids, plasma exchange, intravenous immune globulin (IVIG), and tumor removal. If the patients are poorly responsive to the previous treatment, stronger immunotherapies are applied, such as anti-CD20 therapy, cyclophosphamide, and bortezomib. For the prevention of clinical exacerbation, glucocorticoids, disease-modifying therapy (DMT), and immunosuppressants are suggested for the patients with functional impairment or a high risk of relapse. Anti-CD20 therapy is a highly effective DMT for relapsing-remitting MS (RRMS), and OCR is a unique drug for PPMS. Anti-CD20 drugs are highly effective immune suppressants for refractory patients whose disease fails to respond to traditional immune suppressants. Nowadays, anti-CD20 therapy tends to be used as a first-line treatment for more neuroimmune diseases (Table 1).

CD20 and multiple sclerosis (MS)

MS is the most common chronic inflammatory, demyelinating, and neurodegenerative disease in the CNS [34], and three major phenotypes are observed as MS progresses. Reversible episodes of neurological dysfunction last several days or weeks in the early stages of MS (clinically isolated syndrome, CIS; RRMS). Over time, irreversible progressive clinical manifestations and cognitive deficits develop (secondary progressive MS, SPMS). A small percentage of

TABLE 1 Clinical manifestations and anti-CD20 therapy for neurological and neuromuscular diseases.

	Neuromuscular system					
Location	Muscle	Neuromuscular junction	Peripheral nerve	Central nervous system		
Disease	IIM	MG	CIDP	MS	NMOSD	AE
Epidemiology	Onset peak age: 50 Female: more common in DM, PM, and IMNM Male: more common in IBM Total prevalence: ~2.9–34 per 100,000.	Two onset peak age: 30, 70–80 Female vs male: 3 times in early onset Total prevalence: ~15–25 per 100,000.	Onset age: 40–50 Male vs female: 1.4–4.4 times Total prevalence: ~0.67–10.3 per 100,000.	Onset age: 20–35 in RRMS, 40 or over in PPMS Female vs male: 2–4 times Total prevalence: 2 per 100,000 in Asia, 1–2.5 per 1000 in Western.	Onset age: 28–44 Female vs male: 2.3–7.6 times Prevalence: 0.037 per 100,000 Caucasians in Australia, 2–10 per 100,000 in Asians and Blacks.	Great heterogeneity in onset age and sex Total prevalence: ~13.7 per 100,000.
Clinical manifestations	Proximal muscle weakness, cutaneous and systemic manifestations.	Muscle weakness and fatigability.	Progressive or recurrent weakness and paresthesia with diminished reflexes.	Reversible episodes at initial stages, irreversible clinical/cognitive deficits with development. Progressive disease course occurs at onset in PPMS.	Optic nerve, spinal cord, area postrema of the dorsal medulla, brainstem, diencephalon, or cerebrum.	Psychosis, seizures, cognitive deficits, abnormal movements, dysautonomia, disturbance of consciousness.
Main mechanism	In DM, MAC on the endothelial cells leads to muscle fiber destruction by resembling micro-infarcts; B cells and plasmacytoid cells secrete Abs. In PM and IBM, the CD8-MHC-I complex is a characteristic manifestation. CTL effect, a degenerative component in IBM, IMNM.	Anti-AChR: MAC, blocks the AChR-binding site, after receptor cross-link, and AChR internalization. Anti-Musk: block the interaction between MuSK and LRP4 Anti-LRP4: Not clear.	Classical CIDP: activated T cells and macrophage and Abs go across the blood-nerve barrier to induce demyelination. IgG4-associated CIDP: inhibit the formation of CNTN1/CASPR/NF155 complex; NF186/140 induces the absence of microvilli and reversible proximal conduction block.	In early MS, innate and adaptive immune systems together with resident-activated microglia and astrocytes damage oligodendrocyte through cell contact-dependent mechanisms and soluble factors (Abs and complements, etc.) In late MS, neurodegeneration and CNS-compartmentalized inflammation are the main contributors.	B cells undergo differentiation into AQP4-IgG-specific PCs in the peripheral. AQP4 internalization, decreased expression, modification function, glutamate excitotoxicity, ADCC, and CDC.	In the brain and peripheral, B cells undergo differentiation into Ab-producing PCs. Functional blocking of the target antigen ($GABA_bR$), cross-linking and internalization (NMDAR), and disruption of protein-protein interaction (LGI1).

Anti-CD20 therapy	RTX: usually effective in refractory cases, 78.3% Responsiveness, steroid-sparing, ↓ clinical activity, better response in MSA$^+$ cases, especially in anti-Jo1 or anti-Mi2 IIM.	RTX: usually effective in refractory cases,↑ clinical status, quality of life, ↓ traditional immunomodulatory therapies, and steroid-sparing, especially for anti-MuSK MG.	RTX: usually effective in refractory cases, 75% responsiveness, excellent responses (90%–100%) in IgG4-associated CIDP.	In RRMS, high-efficacy therapy. RTX: ↓ ARR, EDSS score and CELs. OCR: ↓ ARR, EDSS score, CELs, new T2 lesion, brain volume, and disability progression vs IFNβ-1a. OFA: ↓ ARR, EDSS score, CDW, CELs, new T2 lesion, serum neurofilament light chain vs teriflunomide. In PPMS, OCR: ↓ disability progression, walk impairment, T2 lesion, and brain volume.	RTX: prevent clinical exacerbations (first-line treatment), ↓ ARR, EDSS score, without steroid-sparing.	RTX: effective (second-line immunotherapy), applicable (initial treatment). 72.2% responsiveness, ↓ Mean mRS score, and relapses rate.
Supplement	Anti-Jo1 or anti-Mi2 Abs patients achieved significant improvement compared with other MSAs. Reduce cutaneous disease activity. Untreatable in IBM.	Anti-MuSK MG achieved excellent effect with RTX treatment, while the effect is controversial in anti-AChR MG.	–	RTX failed in PPMS. Untreatable in inactive SPMS.	Ub (Phase I open-label study): no serious adverse, ↓ EDSS scores in 90 days.	RTX has better efficacy in Anti-NMADR AE vs others. RTX and tocilizumab combination has better efficacy in refractory cases.

patients present a progressive disease course beginning at onset (PPMS). The representative pathological characteristic of MS is the formation of demyelinating lesions in the brain, spinal cord, and optic nerve [34,61,62].

Current research shows that bidirectional interactions participate in the pathophysiological process of MS among immune cells including T lymphocytes, B lymphocytes, and myeloid cells in the periphery and resident cells including microglia and astrocytes in the CNS [34]. Nonneuronal cells in the CNS secrete diverse inflammatory mediators to recruit inflammatory cells, resulting in demyelination and local inflammation [63,64]. During MS relapse, numerous peripheral immune cells infiltrate the CNS parenchyma [65], and together with resident-activated microglia and astrocytes, lead to subsequent oligodendrocyte injury, demyelination, and neuroaxonal injury through cell contact-dependent mechanisms and soluble factors (immunoglobulin, complements, and cytokines) (Fig. 2A). In the later stages of MS, most infiltrating immune cells into the CNS are diminished [66]. However, CNS-compartmentalized inflammation is still evident, and it involves CNS-resident immune cells and meningeal immune cells ($CD8^+$ T lymphocytes and PCs) forming lymphoid-like structures [67]. In addition to inflammatory mechanisms, neurodegeneration, acute or chronic oxidative stress, mitochondrial dysfunction, ferroptosis, and glutamate homeostasis are all critical contributors to ongoing CNS injury [68].

MS therapies include the management of acute attacks and the prevention of clinical exacerbation. When an acute attack occurs upon initial diagnosis or during relapse, the first-line treatment is high-dose intravenous methylprednisolone, while plasma exchange is reserved for poorly responsive patients or rescue treatment [62]. The latest MS guideline, which was presented in ECTRIMS 2021, suggested that anti-CD20 therapy is an optional strategy for RRMS and inactive SPMS. DMT is used to prevent clinical exacerbation of MS. Two types of initial DMT treatments are optional for RRMS: low-efficacy therapy and high-efficacy therapy. Low-efficacy therapy starts with a safe but moderately effective traditional DMT, while high-efficacy therapy starts with highly effective drugs (such as RTX, OFA, OCR, alemtuzumab, and natalizumab) to prevent the accumulation of CNS damage and clinical exacerbations [69]. Therapeutic options for active SPMS, including all DMTs, are approved for treating RRMS in the United States; but, there is no clear indication for inactive SPMS. On the other hand, OFA and siponimod are the only two drugs with sufficient evidence for active SPMS. For PPMS, OCR is unique based on a large randomized controlled trial (RCT), which is also recommended in Canadian MS Working Group Recommendations [70].

In 2008, the effectiveness of RTX was evaluated by an important randomized, double-blinded, placebo-controlled multicenter clinical trial (HERMES) in 104 patients over 48 weeks. In the RTX group, the proportion of clinical relapses was significantly lower than that in the placebo group at week 24 (14.5% vs 34.3%) and week 48 (20.3% vs 40.0%). Incredibly, a 91% reduction in the cumulative number of gadolinium-enhancing lesions was maintained until week 48 [71]. Later, a large multicenter cohort study ($n=822$) of RTX in RRMS from Sweden showed a significantly low annualized relapse ratio (ARR) of 0.044 and an unaltered median expanded disability status scale (EDSS) score over the follow-up period with RTX [72].

Similar, large clinical trials (OPERA I and OPERA II) of OCR on RMS enrolled 821 and 835 adults respectively, and lasted 96 weeks. Both trials showed a significant decrease in the ARR in patients treated with OCR compared with those treated with IFNβ-1a. Significantly better radiological performance was found for OCR than for IFNβ-1a (94% lower number of lesions with OCR) [47].

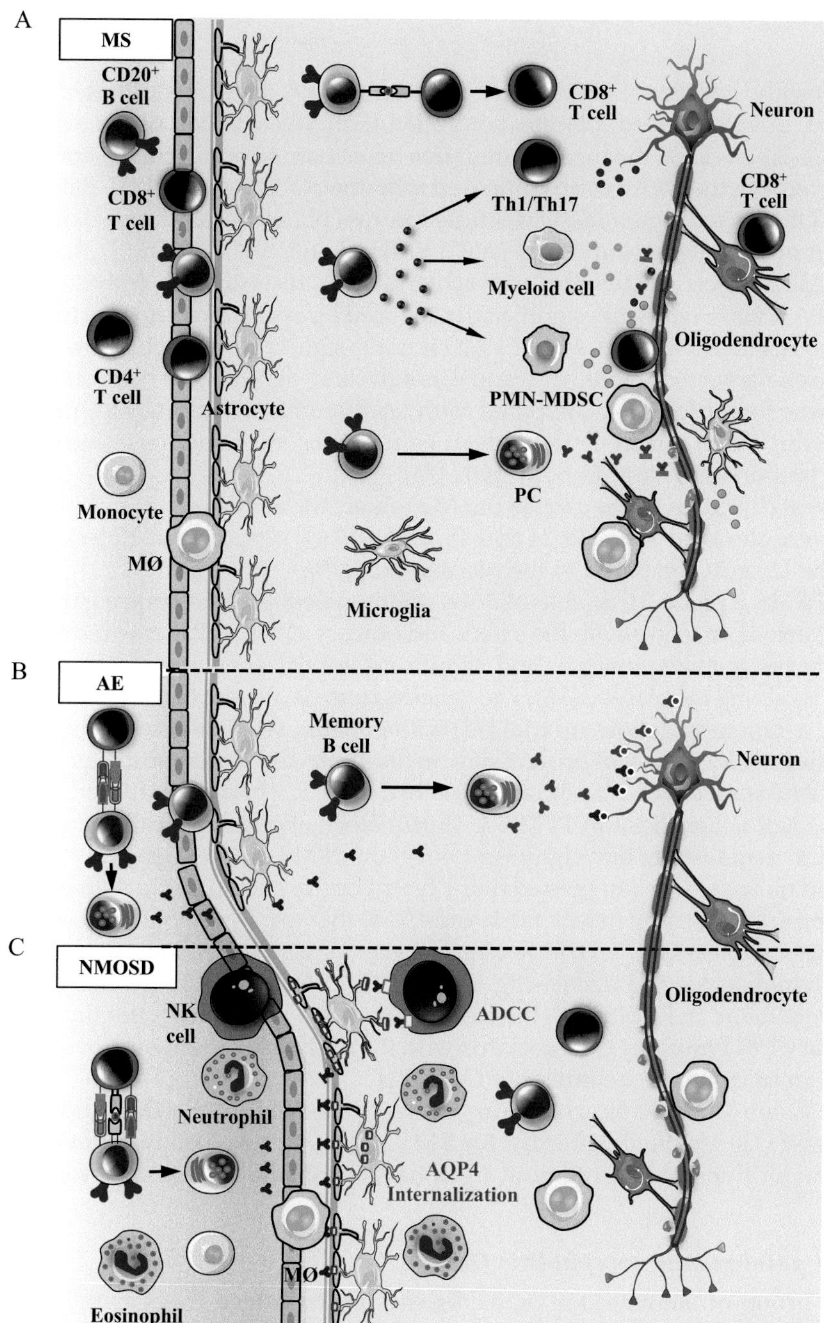

FIG. 2 Different roles of B cells in the pathogenesis of the CNS inflammatory diseases. (A) In MS, B lymphocytes differentiate into PCs and secrete antibodies that contribute to CNS inflammation via opsonization of CNS antigens and complement fixation; B lymphocytes activate CNS-specific pathogenic effector T cells; different subsets of B lymphocytes modulate T lymphocytes, myeloid cells, and PMN-MDSC functions by secreting pro- and antiinflammatory cytokines. (B) In AE, B lymphocytes that are exposed to the processed antigens differentiate into antibody-producing PCs in conjunction with T cells. After entering the brain, memory B cells undergo differentiation into PCs. The presence of antibodies against neuronal surface proteins in the brain may lead to neuronal dysfunction. (C) In NMOSD, B lymphocytes activate T lymphocytes as APCs and produce cytokines. B lymphocytes may also be activated by T lymphocytes and secrete AQP4-antibodies. Circulating AQP4-specific IgG enters the CNS and binds to AQP4 on astrocytes' feet. Various types of infiltrating immune cells are present, including NK cells, macrophages, neutrophils, eosinophils, B lymphocytes, and T lymphocytes.

More recently, additional RRMS treatments have been developed. Phase II, multicenter, randomized, double-blinded, placebo-controlled trials were carried out to evaluate the efficacy of OFA. At week 12, the mean cumulative new contrast-enhancing lesions (CELs) were reduced by 65% in the OFA group compared with the placebo group [73]. Subsequently, the efficacy of OFA vs teriflunomide was studied in two phase III multicenter, double-blinded, double-dummy, parallel-group trials (ASCLEPIOS I and ASCLEPIOS II) that enrolled 927 and 955 RMS subjects (RRMS and few active SPMS), respectively. Both studies explored ARR for OFA arms, which were significantly reduced by over 50% compared to teriflunomide arms. In the ASCLEPIOS I and ASCLEPIOS II trials, significant reductions in confirmed disability worsening were observed at 3 and 6 months and significantly better radiological performance was found for OFA compared with teriflunomide. A significant milestone was a dramatic reduction of serum neurofilament light chain concentrations in the OFA arm relative to the teriflunomide arm in both trials [74].

The newest clinical trial was carried out to evaluate the activity of Ub in 48 RRMS subjects. No CELs were observed at weeks 24 and 48, and a 10.6% reduction in T2 lesion volume was found in the Ub arm compared to the placebo arm [75].

For the PPMS, a phase III, double-blinded, randomized, placebo-controlled trial (ORATORIO) was carried out to evaluate the safety and efficacy of OCR. Patients receiving OCR had significantly better motor function and significant improvements in radiological endpoints than those receiving the placebo [76]. The benefits from OCR were further confirmed in PPMS patients by a long-term, follow-up trial [77] with patients, who initially received OCR, showing a significantly lower risk of progression on disability and better radiological performance than those who started with placebo and switched to OCR. This trial indicated that early treatment with OCR is beneficial in PPMS. Unfortunately, another clinical trial (OLYMPUS) of RTX failed to demonstrate any significant effect on PPMS progression [78].

More and more evidence suggested that T lymphocytes should be considered to be another target of anti-CD20 therapy in MS. First, anti-CD20 therapy was depleting not only $CD20^{+}$ B lymphocytes, but also $CD3^{+}CD20^{+}$ T lymphocytes in MS [9]. Second, increasing control of effector T lymphocytes and decreasing of T lymphocyte autoreactivity and CNS-migratory capacity were found in RRMS with the treatment of OFA [10]. Third, over time a progressive reduction of $CD8^{+}$ lymphocytes associated with the disability progression over the follow-up was found in MS with the treatment of OCR [11].

In general, anti-CD20 therapy has a surprisingly beneficial effect on MS, and different strategies of anti-CD20 are highly effective for RMS and show remarkably better outcomes than IFNβ-1a and teriflunomide. Until now, OCR has remained a unique drug for PPMS.

CD20 and autoimmune encephalitis (AE)

AE is a group of autoimmune brain diseases characterized by prominent neurological symptoms and linked with antibodies against neuronal cell-surface proteins. The most common subtypes are as follows: (i) anti-*N*-methyl-D-aspartate-receptor (NMDAR) encephalitis, (ii) antileucine-rich, glioma-inactivated 1 (LGI1) encephalitis, and (iii) anticontactin-associated protein 2 (CASPR2) encephalitis [79]. Common clinical features include limbic lobe syndrome (psychosis, seizures, memory loss), cognitive deficits, abnormal movements, dysautonomia, and a decreased consciousness [80].

Two major triggers for AE are infection and tumors [81–83]. It is postulated that antigens released by infection-damaged neurons or tumor cells are presented to antigen-presenting cells (APCs) and exposed to naïve B lymphocytes, which in turn differentiate into memory B lymphocytes and antibody-producing PCs in the presence of Th cells. After entering the brain, memory B lymphocytes undergo restimulation and differentiate into antibody-producing PCs [84]. Intrathecal, long-lived, autoantibody-secreting PCs were found in an anti-NMDAR encephalitis study (Fig. 2B) [84]. The different antibodies against neuron-surface proteins may lead to neuronal dysfunction with various clinical manifestations through diverse mechanisms, including antigen (antibody) blocking, cross-linking and internalization, and protein-protein interaction [83,85].

Treatment recommendations for AE are based on retrospective studies and expert opinions. The current treatment includes immunotherapy and tumor removal. For patients showing no clinical response to first-line treatment, RTX and cyclophosphamide are used as second-line treatments in most recommendations [86–88]. RTX is usually effective in refractory AE patients, and it gradually becomes an initial treatment since it reduces clinical relapse and demonstrates excellent clinical performance [80,89]. In 2016, a prospective, controlled trial identified the safety and efficacy of RTX as a second-line immunotherapy for autoimmune limbic encephalitis and showed that it did not have serious adverse effects, regardless of the autoantibody type [89]. A metaanalysis of the efficacy of RTX found that the positive functional outcome rate was 72.2%, the mean modified Rankin Scale (mRS) score was diminished by 2.67, and the percentage of relapse was 14.2% [90].

In (i) anti-NMDAR AE, early treatment with RTX significantly diminished the mRS score compared with delayed treatment. Relative to other subtypes of AE, the diminution of the mean mRS score was significantly higher in anti-NMDAR AE [90]. A similar result was obtained in a real-world trial, which indicated that independent living was achieved with RTX treatment (mRS Score ≤ 2) [91]. RTX treatment has been regarded as an independent factor for nonrelapsing patients in anti-NMDAR AE [92]. In (ii) anti-LGI1 AE, improvement is obtained under first-line treatment, with or without RTX treatment. In (iii) anti-CASPR2 AE, only RTX-treated patients were improved significantly, which was possibly because the IgG of anti-CASPR2 is the IgG4 subtype [91].

RTX can neither pass through the blood-brain barrier (BBB) nor eliminate memory B lymphocytes and long-lived PCs in the bone marrow and intrathecal space, which is the leading cause of its limited effects in refractory and recurrent AE. To enhance its efficacy, Lee et al. combined teratoma removal with SIRT (steroid-intravenous immune globulin-RTX and tocilizumab) treatment for anti-NMDAR AE. SIRT had good therapeutic effects with lower clinical scores than SIR or SI therapy. SIRT treatment within the first month was recommended to achieve the best outcome if the generally delayed course was less effective [93].

In general, RTX is safe and effective as a second-line immunotherapy for AE, especially for anti-NMDAR encephalitis. In addition, RTX could significantly reduce relapse in the long term (Table 1).

CD 20 and neuromyelitis optica spectrum disorder (NMOSD)

NMOSD is a rare inflammatory CNS disease in which the core clinical characteristics involve any of 6 CNS regions: optic nerve, spinal cord, area postrema of the dorsal medulla, diencephalon, cerebrum, or brainstem. The diagnosis of NMOSD is primarily supported by the IgG autoantibody against aquaporin 4 (AQP4), which is mainly expressed in astrocytes and particularly concentrated at the astrocyte end-feet contacting microcapillary endothelial cells [94].

AQP4-IgG is mainly produced by PCs differentiated from B lymphocytes following stimulation with IL6 in the peripheral circulation and rarely found in the CSF [95]. Infection may transiently trigger the breakdown of the BBB, thus allowing AQP4-IgG entry, especially in relatively vulnerable regions and damaged areas (Fig. 2C) [94]. The binding of IgG to AQP4 can result in various functional consequences, such as further amplifying inflammation and contributing to additional oligodendrocyte injury, demyelination, and neuronal loss [96].

Therapy for NMOSD includes the management of acute attacks and the prevention of clinical exacerbations. For the prevention of clinical exacerbation, eculizumab, inebilizumab, or satralizumab are recommended against other traditional immunosuppressive agents [97]. If not available, azathioprine (AZA), mycophenolate mofetil (MMF), and RTX have been considered effective therapies [98].

Some recommendation guidelines suggested that RTX has been used as a first-line therapy for the prevention of clinical exacerbation in NMOSD [98–100]. In a single-blinded placebo-controlled trial (RIN-1), no subject relapsed in the RTX arm, 37% of subjects relapsed in the placebo arm, and steroid sparing was not found in the RTX arm [101]. Other data indicated that the mean ARR was significantly lower after RTX treatment and even lower than that of AZA, although no significant differences were found among RTX, MMF, cyclophosphamide, and cyclosporin A. A similar result was shown for the EDSS scores [102]. RTX can eliminate the $CD20^+$ lymphocytes in peripheral blood and as well disrupt the activity of the germinal centers (lymph nodes) by impacting the affinity of matured B lymphocytes and antibodies in NMOSD. A single-center, phase I, open-label study of Ub add-on therapy was carried out in 5 NMOSD patients, showing the expected decreases in EDSS scores. However, two patients relapsed with residual B lymphocytes [103].

In general, RTX is a safe and effective immunotherapy for preventing clinical exacerbations of NMOSD, and shows significantly reduced relapse but no steroid sparing compared with AZA and placebo (Table 1).

Anti-CD20 therapy is also used in other CNS autoimmune diseases, such as acute disseminated encephalomyelitis [104] and myelin-oligodendrocyte glycoprotein antibody-associated disease [105]. Although RTX could reduce ARR, relapse would still appear, with the total depletion of B lymphocytes. More prospective trials should be carried out to evaluate the efficacy of anti-CD20 therapy for CNS autoimmune diseases.

Clinic implications of CD20 as a therapeutic target in neuromuscular disease

CD20 and myasthenia-gravis (MG)

MG is an autoimmune disorder associated with autoantibodies directed against the acetylcholine receptor (AChR), muscle-specific kinase (MuSK), and lipoprotein-related protein 4 (LRP4) in the postsynaptic membrane at the neuromuscular junction [106–109], with antibodies binding to affect neuromuscular function, which leads to the characteristic manifestations of MG, namely, muscle weakness and fatigability [106–109].

Different subtypes of MG have diverse immune mechanisms. The anti-AChR type has been intensively studied. AChR is presented to $CD4^+$ T lymphocytes by APCs and successively activates mature T and B lymphocytes in the thymus [110]. A large number of germinal centers with B lymphocytes and PCs are found in the hyperplastic thymus. Meanwhile, upregulated regulatory T and Th17 cells induce immune imbalance. Short-lived PCs from peripheral circulation, together with long-lived PCs from bone marrow and thymus, secrete anti-AChR antibodies, thereby promoting the occurrence of MG (Fig. 3A).

Generally, therapy for MG includes a combination of symptomatic therapy, immunosuppressive therapy, short-term therapy, thymectomy, and biologics. With remaining functional impairment after symptomatic treatment, patients should receive immunotherapy, including steroids and other immunosuppressants [108,109]. Eculizumab is approved for the treatment of refractory MG by inhibiting complement activation. RTX has already been widely used in refractory MG due to its remarkable efficacy [110].

In severe MG, such as anti-MuSK MG, RTX can be administered if first-line immunosuppressive therapies fail, effectively depleting the cells that produce IgG4 antibodies [111]. In a multicenter, blinded, prospective clinical review of RTX in anti-MuSK MG, 58% of patients, who reached the primary endpoint with RTX, were significantly better than 16% of controls for 3.5 years. Furthermore, remarkable steroid-sparing and decreasing immunosuppressant usage were found in the RTX group [112]. However, steroid sparing was not found in a randomized, double-blinded, placebo-controlled, multicenter phase-2 trial in mild-moderate anti-AChR MG with RTX [113]. For severe and refractory anti-AChR generalized MG, the primary endpoint was achieved in only one patient, while improvement of muscular function for at least 12 months was observed in half of the patients [114]. Moreover, both anti-MuSK and anti-AChR achieved minimal manifestation or better with RTX, while greater benefits were observed for anti-MuSK [111]. International Consensus Guidance suggested that RTX should be considered as an early therapeutic option in patients with anti-MuSK MG, who have an unsatisfactory response to initial immunotherapy. And the efficacy of RTX in refractory AChR-Ab+ MG is uncertain. It is an option if patients fail or do not tolerate other immunosuppressive agents [115].

In addition, RTX may have a similar effect and lower incidence of adverse events than eculizumab [116]. Significant differences were not observed in the anti-AChR MG patients in terms of clinical status improvements or adverse effects between the low and routine RTX dose groups [117]. Recently, OFA was used for refractory anti-AChR MG patients, who were allergic to RTX and achieved excellent outcomes [118].

In general, RTX is a safe and effective immunotherapy for refractory MG, especially for anti-MuSK MG, and it shows remarkable steroid sparing, improved clinical status, and decreased immunosuppressant usage. However, a steroid-sparing effect was not found in mild-moderate anti-AChR MG (Table 1).

CD20 and chronic inflammatory demyelinating polyradiculoneuropathy (CIDP)

CIDP is an autoimmune disorder that affects the peripheral nerves and nerve roots and often causes chronic progressive or recurrent weakness and paresthesia with diminished reflexes. CIDPs are generally divided into typical and atypical CIDPs. Typical CIDP includes symmetric sensory-motor involvement, while atypical CIDP includes asymmetric, focal, or distal motor and sensory involvement.

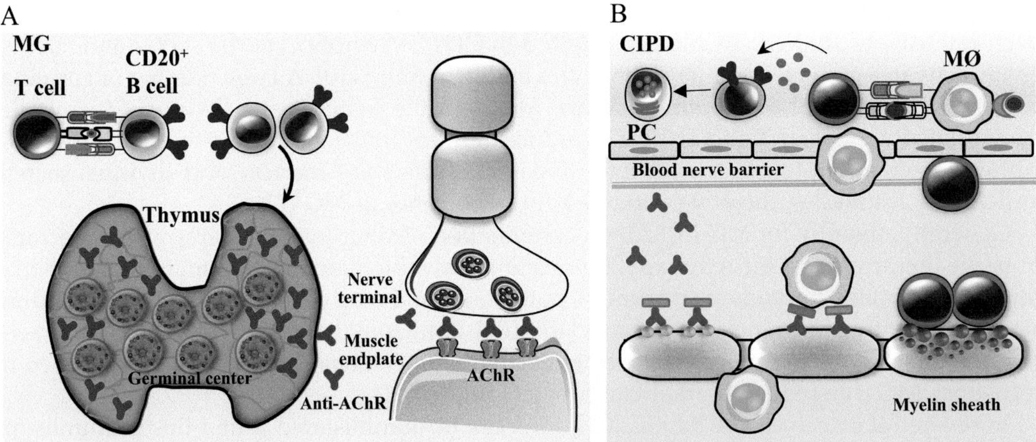

FIG. 3 The pathogenesis of neuromuscular disease. (A) In anti-AChR MG, $CD4^+$ T lymphocytes are activated by antigen-presenting cells. A large number of germinal centers with B lymphocytes and PCs are in the hyperplasia thymus. PCs secrete anti-AChR antibodies, damaging AChR. (B) In typical CIDP, macrophages, with their activated T lymphocytes go through the **blood-nerve barrier** to damage the myelin sheath. Resident T lymphocytes, macrophages, and antibodies secreted by B lymphocytes damage the myelin sheath.

The current hypothesis is that macrophages, activated T lymphocytes, and autoantibodies cross the blood-nerve barrier and work together to induce damage to the peripheral nerve [119]. The classical mechanism of typical CIDP is that macrophages induce the activation of T lymphocytes and both go through the blood-nerve barrier to damage the myelin sheath of the nerve. Resident T lymphocytes and macrophages induce B lymphocytes to secrete antibodies that constitute MACs with complement to damage the myelin sheath (Fig. 3B). One possible mechanism for atypical CIDP is associated with the IgG4 autoantibodies, which act against Ranvier's node proteins, including neurofascin isoform 155 (NF155), contactin-1 (CNTN1), contactin-associated protein-1 (CASPR1), and neurofascin isoforms 140 and 186 (NF140/NF186) [120].

Convincing data from RCTs indicate that two-thirds of patients achieve clinical improvement after treatment with corticosteroids, IVIG, and plasma exchange [119]. Approximately 25% of refractory patients may respond to other immunosuppressive agents, including RTX, AZA, MMF, etc. [121]. AZA, MMF, RTX, cyclophosphamide, and ciclosporin are used in cases of failure or as add-on medication with very low evidence in the European Academy of Neurology/Peripheral Nerve Society consensus guideline of 2021.

RTX is usually effective in refractory cases [122]. However, prospective, randomized, controlled studies for RTX are lacking. A recent metaanalysis found that the rate of responsiveness was 75% after RTX treatment [123]. All of the anti-IgG4 antibody-positive patients showed excellent responses to RTX treatment. In a real-life study, RTX was administered in IgG4 antibody-associated CIDP patients, who did not respond to first-line treatments. Of the 14 patients, 13 patients showed great improvement after 6 months. Unfortunately, one anti-CNTN1 patient with membranous glomerulonephritis died shortly after the first RTX treatment [124]. A retrospective cohort study in chronic immune-mediated sensorimotor neuropathies found excellent outcomes in autoantibody-associated neuropathies and Lewis-Sumner syndrome with RTX [125]. OCR has been used for refractory CIDP patients, resulting in partial recovery without relapses or any adverse events [126].

In general, RTX is a safe and effective immunotherapy for refractory patients with approximately 75% responsiveness, especially for CIDP associated with IgG4 autoantibodies (Table 1).

CD20 and idiopathic inflammatory myopathies (IIMs)

IIMs have been classified into six subtypes based on clinical and pathological characteristics and serological features: dermatomyositis (DM), antisynthetase syndrome (ASS), immune-mediated necrotizing myopathy (IMNM), inclusion body myositis (IBM), polymyositis (PM), and overlap myositis [127,128].

Available data have shown that many adaptive, innate immune mechanisms and nonimmune mechanisms are involved in the pathophysiological processes of IIMs [129]. In DM, the MAC is activated early and deposited on endothelial cells, thus leading to muscle fiber destruction by resembling microinfarcts [128,130,131]. Activated complement and cytokines activate macrophages, $CD4^+$ T lymphocytes, B lymphocytes, and $CD123^+$ plasmacytoid dendritic cells. Antibodies secreted by B lymphocytes and plasmacytoid cells, including Mi-2, melanoma differentiation-associated protein-5, transcriptional intermediary factor-1γ, and nuclear matrix protein-2 participate in myofiber damage and capillary damage in regions of the endomysium [127]. The roles of activated B lymphocytes or plasmacytoid dendritic cells, respectively, in PM and DM are still unknown, perhaps involving antigen presentation or cytokine and antibody release. And the mechanism of IMNM is also unclear; recent studies suggest that antisignal recognition particle (anti-SRP) and anti-hydroxy-3-methylglutaryl-CoA reductase (anti-HMGCR) autoantibodies could bind to the muscle membrane surface to form MAC, subsequently damaging muscle [132].

Glucocorticoids are the first-line therapy in the treatment of IIMs, while immunosuppressive drugs are increasingly used in the early phases. RTX is the only biologic agent widely used in IIMs in refractory cases with recommendations by the guidelines [133].

RTX is usually effective in refractory cases [134–136]. A randomized trial of RTX in myositis (RIM) [137] failed to achieve the primary endpoint. However, the RTX group was able to reduce the clinical activity with significant steroid sparing. A total of 83% of patients received the definition of improvement with RTX. In a post hoc analysis, myositis with autoantibodies was the major predictive factor for clinical improvement after RTX treatment, and patients with anti-Jo1 or anti-Mi2 antibodies presented a significantly higher rate of improvement than patients with other myositis-specific autoantibodies (MSAs). Further analyzing the cutaneous features in the RIM trial, a significant overall improvement in cutaneous disease activity was found in the RTX group [138]. A systematic review evaluating the efficacy of RTX in the treatment of myositis found that the rate of therapeutic response was 78.3% and the majority of patients with MSA showed a beneficial response with long-term remission [134]. In a retrospective case series of nine patients with anti-HMGCR refractory IMNM, who were treated with RTX, only one-third of the patients improved [139].

In general, RTX is a safe and effective immunotherapy for refractory DM, PM, and ASS patients, with nearly 80% improvement and remarkable steroid sparing, especially for patients with MSA. Only one-third of refractory IMNM patients improved with RTX treatment (Table 1).

Anti-CD20 therapy is also used in other autoimmune neuromuscular diseases, such as multifocal motor neuropathy, neuropathy with antimyelin-associated glycoprotein antibodies [140], and Lambert-Eaton myasthenic syndrome [141]. RTX was suggested to be effective and relatively safe in small trials; however, large multicenter RCTs of anti-CD20 therapy need to be carried out for neuromuscular patients.

Based on the pharmacological properties of anti-CD20 therapy, different types of monitoring strategies have been reported. The first strategy is repeating RTX infusions every 6 months without monitoring, because RTX can effectively eliminate the $CD20^+$ cells for 5–8 months; but, after long-time treatment, the RTX may develop resistance due to the antibodies for RTX. The second strategy is monitoring of RTX effects by counting the $CD19^+$ or $CD20^+$ circulating cells; and repeating RTX infusions when $CD19^+$ or $CD20^+$ cells become detectable (over 0.01×10^9/L) [142] or more than 0.1% of total lymphocytes [143]. The third strategy is monitoring RTX effects by counting the $CD19^+$ $CD27^+$ circulating cells, which correspond to memory B cells; and repeating RTX infusions when $CD27^+$ cells are more than 0.05% of total lymphocytes [143]. Some studies think that the recurrent risk of the disease is more correlated with the reemergence of memory B cells than total B cells [144,145]. Other anti-CD20 therapy (such as OFA, OCA), which are mainly used in MS, are monitored using clinical symptoms, imaging, and biomarkers. Nevertheless, none of the monitoring strategies is an absolute guarantee against the risk of relapse [146,147].

Although anti-CD20 therapy is a very effective immunotherapy, the process of the disease still cannot be controlled with appropriate anti-CD20 therapy. The most important reason is that the main target of anti-CD20 is B cells, with plasma cells and T cells. Therefore, defective therapeutic efficacy was found in neuroimmunological diseases in which the main disease mechanism is not B cell, but T cell (paraneoplastic neurological syndromes). In addition, due to long-lived plasma cells, the humoral immune-mediated immune process cannot be completely controlled. Another reason is the BBB, is poorly permeable to CD20 antibody. However, central nervous system's immune diseases exist intrathecal immunoglobulins synthesis, thus intrathecal humoral immunity was not controlled by anti-CD20 therapy. Therefore, in response to the above problems and disease-specific pathogenesis, some new therapeutic methods have been developed and proved to have some effect. First, as the target for plasma cells, anti-CD38 (daratumumab), anti-IL-6R (tocilizumab), and an inhibitor of the 26S proteasome (bortezomib) can inhibit the different physiological processes of plasma cells, so as to achieve the effect of suppressing humoral immunity, which has been more and more used. Second, as the target for BBB, physical breakthrough (intrathecal injection), small molecule (tofacitinib), and biological protocol (chimeric antigen receptor T-cell immunotherapy) have been used in the clinic with good outcome [148]. In addition, as for disease-specific pathogenesis, terminal complement inhibitor such as eculizumab has achieved a significantly lower risk of relapse in $APQ4^+$ NMO patients [149] while FcRn antagonist such as efgartigimod has showed a rapid and long-lasting disease improvement in 75% AChR-Ab+ MG patients [150].

Anti-CD20 therapy-related adverse events

Biological agents have frequently been administered for autoimmune disorders of the nervous and neuromuscular systems. The anti-CD20 mAbs represent a promising therapy for patients, although it is associated with adverse events, including infusion-related reactions (IRRs), infections, hypogammaglobulinemia, and neoplasms.

IRRs are the most common adverse event reported with anti-CD20 mAbs, and they present multiple symptoms, including itching, rash, fever, throat irritation, nausea, headache, dizziness, hypotension, bronchospasms, or angioedema [47]. Moreover, IRRs occur in MS patients treated with distinct anti-CD20 mAbs, whether chimeric, humanized, or human. Compared with the placebo group, IRRs were more frequent after the first infusion in RRMS patients with RTX treatment (78.3% and 40.0%) but less frequent after the second infusion in the RTX group (20.3% and 40%) [71]. Approximately 34.3% of RRMS patients treated with OCR showed IRRs [47], and a similar probability of IRRs was reported in another phase III trial of RRMS and PMS with OCR therapy [48].

Therapeutic anti-CD20 mAbs can activate a variety of effector cells. Effector NK cells also kill healthy CD20$^+$ cells, thus leading to long-lasting cellular immunosuppression in MS or NMOSD patients with anti-CD20 therapies, increasing susceptibility to infections, mainly in the respiratory and urinary systems [40,151], and predisposing patients to opportunistic CNS infections [7]. Although similar incidences of infections were observed in the RTX-treated and placebo groups (71.4% and 69.7%) in the first phase II study of MS, a higher incidence of urinary tract infections and sinusitis was found in the RTX-treated group [47,76].

Human CD20 deficiency results in decreased IgG antibody levels and relatively increased IgM levels, with weak responses against polysaccharides after vaccination [152]. Although CD20 is not presented on PCs, therapeutic anti-CD20 mAbs are associated with reduced immunoglobin levels. RTX may decrease serum IgG levels to some degree [72], and hypogammaglobulinemia may occur in patients with long-term treatment [153].

Immunosuppressive drugs could influence immunological tumor surveillance, resulting in neoplasms. Sporadic cases of malignancies have been reported in RTX-treated or OCR-treated MS patients [72,76]. The pooled prevalence of neoplasms is 1 in 100,000 in RTX-treated MS patients [154]. Compared with the general population, MS patients treated with RTX do not show a greater prevalence of neoplasms over the long term.

Collectively, the current clinical data on MS patient show that, compared with RTX, OCR is competitive and leads to fewer IRRs after the first infusion while OFA is a better choice and presents a relatively lower incidence of IRRs after the first infusion and infections, and significant differences were not observed in serious infection and neoplasm.

Conclusions

Although there is an urgent need for in-depth mechanistic studies, CD20$^+$ lymphocytes have been proven to play a critical role in certain functions associated with BCR signaling and immunopathology. The satisfactory curative effect of anti-CD20 therapy has further demonstrated the prominent position of $CD20^+$ cells in neurological and neuromuscular diseases. RTX is limited in killing $CD20^+$ cells at relatively higher levels and shows weak efficacy with complement shortages in the CNS due to its low penetrability of the BBB. The glycol-engineered Fc domain endows Ub with stronger ADCC than RTX, albeit with similar immunogenic problems. Although humanized OCR and OFA have been approved for use in some types of MS, clinical investigations about their long-term safety are still required to evaluate the risk of certain serious adverse events. OBZ offers better safety and tolerability due to its nature as a fully human anti-CD20 IgG and its unique mechanism of action, although more studies on OBZ as a treatment for neurological and neuromuscular diseases are ongoing.

Moreover, since some $CD20^+$ cells act as antiinflammatory agents, next-generation anti-CD20 mAbs might be developed based on certain synergistic roles to selectively delete inflammatory $CD20^+$ targets while maintaining antiinflammatory $CD20^+$ cells. A bispecific antibody that targets CD20 and CD3 has been created for lymphomas, and they can recruit T lymphocytes to increase the effect and represent a new therapeutic option. In addition, the administration method and cost should be taken into consideration. Overall, anti-CD20 therapy for neurologic autoimmune disease has great promise; however, more basic investigations and clinical trials need to be conducted.

Acknowledgments

This work is supported by the Natural Science Foundation of China (Grant No. 82171452 and No. 82060588); Joint Foundation of Translational Medicine and Interdisciplinary Research (Grant No. ZNJC202230); Translational Medicine and Interdisciplinary Research Joint Fund of Zhongnan Hospital of Wuhan University (Grant No. ZNLH 201909); and the Medical Science Advancement Program of Wuhan University (no. TFJC2018001 and TFLC2018001).

References

[1] Eon Kuek L, et al. The MS4A family: counting past 1, 2 and 3. Immunol Cell Biol 2016;94(1):11–23.

[2] Klein CL, Schafer A, Georges W, Schwaiger G, Mossner M, Hopfner E, Umana KP, Niederfellner G. Epitope interactions of monoclonal antibodies targeting CD20 and their relationship to functional properties. MAbs 2013;5(1):22–33.

[3] Tedder TF, Schlossman SF. Phosphorylation of the B1 (Cd20) molecule by normal and malignant human lymphocytes-B. J Biol Chem 1988;263(20):10009–15.

[4] Valentine MA, Cotner T, Gaur L, Torres R, Clark EA. Expression of the human B-cell surface protein CD20_ alteration by phorbol 12-myristate 13-acetate. Proc Natl Acad Sci U S A 1987;84(22):5.

[5] Pavlasova G, Mraz M. The regulation and function of CD20: an "enigma" of B-cell biology and targeted therapy. Haematologica 2020;105(6):1494–506.

[6] Sellebjerg F, Blinkenberg M, Sorensen PS. Anti-CD20 monoclonal antibodies for relapsing and progressive multiple sclerosis. CNS Drugs 2020;34(3):269–80.

[7] Focosi D, Tuccori M, Maggi F. Progressive multifocal leukoencephalopathy and anti-CD20 monoclonal antibodies: what do we know after 20 years of rituximab. Rev Med Virol 2019;29(6), e2077.

[8] Klasener K, et al. CD20 as a gatekeeper of the resting state of human B cells. Proc Natl Acad Sci U S A 2021;118(7).

[9] Quendt C, et al. Proinflammatory CD20(+) T cells are differentially affected by multiple sclerosis therapeutics. Ann Neurol 2021;90(5):834–9.

[10] von Essen MR, et al. Ofatumumab modulates inflammatory T cell responses and migratory potential in patients with multiple sclerosis. Neurol Neuroimmunol Neuroinflamm 2022;9(4).

[11] Capasso N, Palladino R, Cerbone V, et al. Ocrelizumab effect on humoral and cellular immunity in multiple sclerosis and its clinical correlates: a 3-year observational study. J Neurol 2023;270(1):272–82.

[12] Loken MR, Shah VO, Dattilio KL, Civin CI. Flow cytometric analysis of human bone marrow. II. Normal B lymphocyte development. Blood 1987;70(5):1316–24.

[13] Stashenko P, Nadler LM, Hardy R, Schlossman SF. Expression of cell surface markers after human B lymphocyte activation. Proc Natl Acad Sci U S A 1981;78(6):5.
[14] Hultin LE, et al. Cd20 (Pan-B cell) antigen is expressed at a low-level on a subpopulation of human lymphocytes-T. Cytometry 1993;14(2):196–204.
[15] Schuh E, et al. Features of human CD3+CD20+ T cells. J Immunol 2016;197(4):1111–7.
[16] von Essen MR, et al. Proinflammatory CD20+ T cells in the pathogenesis of multiple sclerosis. Brain 2019;142 (1):120–32.
[17] Mankai A, et al. Purine-rich box-1-mediated reduced expression of CD20 alters rituximab-induced lysis of chronic lymphocytic leukemia B cells. Cancer Res 2008;68(18):7512–9.
[18] Thévenin C, Lucas BP, Kozlow EJ, Kehrl JH. Cell type- and stage-specific expression of the CD20/B1 antigen correlates with the activity of a diverged octamer DNA motif present in its promoter. J Biol Chem 1993;268 (8):5949–56.
[19] Winiarska M, et al. Prenyltransferases regulate CD20 protein levels and influence anti-CD20 monoclonal antibody-mediated activation of complement-dependent cytotoxicity. J Biol Chem 2012;287(38):31983–93.
[20] Batista FD, Harwood NE. The who, how and where of antigen presentation to B cells. Nat Rev Immunol 2009;9 (1):15–27.
[21] Lund FE. Cytokine-producing B lymphocytes-key regulators of immunity. Curr Opin Immunol 2008;20(3):7.
[22] Bubien JK, Zhou LJ, Bell PD, Frizzell RA, Tedder TF. Transfection of the CD20 cell surface molecule into ectopic cell types generates a Ca2+ conductance found constitutively in B lymphocytes. J Cell Biol 1993;121(5):12.
[23] Li H, et al. Store-operated cation entry mediated by CD20 in membrane rafts. J Biol Chem 2003;278(43):42427–34.
[24] Polyak MJ, Li H, Shariat N, Deans JP. CD20 homo-oligomers physically associate with the B cell antigen receptor. Dissociation upon receptor engagement and recruitment of phosphoproteins and calmodulin-binding proteins. J Biol Chem 2008;283(27):18545–52.
[25] Uchida J, et al. Mouse CD20 expression and function. Int Immunol 2004;16(1):119–29.
[26] Walshe CA, et al. Induction of cytosolic calcium flux by CD20 is dependent upon B cell antigen receptor signaling. J Biol Chem 2008;283(25):16971–84.
[27] Rougé L, Chiang N, Steffek M, Kugel C, Croll TI, Tam C, Estevez A, Arthur CP, Koth CM, Ciferri C, Kraft E, Payandeh J, Nakamura G, Koerber JT, Rohou A. Structure of CD20 in complex with the therapeutic monoclonal antibody rituximab. Science 2020;367(6483):7.
[28] Tedder TF, Engel P. CD20: a regulator of cell-cycle progression of B lymphocytes. Immunol Today 1994;15(9):5.
[29] Kneissl S, et al. CD19 and CD20 targeted vectors induce minimal activation of resting B lymphocytes. PLoS One 2013;8(11), e79047.
[30] Kläsener K, Maity PC, Hobeika E, Yang J, Reth M. B cell activation involves nanoscale receptor reorganizations and inside-out signaling by Syk. Elife 2014;3, e02069.
[31] Wise LM, Stohl W. Belimumab and rituximab in systemic lupus erythematosus: a tale of two B cell-targeting agents. Front Med 2020;7:303.
[32] Bar-Or A, et al. Abnormal B-cell cytokine responses a trigger of T-cell-mediated disease in MS? Ann Neurol 2010;67(4):452–61.
[33] Tedder TF, Forsgren A, Boyd AW, Nadler LM, Schlossman S. Antibodies reactive with the B1 molecule inhibit cell cycle progression but not activation of human B lymphocytes. Eur J Immunol 1986;168(8):7.
[34] Filippi M, et al. Multiple sclerosis. Nat Rev Dis Primers 2018;4(1):43.
[35] Li R, Rezk A, Miyazaki Y, Hilgenberg E, Touil H, Shen P, Moore CS, Michel L, Althekair F, Rajasekharan S, Gommerman JL, Prat A, Fillatreau S, Bar-Or A. Proinflammatory GM-CSF-producing B cells in multiple sclerosis and B cell depletion therapy. Sci Transl Med 2015;7(310).
[36] Graf J, et al. Targeting B cells to modify MS, NMOSD, and MOGAD: part 1. Neurol Neuroimmunol Neuroinflamm 2021;8(1).
[37] Cardarelli PM, et al. Binding to CD20 by anti-B1 antibody or F(ab')(2) is sufficient for induction of apoptosis in B-cell lines. Cancer Immunol Immunother 2002;51(1):15–24.
[38] Kumar A, Planchais C, Fronzes R, Mouquet H, Reyes N. Binding mechanisms of therapeutic antibodies to human CD20. Science 2020;369(793):7.
[39] Hofmeister JK, Cooney D, Coggeshall KM. Clustered CD20 induced apoptosis: src-family kinase, the proximal regulator of tyrosine phosphorylation, calcium influx, and caspase 3-dependent apoptosis. Blood Cells Mol Dis 2000;26(2):133–43.
[40] Chisari CG, Sgarlata E, Arena S, Toscano S, Luca M, Patti F. Rituximab for the treatment of multiple sclerosis: a review. J Neurol 2022;269(1):159–83.

[41] Weiner GJ. Rituximab: mechanism of action. Semin Hematol 2010;47(2):115–23.
[42] Lim SH, et al. Fc gamma receptor IIb on target B cells promotes rituximab internalization and reduces clinical efficacy. Blood 2011;118(9):2530–40.
[43] Sabatino JJ, Zamvil SS, Hauser SL. B-cell therapies in multiple sclerosis. Cold Spring Harb Perspect Med 2019;9 (2), a032037.
[44] Florou D, et al. Anti-CD20 agents for multiple sclerosis: spotlight on ocrelizumab and ofatumumab. Brain Sci 2020;10(10).
[45] Sheridan C. Genentech's Ocrevus heralds new chapter in MS treatment. Nat Biotechnol 2017;35(5):393–4.
[46] Kappos L, et al. Ocrelizumab in relapsing-remitting multiple sclerosis: a phase 2, randomised, placebo-controlled, multicentre trial. Lancet 2011;378(9805):1779–87.
[47] Gelfand JM, Cree BAC, Hauser SL. Ocrelizumab and other CD20+ B-cell-depleting therapies in multiple sclerosis. Neurotherapeutics 2017;14(4):835–41.
[48] Mayer L, et al. Ocrelizumab infusion experience in patients with relapsing and primary progressive multiple sclerosis: results from the phase 3 randomized OPERA I, OPERA II, and ORATORIO studies. Mult Scler Relat Disord 2019;30:236–43.
[49] Ellwardt E, et al. Ocrelizumab initiation in patients with MS: a multicenter observational study. Neurol Neuroimmunol Neuroinflamm 2020;7(4).
[50] Teeling JL, et al. Characterization of new human CD20 monoclonal antibodies with potent cytolytic activity against non-Hodgkin lymphomas. Blood 2004;104(6):1793–800.
[51] Teeling JL, et al. The biological activity of human CD20 monoclonal antibodies is linked to unique epitopes on CD20. J Immunol 2006;177(1):362–71.
[52] de Romeuf C, et al. Chronic lymphocytic leukaemia cells are efficiently killed by an anti-CD20 monoclonal antibody selected for improved engagement of FcgammaRIIIA/CD16. Br J Haematol 2008;140(6):635–43.
[53] Bowles JA, et al. Anti-CD20 monoclonal antibody with enhanced affinity for CD16 activates NK cells at lower concentrations and more effectively than rituximab. Blood 2006;108(8):2648–54.
[54] Sawas A, et al. A phase 1/2 trial of ublituximab, a novel anti-CD20 monoclonal antibody, in patients with B-cell non-Hodgkin lymphoma or chronic lymphocytic leukaemia previously exposed to rituximab. Br J Haematol 2017;177(2):243–53.
[55] Le Garff-Tavernier M, et al. Antibody-dependent cellular cytotoxicity of the optimized anti-CD20 monoclonal antibody ublituximab on chronic lymphocytic leukemia cells with the 17p deletion. Leukemia 2014;28(1):230–3.
[56] Gagez AL, Cartron G. Obinutuzumab: a new class of anti-CD20 monoclonal antibody. Curr Opin Oncol 2014;26 (5):484–91.
[57] Decaup E, et al. A tridimensional model for NK cell-mediated ADCC of follicular lymphoma. Front Immunol 2019;10.
[58] Niederfellner G, Lammens A, Mundigl O, Georges GJ, Schaefer W, Schwaiger M, Franke A, Wiechmann K, Jenewein S, Slootstra JW, Timmerman P, Brännström A, Lindstrom F, Mössner E, Umana P, Hopfner K-P, Klein C. Epitope characterization and crystal structure of GA101 provide insights into the molecular basis for type I_II distinction of CD20 antibodies. Blood 2011;118(2):10.
[59] Herter S, et al. Preclinical activity of the type II CD20 antibody GA101 (obinutuzumab) compared with rituximab and ofatumumab in vitro and in xenograft models. Mol Cancer Ther 2013;12(10):2031–42.
[60] Roodselaar J, et al. Anti-CD20 disrupts meningeal B-cell aggregates in a model of secondary progressive multiple sclerosis. Neurol Neuroimmunol Neuroinflamm 2021;8(3).
[61] Reich DS, Lucchinetti CF, Calabresi PA. Multiple sclerosis. N Engl J Med 2018;378(2):169–80.
[62] Thompson AJ, et al. Multiple sclerosis. Lancet 2018;391(10130):1622–36.
[63] Dendrou CA, Fugger L, Friese MA. Immunopathology of multiple sclerosis. Nat Rev Immunol 2015;15(9):545–58.
[64] Minagar A, Alexander JS. Blood-brain barrier disruption in multiple sclerosis. Mult Scler 2003;9(6):540–9.
[65] Ortiz GG, et al. Role of the blood-brain barrier in multiple sclerosis. Arch Med Res 2014;45(8):687–97.
[66] Machado-Santos J, et al. The compartmentalized inflammatory response in the multiple sclerosis brain is composed of tissue-resident CD8+ T lymphocytes and B cells. Brain 2018;141(7):2066–82.
[67] Lassmann H. Multiple sclerosis pathology. Cold Spring Harb Perspect Med 2018;8(3).
[68] Mahad DH, Trapp BD, Lassmann H. Pathological mechanisms in progressive multiple sclerosis. Lancet Neurol 2015;14(2):183–93.
[69] Gross RH, Corboy JR. Monitoring, switching, and stopping multiple sclerosis disease-modifying therapies. Continuum 2019;25(3):715–35.

[70] Freedman MS, et al. Treatment optimization in multiple sclerosis: Canadian MS working group recommendations. Can J Neurol Sci 2020;47(4):437–55.
[71] Hauser SL, Waubant E, Arnold DL, Vollmer T, Antel J, Fox RJ, Bar-Or A, Panzara M, Sarkar N, Agarwal S, Langer-Gould A, Smith CH, HERMES Trial Group. B-cell depletion with rituximab in relapsing-remitting multiple sclerosis. N Engl J Med 2008;358(7):13.
[72] Salzer J, et al. Rituximab in multiple sclerosis: a retrospective observational study on safety and efficacy. Neurology 2016;87(20):2074–81.
[73] Bar-Or A, et al. Subcutaneous ofatumumab in patients with relapsing-remitting multiple sclerosis: the MIRROR study. Neurology 2018;90(20):e1805–14.
[74] Hauser SL, et al. Ofatumumab versus teriflunomide in multiple sclerosis. N Engl J Med 2020;383(6):546–57.
[75] Fox E, et al. A phase 2 multicenter study of ublituximab, a novel glycoengineered anti-CD20 monoclonal antibody, in patients with relapsing forms of multiple sclerosis. Mult Scler 2021;27(3):420–9.
[76] Montalban X, et al. Ocrelizumab versus placebo in primary progressive multiple sclerosis. N Engl J Med 2017;376(3):209–20.
[77] Wolinsky JS, et al. Long-term follow-up from the ORATORIO trial of ocrelizumab for primary progressive multiple sclerosis: a post-hoc analysis from the ongoing open-label extension of the randomised, placebo-controlled, phase 3 trial. Lancet Neurol 2020;19(12):998–1009.
[78] Hawker K, et al. Rituximab in patients with primary progressive multiple sclerosis: results of a randomized double-blind placebo-controlled multicenter trial. Ann Neurol 2009;66(4):460–71.
[79] Shan W, Yang H, Wang Q. Neuronal surface antibody-medicated autoimmune encephalitis (limbic encephalitis) in China: a multiple-center, retrospective study. Front Immunol 2021;12, 621599.
[80] Dalmau J, Graus F. Antibody-mediated encephalitis. N Engl J Med 2018;378(9):840–51.
[81] Lancaster E, et al. Antibodies to the GABA(B) receptor in limbic encephalitis with seizures: case series and characterisation of the antigen. Lancet Neurol 2010;9(1):67–76.
[82] Day GS, et al. Abnormal neurons in teratomas in NMDAR encephalitis. JAMA Neurol 2014;71(6):717–24.
[83] Pruss H. Autoantibodies in neurological disease. Nat Rev Immunol 2021;21(12):798–813.
[84] Malviya M, et al. NMDAR encephalitis: passive transfer from man to mouse by a recombinant antibody. Ann Clin Transl Neurol 2017;4(11):768–83.
[85] Dalmau J, Geis C, Graus F. Autoantibodies to synaptic receptors and neuronal cell surface proteins in autoimmune diseases of the central nervous system. Physiol Rev 2017;97(2):839–87.
[86] Abboud H, et al. Autoimmune encephalitis: proposed recommendations for symptomatic and long-term management. J Neurol Neurosurg Psychiatry 2021;92(8):897–907.
[87] Abboud H, et al. Autoimmune encephalitis: proposed best practice recommendations for diagnosis and acute management. J Neurol Neurosurg Psychiatry 2021;92(7):757–68.
[88] Dale RC, et al. Utility and safety of rituximab in pediatric autoimmune and inflammatory CNS disease. Neurology 2014;83(2):142–50.
[89] Lee WJ, et al. Rituximab treatment for autoimmune limbic encephalitis in an institutional cohort. Neurology 2016;86(18):1683–91.
[90] Nepal G, et al. Efficacy and safety of rituximab in autoimmune encephalitis: a meta-analysis. Acta Neurol Scand 2020;142(5):449–59.
[91] Thaler FS, et al. Rituximab treatment and long-term outcome of patients with autoimmune encephalitis: real-world evidence from the GENERATE registry. Neurol Neuroimmunol Neuroinflamm 2021;8(6).
[92] Nosadini M, et al. Use and safety of immunotherapeutic management of N-methyl-d-aspartate receptor antibody encephalitis: a meta-analysis. JAMA Neurol 2021;78(11):1333–44.
[93] Lee WJ, et al. Teratoma removal, steroid, IVIG, rituximab and tocilizumab (T-SIRT) in anti-NMDAR encephalitis. Neurotherapeutics 2021;18(1):474–87.
[94] Chang VTW, Chang HM. Review: recent advances in the understanding of the pathophysiology of neuromyelitis optica spectrum disorder. Neuropathol Appl Neurobiol 2020;46(3):199–218.
[95] Chihara N, et al. Interleukin 6 signaling promotes anti-aquaporin 4 autoantibody production from plasmablasts in neuromyelitis optica. Proc Natl Acad Sci U S A 2011;108(9):3701–6.
[96] Pittock SJ, Zekeridou A, Weinshenker BG. Hope for patients with neuromyelitis optica spectrum disorders—from mechanisms to trials. Nat Rev Neurol 2021;17(12):759–73.
[97] Levy M, Fujihara K, Palace J. New therapies for neuromyelitis optica spectrum disorder. Lancet Neurol 2021;20(1):60–7.

[98] Sahraian MA, et al. Diagnosis and management of neuromyelitis optica spectrum disorder (NMOSD) in Iran: a consensus guideline and recommendations. Mult Scler Relat Disord 2017;18:144–51.
[99] Carnero Contentti E, et al. Latin American consensus recommendations for management and treatment of neuromyelitis optica spectrum disorders in clinical practice. Mult Scler Relat Disord 2020;45, 102428.
[100] Trebst C, et al. Update on the diagnosis and treatment of neuromyelitis optica: recommendations of the neuromyelitis optica study group (NEMOS). J Neurol 2014;261(1):1–16.
[101] Tahara M, et al. Safety and efficacy of rituximab in neuromyelitis optica spectrum disorders (RIN-1 study): a multicentre, randomised, double-blind, placebo-controlled trial. Lancet Neurol 2020;19(4):298–306.
[102] Banerjee S, Butcher R. Rituximab for the treatment of neuromyelitis optica spectrum disorder. Ottawa (ON): Canadian Agency for Drugs and Technologies in Health; February 2021.
[103] Mealy MA, Levy M. A pilot safety study of ublituximab, a monoclonal antibody against CD20, in acute relapses of neuromyelitis optica spectrum disorder. Medicine 2019;98(25), e15944.
[104] Kacmaz E, et al. Rituximab treatment in acute disseminated encephalomyelitis associated with Salmonella infection. Case Rep Pediatr 2021;2021:5570566.
[105] Whittam DH, et al. Treatment of MOG-IgG-associated disorder with rituximab: an international study of 121 patients. Mult Scler Relat Disord 2020;44, 102251.
[106] Gilhus NE, et al. Myasthenia gravis. Nat Rev Dis Primers 2019;5(1):30.
[107] Gilhus NE. Myasthenia gravis. N Engl J Med 2016;375(26):2570–81.
[108] Gilhus NE, et al. Myasthenia gravis—autoantibody characteristics and their implications for therapy. Nat Rev Neurol 2016;12(5):259–68.
[109] Gilhus NE, Verschuuren JJ. Myasthenia gravis: subgroup classification and therapeutic strategies. Lancet Neurol 2015;14(10):1023–36.
[110] Dalakas MC. Immunotherapy in myasthenia gravis in the era of biologics. Nat Rev Neurol 2019;15 (2):113–24.
[111] Zhao C, et al. Effectiveness and safety of rituximab for refractory myasthenia gravis: a systematic review and single-arm meta-analysis. Front Neurol 2021;12, 736190.
[112] Hehir MK, et al. Rituximab as treatment for anti-MuSK myasthenia gravis: multicenter blinded prospective review. Neurology 2017;89(10):1069–77.
[113] Nowak RJ, et al. Phase 2 trial of rituximab in acetylcholine receptor antibody-positive generalized myasthenia gravis: the BeatMG study. Neurology 2021.
[114] Landon-Cardinal O, et al. Efficacy of rituximab in refractory generalized anti-AChR myasthenia gravis. J Neuromuscul Dis 2018;5(2):241–9.
[115] Narayanaswami P, et al. International consensus guidance for management of myasthenia gravis: 2020 update. Neurology 2021;96(3):114–22.
[116] Feng X, et al. Efficacy and safety of immunotherapies in refractory myasthenia gravis: a systematic review and meta-analysis. Front Neurol 2021;12, 725700.
[117] Li T, et al. Efficacy and safety of different dosages of rituximab for refractory generalized AChR myasthenia gravis: a meta-analysis. J Clin Neurosci 2021;85:6–12.
[118] Waters MJ, Field D, Ravindran J. Refractory myasthenia gravis successfully treated with ofatumumab. Muscle Nerve 2019;60(6):E45–7.
[119] Dalakas MC, Medscape. Advances in the diagnosis, pathogenesis and treatment of CIDP. Nat Rev Neurol 2011;7(9):507–17.
[120] Tang L, et al. Distinguish CIDP with autoantibody from that without autoantibody: pathogenesis, histopathology, and clinical features. J Neurol 2021;268(8):2757–68.
[121] Latov N. Diagnosis and treatment of chronic acquired demyelinating polyneuropathies. Nat Rev Neurol 2014;10(8):435–46.
[122] Muley SA, et al. Rituximab in refractory chronic inflammatory demyelinating polyneuropathy. Muscle Nerve 2020;61(5):575–9.
[123] Hu J, Sun C, Lu J, Zhao C, Lin J. Efficacy of rituximab treatment in chronic inflammatory demyelinating polyradiculoneuropathy: a systematic review and meta-analysis. J Neurol 2022;269(3):1250–63.
[124] Delmont E, et al. Antibodies against the node of Ranvier: a real-life evaluation of incidence, clinical features and response to treatment based on a prospective analysis of 1500 sera. J Neurol 2020;267(12):3664–72.

[125] Motte J, et al. Treatment response to cyclophosphamide, rituximab, and bortezomib in chronic immune-mediated sensorimotor neuropathies: a retrospective cohort study. Ther Adv Neurol Disord 2021;14. p. 1756286421999631.
[126] Casertano S, et al. Ocrelizumab in a case of refractory chronic inflammatory demyelinating polyneuropathy with anti-rituximab antibodies. Eur J Neurol 2020;27(12):2673–5.
[127] Lundberg IE, et al. Idiopathic inflammatory myopathies. Nat Rev Dis Primers 2021;7(1):86.
[128] Dalakas MC. Inflammatory muscle diseases. N Engl J Med 2015;373(4):393–4.
[129] Miller FW, et al. Risk factors and disease mechanisms in myositis. Nat Rev Rheumatol 2018;14(5):255–68.
[130] Dalakas MC. Review: an update on inflammatory and autoimmune myopathies. Neuropathol Appl Neurobiol 2011;37(3):226–42.
[131] Dalakas MC, Hohlfeld R. Polymyositis and dermatomyositis. Lancet 2003;362(9388):971–82.
[132] Allenbach Y, et al. Necrosis in anti-SRP(+) and anti-HMGCR(+)myopathies: role of autoantibodies and complement. Neurology 2018;90(6):e507–17.
[133] de Souza FHC, et al. Guidelines of the Brazilian Society of Rheumatology for the treatment of systemic autoimmune myopathies. Adv Rheumatol 2019;59(1):6.
[134] Fasano S, et al. Rituximab in the treatment of inflammatory myopathies: a review. Rheumatology (Oxford) 2017;56(1):26–36.
[135] Moghadam-Kia S, Aggarwal R, Oddis CV. Biologics for idiopathic inflammatory myopathies. Curr Opin Rheumatol 2017;29(6):645–51.
[136] Kuye IO, Smith GP. The use of rituximab in the management of refractory dermatomyositis. J Drugs Dermatol 2017;16(2):162–6.
[137] Oddis CV, et al. Rituximab in the treatment of refractory adult and juvenile dermatomyositis and adult polymyositis: a randomized, placebo-phase trial. Arthritis Rheum 2013;65(2):314–24.
[138] Aggarwal R, et al. Cutaneous improvement in refractory adult and juvenile dermatomyositis after treatment with rituximab. Rheumatology (Oxford) 2017;56(2):247–54.
[139] Landon-Cardinal O, et al. Rituximab in the treatment of refractory anti-HMGCR immune-mediated necrotizing myopathy. J Rheumatol 2019;46(6):623–7.
[140] Ibrahim H, Dimachkie MM, Shaibani A. A review: the use of rituximab in neuromuscular diseases. J Clin Neuromuscul Dis 2010;12(2):91–102.
[141] Maddison P, et al. The use of rituximab in myasthenia gravis and Lambert-Eaton myasthenic syndrome. J Neurol Neurosurg Psychiatry 2011;82(6):671–3.
[142] Pellkofer HL, et al. Long-term follow-up of patients with neuromyelitis optica after repeated therapy with rituximab. Neurology 2011;76(15):1310–5.
[143] Mealy MA, et al. Comparison of relapse and treatment failure rates among patients with neuromyelitis optica: multicenter study of treatment efficacy. JAMA Neurol 2014;71(3):324–30.
[144] Kim SH, et al. A 5-year follow-up of rituximab treatment in patients with neuromyelitis optica spectrum disorder. JAMA Neurol 2013;70(9):1110–7.
[145] Lebrun C, et al. Therapeutic target of memory B cells depletion helps to tailor administration frequency of rituximab in myasthenia gravis. J Neuroimmunol 2016;298:79–81.
[146] Ciron J, et al. Recommendations for the use of rituximab in neuromyelitis optica spectrum disorders. Rev Neurol 2018;174(4):255–64.
[147] Kim SH, et al. Treatment outcomes with rituximab in 100 patients with neuromyelitis optica: influence of FCGR3A polymorphisms on the therapeutic response to rituximab. JAMA Neurol 2015;72(9):989–95.
[148] Yang J, Liu X. Immunotherapy for refractory autoimmune encephalitis. Front Immunol 2021;12, 790962.
[149] Pittock SJ, et al. Eculizumab in aquaporin-4-positive neuromyelitis optica spectrum disorder. N Engl J Med 2019;381(7):614–25.
[150] Howard Jr JF, et al. Randomized phase 2 study of FcRn antagonist efgartigimod in generalized myasthenia gravis. Neurology 2019;92(23):e2661–73.
[151] Louapre C, Ibrahim M, Maillart E, et al. Anti-CD20 therapies decrease humoral immune response to SARS-CoV-2 in patients with multiple sclerosis or neuromyelitis optica spectrum disorders. J Neurol Neurosurg Psychiatry 2022;93(1):24–31.
[152] Kuijpers TW, Bende RJ, Baars PA, Grummels A, Derks IA, Dolman KM, Beaumont T, Tedder TF, van Noesel CJ, Eldering E, van Lier RA. CD20 deficiency in humans results in impaired T cell–independent antibody responses. J Clin Invest 2010;120(1):9.

[153] Margoni M, Preziosa P, Filippi M, Rocca MA. Anti-CD20 therapies for multiple sclerosis: current status and future perspectives. J Neurol 2022;269(3):1316–34.

[154] Mirmosayyeb O, Shaygannejad V, Ebrahimi N, Ghoshouni H, Ghajarzadeh M. The prevalence of cancer in patients with multiple sclerosis (MS) who received rituximab: a systematic review and meta-analysis [published online ahead of print, 2022 Aug 30]. Neurologia (Engl Ed) 2022.

CHAPTER

18

Reversal of resistance to anti-CD20 antibody therapies: Conclusions and future perspectives

Benjamin Bonavida

Department of Microbiology, Immunology & Molecular Genetics, David Geffen School of Medicine, Jonsson Comprehensive Cancer Center, University of California at Los Angeles, Los Angeles, CA, United States

Abbreviations

ADCC	antibody-dependent cellular cytotoxicity
ALL	acute lymphoblastic leukemia
BsAbs	bispecific antibodies
BTK	bruton tyrosine kinase
CART	chimeric antigen receptor T cells
CDC	complement-dependent cytotoxicity
DLBCL	diffuse large B cell lymphoma
EZH2	enhancer of zeste homolog 2
FL	follicular lymphoma
IO	inotuzumab ozogamicin
LN	upus nephritis
MHCI	major histocompatibility complex I
PD-L1	programmed death ligand 1
R-CHOP	rituximab, cyclophosphamide, adriamycin, vincristine, and prednisone
SLE	systemic lupus erythematosus

Conflict of interest

No potential conflicts of interest were disclosed.

https://doi.org/10.1016/B978-0-443-19200-5.00023-3

Introduction

As the series editor, I am very happy to write a brief summary of the main highlights discussed by the various contributors of this timely volume edited by Dr. William Cho. I also appreciate editor Dr. Cho and the authors of the chapters for their excellent reviews on the therapeutic applications of anti-CD20 antibodies and resistance in both cancers and noncancer-related diseases.

Immunotherapy by antibodies became practical following the milestone discovery of the generation of antigen-specific mAbs by Kohler and Milstein in 1975 [1]. As of 2021, the FDA has approved over 100 monoclonal antibodies (mAbs) for therapeutic use in humans. The first FDA-approved mAb was, in 1997, rituximab a chimeric anti-CD20 mAb for the treatment of B-non-Hodgkin lymphomas. The introduction of antibody-mediated therapy has resulted in significant clinical objective responses and, in many cases, responses in cancers that did not respond to conventional chemotherapies. Further, the combination treatment of mAbs with chemotherapy, immunotherapy, proteasome inhibitors, and other inhibitors has resulted in synergistic antitumor activities with significant objective clinical responses.

Despite their successful clinical use, the underlying mechanisms of rituximab in vivo activities remain elusive. Several mechanisms of action have been reported for the potential in vivo antitumor activities by rituximab including antibody-dependent cellular cytotoxicity (ADCC), complement-dependent cytotoxicity (CDC), and apoptotic activities as well as its cell signaling-mediated effects that are responsible, in part, for its chemo- and immunosensitizing activities. The combination of rituximab and chemo-immunotherapeutic drugs resulted in the reversal of resistance and synergy [2]. However, a subset of patients does not respond to anti-CD20 antibody therapy and the mechanisms of resistance in vivo are not clear. Several mechanisms have been reported including inhibition of ADCC by deposition of C3 activating fragments [3] polymorphism of the FcγRIIIa on cytotoxic cells [4,5], inhibition of CDC [6], loss of CD20 expression on the surface of subclones [7,8], overexpression of antiapoptotic gene products (e.g., Bcl2), CD20 mutations [9], shedding of CD20 rituximab complexes [10], the tumor microenvironment [11], and distribution of rituximab in vivo and its pharmacokinetics and failure to respond to rituximab-mediated cell signaling [2].

Below, are the main highlights contributed in each chapter of this volume.

Therapeutic anti-CD20 antibodies against cancers and escape

In this section, eight chapters are listed in this topic.

Panwar et al.'s Chapter 1 titled *"Therapeutic antibodies against cancer—A step toward the treatment"* reviews in general therapeutic antibodies (structures, activities, new designs, etc.) and the development of resistance and various means to overcome resistance and perspectives of future antibodies. The authors discuss the various forms of mAbs such as chimeric antibodies, humanized antibodies, and human antibodies and their various properties and unique characteristics. The authors also review the various mechanisms underlying resistance and their reversals. For instance, reversal of resistance to anti-CD20 mAbs can be the use of combination therapies, targeting intracellular overactivated survival pathways, altering the dosages, switching to other anti-CD20 mAbs such as drug conjugates, and the use of checkpoint inhibitors. Of interest, the authors discuss various computational techniques for the design of more efficient novel antibodies with enhancements of stability, half-life, and immunogenicity. These are facilitated by the availability of therapeutic antibody databases. Clearly, the cost of development and studies to validate clinical studies must be considered as well as affordability. An important and pivotal factor in resistance is the development of biomarkers that can predict responses or resistance in patients and avoid both refractoriness and relapse as well as the use of alternative therapeutics.

Abubakar et al.'s Chapter 2 titled *"Anti-CD20 antibody treatment for B-cell malignancies"* reviews the classification of B-cell malignancies, available anti-CD20-based therapeutics, mechanisms of action, efficacies, and resistance. The expression of CD20 in the surface of B cells, via its interaction with the B-cell receptor (BCR), acts as a calcium channel and mediates activation. The authors summarized the most common B-cell malignancies [diffuse large B cell lymphoma (DLBCL), follicular lymphoma (FL), chronic lymphocytic leukemia/small lymphocytic lymphoma (CLL/SLL), mantle cell lymphoma (MCL), marginal zone lymphoma (MZL), Burkit lymphoma (BL), lymphoplasmacytic lymphoma (LPL), hairy cell leukemia (HCL), and plasma cell myeloma (PCM)] and treatment guidelines, as monotherapy or combination therapies. The authors review the various anti-CD20 antibodies responses in patients, including rituximab and clinical studies with tositumomab, ofatumumab, veltuzumab, and ublituximab. While various mechanisms of action and resistance have been reported in vivo in patients, it remains unclear which one or more than one mechanisms are responsible and whether different mechanisms play a role in different patients.

Jin et al.'s Chapter 3 titled *"Anti-CD20 antibody treatment for diffuse large B cell lymphoma: Genetic alterations and signaling pathways"* reviews the mechanisms underlying the activities of anti-CD20 mAbs including ADSCC, CDC, apoptosis, the genetic alterations in the two main types of DLBCL, and intracellular molecular signalings (the NF-kB, the MAPK, the Ras/Raf/Mek/ERk, the PI3k/mTOR, and the JAK/Stat pathways). In addition, the authors discuss the B-cell receptor signaling and the Fas/FasL apoptotic pathway. Noteworthy, the authors also discuss additional mechanisms of resistance including immune escape by, for example, mutations in the *Beta2-microglobulin* gene that disrupts the major histocompatibility complex I (MHCI) transport and antigen presentation. The authors conclude that in the absence of a complete and satisfactory treatment for B-cell lymphomas, new approaches are being considered by targeting specific genes.

Clerico et al.'s Chapter 4 titled *"Non-Hodgkin lymphoma treated with anti-CD20 antibody-based immunochemotherapy"* reviews the three anti-CD20 mAbs (rituximab, obinutuzumab, ofatumumab) applications as well the findings with anti-CD20xCD3 bispecific antibodies (BsAbs). In addition, they also discuss mechanisms of resistance. Type I anti-CD20 mAbs, rituximab, and ofatumumab translocate into lipid rafts and activate complement and antibody-dependent cell-mediated cytotoxicity. The type UU anti-CVD20 mAb, obinutuzumab, is a humanized glycoengineered mAb that was developed to overcome the resistance to rituximab. Another anti-CD20 mAb, ublituximab, is a chimeric glycoengineered antibody. Of note, BsAb (mosunetuzumab, glofitamab, epcortamab) are CD20xCD3 mAbs directed against the CD3 on T cells and the CD20 on tumor cells. These

BsAbs activate the T cells to mediate cytotoxicity against the adjacent tumor cells and were reported to show efficacy in patients with refractory/relapse B-NHL. The authors reviewed the clinical applications of the above-approved anti-CD20 mAbs. The authors also discuss the various mechanisms of resistance.

Takiar and Phillips's Chapter 5 titled *"Targeted therapies for follicular lymphoma"* reviews the various options for the treatment of patients with relapsed/refractory FL. It is clear that FL is an incurable disease due to both early and late relapses though a significant improvement has been observed in outcomes over time with the advent of rituximab. The various options discussed include bendamustine and rituximab (BR), lenalidomide and rituximab (R2) and rituximab, cyclophosphamide, adriamycin, vincristine, and prednisone (R-CHOP). Studies have been conducted with PI3K inhibitors and one PI3K inhibitor, copanlisib, is FDA approved. Copanlisib is a pan-class PI3K inhibitor. Several Bruton tyrosine kinase (BTK) inhibitors (ibrutinib, acalabrutinib, and zanubrutinib) have been studied clinically. The response rate of venetoclax (Bcl2 inhibitor) has been modest in FL. The histone methyltransferase, enhancer of zeste homolog 2 (EZH2) is an epigenetic regulator involved in cell-cycle progression, autophagy, and apoptosis, and promotes DNA damage repair. Tazemetostat is an oral inhibitor of EZH2 and was investigated in a phase I study in NHL. Antibody-drug conjugates, bispecific antibodies, and CASR-T cells are also discussed as options for relapsed FL. The authors conclude with an important paragraph on future perspectives.

Montoto's Chapter 6 titled *"Treatment of relapsed follicular lymphoma"* reviews follicular lymphoma FL, the second most frequent subtype of non-Hodgkin lymphoma. Recently, while FL is still considered incurable, novel-targeted drugs were developed that provide several options for treatments. They review the management of patients with FL with a series of principles that are discussed in detail. They also review treatment in challenging situations such as histological transformation. FL transforms into DLBCL and is of poor prognosis. The management of these patients with FL is complicated and many patients have received several lines of treatment at the time of histological transformation, thus limiting the treatment options. The consolidation of the various responses is discussed via maintenance, stem cell transplantation, and cellular therapy. The advent of CAR-T therapy opens new options for high-risk diseases in patients has not been yet incorporated for patients with FL and is being considered currently.

Gurney and Litzow's Chapter 7 titled *"New monoclonal antibodies for the treatment of acute lymphoblastic leukemia."* Acute lymphoblastic leukemia (ALL) is a malignant disease that proliferates and homes in the bone marrow, blood, and extramedullary site and is a predominant cancer in children. The standard therapy for ALL varies according to age. Both molecularly targeted therapies and immunotherapies have been currently in use. The approved clinical studies of antibody-based therapies for B-ALL include rituximab (FDA approved) and a combination of rituximab with bortezomib (phase II), mAbs targeting CD19, blinatumomab (FDA approved) (*B lineage-specific antitumor mouse mAb*) is a bispecific T-cell engager (BITE) (binds both CD19n and CD3 component of the TCR complex), inotuzumab ozogamicin (IO) (targeting CD22 expressed in developing and mature B cells) (humanized, anti-CD22 conjugated to a stable disulfide derivative of cytotoxic calicheamicin). The authors reviewed the resistance to blinatumomab that includes alterations in CD19 expression and suppressed cytotoxic cells as well as expression of the programmed death ligand 1 (PD-L1) on the tumor cells that inactivate the antitumor cytotoxic T cells. The resistance to IO includes the efflux of calicheamicin associated with the P-glycoprotein. The authors present novel approaches that target B-ALL for future evaluation of their therapeutic efficacies in B-ALL.

Veloso and dos Santos's Chapter 8 titled *"Clinical relevance and therapeutic implications of CD20 expression in Hodgkin's lymphoma"* reviews the controversy regarding the role of CD20 expression and response to anti-CD20 treatment. They questioned the efficacy of anti-CD20 therapy in HL and particularly the resistance that develops. Classical Hodgkin lymphoma (cHL) comprises 90% of cases. Four distinct subtypes have been shown for cHL and each subtype features unique immunophenotypes and prognosis. The authors review the pathogenesis of cHL and particularly the role of the tumor microenvironment in the immune escape and clinical studies comparing anti-CD20 with the chemotherapeutic regimen ABVD. Though the anti-CD20 chemotherapy regimen became the mainstream treatment for many B-cell malignancies, anti-CD20 usage has been successful for non-HL used in combination with chemo or radiotherapy. Future studies should address the resistance mechanisms and other anti-CD20 mAbs than rituximab.

Resistance and affinity determination of anti-CD20 antibodies

The above chapters have also discussed the mechanisms of resistance but these were not the main focus. The following three chapters were focused primarily on resistance and their highlights will be discussed.

Wang et al.'s Chapter 9 titled *"Therapeutic options for rituximab-resistant patients"* reviews the subset of patients with B-cell malignancies who are refractory to rituximab treatments and who have a poor prognosis. Hence, several approaches had been undertaken to reinvigorate rituximab as a therapeutic option for resistant patients. These include having a higher affinity of the Fc toward the Fc gamma receptor, improving the antitumor immune effector cells, novel anti-CD20 mAbs, the use of small molecules targeting the survival pathways (e.g., BTK and PI3K inhibitors), combination treatments, the development of bispecific antibodies and chimeric receptor T cells and chimeric antigen receptor T cells (CART). The authors also discuss high-dose chemotherapy and radio-immunotherapy followed by autologous stem cell transplant as a therapeutic option after rituximab resistance. The authors report on the possible use of heterologous iNKT cells in combination with anti-CD20 mAb of higher affinity to the Fc receptor. Aside from CD20 as a target, other receptors can be targeted such as Cd19, Cd22, CD80, Cd30, Cd52, CD40, CD79b, and CD38, and others that are in development. Three anti-CD19 CAR T-cell products have been approved by the FDA for patients (relapsed or refractory) with aggressive B-cell lymphoma. Clearly, the authors speculate that the bridge of pharmacogenetics and personalized therapeutic strategy with individualized gene signature may benefit the patients with an efficient treatment regimen which will lead to improved clinical response and prolongation of survival.

Bordron et al.'s Chapter 10 titled *"Mechanisms of resistance to anti-CD20 antibodies in lymphoid malignancies"* reviews the clinical use of rituximab and the approved obinutuzumab mAb. Obinutuzumab is a type II humanized antibody glycoengineering the Fc region and modified the elbow-hinge amino-acid sequence; these modifications enhance the direct cell death compared to rituximab. The authors reviewed several mechanisms of resistance including the pharmacokinetics (interindividual variability and dosage), alterations of CD20 (shaving, internalization, mutations, and epigenetic dysregulation), ADCC and the Fcgamma receptor polymorphisms, the antibody type, the tumor microenvironment, and resistance to apoptosis.

Grier et al.'s Chapter 11 titled "*Kinetic exclusion assay using cellular membranes for affinity determination of anti-CD20 antibody*" reviews one important mechanism of resistance, namely, the binding affinity of the antibody to the cancer cell which has an impact on the success of the therapy. In this chapter, the authors focused on the methods used to determine binding affinity. The technologies described include surface plasmon resonance (SPR), flow cytometry, the KinExA instrument, analysis using whole cells, and antibody-coated beads.

Therapeutic anti-CD20 antibodies against noncancer diseases

There are six chapters that deal with anti-CD20 antibodies and noncancer-related manifestations. These include (i) monitoring treated patients for autoimmune disorders, (ii) efficacy of anti-CD20 antibodies in autoimmune diseases, (iii) anti-CD20 antibodies in nephrology, (iv) efficacy of anti-CD20 antibodies in neurological and neuromuscular diseases, (v) adverse effects of rituximab in patients with pemphigus, and (vi) depletion of B cells in proliferative lupus nephritis.

Zian et al.'s Chapter 12 titled "*Clinical efficacy of anti-CD20 antibodies in autoimmune diseases*" reviews the underlying molecular mechanisms of autoimmunity, the various anti-CD20 mAbs in clinical use for various autoimmune diseases, and the clinical responses observed in these diseases [rheumatological diseases, neurological diseases (MS), dermatological diseases, and side effects of anti-CD20 treatments in autoimmune diseases].

Snyder and Furie's Chapter 13 titled "*B-cell depletion with obinutuzumab for the treatment of proliferative lupus nephritis*" reviews the current phase 2 clinical trial, the NOBILITY trial, of obinutuzumab in proliferative lupus nephritis (LN). This trial compares obinutuzumab to placebo in patients with LN. The end point of this trial is to increase the rate of CRR when added to standard care compared to standard care alone. It was reported in this trial that 41% (26/43 patients) achieved CRR compared to 23% (14/62 patients) in the placebo group. Hence, a global phase III trial with obinutuzumab is currently being investigated for the treatment of proliferative LN. Other anti-CD20 mAbs are being investigated for systemic lupus erythematosus (SLE) and LN that include ianalumab [a mAb directed against the B-cell activating factor (BAFF) receptor], bispecific antibody (mosuntuzumab targeting both CD3 and CD20), and CAR-T cells.

Kannan's Chapter 14 titled "*Anti-CD20 antibodies in glomerular diseases, their resistance and reversal approaches*" reviews the use of anti-CD20 mAb in renal diseases as an adjunct or alternative treatment to remove autoantibody-producing B cells. The author reviews the role of anti-CD20 mAb in lupus nephritis, Anca-associated vasculitis (AAV), membranous nephropathy, minimal change disease (MCD), focal segmental glomerulosclerosis (FSGS), cryoglobulinemia, thrombotic microangiopathy (TMA), and kidney transplant. Dr. Kannan also discusses resistance and approaches to reverse resistance through the use of new generations of anti-CD20 mAbs and summarizes the clinical trials. This review is updated and with a significant overview of this subject matter.

Dadkhahfar's Chapter 15 titled *"Adverse events following rituximab therapy in pemphigus patients"* reviews the treatment of patients with pemphigus vulgaris (PV) with rituximab and consequent side effects. This disease is the consequence of circulating autoantibodies against transmembrane glycoproteins (desmogleins 1 and 3) leading to the formation of blisters and erosions. Rituximab has been shown to be efficient against PV. However, there are side effects such as infusion-related reactions (IRR) including hypersensitivity reactions and cytokine-releasing syndrome. One unwanted side effect is infections. Furthermore, skin-related side effects are also common adverse effects of rituximab treatment. The author discusses the means to overcome the rituximab-associated side effects.

Brando and Gatti's Chapter 16 titled *"Immune monitoring of patients treated with anti-CD20 therapeutic monoclonals for autoimmune disorders"* reviews the current use of anti-Cd20 antibodies in the majority of autoimmune diseases and consequent manifestations. A thorough review is presented on both the functional and phenotypic development of B cells and CD20 as a marker of mature B cells. The authors also discuss the mechanisms of action of rituximab and other anti-CD20 antibodies and the rationale of B cell depletion in autoimmune disorders. Of interest, they address one mechanism of nonresponsiveness to anti-CD20 antibodies is the circulating plasmablasts that are devoid of CD20 surface expression. Plasmablasts act as effectors in autoimmune disorders and their level is used as an indicator of disease activity. For example, patients with RA and treated with rituximab circulating plasmablasts were associated with nonresponse and bad outcomes. The authors discuss the importance of monitoring patients receiving anti-CD20 therapies for autoimmune disorders.

Fan et al.'s Chapter 17 titled *"Clinical efficacy of anti-CD20 antibodies in neurological and neuromuscular diseases"* reviews the current use of several approved anti-CD20 mAbs in the treatment of neurological and neuromuscular diseases. They discuss CD20 as a therapeutic target in autoimmune diseases in the central nervous system (CNS), in multiple sclerosis (MS), and in neuromyelitis optica spectrum disorder (NMOSD). Also, they review CD20 as a therapeutic target in neuromuscular diseases such as myasthenia gravis (MG), in chronic inflammatory demyelinating polyradiculoneuropathy (CIDP), and in idiopathic inflammatory myopathies (IIMS). The authors suggest that the next generation of anti-CD20 mAbs must selectively delete inflammatory CD20+ targets and maintain antiinflammatory CD20+ cells.

Future perspectives

An additional advancement in the field of antibody-directed therapies consists of the development of antibody-functionalized nanotherapeutics. The generation of nanobioconjugates that are drug-containing nanocarriers is an attractive option for selective cancer therapy. One can also achieve a higher level of selectivity by making these nanostructures respond to additional stimuli such as external radiation. Future oncology-mediated therapeutics are to use antibody-conjugated nanomedicines in which the mAbs will rapidly bind to specific targets and on demand release cytotoxic drugs. Such therapeutics will achieve high efficacy and safety and reverse several mechanisms of resistance to conventional therapeutics. Antibody-conjugated nanomedicine could combine the target-specific binding of mAbs with enhanced delivery and on-demand release of drugs, achieving high efficacy and excellent safety in future oncologic therapeutics.

References

[1] Kohler G, Milstein C. Continuous cultures of fused cells secreting antibody of predefined specificity. Nature 1975;256:495–7.

[2] Bonavida B. Postulated mechanisms of resistance of B-NHL to rituximab treatment: strategies to overcome resistance. Semin Oncol 2014;41:667–77.

[3] Wang M, Han XH, Zhang L, Yang J, Qian JF, Shi YK, et al. Bortezomib is synergistic with rituximab and cyclophosphamide in inducing apoptosis of mantle cell lymphoma cells in vitro and in vivo. Leukemia 2008;22:179–85.

[4] Cartron G, Dacheux L, Salles G, Solal-Celigny P, Bardos P, Colombat P, et al. Therapeutic activity of humanized anti-CD20 monoclonal antibody and polymorphism in IgG Fc receptor FcgammaRIIIa gene. Blood 2002;99:754–8.

[5] Weng WK, Levy R. Two immunoglobulin G fragment C receptor polymorphisms independently predict response to rituximab in patients with follicular lymphoma. J Clin Oncol 2003;21:3940–7.

[6] Macor P, Tripodo C, Zorzet S, Piovan E, Bossi F, Marzari R, et al. In vivo targeting of human neutralizing antibodies against CD55 and CD59 to lymphoma cells increases the antitumor activity of rituximab. Cancer Res 2007;67:10556–63.

[7] Davis TA, Grillo-Lopez AJ, White CA, McLaughlin P, Czuczman MS, Link BK, et al. Rituximab anti-CD20 monoclonal antibody therapy in non-Hodgkin's lymphoma: safety and efficacy of re-treatment. J Clin Oncol 2000;18:3135–43.

[8] Kennedy GA, Tey SK, Cobcroft R, Marlton P, Cull G, Grimmett K, et al. Incidence and nature of CD20-negative relapses following rituximab therapy in aggressive B-cell non-Hodgkin's lymphoma: a retrospective review. Br J Haematol 2002;119:412–6.

[9] Terui Y, Mishima Y, Sugimura N, Kojima K, Sakurai T, Mishima Y, et al. Identification of CD20 C-terminal deletion mutations associated with loss of CD20 expression in non-Hodgkin's lymphoma. Clin Cancer Res 2009;15:2523–30.

[10] Beum PV, Kennedy AD, Williams ME, Lindorfer MA, Taylor RP. The shaving reaction: rituximab/CD20 complexes are removed from mantle cell lymphoma and chronic lymphocytic leukemia cells by THP-1 monocytes. J Immunol 2006;176:2600–9.

[11] Burger JA, Gandhi V. The lymphatic tissue microenvironments in chronic lymphocytic leukemia: in vitro models and the significance of CD40-CD154 interactions. Blood 2009;114:2560.

Index

Note: Page numbers followed by *f* indicate figures and *t* indicate tables.

B

C

D

E

R

S